13. *Existential Generalization (E G)*

$$\Psi\beta$$
$$\therefore \ (\exists\alpha)\Psi\alpha$$

Where (1) 'β' represents any individual constant or free variable; and (2) where $\Psi\beta$ is like $\Psi\alpha$ except for containing free occurrences of β wherever $\Psi\alpha$ contains free occurrences of α.

14. *Existential Instantiation (E I)*

$$(\exists\alpha)\Psi\alpha$$
$$\therefore \ \Psi\beta$$

(1) Where β is a free variable at every place, and only those places, α is free in $\Psi\alpha$; and (2) where β cannot be introduced into the proof by E I if it has already appeared as a free variable in that proof.

II. Definitional Equivalences

D1:   '$p \lor q$' = '$\sim(\sim p \cdot \sim q)$' Df
D2:   '$p \triangle q$' = '$\sim(p \cdot q) \cdot \sim(\sim p \cdot \sim q)$' Df
D3:   '$p \supset q$' = '$\sim(p \cdot \sim q)$' Df
D4:   '$p \equiv q$' = '$\sim(p \cdot \sim q) \cdot \sim(q \cdot \sim p)$' Df
D5:   '$(\exists\alpha)\Psi\alpha$' = '$\sim(\alpha)\sim\Psi\alpha$' Df

III. Logical Equivalences

1. *Double Negation (D N)*

$$p \equiv \sim\sim p$$

2. *Transposition (Trans)*

$$(p \supset q) \equiv (\sim q \supset \sim p)$$

3. *Association (Assoc)*

$$[p \cdot (q \cdot r)] \equiv [(p \cdot q) \cdot r]$$
$$[p \lor (q \lor r)] \equiv [(p \lor q) \lor r]$$

4. *Commutation (Com)*

$$(p \lor q) \equiv (q \lor p)$$
$$(p \cdot q) \equiv (q \cdot p)$$
$$(p \triangle q) \equiv (q \triangle p)$$
$$(p \equiv q) \equiv (q \equiv p)$$

5. *De Morgan's Laws (De M)*

$$(\sim p \lor \sim q) \equiv \sim(p \cdot q)$$
$$(\sim p \cdot \sim q) \equiv \sim(p \lor q)$$

6. *Distribution (Dist)*

$$[p \lor (q \cdot r)] \equiv [(p \lor q) \cdot (p \lor r)]$$
$$[p \cdot (q \lor r)] \equiv [(p \cdot q) \lor (p \cdot r)]$$

7. *Exportation (Exp)*

$$[(p \cdot q) \supset r] \equiv [p \supset (q \supset r)]$$

8. *Material Implication (M I)*

$$(p \supset q) \equiv (\sim p \lor q)$$

9. *Tautology (Taut)*

$$p \equiv (p \cdot p)$$
$$p \equiv (p \lor p)$$

10. *Quantificational Denial (Q D)*

$$(\alpha)\Psi\alpha \equiv \sim(\exists\alpha)\sim\Psi\alpha$$
$$(\alpha)\sim\Psi\alpha \equiv \sim(\exists\alpha)\Psi\alpha$$
$$\sim(\alpha)\Psi\alpha \equiv (\exists\alpha)\sim\Psi\alpha$$
$$\sim(\alpha)\sim\Psi\alpha \equiv (\exists\alpha)\Psi\alpha$$

Deductive Logic
and
Descriptive Language

FRANK R. HARRISON, III

DEPARTMENT OF PHILOSOPHY AND RELIGION
THE UNIVERSITY OF GEORGIA

PRENTICE-HALL, INC. / Englewood Cliffs, N.J.

for DOTTIE

Current printing (last digit):

10 9 8 7 6 5 4 3 2 1

13-197228-6

Library of Congress Catalog Card Number: 69-18891

Printed in the United States of America

PRENTICE-HALL INTERNATIONAL, INC., London
PRENTICE-HALL OF AUSTRALIA, PTY. LTD., Sydney
PRENTICE-HALL OE CANADA, LTD., Toronto
PRENTICE-HALL OF INDIA PRIVATE, LTD., New Delhi
PRENTICE-HALL OF JAPAN, INC., Tokyo

Preface

This book is an *introduction to deductive logic*. It pressupposes no special background or talent. I have attempted to write for you, the beginning logic student—not the professional. Consequently, some of the niceties demanded by a more elegant and formalized approach have been only briefly mentioned or altogether omitted. Neither has any particular philosophical position been set forth or defended. Nor have topics more appropriate to courses in philosophy of science or philosophy of language been pursued. The purpose of this book is to introduce deductive logic and to provide you with techniques useful in analysing many formal structures in descriptive language.

In mastering the material presented you will learn some "rules of logic". For the most part you will find these rules rather simple to learn. But, you will also want to apply these rules of logic to particular arguments—perhaps a more difficult task. To help you develop an "art of doing" logic, I suggest various "rules-of-thumb", which are not rules of logic but aids for applying the rules of logic in particular cases. No claim is made that the suggested rules-of-thumb are the only ones possible or that they are the most efficient. Hopefully, they will help you, as a beginner, "do" logic. As you become more proficient, you will probably develop your own techniques and strategies—your own style.

To add interest to your study of logic, I have drawn from a wide scope of topics in developing the exercises. For example, biology, chemistry, physics, art, history, and music are all used. Contrary to the implications of C. P. Snow, a person can read intelligently both in the liberal arts and the sciences. To appreciate quantum mechanics does not guarantee ignorance of literature; nor does the reverse necessarily hold. Further, the range of topics and disciplines represented in the exercises indicate a justification for viewing logic as the *a priori* study of the forms of descriptive language. After all, we use language to describe things and events in all sorts of diverse areas.

Undoubtedly, this entire book may not be covered in a semester or quarter. There are various parts of the text which, for one reason or another, you may not study. In certain introductory courses, for example, Chapter 9 may be omitted, while perhaps in an introductory "honors course" it may be included. And, you probably will not work all the exercises.

I hope this volume is helpful in your mastery of deductive logic and descriptive language. If the book has some success in reaching this goal, its writing and publication have been worthwhile.

FRANK R. HARRISON, III

The University of Georgia
Athens, Georgia

Acknowledgments

For careful reading and criticism of the manuscript I am indebted to William Beckett, Walter H. O'Briant, and W. E. Tinsley. Bowman L. Clarke, Lawrence G. Jones, Hugues Leblanc, and Richard Severens have greatly helped and influenced me in several sections. I am grateful to Michael A. Payne who, having read several full versions of the manuscript, has offered many useful editorial suggestions. The University of Georgia and the Department of Philosophy have been generous in supplying time and money for writing the text. For this I am thankful. I also acknowledge the advice and, in particular, moral support of the publisher. But, *sine dubitatione*, my deepest gradtude must be reserved for my wife, Dottie. Without her untiring patience and understanding, this book would not yet have been printed. That which is good in it I must attribute to her. And finally, those faults and mistakes remaining are due to my oversight.

"Well! I've often seen a cat without a grin," thought Alice; "but a grin without a cat! It's the most curious thing I ever saw in all my life!"

Contents

Chapter **3**

More About Truth-Tables   65

Chapter **4**

Logical Definitions and Logical Equivalences   99

Chapter **5**

Proofs Validity: Argument Forms   111

Chapter **10**

Chapter **11**

Chapter **12**

Appendices:

1

What Shall We Mean by 'Logic'?

Imagine various situations in which you might use the following sentences:

That's the logical thing to do.

What he said seems logical enough to me.

The evidence logically supports the conclusion.

His conclusion follows logically from the previous remarks.

Politicians do not always reason in a logical way.

Let's think things through logically.

The company follows the logic of better products at lower consumer prices.

The fact that so many different contexts might be built around any one of these examples suggests a wide diversity of use of 'logic' and 'logical'. For example, 'That's the logical thing to do' might be used as another way of saying, 'That's the *right* thing to do' or 'That's the *correct* thing to do'. In such cases the word 'logical' may begin to acquire ethical, or perhaps honorific, overtones. Saying 'The company follows the logic of better products at lower consumer prices' may be understood as 'The company follows the *policy* of better products at lower consumer prices'. Suppose a student asserted 'Since I've studied hard for this quiz and I always make A's when I really study, I'll make an A on this one too'.

We might say, 'His conclusion follows logically'. On the other hand, we might overhear, 'Every time I've ever heard the New York Philharmonic, I've enjoyed it. So, I'll probably also enjoy it this time'. Let us say in this case, 'The evidence logically supports the conclusion'. These examples remind us that 'logic' and 'logical' are words with many uses in our language, some uses being more closely related than others and some not related at all. Consequently, we cannot ask what is meant by 'logic' if we expect one single definition. We can, however, ask what we shall mean by 'logic' in our present studies; that is, we can ask what we shall understand logic to be for our present purposes.

One traditional answer to the question of what is understood by logic—how the word 'logic' is correctly used—is that it is the study of the ways we think about things. From a rather commonsense point of view this notion of logic seems feasible. We do say, 'Let's think things through logically', hoping this activity will result in doing the appropriate thing at the right time and place. Nonetheless, it can be very misleading to suggest that logic is simply the study of the ways we think about things. Logic cannot be *the* study of the ways we think about things, for psychology is concerned directly with finding out how people think, how and why certain thoughts are related, what goes on in the learning process, and the like. So, if we want to say that psychology studies various processes of thinking, we cannot say that logic is *the* study of the ways we think about things.

Perhaps we may say that logic is one of several methods of studying the ways we think about things. But, this is also misleading for at least two very good reasons. *First,* such a notion of logic may lead us to suppose that logic and psychology both belong to the same type of investigation, which is not the case. In attempting to formulate answers to his questions, the psychologist may perform experiments with human beings, mice, and primates. The psychologist is interested in setting up controls and devising empirical techniques in his laboratory. These controls, techniques, and experiments are a critical part of the advancement of psychology. But the logician does not perform such experiments. The work of the logician is neither carried further along nor justified by empirical methods. Logic is not an empirical science, although it is an indispensable tool in all the empirical sciences. *Second,* to maintain that logic is a study of the ways we think about things is to include too much in our concept of logic. From the standpoint of psychology there are many ways we might "think about" things. That family of activities we commonly call 'thinking' is extremely complex. Emotional responses, free associations, daydreaming, and intuition are but a few examples which might fall under the heading of 'thinking'. Logic is interested in none of these activities. We do not want to make logic a branch of psychology any more than we should want to turn psychology into a branch of logic. The two fields are quite distinct. We can suggest that logic is a study of the ways we think about things and this may have some justification in every day uses of the words 'logic', 'logical', and 'thinking', but this view of logic is too misleading for our more technical purposes.

While there is admittedly no one correct answer to 'What is logic?' because there is no one correct meaning of the word 'logic', the following characterization will serve our purposes in this book:

Logic is the a priori study of the forms of descriptive language.

Our overarching goal will be to develop a tool by which we can analyze many formal structures of descriptive language, whether we are describing events on the football field or in the laboratory, in the home or in the office.

To grasp more firmly our definition of 'logic', let us examine briefly the key concepts of *language, descriptive language, form,* and *a priori.* The following remarks certainly do not purport to be a complete discussion of these central notions. Thousands of pages have been written attempting to explicate these concepts. There are still many heated debates being carried out by philosophers, grammarians, philologists, descriptive linguists, and so on concerning the concept of language. Fortunately, we do not need to enter the deep subtleties of these controversies. Our discussion is intended to provide *possible beginning* guideposts and general indicators to a better understanding of logic as the *a priori* study of the forms of descriptive language. Let us now turn our attention to the concept of language.

1. LANGUAGE

Language is one of the—if not *the*—most complicated and important activities of human beings. Science, art, the humanities, and everyday affairs would all be impossible without it. The internationally renowned physicist P. W. Bridgman once wrote

> It would appear that in general a large part of the serious enterprise of the [human] race is precisely to discover how the various things that we want to say can be welded into a verbally consistent whole.*

For example, what is a major purpose of our formal education? Could we not say that a formal education both improves old and familiar uses of language and also gives us new uses so that "the various things that we want to say can be welded into a verbally consistent whole"? To some degree, the ways in which we use language determine our outlook on the world, our political decisions, and our relations with other people. How many pleasant social relations have been marred by an unfortunate choice of words? How many political decisions have run amiss because two people, or two nations, were using such words as 'democracy', 'freedom', 'the people' in vastly different ways? We are persuaded, taught, chided, and molded by language from our earliest years until death. Without language we could not communicate our thoughts, feelings, wants, and desires; we could not worship, enter into ceremonies, tell stories for amusement, or do hundreds of other things that we do daily without a second thought—in fact we could not

---

*Bridgman. P. W., *The Way Things Are* (Cambridge: The Belknap Press of Harvard University Press, 1959), p. 30.

even think without language, much less have a second thought about anything. Indeed, to be human requires language! It is our many linguistic activities that separate us from the various beasts. And to fulfill more completely our human capacities requires more and more mastery of the myriad uses of language. Yet, how often do we take account of the many different languages there are and the diverse ways in which we can and do use them? Probably not very often. We tend to let one of the most important activities of our lives take care of itself willy-nilly.

It is not difficult to suggest examples of what everyone would call 'language'. English, French, and Latin are all common enough. We may, however, also want to claim that mathematics, music, and painting are languages. No one would want to deny that there are very important differences among these various examples. But, there also seem to be important similarities. Each of the examples makes use of certain signs, although in some cases different types of signs are used. In English we find words being built up from letters, sentences from words, paragraphs from sentences. The various notes of a musical score are arranged into phrases and these phrases are woven into musical sentences and complete symphonies. Areas of pigment on a canvas are used to develop a painting, and out of mathematical formulae proofs are constructed.

But it is not enough that any particular language has only a limited supply of signs; these signs must be related to one another in some orderly fashion. A language must have rules, no matter how covert they are, indicating just how the various signs of that language are to be ordered. And there are different ways of ordering the signs in various languages. Thus, the rules of ordering the signs in one language may be different from the rules of another language. Each language must have its grammar. Therefore, we can say a necessary condition for a language is that

> *it has a set of signs and a set of rules which govern how those signs are to be correctly related to one another.*

Someone might want to insist that much more is involved in a language. Our point, however, is that at least the necessary condition above is involved in our concept of language.

2. DESCRIPTIVE LANGUAGE

Logic, as we shall study and understand it, is not concerned with every use or kind of language. For instance, we shall not claim to be dealing with poetry, music, or painting. We shall be interested only in word-languages used descriptively, that is, word-languages which purport to give information. Word-languages are extremely complicated and may be studied from many different viewpoints. Descriptive linguists, for example, are interested in studying different types of sentences of a particular language. Examining English sentences, descriptive linguists often classify them according to their grammatical form or grammatical use, or both. Thus, English sentences may be spoken of as simple, compound, complex, or compound-complex. Or, we may say that English sentences are either declarative, interrogative, imperative, or exclamatory. Furthermore, declarative sentences, let us say, may be simple, compound, complex, or compound-complex. Rules for English grammar can be stated so as to provide us with at least sixteen possible classifications of English sentences.

But we must be careful when speaking of sentences—English or otherwise. Consider these examples:

(1)   Cleanth Brooks was born in 1906.

(2)   *Cleanth Brooks was born in 1906.*

(3)   ***Cleanth Brooks was born in 1906.***

Surely from one point of view (1)—(3) are all the same sentence, but from another they are not. They are each printed on a different line and in a different type font. While a printer or calligrapher might be interested in such features, a descriptive linguist is not. Let us refer to the printed examples (1)-(3) as *speech-tokens* used in performing a speech-act. Roughly, *a speech-token is a particular sound utterance or line of marks used in the act of speaking.* However, the speech-tokens (1)-(3) can also be viewed as instances of one *speech-type. Speech-types are not printed, written, nor uttered; they are neither spatial nor temporal but are exemplified by speech-tokens.* Speech-types may be considered members of different classes (sets, collections) called 'sentences'.

A logician is concerned with speech-tokens (such as you are now seeing on this page) of a particular word-language only insofar as they are used to express statements. *An important feature of statements, distinguishing them from speech-types and sentences, is that they are either true or false but never both.* This property of statements, that they are either true or false, is their *truth-value,* and the truth-value of a given statement is said to be truth or falsity, depending on whether that statement is true or false.

Furthermore, statements are invariant in a way speech-tokens are not. The following are quite distinct, but all express the same statement:

(6)   Litmus paper turns red in an acid solution.

(7)   Litmus paper is turned red in an acid solution.

(8)   Acid solutions turn litmus paper red.

(9)   Le tournesol devient rouge dans une solution acide.

From the logical point of view we are interested only in that invariant statement expressed by (6), (7), (8), and (9). Here, the concept of statement is closely related to that of meaning. We may say that the meanings of (6)-(9) are just those sets of conditions which would make (6)-(9) true or false. Furthermore, if the speech-token 'Litmus paper turns red in an acid solution' indicates a statement which is either true or false given exactly the same conditions which make the statement expressed by the speech-token 'Le tournesol devient rouge dans une solution acide' true or false, then the two speech-tokens express the same statement, have the same meaning.

Even though statements are either true or false and are studied by logicians, a logician is not interested in the *actual* truth or falsity of statements. Nor, in general, does logic offer us any method whereby we may establish whether a given statement is actually true or false. While a statement purportedly describes something, it may fail to do so. A statement may be false. The various empirical sciences are interested in ascertaining if a given statement is actually true or false. The sciences, not logic, are concerned with problems of confirmation and falsification, that is, of establishing the actual truth or falsity of a statement. As students of logic, we shall not be concerned with such empirical procedures. Rather, *we shall study the most general forms of statements and the most general conditions which statements must fulfill if they are to count as true or as false, and this study is quite independent of whether a statement is actually true or not.*

Some important distinctions have been drawn between speech-tokens, speech-types, sentences, and statements. These distinctions are reflected in what we can and cannot say of speech-tokens, speech-types, sentences, and statements. We can say that some written or printed speech-tokens are 2 inches long. We cannot say this of sentences and statements. Speech-types are grammatically correct or they are not, but neither speech-tokens nor statements are spoken of in this way. Statements are true or false; yet speech-tokens and sentences are neither.

Now we shall begin to relax some of these distinctions. A book, such as the one you are reading, uses printed speech-tokens as vehicles for expressing statements. Because you and I probably understand and use English more readily than some other language, our book is printed in English instead of in French, Portuguese, Swahili, or any other currently used language. This is simply a practical consideration. As far as logic is concerned, it makes no difference what speech-tokens we find printed on the various pages or what word-language is used. Therefore, *as logicians*, we may use 'statement' instead of 'speech-token'. This is simply a matter of convenience which should lead to no confusion.

3. FORM

What are we to understand by 'form'? We might say 'The form of the building is basically sound', 'Some people find poetical forms difficult to master', 'The forms of various pieces of Steuben glass are without parallel', and the like. Once more we are faced with a term having various uses, a term which is linked to other terms such as 'structure', 'order', and 'shape'. As a first step, however, in coming to grasp how 'form' is used in our definition of 'logic', we shall say that *the form of anything is the way, or ways, in which the elements of that thing are arranged for a particular purpose.*

This "arranging" of the elements must proceed according to rules—rules either explicitly stated or learned through various processes of imitation, social conditioning, and so forth. English, for example, has a number of different elements such as various letters, words, contractions, abbreviations, and punctuation marks. We put these elements together by following certain rules (although for the most part we follow these rules rather more from habit and training than consciously thinking about them)—rules which comprise English grammar and usage.

The notion of form is often contrasted with that of *content*. In very general terms we may say that

the content of anything is the elements which are ordered by the form of that thing.

In order to elucidate the distinction between form and content, let us consider a few examples:

> Nadja caught a mouse.
>
> Irene sang an aria.
>
> Will read a play.

From the point of view of English grammar these three examples display the same form. Each uses a proper name as its subject and a transitive verb followed by the object of the verb. Consider the following arithmetical expressions:

$$(2 \times 3) = (3 \times 2)$$
$$(\tfrac{1}{2} \times \tfrac{1}{4}) = (\tfrac{1}{4} \times \tfrac{1}{2})$$
$$(\sqrt{3} \times 1) = (1 \times \sqrt{3})$$

Each of these arithmetical examples exhibits the same formal properties. Nevertheless, as in the English examples, the content of these arithmetical expressions is different in each case.

We have already suggested a distinction between sentences and statements. The grammarian is interested in studying the grammatical forms of sentences, and this is an empirical study. On the other hand the logician studies the logical forms of statements. As we proceed in mastering logic, we shall come to see that a given statement may be understood as having several distinct logical forms and that we cannot discuss *the* logical form of a statement outside a particular concrete context determining the purpose, the use, to which we wish to put the statement. We can, however, now make some general comments about form and content.

Logic is understood as the study of the forms of statements, but not their specific content. Viewing logic this way suggests two further points. *First,* since we are interested only in the formal properties of statements, we shall not be concerned with the *specific* meaning of any particular statement, much less whether any particular statement is actually true or false. This is simply to reinforce the suggestion made on page 6. Later, however, we shall notice that the types of statement forms we study are limiting factors of the conditions under which a particular statement may be considered true or false. That is, the form of a statement is necessary, but not sufficient, to determine the conditions under which that statement is to count as true or false. *Second,* because we are concerned with the formal properties of statements, we must devise some method of isolating some form of a statement from its content. We shall do this by constructing a special symbolism. For example, using a grammatical analogy, we might let 'N_s' represent any noun subject of a sentence, 'N_o' any noun object of the action of any transitive verb, and 'V_t' any transitive verb. Then we should be able to represent the grammatical form of

> Nadja caught a mouse.
>
> Irene sang an aria.
>
> Will read a play.

as

$$N_s \, V_t \, N_o$$

Or, suppose we let 'a' and 'b' stand for any number we please. Then *an* arithmetical form of

$$(2 \times 3) = (3 \times 2)$$
$$(\tfrac{1}{2} \times \tfrac{1}{4}) = (\tfrac{1}{4} \times \tfrac{1}{2})$$
$$(\sqrt{3} \times 1) = (1 \times \sqrt{3})$$

could be shown as

$$(a \times b) = (b \times a)$$

The types of symbols we shall adopt in the study of logic will become an obvious aid in making our work much easier, less cumbersome, and more enjoyable.

The special notation we shall employ displays quickly and easily the various forms of statements and the ways in which several statements may be related. This notation is very important, as is the notation of mathematics. For example, consider the following quadratic formula:

$$x = \frac{-b \pm \sqrt{b^2 - 4ac}}{2a}$$

This could be worded in everyday English. But, think how complicated that would be! We would not advance very far in mathematics if limited only to ordinary

English. And, as a matter of historical record, mathematics made little progress until a symbolization, a shorthand, was invented. Such a symbolization has many advantages. It makes life much happier when we do even simple mathematics, for it is no longer necessary to use ordinary language to express mathematical relations. The specialized notation makes life easier in another way, too. It makes it possible *literally to see* various patterns which keep repeating themselves in different problems; consequently, less effort is required. Many times the notation saves us from having to think about a given problem and serves to make such problems quite mechanical. Problems which once took pages to write out, and hours to work, now become vastly simpler and less time-consuming. Problems which could never have been solved without the notation of mathematics are now done with relative ease. The notation is also exact and precise. Each symbol has its own special use, its own special way of being defined. Therefore, the ambiguity and vagueness of ordinary descriptive language are eliminated. So, it was only with the introduction of a specialized notation, a sort of shorthand, that mathematics was able to make any great progress. And what is true of the invention and use of a specialized symbolization in mathematics is equally true of the symbols used in logic today. The symbols we shall adopt are to help us—not hinder us—in mastering logic and studying the forms of descriptive language.

4. A PRIORI

We have spoken of logic as the *a priori* study of the forms of descriptive language. What shall we understand by '*a priori*'? Students of philosophy often speak of empirical statements and *a priori* ones (or of empirical and *a priori* knowledge). Let us examine a few examples of each of these types of statements and then make some general comments about both. Typical examples of empirical statements are the following:

> The musician J. S. Bach died in 1750.
>
> Boston is north of New York.
>
> Hurricanes will strike the east coast of Florida next October.
>
> Lamar Dodd is a world-renowned painter.
>
> Countries which are predominately Roman Catholic have a low rate of suicide.

On the other hand the following are examples of *a priori* statements:

> An octogenarian is a person 80 years of age or older.
>
> Either we shall have heavy snows next year or we shall not.
>
> Since Bill is taller than Michael and Michael is taller than Richard, Bill is taller than Richard.

If litmus paper turns red in an acid solution and this is litmus paper, then this paper will turn red in an acid solution.

What general distinction may we draw between *a priori* and empirical statements? Just this: In order to say whether any *a priori* statement is true or false, it is enough that we know and understand how the various terms in each statement are being used. Thus, to see that 'Either we shall have heavy snows next year, or we shall not' is true, we must understand the use of the terms 'either', 'or', and 'not'. It is not necessary for us to wait until next year and observe the existing weather conditions. Such activities of waiting and observing would play no part in justifying 'Either we shall have heavy snows next year or we shall not'. This is not the case with empirical statements, however. The justification required for these statements is different. In justifying an empirical statement, it is not enough that we know and understand only the use of the terms in the statement, although we certainly must know this. We must also make various sensory observations in order to confirm an empirical statement—or, indeed, to falsify it. We may, therefore, say that the justification of an empirical statement rests on sensory experiences, while the justification of an *a priori* statement does not. No sensory experience, beyond that required in learning one's language, is required in the justification of any *a priori* statement.

> **Thus, the distinction between 'empirical' and 'a priori' draws a distinction between different ways of justifying statements (or knowledge claims).**

The kinds of claims about language we shall encounter in our study are not justified by any sensory experience beyond that required in learning to use *any* descriptive language, be it English, French, or German. Logic is not concerned with the linguistic idiosyncrasies of any one particular descriptive language to the exclusion of any other. Logicians, for example, do not study the grammatical forms of English to the exclusion of those of Swahili. Logicians do not make empirical studies of various languages as a descriptive linguist does. Rather, a logician studies and explicates those rules which any language must follow if that language is to be descriptively meaningful.

5. ARGUMENTS

In that logic is the *a priori* study of the forms of descriptive language, we must consider not only the forms of individual statements but also the various formal ways in which statements may be related to one another in some sort of argument. What do we mean by 'argument'? In ordinary uses of 'argument', many things might be suggested; anything from a slight verbal disagreement to an out-and-out brawl, a discussion, a debate, a summary of a chapter or book, and the like might be called an 'argument'. In our study, however, 'argument' will be used in a technical way. Let us attempt to establish some understanding of this technical use of 'argument'.

Sometimes a person will attempt to establish the truth or falsity of a given statement by presenting evidence which will aid in establishing that statement's truth or falsity. Statements, or a statement, will be used in presenting this evidence. The statement whose truth or falsity is to be established is the *conclusion* of an argument. Statements, or a statement, purporting to present evidence for or against the conclusion are the *premisses* of an argument. The *premiss set* of an argument is the collection of all the premisses of an argument even if there is only one premiss. Furthermore, every fully expressed argument has at least one premiss and exactly one conclusion.

Hence, arguments are sequences of statements used by someone to establish the truth or falsity of a conclusion, given a premiss set. In our use of 'argument', however, the person presenting the argument must also make a claim concerning the *actual* truth of his conclusion; a person claims that all his premisses are actually true. But what if the conclusion is held to be false? In that case the person presenting the argument certainly may claim that at least one of his premisses is actually false. Thus, two claims are made by anyone presenting an argument: *First, such a person claims that the premisses help to establish the truth or falsity of the conclusion and, second, a person claims something about the actual truth or falsity of his premisses.* Let us notice at once, then, that arguing is a human activity. Machines, for example, do not argue, although we may use machines to help substantiate some of the claims made by a person who is arguing.

Our characterization of 'argument' suggests that an argument may go astray in two ways. *First*, as a matter of fact, the claims concerning the actual truth or falsity of the premisses may be mistaken. We, however, have already noted that as logicians we are not concerned with ascertaining whether any statement is actually true or false, although we shall be interested in some very general logical conditions concerning the truth and falsity of statements. The *second* way in which an argument might go astray is this: While the claim is made that the premisses support the truth or falsity of the conclusion; nevertheless, they do not. It is this claim which will be of interest to us as logicians. We shall be interested in analyzing the relationship holding—or not holding—between a premiss set and conclusion of a given argument. A great deal of time will be devoted to developing and learning both rules and methods permitting us to carry out this type of analysis.

In passing we may notice that certain English words often are used as flags or indicators of a premiss. Some of these are 'as', 'because', 'for', and 'since'. Other words are sometimes used to indicate a conclusion: 'accordingly', 'consequently', 'hence', 'so', 'therefore', 'thus', and 'wherefore' are examples. Not all arguments make use of such flag words—and this list does not pretend to be exhaustive—but enough arguments do use these words for them to be very helpful in distinguishing premisses and conclusions.

Generally speaking, there are several types of relationships which may be said to hold between premiss sets and conclusions. Consequently, we may isolate several distinct types of arguments.

The first general type of argument we may notice is a *deductive argument*. There are many particular examples of deductive arguments, of which the following are but three:

> I'm either going to the movies or staying home and studying. But, I can't go to the movies. Therefore, I'm going to stay home and study.

> The rate of suicide is high in a given country only if the number of Roman Catholics in that country is low. However, America is a country with a high rate of suicide. Hence, the number of Roman Catholics in America is low.

> Because I have put this paper in acid, I have followed the experiment correctly if it is litmus paper. Since this is litmus paper, I have followed the experiment correctly only if it turns red. Consequently, since I put this paper in acid, it turns red if it is litmus paper.

Let us examine more closely the relationship which supposedly holds between the premisses and the conclusion in each case. In these examples the relationship holding between the premisses and the conclusions is one of *logical entailment*. By 'logical entailment' we shall understand that

if all the premisses are true, then the conclusion must also be true.

Of course, as far as logical entailment is concerned, we have not claimed that the premisses in any one of the examples above *are* all true. But, that is beside the point. What is important is the claim that *if* all of the premisses were true, *then* the conclusion would also be true. In other words, the claim is made that

in a deductive argument the truth of its premisses is sufficient to establish the truth of its conclusion if the premisses do logically entail the conclusion.

Hence, if we were to accept the premisses of any of the examples above as all being true and at the same time deny the truth of the conclusion, we would be contradicting ourselves. In this case someone could justly accuse us of not knowing how to use descriptive language correctly.

An *inductive argument* differs from a deductive one in that there is no claim to establish the truth of the conclusion solely from the truth of the premisses. Even if all the premisses of an inductive argument were true, this would not be sufficient to establish the truth of the conclusion. For in any inductive argument we might accept all the premisses as true and still deny the truth of the conclusion without involving ourselves in any contradiction. Of course in some cases we may be rather foolish to accept the premisses and deny the conclusion. But, being foolish and being involved in a contradiction are two different things. Consider someone saying, 'In the majority of times I've gambled, I've lost a great deal of money'. This may be a true statement about the person making the remark. He may continue, 'I just can't resist it—I'm going to find a game going now'. Again, this may be accepted as true. From these two statements we might expect our luckless friend to say, 'I'll probably lose a good deal this time, too'. Yet, he might not say this. He might say instead—as habitual gamblers often do—'But *this time* I'll no doubt win'. While it may be silly for the person in question to say this unless he knew, for example, the tables were rigged in his favor, nevertheless, he would not be contradicting himself. The following are further examples of inductive arguments:

> It has been established—by infallible television commercials—that Brand Z toothpaste prevents more cavities for most people. Consequently, Brand Z will probably prevent more cavities for me too.

> Most conservative, upper middle-class Americans vote a conservative ticket. Certainly Bowman Lafayette is an upper middle-class American. Therefore, he also will no doubt vote a conservative ticket.

> The majority of nineteenth-century rural Americans was Puritanical in ethical outlook. My great-great-grandfather was a nineteenth-century rural American. So, he was also probably Puritanical in his ethical outlook.

At best the premisses of these inductive arguments give only probable reasons for supposing that the conclusions are true if the premisses all are. The truth of all the premisses of an inductive argument does not guarantee the truth of the conclusion of that argument.

In order to establish the truth of the conclusion of an inductive argument, we need to find evidence which will tend to confirm that conclusion. It becomes necessary to employ empirical observations to confirm or falsify the conclusion of an inductive argument; moreover, this is done independently of the truth of the premisses. In this sense the information presented in the conclusion of an inductive argument "goes beyond" the information given in the premisses.

Very often inductive arguments are used to make predictions about some future event. The concluding statements in the first two examples above make predictions. We are predicting that something will be the case when we say 'Consequently, Brand Z will probably prevent more cavities for me too', and 'Therefore, Bowman Lafayette also will no doubt vote a conservative ticket'. Yet not all inductive arguments make predictions. Our third example predicts nothing when it concludes 'So, my great-great-grandfather *was* also probably Puritanical in his ethical outlook'. We must not confuse an inductive argument concluding with a prediction and the conclusion of an inductive argument being such that future events or evidence to be found may tend to confirm or falsify it. And, in that future events, future evidence, may tend to confirm or falsify the conclusion of an inductive argument, we say that the truth of the premisses of such an argument does not guarantee the truth of the conclusion. In sum,

> **the truth of the conclusion of an inductive argument is never guaranteed solely by the truth of the premisses of that argument.**

Analogical arguments comprise a third type of argument we may distinguish. While some logicians claim that analogical arguments are a special sort of inductive argument, and some say that they are incomplete deductive arguments, we shall maintain that deductive, inductive, and analogical arguments differ in important respects.

Suppose we had a friend who was a specialist in marine biology, and he said, 'The whale swims in the sea like a fish'. We might think this assertion hardly counts as exciting news; but we would not hesitate to accept it as true. Furthermore, our friend tells us, 'The whale is also air-breathing, warm-blooded, and viviparous'. We should no doubt also accept this statement as true. Now our friend might continue by saying, 'Thus, the whale is an animal and not a fish'.

Such an argument is *similar to* an inductive argument in that we could accept all the premises as true, reject the conclusion, and not involve ourselves in a contradiction. Captain Ahab might well accept the premises concerning whales as being true and still insist on calling Moby Dick the 'big fish' without contradicting himself. Yet the analogical argument is also *similar to* a deductive argument. Why? Because in order to establish the truth of the conclusion of an analogical argument, we do not depend on any information other than that mentioned in the premises. Having been given the two initial premises concerning whales, it does not help us in the least to go out and observe further particular whales in order to determine whether a whale is "really" a fish or a mammal. Such further empirical observations are simply not to the point in confirming or falsifying the conclusions of analogical arguments.

Besides being used in the sciences to classify various objects, analogical arguments are also used in the courtroom. Consider two lawyers debating a matter of some concern—a tax issue. The state wants to impose higher taxes on a certain business. The argument from the point of view of the state may proceed something like this:

> While it is a motor vehicle used to transport people—there can be no doubt of that—the major part of its use is to transport *dead* people. Therefore, we must not consider a hearse in the same tax category as an automobile. Rather, we must classify hearses as pickup and delivery trucks and tax them accordingly.

Once again this is an arguent in which all the premises may be accepted as true and the conclusion denied without generating any contradiction. Yet, in order to confirm or falsify the conclusion, we need no evidence other than that already presented in the premises. We have all seen hearses and know to what uses they are put. We do not need to examine more of them to say whether the piece of reasoning above is correct or not or whether the conclusion is true or not. As in the case of whales, this is simply not to the point. In sum an analogical argument is one in which

> ***the truth of the premises is not held logically to entail the truth of the conclusion, but neither is the truth of the conclusion established by any investigations other than those used in establishing the truth of the premises.***

Of these three types of arguments, the deductive, inductive, and analogical, we shall study exclusively the deductive argument. We shall study only those arguments in which the claim is made that *if* all the premisses are true, *then* the conclusion must also be true. We shall be concerned with the rules of *deductive logic*, while we realize that there are other very important branches of logic.

6. VALIDITY, INVALIDITY, AND SOUNDNESS

In a deductive argument either the premisses may not support the conclusion in the required manner or all the statements in the argument may not be true. We are now led to the distinction of truth and falsity on the one hand and validity and invalidity on the other. Statements are said to be true or false, but not both. We do not speak of arguments as being either true or false. A deductive argument is spoken of as being valid or invalid. The conclusion of a deductive argument is supposedly related to its premisses according to various rules which guarantee that if all the premisses are true, the conclusion must also be true. If the conclusion is indeed related to the premisses according to the rules of deductive logic, that argument is said to be valid; otherwise it is said to be invalid. *Thus, we speak of deductive arguments as being either valid or invalid and statements as being either true or false.*

For example, all the statements—premisses and conclusions—in the following argument are true; yet, the argument is invalid:

> Some dogs are vicious animals. Some vicious animals provide excellent protection. Consequently, some dogs provide excellent protection.

The truth of the premisses of this argument does not guarantee the truth of the conclusion. In order to point this out, we can construct another argument *which has the same logical form as the previous one.* Only now, while all the premisses are true, the conclusion is false:

> Some acids are soluble in water. Some things which are soluble in water are sweet to the taste. Accordingly, some acids are sweet to the taste.

Now consider the following argument:

> Some reptiles are viviparous creatures. All viviparous creatures are warm-blooded. Hence, some reptiles are warm-blooded.

In this case the conclusion is false, but the first premiss is also false. Nevertheless, if all the premisses were true, then the conclusion would of logical necessity also be true. Here we have a *valid argument* made up of some *false statements.* On the other hand the next argument is not only valid, but it is also composed of all true statements:

Some animals are cats. All cats are viviparous. Hence, some animals are viviparous.

While the notions of *truth* and *falsity* and of *validity* and *invalidity* are quite distinct, there is an important relation holding between them in deductive arguments.

> **If a deductive argument is valid and if all the premisses of that argument are true, then the conclusion must also be true.**

In a valid deductive argument there may be at least one (and perhaps all) false premiss and a false conclusion. There may even be at least one (and perhaps all) false premiss and a true conclusion. *There can never be, in a valid deductive argument all true premisses and at the same time a false conclusion.* Further, an *invalid* deductive argument may have at least one (and perhaps all) false premiss and a false conclusion. Indeed, in an invalid deductive argument all the premisses and the conclusion may be true. *If, however, all the premisses of a deductive argument are true and the conclusion false, that deductive argument is invalid.*

These possible combinations of truth and falsity on the one hand and of validity and invalidity on the other may be grouped into two classes. A deductive argument may be either *sound* or *unsound*. A deductive argument is called '*sound*' if, and only if, all the premisses of the argument are true and the argument is also valid. Otherwise a deductive arguent is called '*unsound*'. Thus, we can have a valid argument which is, nevertheless, unsound.

7. USE AND MENTION

Another set of distinctions which is important in our study of logic, and in other areas as well, is indicated by 'use' and 'mention'. In the majority of cases descriptive language is used to talk about events and objects in the world around us. A person purports—though sometimes unsuccessfully—to describe various areas of the world and his experiences, to present information about the world, to learn things about it from others. He wants to talk about his latest escapades, the big fish that got away, chemical compounds, the atomic properties of the various elements, and so on. In such talk about the world we must *use* words which *mention* the objects or events we wish to talk about. If, for example, we want to talk about the relation of Mars to Venus and Earth during a given geocentric time period, we must use the names of the planets we mention in our talk. It would be foolish to suppose that our assertions actually contained the planets themselves. Statements do not literally contain the objects, as such, which they mention. Rather, we should say that statements contain names which are used to mention objects or events. Thus, when we say that

(1)   England is to the west of France.

we do not use the nations of England and France in our assertion about them. We mention these nations by *using* names for them. This is an obvious point. But, being so obvious, the point is sometimes overlooked. Often we fail to notice something because it is too close, not because it is too far away!

But, suppose we do not want to talk about planets or nations. Suppose we wish to talk about the *names* of planets and nations. Then we must mention these names in our statements about them. In this case we must distinguish between the name of an object and the name of the name of an object. In some instances this is clearly accomplished by the use of different words. For example, if we wish to call upon the Deity, we might use one of His names. We might call upon Yahweh. Yet, this name of the Deity also has a name, which is the Tetragrammaton. In this case we are able to use a different word for the name of the name of an object. The number of such cases is limited, however. *Usually, we name a linguistic element by putting semi-quotes* (single quotation marks) *around the element to be named.* The following examples illustrate this point:

(2)   Mars is the fourth planet from the sun.
(3)   'Mars' has four letters and rhymes with 'stars'.

In (2) we are clearly referring to the planet, Mars; but in (3) we are saying something about the word used to name the planet. It would be ungrammatical and meaningless to assert

(4)   Mars has four letters and rhymes with stars.

Planets are not composed of letters of the alphabet; neither do they rhyme with other celestial bodies.

In sum, in (1) and (2), words are used in order to mention objects. In (3), however, words are used to mention other words. Let us, therefore, adopt this rule:

> *The name of an object is formed, when that object is itself any linguistic element, by flanking that element on its left- and right-hand sides with semi-quotes.*

As a convenience in writing, we shall also say that

> *any linguistic element appearing on a line by itself may be counted as the name of that element.*

As we proceed, many potential pitfalls will be avoided in our studies if we draw a distinction between a linguistic element and the name of that element.

8. TIPS ON STUDYING LOGIC

In order to make the study of logic simpler, a few helpful suggestions should be heeded. Two of these are "psychological" in nature. To begin with, *do not be afraid of logic*. Some students do poorly in logic, as well as in mathematics and foreign languages, simply because they fear these subjects. Even before beginning a course, some students have already made up their minds that they will not do well, that they cannot do well. In many cases these students feel that there is something unnatural, something odd, strange, and mysterious, about logic, mathematics, or foreign languages. But, there is nothing of the occult here. It is simply a matter of being at first unfamiliar with the notations of logic and mathematics or with the words and grammar of German or Greek. In many ways logic is no more "unnatural" than English. It is less familiar to many people. There will be a specialized notation to be learned—a technical vocabulary—but the symbols used are few and they are well defined. There will also be some rules to master, but their number is small. It is for you to master the symbols and rules of logic. They are the tools of your trade; they are designed, in part, to make your work easier. Become familiar with the symbols and rules. *Do not be afraid of them!*

The second psychological point is this: *Train yourself to look for patterns, forms, and structures which reoccur in various particular cases and ways.* After all, we are approaching logic as the *a priori* study of the forms of descriptive language. You will soon learn that in descriptive language there are various forms, various patterns, which are used repeatedly in different particular cases and for different ends. Many of these forms *can be seen, quite literally, just by looking.* Therefore, train yourself to look for these patterns and how and why they are used the way they are in a given case. Psychologically speaking, some people find it very difficult to see relations, to grasp analogies, to notice formal similarities between different particular events or objects. Sometimes it is equally difficult for these people to see structures in language. For example, some people may read and reread several poems all having the same poetic pattern without noticing this fact. Or, in music it is all too often that people will listen to several compositions without realizing all the compositions made use of the fugue form or the sonata-allegro form or the saraband form. It is not that such people do not know the names of various poetical or musical forms. It is, sadly, the fact that they simply do not notice them at all. In the study of logic, however, you must train yourself to be aware of formal patterns. Here, it is the formal similarities which are important. Attempt always to notice general forms; *concentrate on structure.*

Like mathematics and other languages, logic is built up piece by piece. Your study will commence with intuitively simple steps, steps which may at first seem hardly worth the bother to learn. But, as you progress, you will find that new material will be quite incomprehensible unless you have thoroughly mastered all that went before. You will not be able to omit one section and hope to understand the ones which follow. You will not be able to do poorly in one section and hope to do well in the following ones. You must learn to do each lesson very carefully and to understand it completely before going on to the next.

There are two ways in which such learning and understanding may be accomplished. There is a body, or group, of rules to be learned and there is the application of these rules to particular problems. Logic comprises a series of rules which you must learn. You must be completely familiar with these rules. You must be able to recognize them in varying situations. You must know them thoroughly. But it is not enough just to learn the rules of logic, you must also be able to apply them in particular situations. Rules without practice are vacuous; practice without rules is blind. Only when you are successfully able to do various exercises and to understand each one completely will you have mastered those areas of logic which you are about to study.

EXERCISES

Complete the exercises in your own words, without referring back to the text of the chapter. If you have to look back at the chapter, you probably have not mastered the material as well as you should have. Of course after you have finished all the exercises, you may then want to check your work with the text.

Group A:

Define the following technical terms in your own words.

(1) logic	**(9)** deductive argument
(2) language	**(10)** inductive argument
(3) statement	**(11)** analogical argument
(4) form	**(12)** logical entailment
(5) content	**(13)** validity
(6) argument	**(14)** invalidity
(7) premiss	**(15)** soundness
(8) conclusion	

Group *B*:

In the following, each may be understood in several ways because of the underlined words. Give at least two distinct interpretations for each of the examples.

Example: **(1)** John is *mad*.
  a) John is insane.
  b) John is angry.

(2) The *board* was here yesterday.

(3)   Is the *file* in the other room?

(4)   That's a *fine* piece of glass.

(5)   Break the *record*!

(6)   Lord Palmerston's *carriage* was impressive.

(7)   Are the *plants* flourishing?

(8)   I use *tables* in my work.

(9)   Go to the *bank*!

(10)   *Cabinets* are useful in our government.

(11)   Is that really a *logical* argument?

Group C:

Using semi-quotes, correctly punctuate the following.

Example: (1)   Athens begins with an A.
              'Athens' begins with an 'A'.

(2)   John is a proper name.

(3)   The name of Boston is Boston.

(4) $(a \times b) = (b \times a)$ is an algebraic formula.

(5)   Let us define logic as the *a priori* study of the forms of descriptive language.

(6)   The sum of $5 + 7$ is 12.

(7)   Saul wrote a term paper uses the active voice of the verb, while A term paper was written by Saul uses the passive voice.

(8)   Let the letter p stand for any statement you please, then p or not p is always a true statement.

(9) $P(x, y)$ is to be read the probability of x, given y.

(10)   Saul was later named Paul.

(11)   The curve of any elliptical motion can be depicted by $\dfrac{(x - h)^2}{a^2} + \dfrac{(y - k)^2}{b^2} = 1$.

Group D:

Which of the following statements are empirical and which *a priori*? Why?

(1)   Of the two East African tribes, the Galla have a more complicated age class than the Kipsigis.

(2)   Every empirical statement is justified by an appeal to sense-experience.

(3)   If it isn't true that all animals are carnivorous, then some aren't.

(4)   Mars is the fourth planet from the sun.

(5)   Russell Sage built the La Crosse & Milwaukee Railroad in 1852.

(6) If it isn't true that some hydrogen atoms do not contain only one proton and one electron, all hydrogen atoms do.

(7) A seven under par was shot by Peter Thomson at the 1965 British Open.

(8) Either we shall go to Easthampton next summer or we shall not.

(9) There is substantial medical evidence to indicate that many nonnarcotic drugs can lead to addiction.

(10) The first bank in North America was established at Philadelphia.

(11) Samuel Insull was the founder of the Insull Utilities Investments Incorporation of Illinois.

(12) My pain is mine and not yours.

(13) All men strive after that which they hold to be good.

(14) Some men are more ambitious than others.

(15) It's a sin to tell a lie.

Group E:

In each of the following arguments, indicate which statements are premisses and which conclusions.

(1) In a freshman course in chemistry Tom discovered his litmus paper turned red whenever he put it into an acidic solution; if, however, he put it into a basic medium, it turned blue. Tom put his lithmus paper into either an acidic solution or a basic medium. Having done this, he noticed that his litmus paper did not turn blue. Therefore, the litmus paper turned red.

(2) No employee who is either slovenly or discourteous can be promoted. Accordingly, no discourteous employee can be promoted.

(3) Even though it has a duck-like bill and webbed feet and swims like a duck, nevertheless, the platypus bears its young live and suckles them. Hence, the platypus is a mammal and not a fowl.

(4) We know that the curve of planetary motion can be depicted by

$$\frac{(x - h)^2}{a^2} + \frac{(y - k)^2}{b^2} = 1$$

This is certain since planetary motion is elliptical, and the curve of any elliptical motion can be depicted by

$$\frac{(x - h)^2}{a^2} + \frac{(y - k)^2}{b^2} = 1$$

(5) Most of the members of Congress have supported the President on his various bills and appointments. So, it stands to reason that they will probably support him on this appointment, too.

(6) Any nation has either a large population of poverty or a substantial middle class. Every large population of poverty is accompanied by a high rate of suicide. It's a fact that some nations do not have a high rate of suicide. Thus, some nations have a substantial middle class.

(7)   All exergonic reactions are heat-producing reactions. This is based on the following considerations. All exergonic reactions are spontaneous, and spontaneous exergonic reactions are all $-\Delta F°$ reactions. And, further, any spontaneous exergonic reaction which is $-\Delta F°$ is a heat-producing reaction.

(8)   If someone is going to be thrown out of school because of cheating, he should also be thrown out for knowingly passing bad checks. After all, passing a bad check knowingly is very much like cheating.

(9)   Thinking might be viewed solely as the manipulation of symbols according to certain rules. And, we also might want to claim that man's ability to think distinguishes him from the other animals. But, on this account, computers are also able to think and are, as man, distinguished from the lower animals because of this ability.

(10)   Brand X toothpaste has been proved statistically to lessen the possibility of cavities more than any other brand on the market. This means that if I use Brand X, I'll probably have fewer cavities than if I use Brand Z.

Group F:

Which of the arguments in Group E do you suppose are deductive, inductive, or analogical? What reasons led you to your decisions?

Group G:

(1)   Write five sentences in which you use either the word 'logic' or 'logical' differently in each case. Then describe how you are using the word 'logic' or 'logical' in each of these sentences.

(2)   Write a short essay pointing out the difficulties in which someone might become involved if he said that logic is the study of how we think about things.

(3)   Carefully describe why we do not want to say merely that logic is the study of the forms of descriptive language.

(4)   Explain how you might use the distinctions denoted by the words 'use' and 'mention' in courses you have taken, or are taking, other than this course in logic.

(5)   Construct three deductive arguments, three inductive arguments, and three analogical arguments which are relevant to your special fields of interest.

2

Minding Our P's and Q's

We might think of deductive logic as a tall building, each floor resting on the one immediately below and at last coming to the ground level. Like such a building, logic is made up of many levels, each "higher" level using all the logical apparatus introduced at any "lower" level but also introducing new logical devices that cannot be explained solely in terms of old ones. In the previous chapter we laid the foundations on which to build the first floor of our edifice. Let us quickly review some of the more salient points.

'Logic' has been defined as 'the *a priori* study of the forms of descriptive language'. We are not interested in every language, in all the myriad uses of language, but only in statements. Statements are roughly denoted by saying that they may be expressed by speech-tokens and are either true or false, but not both. As logicians, we are not interested in any one particular descriptive language, such as English, to the exclusion of any other. The rules of logic are not justified by empirical appeals to particular descriptive languages. Particular descriptive languages, however, often suggest rules of logic to us. While we are not interested in the specific content of any particular statement, we are interested in its logical form, the general truth conditions which must be satisfied for statements to count as either true or false (but not both), and the ways statements can be formally related to one another in arguments. Of the three types of arguments discussed in the last chapter—deductive, inductive, and analogical—let us restate

23

that we shall study only deductive arguments. We shall study only those arguments which claim that *if* all the premises are true, *then* the conclusion must also be true. Again, deductive logic is our sole area of interest in this book.

1. THE TRUTH-FUNCTIONAL CALCULUS

The first level, the ground floor, of deductive logic is called the '*Truth-Functional Calculus*'. This tag might seem a bit foreboding to the beginner, but there is no reason for any misgivings. We do not want to let a name worry us! To understand better the types of statements we shall be studying in the Truth-Functional Calculus, consider these examples:

(1)   Rome is the capital of Italy, and Paris is the capital of France.

(2)   I'm going to visit David in New York or Milton in Boston.

(3)   If Stalin was a capitalist, then I'm a monkey's uncle.

(4)   The Tenasserim River doesn't flow north to the Andaman Sea.

As we all know, English grammar provides rules for classifying any sentence as either simple or compound, but not both. A simple sentence contains no independent clause as a component part, whereas a compound sentence does. All four of the examples above are compound sentences. Sentence (1) has two independent clauses: 'Rome is the capital of Italy' and 'Paris is the capital of France'. These independent clauses are joined together by the word 'and'. Sentence (2) also has two independent clauses: 'I'm going to visit David in New York' and 'I'm going to visit Milton in Boston'. Unlike (1), the independent clauses in (2) are joined together by 'or'. The independent clauses out of which (3) is compounded are 'Stalin was a capitalist' and 'I'm a monkey's uncle'. Sentence (4) is another way of expressing 'The following is not the case: The Tenasserim River flows north to the Andaman Sea'. In this case 'The Tenasserim River flows north to the Andaman Sea' is an independent clause.

Each of these four compound sentences expresses statements such that the truth-value of the statement expressed is determined entirely by the truth-values of its independent clauses, or clause, and the use of words such as 'and', 'either · · · or – – – ', 'if · · ·, then – – – ', and 'the following is not the case'. To clarify this claim, let us return to the examples. The *statement* 'Rome is the capital of Italy, and Paris is the capital of France' is true just when 'Rome is the capital of Italy' and 'Paris is the capital of France' are both true. If either one, or both, of these independent clauses were false, the entire compound statement 'Rome is the capital of Italy, and Paris is the capital of France' would also be false. On the other hand, 'I'm going to visit David in New York or Milton in Boston' would be false just when both 'I'm going to visit David in New York' and 'I'm going to visit Milton in Boston' are false. 'If Stalin was a capitalist, then I'm a monkey's uncle' is true except in that case in which 'Stalin was a capitalist' is true while 'I'm a monkey's uncle' is false. And 'The Tenasserim River does not flow north to the Andaman Sea' is true only if 'The Tenasserim River flows north to the Andaman Sea' is false. Thus, *the truth or falsity of any one of these compound statements depends on the truth or falsity of the independent clauses from which the compound statement is built.* This notion can be put into more technical jargon by saying that the truth-value of these compound statements is a function of the truth-value of their independent clauses and that we can calculate the possible truth-value of these compound statements by giving the possible truth-values of the independent clauses. In general we may say now that

> *the Truth-Functional Calculus is a logical study of those statements whose truth-values are determined by the truth-values of their component parts.*

We must also notice that a simple statement is in a sense its own independent clause and is automatically either true or false, but not both. This is to say, a simple statement is purely truth-functional.

There are some compound statements which are not truth-functional, however:

(5)   I believe Rome is the capital of Italy.

(6)   I hope to visit David in New York.

(7)   I think the Tenasserim River flows south to the Andaman Sea.

What if 'Rome is the capital of Italy' is true? Does this determine the truth of 'I believe Rome is the capital of Italy'? No, for beliefs are often mistaken. What if I do hope to visit David in New York? Does it follow from this that I actually shall? Certainly not! And similar remarks can be made about (7). For surely thinking something to be the case does not make it so. There are examples of compound statements which are not truth-functional. The truth-values of these statements are not functions of the truth-values of their independent clauses.

There are other examples of compound statements which, strictly speaking, are not truth-functional. For example,

(8)   Achilles slew Hector and dragged him around the walls of ancient Troy.

(9)   If I pour water into sulfuric acid, there will be an explosion.

The truth-value of (8) does not depend *solely* on the truth-values of its independent clauses, as is the case in (1). Statement (8) suggests a temporal relation between the slaying of Hector and the sorry spectacle outside the city walls. The 'and' in (8) is to be read 'and then'. In a word, (8) could not be asserted in the following way and still retain its same truth-value:

(10)   Achilles dragged Hector around the walls of ancient Troy and slew him.

On the other hand we could express (1) in the following manner without changing its truth-value:

(11) Paris is the capital of France, and Rome is the capital of Italy.

Further, (9) not only suggests the temporal priority of my pouring water into sulfuric acid, followed by an explosion, but it also suggests that my pouring water into sulfuric acid is a causal factor of the explosion. The truth-value of (9) is not retained by the statement

(12) If there will be an explosion, then I pour water into sulfuric acid.

In a purely truth-functional statement, such relations as temporal or causal ones are not found. *In a purely truth-functional statement, the truth-value of that statement is determined solely by the truth-values of its component parts.*

'But isn't it the case that many statements *do* assert temporal and causal relations?' someone might ask. 'And isn't it also the case that these statements are more important in carrying out our daily affairs and in studying specialized areas of knowledge than purely truth-functional statements?'

Undoubtedly both of these questions may be answered affirmatively. We do want to realize, however, that statements like (8) and (9) have a truth-functional element. For example, (8) could not be counted as a true statement unless the statements 'Achilles slew Hector' and 'Achilles dragged Hector around the walls of ancient Troy' were both true, no matter what temporal relation is also being suggested by the entire compound statement. And similar comments may be made, as we shall see presently, in relation to (9). Many statements are not purely truth-functional, but many of these very same statements enjoy a truth-functional element. For the present we shall make it our business *to study only this truth-functional element.* Furthermore, for the time being, we shall study deductive arguments from a truth-functional point of view. Rules will be established guaranteeing that if some statements, or a statement, are truth-functionally true, then any further statement deduced in accordance with these rules must also be truth-functionally true. Such rules can be developed without considering temporal or causal relations, and so for our present purposes we shall ignore these relations.

EXERCISES

Which of the following statements would you say are purely truth-functional and which not? For those statements you claim are not purely truth-functional, give your reasons.

(1) It's going to rain or snow.

(2) If John doesn't come, Bill will leave.

(3) Wine is a mocker and strong drink a maker of fools.

(4)   Bedloe's Island is in New York Bay.

(5)   The lab will blow up if the experimenters are careless.

(6)   Either individuals will all learn to live with one another or we shall not live at all.

(7)   That stocks fall off is a necessary condition for a financial recession.

(8)   Military production is going to increase, and, therefore, the supply of consumer goods will be curtailed.

(9)   Either we build up our military strength to protect our national interests or we shall have to fight an all-out war.

(10)   Xanthippe was the overbearing wife of Socrates.

(11)   Mrs. Jordan was asleep at the wheel when she collided with another car.

(12)   Either the oxygen in the tube combined with the filament to form an oxide or else it completely vanished.

(13)   The thoughts of the diligent tend only to plenteousness, but of everyone that is hasty only to want.

(14)   I'm going to San Francisco and Los Angeles next summer.

(15)   David is going perforce to join the Air National Guard or the Navy.

(16)   If frozen plasma is slowly thawed, a rich residue of antihemophilic globulin remains.

(17)   Solving the complex problems of space travel is a massive and expensive undertaking.

(18)   If the distance between two electrical charges is doubled, the force between them is decreased to one-quarter its original value.

(19)   The motion of an electron or of any other particle is associated with a wave motion or wave length.

(20)   Protons have energy, momentum, and wave length; moreover, so do matter particles.

(21)   The axiomatic approach to algebra yields many unexpected theorems while also contributing powerful tools necessary in topology, integration theory, and theory of numbers.

(22)   Unless the Kinsey Reports are read seriously by our lawmakers, many now existing laws will not be modified or abrogated completely.

(23)   C. L. Hull holds that behavior at any given time is always the result of some stimulation at an instantly preceding moment.

(24)   If a given society is to maintain its structural cohesion, there must be conformity among the members of that society; but if a society is not to lapse into a mediorce existence, it must protect and encourage the nonconformist.

(25)   If we know a man's anatomy and physiology in great detail and also the way in which the environment acts on detailed structures, then we should be able to explain why, under certain conditions, a man behaved the way he did.

2. ATOMIC AND MOLECULAR STATEMENTS

Logicians often refer to *atomic* and *molecular* statements instead of simple and compound ones, and we shall also follow this practice.

There are good reasons for speaking of statements as either atomic or molecular. *First*, to distinguish between atomic and molecular statements, instead of simple and compound ones, will help remind us that we are not concerned with English grammar, or descriptive linguistics, as such. We are engaged in an *a priori* study, not an empirical one. *Second*, we shall understand the concepts of atomic and molecular to refer to truth-functional statements, or those aspects of statements which are truth-functional. *Third*, as understood by logicians, the notions of atomic and molecular statements are relative ones, there being no absolute atomic statements. On the other hand, according to the rules of English grammar, there are absolute simple sentences. For example, consider the following, which appeared in the previous Exercise:

(1) If a given society is to maintain its structural cohesion, there must be conformity among the members of that society; but if a society is not to lapse into a mediocre existence, it must protect and encourage the nonconformist.

If we were asked to write the simple sentences from which (1) is built, English grammar would dictate that we proceed in this way:

(2) A given society is to maintain its structural cohesion.

(3) There must be conformity among the members of that society.

(4) A society is not to lapse into a mediocre existence.

(5) A society must protect and encourage the nonconformist.

Are we finished? Have we disjointed (1) into its most simple sentences? No, for (4) and (5) still contain independent clauses. From (4) we must extract

(6) A society is to lapse into a mediocre existence.

and (5) is compounded out of these:

(7) A society must protect the nonconformist.

(8) A society must encourage the nonconformist.

Now we are finished. Sentences (2), (3), (6), (7), and (8) represent the absolute simple sentences from which the compound sentence, (1), is constructed. Yet, for purposes of a particular *logical* analysis, we might want to say that (1) is constructed from only two parts; namely,

(9)   If a given society is to maintain its structural cohesion, there must be con-
          formity among the members of that society.

(10)   If a society is not to lapse into a mediocre existence, it must protect and encour-
          age the nonconformist.

It is quite possible that in relation to some particular case, or for some particular
purpose, a logician would say that (9) and (10) are atomic statements.

> *What statements are to count as atomic or molecular depends upon the*
> *immediate purposes or goals we wish to accomplish and the rules we have*
> *to accomplish these goals.*

Furthermore, a sentence which is simple from the point of view of English
grammar might be interpreted as expressing a statement which is molecular for
purposes of logical analysis. The statement 'Dave came into the room' might be
analyzed as 'Dave's head came into the room, and Dave's neck came into the
room, and Dave's torso came into the room, and Dave's arms came into the room,
and . . . '. Once again the immediate purposes or goals we wish to accomplish by
our logical analysis are relevant.

For the reasons above we shall adopt the terms 'atomic' and 'molecular' rather
than 'simple' and 'compound'. As a matter of practice, however, in many instances
of logical analysis a particular sentence will be simple from the point of view of
English grammar as well as expressing a statement which is atomic from the stance
of logic. Nevertheless, we shall draw a theoretical boundary between the simple-
compound distinction and the atomic-molecular, using the first when we wish to
talk in terms of English grammar and the second when we wish to talk in terms
of logic.

Our discussion of atomic and molecular statements reinforces remarks found
on page 7, Chapter 1. There we said that

> *the form of anything is the way, or ways, in which the elements of that thing*
> *are arranged for a particular purpose.*

Like the notions of atomic and molecular statements, the concept of the logical
form of a statement cannot be meaningfully discussed outside some concrete
context. In fact, from a logical point of view, we cannot speak of *the* form of a
particular statement unless we lay down some convention governing what we mean
by '*the* form'. We can no more say what *the* logical form of 'If Vance reads *Ushant*,
he is a student of Conrad Aiken' is than we can say whether the statement is atomic
or molecular. Such questions can be resolved only in some concrete context, for
a particular purpose.

Group A:

Consider the following statements as atomic:

Tony is coming.

Jane is happy.

The weather is warm.

The party is called off.

Now using

not

and

either $\cdots$ or $---$

if $\cdots$, then $---$

and the four atomic statements, construct at least fifteen different molecular statements.

Examples: a) Tony is coming and Jane is happy.

b) If either the weather is warm or the party is not called off, then Tony is coming and Jane is happy.

Group B:

In the previous set of exercises on page 26, analyze all the even-numbered compound sentences into the simple sentences from which they are constructed.

3. *STATEMENT VARIABLES AND LOGICAL CONSTANTS*

Having defined 'logic' as 'the *a priori* study of the forms of descriptive language', we suggested that it would be necessary to develop a way of isolating these forms. The first step in doing this is to introduce the concepts of *variables* and *constants*.

The uses of variables and constants should be quite familiar to anyone who has taken a course in, say, elementary algebra or geometry. For example, you probably remember this algebraic formula:

(1) $\qquad (a \times b) = (b \times a)$

This is a law of commutation. Example (1) shows us that the arrangement of any two numbers does not affect the product of these two numbers. In (1), 'a' and 'b' are numerical variables. They serve the purpose of space holders, or blank spots, which may be filled by any number we please. The only restriction is that the same number is to be asserted at each occurrence of the same numerical variable. Following this restriction, we can easily obtain

(2) $(1 \times 2) = (2 \times 1)$

(3) $(\frac{1}{4} \times \frac{1}{2}) = (\frac{1}{2} \times \frac{1}{4})$

(4) $(-3 \times 4) = (4 \times -3)$

(5) $(2 \times \sqrt{4}) = (\sqrt{4} \times 2)$

Statements (2)–(5) are *replacement values* or *instances* of (1). Each of the examples replaces the variables in (1) by some definite number. Each may be said to have the same form depicted by (1); that is, each of the examples is an instance of the form depicted by (1).

Referring to the type of thing which may be substituted for a variable as '*the range*' of the variable, and the particular thing which is substituted for the variable as '*the value*' of that variable, we may say

a variable is some sign having a range but whose value may change in different contexts of use.

Thus, in (1), 'a' is a variable whose range is numbers. The *value* of 'a', however, is different in each example, (2)–(5).

It should be understood quite clearly that (1) serves the function of a *picture*. (1) pictures, or displays, an algebraic form common to examples (2)–(5). And there is an indefinitely large number of further numerical statements we could write, all being instances of the same algebraic formula. We can picture a form common to all these numerical statements because we make use of numerical variables.

In logic we also use variables. But none of these variables will be replaced by numbers. *Statement variables* are the first type of variables we shall use. The range of these variables, that is, the things that may replace them, are statements. Let us arbitrarily select the lowercase letters 'p', 'q', 'r', and 's' as our statement variables.

A very important formula we shall use in our study of logic is

(6)   not p

Here, 'p' represents any statement we please, and 'not p' represents the denial of that statement. All the following statements may be viewed as instances of the statement form 'not p'.

(7)   The atomic number of sulfur is not 18.

(8)   It is unwise to allow a great deal of freedom to newly emerging nations.

(9)   The KKK is nonrepresentative of a large segment of the South.

(10)   Joan is incapable of deep affection.

Using the phrase 'The following is not the case', the four examples above can be reexpressed.

(11)   The following is not the case: The atomic number of sulfur is 18.

(12)   The following is not the case: It is wise to allow a great deal of freedom to newly emerging nations.

(13)   The following is not the case: The KKK is representative of a large segment of the South.

(14)   The following is not the case: Joan is capable of deep affection.

In each case, let the statement on the right-hand side of the colon be replaced by 'p', and let the phrase 'The following is not the case' be shortened to 'not'. Then we quite literally see how all these examples may be read as instances of the same molecular statement form

$$\text{not } p$$

Just as we replaced the 'a' and 'b' in (1) by various numbers, so we can replace the 'p' in (6) by various statements. Also like (1), 'not p' pictures a form, or structure. Here, *it is very important that we distinguish statements and statement forms.* We shall say that

> *a statement form always contains at least one variable of some sort; a statement contains no variables.*

Because statement forms contain at least one variable, at least one blank spot, it makes no sense to say that they are either true or false; however, statements are said to be either true or false, but not both. But, statement forms can be turned into statements when *all* the variables in the statement form are replaced by their proper values, namely, in the Truth-Functional Calculus, *statements.* And this is just what we did in (7)–(10) in relation to 'not p'.

Remember that 'p', 'q', 'r', and 's' are *statement* variables, which may be replaced by any statement we please. In that 'p', 'q', 'r', and 's' are statement *variables*, their values—just which statements we do replace at these variables— may change in different contexts.

Let us now turn our attention to the concept of a constant. Roughly,

> *a constant is a sign which has a fixed specific meaning.*

There are several types of constants we wish to distinguish. Consider the following algebraic example:

(15) $(2 + \sqrt{a}) = (\sqrt{a} + 2)$

While 'a' in (15) is a numerical variable, all the other signs are various types of constants—signs which have a fixed specific meaning. In general we may distinguish between algebraic and nonalgebraic constants. By 'algebraic constant' we mean 'a sign indicating a set of rules to be used': by 'nonalgebraic constant' we understand 'a sign which has some determinate referent'. We may also suggest that algebraic constants are used to express the algebraic form of, say, (15), whereas nonalgebraic constants are used to express the content of such expressions. Characterizing algebraic and nonalgebraic constants in this fashion, we say that '(', ')', '$\sqrt{}$', '+', and '=' are algebraic constants, while '2' is nonalgebraic. Furthermore, we may distinguish three different types of algebraic constants. *First*, there are *constants of punctuation* which are used to group elements in an algebraic expression. The signs '(' and ')' are examples of constants of punctuation. *Second*, we may notice *algebraic operators* which while they are algebraic constants, are not constants of punctuation. The sign '$\sqrt{}$' is an algebraic operator indicating a set of rules which may be used on any number it governs. *Third*, there are the signs '+' and '='. These are also algebraic constants, but they differ from algebraic operators because they must be flanked on both their left- and right-hand sides by complete algebraic expressions. These signs resemble algebraic operators in that they also indicate a set of rules to be used. Such constants as these are *algebraic connectives*. Thus, all algebraic connectives are operators, but not all operators are connectives.

In logic we shall make a distinction between logical and nonlogical constants which is analogous to algebraic and nonalgebraic constants. Also, following the suggestions of (15), we shall distinguish among constants of punctuation, logical operators, and logical connectives as different types of logical constants. Notice that logical constants in no way determine the specific content of any statement, for they have no referents. Rather, logical constants are closely connected with expressing the logical form of a statement.

4. TRUTH-FUNCTIONAL DENIAL

The first logical constant we shall introduce is a logical operator but not a logical connective. The concept of denial holds a central place in descriptive language. In English we often express denial by inserting 'not' into the statement we wish to deny. For instance, the statement

(1)   The role of oxygen in burning, rusting, and respiration was *not* understood before this substance had been prepared in a relatively pure state.

is the denial of

(2)   The role of oxygen in burning, rusting, and respiration was understood before this substance had been prepared in a relatively pure state.

From the point of view of the truth-values of (1) and (2), when one is true, the other is false.

Letting '*p*' represent any statement we wish, the logical form of truth-functional denial may be expressed as

(3) $\sim p$

The logical constant '$\sim$' is called '*tilde*' and is nothing more than a modified 'N' (for '*nein*' or 'not'.)

It is very important to distinguish between a statement which may be represented as '$\sim A$' and a statement form such as '$\sim p$'. Let us roughly characterize a *statement form as always using at least one variable* (of some sort or another), *whereas no variables* (of any sort) *are used in a statement*.

Since only statements have a truth-value—are true or false—strictly speaking, we can never speak of the truth-value of any statement form, for variables do not have a truth-value. Yet, because any statement may be substituted for a given statement variable and because any statement is either true or false, we may speak *as if* a statement variable itself were true or false. We shall often employ this "as if" manner of speaking not only in this chapter but also in subsequent ones. Hence, we shall speak as if '*p*', a statement variable, were true or false.

Consider the statement '$\sim A$' and the statement form '$\sim p$'. Because '$\sim A$' may be considered an instance of either '*p*' or '$\sim p$', it is misleading to suggest that '$\sim A$' is either an atomic or molecular statement is any absolute sense of 'atomic statement' and 'molecular statement'. We shall speak of atomic statement forms and molecular statement forms in an absolute sense, however. *An atomic statement form will always be depicted by some single variable*, such as '*p*', '*q*', '*r*', or '*s*'; whereas a *molecular statement form is always depicted by at least one variable coupled with at least one logical operator*, such as '$\sim p$'.

'$\sim p$' is a molecular statement form in which the tilde, '$\sim$', is always used in accordance with this rule:

> **Given any statement '*p*', if '*p*' is true, '$\sim p$' is false; but if '*p*' is false, '$\sim p$' is true.**

This rule, and only this rule, determines how we shall use the tilde in our symbolism.

It is possible to construct a table, or matrix, which corresponds to the rule governing the use of the tilde. Letting '*p*' stand for any statement, '1' for 'is true', and '0' for 'is false', we may write

$$p$$

$$1$$

$$0$$

But, our rule concerning '$\sim p$' tells us that if 'p' is true, '$\sim p$' is false. So we draw

$$
\begin{array}{ccc}
p & & \sim p \\
1 & \rightarrow & 0 \\
0 & &
\end{array}
$$

Further, we also know that if 'p' is false, '$\sim p$' is true; or

$$
\begin{array}{ccc}
p & & \sim p \\
1 & \rightarrow & 0 \\
0 & \rightarrow & 1
\end{array}
$$

A more common way of writing the table above is

(4)

p	$\sim p$
1	0
0	1

Truth-Table I

Example (4) is called a '*truth-table*'. This particular truth-table quite literally *shows* us the conditions under which any statement interpreted as having the form '$\sim p$' is true and the conditions under which such a statement is false.

We have already mentioned in the previous section that there is more than one way in English to express the concept of denial.

(5)   He is unsystematic in his work.

(6)   She is incapable of grasping what you are saying.

(7)   The board of trustees was noncommittal in its report on recent student uprisings.

On the other hand, 'not' sometimes appears in phrases which need not suggest denial. Here are some examples:

(8)   Not only are we going to dinner, we are also going to the theater.

(9)   Not only will he be promoted in rank, but further he will receive a substantial salary increase.

(10)   Bo is not coming unless John brings the refreshments.

The moral to be learned from these examples is this: We cannot rely on the appearance, or nonappearance, of the word 'not' to indicate that a statement is being denied. *What is always required is a careful and sensitive reading in order to grasp what is being asserted.* And this advice should be heeded whenever we read, write, or speak—whether we are actually engaged in a study of logic or not!

Suppose we wished to use the tilde to express the statement 'The atomic number of sulfur is not 18'. We might write

(11)   ~ the atomic number of sulfur is 18.

Here, '~' is read 'The following is not the case', as in (11) of Section 3. It would be a waste of time and energy to write out 'The atomic number of sulfur is 18' all the time. Therefore, let us be a bit lazy and introduce a shorthand notation. Instead of writing out 'The atomic number of sulfur is 18', let us arbitrarily select and write '*N*'. This is certainly much simpler than writing the full statement! Now, the capital letter '*N*' functions as an initial of the statement being denied by the tilde in (11). This convention is very much like signing a note with an initial rather than writing out our full name. Such capital letters in the Truth-Functional Calculus may be viewed as nonlogical constants for a particular example. In order to save ourselves time and energy, let us say that whenever we symbolize statements, we shall adopt the convention of using capital letters as initials of statements.

Now (11) is symbolized as

$$\sim N$$

And what are the truth-conditions of '$\sim N$'? To ask this question is to ask for the conditions under which '$\sim p$' is true and the conditions under which it is false. The question is straightforwardly answered by the following truth-table:

(12)

N	$\sim N$
1	0
0	1

This truth-table shows us that when '*N*' is true, '$\sim N$' is false; however, when '*N*' is false, '$\sim N$' is true.

EXERCISES

Group A:

Why do you suppose the tilde is a logical operator, yet not a logical connective?

Group B:

Turn back to (8)–(10) of Section 3. Letting '*F*' stand for 'It is wise to allow a great deal of freedom to newly emerging nations', '*K*' for 'The KKK is representative of a large segment of the South', and '*J*' for 'Joan is capable of deep affection', symbolize (8)–(10) with the use of the tilde.

Group C:

Using the suggested notation following each of the statements below, translate them into truth-functional symbolism.

Example: She never *w*orks on Sunday. (*W*)

$$\sim W$$

(1) Many *p*sychologists are not interested in theory construction. (*P*)

(2) It is well-nigh impossible to approach observed *d*ata without a theory of some sort. (*D*)

(3) The danger of reading one's *p*rejudices into observed data cannot be avoided by refusing to theorize. (*P*)

(4) Deductive *l*ogic does not provide a method for establishing the empirical truth of premises. (*L*)

(5) *L*ogic is unconcerned with how we actually think about things. (*L*)

(6) The principle of the steady increase of military *p*ower as a deterrent to war is never sound. (*P*)

(7) Nguyen Cao *K*y was not pleased with Henry Cabot Lodge's appointment as ambassador. (*K*)

(8) Communistic *g*overnments are often insincere in their political promises. (*G*)

(9) It is fallacious to suppose any one *g*overnment is equally well suited for every people. (*G*)

(10) Economics and political *p*ower are inseparable. (*P*)

Group D:

Using (4) and (12) of this section as your models, construct a truth-table for each of the statements in Group B.

5. *TRUTH-FUNCTIONAL CONJUNCTION*

In Section 4 we introduced a logical operator, that is, a sign indicating a set of rules which will allow certain moves to be made with the statement variables, or statements, coupled with the sign in question. The tilde is not a logical connective because it does not serve to join together two or more statement variables or statements. Another way of saying this is that the tilde is always flanked on its right-hand side by a statement form, or statement; it is never flanked on its left-hand side by either a statement form or statement. Our next logical constant, however, is a logical connective. It must always be flanked on both its left- and right-hand sides by either statement forms or statements.

We have already seen that the concept of *conjunction* is unclear.

(1)   Ramon Lull (1232–1315) used a mechanical device for operating a logical system *and* attempted to use geometrical diagrams for establishing the truth of nonnumerical statements.

(2)   Achilles slew Hector *and* dragged him around the walls of ancient Troy.

(3)   I poured water into sulfuric acid, *and* there was an explosion.

Statement (1) represents a straightforward truth-functional use of 'and'. Statement (2) indicates a temporal relation, and (3) suggests both a temporal and causal relation. Of course we shall be interested only in truth-functional conjunctions or those elements of conjunctive statements which are truth-functional.

We shall adopt the *dot* in our symbolization to indicate the notion of truth-functional conjunction. Thus, (1)–(3) may be symbolized as

$$D \cdot G$$
$$A \cdot T$$
$$W \cdot E$$

and, in general, the truth-functional conjunction is pictured by the *molecular statement form*

(4) $p \cdot q$

Further, the rule determing the use of truth-functional conjunction is

> **Given any statements 'p' and 'q', then 'p·q' is true if, and only if, both 'p' and 'q' are true. In all other cases, 'p·q' is false.**

This rule, and only this rule, determines what we mean by 'truth-functional conjunction', and how the dot is used in our notation.

As with the tilde, it is also possible to construct a truth-table corresponding to the rule governing '$p \cdot q$'. If 'p' is true, it is obvious that 'q' may be either true or false, but not both. And if 'p' is false, 'q' may be either true or false, but not both. Again, let '1' stand for 'is true' and let '0' stand for 'is false'. Then we may draw

$$
\begin{array}{cc}
p & q \\
& 1 \\
1 \Big< & \\
& 0 \\
& 1 \\
0 \Big< & \\
& 0
\end{array}
$$

But '$p \cdot q$' is true only when *both* 'p' and 'q' are true.

$$
\begin{array}{ccc}
p & q & p \cdot q \\
\end{array}
$$

1 $\big<$ 1 $\longrightarrow$ 1
        0 $\longrightarrow$ 0

0 $\big<$ 1 $\longrightarrow$ 0
        0 $\longrightarrow$ 0

A more common way of representing the above is

(5)

p	q	$p \cdot q$
1	1	1
1	0	0
0	1	0
0	0	0

Truth-Table II

A word of warning concerning 'and' is in order. While 'and' is often used to indicate conjunction, it also has other uses.

(6)   Peaches and cream are excellent for breakfast.

(7)   John and David are pals.

In (6) 'and' is used to form the compound subject of the statement. It would be incorrect to read (6) as 'Peaches are excellent for breakfast, and cream is excellent for breakfast'. What is excellent for breakfast is the combination of peaches and cream. On the other hand the use of 'and' in (7) indicates a relation holding between John and David. It would be incorrect to read (7) as 'John is a pal, and David is a pal'. Therefore, we must not suppose that an occurrence of 'and' is a guarantee that conjunction is being suggested.

Furthermore, other terms besides 'and' often are used to indicate a conjunction. *Examine the following list very carefully*:

(8)   a) p and q
       b) p and then q
       c) p, albeit q
       d) p although q
       e) p as well as q
       f) p at the same time that q
       g) p but q
       h) p, but also q
       i) p, but so is q
       j) p despite the fact that q

    k)   *p* even though *q*
    l)   not only *p*, but also *q*
    m)   not only *p*, but further *q*
    n)   not only *p*, but *q* as well
    o)   *p*; further *q*
    p)   *p*; however, *q*
    q)   *p*; in addition *q*
    r)   *p* in spite of *q*
    s)   *p*; moreover *q*
    t)   *p*; nevertheless *q*
    u)   *p* regardless of *q*
    v)   *p*, still *q*
    w)   *p* when *q*
    x)   *p*, whereas *q*
    y)   *p*, while *q*
    z)   *p*, yet *q*

Although this list does not claim to exhaust the various expressions indicating conjunction, it does suggest the many ways we can express the concept of conjunction. Nor is it the case that every word or phrase in this list is used only to express conjunction. Nevertheless, this list of expressions should prove helpful in indicating how a conjunction may be expressed.

    Certainly, in our conversation and writing, it very often does make a difference just how we express a conjunction. There is an important difference indicated in each of these:

(9)   She loves me, and she also loves my brother.

(10)   She loves me; nevertheless she also loves my brother.

(11)   She loves me despite the fact that she also loves my brother.

But, no matter what else is being suggested by (9)–(11), this much is: If each is to count as true, then 'She loves me' and 'She also loves my brother' must both be true. No matter what else is involved in these three conjunctions, they must at least satisfy the condition of a *truth-functional* conjunction if they are to be counted as true. Of course these remarks also hold for (2) and (3) of the present section. As (2) and (3) were both translated into truth-functional conjunctions,

(12) $A \cdot T$

(13) $W \cdot E$

so we might also translate (9)–(11) as

(14) $M \cdot B$

    What are the truth-functional conditions under which (12), (13), and (14) would be true? What are the conditions under which they would be false? To answer this question, we may construct a truth-table for each of them based on Truth-Table II.

A	T	$A \cdot T$	W	E	$W \cdot E$	M	B	$M \cdot B$
1	1	1	1	1	1	1	1	1
1	0	0	1	0	0	1	0	0
0	1	0	0	1	0	0	1	0
0	0	0	0	0	0	0	0	0

EXERCISES

Group A:

Write out at least one complete statement for each of the expressions in (8) above.

Group B:

Using the suggested notation at the end of each of the following statements, translate them into truth-functional symbolism. Be certain to observe denial by using the tilde.

Example: John isn't going to the fair, but Mary will be there. (J, M)

$$\sim J \cdot M$$

(1)   Many religious fanatics preach universal love, although they certainly do not love members of religious organizations other than their own. (F, O)

(2)   Birth control continues to be a religious issue regardless of the fact that recent scientific findings are often at variance with the beliefs of religious groups. (C, F)

(3)   Not only is the whale air-breathing, but it is viviparous as well. (A, V)

(4)   It is not necessary to give up Newtonian mechanics even though we accept quantum theory. (M, T)

(5)   The government declared war in spite of the fact that it did not want to do so. (G, W)

(6)   Most of the President's legislation was passed; nevertheless, it met strong opposition from some quarters. (L, O)

(7)   Barry Goldwater lost the presidential election; yet he was still a powerful figure in the Republican Party. (G, R)

(8)   The nuclear fallout rate is not so high as it once was; this is attributed to the moritorium on testing. (R, M)

(9)   Government funds have often been distributed in an unequitable way among

institutions of higher learning, but of course Washington does not admit this. (*F, W*)

(10) At one time the center of American intellectual life was the Northeast; however, the center now seems to be moving to the West (*N, W*)

(11) Jones is not listed in *Who's Who in America,* but neither is Smith. (*J, S*)

(12) We are witnessing the definitive triumph of regionalism—the adoption of regional equalization as an undisputed national goal; at the same time we are witnessing the death of regionalism as the political expression of a way of life. (*R, D*)

(13) In a binary number system we may find '1 + 1 = 1', while '1 × 0 = 0' may also be a part of the system. (*B, S*)

(14) Any body may be electrically charged under proper conditions, but not every body seems to have very strong magnetic properties. (*C, P*)

(15) The volume of a gas is inversely proportional to the pressure—the temperature of the gas remaining constant; furthermore, the pressure of a gas is proportional to the average kinetic energy of its molecules. (*V, P*)

(16) C. L. Hull proposed his original derivation of reasoning in 1935 and then repeated the proofs in 1952. (*D, P*)

(17) Within the last decade or so, social psychology has increased the quality of its research in addition to the quantity of articles put out by researchers in the field. (*R, A*)

(18) Not only does theory serve as a tool in scientific investigation but also as a goal in its own right. (*T, G*)

(19) While theory construction is often seen as a goal in its own right, still it must be related to empirical research. (*C, R*)

(20) Not only must the scientist carefully observe various data, he must further construct theories whereby his observations can be organized into a body of knowledge. (*D, T*)

Group C:

Using Truth-Table II as a model, construct truth-tables for (2), (3), (6), (10), (12), (13), (15), (16), (18), and (20) in Group B.

6. *TRUTH-FUNCTIONAL DISJUNCTION*

So far in our study of the Truth-Functional Calculus we have become acquainted with two logical constants used in formulating truth-functional statements—the *tilde* and the *dot.* We have also seen that the tilde is a logical operator, whereas the dot is a logical connective. There are other types of statements besides denials and conjunctions, statements which use logical constants other than the tilde and dot. The *disjunctive statement* is an example. In English we find regularly the phrase 'either . . . or – – –' used to denote a disjunctive statement. A few examples of disjunctive statements are

(1) According to Werner Heisenberg, we know either the position of a subatomic particle or its velocity.

(2) Dottie will be at Carrs Hill Plantation or Recording for the Blind.

(3) I'm going to dine with Irene or go to the concert.

(4) Either you give me the money or I'll tell the whole nasty story.

Each of these four statements makes use of the phrase 'either $\cdots$ or – – –', although 'either' is not explicitly written in the second and third examples. Using statement initials, we may begin to isolate logical forms of (1)–(4).

(5) Either P or V

(6) Either P or B

(7) Either I or C

(8) Either M or S

Using statement variables in place of statement initials, let us write

(9) Either p or q

Of course (9) is not itself a statement, but it *pictures* a form of an indefinitely large number of statements. We must be on our guard, however, for 'Either p or q' may be interpreted in two distinct ways.

Read carefully (1) and (2). The first example asserts that the position of a subatomic particle can be known or the velocity of the particle can be known, but both its position and velocity cannot be known under exactly the same circumstances. The second example states thet Dottie will be either at Carrs Hill or Recording for the Blind. Now, if we know that Carrs Hill and the location for Recording for the Blind are several miles apart, we know (2) is *not* asserting that Dottie is in both places at once. Rather, the second example tells us that Dottie is at one place or the other, *but not both*. Statement (3), on the other hand, is rather unlike (1) and (2). The third example asserts either that I am going to dine with Irene or that I am going to the concert; and if I am fortunate, I *may do both*. It may be that Irene and I dine together and then both of us go to the concert. And the last example? This smacks of blackmail! The blackmailer is telling his hapless victim either to hand over the money or the whole mess will be brought into the open. The victim may optimistically believe that if he does turn over the money, the story will not be told and he will be spared. But, as we have seen, believing something does not make it so! In the present case the unfortunate victim is interpreting 'either p or q' in the sense of (1) and (2). The blackmailer has other intentions, however. He is going to collect the money and also sell the story to the local newspaper. Hence, the blackmailer is using 'either *p* or *q*' in the sense of (3). In sum there are two distinct truth-functional interpretations of 'either *p* or *q*':

(10)   Either *p* or *q*, and perhaps both

(11)   Either *p* or *q*, but not both.

Statement (10) is the *inclusive*, or weak, use of 'either *p* or *q*' because it includes the logical possibility of both the statements represented by '*p*' and '*q*' being true and 'either *p* or *q*' also being true. Statement (11) is the *exclusive*, or strong, use of 'either *p* or *q*' because it excludes the logical possibility of both the statement represented by '*p*' and '*q*' being true and 'either *p* or *q*' also being true.

In Latin we find inclusive disjunctive statements expressed by '*vel* ··· *vel* – – –' and exclusive disjunctive statements by '*aut* ··· *aut* – – –'. Using a '∨', from '*vel*', we shall symbolize the inclusive use of 'either *p* or *q*' by the *molecular statement form*

(12)   *p* ∨ *q*

The '∨' often is called '*wedge*'. And using a delta, '△' (which looks like the upper part of an 'A'), we shall symbolize the exclusive 'either *p* or *q*' by the *molecular statement form*

(13)   *p* △ *q*

It is obvious that '∨' and '△' are both logical connectives. They must be flanked on both their left-hand side (the left-hand disjunct) and their right-hand side (the right-hand disjunct) by statement forms or statements.

The rule governing the use of the inclusive disjunctive 'either *p* or *q*' is

> ***Given any statements 'p' and 'q', then any statement 'p ∨ q' is true if, and only if, at least one—AND PERHAPS BOTH—of its disjuncts is true.***

A truth-table may be constructed corresponding to this rule.

p	*q*	*p* ∨ *q*
1	1	1
1	0	1
0	1	1
0	0	0

Truth-Table III

This truth-table literally shows us that only when both the statements at '*p*' and '*q*' are false is '*p* ∨ *q*' also false.

On the other hand the exclusive use of 'either p or q' is governed by the rule

Given any statements 'p' and 'q', then any statement '$p \triangle q$' is true if, and only if, one—BUT NOT BOTH—of its disjuncts is true.

We may also construct a truth-table corresponding to the rule of exclusive disjunction.

p	q	$p \triangle q$
1	1	0
1	0	1
0	1	1
0	0	0

Truth-Table IV

Here, we see when the statements 'p' and 'q' are both false, '$p \triangle q$' is false; moreover, when the statements 'p' and 'q' are both true, '$p \triangle q$' is false.

In carefully worded business letters, legal briefs, wills, and the like, it is not uncommon to find such phrases as 'and/or' and 'but not both'. These phrases are frequently employed to distinguish the two uses of 'either p or q' when there may be some reasonable doubt about correct interpretation. We shall follow a simple practice. When it is not reasonably clear that 'either p or q' is to be understood in its exclusive use, we shall write, for example, 'but not both'. Ambiguous 'either p or q' statements which are to have an inclusive interpretation will be clarified by 'and/or', 'and perhaps both', or the like. And, finally, *if in doubt, always use the inclusive sense of 'either p or q'.*

EXERCISES

Group A:

Finish symbolizing (5)–(8) using 'V' and '$\triangle$'. Symbolize (8) first as an inclusive disjunctive statement and then as an exclusive one.

Group B:

Using the suggested statement initials at the end of each of the following statements, translate the statements into truth-functional notation. Be certain to observe any notion of denial by using the tilde.

Example: a) I'll go to the beach with you or to the mountains. (B, M)

$$B \lor M$$

b) Either you'll not be drafted by the Army or you'll certainly go into some other branch of the armed services, but not both. (A, S)

$$\sim A \triangle S$$

(1)   When I'm in New Orleans I always go to hear Al Hirt or Pete Fountain. (H, F)

(2)   Either William Shakespeare was not a literary fraud or someone else wrote the plays attributed to him. (F, P)

(3)   You must pass this course or make up your credit hours in some other way. (C, H)

(4)   Either young lovers are miserable or they do not stay at home, and perhaps both. (M, H)

(5)   Either dividends are paid on bonds or the production prices of consumer goods increase, but not both. (D, P)

(6)   We accept '$\Delta p \, \Delta q \geq h/4\pi$' or we do not study quantum mechanics (but not both). (A, S)

(7)   Either we accept quantum mechanics or we study objects larger than atomic size. (M, O)

(8)   The wave theory and/or the quantum theory of light is used in contemporary physics. (W, Q)

(9)   Either AB is an arc segment in Euclidean geometry or it is a line segment. (A, L)

(10)   Euclid's "parallel line" postulate holds or we do not accept Euclidean geometry. (P, G)

(11)   A man has a great deal of dynamic self-assertion or he is mentally healthy; and, if he is fortunate, both. (S, H)

(12)   Either a person is not mentally deficient or new avenues of behavior do not open themselves to him as he reconstructs the course of events surrounding him. (D, A)

(13)   A successful man is either intellectually creative and/or mentally dynamic. (C, D)

(14)   Human behavior is viewed as basically anticipatory rather than reactive or a man is environmentally controlled (but not both). (B, M)

(15)   A man is either mentally deficient or mentally healthy. (D, H)

(16)   Socrates was either an active seducer of the youth or not a very good philosopher. (S, P)

(17)   Immanuel Kant believed that he had to reject the philosophical position of David Hume or the truths of mathematics. (H, M)

(18)   Logical Positivists maintain that meaningful statements are either empirical or analytic, but not both. (E, A)

(19)   We must do away with narrow-minded Puritanism or accept an ethical absolutism imposed by a small vocal group. (P, A)

(20)   We shall have to modify our attitudes toward many activities of individuals or give up contemporary science as hocus-pocus. (A, S)

Group C:

Using Truth-Tables III and IV as models, construct a truth-table for each of the odd-numbered statements in Group B.

Group D:

Twelve of the statements in Group B do not make use of the term 'and/or', 'but not both', or some equivalent phrase. Therefore, why did you translate these statements as you did? You might want to discuss your reasons with your friends and/or in class.

7. CONSTANTS OF PUNCTUATION AND THE NOTION OF SCOPE

We must now consider constants of punctuation. Suppose someone were to tell us

(1)   We shall define 'heat' as either 'that phlogiston which causes a body to rise in temperature' or 'that form of energy which is exchanged between bodies because they are at different temperatures' and proceed with our experiments.

Well and good! But what are we to understand by (1), for as it stands is it not ambiguous? Sentence (1) may be interpreted either as having the form of an overall disjunction or of an overall conjunction. Of course the use of a comma would clarify matters.

(2)   We shall define 'heat' as either 'that phlogiston which causes a body to rise in temperature', or 'that form of energy which is exchanged between bodies because they are at different temperatures' and proceed with our experiments.

(3)   We shall define 'heat' as either 'that phlogiston which causes a body to rise in temperature' or 'that form of energy which is exchanged between bodies because they are at different temperatures', and proceed with our experiments.

Using statement variables, the overall truth-table picture of (2) may be expressed

p	q	$p \lor q$
1	1	1
1	0	1
0	1	1
0	0	0

but of (3)

p	q	$p \cdot q$
1	1	1
1	0	0
0	1	0
0	0	0

Comparing the truth-table of '$p \lor q$' with '$p \cdot q$', we see literally the different interpretations of (1):

$p \lor q$	$p \cdot q$
1	1
1	0
1	0
0	0

Also consider the following arithmetical example:

(4) $2 \times 3 + 4 = x$

There are two distinct values for 'x'. We might write '14' or '10', depending on how we interpret '$2 \times 3 + 4$', for we might understand (4) in either one of the following ways:

$$2 \times (3 + 4) = 14$$
$$(2 \times 3) + 4 = 10$$

Once again the ambiguity involved in the original example is dispelled by appropriate punctuation marks.

We also need constants of punctuation in our logical symbolism. The punctuation marks we shall use are *parentheses*, *brackets*, and *braces*. These constants will always be written in pairs. Thus, a left-hand parenthesis will *never* be written without a right-hand one. Furthermore, these constants of punctuation will be understood as having an order of strength. Parentheses will count as indicating a weaker break in a statement form or statement than brackets, and brackets a weaker break than braces. The idea of punctuation marks having an order of strength is also common in English grammar. We all know that the comma is the weakest of such marks, then the semicolon, followed by the colon, and finally the period. In fact, *in translating particular English sentences into our logical notation, we often find the grammatical punctuation marks of the sentences helpful in grouping elements in the logical notation.* Grammatical form may help suggest the appropriate logical form.

> *Our constants of punctuation are, therefore,*
>
> $$\{ \, [\, (\,) \,] \, \}$$
>
> *And if we ever need more punctuation marks, we shall simply start over again with parentheses.*
>
> $$\{ \, [\, (\, \{ \, [\, (\,) \,] \, \} \,) \,] \, \}$$

We are now in a position to clarify (1) by showing the distinct possible truth-functional interpretations it may have. We first simply replace 'or' by '$\vee$' and 'and' by '$\cdot$' and use statement initials in place of statements:

(5) $T \vee B \cdot E$

Using constants of punctuation, (5) may be written as either

(6) $T \vee (B \cdot E)$

or

(7) $(T \vee B) \cdot E$

As (5) stands without a specific context, we do not know whether (6) or (7) is intended. But, we have been able by means of constants of punctuation to render (5) unambiguous in two ways. And this is an important step toward clarity!

Constants of punctuation, in dispelling ambiguity, indicate the *scope* of a given logical operator or connective. The scope of an operator or connective may be roughly described as that part of a statement, or statement form, which falls under the control of the operator or connective. An example will be helpful. Consider the statement

(8)   Grant is not either coming or going.

Suppose we were asked to translate (8) into our logical notation. We might want to write

(9) $\sim C \vee G$

or, perhaps, even

(10) $\sim C \vee \sim G$

But let us be careful. What have we denied in (9) and (10)? In (9) we have denied only that Grant is coming. We have not denied that he is going. But (8) asserts both that Grant is not coming and he is not going. Consequently, (9) could not be a correct translation of (8). Then, too, (10) is not a correct translation of (8). Statement (10) asserts that Grant is not coming or he is not going, but he might do one or the other. Yet, (8) is denying both that Grant is coming and going. Statement (8) is denying the whole of 'Grant is either coming or going'. And this denial is symbolized as

(11) $\sim (C \vee G)$

Statement (11), by using parentheses, clearly shows that the entire statement 'Grant is either coming or going' is being denied. In more technical jargon we may say that 'Grant is either coming or going' falls under the scope of the tilde.

Concerning specifically the scope of the tilde, we shall introduce a few conventions.

> *The tilde shall operate over the smallest possible statement, or statement form, following it. This statement, or statement form, shall be indicated by parentheses, brackets, or braces. By convention, however, when the statement, or statement form, following the tilde employs no logical connectives, the punctuation marks will be omitted.*

Let us apply these conventions to several examples. Consider the statement

(12)   Symbolic logic is unfamiliar to Tony. (F)

Using 'F', we may translate (12) as

(13) $\sim F$

Suppose we denied (12):

(14)   Symbolic logic is not unfamiliar to Tony. (F)

We translate (14) as

(15) $\sim(\sim F)$

But, do we need the parentheses in (15)? No, for our conventions dealing with the scope of the tilde tell us when the statement following the tilde employs no logical connectives, the punctuation marks will be omitted. '$\sim F$' employs no logical connectives—only an operator. Therefore, by convention, (14) is correctly symbolized as

(16) $\sim\sim F$

Another example we may consider is

(17)   Neither logic nor mathematics is familiar to Tony. (L, M)

Since 'neither p nor q' may be translated as '$\sim(p \lor q)$', we render (17) as

(18) $\sim(L \lor M)$

Could we have written '$\sim L \lor M$' instead of '$\sim(L \lor M)$'? No, because the statement being denied, '$L \lor M$', uses a logical connective. Nor could (17) be translated as '$\sim L \lor \sim M$'. It must be noted that the tilde does *not* function like the minus sign in algebra. And in particular we can *never* "multiply through" any set of punctuation marks with the tilde.

Someone might also say

(19)   Neither is logic unfamiliar nor mathematics familiar to Tony. (*L, M*)

A correct way of translating (19) is

(20) $\sim(\sim L \vee M)$

It would not be correct to write '$\sim \sim L \vee M$', because '$\sim L \vee M$' makes use of a logical connective.

The notion of scope is also applicable to logical connectives. For example, the scope of the '$\vee$' is the statements, or statement forms, to its left- and right-hand sides. Exactly what these statements are in any particular case is indicated by appropriate punctuation marks. Thus, in (6) the scope of the '$\vee$' is '*T*' and '*B·E*'. In general, then,

> *a logical connective shall operate over the smallest statement, or statement form, flanking it on both its left- and right-hand sides. These statements, or statement forms, are indicated by constants of punctuation. By convention, however, when these statements, or statement forms, employ no logical connectives themselves, the punctuation marks will be omitted.*

EXERCISES

Using the suggested statement initials, translate each of the following statements into truth-functional notation.

Examples: a) It isn't the case that Jones both doesn't run for office and isn't elected. (*R, E*)

$$\sim(\sim R \cdot \sim E)$$

b) Either the litmus paper is put into an acid solution and doesn't turn red or the experiment is a failure. (*S, R, F*)

$$(S \cdot \sim R) \vee F$$

c) The given number can be factored into two odd numbers and yet also be a natural number, or we can assume the given numbers; however, the given number cannot be factored into two even numbers. (*O, N, E*)

$$[(O \cdot N) \vee E] \cdot \sim E$$

(1) Either John is not coming or he's going. (*C, G*)

(2) Either John is not coming or he's not going. (*C, G*)

(3) It is not the case that John either is coming or not going. (*C, G*)

(4) Neither is John not coming nor is he going. (*C, G*)

(5) People are not both altruistic and yet selfish. (*A, S*)

(6)   It isn't the case both that I don't know logic thoroughly albeit my knowledge of logic is not weak. (T, W)

(7)   It's not true both that I don't apply logic to my studies whereas I am able to do well with intricate problems. (S, P)

(8)   The following is not the case: The synodic month is the time interval between successive identical phases of the moon and also the time required for one rotation of the moon on its axis. (M, R)

(9)   It isn't the case both that acetic acid doesn't react with sodium whereas ethane does. (A, E)

(10) CH$_3$COOH is acetic acid, and it is neither a base nor a salt. (A, B, S)

(11) Either a planet is at its closest distance to the sun, or it is not at its perihelion and isn't moving as rapidly as when at its perihelion. (D, P, M)

(12) One revolution of the earth around the sun is a sidereal year but not a tropical year, while the interval between successive spring equinoxes is a tropical year. (S, T, E)

(13) We may either assume a geocentric cosmology when accepting the concept of epicycles, or assume a heliocentric cosmology, but not both. (G, E, H)

(14) Either a number is odd or even, or it isn't a natural number. (O, E, N)

(15) It isn't the case that a given number is odd and even or that it is not a natural number. (O, E, N)

(16) The following doesn't hold: A given number is both odd and even, and it is also a natural number. (O, E, N)

(17) People are both kind and altruistic, or they are selfish (but hardly both). (K, A, S)

(18) Either Joan doesn't smoke Home Runs and doesn't drink Colt 45, or she is quite healthy. (S, D, H)

(19) Neither does Joan smoke Home Runs nor drink Colt 45, or Joan is quite healthy. (S, D, H)

(20) The following isn't the case: Joan smokes Home Runs or drinks Colt 45, and she isn't healthy. (S, D, H)

(21) The following doesn't hold: It is not the case both that Joan doesn't smoke Home Runs and doesn't drink Colt 45, and further Joan isn't healthy. (S, D, H)

(22) Either I don't know logic thoroughly or I'm able to apply it to my studies; moreover, it is not the case both that my knowledge of logic is weak and I am able to do well with intricate problems. (T, S, W, P)

(23) Either theories are constructed in psychology, or neither experimental nor clinical psychologists are interested in this type of work or neither statistical nor quantitative measurement is satisfactory for representing psychological data. (T, E, C, S, Q)

(24) The following isn't the case: Theories aren't constructed in psychology; further, it isn't true that neither experimental nor clinical psychologists are interested in this type of work or that neither statistical nor quantitative measurement is satisfactory for representing psychological data. (*T, E, C, S, Q*)

(25) The following isn't true: Theories aren't constructed in psychology; moreover, it isn't true both that experimental or clinical psychologists are interested in this type of work and that statistical or quantitative measurement is satisfactory for representing psychological data. (*T, E, C, S, Q*)

8. *TRUTH-FUNCTIONAL HYPOTHETICALS*

Approaching logic as the *a priori* study of the forms of descriptive language, we have found it necessary to devise ways of isolating and discussing these forms. Thus far we have investigated truth-functional conjunction, truth-functional negation, and two types of truth-functional disjunction, namely inclusive and exclusive disjunctions. We must now consider another type of truth-functional statement—the *truth-functional hypothetical*, or conditional, statement.

Let us consider the following straightforward English examples:

(1)   If Heliotrope marries Andrew, then Andrew will be elated.

(2)   If Jones is a United States senator, then he is at least 30 years old.

(3)   If the statement 'It is either going to rain or snow and we know that it isn't going to rain' is true, then the statement 'It is going to snow' is also true.

(4)   If the moon is made of green cheese, then I'm a monkey's uncle.

In an obvious way each of these examples differs from the others. They each mention some different state of affairs; each has a different content. But, is there some element which (1)–(4) all share? To answer this question, we must start with a few rather basic observations. First, each of the examples uses the phrase 'If · · ·, then – – –'. They all express hypothetical statements. Second, in each case a complete statement follows both the term 'If' and the term 'then'. The statement following 'If' is the *antecedent* of the overall hypothetical statement, and the statement following 'then' is the *consequent*. The antecedent of a hypothetical statement is also sometimes called the 'protasis' or 'implicans', and the consequent the 'apodosis' or 'implicate'. Therefore, in each of the four examples we discover this sort of arrangement:

(5)   If *antecedent*, then *consequent*.

Since both the antecedent and consequent are always statements, we may represent them by statement variables:

(6)   If *p*, then *q*.

It might now be very tempting to suggest that (6) represents what is common to all four of the examples. We must be extremely careful with such a suggestion, however, for 'If p, then q' is ambiguous. To appreciate the ambiguity of hypothetical English sentences, let us return to our four examples. While the phrase 'If $\cdots$, then $---$' is used in each of the examples, it is used somewhat differently in every case. In each case 'If $\cdots$, then $---$' suggests a somewhat different relation holding between the antecedent and consequent.

The first example suggests that Heliotrope's marriage to Andrew will be temporally prior to Andrew's elation; moreover, the marriage will be a causal factor of this elation. In the second example the consequent provides, at least in part, the definition of 'United States senator'. Sentence (2) is not suggesting that the state of affairs mentioned by the antecedent is either temporally prior or a causal factor to the state of affairs mentioned by the consequent. As a matter of fact, Jones must be at least 30 years old before he can be a senator. The relation suggested in (2) is one of definition. Neither does the third example suggest a temporal or causal relation holding between the state of affairs mentioned by the antecedent and that mentioned by the consequent. Nor is some sort of definitional relation being suggested. In (3), we find an example of logical entailment; that is, the truth of the antecedent logically guarantees the truth of the consequent. And what of the fourth example? Certainly the moon being made of green cheese is not a causal factor of my being a monkey's uncle, nor is it temporally prior—if, indeed, I did have a sibling who had a primate as a child. Neither is a definitional relation being suggested in (4) nor do we find logical entailment. The fourth example does suggest this: If the antecedent were true and at the same time the consequent false, the entire hypothetical statement would count as false.

The important moral to be drawn from our discussion is that an English sentence making use of the phrase 'If $\cdots$, then $---$' may indicate quite different relations holding between the antecedent and consequent. There is, nevertheless, a *truth-functional* interpretation in terms of truth and falsity common to all the statements asserted in (1)–(4). The common truth-functional interpretation is this:

> **It is not the case both that the antecedent is true and that the consequent not true if the entire hypothetical statement is to count as true.**

Suppose Heliotrope did marry Andrew, and yet after the wedding Andrew was not elated. Certainly, then, the statement 'If Heliotrope marries Andrew, then Andrew will be elated' is false. Or even suppose, in some wild way, that the moon were made of green cheese but, also, that I am not a monkey's uncle. Then, it is false to say 'If the moon is made of green cheese, then I'm a monkey's uncle'.

The common truth-functional element of all hypothetical statements is that it is not the case both that the antecedent is true and the consequent is not true if the entire hypothetical statement is to count as true. Let us construct a truth-table corresponding to this common truth-functional element.

First, let 'p' stand for any antecedent you please and 'q' for any consequent. Second, let us symbolize the antecedent as being true *and* the consequent as *not* being true by the following:

$$p \cdot \sim q$$

But, we have agreed that it is not the case both that the antecedent is true and the consequent not true if the entire hypothetical statement is to count as true. Using the tilde and parentheses to indicate the tilde's scope, we can render 'It is not the case both that . . .' by

(7) $\sim (p \cdot \sim q)$

(7) corresponds to "It is not the case both that 'p'—the antecedent—is true, and 'q'—the consequent—is false".

We now want to construct a truth-table for (7). Such a truth-table will depict under what conditions any statement having the form '$\sim (p \cdot \sim q)$' is true and under what conditions such a statement is false. Again, using '1' for 'is true' and '0' for 'is false', we may interpret 'p' and 'q' as

(8)

p	q	
1	1	
1	0	
0	1	
0	0	

Remembering the rule governing the tilde, we know if the statement at 'q' is true, '$\sim q$' is false and if the statement at 'q' is false, '$\sim q$' is true. We may represent this information while continuing our truth-table.

(9)

p	q	$\sim q$
1	1	0
1	0	1
0	1	0
0	0	1

We notice in (9) there is a '0' under '$\sim q$' in every case where there is a '1' under 'q' and a '1' under '$\sim q$' in just those cases where there is a '0' under 'q'.

Knowing a truth-functional conjunction is true if, and only if, all its conjuncts are true, we are now ready to calculate the truth-conditions of '$p \cdot \sim q$'.

(10)

p	q	$\sim q$	$p \cdot \sim q$
1	1	0	0
1	0	1	1
0	1	0	0
0	0	1	0

In (10) we notice a '1' appears under '$p \cdot \sim q$' only in that case where a '1' appears both under 'p' and '$\sim q$'. Again, appealing to the rule governing the use of the tilde, our truth-table is completed.

(11)

p	q	$\sim q$	$p \cdot \sim q$	$\sim(p \cdot \sim q)$
1	1	0	0	1
1	0	1	1	0
0	1	0	0	1
0	0	1	0	1

A '1' appears under '$\sim(p \cdot \sim q)$' only when a '0' appears under '$p \cdot \sim q$', and a '0' appears under '$\sim(p \cdot \sim q)$' only when a '1' appears under '$p \cdot \sim q$'.

It is extremely important that we follow clearly the discussion of truth-functional hypotheticals to this point. We first carefully examined four hypothetical English sentences. This examination led us to see that the phrase 'If $\cdots$, then $---$' has several uses. Nevertheless, there is one feature common to all hypothetical statements; namely, if the antecedent is true and at the same time the consequent false, then the entire hypothetical statement will be false. Hence, we said that it is not the case both that the antecedent of a hypothetical statement is true and the consequent not true if the entire hypothetical statement is true. Symbolizing this information as '$\sim(p \cdot \sim q)$', we constructed the truth-table appearing in (11).

The truth-table in (11) shows us that whenever some statement at 'q' is true, '$\sim(p \cdot \sim q)$' is also true whether the statement at 'p' is true or false. We also see that whenever 'p' is false, '$\sim(p \cdot \sim q)$' is true whether 'q' is true or false. Only when 'p' is true and 'q' false is '$\sim(p \cdot \sim q)$' false. That is, *only when the antecedent of a hypothetical statement is true and at the same time the consequent false will the entire hypothetical statement be false.*

Instead of writing '$\sim(p \cdot \sim q)$' to indicate that truth-functional element common to all hypothetical statements, logicians often introduce a new logical connective into their symbolism. We shall follow this procedure and introduce the following *molecular statement form* as an abbreviation of '$\sim(p \cdot \sim q)$':

$$p \supset q$$

The '$\supset$' is called '*horseshoe*' and is a logical connective which must be flanked on both its left- and right-hand sides by statement forms or statements.

While '$p \supset q$' may be read 'If p, then q', it is necessary always to remember that the only relation holding between the antecedent, 'p' and the consequent, 'q', is that if the antecedent is true and the consequent false, then '$p \supset q$' is false. Since neither a temporal, causal, or definitional relation nor logical entailment is being indicated by the horseshoe, it is called '*material implication*'. In sum we present the rule governing the use of the horseshoe:

> **Given any statements 'p' and 'q', then any statement '$p \supset q$' is true except when 'p' is true and 'q' false.**

This rule may be depicted by Truth-Table V:

p	q	$p \supset q$
1	1	1
1	0	0
0	1	1
0	0	1

Truth-Table V

In our present study of logic, we shall translate all hypothetical statements into our horseshoe notation. We shall consider all hypothetical statements solely as material implications and deal only with their truth-functional element.

While we shall always translate hypothetical statements into the general form '$p \supset q$', there are many ways of expressing 'If p, then q' in ordinary English. In some cases the antecedent is written after the consequent. Often the word 'then' is omitted. And in many cases the phrase 'If $\cdots$, then $--$' is not used at all. Continuing to let 'p' represent any antecedent and 'q' any consequent, the following are some of the more common ways of expressing a hypothetical statement in ordinary English. Realizing that this list does not purport to be complete, nevertheless, you should become thoroughly familiar with these expressions, remembering that they all may be translated into the form '$p \supset q$'.

(12)   a)   if p, q
      b) q if p
      c)   if p, this means q
      d) p only if q
      e)   had p, q
      f) q, had p
      g) p provided that q
      h)   not q unless p
      i)   unless p, not q
      j) p implies q
      k) q is implied by p
      l)   whenever p, q

m)   *q* whenever *p*
n)   a necessary condition for *p* is *q*
o)   *q* is a necessary condition for *p*
p)   that *q* is a necessary condition for *p*
q)   a sufficient condition for *q* is *p*
r)   *p* is a sufficient condition for *q*
s)   that *p* is a sufficient condition for *q*

Notice that while 'if' always introduces the antecedent of a hypothetical statement, 'only if' always introduces the consequent. Furthermore, the sufficient condition of any state of affairs is always mentioned by the antecedent of a hypothetical statement. On the other hand, a necessary condition for any state of affairs is always mentioned by the consequent of a hypothetical statement. Now, some state of affairs, *A*, is a sufficient condition for another state of affairs, *B*, if, and only if, any occurrence of *A* guarantees an occurrence of *B*. On the other hand, some state of affairs, *B*, is a necessary condition for another state of affairs, *A*, if, and only if, *B* always occurs when *A* does but the occurrence of *B* does not guarantee the occurrence of *A*.

The list of expressions above, often used to indicate hypothetical statements, does not pretend to be complete, nor does it suggest that these expressions are used only to indicate hypothetical statements. Nevertheless, hypothetical statements often are indicated by the expressions found in this list.

EXERCISES

Group A:

Write out at least one complete statement for each of the expressions in (12) above.

Group B:

Using the suggested notation at the end of each of the following statements, translate them into truth-functional symbolism.

Examples: a)   Had the Kashmir problem been solved in 1947, there would be better diplomatic relations between India and Pakistan. (*K, R*)

$$K \supset R$$

b)   Unless he follows the instructions carefully or is very lucky, the experiment will not be a success. (*F, L, E*)

$$(F \lor L) \supset E$$

Why would it be incorrect to symbolize example (b) as '$(F \lor L) \supset {\sim} E$' even though the word 'not' appears in the English statement?

(1)   A sufficient condition for a society quickly dissolving for lack of social cohesion is that it is made up of a majority of self-centered persons. (*D, P*)

(2) That an individual can be parasitic on a society is a sufficient condition for that society to be made up of a majority of self-centered persons. (*I, P*)

(3) An individual can be self-centered only if the society in which he lives is altruistic, while he can be parasitic on that society. (*I, A, P*)

(4) Whenever a person's moral practices are often quite different from his claimed ethical systems, he is fundamentally psychopathic. (*M, P*)

(5) A person is not fundamentally psychopathic unless he is not able to function at his best capacity in a given society. (*P, C*)

(6) That a man is environmentally controlled is a sufficient condition for his being mentally deficient. (*C, D*)

(7) A person may become paranoid if he is not able to function at his best capacity in a given society. (*P, C*)

(8) That human behavior is viewed as basically anticipatory rather than reactive implies that each person sets up his own network of pathways leading into the future. (*B, N*)

(9) A necessary condition for a man not being mentally deficient is that either he is not environmentally controlled or human behavior is viewed by him as basically anticipatory rather than reactive. (*D, C, B*)

(10) If a man is either intellectually creative or mentally dynamic, he is intellectually creative only if he adds to environmental change. (*C, D, A*)

(11) Unless we accept Newtonian mechanics, we don't accept the formula '$F = G(m_1 m_2/R^2)$'; moreover, accepting quantum theory is a sufficient condition for accepting the statistical formula '$\Delta p \, \Delta q = h/4\pi$'. (*N, F, Q, S*)

(12) Whenever it is not the case that we either accept Newtonian mechanics or accept quantum theory, we do not accept the best systems physicists have to offer. (*N, Q, S*)

(13) That we are followers of Werner Heisenberg is a necessary condition for accepting the statistical formula '$\Delta p \, \Delta q = h/4\pi$', whereas accepting the formula '$F = G(m_1 m_2/R^2)$' implies that we accept seventeenth-century mechanics. (*H, S, F, M*)

(14) If we wish to study subatomic particles, we accept quantum theory; furthermore, we do not consider Newtonian mechanics adequate for our present purposes if we accept quantum theory. (*P, Q, N*)

(15) If we accept either Newtonian mechanics or quantum theory, then accepting Newtonian mechanics is a sufficient condition for asserting that both the velocity and position of a Newtonian particle can be simultaneously determined. (*N, Q, P*)

(16) Not being able to use the statistical formula '$\Delta p \, \Delta q = h/4\pi$' in our system is a necessary condition for asserting that both the velocity and position of a Newtonian particle can be simultaneously determined, or we neither accept quantum theory nor assert that both the velocity and position of a Newtonian particle can be simultaneously determined. (*S, P, Q*)

(17)   Had we accepted the idea of instantaneous motion we could have accepted Newtonian mechanics, but we accept quantum theory instead. (*M, N, Q*)

(18)   That there will be a financial recession is a necessary condition for both the production prices of consumer goods to increase and for consumer spending not to increase. (*R, P, S*)

(19)   If stocks fall off or there is not a financial recession (but not both), it will not be the case both that dividends will be paid on bonds and personal savings won't increase. (*S, R, D, P*)

(20)   A given number *x* is neither odd nor even only if isn't a natural number. (*O, E, N*)

(21)   If the given number *x* is even, it can be divided by two without leaving a remainder; but if the given number *x* can be divided by two without leaving a remainder, it cannot be factored into two odd numbers. (*E, D, F*)

(22)   It not being the case both that the given number *x* can be factored into two odd numbers and also be a natural number is a sufficient condition for assuming the given number *x* can be factored into two even numbers, but the given number *x* cannot be factored into two even numbers. (*O, N, E*)

(23)   It is not the case that if theories in psychology are constructed then not both clinical psychologists are interested in this type of work while experimental psychologists are not. (*T, C, E*)

(24)   A necessary condition for theories in psychology not being constructed is the following: Neither experimental nor clinical psychologists are interested in this type of work, or neither statistical nor quantitative measurement is satisfactory in representing psychological data. (*T, E, C, S, Q*)

(25)   That statistical measurement is satisfactory in representing psychological data is a necessary condition for either it not being the case both that clinical and experimental psychologists are not interested in this type of work or that quantitative measurement is not satisfactory in representing psychological data (but not both). (*S, C, E, Q*)

Group C:

Using Truth-Table V as your model, construct truth-tables for the logical symbolizations of (1), (2), (4), (6), and (8) in Group B.

9. MATERIAL EQUIVALENCE

Descriptive language sometimes makes use of such statements as

(1)   I'll go to the concert if, and only if, you'll go.

(2)   That a given natural number is even is both a sufficient and necessary condition for it not being odd.

Beginning with (1), let us express both of these examples in logically equivalent, but grammatically different, forms.

(3)   I'll go to the concert *IF* you'll go, *AND* I'll go to the concert *ONLY IF* you'll go.

Statement (3) is simply (1) rewritten and is an overall conjunction of two hypothetical statements. Now, we may render the left-hand conjunct of (3) as

(4)   If you'll go (to the concert), then I'll go to the concert.

The right-hand conjunct of (3) is certainly equivalent to

(5)   If I'll go to the concert, then you'll go (to the concert).

Putting (4) and (5) back into conjunction, we have

(6)   If you'll go (to the concert), then I'll go to the concert; and if I'll go to the concert, then you'll go (to the concert).

Since (6) is a rewriting of (3) and (3) of (1), it follows that (6) is a rewriting of (1). Now, let us examine (2), which can also be rendered as a conjunction:

(7)   That a given number is even is a *SUFFICIENT CONDITION* for it not being odd, *AND* that a given number is even is a *NECESSARY CONDITION* for it not being odd.

The two conjuncts in (7) are both hypothetical statements, as was the case in (3). The left-hand conjunct in (7) is rewritten as

(8)   If a given number is even, then it is not odd.

And the right-hand conjunct of (7) may be rewritten as

(9)   If a given number is not odd, then it is even.

Putting (8) and (9) into conjunction, we have

(10)   If a given number is even, then it is not odd; and if a given number is not odd, then it is even.

Since (10) is only another way of writing (7) and (7) is a rewriting of (2), (10) is a rewriting of (2).

Using appropriate statement initials and truth-functional constants, we may symbolize (6) and (10), respectively, in the following ways:

(11) $(Y \supset I) \cdot (I \supset Y)$

(12) $(E \supset \sim O) \cdot (\sim O \supset E)$

Utilizing statement variables, we may represent a molecular statement form common to both (11) and (12) as

(13) $(p \supset q) \cdot (q \supset p)$

Since (11) and (12) are rewritings of (1) and (2), respectively, and (13) is a statement form common to both (11) and (12), if we could determine the truth conditions of (13), we would automatically have the truth conditions of (1) and (2).

In that '$(p \supset q) \cdot (q \supset p)$' is the form of an overall conjunction, it may be counted as true if, and only if, both '$p \supset q$' and '$q \supset p$' are true. But any hypothetical statement is truth-functionally true if, and only if, it is not the case that the antecedent is true and the consequent false. These truth conditions are met in the following truth-table:

(14)

p	q	$p \supset q$	$q \supset p$	$(p \supset q) \cdot (q \supset p)$
1	1	1	1	1
1	0	0	1	0
0	1	1	0	0
0	0	1	1	1

(14) literally shows us that any statement of the form '$(p \supset q) \cdot (q \supset p)$' is true if, and only if, *both* the statements at 'p' and 'q' are true or *both* false.

Instead of writing (1) and (2) as conjunctions of two hypothetical statements, we shall introduce a new logical connective into our symbolism. This connective is sometimes known as the '*triple-bar*' or the '*biconditional*' and is pictured in the *molecular statement form*

(15) $p \equiv q$

The triple-bar is a logical connective and must be flanked on both its left- and right-hand sides by statement forms or statements. The statement form at (15), or any instance of it, shall be known as '*material equivalence*', or the '*biconditional*'.

From our previous discussion we know that '$p \equiv q$' is only a rewriting of '$(p \supset q) \cdot (q \supset p)$'. Hence, the conditions which make '$(p \supset q) \cdot (q \supset p)$' true or false also render '$p \equiv q$' true or false. Consequently, the rule determining the use of the triple-bar may be given in this manner:

> **Given any statements 'p' and 'q', '$p \equiv q$' is true if, and only if, both 'p' and 'q' are true or both false.**

The truth-table corresponding to the rule of material equivalence above is drawn as follows:

p	q	$p \equiv q$
1	1	1
1	0	0
0	1	0
0	0	1

Truth-Table VI

Remember always to symbolize any statement using such phrases as 'if, and only if', or 'is both a sufficient and necessary condition for' with the triple-bar.

We now have been introduced to all the logical constants we shall use in the Truth-Functional Calculus. The next chapter will expand the use of truth-tables so that we may demonstrate the validity or invalidity of deductive arguments composed of truth-functional statements.

EXERCISES

Group A:

Using the suggested notation, translate each of the following statements into truth-functional symbolism. Be certain to use the triple-bar when appropriate.

(1) A precipitate will form in the solution whenever, and only whenever, the solubility product constant is exceeded. (P, C)

(2) That something is a sea creature is both a necessary and sufficient condition for it living in salt or brackish water. (C, S, B)

(3) Mollusks live in the ocean or near the shore if, and only if, they are bivalves. (O, S, B)

(4) If a mandrill is a mammal and has a spine then it is a primate if, and only if, it stands erect and has a true cerebrum. (M, S, P, E, C)

(5) A tree is either coniferous or deciduous (but not both) when, and only when, it has either broad, veined leaves or needles (but not both). (C, D, L, N)

(6) Equilibrium is reached in a solution if, and only if, the equilibrium constant is reached and neither the temperature nor pressure is changed. (S, C, T, P)

(7) That it is not the case that this is an acid or a base (but not both) is both a sufficient and necessary condition for it not being water and not having a pH of 7. (A, B, W, P).

(8) If water is neutral it has a pH of 7 when, and only when, basic properties do not begin before 7 and acidic properties do not exceed 7. (W, P, B, A)

(9)   If this substance is an acid, then it contains free hydrogen ions; which is a necessary and sufficient condition for this substance to be stinging to the touch and sour to the taste, only if it is in fact an acid and not a base. (*A, I, S, T, B*)

(10) A cell will neither lyse nor plasmolyse if, and only if, in the case that whenever a cell is in an isotonic solution or has an impermeable membrane to water, then water is unable to migrate and the cytoplasmic volume stays constant. (*L, P, S, M, W, V*)

Group B:

Construct at least twenty truth-functional statements, being certain to use all the logical operators you have learned. Then symbolize these statements in our logical notation.

3

More About Truth-Tables

In the previous chapter all the various truth-functional operators to be used in our study of the Truth-Functional Calculus were discussed. Reviewing, we recall the statement forms using these operators:

$$\sim p$$
$$p \cdot q$$
$$p \vee q$$
$$p \triangle q$$
$$p \supset q$$
$$p \equiv q$$

Truth-tables were introduced as devices showing the conditions under which statements interpreted as displaying these forms are to count as true and the conditions under which such statements are to count as false.

p	$\sim p$		p	q	$p \cdot q$		p	q	$p \vee q$
1	0		1	1	1		1	1	1
0	1		1	0	0		1	0	1
			0	1	0		0	1	1
			0	0	0		0	0	0

p	q	$p \triangle q$	p	q	$p \supset q$	p	q	$p \equiv q$
1	1	0	1	1	1	1	1	1
1	0	1	1	0	0	1	0	0
0	1	1	0	1	1	0	1	0
0	0	0	0	0	1	0	0	1

Truth Tables I–VI

Now, let us begin to expand our use of truth-tables, noting ways in which they can be employed to picture very important features about not only truth-functional statements, but also *arguments* composed of truth-functional statements.

1. CONSTRUCTING TRUTH-TABLES

Consider the following statements, asking under what conditions they would count as true and under what conditions false. We want to determine the *truth-conditions* of these statements. Of course this is a different matter from asking whether these statements are actually true or not. Nevertheless, the two questions are related, for we could never say whether any statement is actually true or false unless we first knew the general conditions which would make it true or false.

(1)   We don't consider Newtonian mechanics adequate whenever we wish to study subatomic particles. (*M, P*)

(2)   CH₃COOH is acetic acid and neither a base nor a salt. (*A, B, S*)

(3)   Mollusks live in the ocean or near the ocean's shore if, and only if, they are bivalves. (*O, S, B*)

These statements may be symbolized as

(4) $P \supset \sim M$

(5) $A \cdot \sim (B \vee S)$

(6) $(M \vee S) \equiv B$

We see that (4) may be viewed as an overall hypothetical statement. The truth-table of '$p \supset q$' shows a hypothetical statement counts as true in every case except when its antecedent is true and its consequent false. Hence, '$P \supset \sim M$' will count as true in every case except when 'P' is true and '$\sim M$' is false, '$\sim M$' being false only when 'M' is true. This information can be put into a truth-table.

(7)

P	M	$\sim M$	$P \supset \sim M$
1	1	0	0
1	0	1	1
0	1	0	1
0	0	1	1

(7) literally shows us that only when both 'P' and 'M' are true is '$P \supset \sim M$' false.

(5) may be interpreted as an overall conjunction which is true if, and only if, both 'A' and '$\sim (B \vee S)$' are true. Further, '$\sim (B \vee S)$' is true only when '$B \vee S$' is false; moreover, '$B \vee S$' is false in only that case where both 'B' and 'S' are false. All this information is dependent on the truth-tables of '$p \cdot q$', '$\sim p$', and '$p \vee q$'. We can now construct a truth-table displaying the conditions under which '$A \cdot \sim (B \vee S)$' will count either as true or false.

(8)

A	B	S	$B \vee S$	$\sim (B \vee S)$	$A \cdot \sim (B \vee S)$
1	1	1	1	0	0
1	1	0	1	0	0
1	0	1	1	0	0
1	0	0	0	1	1
0	1	1	1	0	0
0	1	0	1	0	0
0	0	1	1	0	0
0	0	0	0	1	0

Clearly, only when 'A' is true, 'B' false, and 'S' false is '$A \cdot \sim (B \vee S)$' true.

We read (6) as an instance of material equivalence. From the truth-table of '$p \equiv q$' we notice that any statement of this form is true if, and only if, the statements at 'p' and 'q' have exactly the same truth-value. The statements at 'p' and 'q' must both be true or both false for a statement of the form '$p \equiv q$' to be true. In (6), let us read '$M \vee S$' as an instance of 'p' and 'B' as an instance of 'q'. Therefore, '$(M \vee S) \equiv B$' is true only when both '$M \vee S$' and 'B' are true or both false. Of course we know that '$M \vee S$' is true in every case except when 'M' and 'S' are both false. This information may be exhibited in the following manner:

(9)

M	S	B	$M \vee S$	$(M \vee S) \equiv B$
1	1	1	1	1
1	1	0	1	0
1	0	1	1	1
1	0	0	1	0
0	1	1	1	1
0	1	0	1	0
0	0	1	0	0
0	0	0	0	1

(9) shows us that '$(M \lor S) \equiv B$' counts as true in four different cases: when 'M', 'S', and 'B' are all true; when 'M' and 'B' are true but 'S' false; when 'M' is false and 'S' and 'B' are both true; and when 'M', 'S', and 'B' are all false. In every other case '$(M \lor S) \equiv B$' is to be understood as false. These are the truth-conditions of (9).

Now, how can we actually go about constructing truth-tables? As in many discussions, a little technical jargon will prove helpful. Let us refer to any string of '1's and '0's going horizontally across the page in a truth-table as a '*row*' of that truth-table, any string of '1's and '0's running vertically as a '*column*', and the columns to the *left-hand* side of the double vertical lines as '*lead columns*' of the truth-table. Each row of the lead columns in a truth-table is understood as representing a distinct truth-condition of the statement being analyzed.

Since a truth-table of a particular statement presents a picture of all the possible conditions which would make the statement true or false, we must establish a way of depicting all possible combinations of '1's and '0's for that statement. In turn this requires that we know how many lead columns and rows a particular truth-table must have and also how to arrange initially the numerals '1' and '0' of the lead columns.

Let us say, as a matter of convention, that each single letter in (4), (5), and (6) represents a statement which may be counted as atomic in relation to the overall statement in which it appears. Thus, in (5), 'A', 'B', and 'S' are considered atomic relative to '$A \cdot \sim (B \lor S)$'. The number of lead columns in any truth-table is determined by the number of distinct atomic statements in the statement we wish to analyze. There is one lead column for each distinct atomic statement. Notice in (4) we find two lead columns, while in (5) and (6) there are three.

In order to avoid possible confusion, consider the following:

(10) $(A \lor B) \triangle (C \cdot B)$

How many lead columns would a truth-table for this statement have? *Three*, because there are three *distinct*, atomic, statements—'A', 'B', and 'C'—atomic relative to '$(A \lor B) \triangle (C \cdot B)$'. While '$B$' appears twice in (10), we do not count the number of appearances of atomic statements in order to determine the number of lead columns of a particular truth-table. *To determine the number of lead columns for a truth-table of a given statement, we count the number of distinct statements atomic relative to the statement we wish to analyze.*

We also must be able to fix the number of rows in any truth-table. This is determined by two considerations: *first*, the number of distinct atomic statements in the overall statement we wish to analyze, and, *second*, that each of these relative atomic statements may be assigned a '1' or a '0' but not both in the same row. These two considerations are reflected in the following:

$$\textit{number of rows} = 2^n$$

where 'n' represents the number of distinct atomic statements relative to the particular statement we wish to analyze and where '2' represents the number of distinct truth-values such a statement has.

Statement (4) has two distinct statements, 'P' and 'M', which count as atomic relative to '$P \supset \sim M$'. Using our formula, and substituting '2' for 'n', we have

$$\text{number of rows} = 2^2 = 4$$

where, of course, '2^2' is read '2×2'. On the other hand, both (5) and (6) have three distinct statements counting as relatively atomic. Hence, the number of rows needed in a truth-table of these statements is eight. This is easily determined by our formula, substituting '3' for 'n'.

$$\text{number of rows} = 2^3 = 8$$

where '2^3' is read '$2 \times 2 \times 2$'.

Whenever the overall statement we wish to analyze by truth-table means is not interpreted as molecular, but atomic, then that statement's truth-table has exactly two rows and one column. The truth-table constructed for 'Winter is icummen in' is

$$W$$

$$1$$

$$0$$

Such a statement is either true or false, but not both, and this is displayed by its appropriate truth-table.

Since a particular truth-table must exhibit all the conditions which would make a given statement true and all the conditions which would make it false, it is necessary to determine a way of arranging the '1's and '0's of the lead columns so that all possible combinations of these numerals are realized. One effective way of doing this is to alternate the '1's and '0's at every row in the lead column next to the double lines until we exhaust the number of rows—2^n—required in the truth-table. In the next lead column the '1's and '0's are alternated by twos; in the third lead column, by fours; in the next, by eights; in the fifth, by sixteens; and so on. Referring to (7), (8), and (9), notice how the '1's and '0's have been alternated in the lead columns.

But how are we to construct the columns beyond the lead columns? Consider again the statement

(2) CH_3COOH is acetic acid and neither a base nor a salt. (A, B, S)

Symbolizing (2), we may write

(5) $A \cdot \sim (B \vee S)$

In this overall statement there are three relative atomic statements. Consequently, to construct a truth-table for (2), we need three lead columns and eight rows.

A	B	S	
1	1	1	
1	1	0	
1	0	1	
1	0	0	
0	1	1	
0	1	0	
0	0	1	
0	0	0	

The symbolization of (5) shows its gross structure is a conjunction, which is true only when all its conjuncts are true. One of the conjuncts of (5), 'A', is a lead column and has already been assigned various '1's and '0's. The other conjunct of (5) is the denial of '$B \lor S$'. Let us construct a new column in our truth-table—a column showing the truth-values of '$B \lor S$', given the lead columns.

A	B	S	B ∨ S
1	1	1	1
1	1	0	1
1	0	1	1
1	0	0	0
0	1	1	1
0	1	0	1
0	0	1	1
0	0	0	0

In order to construct the column of '1's and '0's under '$B \lor S$', we look under the columns 'B' and 'S'. In each row where there is a '1' under 'B' or under 'S', or both, we put a '1' under '$B \lor S$'. If there is a '0' under both 'B' and 'S' in the same row, we put a '0' under '$B \lor S$'. We can now expand our truth-table by constructing a column for the right-hand conjunct of (5), '$\sim(B \lor S)$'.

A	B	S	B ∨ S	∼(B ∨ S)
1	1	1	1	0
1	1	0	1	0
1	0	1	1	0
1	0	0	0	1
0	1	1	1	0
0	1	0	1	0
0	0	1	1	0
0	0	0	0	1

'$\sim(B \lor S)$' is given a '0' in each row in which '$B \lor S$' is assigned a '1' and a '1' in each row in which '$B \lor S$' is assigned a '0'. We are now ready to complete the truth-table analysis of '$A \cdot \sim(B \lor S)$':

A	B	S	$B \lor S$	$\sim(B \lor S)$	$A \cdot \sim(B \lor S)$
1	1	1	1	0	0
1	1	0	1	0	0
1	0	1	1	0	0
1	0	0	0	1	1
0	1	1	1	0	0
0	1	0	1	0	0
0	0	1	1	0	0
0	0	0	0	1	0

Since '$A \cdot \sim(B \lor S)$' is a conjunction, it will count as true in just those cases in which both 'A' and '$\sim(B \lor S)$' are true. Hence, we put a '1' under the column '$A \cdot \sim(B \lor S)$' in only those rows in which 'A' is assigned a '1' and '$\sim(B \lor S)$' is also assigned a '1'. The fourth row is the only one which fulfills these conditions. Only when 'A' is true and 'B' and 'S' both false will '$A \cdot \sim(B \lor S)$' be true.

Metaphorically, we might view truth-functional statements such as (4), (5), and (6) as composed of "bits and pieces" "held together" by the logical constants '$\sim$', '$\cdot$', '$\lor$', '$\triangle$', '$\supset$', and '$\equiv$'. In constructing a truth-table, we start with the relatively smallest bits and pieces—smallest in relation to the overall statement we are analyzing. Then we compute the next smallest bits and pieces, making use of the truth-table definitions of '$\sim p$', '$p \cdot q$', '$p \lor q$', '$p \triangle q$', '$p \supset q$', and '$p \equiv q$'. Continuing in this manner, we finally analyze the entire statement in question. Starting from the "center" of a particular statement, we work outward step-by-step until we have completed our truth-table. Having finished the truth-table, we can say under just what truth-conditions the analyzed truth-functional statement would be true and under what conditions false. Of course we make no pretense to know which of these truth-conditions actually holds, but as logicians we are not concerned with this.

EXERCISES

Group A:

Construct a truth-table for each of the following.

(1) A

(2) $A \cdot B$

(3) $\sim(A \cdot B)$

(4) $\sim A \cdot \sim B$

(5) $A \lor B$

(6) $\sim (A \lor B)$

(7) $\sim A \lor \sim B$

(8) $\sim (A \supset B)$

(9) $\sim \sim (A \cdot \sim B)$

(10) $\sim (\sim A \lor B)$

(11) $A \supset (\sim B \supset \sim C)$

(12) $(A \cdot C) \supset B$

(13) $A \bigtriangleup (B \cdot C)$

(14) $A \supset (B \equiv C)$

(15) $(A \lor B) \lor \sim (A \cdot C)$

(16) $(A \bigtriangleup B) \cdot (B \equiv C)$

(17) $\sim [A \supset (B \supset C)] \bigtriangleup [(A \cdot B) \supset C]$

(18) $[A \lor (B \cdot C)] \equiv [(A \lor B) \cdot (A \lor C)]$

(19) $[A \supset \sim (B \lor C)] \lor (C \cdot D)$

(20) $A \bigtriangleup [B \supset (C \lor \sim D)]$

Group B:

Translate each exercise in Group A into an English statement, interpreting 'A' as 'taxes are augmented', 'B' as 'bank savings increase', 'C' as 'spending is curtailed', and 'D' as 'production rates are dropping'.

Group C:

Symbolize the following statements using the suggested notation and then construct a truth-table for each.

(1) ATP contains oxygen but not nitrogen. (O, N)

(2) ATP doesn't contain oxygen; still it does contain nitrogen. (O, N)

(3) It isn't true that ATP contains a peptide bond despite the fact that it doesn't contain a peptide bond. (B)

(4) Rudolf Virchow believed in spontaneous generation or he believed in cellular division. (G, D)

(5) It isn't the case that Rudolf Virchow believed in spontaneous generation or cellular division. (G, D)

(6) If oxidation is the removal of electrons, then if reduction is the addition of electrons, oxidation is the removal of electrons. (O, R)

(7) If oxidation is the removal of electrons but reduction is the addition of them, then the removal of electrons is not oxidation only if the addition of electrons is not reduction. (*O, R*)

(8) Unless this insect has a false vein, it isn't of the family Syrphus; but if it doesn't have wings, it isn't of the family Syrphus. (*V, S, W*)

(9) That it isn't the case that this insect is a squash bug if, and only if, it is not of the order Hemiptera is a necessary and sufficient condition that it is a squash bug if, and only if, it is of the order Hemiptera. (*B, H*)

(10) Either this is an insect and is of the order Hemiptera or it is an insect and of the order Diptera, but not both. (*I, H, D*)

(11) If this element is ytterbium, then its atomic number is 70 if, and only if, its atomic weight is 173.04. (*Y, N, W*)

(12) That this element is ytterbium is a sufficient condition for either its atomic number not being 70 or its atomic weight being 173.04, but not both. (*Y, N, W*)

(13) West opens with one no-trump while North passes or West opens with one no-trump but East responds, or West neither opens with one no-trump nor does South pass. (*W, N, E, S*)

(14) If South must open whenever he has a fourteen honor point count but North cannot respond to South whenever he has a three honor point count, and further it isn't true both that North cannot respond to South and South must open, then either South doesn't have a fourteen honor point count or North doesn't have a three point honor count. (*S, F, N, T*)

(15) That West leads the queen is sufficient to lose the trick to North's king, but if West leads the ace, South will trump; moreover, West makes game if, and only if, neither he loses the trick to North's king nor South trumps. (*Q, K, A, T, G*)

2. SHORTENED FORM TRUTH-TABLES

Although quite mechanical in their construction, truth-tables often become rather cumbersome. For example, the following statement would require a truth-table having sixteen rows and nine columns!

(1)   If water is neutral it has a pH of 7 when, and only when, basic properties do not begin before 7 and acid properties do not exceed 7. (*W, P, B, A*)

In our symbolization, (1) may appear as

(2) $(W \supset P) \equiv (\sim B \cdot \sim A)$

The truth-table for (2) would have the following columns:

(3)	W	P	B	A	$\sim B$	$\sim A$	$\sim B \cdot \sim A$	$W \supset P$	$(W \supset P) \equiv (\sim B \cdot \sim A)$

Unfortunately, we cannot reduce the number of rows required for a given truth-table, that number always being equal to 2^n, but we can reduce some of our effort in writing out columns. How?

You will notice there are four statements relatively atomic to the overall statement symbolized in (2). These atomic statements—'W', 'P', 'B', and 'A'—comprise the lead columns in (3). Following our conventional method of assigning '1's and '0's in lead columns, we would alternate the '1's and '0's at every row under 'A', by twos under 'B', fours under 'P', and eights under 'W'. But, instead of writing lead columns as such, simply jot down these configurations of '1's and '0's under the atomic statements as they appear in (2) from left to right.

(4) $(W \supset P) \equiv (\sim B \cdot \sim A)$

1	1	1	1
1	1	1	0
1	1	0	1
1	1	0	0
1	0	1	1
1	0	1	0
1	0	0	1
1	0	0	0
0	1	1	1
0	1	1	0
0	1	0	1
0	1	0	0
0	0	1	1
0	0	1	0
0	0	0	1
0	0	0	0

Furthermore, if 'B' has a '1' under it at some row, '$\sim B$' will have a '0'; and if 'B' has a '0' under it, '$\sim B$' will have a '1'. The same holds for 'A'. We continue (4) by writing the appropriate '1's and '0's under the tildes governing 'B' and 'A'.

(5) $(W \supset P) \equiv (\sim B \cdot \sim A)$
  1   1   01 01
  1   1   01 10
  1   1   10 01
  1   1   10 10
  1   0   01 01
  1   0   01 10
  1   0   10 01
  1   0   10 10
  0   1   01 01
  0   1   01 10
  0   1   10 01
  0   1   10 10
  0   0   01 01
  0   0   01 10
  0   0   10 01
  0   0   10 10

Under the dot in '$\sim B \cdot \sim A$', we shall write a '1' in only those rows having a '1' under both the tilde in '$\sim B$' and '$\sim A$'.

(6) $(W \supset P) \equiv (\sim B \cdot \sim A)$
  1   1   0 1 0 0 1
  1   1   0 1 0 1 0
  1   1   1 0 0 0 1
  1   1   1 0 1 1 0
  1   0   0 1 0 0 1
  1   0   0 1 0 1 0
  1   0   1 0 0 0 1
  1   0   1 0 1 1 0
  0   1   0 1 0 0 1
  0   1   0 1 0 1 0
  0   1   1 0 0 0 1
  0   1   1 0 1 1 0
  0   0   0 1 0 0 1
  0   0   0 1 0 1 0
  0   0   1 0 0 0 1
  0   0   1 0 1 1 0

Continuing, '$W \supset P$' is assigned the truth-value '1' in every row except those in which 'W' is assigned '1' and 'P' is assigned '0', as shown in this truth-table:

(7) $(W \supset P) \equiv (\sim B \cdot \sim A)$
         1 1 1   0 1 0 0 1
         1 1 1   0 1 0 1 0
         1 1 1   1 0 0 0 1
         1 1 1   1 0 1 1 0
         1 0 0   0 1 0 0 1
         1 0 0   0 1 0 1 0
         1 0 0   1 0 0 0 1
         1 0 0   1 0 1 1 0
         0 1 1   0 1 0 0 1
         0 1 1   0 1 0 1 0
         0 1 1   1 0 0 0 1
         0 1 1   1 0 1 1 0
         0 1 0   0 1 0 0 1
         0 1 0   0 1 0 1 0
         0 1 0   1 0 0 0 1
         0 1 0   1 0 1 1 0

We are now ready to complete a truth-table for (2). Being a biconditional, (2) will be assigned a '1' in just those rows where both '$W \supset P$' and '$\sim B \cdot \sim A$' are '1' or both are '0'. In every other row, (2) will be assigned a '0'. The vertical arrow beneath the truth-table indicates the final column of the analysis.

(8) $(W \supset P) \equiv (\sim B \cdot \sim A)$
          1 1 1   0   0 1 0 0 1
          1 1 1   0   0 1 0 1 0
          1 1 1   0   1 0 0 0 1
          1 1 1   1   1 0 1 1 0
          1 0 0   1   0 1 0 0 1
          1 0 0   1   0 1 0 1 0
          1 0 0   1   1 0 0 0 1
          1 0 0   0   1 0 1 1 0
          0 1 1   0   0 1 0 0 1
          0 1 1   0   0 1 0 1 0
          0 1 1   0   1 0 0 0 1
          0 1 1   1   1 0 1 1 0
          0 1 0   0   0 1 0 0 1
          0 1 0   0   0 1 0 1 0
          0 1 0   0   1 0 0 0 1
          0 1 0   1   1 0 1 1 0
                    ↑

Let us review, in general terms, how we constructed the shortened form truth-table, (8). We first symbolized (1), using the suggested notation. Here, we carefully showed the scope of the operators by punctuation marks. Next, we counted the number of distinct statements relatively atomic to (2). We determined the number of rows needed, using the formula 'number of rows $= 2^n$'. Starting with the extreme lefthand atomic statement, we wrote a column of '1's and '0's, alternating by half the number of the total number of rows; then, under the next distinct atomic statement, we constructed a column, alternating by fours, and so on. Having constructed columns under all the atomic statements in (2), we commenced to calculate the truth-values of the next smallest statements, in this case '$\sim B$' and '$\sim A$', given the truth-conditions of a particular row. We wrote the appropriate '1' or '0' of these statements under the logical operator governing them, namely the tilde. Completing these columns, we moved to the next smallest statement in (2). Actually, in our present example we could have constructed a column for either '$W \supset P$' or '$\sim B \cdot \sim A$' first, although in this case we analyzed '$\sim B \cdot \sim A$' first and then '$W \supset P$'. Finally, we formulated a column of '1's and '0's under the major connective in (2), the triple-bar, this final truth-table representing all the possible truth-conditions of (2).

This entire procedure might be viewed as simply starting with the smallest "pieces" of a given statement and working in a step-by-step fashion until the entire statement is analyzed.

EXERCISES

Group A:

(1) If you had a molecular statement made up of exactly three distinct atomic statements, how many rows would you need for a truth-table of that molecular statement and how would you alternate the '1's and '0's in the column under the extreme left-hand atomic statement?

(2) Suppose you had a molecular statement built up from exactly six distinct atomic statements. How many rows would you need for its truth-table? How would you alternate the '1's and '0's in the column under the extreme left-hand atomic statement, under the next atomic statement?

Group B:

Construct shortened form truth-tables for the exercises in Groups A and C, Section 1, Chapter 3.

3. TAUTOLOGICAL, CONTRADICTORY, AND CONTINGENT STATEMENTS

It is often useful to categorize truth-functional statements as *'tautological'*, *'contradictory'*, or *'contingent'*. To understand what these terms mean, let us consider some examples of truth-functional statements, first symbolizing them and then constructing a shortened form truth-table for each.

(1) If the computer is able to change its goals whenever it is helpful to psychologists interested in learning theory and also it is helpful, then the computer is indeed able to change its goals. (*C, H*)

(2) That the computer is able to change its goals or is helpful to psychologists interested in learning theory is both a necessary and sufficient condition for it not being true that the computer is not able to change its goals only if it is helpful to psychologists interested in learning theory. (*C, H*)

(3) Considering that the computer is helpful to psychologists interested in learning theory only if it is able to change its goals and also the computer is able to change its goals, it follows that the computer is helpful to psychologists interested in learning theory. (*H, C*)

(4) Had the computer been able to change its goals, it would not have been helpful to psychologists interested in learning theory; but the computer is able to change its goals and is helpful to psychologists interested in learning theory. (*C, H*)

(5) That the computer is helpful to psychologists interested in learning theory when, and only when, it is able to change its goals is both a sufficient and necessary condition for either the computer not being of help to psychologists interested in learning theory or its being able to change its goals, but certainly not both. (*H, C*)

(6) If the computer is able to change its goals whenever it is helpful to psychologists interested in learning theory and it is not helpful, then the computer is not able to change its goals. (*C, H*)

Symbolizing each of these examples and constructing a shortened form truth-table, we have

(7) $[(H \supset C) \cdot H] \supset C$

```
1 1 1  1 1  1  1
1 0 0  0 1  1  0
0 1 1  0 0  1  1
0 1 0  0 0  1  0
        ↑
```

(8) $(C \lor H) \equiv \sim(\sim C \supset H)$

1 1 1   0   0 0 1 1   1
1 1 0   0   0 0 0 1 1   0
0 1 1   0   0 1 0 1   1
0 0 0   0   1 1 0 0 0   0
           ↑

(9) $[(H \supset C) \cdot C] \supset H$

1 1 1 1 1 1 1
1 0 0 0 0 1 1
0 1 1 1 1 0 0
0 1 0 0 0 1 0
        ↑

(10) $(C \supset \sim H) \cdot (C \cdot H)$

1 0 0 1 0 1 1 1
1 1 1 0 0 1 0 0
0 1 0 1 0 0 0 1
0 1 1 0 0 0 0 0
        ↑

(11) $(H \equiv C) \equiv (\sim H \triangle C)$

1 1 1   1   0 1 1   1
1 0 0   1   0 1 0 0
0 0 1   1   1 0 0   1
0 1 0   1   1 0 1 0
        ↑

(12) $[(H \supset C) \cdot \sim H] \supset \sim C$

1 1 1   0 0 1   1 0 1
1 0 0   0 0 1   1 1 0
0 1 1   1 1 0   0 0 1
0 1 0   1 1 0   1 1 0
           ↑

Let us make several observations about (7)–(12). Notice first (7) and (11).
Although (7) is an overall hypothetical and (11) a biconditional statement, both
statements have a common feature. Their truth-tables clearly depict this shared
element. Under the main horseshoe in (7), we find a column made up entirely of
'1's; moreover, under the main triple-bar in (11) we find all '1's. This means that
no matter whether 'H' and 'C' are true or false, the statements '$[(H \supset C) \cdot H] \supset C$'
and '$(H \equiv C) \equiv (\sim H \triangle C)$' must always be true. Both of these statements are
tautologies. In general,

> *a truth-functional statement is called 'tautological' if, and only if, it has a*
> *'1' in every row in the final column of its truth-table analysis.*

A tautology can never be false but must always be true because of its logical form, because of the way in which the logical constants are used.

On the other hand, inspecting (8) and (10), we notice at once that in both cases the final column of these truth-tables is composed of only '0's. Not a single '1' appears under the triple-bar in (8) or under the main dot in (10). No matter, then, whether '*C*' or '*H*' are true or false, '$(C \lor H) \equiv \sim (\sim C \supset H)$' and '$(C \supset \sim H) \cdot (C \cdot H)$' must always be false. In general,

> *a truth-functional statement is called 'contradictory' if, and only if, it has a '0' in every row in the final column of its truth-table analysis.*

We can notice at once that the denial of any tautology is a contradictory statement, and the denial of any contradictory statement is a tautology. For example, since '$[(H \supset C) \cdot H] \supset C$' is a tautology, '$\sim \{[(H \supset C) \cdot H] \supset C\}$' is contradictory; whereas, because '$(C \lor H) \equiv \sim (\sim C \supset H)$' is contradictory, '$\sim [(C \lor H) \equiv \sim (\sim C \supset H)]$' is tautological.

In the final columns of (9) and (12), we discover both the numerals '1' and '0'. Consequently, we know that under some conditions (3) and (6) are true and under some other conditions false. Whether, for example, '$[(H \supset C) \cdot C] \supset H$' is true or false is contingent upon the particular truth-values assigned to '*H*' and '*C*'. In contrast, the truth of a tautology is not contingent upon the truth-values of its component statements; moreover, neither is the falsity of a contradiction dependent upon the truth-values of its component statements. Tautologies are always true and contradictions always false—because of their logical form, because of the ways in which we use such terms as 'not', 'and', and 'if · · · then   —' in English or their equivalents in any other descriptive language you please. The truth or falsity of a contingent statement is dependent not only upon our use of such terms as 'if · · · then – – –' but also upon the truth or falsity of the component statements involved. Under some conditions a contingent statement will be true and under others, false. In general,

> *a truth-functional statement is called 'contingent' if, and only if, it has at least one '1' and one '0' in the final column of its truth-table analysis.*

EXERCISES

Group A:

In Group C of the exercises in Section 1, Chapter 3, which statements are tautologies, which contradictory, and which contingent?

Group B:

Determine by shortened-form truth-tables which of the following statements are tautologies, which contradictory, and which contingent. Use the suggested notation in symbolizing the statements.

(1) Either Arnold Schoenberg's *Verkaert Nacht* is his most popular work, or it isn't. (*S*)

(2) It is not the case that either Arnold Schoenberg was a man interested in whole-tone scales or he wasn't interested in whole-tone scales. (*S*)

(3) If Arnold Schoenberg's music is easy to understand, Alban Berg's music isn't. (*S, B*)

(4) If DNA is a nucleic acid, then it isn't true that it isn't a nucleic acid. (*A*)

(5) It isn't the case both that sodium chloride is an enzyme and a neutral only if sodium chloride is either not an enzyme or not a neutral. (*E, N*)

(6) Sodium chloride is an acid or a salt; moreover, sodium chloride is a salt or it is neutral. (*A, S, N*)

(7) Either Maurice Ravel's style suddenly appeared or it slowly evolved; but it didn't suddenly appear, and moreover, it didn't slowly evolve. (*A, E*)

(8) Antonio Vivaldi and J. S. Bach are musical giants or we can't trust the best of critics (but not both) only if we can't trust the best of critics and either Bach or Vivaldi is a musical giant. (*V, B, C*)

(9) That J. S. Bach lived in the baroque period and composed either fugues or toccatas implies that Bach lived in the baroque period and composed fugues or he lived in the baroque period and composed toccatas. (*B, F, T*)

(10) J. S. Bach studied with Dietrich Buxtehude only if he mastered the organ and he mastered the organ only if he was well received in the social circles of his day; but Bach did study with Buxtehude and yet wasn't well received in the social circles of his day. (*B, O, C*)

(11) Unless J. S. Bach studied with Dietrich Buxtehude, he didn't master the organ, and if he studied the compositions of Antonio Vivaldi, he mastered chamber music; moreover, it isn't the case that if Bach studied with Buxtehude, he mastered chamber music. (*B, O, V, C*)

(12) Either it isn't the case that West takes the bid and East is dummy, or West must play against South's strength in spades or overcome North's fourteen honor point count. (*W, E, S, N*)

(13) That East or North will bid at the one-suit level, or South will mention one no-trump is a necessary and sufficient condition for West not opening with a bid of two. (*E, N, S, W*)

(14) That the First and Third Estates were each a part of the National Assembly was a sufficient condition for the following: That the First Estate was not a part of the National Assembly implied the support of the King and that the Third Estate was not a part of the National Assembly implied the support of the nobility, or both the nobility and the King supported the National Assembly. (*F, T, K, N*)

(15)   The following isn't the case: It isn't true that either the King and nobility were left helpless or it didn't happen that both the members of the Third Estate took matters into their own hands and declared themselves the National Assembly; or if the members of the Third Estate took matters into their own hands and declared themselves the National Assembly, then the nobility and King were left helpless. (*K, N, T, A*)

4. ESTABLISHING VALIDITY
AND INVALIDITY

Often statements are related to one another in an argument, as suggested in Chapter 1. We find some statements, or statement, the premiss set, claiming to establish the truth or falsity of another statement, the conclusion. The relation holding between the premiss set and conclusion in a deductive argument is indicated by the terms '*valid*' and '*invalid*'.

> *A deductive argument is valid if, when all its premises are true, then its conclusion must also be true. If all the premises of a deductive argument are true and the conclusion false, that argument is invalid.*

Truth-tables can be used to establish the validity, or invalidity, of any truth-functional deductive argument.

Let us consider a rather simple example of a truth-functional argument:

(1)   Unless food prices continue to rise or building costs soar, the general living index will not remain in an inflationary trend. We read in the papers that food prices continue to rise. So, we must conclude that the general living index will remain inflationary. (*F, B, I*)

Symbolizing the premisses of (1), we write

(2)   1) $(F \lor B) \supset I$ Pr
     2) F Pr

Notice to the left of the symbolized premisses the numerals '1' and '2' are written, and to the right, 'Pr'. The numerals serve simply as names of the premisses and 'Pr' says only that these statements are premisses and are accepted *as if* they were true. To our symbolized premisses we add our symbolized conclusion.

(3) $\therefore I$
     1) $(F \lor B) \supset I$ Pr
     2) F Pr

The conclusion is symbolized immediately after we symbolize the premisses and is put to the upper right-hand edge of the symbolized premiss set. The three dots, '∴', form a sign claiming that the premisses logically entail the conclusion; that is, if all the premisses are true, then so is the conclusion.

Is our argument valid? Does the truth of all the premisses guarantee the truth of the conclusion? How can we tell? Simple! Remember an argument is valid *if* when *all* the premisses are true, *then* the conclusion is also true. We have just used an 'if · · · then – – –' statement to describe validity in general. But we can also use the same sort of statement to describe the possible validity of (3).

(4)   If the premisses '$(F \lor B) \supset I$' and 'F' are both true, then 'I' must be true if (3) is a valid argument.

Here (4) is a statement about (3), but it indicates how to proceed in formulating a truth-table method for establishing validity. Take the premisses of (3) and put them into conjunction. Let this conjunction become the antecedent of a hypothetical statement of which the conclusion of (3) is the consequent.

(5) $\{[(F \lor B) \supset I] \cdot F\} \supset I$

Then (5) is a *statement* which corresponds to the *argument* (3).

Let us construct a shortened form truth-table for (5). Since we count 'F', 'B', and 'I' as atomic statements relative to (5), we need eight rows in our truth-table.

(6) $\{[(F \lor B) \supset I] \cdot F\} \supset I$

1	1 1	1 1 1 1	1 1
1	1 1	0 0 0 1	1 0
1	1 0	1 1 1 1	1 1
1	1 0	0 0 0 1	1 0
0	1 1	1 1 0 0	1 1
0	1 1	0 0 0 0	1 0
0	0 0	1 1 0 0	1 1
0	0 0	1 0 0 0	1 0

↑

Is (6) a tautological, contingent, or contradictory statement? A quick inspection reveals that the statement is a tautology. This also indicates that the argument, (1), is valid. How do we know? The only combination of '1' and '0' making a statement of the form '$p \supset q$' false is when 'p' is assigned a '1' and 'q' a '0'. If the antecedent, as in (6), is the conjunction of all the premisses of an argument and the consequent is the conclusion of that argument, then the only case in which the entire hypothetical statement could be false is when the antecedent, that is, the *conjunction of all the premisses*, is true and the consequent, that is, *the conclusion*, is false. There is no such case in (6), however. In (6) we find no row in which the antecedent—all the premisses—is true and the consequent—the conclusion—false. If there were such a case, (6) would not be a tautology. Hence, the argument symbolized at (3) is valid; there is no way to make all the premises true and the conclusion false.

Consider the following argument, which is similar to (1):

(7)   If food prices continue to rise and building costs soar, the general living index will remain in an inflationary trend. We read in the papers that food prices continue to rise. So, we must conclude that the general living index will remain inflationary. (*F, B, I*)

Symbolizing (7), we write the following:

(8)   ∴ *I*
   1) (*F·B*) ⊃ *I*   Pr
   2) *F*   Pr

Is this a valid truth-functional argument? To answer this question, we construct a hypothetical statement whose antecedent is the conjunction of all the premises of the argument and whose consequent is the argument's conclusion.

(9)   {[(*F·B*) ⊃ *I*]·*F*} ⊃ *I*

We next construct a truth-table for (9).

(10)   {[(*F* · *B*) ⊃ *I*] · *F*} ⊃ *I*
           1 1 1   1 1 1 1   1 1
           1 1 1   0 0 0 1   1 0
           1 0 0   1 1 1 1   1 1
           1 0 0   1 0 1 1   0 0
           0 0 1   1 1 0 0   1 1
           0 0 1   1 0 0 0   1 0
           0 0 0   1 1 0 0   1 1
           0 0 0   1 0 0 0   1 0
                              ↑

Statement (9) is not a tautology; it is a contingent statement! But, this tells us that (7) is not a valid argument, for there is at least one case in which all the premises can be true and the conclusion false. This case is precisely when '*F*' is true and both '*B*' and '*I*' are false.

Notice the next example:

(11)   Either Wystan Auden or Fred Pottle attended the meeting. So, either Pottle or Auden attended the meeting.

We may symbolize (11) as

(12)   ∴ *P* ∨ *A*
   1) *A* ∨ *P*   Pr

If we should like to determine by truth-table methods whether or not (11) is valid, we must first construct a hypothetical statement corresponding to (12). Heretofore, in building up a hypothetical statement corresponding to a given argument, we have said first to put all the premisses into conjunction. In the present example it does not make sense to speak of putting all the premisses into conjunction, there being only one premiss in the premiss set. When cases of this sort occur, the single premiss becomes the antecedent of the hypothetical statement corresponding to the original argument:

(13) $(A \vee P) \supset (P \vee A)$

In general, to establish the validity or invalidity of a truth-functional argument by means of truth-tables, proceed through these steps:

(1) *Symbolize the argument.*
(2) *Construct a hypothetical statement whose antecedent, in the appropriate cases, is the conjunction of all the premisses of the argument in question and whose consequent is the conclusion.*
(3) *Run a truth-table analysis on the hypothetical statement.*
(4) *If that hypothetical statement is a tautology, the argument from which it was constructed is valid; if that hypothetical statement is contingent or contradictory, the original argument is invalid.*

In using truth-table methods to demonstrate validity or invalidity, it is not uncommon to find an argument with a relatively complicated premiss set; for example,

(14) $\therefore C \supset B$

     1) $[A \supset (B \supset C)] \cdot [D \supset (C \supset B)]$ Pr
     2) $D \vee A$ Pr
     3) B Pr
     4) $\sim C$ Pr

Putting all the premisses of (14) into conjunction presents us with a problem of punctuation. Our punctuation markings must accomplish two things: *First,* they must clearly exhibit each distinct conjunct as corresponding to a separate premiss; *second,* the punctuation markings must clearly manifest the form '$p \cdot q$'. (15), following, does not fulfill the first requirement nor does (16) fulfill the second.

(15) $\{[A \supset (B \supset C)] \cdot [D \supset (C \supset B)] \cdot [(D \vee A) \cdot (B \cdot \sim C)]\} \supset (C \supset B)$

(16) $\big(\{[A \supset (B \supset C)] \cdot [C \supset (C \supset B)]\} \cdot (D \vee A) \cdot B \cdot \sim C\big) \supset (C \supset B)$

To avoid such pitfalls, we shall adopt this convention for punctuation, calling it '*associating to the left*':

Place into conjunction the first and second premises of the argument, clearly showing by appropriate punctuation markings the conjuncts corresponding to the distinct premises, while also retaining the overall form 'p·q'; to this conjunction, place into conjunction the third premise of the argument, again clearly showing by appropriate punctuation markings the conjuncts corresponding to the distinct premises, while also retaining the overall form 'p·q'; proceed in this manner until all the premises are put into conjunction.

Following the convention of associating to the left, we may return to (14) and put all the premises into conjunction:

(17) $\overbrace{\{[A \supset (B \supset C)]\cdot[D \supset (C \supset B)]\}}^{p}\cdot\overbrace{(D \vee A)}^{q}$

$\overbrace{(\{[A \supset (B \supset C)]\cdot[D \supset (C \supset B)]\}\cdot(D \vee A))}^{p}\cdot\overbrace{B}^{q}$

$\overbrace{[(\{[A \supset (B \supset C)]\cdot[D \supset (C \supset B)]\}\cdot(D \vee A))\cdot B]}^{p}\cdot\overbrace{\sim C}^{q}$

We may now form the hypothetical statement corresponding to (14):

(18) $\big\{\big[(\{[A \supset (B \supset C)]\cdot[D \supset (C \supset B)]\}\cdot(D \vee A))\cdot B\big]\cdot \sim C\big\} \supset (C \supset B)$

EXERCISES

Symbolize the following arguments using the suggested notation, and then by truth-table methods determine whether each argument is valid or invalid.

(1) Epilepsy is referred to as "genetic" or "acquired". Hence, it is correct to refer to epilepsy as "acquired". (*G*, *A*)

(2) If convulsions are called "symptomatic", they are attributable to organic brain pathology. Convulsions are attributable to organic brain pathology. So, convulsions are called "symptomatic". (*S*, *P*)

(3) Dilantin isn't an effective anticonvulsive agent or it is prescribed for epileptic patients. Dilantin is an effective anticonvulsive agent. Therefore, Dilantin is prescribed for epileptic patients. (*D*, *P*)

(4) Whenever an inadequate dose of Tridione is given, it can be reinforced by the adjunctive use of phenobarbital. An inadequate dose of Tridione is not given. So, it isn't true that Tridione can be reinforced by the adjunctive use of phenobarbital. (*T*, *P*)

(5) Samuel Clemens wrote either *Huckleberry Finn* or *Leaves of Grass*, but not both. He didn't write *Leaves of Grass*. Hence, it isn't the case both that Clemens wrote *Huckleberry Finn* and didn't write *Leaves of Grass*. (*F, G*)

(6) That Thomas Wolfe wasn't from the South is a sufficient reason to say that he wasn't from North Carolina. Yet, Wolfe was from North Carolina. Consequently, Wolfe was from the South. (*S, C*)

(7) Thomas Wolfe was either a northern novelist or a southerner, but not both. He was a southerner if, and only if, he was born below the Mason-Dixon Line. Thus, either Wolfe was a northern novelist or he was born below the Mason-Dixon Line, but not both. (*N, S, L*)

(8) Thomas Wolfe described real people; but also if Wolfe lived in Asheville, he described southerners. So, that Wolfe described real people is a sufficient condition for his describing southerners. (*P, A, S*)

(9) Robert Frost was a poet but James Adams wasn't. Either Carl Sandburg was a poet or Adams was, but not both. Hence, both Sandburg and Frost were poets. (*F, A, S*)

(10) If we're interested in northern literature, then we'll read Robert Frost whenever we read poetry. We'll not read Frost, however. Therefore, we aren't interested in northern literature even though we do read poetry. (*L, F, P*)

(11) If you like modern poetry, then you've read Robert Frost only if you've read "Birches". You don't like modern poetry. You like modern poetry or you haven't read Frost. So, you haven't read "Birches". (*P, F, B*)

(12) Henry James wrote short stories or poems. James wrote short stories or novels. He didn't write poems. Consequently, he wrote novels. (*S, P, N*)

(13) Sinclair Lewis wrote *Main Street* or *Look Homeward, Angel*, but not both. He wrote *Main Street*. If he didn't write *Look Homeward, Angel*, Lewis didn't write about North Carolina. Hence, he wrote neither *Look Homeward, Angel* nor about North Carolina. (*S, A, C*)

(14) Eugene O'Neill wrote plays, or he wrote novels and short stories. He wrote short stories or he didn't write novels. Thus, O'Neill wrote plays. (*P, N, S*)

(15) If the choroid absorbs light but doesn't make a reflection, we see a clear image. There isn't a clear image or the choroid absorbs light. The choroid doesn't absorb light. Hence, that the choroid doesn't make a reflection is a necessary condition that it absorbs light. (*L, R, I*)

(16) That the choroid absorbs light is a sufficient condition that it reduces reflection if, and only if, the image is clear. If it doesn't cut down reflection, it absorbs light. But, a choroid doesn't absorb light. Therefore, the image is clear. (*L, R, I*)

(17) The choroid doesn't absorb light. Either it isn't the case both that the choroid reduces reflection and doesn't blur the image, or the choroid does absorb light. The choroid doesn't absorb light if, and only if, it isn't the case both that it does blur the image and doesn't reduce reflection. Hence, the choroid reduces reflection or it blurs the image, but not both. (*L, R, I*)

(18) If actin is in the myofibril, so is myosin; also if the muscle contracts, ATP is part of the contraction complex. It isn't true that both myosin is in the myofibril and ATP is part of the contraction complex. The muscle contracts. Consequently, actin is in the myofibril. (*A, M, C, T*)

(19) It isn't true that both actin and not myosin are in the muscle filament bands. Further, it isn't true that both myosin but not actin are in the muscle filament bands. If a contraction occurs, then actin is in the muscle filament bands when, and only when, myosin is also in the bands. A relaxation or contraction occurs. Therefore, a relaxation occurs. (*A, M, C, R*)

(20) If actin is in the myofibril, then so is myosin; moreover, if ATP is split, the muscle contracts. It isn't the case both that actin isn't in the myofibril and ATP isn't split. The muscle doesn't contract. So, myosin isn't in the myofibril. (*A, M, T, C*)

5.   ANOTHER TRUTH-TABLE METHOD OF ESTABLISHING VALIDITY AND INVALIDITY

In the previous section we demonstrated the validity of a rather simple argument—simple in the sense that there were only eight rows in the truth-table of the hypothetical statement corresponding to that argument. Similar remarks were in order concerning our second argument, which was shown invalid by truth-table techniques. The same methods can be used for longer, more complicated arguments.

(1)   Grant won't be elected or he complies with the policies of the party boss. Now, Grant may preserve his personal integrity or not comply. Grant won't be in a position, however, to serve the needy people of his district if he preserves his personal integrity. If he isn't in a position to serve the needy people of his district, Grant is letting political corruption spread further. By his very nature Grant cannot allow political corruption to spread further. Hence, Grant is in the quandary of not being elected. (*E, C, I, S, P*)

In our symbolic notation, (1) reads

(2)   ∴ ~*E*
    1) ~*E* ∨ *C*   Pr
    2) *I* ∨ ~*C*   Pr
    3) *I* ⊃ ~*S*   Pr
    4) ~*S* ⊃ *P*   Pr
    5) ~*P*   Pr

We could now construct the required hypothetical statement, *grouping the premisses forming the antecedent by twos to the left.*

(3) $[(\{[(\sim E \vee C) \cdot (I \vee \sim C)] \cdot (I \supset \sim S)\} \cdot (\sim S \supset P)) \cdot \sim P] \supset \sim E$

The truth-table analysis of (3) would require thirty-two rows. Constructing thirty-two rows for (3) is not an impossible task, but it is tedious. There are easier ways of doing things!

We want to ascertain whether (1) is valid or not. Let us assume that it is not valid. If it is not valid, that is, if (1) is invalid, there will be *at least one way*—there may be more—of making the conclusion false and all the premisses true. If we cannot do this, (1) is not invalid, which is to say (1) is valid. *Can we interpret the conclusion as false and all the premisses true?*

'$\sim E$' is false only if 'E' is true. Since '$\sim E$' is the conclusion and we want to make the conclusion false, let us assume 'E' to be true. At every occurrence of 'E' in our premiss set we must assume it to be true since it is assumed true in the conclusion. A '$\sim E$' appears in the first premiss, but since 'E' has to be true—if the conclusion is to be false—this '$\sim E$' must be false. We are still attempting to make all the premisses true and the conclusion false. Since '$\sim E$' is false in the first premiss and since the first premiss is an inclusive disjunctive statement, the other disjunct, 'C', must be assumed true. A '$\sim C$' appears in the second premiss and must be false if the 'C' of the first premiss is true. This leads us to assume 'I' of the second premiss is true so that '$I \vee \sim C$' will be true. The antecedent of the third premiss, 'I', must therefore be true. Yet, if 'I' is true, and we hope to interpret all the premisses as true and the conclusion false, '$\sim S$' of the third premiss must be true. We are now led to the fourth premiss. Since 'S' is false in the third premiss, to make '$\sim S$' true, 'S' must also be false in the fourth premiss making '$\sim S$' true in the fourth premiss. But, if the antecedent of the fourth premiss is true, its consequent, 'P', must be true for that premiss to be true. Unfortunately, this makes the fifth premiss, '$\sim P$', false. In effect we have shown that there is no way to interpret the conclusion of (1) as false and all the premisses true. Since (1) cannot be invalid, it must be valid!

We can exhibit the information of the preceding paragraph like this:

(4)   *Where:*

1)	$\sim E \vee C$	$0 \vee 1$		$C = 1$
2)	$I \vee \sim C$	$1 \vee 0$		$E = 1$
3)	$I \supset \sim S$	$1 \supset 1$		$I = 1$
4)	$\sim S \supset P$	$1 \supset 1$		$P = 1$
5)	$\sim P$	~ 1	X	$S = 0$
	$\therefore \sim E$	$\therefore 0$		

where 'X' indicates the false premiss.

Or suppose we wished to demonstrate the validity or invalidity of this argument:

(5)   A person's moral practices are often not different from his claimed ethical
system. Yet, whenever a person's moral practices are often different from his
claimed ethical system, he may easily become psychopathic. That a person
may easily become psychopathic is a sufficient condition for not being able
to function at his best capacity. Now, a person may become mentally unbalanced whenever he is not able to function at his best capacity; furthermore,
if a person's moral practices are often different from his claimed ethical system,
local social conditions are usually the fundamental cause. Consequently, if a
person becomes mentally unbalanced, local social conditions are usually the
fundamental cause. (M, P, C, U, S)

In symbols, (5) may be expressed as

(6) $\therefore U \supset S$
   1) $\sim M$ Pr
   2) $M \supset P$ Pr
   3) $P \supset \sim C$ Pr
   4) $(\sim C \supset U) \cdot (M \supset S)$ Pr

Once more we *assume* the invalidity of (5), thereby interpreting '$U \supset S$' as
false while attempting to interpret all the premisses as true. If '$U \supset S$' is false,
'U' must be true and 'S' false. Furthermore, because we are trying to make all
the premisses true, '$\sim M$', the first premiss, must be true, which makes 'M' false.
Because 'M' is false, 'P' in the second premiss may be either true or false, leaving
the second premiss true. If we interpret 'P' as true, 'C' must be false and '$\sim C$'
true in the third premiss. This would also make '$\sim C$' true in the fourth premiss,
and since 'U' is true, '$\sim C \supset U$' would be true. Because we have said that 'M'
is false, '$M \supset S$' is true, and hence the fourth premiss is also true. Consequently,
there is at least one way to interpret all the premisses of (5) as true and the conclusion false. The argument is invalid. This information may be pictured in this
way:

(7)   *Where:*
  1) $\sim M$ ~ 0 $C = 0$
  2) $M \supset P$ $0 \supset 1$ $M = 0$
  3) $P \supset \sim C$ $1 \supset 1$ $P = 1$
  4) $(\sim C \supset U) \cdot (M \supset S)$ $(1 \supset 1) \cdot (0 \supset 0)$ $S = 0$
     $\therefore U \supset S$ $\therefore 1 \supset 0$ $U = 1$

It should be noticed that there may be several ways of assigning truth-values to
the statements in a given truth-functional argument showing the invalidity of that
argument. For example, instead of (7) we may have written

(8)   *Where:*

1)	$\sim M$	~ 0	$C = 0$
2)	$M \supset P$	$0 \supset 0$	$M = 0$
3)	$P \supset \sim C$	$0 \supset 1$	$P = 0$
4)	$(\sim C \supset U)\cdot(U \supset S)$	$(1 \supset 1)\cdot(0 \supset 0)$	$S = 0$
	$\therefore\ U \supset S$	$\therefore\ 1 \supset 0$	$U = 1$

The important point is that *we need show only one such interpretation to show the argument invalid.*

Many arguments have conclusions which might be falsified in a number of different ways. If a particular conclusion is a conjunction, it might be falsified in three distinct ways; if a biconditional, in two; and so on. Furthermore, some ways of falsifying the conclusion might not yield all true premises. To demonstrate a truth-functional argument invalid, it is enough to show at least one way of falsifying the conclusion and having all true premises, although our first attempts might fail. If, on the other hand, there is *no way* of showing the conclusion false and all the premisses true, we have demonstrated the validity of that argument.

EXERCISES

Group A:

Use the truth-table techniques developed in this section to establish the validity or invalidity of the arguments in the exercises of the preceding section.

Group B:

Using the truth-table techniques developed in this section, determine which of the following are valid and which invalid.

(1) $\therefore\ B \supset A$
    1) A Pr

(2) $\therefore\ A \supset B$
    1) A Pr

(3) $\therefore\ B$
    1) $(A \supset B)\cdot A$ Pr

(4) $\therefore\ B$
    1) $(A \supset B)\vee A$ Pr

(5) $\therefore\ B$
    1) $(A \supset B)\vee \sim A$ Pr

(6) $\therefore\ A \supset C$
    1) $\sim A \vee (B\cdot C)$ Pr

(7) $\qquad\qquad\qquad\qquad\qquad\qquad\therefore\ C \supset B$

   1) $(A \cdot B) \supset C$ Pr

   2) A Pr

(8) $\qquad\qquad\qquad\qquad\qquad\qquad\therefore\ C \vee B$

   1) $(A \equiv B) \supset [C \vee (A \cdot B)]$ Pr

   2) $(A \supset C) \cdot (C \supset B)$ Pr

   3) $(B \supset C) \cdot (C \supset A)$ Pr

(9) $\qquad\qquad\qquad\qquad\qquad\qquad\therefore\ A \cdot B$

   1) $C \supset (A \cdot C)$ Pr

   2) $(A \cdot B) \vee B$ Pr

   3) $\sim B \triangle C$ Pr

(10) $\qquad\qquad\qquad\qquad\qquad\qquad\therefore\ C \triangle B$

   1) $\sim[(B \cdot \sim C) \cdot \sim A]$ Pr

   2) $\sim(A \cdot \sim B)$ Pr

   3) $\sim(\sim C \cdot \sim B)$ Pr

(11) $\qquad\qquad\qquad\qquad\qquad\qquad\therefore\ C \equiv D$

   1) $A \supset (C \supset D)$ Pr

   2) $B \triangle (D \cdot B)$ Pr

   3) $(D \cdot \sim C) \supset B$ Pr

   4) $D \cdot A$ Pr

(12) $\qquad\qquad\qquad\qquad\qquad\qquad\therefore\ A \cdot (C \cdot B)$

   1) $(D \vee B) \supset C$ Pr

   2) $A \triangle D$ Pr

   3) $(C \vee B) \supset D$ Pr

   4) $D \supset (B \cdot \sim D)$ Pr

(13) $\qquad\qquad\qquad\qquad\qquad\qquad\therefore\ A \supset (B \equiv C)$

   1) $\sim(D \cdot A)$ Pr

   2) $A \supset (\sim D \equiv \sim B)$ Pr

   3) $(D \cdot A) \supset C$ Pr

(14) $\qquad\qquad\qquad\qquad\qquad\qquad\therefore\ (C \supset B) \vee \sim(B \vee C)$

   1) $(A \supset B) \supset (C \supset B)$ Pr

   2) $(D \supset C) \supset \sim(B \vee C)$ Pr

(15) $\qquad\qquad\qquad\qquad\qquad\qquad\therefore\ (\sim B \vee D) \cdot (D \vee \sim A)$

   1) $A \equiv B$ Pr

   2) $\sim C \equiv B$ Pr

   3) $(A \vee D) \cdot \sim C$ Pr

(16) $\qquad\qquad\qquad\qquad\qquad\qquad\therefore\ C \vee \sim F$

   1) $A \supset (B \supset C)$ Pr

   2) $\sim D \supset (E \supset \sim F)$ Pr

   3) $\sim(A \cdot D) \supset \sim(B \vee E)$ Pr

   4) $E \vee B$ Pr

(17) $\therefore \sim(\sim B \cdot \sim F)$

     1) $\sim(A \supset B) \supset C$ Pr
     2) $D \supset \sim(E \cdot \sim F)$ Pr
     3) $A \triangle E$ Pr
     4) $\sim(\sim C \cdot D) \supset E$ Pr
     5) $\sim E$ Pr

(18) $\therefore F \vee G$

     1) $(A \supset B) \cdot (C \supset D)$ Pr
     2) $\sim(A \vee C) \supset \sim E$ Pr
     3) $(D \supset F) \cdot (B \supset G)$ Pr
     4) E Pr

(19) $\therefore (B \vee C) \cdot (E \vee H)$

     1) $\sim A \equiv \sim B$ Pr
     2) $\sim A \equiv C$ Pr
     3) $(D \supset E) \cdot B$ Pr
     4) $F \supset G$ Pr
     5) $\sim(\sim D \cdot \sim F)$ Pr
     6) $\sim G$ Pr

(20) $\therefore \sim F \supset J$

     1) $\sim A \supset \sim B$ Pr
     2) $A \supset (C \triangle D)$ Pr
     3) $E \supset (C \supset F)$ Pr
     4) $\sim(G \cdot E)$ Pr
     5) $G \triangle \sim H$ Pr
     6) $H \triangle I$ Pr
     7) $I \supset (D \supset J)$ Pr
     8) $H \cdot B$ Pr

6.   CONSISTENCY AND INCONSISTENCY

Arguments are often spoken of as '*consistent*' or '*inconsistent*'. Briefly

> *for a consistent argument there is at least one assignment of '1's and '0's to the premiss set of that argument which would make the premisses all true. For an inconsistent argument there is no assignment of '1's and '0's to the premiss set of that argument which would make all the premisses true.*

Consequently, when we use the terms 'consistency' and 'inconsistency', we really are saying something about the premiss set of an argument. Only in that arguments have premisses are we justified in calling arguments 'consistent' or 'inconsistent'.

Our mastery of truth-tables allows us to demonstrate whether a truth-functional argument is consistent or inconsistent. The procedure is very simple:

(1)   *Symbolize all the premisses of the argument in question.*
(2)   *Put these premisses in conjunction—if there is more than one—by pairs, associating to the left.*
(3)   *Construct a truth-table for this conjunction.*
(4)   *If the conjunction is either tautological or contingent, the premisses are consistent; if the conjunction is contradictory, the premisses are inconsistent.*

It is suggested that the premisses of an argument are consistent if there is at least one interpretation making them all true. Hence, if the conjunction formed from the premisses is either contingent or tautological, there will be one such interpretation, for a conjunction is true when, and only when, all its conjuncts are true. But, the premisses are the conjuncts! If the conjunction formed from the premisses is contradictory, the premisses are inconsistent. In this case there would be always at least one conjunct—at least one premiss—false in order for the conjunction to be false in every row of its truth-table analysis.

Consider this argument:

(1)   Either my Zipper Gripper will hold or I'll be most embarrassed, but not both. It isn't true that my Zipper Gripper will hold and I shall not be most embarrassed. Further, either I shall not be most embarrassed or my Zipper Gripper will hold. My Zipper Gripper isn't going to hold. Therefore, I'll be most embarrassed. (G, E)

Using statement initials and our logical constants, (1) may be symbolized as

(2) $\therefore E$
   1) $G \triangle E$ Pr
   2) $\sim(G \cdot \sim E)$ Pr
   3) $\sim E \lor G$ Pr
   4) $\sim G$ Pr

Is the premiss set of (1) consistent? This is easily determined by putting all the premisses in conjunction and then constructing a truth-table for that statement.

(3) $\{[(G \triangle E) \cdot \sim (G \cdot \sim E)] \cdot (\sim E \lor G)\} \cdot \sim G$
           1 0 1   0 1   1 0 0 1   0   0 1 1 1   0 0 1
           1 1 0   0 0   1 1 1 0   0   1 0 1 1   0 0 1
           0 1 1   0 1   0 0 0 1   0   0 1 0 0   0 1 0
           0 0 0   0 1   0 0 1 0   0   1 0 1 0   0 1 0
                                                 ↑

At once we see that the column under the farthermost right-hand dot has a '0' in every row. Since this final column of the truth-table analysis consists entirely of '0's, the overall conjunction is shown to be contradictory. The premisses of (1) must, therefore, be inconsistent. *There is no way of interpreting these premisses such that they would all be true.*

We might ask ourselves if the following argument is consistent or inconsistent:

(4)   It isn't true that this litmus paper is put into an acid solution but at the same time doesn't turn red. Had this litmus paper turned red, the experiment wouldn't have been a failure. Either this litmus paper is put into an acid solution and doesn't turn red, or the experiment is a failure. The litmus paper, therefore, doesn't turn red and the experiment is a failure. (S, R, F)

Symbolizing (4), we have

(5) $\therefore \sim R \cdot F$

1) $\sim (S \cdot \sim R)$ Pr
2) $R \supset \sim F$ Pr
3) $(S \cdot \sim R) \vee F$ Pr

Next, we place the premisses of (5) into conjunction, associate to the left, and construct a truth-table:

(6) $[\sim (S \cdot \sim R) \cdot (R \supset \sim F)] \cdot [(S \cdot \sim R) \vee F]$

```
1 1 0 0 1  0  1 0 0 1  0  1 0 0 1 1 1
1 1 0 0 1  1  1 1 1 0  0  1 0 0 1 0 0
0 1 1 1 0  0  0 1 0 1  0  1 1 1 0 1 1
0 1 1 1 0  0  0 1 1 0  0  1 1 1 0 1 0
1 0 0 0 1  0  1 0 0 1  0  0 0 0 1 1 1
1 0 0 0 1  1  1 1 1 0  0  0 0 0 1 0 0
1 0 0 1 0  1  0 1 0 1  1  0 0 1 0 1 1
1 0 0 1 0  1  0 1 1 0  0  0 0 1 0 0 0
                      ↑
```

Inspecting our truth-table, we discover that (6) is a contingent statement, having at least one '1' and at least one '0' in its final truth-table column. However, since the conjuncts of (6) are the premisses of our original argument, (4), we know there is at least one interpretation making all the premisses true. Of course this interpretation is when 'S' and 'R' are set at '0' and 'F' at '1'. Therefore, our premisses are consistent.

It should not be surprising to notice that *any argument having an inconsistent premiss set is valid no matter what the conclusion of that argument might be.* Given inconsistent premisses, any conclusion is logically entailed by them. Why? We remember that any argument is valid if, and only if, a certain hypothetical statement constructed from the argument is tautological. The antecedent of the hypothetical statement in question is nothing more than the conjunction of all the premisses of the argument. If the premisses of an argument are inconsistent, their conjunction is always contradictory—'0', or false, in every row. A hypothetical statement is false, however, only when the antecedent is true and the consequent false. In the case of inconsistent premises the antecedent can never be true, and, consequently, the hypothetical statement can never be false. The hypothetical statement must be tautological regardless of its consequent! The argument must be valid regardless of its conclusion!

Because any conclusion whatsoever is logically entailed by an inconsistent premiss set, in one sense such a premiss set is rather uninteresting. It allows us "to say too much". In another sense it is extremely important to ascertain whether or not a given premiss set is consistent or inconsistent. What if Newton's laws of motion were inconsistent? Anything could then be proved, given these laws. What if various premisses in finance happened to be inconsistent? Anything could be shown to follow from those premisses. Or, what if a person holds certain political beliefs which are inconsistent? He may strictly prove anything he wishes. The notions of consistency and inconsistency become very important, then, in our lives. And while we have developed only a method for determining whether truth-functional arguments are consistent or inconsistent, this is an important step forward.

One final word: While all inconsistent arguments are valid no matter what the conclusion, *no inconsistent argument can ever be sound.* A sound argument is not only valid but also has nothing but true premisses—something which can never be enjoyed by an inconsistent argument.

EXERCISES

Symbolize the following arguments using the suggested notation. Then determine by shortened-form truth-tables which of these arguments has a consistent premiss set and which an inconsistent premiss set. Further, determine by shortened-form truth-tables whether those arguments having consistent premiss sets are valid or invalid.

(1) John Steinbeck wrote about itinerant farmers if, and only if, his works contain stories about people traveling from place to place in search of agricultural jobs. So, either Steinbeck wrote about itinerant farmers or his works contain stories about people traveling from place to place in search of agricultural jobs. (*F, W*)

(2) William Faulkner was awarded the Nobel Prize. If Faulkner was awarded the Nobel Prize, he is considered a successful writer. Hence, Faulkner is considered a successful writer. (*P, W*)

(3) Edgar Allan Poe wrote either *The Pit and the Pendulum* or *Chrome Yellow.* He didn't write *Chrome Yellow.* Therefore, Poe's having written *The Pit and the Pendulum* is a sufficient reason for his having written *Chrome Yellow.* (*P, Y*)

(4) Lord Byron wrote "Don Juan", or he wrote "The Battle of Blenheim" but not "Don Juan". So, Byron wrote "Don Juan". (*J, B*)

(5) That Percy Bysshe Shelley wrote "Adonais" implies he wrote "Don Juan". But it isn't true that Shelley wrote "Adonais" and "Don Juan". Shelley didn't write "Don Juan". Consequently, he wrote either "Adonais" or "Don Juan". (*A, J*)

(6) The League of Nations would have been valuable had Woodrow Wilson been right. If the League of Nations had been valuable, America would not have followed an isolationist policy and, moreover, Wilson would have been right. So, if Wilson had been right, America would not have followed an isolationist policy. (*L*, *W*, *A*)

(7) If Woodrow Wilson and advocates of world government were correct, then the Senate should have accepted the League of Nations. The advocates of world government having been correct was a necessary condition for the Senate having accepted the League of Nations. Therefore, if Wilson was correct, the advocates of world government were also correct. (*W*, *A*, *S*)

(8) Either the Senate or Woodrow Wilson was correct in their opinion of the League of Nations. It isn't the case that if Wilson wasn't correct in his opinion, then the Senate was. Hence, either Wilson was correct in his opinion of the League of Nations or America wasn't prepared to have an isolationist policy. (*S*, *W*, *A*)

(9) Aristotle was a student of Plato; moreover, either Empedocles or Plato followed Socrates. It isn't true both that Empedocles didn't follow Socrates while Aristotle was a student of Plato. Hence, Empedocles didn't follow Socrates; yet Aristotle was a student of Plato. (*A*, *E*, *P*)

(10) Either pleasure or happiness (but not both) is the chief end of man; moreover, happiness is man's chief end. That pleasure is the chief end of man is a necessary and sufficient condition for Aristotle's *Nicomachean Ethics* being wrong. So, Aristotle's *Nicomachean Ethics* is wrong. (*P*, *H*, *E*)

(11) If the most important problem of any individual is not merely to live but to live well, we may want to study Plato. Of course the most important problem of any individual *is* to live well. We may not want to study Plato even though the most important problem of any individual is not merely to live. Therefore, if the most important problem of any individual is not merely to live, then we may want to study Plato. (*L*, *W*, *P*)

(12) It isn't the case both that Socrates is correct in his position and we should be unjust. Either Socrates or Thrasymachus is correct. Socrates is correct. So, we should be just despite the fact that Thrasymachus is correct. (*S*, *J*, *T*)

(13) That we don't ignore both Plato and Aristotle suggests we're concerned with leading a good life. Not being concerned with leading a good life is a necessary condition for ignoring Aristotle. Now, we don't ignore both Aristotle and Plato. Therefore, we're concerned with leading the good life while also not ignoring Aristotle. (*P*, *A*, *L*)

(14) If "Portrait of Leander" was written in the sixteenth century, then if "Loved by a God" was also written in the sixteenth century, the poems were written by Christopher Marlowe. Of course "Loved by a God" was written in the sixteenth century. Furthermore, that the poems were written by Marlowe is a sufficient reason for claiming that "Loved by a God" and "Portrait of Leander" were both written in the sixteenth century. So, that Marlowe wrote these poems is a necessary and sufficient condition that "Portrait of Leander" was written in the sixteenth century. (*L, G, M*)

(**15**)   Aldous Huxley wrote *Hadrian's Memoirs* or *Brave New World* (but not both), or he was a poet and wrote "Desiderato". Huxley wrote both *Brave New World* and *Hadrian's Memoirs*, although he didn't write "Desiderato". Consequently, if he wrote "Desiderato", he wrote *Brave New World* and was also a poet. (*M, W, P, D*)

(**16**)   John Keats is not a Romantic writer if, and only if, Robert Browning is. If Keats is a Romantic writer, he isn't a Victorian author. The poetry of Keats has Victorian characteristics or he isn't a Victorian author, but not both. Therefore, it isn't the case both that Browning isn't a Romantic writer while Keats' poetry has Victorian characteristics. (*K, B, A, C*)

(**17**)   If adenine is a purine while uracil isn't, then guanine is a purine. It isn't true that adenine isn't a purine and guanine is. Neither uracil nor guanine is a purine. Further, it isn't the case both that guanine is a purine and thymine isn't. So, thymine is a purine. (*A, U, G, T*)

(**18**)   If adenine is a purine, so is guanine. While adenine is a purine, uracil isn't. That thymine is a pyrimidine is a sufficient condition for the following not being the case; namely, if adenine is a purine, uracil isn't. That uracil is a purine is a necessary condition for guanine being a purine. Hence, thymine is a pyrimidine and if uracil is a purine then so is guanine. (*A, G, U, T*)

(**19**)   Madge will come to the Halloween party if, and only if, Grace isn't there. If Louise doesn't come to the party, Grace is there. Either Madge comes to the Halloween party or everyone goes to Peachtree Street; moreover, Louise doesn't come. So Grace doesn't come to the Halloween party and everyone goes to Peachtree Street. (*M, G, L, P*)

(**20**)   That Julia will stay at her cottage is a necessary condition for the following: It's raining or cold (but not both), while it isn't the case that she isn't listening to Bach and isn't reading *Peanuts*. Therefore, that it isn't the case that she is listening to Bach and it isn't raining is a sufficient condition for Julia staying at her cottage. (*J, R, C, B, P*)

4

Logical Definitions

and

Logical Equivalences

In our study of the *a priori* forms of descriptive language we have examined statements exhibiting the forms

$$\sim p$$
$$p \cdot q$$
$$p \vee q$$
$$p \triangle q$$
$$p \supset q$$
$$p \equiv q$$

From the viewpoint of deductive logic, some of these forms could be eliminated. This remark is not only important for the development of deductive logic, it is also important because it indicates how closely related certain statements of descriptive language are. Suppose I said to you

(1)   If Niels Bohr is correct, classical physics must be augmented.

From a logical point of view I could have said the same thing by asserting

(2)   Either Niels Bohr is not correct or classical physics must be augmented.

Or perhaps I might even have claimed

(3)   It isn't true that Niels Bohr is correct and classical physics must not be augmented.

Certainly, the sentences expressed by (1), (2), and (3) differ grammatically, rhetorically, in their number of words, and so on. But they all share a common feature: Whatever makes one of these, as statements, truth-functionally true makes them all truth-functionally true, and whatever makes one truth-functionally false makes them all truth-functionally false. Sentences (1) and (2) suggest that we could eliminate statements of the forms '$p \supset q$' and '$\sim p \lor q$', reexpressing them in terms of 'not' and 'and' as in (3).

This suggestion is correct; moreover, it can be expanded. We can reexpress any truth-functional statement in terms of only the tilde and dot or only the tilde and wedge or only the tilde and horseshoe. From the point of view of our deductive logic we could do away with any two of these: the dot, the wedge, or the horseshoe. That we retain all these logical operators in our symbolization is a matter of convenience in rendering ordinary descriptive language into our logical notation. More technically, let us say that the tilde and dot, the tilde and wedge, and the tilde and horseshoe are *functionally complete sets of operators for the Truth-Functional Calculus*. Symbolically, we write

$$\{\sim, \cdot\} \qquad \{\sim, \lor\} \qquad \{\sim, \supset\}$$

where the braces mean 'functionally complete set of operators'.

Any truth-functional statement can be rewritten in terms of $\{\sim, \cdot\}$ or $\{\sim, \lor\}$ or $\{\sim, \supset\}$. No matter which set we select, the logical operators in that set will be known as '*primitive operators*'. Within the system we select, all logical operators which are not primitive will be defined in terms of the primitive operators. Hence, any statement using a nonprimitive operator may be looked upon simply as an *abbreviation* of a statement written entirely in terms of primitive operators. The primitive operators are not defined within the system; all other logical operators are defined by means of the primitives.

In our three functionally complete sets of operators for the Truth-Functional Calculus, the tilde appears in each set and is said to be *absolutely primitive*. On the other hand, the dot, the wedge, and the horseshoe are said to be *relatively primitive* for the functionally complete set in which each appears.

Suppose we wanted to define statements of the forms '$p \lor q$', '$p \triangle q$', '$p \supset q$', and '$p \equiv q$' in terms of the tilde and dot. Let us see how this might be accomplished.

The truth-table for any statement of the form '$p \lor q$' is

(4) $p \lor q$
           1 1 1
           1 1 0
           0 1 1
           0 0 0
             ↑

A statement of the form '$p \lor q$' is false, '0', just in that case when both the statements at 'p' and 'q' are false. Symbolically, we may write this as

(5) $\sim p \cdot \sim q$

Now, let us deny (5):

(6) $\sim (\sim p \cdot \sim q)$

Constructing a truth-table for (6), we have

(7) $\sim (\sim p \ \cdot \ \sim q)$
           1 0 1 0 0 0 1
           1 0 1 0 1 0
           1 1 0 0 0 1
           0 1 0 1 1 0
           ↑

Notice that (6) is written entirely in terms of the tilde and dot—*one* possible set of primitive operators. But also notice that the final truth-table column of (4) is exactly the same as the final truth-table column of (7):

                                1

                                1

                                1

                                0

Therefore '$p \lor q$' is defined in terms of '$\sim (\sim p \cdot \sim q)$'.

To assert that one statement, or statement form, is defined in terms of another statement, or statement form, let us use the notation '$- - - = \cdots$ Df'. Further, that statement, or statement form, to the left of the equals sign is called the '*definiendum*', or 'that which is to be defined'. The statement, or statement form, to the right of the equals sign is known as the '*definiens*', or 'that which defines'. In a correctly constructed logical definition, only primitive operators are found in the *definiens*, while any other logical operator is found in the *definiendum*. All this information is expressed in the following definition of '$p \lor q$' in terms of '$\sim(\sim p \cdot \sim q)$'.

(8)   '$p \lor q$' = '$\sim(\sim p \cdot \sim q)$'   Df

Following the procedure above, we construct a definition for '$p \triangle q$'. First we notice the truth-table for '$p \triangle q$':

(9) $p \triangle q$
   1 0 1
   1 1 0
   0 1 1
   0 0 0
     ↑

Any statement of the form '$p \triangle q$' is false when both the statements at 'p' and 'q' are true or when both are false. This is to say, in our notation,

(10) $(p \cdot q) \cdot (\sim p \cdot \sim q)$

Denying separately both possibilities for falsifying a statement of the form '$p \triangle q$', we write

(11) $\sim(p \cdot q) \cdot \sim(\sim p \cdot \sim q)$

Constructing a truth-table for (11), we have

(12) $\sim(p \cdot q) \cdot \sim(\sim p \cdot \sim q)$
   0 1 1 1 0 1 0 1 0 0 1
   1 1 0 0 1 1 0 1 0 1 0
   1 0 0 1 1 1 1 0 0 0 1
   1 0 0 0 0 0 1 0 1 0 1 1 0
       ↑

Not only is (12) rendered solely in terms of the tilde and dot, but also its final truth-table column is the same as that of (9). Therefore, we say

(13)   '$p \triangle q$' = '$\sim(p \cdot q) \cdot \sim(\sim p \cdot \sim q)$'   Df

The truth-table for '$p \supset q$' is

(14) $p \supset q$
   1 1 1
   1 0 0
   0 1 1
   0 1 0
     ↑

which shows that a statement of the form '$p \supset q$' is false if, and only if, the statement at 'p' is true and at 'q' false, or

(15) $p \cdot \sim q$

Denying (15) yields

(16) $\sim(p \cdot \sim q)$

If we construct a truth-table for (16),

(17) $\sim(p \quad \cdot \quad \sim q)$
         1 1 0   0 1
         0 1 1   1 0
         1 0 0   0 1
         1 0 0   1 0
         ↑

we discover that the final truth-table column of (17) is the same as the final column of (14). Thus, we assert

(18)   '$p \supset q$' = '$\sim(p \cdot \sim q)$'   Df

Finally, we build a truth-table for '$p \equiv q$':

(19) $p \equiv q$
         1 1 1
         1 0 0
         0 0 1
         0 1 0
           ↑

and notice that only when the statements at 'p' and 'q' have opposite truth-values is '$p \equiv q$' false; that is,

(20) $(p \cdot \sim q) \cdot (q \cdot \sim p)$

Denying separately both of these possibilities, we write

(21) $\sim(p \cdot \sim q) \cdot \sim(q \cdot \sim p)$

And now, let us construct a truth-table for (21):

(22) $\sim(p \quad \cdot \quad \sim q) \quad \cdot \quad \sim(q \quad \cdot \quad \sim p)$
         1 1 0   0 1   1 1 1   0 0 1
         0 1 1   1 0   0 1 0   0 0 1
         1 0 0   0 1   0 0 1   1 1 0
         1 0 0   1 0   1 1 0   0 1 0
             ↑

We quickly see that the final column of the truth-table in (22) is exactly the same as that of (19). Furthermore, (22) is expressed by using only the tilde and dot. We therefore say

(23)   '$p \equiv q$' $=$ '$\sim(p \cdot \sim q) \cdot \sim(q \cdot \sim p)$'   Df

Reviewing our four definitions, we have

(24)   '$p \vee q$' $=$ '$\sim(\sim p \cdot \sim q)$'   Df
        '$p \triangle q$' $=$ '$\sim(p \cdot q) \cdot \sim(\sim p \cdot \sim q)$'   Df
        '$p \supset q$' $=$ '$\sim(p \cdot \sim q)$'   Df
        '$p \equiv q$' $=$ '$\sim(p \cdot \sim q) \cdot \sim(q \cdot \sim p)$'   Df

In each case the *definiendum* (that expression containing only nonprimitive operators) is defined in terms of an appropriate *definiens* (that expression containing only primitive operators).

Which set of logical operators we select as primitives is a matter of some freedom. For example, if we were to opt for the tilde and wedge as comprising our set of primitive operators, we could construct these definitions:

(25)   '$p \cdot q$' $=$ '$\sim(\sim p \vee \sim q)$'   Df
        '$p \supset q$' $=$ '$\sim p \vee q$'   Df

Or, having chosen the tilde and horseshoe as our primitive operators, we could use the following as definitions:

(26)   '$p \cdot q$' $=$ '$\sim(p \supset \sim q)$'   Df
        '$p \vee q$' $=$ '$\sim p \supset q$'   Df

It is now possible in an orderly manner to transform any truth-functional statement into a statement using only truth-functional denial and conjunction. First, symbolize the statement, and then change the various operators that are not a tilde or a dot by appealing to our definitions in (24). For example, consider this statement:

(27)   If it's cold or the fire is burning, and it's raining or snowing (but not both), then we'll stay home tonight. (C, F, R, S, H)

    $[(C \vee F) \cdot (R \triangle S)] \supset H$

We may first transform '$C \vee F$' into its definitional equivalence:

(28) $[\sim(\sim C \cdot \sim F) \cdot (R \triangle S)] \supset H$

Next working with '$R \triangle S$', we obtain

(29) $\{\sim(\sim C \cdot \sim F) \cdot [\sim(R \cdot S) \cdot \sim(\sim R \cdot \sim S)]\} \supset H$

Finally, we convert the overall hypothetical statement, (29), into terms of the tilde and dot:

(30) $\sim\big(\{\sim(\sim C\cdot\sim F)\cdot[\sim(R\cdot S)\cdot\sim(\sim R\cdot\sim S)]\}\cdot\sim H\big)$

Statement (30), from a truth-functional point of view, is simply (27) reexpressed in terms of $\{\sim,\,\cdot\}$.

EXERCISES

Group A:

What do we mean by '*definiendum*', by '*definiens*'?

Group B:

(1) Using only the tilde and wedge, construct definitions for '$p \triangle q$' and '$p \equiv q$'. Use truth-tables to check your work.

(2) Using only the tilde and horseshoe, construct definitions for '$p \triangle q$' and '$p \equiv q$'. Use truth-tables to check your work.

Group C:

Symbolize the following statements using the suggested notation, and then transform each symbolized statement into one using only the tilde and the dot.

(1) To be well educated, you must be familiar with the writings of W. H. Auden or T. S. Eliot. (A, E)

(2) Having carefully read the works of Plato, then you'll be in a better position to understand T. S. Eliot. (P, E)

(3) Either you've not read *Ushant* or you're well versed in contemporary literature, but not both. (U, L)

(4) It isn't true that you've ignored Sigmund Freud if you're interested in Conrad Aiken. (F, A)

(5) Neither did T. S. Eliot not write "Old Deuteronomy" nor did he not write "Mr. Mistoffelees". (D, M)

(6) If Conrad Aiken was greatly influenced by the death of his parents, then he was influenced by Sigmund Freud only if his writings are introspective. (D, F, W)

(7) That you are interested in Dylan Thomas is a sufficient reason to read both "A Child's Christmas in Wales" and "Under Milk Wood". (T, C, W)

(8) Appreciating W. H. Auden is a necessary condition for appreciating fine balance of sound and rhythm. (A, S, R)

(9) Either you find E. E. Cummings exciting, or if you read his poetry, you become bewildered. (*C, P, B*)

(10) Dylan Thomas was a burly man or a bit of a ham, but always a great poet. (*M, H, P*)

(11) It isn't the case that being interested in second-rate literature and not knowing Greek mythology is a necessary condition for reading the works of Robert Graves. (*L, M, W*)

(12) Either you're acquainted with Ernest Hemingway's writings or you're neither interested in American literature nor the short story—but not both. (*H, L, S*)

(13) If William Faulkner may be considered either a Mississippian or Virginian, but surely a world-famous author, then he may be considered a world-famous author and a Mississippian, or he may be considered a world-famous author and a Virginian. (*M, V, A*)

(14) You're not interested in southern literature or you've read both the works of Truman Capote and Carson McCullers if, and only if, you're not interested in southern literature or you've read the works of McCullers. (*L, C, M*)

(15) If you're familiar with southern literature when, and only when, you've read the major southern writers whenever you've read broadly, then you've both read broadly and read the major southern writers only if you're familiar with southern literature. (*L, W, R*)

2. LOGICAL EQUIVALENCES

In our study of logic we shall say that two statements, or statement forms, are logically equivalent if, and only if, they are both true under exactly the same conditions and both false under exactly the same conditions, that is, if they have identical truth-values given identical truth-conditions. For example, the following statements are logically equivalent:

(1) If the neuron is alive and fires, then it has a given minimum number of excitatory fibers.

(2) If the neuron is alive, it has a given number of excitatory fibers whenever it fires.

The truth-conditions making (1) true are the very same conditions guaranteeing the truth of (2), and vice versa. Further, whatever conditions make (1) false are the same as those which guarantee the falsity of (2), and vice versa. This being the case, we can devise a truth-table method for determining whether any two truth-functional statements are logically equivalent or not:

(1) *Symbolize the truth-functional statements in question.*

(2) *From these two symbolized statements, construct a third statement of the form 'p ≡ q' where 'p' is one of the original symbolized statements and 'q' the other.*

(3) *Construct a truth-table analysis of this biconditional.*

(4) *If the biconditional is either contingent or contradictory, the original two statements are **not** logically equivalent; but if the biconditional is tautological, the original two statements **are** logically equivalent.*

For example, returning to (1) and (2), we can illustrate these four steps:

(1) $(A \cdot F) \supset N$

        $A \supset (F \supset N)$

(2) $[(A \cdot F) \supset N] \equiv [A \supset (F \supset N)]$

(3) $[(A \cdot F) \supset N] \equiv [A \supset (F \supset N)]$

```
1 1 1   1 1   1   1 1   1 1 1
1 1 1   0 0   1   1 0   1 0 0
1 0 0   1 1   1   1 1   0 1 1
1 0 0   1 0   1   1 1   0 1 0
0 0 1   1 1   1   0 1   1 1 1
0 0 1   1 0   1   0 1   1 0 0
0 0 0   1 1   1   0 1   0 1 1
0 0 0   1 0   1   0 1   0 1 0
              ↑
```

(4)   Since only '1's appear under the triple-bar, we know that '[(A·F) ⊃ N] ≡ [A ⊃ (F ⊃ N)]' is tautological and, therefore, '[(A·F) ⊃ N]' and '[A ⊃ (F ⊃ N)]' are logically equivalent statements.

Note that corresponding to every definitional equivalence there is a logical equivalence. It is not the case, however, that corresponding to every logical equivalence there is a definitional equivalence.

You will find both definitional and logical equivalences playing an important role in successive chapters.

EXERCISES

Symbolize the following pairs of statements using the suggested notation. By truth-table methods, determine which statements are logically equivalent and which are not.

Example: a) Either the sky fell on Chicken Little or Mother Hen was happy; moreover, it isn't the case both that the sky fell on Chicken Little but Mother Hen was happy. (*L, H*)

           b) The sky falling on Chicken Little implies that Mother Hen wasn't happy; despite which Mother Hen was happy or the sky fell on Chicken Little. (L, H)

$$(L \lor H) \cdot \sim (L \cdot H)$$

$$(L \supset \sim H) \cdot (H \lor L)$$

$$[(L \lor H) \cdot \sim (L \cdot H)] \equiv [(L \supset \sim H) \cdot (H \lor L)]$$

```
1 1 1  0 0 1 1 1   1  1 0 0 1 0 1 1 1
1 1 0  1 1 1 0 0   1  1 1 1 0 1 0 1 1
0 1 1  1 1 0 0 1   1  0 1 0 1 1 1 1 0
0 0 0  0 1 0 0 0   1  0 1 1 0 0 0 0 0
                   ↑
```

Since the biconditional formed from the original two statements is a tautology, these statements are logically equivalent.

(1) a) Charles Baudelaire is a familiar French poet. (B)
    b) Charles Baudelaire isn't an unfamiliar French poet. (B)

(2) a) You are fond of either André Gide or Paul Claudel. (G, C)
    b) You are fond of either Paul Claudel or André Gide. (C, G)

(3) a) It isn't true that Stephane Mallarmé and Rainer Rilke are both French poets. (M, R)
    b) Either Stephane Mallarmé is not a French poet or Rainer Rilke isn't. (M, R)

(4) a) Either you aren't interested in Naturalism or you've read Émile Zola. (N, Z)
    b) You aren't interested in Naturalism; however, you've read Émile Zola. (N, Z)

(5) a) Neither Victor Hugo nor Théophile Gautier belong to the eighteenth century. (H, G)
    b) Théophile Gautier doesn't belong to the eighteenth century, but also Victor Hugo doesn't belong to it. (G, H)

(6) a) It isn't the case both that a person of letters hasn't read François-René de Chateaubriand and also hasn't read Alphonse de Lamartine. (C, L)
    b) A person of letters has read either Alphonse de Lamartine or François-René de Chateaubriand. (L, C)

(7) a) Either you have read *Le Petit Prince* or you understand Antoine de Saint-Exupéry, but not both. (P, E)
    b) You understand Antoine de Saint-Exupéry when, and only when, you have read *Le Petit Prince*. (E, P)

(8) a) An educated person has read Marcel Proust and Colette. (P, C)
    b) An educated person neither has not read Marcel Proust nor has not read Colette. (P, C)

(9) a) If you have felt ennui, you can understand Charles Baudelaire. (E, B)
    b) Not understanding Charles Baudelaire is a sufficient reason for not having felt ennui. (B, E)

(10) a) You hold Gustave Flaubert to be a Realist or Paul Verlaine to be a Naturalist;

moreover, you don't hold both that Flaubert is a Realist and Verlaine a Naturalist. (*F, V*)

b) You don't hold Paul Verlaine to be a Naturalist whenever you hold Gustave Flaubert to be a Realist, even though you hold Verlaine to be a Naturalist or Flaubert a Realist. (*V, F*)

(11) a) Arthur Rimbaud is an exciting poet and wrote "Une Saison en enfer" or "Le Bateau ivre". (*R, S, B*)

b) Arthur Rimbaud is an exciting poet and wrote "Une Saison en enfer", or he is an exciting poet and wrote "Le Bateau ivre". (*R, S, B*)

(12) a) If we wish to comprehend Charles Baudelaire, then we must at least read "Correspondances" and "Les Fleurs du mal". (*B, C, F*)

b) We must at least read Charles Baudelaire's "Les Fleurs du mal"; moreover, if we wish to comprehend Baudelaire, then we must at least read "Correspondances". (*F, B, C*)

(13) a) We'll study André Gide, but if we read French literature, we may be shocked. (*G, L, S*)

b) If we study André Gide and read French literature, we shall study Gide and may be shocked. (*G, L, S*)

(14) a) You'll appreciate Paul Verlaine or you're dense and hardened. (*V, D, H*)

b) You'll appreciate Paul Verlaine or you're dense; moreover, you'll appreciate Verlaine or you're hardened. (*V, D, H*)

(15) a) Reading both "Les Fenêtres" and "L'Azur" is a necessary condition for studying Stephane Mallarmé. (*F, A, M*)

b) Having both studied Stephane Mallarmé and read "Les Fenêtres" is a sufficient condition for having read "L'Azur". (*M, F, A*)

(16) a) You have a romantic spirit only if you grasp Alfred de Musset and Alfred de Vigny. (*S, M, V*)

b) Unless you have a romantic spirit, you don't grasp Alfred de Vigny; but also you grasp Alfred de Musset if you've a romantic spirit. (*S, V, M*)

(17) a) If we believe history, then Paul Verlaine went to prison if, and only if, he shot Arthur Rimbaud. (*H, V, R*)

b) If we're to believe both history and that Paul Verlaine went to prison, then he shot Arthur Rimbaud. (*H, V, R*)

(18) a) Either Victor Hugo and Alfred de Musset are Romanticists or Paul Verlaine and Arthur Rimbaud are *poètes maudits*. (*H, M, V, R*)

b) Either Victor Hugo and Alfred de Musset are Romanticists or Paul Verlaine is a *poète maudit*; moreover, Arthur Rimband is also a *poète maudit*. (*H, M, V, R*)

(19) a) We listen to André Gide, "Le mal n'est jamais dans l'amour", or to Jean-Paul Sartre, "L'enfer, c'est l'autre", despite the fact that we also read François Mauriac or Colette. (*G, S, M, C*)

b) Either we read Colette and François Mauriac or we listen either to André

Gide, "Le mal n'est jamais dans l'amour", or to Jean-Paul Sartre, "L'enfer, c'est l'autre". (*C, M, G, S*)

(20) a) We may discover ourselves in studying Marcel Proust and Albert Camus, or we neither reflect on our inner world nor do justice to our lives. (*P, C, R, J*)

b) If we reflect on our inner world, we may discover ourselves in studying Albert Camus and Marcel Proust; but also we may discover ourselves in studying Albert Camus and Marcel Proust if we do justice to our lives. (*R, C, P, J*)

5

Proofs of Validity:

Argument Forms

While truth-tables can be used successfully to show the validity of some deductive arguments, they have serious limitations. *First*, they are tedious to construct and also easily allow for mistakes. Who wants to write thirty-two, sixty-four, or more rows, to say nothing of possible scores of columns? And who has not read a '0' for a '1' in some maze of '1's and '0's? *Second*, while the validity of valid *truth-functional* arguments can be established by truth-tables, there are other types of valid deductive arguments whose validity cannot be displayed this way. Consequently, we must learn other methods for establishing validity. Briefly, we want to devise methods, other than truth-table ones, which will assure us that if the premises of an argument are true, then the conclusion must also be true.

1. PURPOSE AND GENERAL CHARACTERISTICS
OF PROOFS OF VALIDITY

The concept of a *proof of validity* should not be unfamiliar to anyone who has studied geometry or algebra. In both disciplines we begin with a set of "statements"

—the axioms—and move in a line-by-line fashion, according to well-prescribed rules, to some concluding line—a theorem. We then claim that, assuming the truth of the axioms, the theorem is also true.

Beginning with the premiss set of an argument, we shall move through a finite number of statements, according to well-prescribed rules, to the conclusion of the argument. The well-prescribed rules—the *Rules of Transformation*—are each designed to guarantee that if the premisses of an argument are all true, then any new statement generated from the premisses by these rules must also be true. In particular, the last statement in the finite sequence of statements must be true. Of course if the argument is valid, the last statement in the sequence will be the conclusion of the argument. Such a procedure which establishes the validity of a valid argument will be known as a '*proof of validity*'.

In any proof of validity every statement must be justified; every statement must have its *raison d'être*. Premisses are justified by writing 'Pr' to the extreme right-hand side of the statement. 'Pr' simply means that this statement is a premiss, and we accept it as such, with no further justification. If a particular statement is not a premiss, it must be justified by writing at the extreme right-hand side *where* it came from and *how*. In short, every statement in a proof of validity which is not a premiss must be justified by answering the questions (1) '*from where?*' and (2) '*how?*'. No statement in a proof can go unjustified; no statement can be "slipped in by the back door". *No matter how obvious or trivial a move in a proof might seem to you, that move cannot be omitted or left unjustified.*

When constructing proofs of validity, we shall find it most helpful to give every statement in a proof a name; then we may refer to any statement in a proof by its name. We could use names such as 'Hezekiah', 'Heliotrope', and 'Hannibal'. But this procedure would at best become burdensome and taxing. It is better to be less creative and more pedantic in naming statements of a proof. *The numerals* '1', '2', '3', *and so on, will be used to name the statements of a proof.* These names shall be assigned as follows: The first statement in a proof will be named '1', the second '2', the third '3', and so on through the last statement of the proof. These names will be written to the left-hand side of the statement being named.

As we proceed in our studies, there will be two areas of "doing logic" to master. *First*, we must establish and learn thoroughly the Rules of Transformation. This will require a small amount of memory work. We must become very familiar with the rules, being able to recall them quickly and accurately. *Second*, we must be able to apply these rules to particular arguments. Obviously, we cannot apply the Rules of Transformation unless we know them; but knowing the rules does not guarantee that we can use them in concrete cases. The application of general rules to concrete cases may well be viewed as an art. There are no strict "rules of application" available for correctly using our Rules of Transformation. There are, however, techniques and strategies which are often—*though by no means always*—helpful in constructing proofs of validity. These techniques will be suggested as we proceed.

2. ARGUMENT FORMS

Generally speaking, Rules of Transformation will fall into two types: Argument Forms and Definitional and Logical Equivalences. Both types of Rules of Transformation are designed to guarantee validity but are used in different ways in constructing proofs of validity. We shall first discuss, and master the use of, Argument Forms.

Again it is necessary to stress the distinctions between arguments and argument forms. Arguments are series of particular statements, where at least one of these statements is claimed to support the truth or falsity of another. *How* these statements are related to one another may be considered the form of the argument. While a particular argument is made up of a sequence of statements, there are no statements whatsoever in an argument form, although there are statement forms. This feature of argument forms is underscored by using statement variables in their symbolic representation. Since argument forms contain no statements, we cannot, strictly speaking, refer to the premises and conclusion of any argument form as either true or false. Consequently, strictly speaking, it is inappropriate to call an argument form 'valid' or 'invalid'. Arguments are valid or invalid; argument forms of a certain sort guarantee the validity of valid arguments.

When speaking very informally, we may call argument forms 'valid'. Here we mean that if some statement is substituted for a statement variable in the argument form and a statement is substituted for each statement variable—the same statement appearing at each occurrence of the same statement variable throughout the argument form—the resulting argument would be valid. Furthermore, such an argument is called an '*instance*' of the argument form in question. Similar remarks can be made about the phrase 'invalid argument forms'. If some statement is substituted for a statement variable in the argument form and a statement is substituted for each statement variable—the same statement appearing at each occurrence of the same statement variable throughout the argument form—the resulting argument would be invalid. Thus, there are argument forms which guarantee validity and argument forms which do not. Now, there is an indefinitely large number of valid argument forms, and for each single valid argument form there is an indefinitely large number of valid arguments having that form. It would be quite impossible to memorize all valid argument forms, let alone all possible instances of each valid form. So, we shall learn a rather small collection of valid argument forms. With their help we may prove the validity of valid arguments.

The preceding paragraph suggests a *rule of substitution* for statements into statement and argument forms. Indeed, the notion of substitution has been implicit throughout our previous work. Let us make this concept more explicit—first in relation to statement forms and second as used with argument forms.

In any statement form we may substitute any statement at any occurrence of a single statement variable provided we substitute the same statement at

> *each occurrence of that single statement variable in the entire statement form.*

Consider this statement form:

(1) $p \supset (q \lor \sim q)$

A truth-table analysis will show that (1) is tautological; that is, any statement interpreted as having this form is tautological. Our rule of substitution must preserve the truth-value of (1). The tautological character of (1) is maintained if we substitute, say, 'L' for 'q'.

(2) $p \supset (L \lor \sim L)$

'L' is substituted at every occurrence of 'q' in (1), resulting in (2). However, the following substitution of 'L' in (1) is incorrect.

(3) $p \supset (q \lor \sim L)$

Statement (3) is incorrect because we have *not* substituted 'L' for every occurrence of 'q' in (1). Notice, from (3) we might proceed to

(4) $p \supset (M \lor \sim L)$

But surely neither (3) nor (4) are tautological, whereas (1) is.

Neither can we substitute statements for molecular statement forms. For example, while (1) is tautological, the following is not:

(5) $p \supset L$

We cannot substitute 'L' for '$q \lor \sim q$'. We can substitute only a statement for a *single* statement variable, provided the same statement replaces the same statement variable throughout the entire statement form.

Roughly, an argument form is a *sequence* of statement forms. Some argument forms are valid and some not. Any rule of substitution of statements into argument forms must maintain the validity or invalidity of the particular argument form in the argument resulting from the substitutions. With this in mind we say

> *in any argument form we may substitute any statement at any occurrence of a single statement variable provided we substitute the same statement at each occurrence of that single statement variable throughout the entire argument form.*

Consider the following valid argument form, where '$\therefore$' is understood to mean 'therefore'.

(6) $p \vee (q \vee \sim q)$

               $\sim p$

               $\therefore q \vee \sim q$

Now, suppose we wish to substitute '$A \supset B$' for 'p' and '$B \supset C$' for 'q'. Following our rule for substituting statements for statement variables in argument forms, we write

(7) $(A \supset B) \vee [(B \supset C) \vee \sim (B \supset C)]$

               $\sim (A \supset B)$

               $\therefore (B \supset C) \vee \sim (B \supset C)$

The following examples are incorrect attempts which substitute '$A \supset B$' for 'p' and '$B \supset C$' for 'q' in (6). Why are these examples incorrect?

(8) $p \vee [(B \supset C) \vee \sim (B \supset C)]$

               $\sim (A \supset B)$

               $\therefore q$

(9) $(A \supset B) \vee (B \supset C)$

               $\sim (A \supset B)$

               $\therefore B \supset C$

EXERCISES

Group A:

In each of the following statement forms, first substitute 'A' for 'p', 'B' for 'q', and 'C' for 'r'. Next, in each of the statement forms, substitute '$A \supset B$' for 'p', '$\sim (C \cdot \sim B)$' for 'q', and '$(D \supset B) \cdot (E \supset B)$' for '$r$'. Be certain to maintain proper punctuation.

(1) $p \supset (q \supset r)$

(2) $(p \cdot q) \vee \sim r$

(3) $p \equiv (q \cdot r)$

(4) $p \vee (q \vee r)$

(5) $\sim (p \supset q) \cdot r$

(6) $(p \supset q) \supset r$

(7) $(p \triangle \sim q) \triangle r$

(8) $\sim [p \supset (q \cdot r)]$

(9) $\sim [p \supset (q \vee \sim r)]$

(10) $\sim[p \supset \sim(q \equiv \sim r)]$

Group B:

In each of the following argument forms, substitute 'A' for 'p', 'B' for 'q', and 'C' for 'r'. Next, in each of the argument forms, substitute '$A \lor B$' for 'p', '$\sim(C \lor D)$' for 'q', and '$\sim[C \supset (D \supset B)]$' for '$r$'.

(1) $p \cdot (q \cdot r)$
       $\therefore p$

(2) $(p \lor q) \lor r$
       $\sim(p \lor q)$
       $\therefore r$

(3) $(p \cdot q) \lor r$
       $\therefore q \lor r$

(4) $(p \equiv q) \supset r$
       $q \equiv p$
       $\therefore r \lor p$

(5) $p \supset (q \supset r)$
       $\sim(q \supset r)$
       $\therefore \sim p$

(6) $p \supset (q \supset r)$
       $\therefore (p \cdot \sim r) \supset \sim q$

(7) $(p \lor q) \cdot \sim r$
       $\therefore \sim r \cdot (p \lor q)$

(8) $p \supset (q \cdot \sim q)$
       $(q \cdot \sim q) \supset r$
       $\therefore \sim r \supset \sim p$

(9) $p \lor q$
       $\therefore \sim r \lor (q \lor p)$

(10) $\sim p \cdot (q \cdot r)$
       $\therefore (\sim p \cdot q) \cdot r$

3. SIMPLIFICATION, COMMUTATION OF THE DOT, AND CONJUNCTION

Let us now turn to the first of those argument forms we shall utilize in constructing proofs of validity. Many of these argument forms permit us to "take apart" molecular statements; others allow us to "put together" separate statements in different ways. For example, suppose we were told

(1)   Atlanta is the capital of Georgia and the largest city in the state.

If (1) is true, then surely the following statement is also true:

(2)   Atlanta is the capital of Georgia.

Recalling the conditions making any statement of the form '$p \cdot q$' true, we see that if a statement of the form '$p \cdot q$' is true, then 'p' must also be true. We may express this logical fact as the following argument form:

Simplification (*Simp*)

$$p \cdot q$$
$$\therefore p$$

Simplification, referred to by 'Simp' in proofs of validity, states that if any truth-functional conjunction is true, the *left-hand* conjunct of that conjunction is also true. But surely if (1) is true, the following is also true:

(3)   Atlanta is the largest city in the state.

This is certainly the case, although we *cannot* deduce (3) directly from (1) by an appeal to Simplification. We cannot make such a direct appeal because Simplification guarantees the truth of only the *left-hand* conjunct of the overall conjunction. Statement (3) is the *right-hand* conjunct of (1).

But, consider, if (1) is true, the following must also be true:

(4)   Atlanta is the largest city in the state and the capital of Georgia.

In general, if any statement of the form '$p \cdot q$' is true, then '$q \cdot p$' must also be true. We may express this as

Commutation (*Com*)

$$p \cdot q$$
$$\therefore q \cdot p$$

Commutation, or 'Com' when referred to in proofs, asserts that the truth-value of a truth-functional conjunction is not affected by the ordering of the separate conjuncts.

If the statement (1) is true, Commutation guarantees the truth of (4); but if (4) is true, Simplification guarantees the truth of (3).

There is another argument form establishing validity to consider. Let us imagine the next statement is true:

(5)   Atlanta is a city of well over a million people.

Also, assume the truth of (6):

(6)   Atlanta is the financial center of the Southeast.

If we assume both (5) and (6) are true, we must also assume (7) true:

(7)   Atlanta is a city of well over a million people and it is the financial center of
the Southeast.

Or, when two separate statements are true, their truth-functional conjunction is
also true:

Conjunction (Conj)

$$p$$
$$q$$
$$\therefore p \cdot q$$

Now, by examining a particular argument, let us see how we may use the argument forms Simplification, Commutation, and Conjunction in constructing a
proof of validity.

(8)   The party is in full swing, although Kerr is leaving; moreover, it is still early
so Dale is coming. Consequently, Dale is coming even though Kerr is leaving.
(P, K, E, D)

First, we must symbolize the argument using the suggested notation:

(9) $\therefore D \cdot K$
 1) $(P \cdot K) \cdot (E \cdot D)$ P_1

Next, inspect the conclusion, '$D \cdot K$'. What kind of statement is it? And, how does
the conclusion appear in the premiss set of (9)? In (9) literally we see the conclusion
as an overall conjunction. Since there is only one premiss in the premiss set, the
conclusion must be deduced from that statement if the argument is valid. The
premiss is, like the conclusion, viewed as an overall conjunction. The 'K' of our
conclusion is found in the left-hand conjunct of the premiss, while the 'D' is in
the right-hand conjunct. Obtaining 'K' and 'D' on separate lines of our proof,
we could then assert '$D \cdot K$' on a new line by Conjunction. Working toward this
end, we disjoint the premiss into its separate conjuncts.

(10) $\therefore D \cdot K$
   1) $(P \cdot K) \cdot (E \cdot D)$ Pr
   2) $P \cdot K$ 1, Simp
   3) $(E \cdot D) \cdot (P \cdot K)$ 1, Com
   4) $E \cdot D$ 3, Simp

Using Simplification, we isolate '$P \cdot K$' from the premiss. We then obtain '$E \cdot D$' on a separate line. But, before we can do this, it is necessary to use Commutation. Why? Because Simplification allows us to isolate only the left-hand conjunct of an overall conjunction, but '$E \cdot D$' is the right-hand conjunct of the first statement in our proof. We must now deduce 'D' from the fourth statement and 'K' from the second statement in the proof:

   5) $K \cdot P$ 2, Com
   6) $D \cdot E$ 4, Com
   7) K 5, Simp
   8) D 6, Simp
   9) $\therefore D \cdot K$ 8, 7, Conj

In the proof of validity, (10), every statement is justified; the premiss by 'Pr' and the other statements by answering the questions (1) *'from where?'* and (2) *'how?'* For example, the justification of the seventh statement reads '5, Simp'. We are assured that the seventh statement is obtained from the fifth by Simplification. Since Simplification is an argument form guaranteeing validity, if the fifth statement is true, the seventh must also be true.

Also carefully notice the justification of the ninth statement, '8, 7, Conj'. Why have we written '8, 7, Conj' instead of '7, 8, Conj'? In the argument form, Conjunction,

$$p$$
$$q$$
$$\therefore p \cdot q$$

the left-hand conjunct of the conclusion is the same as the first premiss, whereas the right-hand conjunct of the conclusion is the same as the second premiss. In our proof of validity, (10), the eighth statement is an instance of the *first* premiss of Conjunction, while the seventh statement is an instance of the *second* premiss. We indicate this by writing '8' to the left-hand side of '7' in the justification of the ninth line.

We shall adopt the following convention governing the justifications of non-premiss statements in a proof of validity:

> **In general the order of the numerals, left to right, in justifications of statements in proofs of validity will indicate which statement in the proof is an instance of which premiss in the argument form being used.**

We also might have completed (10) as follows; however, our proof would have been one statement longer.

7)	K	5, Simp
8)	D	6, Simp
9)	$K \cdot D$	7, 8, Conj
10)	$\therefore D \cdot K$	9, Com

As far as constructing a proof for (8), the sequence of statements above is perfectly acceptable. This sequence is, however, an extra statement longer—an extra statement which can be avoided.

In Chapter 2 we discovered

> **which statements are to count as atomic or molecular depends upon the immediate purposes or goals we wish to accomplish and the various methods we have of accomplishing these goals.**

The relative nature of the concepts of atomic and molecular statements becomes clearer in (10). There the premiss is read as a molecular statement of the form '$p \cdot q$', where '$P \cdot K$' is interpreted as an instance of 'p' and '$E \cdot D$' as an instance of 'q'. Here both '$P \cdot K$' and '$E \cdot D$' are understood as atomic statements *in relation to the statement form* '$p \cdot q$'. By Simplification, however, '$P \cdot K$' becomes the second statement of (10) and is then reread as an instance of '$p \cdot q$' and not as an instance of 'p'. Consequently, as **coming from** the first statement in the proof, '$P \cdot K$' is thought of as atomic. Viewed as **leading to** the fifth statement in the proof, '$P \cdot K$' is thought of as molecular. Whether a statement in a proof is interpreted as atomic or molecular depends on *how it is being used* in that proof. Let us say that

> **any statement which is understood as an instance of a single statement variable will be called 'atomic' in relation to that statement variable; while any statement which is understood as an instance of a statement variable governed by some logical operator will be called 'molecular' in relation to that statement variable.**

Thus, when '$P \cdot K$' is read as an instance of 'p', it is considered atomic; but as an instance of '$p \cdot q$', it is thought of as molecular.

Any proof of the validity of a valid argument may be constructed in a finite sequence of statements, but as either the number of premisses or Rules of Transformation increase, so does the number of possible statements allowed by the rules. No matter how large the number of possible statements in a proof of validity becomes, however, it will always be a finite number. Thus, the conclusion of a valid argument is always deduced in a finite number of steps.

Now, given a premiss set and our Rules of Transformation, we may construct many new statements in a proof of validity. However, *only some of these statements may lead to the desired conclusion.* So a major problem in constructing proofs of validity is the quick elimination of possible steps, which indeed are logically correct but which would not lead to a desired conclusion; at the same time we must also generate statements which do lead to the desired conclusion. Here we have to learn how to apply our Rules of Transformation to particular arguments. As the number of rules increases and more complicated premiss sets are found, the application problem becomes more acute. But if we make it a practice (1) to commence with the conclusion of an argument and work "backward" to the premisses and (2) to apply certain "rules of thumb" to premisses when we can, the construction of proofs will become relatively easy.

The first rule of thumb is this: When a premiss is an overall conjunction, separate it into its various conjuncts unless there is an obvious reason for not doing so. An overall conjunction can always be disjointed by appealing to Simplification, Commutation, and then again Simplification. Following this rule of thumb may lead you to a few unnecessary statements in the proof; nevertheless, this rule of thumb will never lead you to a logically incorrect step and it will very likely help you gain the desired conclusion.

In beginning with the conclusion of an argument and working toward the premiss set, ask yourself the following sorts of questions:

(1)   *What kind of overall statement is the conclusion: a conjunction, disjunction, etc.?*

(2)   *Does the conclusion appear as a whole in any premiss?*

If the answer to the second question is 'yes', then ask

(3)   *In what kind of statement does the conclusion appear?*

(4)   *Given that kind of statement, what Rules of Transformation do I know which can isolate the conclusion on a line by itself?*

(5)   *But in order to use one of these rules to isolate the conclusion, do I need some further statement on a separate line in the proof?*

(6)   *If so, what is that statement?*

Next, let the statement suggested by the sixth question become, as it were, the conclusion you want and ask the six questions about it. Continue in this "backward" manner until one or more of the premisses yields a statement needed in the sequence of statements leading to the actual conclusion of the argument.

Suppose your answer to the second question was 'no'; suppose the conclusion does not appear as a whole in any premiss. Then proceed in this fashion:

(3-a)   *Where do the "pieces" of the conclusion appear in the premiss set?*

(4-a)   *In what kind(s) of statement(s) do these "pieces" appear and how?*

Of each "piece", or part, of the conclusion, ask

(5-a)   *Given that kind of statement and the type of statement that is the conclusion, what Rules of Transformation do I have either to isolate the part of the conclusion on a line by itself or to combine it with another statement and thus obtain the conclusion?*

(6-a)   *But in order to carry out this plan do I need some further statement on a separate line in the proof?*

(7-a)   *If so, what is that statement?*

And so on.

Such series of questions are designed to help you discover a fairly economical way of obtaining the conclusion of a particular argument. *You should not feel bound to use just this series of questions*; but, at this beginning stage of learning to construct proofs of validity, questions like these may be very helpful.

EXERCISES

Group A:

Give the correct justification for each unjustified statement in the following.

(1)   ∴ *A*

    1) $A \cdot (B \supset C)$ Pr

    2) ∴ *A*

(2)   ∴ *E*

    1) $(B \lor C) \cdot E$ Pr

    2) $E \cdot (B \lor C)$

    3) ∴ *E*

(3)   ∴ *D*

    1) $C \cdot (D \cdot E)$ Pr

    2) $(D \cdot E) \cdot C$

    3) $D \cdot E$

    4) ∴ *D*

(4)   ∴ $C \cdot (A \lor D)$

    1) $A \lor D$ Pr

    2) $B \cdot C$ Pr

    3) $C \cdot B$

    4) C

    5) ∴ $C \cdot (A \lor D)$

(5)   ∴ $B \cdot C$

    1) $(A \cdot B) \cdot C$ Pr

    2) $A \cdot B$

    3) $C \cdot (A \cdot B)$

    4) C

    5) $B \cdot A$

    6) B

    7) ∴ $B \cdot C$

(6) $\therefore$ $[D\cdot(B \supset C)]\cdot(A \supset B)$

   1) $[(A \supset B)\cdot(B \supset C)]\cdot D$ Pr
   2) $(A \supset B)\cdot(B \supset C)$
   3) $D\cdot[(A \supset B)\cdot(B \supset C)]$
   4) D
   5) $A \supset B$
   6) $(B \supset C)\cdot(A \supset B)$
   7) $B \supset C$
   8) $D\cdot(B \supset C)$
   9) $\therefore$ $[D\cdot(B \supset C)]\cdot(A \supset B)$

(7) $\therefore$ $(E\cdot F)\cdot[(A \lor B) \supset D]$

   1) $(A \lor B) \supset D$ Pr
   2) $(C\cdot E)\cdot F$ Pr
   3) $C\cdot E$
   4) $F\cdot(C\cdot E)$
   5) F
   6) $E\cdot C$
   7) E
   8) $E\cdot F$
   9) $\therefore$ $(E\cdot F)\cdot[(A \lor B) \supset D]$

(8) $\therefore$ $[\sim(C\cdot \sim E)\cdot \sim(A\cdot \sim B)]$
                                             $\cdot[A\cdot \sim(B\cdot \sim C)]$

   1) $\sim(A\cdot \sim B)\cdot[\sim(B\cdot \sim C)\cdot \sim(C\cdot \sim E)]$ Pr
   2) $(E \supset D)\cdot A$ Pr
   3) $\sim(A\cdot \sim B)$
   4) $[\sim(B\cdot \sim C)\cdot \sim(C\cdot \sim E)]\cdot \sim(A\cdot \sim B)$
   5) $\sim(B\cdot \sim C)\cdot \sim(C\cdot \sim E)$
   6) $\sim(B\cdot \sim C)$
   7) $\sim(C\cdot \sim E)\cdot \sim(B\cdot \sim C)$
   8) $\sim(C\cdot \sim E)$
   9) $A\cdot(E \supset D)$
  10) A
  11) $\sim(C\cdot \sim E)\cdot \sim(A\cdot \sim B)$
  12) $A\cdot \sim(B\cdot \sim C)$
  13) $\therefore$ $[\sim(C\cdot \sim E)\cdot \sim(A\cdot \sim B)]\cdot[A\cdot \sim(B\cdot \sim C)]$

(9) $\therefore$ $[(\sim F \cdot D) \cdot (\sim B \cdot C)]$
                                                                  $\cdot [(E \lor F) \cdot (A \lor B)]$

   1) $[(A \lor B) \cdot (\sim B \cdot C)] \cdot [(E \lor F) \cdot (\sim F \cdot D)]$ Pr
   2) $(A \lor B) \cdot (\sim B \cdot C)$
   3) $[(E \lor F) \cdot (\sim F \cdot D)] \cdot [(A \lor B) \cdot (\sim B \cdot C)]$
   4) $(E \lor F) \cdot (\sim F \cdot D)$
   5) $A \lor B$
   6) $(\sim B \cdot C) \cdot (A \lor B)$
   7) $\sim B \cdot C$
   8) $E \lor F$
   9) $(\sim F \cdot D) \cdot (E \lor F)$
  10) $\sim F \cdot D$
  11) $(\sim F \cdot D) \cdot (\sim B \cdot C)$
  12) $(E \lor F) \cdot (A \lor B)$
  13) $\therefore$ $[(\sim F \cdot D) \cdot (\sim B \cdot C)] \cdot [(E \lor F) \cdot (A \lor B)]$

(10) $\therefore$ $(D \cdot C) \cdot [(E \lor F) \cdot (A \lor B)]$

   1) $[(A \lor B) \cdot (\sim B \cdot C)] \cdot [(E \lor F) \cdot (\sim F \cdot D)]$ Pr
   2) $(A \lor B) \cdot (\sim B \cdot C)$
   3) $[(E \lor F) \cdot (\sim F \cdot D)] \cdot [(A \lor B) \cdot (\sim B \cdot C)]$
   4) $(E \lor F) \cdot (\sim F \cdot D)$
   5) $A \lor B$
   6) $(\sim B \cdot C) \cdot (A \lor B)$
   7) $\sim B \cdot C$
   8) $C \cdot \sim B$
   9) C
  10) $E \lor F$
  11) $(\sim F \cdot D) \cdot (E \lor F)$
  12) $\sim F \cdot D$
  13) $D \cdot \sim F$
  14) D
  15) $(E \lor F) \cdot (A \lor B)$
  16) $D \cdot C$
  17) $\therefore$ $(D \cdot C) \cdot [(E \lor F) \cdot (A \lor B)]$

Group B:

Construct a proof of validity for each of the following.

(1) $\therefore$ A
  1) $A \cdot B$ Pr

(2) $\therefore$ $B \cdot A$
  1) $A \cdot B$ Pr

(3) $\therefore$ B
  1) $A \cdot B$ Pr

(4) $\therefore A \cdot B$
   1) A Pr
   2) B Pr

(5) $\therefore C \cdot B$
   1) $A \cdot B$ Pr
   2) C Pr

(6) $\therefore A \lor B$
   1) $(A \lor B) \cdot (C \lor D)$ Pr

(7) $\therefore (C \lor D) \cdot (A \lor B)$
   1) $(A \lor B) \cdot (C \lor D)$ Pr

(8) $\therefore \sim(B \cdot \sim A)$
   1) $\sim(A \cdot \sim B) \cdot \sim(B \cdot \sim A)$ Pr

(9) $\therefore (B \supset C) \cdot (C \supset D)$
   1) $(A \supset B) \cdot (B \supset C)$ Pr
   2) $C \supset D$ Pr

(10) $\therefore \sim(B \cdot \sim C) \cdot [\sim(C \cdot \sim D) \cdot \sim(\sim A \cdot \sim B)]$
   1) $\sim(\sim A \cdot \sim B) \cdot \sim(B \cdot \sim C)$ Pr
   2) $\sim(C \cdot \sim D)$ Pr

Group C:

Give every exercise in Group B an interpretation by writing for each of the capital letters in a particular exercise an English statement—the same statement at each occurrence of the same capital letter in any given exercise—while also using appropriate English phrases for the logical operators.

Group D:

Symbolize the following arguments using the suggested notation, and then construct a proof of validity for each.

(1) Game theory can be useful in learning theory, but we must understand first the connection between game theory and logical networks. Hence, game theory can be useful in learning theory. (T, N)

(2) General descriptions of game theory involve infinite, nonzero sum, n-person games; moreover, these descriptions can be developed in considerable detail. Thus, general descriptions of game theory can be developed in considerable detail. (T, D)

(3) The need for learning theory is recognized by many psychologists. Further, models for learning theory are also recognized to be needed. Consequently, many psychologists recognize a need for learning theory and models for that theory. (T, M)

(4) Several different models can be constructed in the area of learning theory, but the difficulty is to select an appropriate model and this must be done in relation to the theory. Therefore, several different models can be constructed in the area of learning theory, although the difficulty is to select an appropriate model. (*C, S, R*)

(5) Game theory and logical networks can be used as models in learning theory, although there are other devices which may be employed. So although there are other devices which may be employed, nevertheless logical networks can be used as models in learning theory. (*T, N, D*)

(6) Information science is a relatively new area of study; but although it needs a more theoretical foundation, nevertheless it has generated a great deal of interest and produced some useful results. Thus, while information science is a relatively new area of study, it has generated a great deal of interest. (*A, F, I, R*)

(7) You've a regard for concrete detail and study computer programming; yet you also enjoy abstract thinking and do well in mathematics. Therefore, you study computer programming and do well in mathematics; but moreover you also enjoy abstract thinking as well as having a regard for concrete detail. (*R, P, T, M*)

(8) If you're interested in information retrieval systems, you'll enjoy information science; also if you enjoy information science, you'll need matrix algebra. However, you'll need matrix algebra only if you pursue systems design; but if you pursue systems design, you must study computers. Consequently, if you're interested in information retrieval systems, you'll enjoy information science; yet if you pursue systems design, you must study computers. (*I, E, N, P, S*)

(9) A strong background in mathematics is desirable if you plan to study information science; moreover, you should also have a working knowledge of computers. You might also find a knowledge of neurological networks helpful along with a careful study of logic. Consequently, a strong background in mathematics is desirable if you plan to study information science, and you should also have a working knowledge of computers and a careful study of logic. (*M, S, C, N, L*)

(10) We'll take either game theory or matrix algebra our first year and also study either systems design or numeric processing; moreover, we'll study mathematical linguistics and semantics. Wherefore, we'll study semantics as well as take either game theory or matrix algebra our first year; but even so we'll also study mathematical linguistics while studying systems design or numeric processing. (*T, A, D, P, L, S*)

4. DISJUNCTIVE SYLLOGISM,
COMMUTATION OF THE WEDGE,
AND ADDITION

The group of argument forms we shall now consider all apply to inclusive disjunctive statements. Suppose we are told

(1)   The atomic number of thulium is 96 or 69.

Inspecting the standard list of elements, we discover

(2)   The atomic number of thulium is *not* 96.

Assuming the truth of (1) and (2), it follows at once

(3)   The atomic number of thulium is 69.

Statements (1), (2), and (3) comprise an instance of a valid argument form. Of any argument having this form, if all the premisses are true, the conclusion must also be true:

Disjunctive Syllogism (DS)

$$p \lor q$$
$$\sim p$$
$$\therefore q$$

The argument form, Disjunctive Syllogism, has two premisses which may be described in this way. The first premiss is an inclusive disjunctive statement form; the second premiss has exactly one more tilde than the left-hand disjunct of the first premiss; and the conclusion is the same as the right-hand disjunct of the first premiss. This argument form, and only this argument form, is Disjunctive Syllogism.

But, imagine we are told

(4)   The atomic number of thulium is 69 or the atomic number of berkelium is 96.

Also, we accept (5) as true:

(5)   The atomic number of berkelium is *not* 96.

Given the truth of both (4) and (5), we still *cannot* assert by Disjunctive Syllogism

(6)   The atomic number of thulium is 69.

We cannot assert (6), given only (4) and (5), because (5) is not the denial of the *left-hand* disjunct of (4); moreover, (6) is not the same as the *right-hand* disjunct of (4). Nevertheless, if (4) is true, then (7) is also true:

(7)   The atomic number of berkelium is 96 or the atomic number of thulium is 69.

Moving from (4) to (7), we appeal to this valid argument form:

Commutation (Com)

$$p \lor q$$
$$\therefore q \lor p$$

Here Commutation tells us the ordering of the disjuncts in an inclusive disjunctive statement does not affect the truth-value of that statement. Now, (7), (5), and (6) are an instance of Disjunctive Syllogism.

Another important argument form we shall use in constructing proofs of validity is called '*Addition*'. Let it be taken for granted (8) is true:

(8)   The atomic weight of neptunium is 237.

Yet, if (8) is true, so is (9):

(9)   The atomic weight of neptunium is 237 or there are round squares.

We remember an inclusive disjunctive statement is truth-functionally true if *at least one* of its disjuncts is true. Since (8) is both true and also one of the disjuncts of (9), (9) must be true. Statement (8) and (9) may be interpreted as displaying this valid argument form:

Addition (Add)

$$p$$
$$\therefore p \lor q$$

It is very important to notice that we may substitute *any* statement (true or false) we please at '*q*' in the argument form above. The statement replacing '*q*' may not even be mentioned in the proof we are constructing—although it may have been— before using Addition. Addition is the *only* argument form we have allowing us to introduce statements not mentioned in the premiss set into a proof. Conse- quently, *if a given conclusion of a proof ever contains a statement not found in the premiss set, we shall always use Addition somewhere in constructing that proof.*

A common mistake beginners in logic often make is exemplified in the next example:

(10)   The atomic weight of neptunium is 237. Therefore, the atomic weight of neptunium is 237 *and* there are round squares.

This is an invalid argument, for the premiss is true and the conclusion false. The conclusion of (10) is a conjunction. Conjunctions are true only when all their conjuncts are true. But 'there are round squares' is certainly false. Hence, 'the atomic weight of neptunium is 237 *and* there are round squares' must also be false. The moral here is that *Addition is appropriate only with the wedge and never with the dot.*

Let us analyze this argument:

(11)   We shall either study quantum mechanics or admit to being bound by aca- demic tradition. Yet, we are a progressive nation which is not bound by academic tradition. Hence, we shall not progress in our work or we shall study quantum mechanics. (*M, T, N, W*)

Using the suggested notation, we may symbolize (11) as

(12) $\therefore \sim W \lor M$
   1) $M \lor T$ Pr
   2) $N \cdot \sim T$ Pr

Noticing the second premiss of (12) is an overall conjunction, we may wish to follow our rule of thumb and generate three more statements in the proof:

   3) N 2, Simp
   4) $\sim T \cdot N$ 2, Com
   5) $\sim T$ 4, Simp

Now, examining the conclusion of the argument, we may want to ask the following sorts of questions:

  (1)   What kind of overall statement is the conclusion? *An inclusive disjunctive statement.*

  (2)   Does the conclusion appear as a whole in any premiss? *No.*

(3-a)   Where do the "pieces" of the conclusion appear in the premiss set? *'M' appears in the first premiss, but neither '$\sim W$' nor 'W' appear anywhere in the premiss set.*

(4-a)   In what kind of statement does 'M' appear and how? *'M' appears as the left-hand disjunct of an inclusive disjunctive statement.*

(5-a)   Given that 'M' appears as the left-hand disjunct in an inclusive disjunctive statement and that the conclusion is '$\sim W \lor M$', what argument forms do we have to isolate 'M' on a line by itself to obtain the conclusion? *Using Commutation followed by Disjunctive Syllogism, we could assert 'M' on a separate line in the proof. Having 'M', we could then use Addition followed by Commutation to reach the conclusion.*

(6-a)   But, in order to carry out this plan, do we need some further statement in our proof? *Yes.*

(7-a)   If so, what is that statement? *We need '$\sim T$' in order to carry out the proposed Disjunctive Syllogism move.*

(8-a)   But, where can we obtain '$\sim T$'? *'$\sim T$' is the fifth statement in the proof.*

We now have all the information necessary to complete our proof of (11):

(13) $\therefore \sim W \lor M$
   1) $M \lor T$ Pr
   2) $N \cdot \sim T$ Pr
   3) N 2, Simp
   4) $\sim T \cdot N$ 2, Com
   5) $\sim T$ 4, Simp
   6) $T \lor M$ 1, Com

7)	M	6, 5, DS
8)	$M \lor \sim W$	7, Add
9)	$\therefore \sim W \lor M$	8, Com

The third, fourth, and fifth statements are asserted quite automatically by following our rule of thumb concerning overall conjunctions. Notice, however, that 'N', the third statement, is not used in (13) to reach the conclusion. We find no justification in the proof referring to the third statement. Consequently, a shorter proof of the validity of (11) is

(14) $\therefore \sim W \lor M$

1)	$M \lor T$	Pr
2)	$N \cdot \sim T$	Pr
3)	$\sim T \cdot N$	2, Com
4)	$\sim T$	3, Simp
5)	$T \lor M$	1, Com
6)	M	5, 4, DS
7)	$M \lor \sim W$	6, Add
8)	$\therefore \sim W \lor M$	7, Com

EXERCISES

Group Λ:

Give the correct justification for each statement not already justified.

(1) $\therefore A$

1)	$\sim B$	Pr
2)	$A \lor B$	Pr
3)	$B \lor A$	
4)	$\therefore A$	

(2) $\therefore D \lor E$

1)	$C \cdot D$	Pr
2)	$D \cdot C$	
3)	D	
4)	$\therefore D \lor E$	

(3) $\therefore A$

1)	$(A \lor B) \cdot \sim B$	Pr
2)	$A \lor B$	
3)	$\sim B \cdot (A \lor B)$	
4)	$\sim B$	
5)	$B \lor A$	
6)	$\therefore A$	

(4) $\therefore (C \supset D)\cdot(E \vee \sim D)$

   1) $\sim(A \vee B)$ Pr

   2) $(C \supset D) \vee (A \vee B)$ Pr

   3) $\sim D$ Pr

   4) $(A \vee B) \vee (C \supset D)$

   5) $C \supset D$

   6) $\sim D \vee E$

   7) $E \vee \sim D$

   8) $\therefore (C \supset D)\cdot(E \vee \sim D)$

(5) $\therefore (D \vee A)\cdot(E \supset D)$

   1) $\sim(B \supset C)\cdot A$ Pr

   2) $(E \supset D) \vee (B \supset C)$ Pr

   3) $\sim(B \supset C)$

   4) $A\cdot \sim(B \supset C)$

   5) A

   6) $(B \supset C) \vee (E \supset D)$

   7) $E \supset D$

   8) $A \vee D$

   9) $D \vee A$

  10) $\therefore (D \vee A)\cdot(E \supset D)$

(6) $\therefore D\cdot A$

   1) $(A \vee B)\cdot \sim C$ Pr

   2) $\sim B\cdot(C \vee D)$ Pr

   3) $A \vee B$

   4) $\sim C\cdot(A \vee B)$

   5) $\sim C$

   6) $\sim B$

   7) $(C \vee D)\cdot \sim B$

   8) $C \vee D$

   9) $B \vee A$

  10) A

  11) D

  12) $\therefore D\cdot A$

(7) $\therefore G \vee [F \vee (C \vee E)]$

   1) $(C \vee D) \vee (A \supset B)$ Pr

   2) $\sim D\cdot \sim(A \supset B)$ Pr

   3) $\sim D$

   4) $\sim(A \supset B)\cdot \sim D$

   5) $\sim(A \supset B)$

   6) $(A \supset B) \vee (C \vee D)$

   7) $C \vee D$

   8) $D \vee C$

   9) C

10) $C \lor E$

11) $(C \lor E) \lor F$

12) $F \lor (C \lor E)$

13) $[F \lor (C \lor E)] \lor G$

14) $\therefore\ G \lor [F \lor (C \lor E)]$

(8) $\therefore\ (A \lor C) \cdot F$

  1) $\sim(A \lor B) \cdot \sim(B \lor C)$ Pr

  2) $(A \lor B) \lor (C \lor E)$ Pr

  3) $(F \lor E) \lor (B \lor C)$ Pr

  4) $\sim E$ Pr

  5) $\sim(A \lor B)$

  6) $\sim(B \lor C) \cdot \sim(A \lor B)$

  7) $\sim(B \lor C)$

  8) $C \lor E$

  9) $E \lor C$

10) C

11) $C \lor A$

12) $A \lor C$

13) $(B \lor C) \lor (F \lor E)$

14) $F \lor E$

15) $E \lor F$

16) F

17) $\therefore\ (A \lor C) \cdot F$

(9) $\therefore\ (H \lor C) \cdot (G \lor I)$

  1) $\sim A \cdot \sim F$ Pr

  2) $A \lor (B \lor C)$ Pr

  3) $E \lor (F \lor G)$ Pr

  4) $\sim B \cdot \sim E$ Pr

  5) $\sim A$

  6) $\sim F \cdot \sim A$

  7) $\sim F$

  8) $\sim B$

  9) $\sim E \cdot \sim B$

10) $\sim E$

11) $B \lor C$

12) C

13) $C \lor H$

14) $H \lor C$

15) $F \lor G$

16) G

17) $G \lor I$

18) $\therefore\ (H \lor C) \cdot (G \lor I)$

(10) $\therefore (E \cdot C) \vee (E \cdot D)$

    1) $(\sim A \vee B) \cdot (\sim B \cdot \sim D)$ Pr

    2) $[(A \vee C) \vee D] \cdot [(E \vee B) \vee A]$ Pr

    3) $\sim A \vee B$

    4) $(\sim B \cdot \sim D) \cdot (\sim A \vee B)$

    5) $\sim B \cdot \sim D$

    6) $\sim B$

    7) $\sim D \cdot \sim B$

    8) $\sim D$

    9) $(A \vee C) \vee D$

    10) $[(E \vee B) \vee A] \cdot [(A \vee C) \vee D]$

    11) $(E \vee B) \vee A$

    12) $D \vee (A \vee C)$

    13) $A \vee C$

    14) $B \vee \sim A$

    15) $\sim A$

    16) C

    17) $A \vee (E \vee B)$

    18) $E \vee B$

    19) $B \vee E$

    20) E

    21) $E \cdot C$

    22) $\therefore (E \cdot C) \vee (E \cdot D)$

Group B:

Construct a proof of validity for each of the following.

(1) $\therefore B \vee A$

    1) $A \vee B$ Pr

(2) $\therefore B$

    1) $\sim A$ Pr

    2) $A \vee B$ Pr

(3) $\therefore A$

    1) $A \vee B$ Pr

    2) $\sim B$ Pr

(4) $\therefore C \vee B$

    1) $A \vee B$ Pr

    2) $\sim A$ Pr

(5) $\therefore (C \vee D) \vee (B \vee A)$

    1) $A \vee B$ Pr

(6) $\therefore (A \cdot C) \vee D$

    1) $A \cdot \sim B$ Pr

    2) $C \vee B$ Pr

(7) $\therefore\ D \vee C$
   1) $A \vee [B \vee (C \vee D)]$ Pr
   2) $\sim B \cdot \sim A$ Pr

(8) $\therefore\ (C \vee A) \cdot (B \vee D)$
   1) $(D \cdot C) \vee (A \cdot B)$ Pr
   2) $\sim (A \cdot B)$ Pr

(9) $\therefore\ (B \vee E) \cdot (C \vee F)$
   1) $(A \vee B) \cdot (C \vee D)$ Pr
   2) $\sim A \cdot \sim D$ Pr

(10) $\therefore\ [(B \cdot \sim A) \vee E] \cdot [(C \cdot \sim D) \vee F]$
   1) $(B \vee A) \cdot \sim A$ Pr
   2) $(D \vee C) \cdot \sim D$ Pr

Group C:

Give every exercise in Group B an interpretation by substituting for each of the capital letters in a particular exercise an English statement—the same statement at each occurrence of the same capital letter in any given exercise—while also writing appropriate English phrases for the logical operators.

Group D:

Symbolize the following arguments using the suggested notation, and then construct a proof of validity for each.

(1) We'll study either Plato or Aristotle. So, we'll study either Aristotle or Plato. (P, A)

(2) Aristotle doesn't have the best literary style of the great ancient philosophers, but either Plato or Aristotle does. Thus, Plato has the best literary style of the great ancient philosophers. (A, P)

(3) Plato wrote either the *Symposium* or the *Eudemian Ethics*; yet he didn't write the *Eudemian Ethics*. Hence, Plato wrote the *Lysis* or the *Symposium*. (S, E, L)

(4) Either Eryximachus doesn't understand love as some cosmic principle or both Phaidrus and Alcibiades think of love in its more physical forms. Socrates declares that he isn't ignorant about love matters, and further it isn't true that Eryximachus doesn't understand love as some sort of cosmic principle. Therefore, either Phaidrus or Alcibiades think of love in its more physical forms, while Socrates declares that he isn't ignorant about love matters. (E, P, A, S)

(5) In the *Symposium*, Phaidrus doesn't have a correct concept of love but neither does Eryximachus, and moreover Agathon doesn't know what he's talking about or Phaidrus does have a correct concept of love. Either Agathon knows what he's talking about or we must listen carefully to Diotima. Consequently, Eryximachus has a correct notion of love or we must listen carefully to Diotima. (P, E, A, D)

(6) The *Republic* or *Ion* are early dialogues of Plato, but the *Lysis* or *Timaeus* are late works. The *Republic* isn't an early dialogue and the *Lysis* isn't a late work. So, either the *Ion* or *Charmides* are early dialogues of Plato, while the *Statesman* or *Timaeus* are late works. (*R, I, L, T, C, S*)

(7) We aren't interested in ancient Greek philosophy, or we'll read at least the *Timaeus* and the *Republic*. Also we'll read either the *Republic* or *Laws*, or the *Meno*. It isn't the case that we'll read at least the *Timaeus* and the *Republic*. Either we don't read the *Meno* and don't read the *Republic*, or we're interested in ancient Greek philosophy. Hence, either it isn't true that we are interested in ancient Greek philosophy and read the *Republic*, or else we'll read the *Republic* or *Laws*. (*P, T, R, L, M*)

(8) It isn't true that the activities of Meletus were both necessary and sufficient conditions for there being a public condemnation of Socrates; but also, Anytus didn't interfere or, indeed, the activities of Meletus were both necessary and sufficient conditions for the public condemnation of Socrates. Anytus interfered, or it isn't the case that Lycon didn't step in but yet there was a public condemnation of Socrates. Either we must believe Plato's report of the trial, or Lycon didn't step in even though there was a public condemnation of Socrates. So, we must believe Plato's report of the trial. (*M, S, A, L, P*)

(9) Thrasymachus wasn't at Socrates' execution but Crito was; further, while Echecrates wasn't there, Simmias was. Now, either Xanthippe didn't stay at the prison or Thrasymachus was at the execution. Furthermore, either Echecrates was at Socrates' execution, or Apollodoros was with Socrates or Xanthippe stayed at the prison. Consequently, we must not believe Plato if Echecrates was at Socrates' execution, or both Apollodoros and Simmias were with Socrates. (*T, C, E, S, X, A, P*)

(10) Either we don't understand our contemporary world, or if we do then we don't need to study the ancient philosophers. We don't need to study the ancient philosophers despite the fact that we'll lose our cultural heritage, or we understand our contemporary world. It isn't the case that we don't need to study the ancient philosophers whenever we understand our contemporary world; furthermore if we don't need to study the ancient philosophers, we ignore a vital historical source of our civilization. Hence, we don't need to study the ancient philosophers only if we ignore a vital historical source of our civilization; and also either we return to the writings of the ancient Greeks or we lose our cultural heritage. (*W, P, H, S, G*)

5. MODUS PONENS AND MODUS TOLLENS

Perhaps we have mused to ourselves

(1)   Unless I am more tolerant of others, they won't be more understanding of me.

And, we honestly strive to bring about the conditions to make (2) true:

(2)   I am more tolerant of others.

If both (1) and (2) are true, then we can say that (3) is also true:

(3)   They—others—will be more understanding of me.

[Unfortunately, while (1), (2), and (3) form an instance of a valid argument, this argument is usually not sound. The "hitch" appears in the first premiss. While the antecedent may be true, the consequent in reality often is not.] The argument form guaranteeing the validity of the argument above is

Modus Ponens (*MP*)

$$p \supset q$$
$$p$$
$$\therefore q$$

'*Modus Ponens*' simply means 'the mode of affirming', from the Latin '*modus*'—'mode'—and '*ponere*'—'to affirm'. This valid argument form is also sometimes referred to as '*Modus Ponendo Ponens*'—'the mode which, by affirming, affirms'. The name 'Modus Ponens' is descriptive of the argument form: The second premiss does affirm the antecedent of the first premiss, while the conclusion does affirm the consequent of the first premiss. Any argument which is an instance of this argument form is valid; that is, if all the premisses of the argument are true, the conclusion must also be true.

Consider this example:

(4)   In our society a person's moral practices are often different from the ethical code he claims to follow. But certainly a person is fundamentally distressed whenever his moral practices are often different from the ethical code he claims to follow. Furthermore, that a person is fundamentally distressed is a sufficient condition for his not being able to function at his best capacity. A person may become mentally ill whenever he isn't able to function at his best capacity; moreover, if a person's moral practices are often different from the ethical code he claims to follow, prevailing social conditions are usually one cause of this. Hence, we may conclude that a person may become mentally ill; moreover, prevailing social conditions are usually one cause of this. (*P, D, F, I, C*)

As always, we first symbolize the argument:

(5) $\therefore I \cdot C$

    1) P Pr

    2) $P \supset D$ Pr

    3) $D \supset \sim F$ Pr

    4) $(\sim F \supset I) \cdot (P \supset C)$ Pr

Noticing that the fourth premiss may be read as an overall conjunction, we may proceed quite mechanically through the seventh line:

    5) $\sim F \supset I$ 4, Simp

    6) $(P \supset C) \cdot (\sim F \supset I)$ 4, Com

    7) $P \supset C$ 6, Simp

Now, moving from the conclusion toward the premiss set of (5), we ask such questions as

    (1)   What kind of overall statement is the conclusion? *The conclusion may be interpreted as an overall conjunction.*

    (2)   Does the conclusion appear as a whole in any premiss, and, if not, what rule might we use to obtain the conclusion? *The conclusion does not appear as a whole in any premiss, but it may be reached by an appeal to Conjunction.*

  (3-a)   Where do the "pieces" of the conclusion appear in the premiss set? *Both 'I' and 'C' appear in the fourth premiss. However, the fourth premiss has been disjointed into the fifth and seventh statements.*

  (4-a)   In what kinds of statements do 'I' and 'C' appear and how? *'I' and 'C' both appear as consequents in overall hypothetical statements, namely, in lines 5 and 7.*

  (5-a)   Since both 'I' and 'C' appear as consequents, how may we isolate them on separate lines? *We might use Modus Ponens.*

  (6-a)   To obtain 'I' and 'C' by *Modus Ponens*, do we need any other statements in the proof, and, if so, what? *Yes, we need as separate statements the antecedents of statements in lines 5 and 7, namely, '$\sim F$' and 'P'.*

  (7-a)   Where do we find '$\sim F$' and 'P' in the proof? *'P' is the first premiss of the proof, while '$\sim F$' appears in the third statement.*

The series of questions is continued, now asking them in relation to '$\sim F$', for we must have '$\sim F$' in order to obtain 'I', and 'I' is needed to establish '$I \cdot C$' by Conjunction. A finished proof of the validity of (4) may now be constructed:

(6) $\therefore I \cdot C$

    1) P Pr

    2) $P \supset D$ Pr

    3) $D \supset \sim F$ Pr

    4) $(\sim F \supset I) \cdot (P \supset C)$ Pr

    5) $\sim F \supset I$ 4, Simp

6)	$(P \supset C) \cdot (\sim F \supset I)$	4, Com
7)	$P \supset C$	6, Simp
8)	C	7, 1, MP
9)	D	2, 1, MP
10)	$\sim F$	3, 9, MP
11)	I	5, 10, MP
12)	$\therefore I \cdot C$	11, 8, Conj

You will notice that 'P' has been used twice in (6)—once to obtain line 8 and again to secure the statement in line 9. *Any statement in a proof may be used as often as it is needed to obtain the desired conclusion provided it is correctly used each time in accordance with some Rule of Transformation.*

Another valid argument form we shall find very helpful in constructing proofs of validity is called '*Modus Tollens*' from the Latin '*modus*'—'mode'—and '*tollere*' —'to deny'. This particular argument form is sometimes referred to as '*Modus Tollendo Tollens*', or 'the mode which, by denying, denies'. For example, suppose we were told

(7)   If Kenneth MacCorquordale is correct, hypothetical constructs require certain entities to exist.

Yet also assume the truth of

(8)   Hypothetical constructs don't require certain entities to exist.

So we may now assert

(9)   MacCorquordale isn't correct.

We have in (7), (8), and (9) an instance of the valid argument form

Modus Tollens (MT)

$$p \supset q$$
$$\sim q$$
$$\therefore \sim p$$

In Modus Tollens the first premiss is the form of a hypothetical statement, the second premiss denies the consequent of the first, and the conclusion is the same as the denial of the antecedent of the first premiss. We may also say that the second premiss of Modus Tollens always has exactly one more tilde than the consequent of the first premiss; also, the conclusion always has exactly one more tilde than the antecedent of the first premiss.

Let us examine an argument whose proof of validity makes use of Modus Tollens:

(10)   In an introductory chemistry course Dottie discovered her litmus paper turned red whenever she put it in an acidic solution; however, if she put it in a basic medium, it turned blue. Now, Dottie put her litmus paper in either an acidic solution or a basic medium. Having done this, she noticed that the litmus paper didn't turn blue. Therefore, her litmus paper turned red. (R, A, M, B)

Symbolizing (10), we may write

(11) $\therefore R$

     1) $(A \supset R) \cdot (M \supset B)$ Pr
     2) $A \lor M$ Pr
     3) $\sim B$ Pr

Because the first premiss is read as an overall conjunction, we may want to break it down at once into its separate conjuncts:

     4) $A \supset R$ 1, Simp
     5) $(M \supset B) \cdot (A \supset R)$ 1, Com
     6) $M \supset B$ 5, Simp

We see that 'R', the conclusion, appears in the left-hand conjunct of the first premiss, that conjunct also being the fourth statement in (11). Examining the fourth statement, we notice it is a hypothetical with 'R' as its consequent. How could we isolate 'R' on a separate line? Using Modus Ponens with '$A \supset R$', we could assert the desired conclusion. Such a move, however, requires 'A' to appear as a distinct statement in the proof. Again, inspecting the premiss set, we find 'A' as the left-hand disjunct of the second premiss. Employing Commutation and then Disjunctive Syllogism, we could deduce 'A'. But in order to use Disjunctive Syllogism, we must have '$\sim M$'. While '$\sim M$' does not appear in the premiss set, 'M' is found in the right-hand conjunct of the first premiss. Proceeding, the right-hand conjunct of the first premiss is also the sixth statement in (11). Here we find 'M' as the *antecedent* of a hypothetical statement. If we could utilize Modus Tollens with '$M \supset B$', '$\sim M$' would be reached at once. This use of Modus Tollens demands '$\sim B$', which is the third premiss. All we need to construct a proof for (10) is now at hand:

(12) $\therefore R$

     1) $(A \supset R) \cdot (M \supset B)$ Pr
     2) $A \lor M$ Pr
     3) $\sim B$ Pr
     4) $A \supset R$ 1, Simp
     5) $(M \supset B) \cdot (A \supset R)$ 1, Com
     6) $M \supset B$ 5, Simp
     7) $\sim M$ 6, 3, MT

8)	$M \lor A$	2, Com
9)	A	8, 7, DS
10)	$\therefore R$	4, 9, MP

Modus Ponens and Modus Tollens are often confused with two argument forms which *are not valid*. These worthless *deductive* argument forms are known as the *'Fallacy of Affirming the Consequent'* and the *'Fallacy of Denying the Antecedent'*. These argument forms are called 'fallacies' because the truth of the premisses of any instance of them does **not** guarantee the truth of the conclusion of that argument.

Imagine that a business man had been able to salvage some capital after October, 1929. Around the first of 1930 he might have investigated various ways to recoup at least part of his losses. After studying many companies and corporations, our business man decides to invest his remaining resources in the Insull Utilities Investments Incorporation of Illinois. After all, Samuel Insull was the president of this immense holding company of various utilities. This seemed guarantee enough of a successful venture. Thus, in a straightforward way our friend is thinking to himself:

(13)   I better invest all I have left in the Insull Utilities Investments Incorporation
         if I'm to regain any of my financial losses.

He does invest but, unfortunately, common shares that had been around $500.00 in 1930 were valued at less than four cents on the dollar by May, 1932.

The example above is an instance of this invalid argument form:

Fallacy of Affirming the Consequent

$$p \supset q$$
$$q$$
$$\therefore p$$

Remember, no deductive argument of this form is valid! The truth of the premisses does not guarantee the truth of the conclusion.

Or, we might hear a sociologist arguing in the following way, claiming that the truth of his premisses establishes the truth of his conclusion.

(14)   If the rate of suicide in France and Spain is low, the rate of suicide is inversely
         proportional to the number of Roman Catholics in a given country. Yet
         the rate of suicide in France and Spain isn't low. The rate of suicide, there-
         fore, isn't inversely proportional to the number of Roman Catholics in a
         given country.

Whether or not the conclusion of (14) is true is not in question. What is in question is the *claim* that the truth of the premisses guarantees the truth of the conclusion;

and this claim does not stand. *No argument of the following argument form is valid:*

Fallacy of Denying the Antecedent

$$p \supset q$$
$$\sim p$$
$$\therefore \ \sim q$$

EXERCISES

Group A:

Give the correct justification for each unjustified statement.

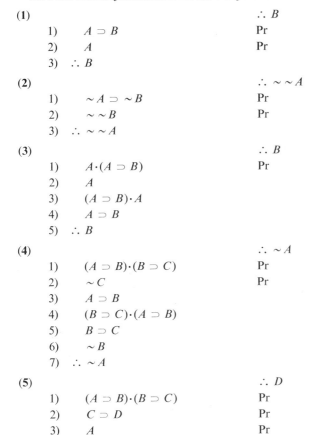

(1) $\therefore$ B
    1) $A \supset B$ Pr
    2) A Pr
    3) $\therefore$ B

(2) $\therefore \ \sim \sim A$
    1) $\sim A \supset \sim B$ Pr
    2) $\sim \sim B$ Pr
    3) $\therefore$ $\sim \sim A$

(3) $\therefore$ B
    1) $A \cdot (A \supset B)$ Pr
    2) A
    3) $(A \supset B) \cdot A$
    4) $A \supset B$
    5) $\therefore$ B

(4) $\therefore \ \sim A$
    1) $(A \supset B) \cdot (B \supset C)$ Pr
    2) $\sim C$ Pr
    3) $A \supset B$
    4) $(B \supset C) \cdot (A \supset B)$
    5) $B \supset C$
    6) $\sim B$
    7) $\therefore$ $\sim A$

(5) $\therefore$ D
    1) $(A \supset B) \cdot (B \supset C)$ Pr
    2) $C \supset D$ Pr
    3) A Pr
    4) $A \supset B$

5)		$(B \supset C) \cdot (A \supset B)$
6)		$B \supset C$
7)		B
8)		C
9)	$\therefore$	D

(6) $\therefore E \cdot B$

1)	$\sim A \supset B$	Pr
2)	$\sim C$	Pr
3)	$A \supset D$	Pr
4)	$\sim C \supset \sim D$	Pr
5)	$B \supset E$	Pr
6)	$\sim D$	
7)	$\sim A$	
8)	B	
9)	E	
10)	$\therefore E \cdot B$	

(7) $\therefore E \lor D$

1)	$A \supset B$	Pr
2)	$A \lor C$	Pr
3)	$B \supset D$	Pr
4)	$\sim C$	Pr
5)	$C \lor A$	
6)	A	
7)	B	
8)	D	
9)	$D \lor E$	
10)	$\therefore E \lor D$	

(8) $\therefore (B \cdot A) \cdot (C \cdot E)$

1)	$A \supset (B \supset C)$	Pr
2)	$(D \lor E) \supset A$	Pr
3)	$E \cdot B$	Pr
4)	E	
5)	$B \cdot E$	
6)	B	
7)	$E \lor D$	
8)	$D \lor E$	
9)	A	
10)	$B \supset C$	
11)	C	
12)	$C \cdot E$	
13)	$B \cdot A$	
14)	$\therefore (B \cdot A) \cdot (C \cdot E)$	

(9) $\therefore\ G \vee E$

    1) $\sim A \supset \sim C$ Pr
    2) $\sim A \cdot B$ Pr
    3) $[A \vee (C \vee D)] \cdot [(B \cdot D) \supset E]$ Pr
    4) $\sim A$
    5) $B \cdot \sim A$
    6) B
    7) $A \vee (C \vee D)$
    8) $[(B \cdot D) \supset E] \cdot [A \vee (C \vee D)]$
    9) $(B \cdot D) \supset E$
  10) $\sim C$
  11) $C \vee D$
  12) D
  13) $B \cdot D$
  14) E
  15) $E \vee G$
  16) $\therefore\ G \vee E$

(10) $\therefore\ \sim B$

    1) $A \supset (B \supset C)$ Pr
    2) $A \vee D$ Pr
    3) $(D \supset E) \cdot (E \supset F)$ Pr
    4) $G \supset (\sim F \cdot \sim C)$ Pr
    5) G Pr
    6) $D \supset E$
    7) $(E \supset F) \cdot (D \supset E)$
    8) $E \supset F$
    9) $\sim F \cdot \sim C$
  10) $\sim F$
  11) $\sim C \cdot \sim F$
  12) $\sim C$
  13) $\sim E$
  14) $\sim D$
  15) $D \vee A$
  16) A
  17) $B \supset C$
  18) $\therefore\ \sim B$

Group B:

Construct a proof of validity for each of the following.

(1) $\therefore\ C \cdot \sim A$

  1) $(A \supset B) \cdot C$ Pr
  2) $\sim B$ Pr

(2) $\therefore C$

   1) $A \lor B$ Pr

   2) $(B \supset C) \cdot \sim A$ Pr

(3) $\therefore D \lor C$

   1) $(A \lor B) \lor C$ Pr

   2) $(A \lor B) \supset E$ Pr

   3) $\sim E$ Pr

(4) $\therefore \sim B \cdot \sim A$

   1) $\sim (B \lor C) \lor A$ Pr

   2) $\sim A$ Pr

   3) $(D \lor E) \supset (B \lor C)$ Pr

   4) $\sim B \lor (D \lor E)$ Pr

(5) $\therefore C$

   1) $(A \cdot B) \supset C$ Pr

   2) $(D \supset A) \cdot (E \supset B)$ Pr

   3) $E \cdot D$ Pr

(6) $\therefore (\sim A \cdot \sim B) \cdot (C \cdot D)$

   1) $(B \supset A) \cdot (\sim B \supset C)$ Pr

   2) $(C \supset D) \cdot \sim A$ Pr

(7) $\therefore (A \lor B) \cdot (A \cdot E)$

   1) $(A \lor \sim B) \supset \sim (C \lor D)$ Pr

   2) $(C \lor D) \lor (A \cdot E)$ Pr

   3) $(B \supset F) \cdot \sim F$ Pr

(8) $\therefore F \lor E$

   1) $(A \supset B) \cdot (C \supset D)$ Pr

   2) $A \cdot \sim D$ Pr

   3) $(\sim C \cdot B) \supset (E \lor D)$ Pr

(9) $\therefore \sim G$

   1) $(A \cdot B) \cdot (C \cdot D)$ Pr

   2) $[(B \cdot D) \supset E] \cdot [(A \cdot C) \supset F]$ Pr

   3) $(E \cdot F) \supset \sim G$ Pr

(10) $\therefore A \cdot D$

   1) $(A \lor B) \cdot (C \lor D)$ Pr

   2) $(B \supset E) \cdot (C \supset F)$ Pr

   3) $[(\sim E \cdot \sim F) \lor G] \cdot \sim G$ Pr

Group C:

Give every exercise in Group B an interpretation by substituting for each of the capital letters in a particular exercise an English statement—the same statement at each occurrence of the same capital letter in any given exercise—while also writing appropriate English phrases for the logical operators.

Group D:

Symbolize the following arguments using the suggested notation, and then construct a proof of validity for each.

(1)   That we're interested in Samuel Beckett is a sufficient reason for reading *Molloy*. We are interested in Beckett. So we'll read *Molloy*. (*B, M*)

(2)   Samuel Beckett is unfamiliar only if we aren't well educated. Now, we aren't acquainted with "Waiting for Godot" if we aren't well educated. Of course we aren't unacquainted with "Waiting for Godot". Consequently, Beckett isn't unfamiliar to us. (*F, E, A*)

(3)   Unless we enjoy contemporary literature, we shall not read the works of Samuel Beckett. Yet we'll read Beckett's works only if we've the time. We certainly do enjoy contemporary literature, and also we'll read *The Unnamable* whenever we've the time. Hence, we enjoy contemporary literature and read *The Unnamable*. (*L, B, T, U*)

(4)   Samuel Beckett is an Irish, and not an English, playwright. Had he been born in London, Beckett would've been an English playwright. Now, Beckett is an Irish playwright and wasn't born in London only if he was a fellow countryman of Dylan Thomas. So Beckett, who is an Irish playwright, is also a fellow countryman of Thomas. (*I, E, L, T*)

(5)   Prices continue to increase despite the fact that buying dwindles. That Wall Street may suffer is a necessary condition that either money becomes scarcer or prices continue to rise. Thus, buying dwindles despite the fact that Wall Street may also suffer. (*P, B, S, M*)

(6)   If inflation continues, taxes will increase; moreover, if taxes increase, money will become scarcer. Now, either money doesn't become scarcer or business will continue to recede. That money doesn't become scarcer is a sufficient condition for the worker being happier. Business won't continue to recede. Therefore, the worker will be happier while inflation won't continue. (*I, T, M, B, W*)

(7)   If prices rise whenever there is an inflationary spiral, the market won't be stable. Either the market won't be unstable or bonds fluctuate; moreover, bonds don't fluctuate or government controls are affected. Government controls won't be affected. Either there's an inflationary spiral only if prices rise or we find a sound economy. So we find a sound economy even though government controls won't be affected. (*P, S, M, B, C, E*)

(8)   Salaries or dividends remain constant, despite the fact that business isn't controlled. Business is controlled whenever government intervenes. Salaries remain constant but government doesn't intervene only if the economy balances itself. That dividends remain constant is a sufficient condition for business being controlled. Hence, either the economy balances itself and dividends don't remain constant, or the economy balances itself and dividends remain constant. (*S, D, B, G, E*)

(9) It's neither the case that time is an unimportant factor nor we aren't interested in maximizing our economic theory research only if we find computers interesting. That we aren't interested in maximizing our economic theory research or we find computers interesting is a sufficient condition for pursuing applied mathematics. Neither is time an unimportant factor nor are we not interested in maximizing our economic theory research, or either we are bound to old techniques of economic analysis or recent developments in logic are unfamiliar. Yet it isn't the case that either we are bound to old techniques of economic analysis or recent developments in logic are unfamiliar. If we either pursue applied mathematics or aren't bound to old techniques of economic analysis, then we should acquaint ourselves with the research of Richard Stone. Therefore, it isn't the case that we should both acquaint ourselves with the research of Stone and also find computers interesting; or while finding computers interesting, we should acquaint ourselves with the research of Stone. (*T, R, C, M, A, D, S*)

(10) If we're interested in contemporary economic theory, we must study mathematical models. It isn't true that we must study mathematical models or be familiar with mathematical analysis, but not both. That we need to study Boolean algebras is a necessary condition for being interested in either axiomatic systems or computer research. We're interested in axiomatic systems only if we're acquainted with contemporary systems of logic despite the fact that we're not unfamiliar with mathematical analysis. Either we're interested in contemporary economic theory or we're unfamiliar with mathematical analysis, or we either must study mathematical models or be familiar with mathematical analysis, but not both. We're interested in axiomatic systems. Thus, we're interested in contemporary economic theory and are acquainted with contemporary systems of logic while also being interested in axiomatic systems and needing to study Boolean algebras; and, moreover, we must also study mathematical models. (*T, M, A, B, S, R, L*)

6. HYPOTHETICAL SYLLOGISM AND CONSTRUCTIVE DILEMMA

Let us accept these statements as true:

(1)   We don't need quantum mechanics unless we wish to study subatomic particles.

and

(2)   If we need quantum mechanics, we cannot consider Newton's theories adequate for our purposes.

At once we can assert the truth of

(3)   If we wish to study subatomic particles, we cannot consider Newton's theories adequate for our purposes.

The truth of (1) and (2) guarantees the truth of (3), and these three statements comprise an instance of

Hypothetical Syllogism (HS)

$$p \supset q$$
$$q \supset r$$
$$\therefore p \supset r$$

Hypothetical Syllogism relates two premisses and a conclusion, all being hypothetical statement forms. Carefully notice that the consequent of the first premiss is the same as the antecedent of the second; the antecedent of the conclusion is the same as the antecedent of the first premiss; and the consequent of the conclusion is the same as the consequent of the second premiss. This, and only this, argument form is called 'Hypothetical Syllogism'.

To see Hypothetical Syllogism "in action", let us construct a proof of validity for this argument:

(4)   New's concern with decent government is a sufficient condition for his entering the coming political race. If New wins in the elections, then he will keep the highest moral standards if he enters the political race. That New has the confidence of the voters is a sufficient condition for his winning in the elections. New certainly does have the confidence of the voters. Consequently, New is concerned with decent government only if he keeps the highest moral standards. (N, R, E, S, V)

We may symbolize (4) in this way:

(5) $\therefore N \supset S$
    1) $N \supset R$ Pr
    2) $E \supset (R \supset S)$ Pr
    3) $V \supset E$ Pr
    4) V Pr

In that our conclusion can be read as a hypothetical statement, we may suppose it will be reached by Hypothetical Syllogism. This supposition is strengthened when we examine the premiss set, for nowhere do we find '$N \supset R$' appearing as a whole. However, 'N' is found as the antecedent of the first premiss, while 'S' appears in the consequent of the second premiss. To reach our conclusion, we need *both* '$N \supset R$' and '$R \supset S$' on separate lines in the proof. Since '$N \supset R$' is the first premiss of (5), we may turn our attention to '$R \supset S$'. '$R \supset S$' is the consequent of the second premiss and could be asserted as a distinct statement in the proof if we could utilize Modus Ponens. In order to carry out this plan, 'E', the antecedent of the second premiss, is needed as a separate statement. 'E' may be deduced from the third and fourth statements by Modus Ponens. We may complete a proof of the validity of (4):

(6) $\therefore N \supset S$

1)	$N \supset R$	Pr
2)	$E \supset (R \supset S)$	Pr
3)	$V \supset E$	Pr
4)	V	Pr
5)	E	3, 4, MP
6)	$R \supset S$	2, 5, MP
7)	$\therefore N \supset S$	1, 6, HS

Another proof we may construct for (4) is

(7) $\therefore N \supset S$

1)	$N \supset R$	Pr
2)	$E \supset (R \supset S)$	Pr
3)	$V \supset E$	Pr
4)	V	Pr
5)	$V \supset (R \supset S)$	3, 2, HS
6)	$R \supset S$	5, 4, MP
7)	$\therefore N \supset S$	1, 6, HS

You may have seen literally the relationship of Hypothetical Syllogism between the third and second premisses, thereby yielding the fifth statement in (7). Our task is still to isolate '$R \supset S$' as a separate statement, but we do this by using Modus Ponens at line 6. It is important to appreciate that both (6) and (7) are acceptable proofs of the validity of (4). As we proceed in mastering deductive logic, it will not be unusual to discover several distinct proofs of validity for the same argument.

The remaining argument form establishing validity we shall introduce here is called '*Constructive Dilemma*'. Let us assume it is true that

(8)   Unless I know logic well, I am not able to apply it to my studies.

Furthermore, we shall suppose that (9) is also true:

(9)   If my knowledge of logic is weak, I do not do well in constructing proofs.

We also accept the truth of

(10)   Either I know logic well or my knowledge of logic is weak.

Given the truth of (8), (9), and (10), we may assert the truth of

(11)   So either I am able to apply logic to my studies or I do not do well in constructing proofs.

The statements (8), (9), (10), and (11) comprise a straightforward instance of this argument form:

Constructive Dilemma (CD)

$$p \supset q$$
$$r \supset s$$
$$p \lor r$$
$$\therefore q \lor s$$

The argument form, Constructive Dilemma, is composed of three premisses and a conclusion. The first two premisses are hypothetical statement forms; the third, the form of an inclusive disjunctive statement; while the conclusion is also an inclusive disjunctive statement form. Be very careful to notice that the antecedent of the first premiss is exactly the same as the left-hand disjunct of the third premiss and that the antecedent of the second premiss and the right-hand disjunct of the third premiss are the same. Further, the consequent of the first premiss and the left-hand disjunct of the conclusion are the same; and the consequent of the second premiss is the same as the right-hand disjunct of the conclusion. This, and only this, argument form is called 'Constructive Dilemma'.

How is Constructive Dilemma used in constructing a proof of validity? Consider this argument:

(12)   If Thomas has good grades, he is industrious if he has worked long hours; and if he isn't careless, he won't repress his abilities if he learns a great deal. Thomas will learn a great deal only if he has good grades while not being careless. Thomas does learn a great deal. Wherefore, he either is industrious or doesn't repress his abilities. (G, I, W, C, R, L)

Beginning a proof of validity by symbolizing (12), we then notice that the first premiss may be read as an overall conjunction. Breaking the first premiss into its component conjuncts, we obtain

(13) $\therefore I \lor \sim R$

1)	$[G \supset (W \supset I)] \cdot [\sim C \supset (L \supset \sim R)]$	Pr
2)	$L \supset (G \cdot \sim C)$	Pr
3)	L	Pr
4)	$G \supset (W \supset I)$	1, Simp
5)	$[\sim C \supset (L \supset \sim R)] \cdot [G \supset (W \supset I)]$	1, Com
6)	$\sim C \supset (L \supset \sim R)$	5, Simp

Examining the conclusion and reading it as an inclusive disjunctive statement, we see that it appears nowhere as a whole in the premiss set of (13). How, then, shall we obtain this conclusion; what Rule of Transformation may we use to assert '$I \lor \sim R$'? There are three argument forms we know yielding an inclusive disjunctive conclusion: Commutation, Addition, and Constructive Dilemma. If we obtain '$I \lor R$' by Commutation, we first must have '$\sim R \lor I$' which would be obtained by Addition or Constructive Dilemma. If we attempt to reach '$I \lor \sim R$' (or, indeed, '$\sim R \lor I$') by Addition, we must assert first either 'I' or '$\sim R$' as a separate statement in our proof. Finally, '$I \lor \sim R$' (or '$\sim R \lor I$') may be deduced by Constructive Dilemma. Moving to '$I \lor \sim R$' by Constructive Dilemma, we shall need two hypothetical statements such that 'I' is the consequent of one and '$\sim R$' the consequent of the other. Further, we shall need an inclusive disjunctive statement such that its two disjuncts are the same as the antecedents of the two hypothetical statements. Schematically, we want to discover the following if we plan to use Constructive Dilemma:

$$p \supset I$$
$$r \supset \sim R$$
$$p \lor r$$
$$\therefore I \lor \sim R$$

Inspecting the premiss set of (13), we find both 'I' and '$\sim R$' in the first premiss which we have already disjointed into lines 4 and 6 of the proof. Both the fourth and sixth statements are hypotheticals, 'I' appearing in the consequent of line 4 and '$\sim R$' in the consequent of line 6. The consequents of lines 4 and 6 are themselves consequents; namely,

$$W \supset I$$
$$L \supset \sim R$$

Having these lines, if we obtain '$L \lor W$', we can then use Constructive Dilemma. But we deduce '$L \lor W$' from the third premiss by Addition.

We still need '$W \supset I$' and '$L \supset \sim R$' as separate statements in the proof. Since these statements are consequents of hypothetical statements, they may be asserted by using Modus Ponens. To complete this plan, we must have 'G' and '$\sim C$' as isolated statements in the proof. How are we to derive 'G' and '$\sim C$'? Simple enough! By Modus Ponens, the statements in lines 2 and 3 produce '$G \cdot \sim C$'. Simplification, Commutation, and another use of Simplification then give us 'G' and '$\sim C$'. A completed proof of the validity of (12) is

(14) $\therefore I \lor \sim R$

1)	$[G \supset (W \supset I)] \cdot [\sim C \supset (L \supset \sim R)]$	Pr
2)	$L \supset (G \cdot \sim C)$	Pr
3)	L	Pr
4)	$G \supset (W \supset I)$	1, Simp
5)	$[\sim C \supset (L \supset \sim R)] \cdot [G \supset (W \supset I)]$	1, Com
6)	$\sim C \supset (L \supset \sim R)$	5, Simp
7)	$G \cdot \sim C$	2, 3, MP
8)	G	7, Simp
9)	$\sim C \cdot G$	7, Com
10)	$\sim C$	9, Simp
11)	$W \supset I$	4, 8, MP
12)	$L \supset \sim R$	6, 10, MP
13)	$L \lor W$	3, Add
14)	$W \lor L$	13, Com
15)	$\therefore I \lor \sim R$	11, 12, 14, CD

EXERCISES

Group A:

Give the correct justification for each unjustified line in the following exercises.

(1) $\therefore C \supset B$

1)	$A \supset B$	Pr
2)	$C \supset A$	Pr
3)	$\therefore C \supset B$	

(2) $\therefore B \lor D$

1)	$A \supset B$	Pr
2)	$A \lor C$	Pr
3)	$C \supset D$	Pr
4)	$\therefore B \lor D$	

(3) $\therefore E \supset B$

1)	$D \supset (A \supset B)$	Pr
2)	$D \cdot C$	Pr
3)	$C \supset (E \supset A)$	Pr
4)	D	
5)	$C \cdot D$	
6)	C	
7)	$E \supset A$	
8)	$A \supset B$	
9)	$\therefore E \supset B$	

(4) $\therefore \sim (D \lor E) \lor (E \lor D)$

  1) $A \lor B$ Pr

  2) $(B \supset D) \cdot (A \supset E)$ Pr

  3) $B \supset D$

  4) $(A \supset E) \cdot (B \supset D)$

  5) $A \supset E$

  6) $E \lor D$

  7) $(E \lor D) \lor \sim (D \lor E)$

  8) $\therefore \sim (D \lor E) \lor (E \lor D)$

(5) $\therefore B \lor E$

  1) $(A \supset B) \cdot C$ Pr

  2) $D \supset E$ Pr

  3) $C \supset D$ Pr

  4) $A \supset B$

  5) $C \cdot (A \supset B)$

  6) C

  7) $C \supset E$

  8) $C \lor A$

  9) $E \lor B$

 10) $\therefore B \lor E$

(6) $\therefore F \lor \sim E$

  1) $A \lor (B \lor C)$ Pr

  2) $D \supset \sim E$ Pr

  3) $\sim A \supset (C \supset F)$ Pr

  4) $B \supset D$ Pr

  5) $\sim A$ Pr

  6) $B \lor C$

  7) $C \supset F$

  8) $B \supset \sim E$

  9) $\sim E \lor F$

 10) $\therefore F \lor \sim E$

(7) $\therefore D \lor F$

  1) $A \cdot B$ Pr

  2) $B \supset (C \supset D)$ Pr

  3) $A \supset (C \lor E)$ Pr

  4) $E \supset F$ Pr

  5) A

  6) $B \cdot A$

  7) B

  8) $C \supset D$

  9) $C \lor E$

 10) $\therefore D \lor F$

(8) $\therefore C \lor E$

1)	$(A \supset B) \cdot (B \supset C)$	Pr
2)	$(D \supset E) \cdot (D \lor A)$	Pr
3)	$A \supset B$	
4)	$(B \supset C) \cdot (A \supset B)$	
5)	$B \supset C$	
6)	$D \supset E$	
7)	$(D \lor A) \cdot (D \supset E)$	
8)	$D \lor A$	
9)	$A \supset C$	
10)	$E \lor C$	
11)	$\therefore C \lor E$	

(9) $\therefore H \lor C$

1)	$A \supset (B \supset C)$	Pr
2)	$D \supset (A \cdot E)$	Pr
3)	$(G \cdot E) \supset (B \lor F)$	Pr
4)	$G \cdot D$	Pr
5)	$F \supset H$	Pr
6)	G	
7)	$D \cdot G$	
8)	D	
9)	$A \cdot E$	
10)	A	
11)	$E \cdot A$	
12)	E	
13)	$B \supset C$	
14)	$G \cdot E$	
15)	$B \lor F$	
16)	$F \lor B$	
17)	$\therefore H \lor C$	

(10) $\therefore B \supset F$

1)	$A \supset (B \supset C)$	Pr
2)	$D \supset (C \supset F)$	Pr
3)	$\sim G \supset D$	Pr
4)	$\sim H \supset A$	Pr
5)	$H \supset I$	Pr
6)	$\sim I \lor J$	Pr
7)	$\sim G \cdot \sim J$	Pr
8)	$\sim G$	
9)	$\sim J \cdot \sim G$	
10)	$\sim J$	
11)	D	
12)	$C \supset F$	

13) $J \lor \sim I$
14) $\sim I$
15) $\sim H$
16) A
17) $B \supset C$
18) $\therefore B \supset F$

Group B:

Construct a proof of validity for each of the following.

(1) $\therefore B \lor D$

  1) $A \supset B$ Pr
  2) $C \supset D$ Pr
  3) $A \lor C$ Pr

(2) $\therefore A \supset D$

  1) $A \supset B$ Pr
  2) $B \supset C$ Pr
  3) $C \supset D$ Pr

(3) $\therefore D \lor B$

  1) $A \supset B$ Pr
  2) $A \lor C$ Pr
  3) $C \supset D$ Pr

(4) $\therefore B \supset E$

  1) $A \lor (B \supset C)$ Pr
  2) $(C \supset E) \cdot \sim A$ Pr

(5) $\therefore C \lor E$

  1) $(A \supset B) \cdot (B \supset C)$ Pr
  2) $D \supset E$ Pr
  3) $D \lor A$ Pr

(6) $\therefore E \lor F$

  1) $(A \supset B) \cdot (C \supset D)$ Pr
  2) $A \lor C$ Pr
  3) $(D \supset F) \cdot (B \supset E)$ Pr

(7) $\therefore (G \cdot H) \lor (G \lor H)$

  1) $[A \supset \sim(B \cdot \sim C)] \supset (D \lor E)$ Pr
  2) $[A \supset (B \supset F)] \cdot [(B \supset F) \supset (B \cdot \sim C)]$ Pr
  3) $(D \lor E) \supset [(D \supset G) \cdot (E \supset H)]$ Pr

(8) $\therefore \{[C \lor (\sim E \lor \sim F)] \cdot [\sim(\sim G \cdot \sim H) \lor I]\} \lor [C \cdot \sim(\sim G \cdot \sim H)]$

  1) $[\sim(A \cdot B) \supset C] \cdot [D \supset (\sim E \lor \sim F)]$ Pr
  2) $[\sim(A \cdot B) \lor D] \cdot [E \lor \sim(\sim A \cdot \sim B)]$ Pr
  3) $[E \supset \sim(\sim G \cdot \sim H)] \cdot [\sim(\sim A \cdot \sim B) \supset I]$ Pr

(9) $\therefore G \lor E$
  1) $[A \lor (B \cdot \sim C)] \cdot \sim A$ Pr
  2) $[B \supset (D \supset E)] \cdot [\sim C \supset (F \supset G)]$ Pr
  3) $(\sim A \lor F) \supset (F \lor D)$ Pr

(10) $\therefore H \lor F$
  1) $(A \lor \sim B) \supset (C \lor D)$ Pr
  2) $[\sim E \supset (C \supset F)] \cdot [\sim G \supset (D \supset H)]$ Pr
  3) $[E \supset (H \lor I)] \cdot [G \supset (I \lor J)]$ Pr
  4) $\sim (H \lor I) \cdot \sim (I \lor J)$ Pr
  5) $(I \lor J) \lor [(H \lor I) \lor (A \lor \sim B)]$ Pr

Group C:

Give every exercise in Group B an interpretation by writing for each of the capital letters in a particular exercise an English statement—the same statement at each occurrence of the same capital letter in any given exercise—while also using appropriate English phrases for the logical operators.

Group D:

Symbolize the following arguments using the suggested notation, and then construct a proof of validity for each.

(1) Unless we read the works of Jean Anouilh, we shall not read *The Lark*. Yet we'll read the works of either Anouilh or Jacinto Benavente. Reading Benavente's works implies we'll read *The Passion Flower*. Wherefore, we'll read neither *The Lark* nor *The Passion Flower*, or we'll read *The Passion Flower* or *The Lark*. (A, L, B, F)

(2) Reading *The Madwoman of Chaillot* or *No Exit* implies an interest in contemporary French theater. We're familiar with the works of Jean Giraudoux only if we've read *The Madwoman of Chaillot;* whereas we're familiar with the works of Jean-Paul Sartre provided we've read *No Exit*. Now, we're familiar with the works of Sartre or Giraudoux. Accordingly, we've an interest in contemporary French theater or we're merely attempting to be culturally adept. (C, E, T, G, S, A)

(3) Not only is a study of Jean-Paul Sartre implied by a study of contemporary French theater, but further a reading of *The Flies* is implied by a study of Sartre. A reading of *The Flies* implies a comprehension of ancient Greek mythology, whereas a comprehension of ancient Greek mythology implies a liberal education. Thus, a study of contemporary French theater implies a liberal education. (S, T, F, M, E)

(4) In a course in contemporary European literature Franz Kafka or Albert Camus will be studied; moreover, if Kafka is studied, *The Trial* will be read. A sense of the absurd is conveyed to us whenever *The Trial* is read, while a study of Camus conveys the hope of hopelessness. Consequently, the hope of hopelessness or a sense of the absurd is conveyed to us. (K, C, T, A, H)

(5) Studying Franz Kafka is a sufficient condition for appreciating *The Trial* and *The Castle*. We fully appreciate *The Trial* only if we feel our absurd moral position whenever we fully appreciate *An Imperial Message*. If we appreciate *The Castle*, then unless we feel our absurd moral position, we don't understand the absence of Count Westwest. We study Kafka. So, if we fully appreciate *An Imperial Message*, we understand the absence of Count Westwest. (*K, T, C, P, M, W*)

(6) If J. S. Bach didn't compose in the Romantic Period, then the music of Bach should be played in its appropriate style whenever this music is correctly appreciated. Bach wrote in the Romantic Period only if he made extensive use of the pianoforte. If Bach didn't compose in the Romantic Period, this means that the music of Bach is misunderstood only if it is performed in the style of Richard Wagner. Bach didn't make extensive use of the pianoforte; nevertheless, the music of Bach is misunderstood or correctly appreciated. Therefore, Bach's music should be played in its appropriate style or in the style of Wagner. (*R, S, A, P, U, W*)

(7) If it isn't true both that J. S. Bach is a man of great musical genius while yet living in the contemporary age, then if Bach composed *Le Sacre du Printemps*, he is a contemporary composer. That Bach's works are replete with contemporary musical idioms is a necessary condition for his being both a man of great musical genius as well as living in the contemporary age. Bach's works aren't replete with contemporary musical idioms; moreover, Bach composed the *B minor Mass* or *Le Sacre du Printemps*. Now, that Bach is a contemporary composer implies that his works are replete with contemporary musical idioms; on the other hand, unless he composed the *B minor Mass*, his works aren't replete with ornamentations. So, the works of Bach are replete with contemporary musical idioms or ornamentations. (*G, A, P, C, I, M, O*)

(8) If Heinrich Schütz was influenced by Claudio Monteverdi, then if he was also influenced by Andrea Gabrieli, his music reflects the influence of Italian composers; yet if Schütz paid little attention to the Italians, then whenever he uses an Italianate style, it is quite accidental. Either Schütz paid little attention to the Italians or he was influenced by Monteverdi, or he was influenced by Dietrich Buxtehude. Not only wasn't Schütz influenced by Buxtehude while he was influenced by Gabrieli, further it isn't true that whenever Schütz used an Italianate style, it was quite accidental. Consequently, the music of Schütz reflects the influence of Italian composers. (*M, G, C, I, S, A, B*)

(9) We certainly must recognize the importance of the toccata if we wish to characterize the forms of early baroque organ; moreover, we shall not comprehend the early toccata style unless we understand the toccatas of Girolamo Frescobaldi. Either we wish to characterize the forms of early baroque organ or we understand the toccatas of Frescobaldi; while yet either we also understand the organ works of Buxtehude or we don't study the earlier baroque period of music. Unless we understand the organ works of Buxtehude, we cannot appreciate fully later developments in organ composition; but nevertheless the music of Buxtehude may remain mysterious if we don't study the earlier baroque period. Hence, even though we certainly must recognize the importance of the toccata, or comprehend the early toccata style, nonetheless, we also can appreciate fully later developments in organ composition or the music of Buxtehude may remain mysterious. (*T, O, S, F, B, P, C, M*)

(10) If either the majority of music historians is in error or in fact Antonio Vivaldi is the master of the concerto form, then if one of Vivaldi's major concerti is *The Seasons,* David Johnson is quite correct in speaking of its greatness. Yet, on the other hand, if either music critics aren't mistaken or Vivaldi's choral works aren't well-known, then *The Gloria* is an unimportant work if Vivaldi really wasn't interested in choral music. While Vivaldi's choral works aren't well-known, nevertheless he is the master of the concerto form. Furthermore, *The Gloria* is not an unimportant work despite the fact that either Vivaldi wasn't interested in choral music or *The Seasons* is one of his major concerti. So, the concert-going public might do well to ignore *The Seasons* or David Johnson is quite correct in speaking of its greatness. (*H, F, S, J, C, W, G, M, P*)

7. DEMONSTRATING THAT OUR ARGUMENT FORMS GUARANTEE VALIDITY

In Chapter 3 truth-table techniques were introduced to exhibit validity and invalidity of truth-functional arguments. Corresponding to every truth-functional argument is a hypothetical statement such that the antecedent of this statement is formed by putting all the premises of the argument into conjunction, and the consequent of the statement is the conclusion of the argument. If this hypothetical statement is found to be tautological, the original argument is valid. If, on the other hand, the hypothetical statement is either contingent or contradictory, the original argument is invalid.

Whereas in Chapter 3 we talked, for the most part, of arguments and statements, let us now talk of argument forms and statement forms. Corresponding to every argument form is a hypothetical statement form. Here all the premises are placed in conjunction to form the antecedent of the hypothetical statement form, and the conclusion of the argument form is the consequent of the hypothetical statement form.

Strictly speaking, argument forms are not valid or invalid, and neither are statement forms tautologies or not. But some statement forms guarantee tautological statements in that no matter what statements are substituted for the statement variables in the statement form—the same statement being substituted at each occurrence of the same variable—the result is a tautology. Since it does not matter which statement is substituted for a statement variable, and since any statement is either true or false, we speak *as if* our statement variables were either true or false. We can now construct truth-tables for statement forms corresponding to argument forms. Furthermore, if the last column of the truth-table for the statement form consists solely of '1's, that statement form guarantees tautological statements and the argument form to which it corresponds guarantees validity.

We have maintained that Modus Ponens guarantees validity; no argument showing this form can have all true premises and a false conclusion. Let us substantiate this claim:

$$p \supset q$$

$$p$$

$$\therefore q$$

$$[(p \supset q) \cdot p] \supset q$$

$$
\begin{array}{ccccccc}
1 & 1 & 1 & 11 & 1 & 1 \\
1 & 0 & 0 & 01 & 1 & 0 \\
0 & 1 & 1 & 00 & 1 & 1 \\
0 & 1 & 0 & 00 & 1 & 0 \\
& & & & \uparrow &
\end{array}
$$

Since in the final column of the truth-table analysis of '$[(p \supset q) \cdot p] \supset q$' we find only '1's, this statement form guarantees that any statement exhibiting this form will be a tautology. In turn, any argument having the form Modus Ponens will be valid.

EXERCISES

Group A:

Using shortened form truth-table means, establish which of the following argument forms guarantee validity and which do not.

(1) $p \supset q$	**(11)** $p \lor q$
$\sim q$	$\therefore q \lor p$
$\therefore \sim p$	
(2) $p \supset q$	**(12)** p
q	q
$\therefore p$	$\therefore p \cdot q$
(3) $p \supset (p \cdot q)$	**(13)** p
$\therefore p \supset q$	$\therefore p \lor q$
(4) $\sim (p \lor q)$	**(14)** $p \supset q$
$\therefore \sim q$	$\sim p$
	$\therefore \sim q$

(5) $p \supset q$

       $r \supset s$

       $p \vee r$

      $\therefore q \vee s$

(6) $q \vee p$

       $\sim p$

      $\therefore q$

(7) $p \cdot q$

      $\therefore q \cdot p$

(8) p

      $\therefore q \cdot p$

(9) $p \vee q$

       p

      $\therefore \sim q$

(10) $\sim(p \cdot q)$

      $\therefore \sim p$

(15) $\sim(p \vee q)$

       p

      $\therefore q$

(16) $\sim(p \supset q)$

      $\therefore \sim q \cdot p$

(17) $\sim(p \supset q)$

      $\therefore p$

(18) $p \cdot q$

      $\therefore p$

(19) $p \vee q$

       $\sim p$

      $\therefore q$

(20) $p \supset q$

       $q \supset r$

      $\therefore p \supset r$

Group B:

Are any of the argument forms in Group A which guarantee validity not used in Chapter 5 to construct proofs of validity? If so, which ones? How many argument forms guaranteeing validity do you suppose there are? Should we not learn all of them? If not, why not?

6

Proofs of Validity:
Definitional Equivalences

In Chapter 5, Section 2, we discovered that there are two types of Rules of Transformation which may be used in constructing proofs of validity: argument forms and equivalences. The purpose of Rules of Transformation is to guarantee validity. These rules must guarantee if all the premisses of an argument are true, then any statement obtained from these premisses by the Rules of Transformation must also be true; and, in particular, the concluding statement must be true.

In Chapter 4 the notions of definitional and logical equivalences were introduced and developed. As pointed out in Chapter 4, Section 1, there are several sets of logical operators in terms of which we may write any truth-functional statement or statement form. For our purposes, however, let us select $\{\cdot, \sim\}$ as our set of primitive operators. Consequently, the four following expressions are adopted as definitional equivalences:

D1:   '$p \vee q$' = '$\sim(\sim p \cdot \sim q)$'   Df

D2:   '$p \triangle q$' = '$\sim(p \cdot q) \cdot \sim(\sim p \cdot \sim q)$'   Df

D3:   '$p \supset q$' = '$\sim(p \cdot \sim q)$'   Df

D4:   '$p \equiv q$' = '$\sim(p \cdot \sim q) \cdot \sim(q \cdot \sim p)$'   Df

We know that any statement of the form '$p \lor q$' is true if, and only if, a statement of the form '$\sim(\sim p \cdot \sim q)$' is true (and vice versa), where 'p' is replaced by the same statement in both the *definiendum* and *definiens* and 'q' is replaced by the same statement in both the *definiendum* and *definiens*. Consequently, if 'Either William Shakespeare wrote his plays or Christopher Marlowe wrote the plays attributed to Shakespeare' is true, then so is the statement 'It isn't true both that William Shakespeare didn't write his plays and Christopher Marlowe didn't write the plays attributed to Shakespeare'. In sum our definitional equivalences retain the truth-value of statements.

Once more haunting our discussion is an implicit notion of substitution. We can substitute any statement for a single statement variable in a definition form provided we substitute the same statement for the same single statement variable throughout the entire definition form.

But substitution is not the only rule governing our use of definition forms. There is another rule which *is in no way applicable to argument forms*. This is the notion of *replacement*. While we may substitute statements for single statement variables, *we may replace any statement by a definitionally equivalent statement*. Let us suppose the following is a true statement:

(1) $\sim[(A \supset B) \cdot \sim(C \supset D)]$

Further, if we imagine '$A \supset B$' as an instance of 'p' and '$C \supset D$' of 'q', then we may say (1) exhibits the form '$\sim(p \cdot \sim q)$'. If this is the case, we can now assert the truth of

(2) $(A \supset B) \supset (C \supset D)$

where (2) is understood as displaying the form '$p \supset q$'.

Then unlike substitution, replacement allows us to replace one statement for another if those statements are definitionally equivalent. Yet replacement provides more freedom of movement than simply permitting us to replace one *whole* statement by another *whole* statement which is definitionally equivalent. Consider this example:

(3) $A \supset (B \supset C)$

Let us suppose (3) is a true statement and, furthermore, 'A' is an instance of 'r', 'B' an instance of 'p', and 'C' of 'q'. This being the case, we may now assert

(4) $A \supset \sim(B \cdot \sim C)$

We are permitted to replace a "*part*" of an overall statement by another "*part*", provided the two "parts"—for example, the consequents of (3) and (4)—are definitionally equivalent. *Whereas our argument forms apply to whole statements, definitional equivalences may be used on parts of statements.*

There is another important difference between substitution and replacement. When we substitute some statement for a single statement variable—either in a statement form or an argument form—we must substitute the same statement at every occurrence of the same single statement variable. Replacement does not require that we replace every occurrence of the same statement, in a larger statement, by its definitional equivalence. Observe the next example, considering it a true statement:

(5) $(A \supset B) \supset [C \supset (A \supset B)]$

We notice '$A \supset B$' occurs twice in (5). Nevertheless, replacement and our definitional equivalences permit us to write, for example,

(6) $(A \supset B) \supset [C \supset \sim (A \cdot \sim B)]$

We are not required to make the replacement throughout (5).

We shall now understand the notion of replacement in this manner:

> *Any statement may be replaced by its definitional equivalence. Such a replacement of definitionally equivalent statements may be performed on "parts" (these "parts" themselves being statements) of statements; moreover, such replacement need not be performed at every occurrence of the same "part" of a statement.*

1. USING DEFINITION 1 IN PROOFS OF VALIDITY

D1:   '$p \lor q$' $=$ '$\sim (\sim p \cdot \sim q)$'   Df

Imagine someone presented this argument:

(1)   It isn't accepted that cancer isn't always fatal and some patients don't recover. Cancer isn't always fatal, and in fact if some patients recover, this indicates the significance of an early discovery of the disease. Therefore, the early discovery of the disease is significant. (*F, R, D*)

In constructing a proof of (1), we first symbolize the argument:

(2) $\therefore S$
   1) $\sim (\sim F \cdot \sim R)$ Pr
   2) $\sim F \cdot (R \supset S)$ Pr

Noticing the second premiss is a conjunction and not having any obvious reason to keep it in that form, we simplify it:

3)	$\sim F$	2, Simp
4)	$(R \supset S) \cdot \sim F$	2, Com
5)	$R \supset S$	4, Simp

Having proceeded through line 5, we see at once that the conclusion, 'S', appears as the consequent of a hypothetical statement at line 5. 'S' may be obtained from the fifth statement if we could use Modus Ponens. Yet, before we can use Modus Ponens with the statement on line 5, we must have asserted 'R', the antecedent of the statement, as a separate statement in our proof.

Other than in the second premiss, 'R' appears in the first premiss of the argument. How are we to isolate 'R' from this premiss? The answer is really quite simple. If we interpret the first premiss as displaying the form '$\sim(\sim p \cdot \sim q)$', Definition 1 and our notion of replacement allow us to assert line 6 in (3)—'$F \lor R$'. Having '$\sim F$' at line 3, by Disjunctive Syllogism we obtain 'R'. The complete proof may be written as

(3) $\therefore S$

1)	$\sim(\sim F \cdot \sim R)$	Pr
2)	$\sim F \cdot (R \supset S)$	Pr
3)	$\sim F$	2, Simp
4)	$(R \supset S) \cdot \sim F$	2, Com
5)	$R \supset S$	4, Simp
6)	$F \lor R$	1, D1
7)	R	6, 3, DS
8)	$\therefore S$	5, 7, MP

Now, examine this argument:

(4)   Whenever we travel directly south, we don't travel east and west. However, our compass shows we are traveling west. So, we aren't traveling south. (S, E, W)

Symbolizing (4), we write

(5) $\therefore \sim S$

1)	$S \supset (\sim E \cdot \sim W)$	Pr
2)	W	Pr

The conclusion, '$\sim S$', does not appear in the premiss set; yet 'S' appears as an antecedent of a hypothetical statement in line 1. A use of Modus Tollens would guarantee '$\sim S$'. But before Modus Tollens can be used, the denial of the consequent of the first premiss must be asserted as a separate statement in (5). Clearly, the denial of '$\sim E \cdot \sim W$' is '$\sim(\sim E \cdot \sim W)$'. How are we to obtain '$\sim(\sim E \cdot \sim W)$' from our premisses? In a very straightforward way! If we understand '$\sim(\sim E \cdot$

$\sim W)$' as exhibiting the form '$\sim(\sim p \cdot \sim q)$', then we know that by obtaining '$E \vee W$' we could assert '$\sim(\sim E \cdot \sim W)$' by Definition 1. And '$E \vee W$' may be deduced from the second premiss by using Addition and then Commutation. The completed proof may now be written:

(6) $\therefore \sim S$

1)	$S \supset (\sim E \cdot \sim W)$	Pr
2)	W	Pr
3)	$W \vee E$	2, Add
4)	$E \vee W$	3, Com
5)	$\sim(\sim E \cdot \sim W)$	4, D1
6)	$\therefore \sim S$	1, 5, MT

The proofs of validity constructed at (3) and (6) suggest two important points to remember. *First*, an instance of '$p \vee q$' may be replaced by the corresponding instance of '$\sim(\sim p \cdot \sim q)$' and vice versa. Logical definitions are read from left to right and from right to left in constructing proofs of validity. *Second*, as a general —but not unbreakable—rule of thumb in the art of constructing proofs, *whenever you have a tilde on the outside of a set of punctuation marks, remove that tilde.* In (3) this is exactly what we did in proceeding from lines 1 to 6. There are cases, of course, when we shall want to have a tilde on the outside of a set of punctuation marks, as in moving from line 4 to 5 in (6). But, in such cases, it is usually relatively clear why we need a tilde located on the outside of a set of punctuation marks. As a general rule of thumb, remove tildes from the outside of punctuation marks. Our various logical definitions will often be helpful in observing this rule of thumb.

EXERCISES

Group A:

Give the correct justification for each unjustified line.

(1) $\therefore C$

1)	$\sim(\sim A \cdot \sim B)$	Pr
2)	$(B \vee A) \supset C$	Pr
3)	$A \vee B$	
4)	$B \vee A$	
5)	$\therefore C$	

(2) $\therefore A$

1)	$\sim(\sim A \cdot \sim B)$	Pr
2)	$\sim B$	Pr
3)	$A \vee B$	
4)	$B \vee A$	
5)	$\therefore A$	

(3) $\therefore\ C$

    1) $\sim A \cdot \sim B$ Pr

    2) $(\sim B \cdot \sim C) \supset A$ Pr

    3) $\sim A$

    4) $\sim B \cdot \sim A$

    5) $\sim B$

    6) $\sim(\sim B \cdot \sim C)$

    7) $B \lor C$

    8) $\therefore\ C$

(4) $\therefore\ \sim(\sim B \cdot \sim \sim D)$

    1) $(A \supset B) \cdot (C \supset \sim D)$ Pr

    2) $\sim(\sim A \cdot \sim C)$ Pr

    3) $A \supset B$

    4) $(C \supset \sim D) \cdot (A \supset B)$

    5) $C \supset \sim D$

    6) $A \lor C$

    7) $B \lor \sim D$

    8) $\therefore\ \sim(\sim B \cdot \sim \sim D)$

(5) $\therefore\ \sim(\sim D \cdot \sim C)$

    1) $\sim(\sim A \cdot \sim B) \supset C$ Pr

    2) B Pr

    3) $B \lor A$

    4) $A \lor B$

    5) $\sim(\sim A \cdot \sim B)$

    6) C

    7) $C \lor D$

    8) $D \lor C$

    9) $\therefore\ \sim(\sim D \cdot \sim C)$

(6) $\therefore\ \sim[\sim C \cdot \sim(E \cdot F)]$

    1) $(A \supset B) \cdot (B \supset C)$ Pr

    2) $\sim(\sim A \cdot \sim D)$ Pr

    3) $D \supset (E \cdot F)$ Pr

    4) $A \supset B$

    5) $(B \supset C) \cdot (A \supset B)$

    6) $B \supset C$

    7) $A \lor D$

    8) $A \supset C$

    9) $C \lor (E \cdot F)$

   10) $\therefore\ \sim[\sim C \cdot \sim(E \cdot F)]$

(7) $\therefore D \lor G$

   1) $A \supset (B \lor C)$ Pr
   2) $\sim(\sim B \cdot \sim C) \supset D$ Pr
   3) $\sim(\sim A \cdot \sim E)$ Pr
   4) $(E \supset F) \cdot (F \supset G)$ Pr
   5) $E \supset F$
   6) $(F \supset G) \cdot (E \supset F)$
   7) $F \supset G$
   8) $(B \lor C) \supset D$
   9) $A \lor E$
 10) $A \supset D$
 11) $E \supset G$
 12) $\therefore D \lor G$

(8) $\therefore \sim(\sim \sim F \cdot \sim G)$

   1) $\sim[\sim A \cdot \sim \sim (\sim B \cdot \sim C)]$ Pr
   2) $(B \supset D) \cdot (C \supset E)$ Pr
   3) $\sim A$ Pr
   4) $F \supset (\sim D \cdot \sim E)$ Pr
   5) $B \supset D$
   6) $(C \supset E) \cdot (B \supset D)$
   7) $C \supset E$
   8) $A \lor \sim(\sim B \cdot \sim C)$
   9) $\sim(\sim B \cdot \sim C)$
 10) $B \lor C$
 11) $D \lor E$
 12) $\sim(\sim D \cdot \sim E)$
 13) $\sim F$
 14) $\sim F \lor G$
 15) $\therefore \sim(\sim \sim F \cdot \sim G)$

(9) $\therefore \sim(\sim F \cdot \sim E) \lor (\sim E \cdot \sim F)$

   1) $(\sim A \cdot \sim B) \supset \sim(\sim C \cdot \sim D)$ Pr
   2) $\sim(C \lor D)$ Pr
   3) $\sim B \cdot (A \supset E)$ Pr
   4) $\sim B$
   5) $(A \supset E) \cdot \sim B$
   6) $A \supset E$
   7) $(\sim A \cdot \sim B) \supset (C \lor D)$
   8) $\sim(\sim A \cdot \sim B)$
   9) $A \lor B$
 10) $B \lor A$
 11) A
 12) E
 13) $E \lor F$
 14) $F \lor E$
 15) $\sim(\sim F \cdot \sim E)$
 16) $\therefore \sim(\sim F \cdot \sim E) \lor (\sim E \cdot \sim F)$

(10)　　　　　　　　　　　　　　　　　　　$\therefore \sim[\sim\sim(\sim H \cdot \sim G) \cdot \sim\sim(\sim I \cdot \sim J)]$

1)　$A \supset [B \vee (C \vee D)]$　　　　Pr
2)　$\sim[B \vee \sim(\sim C \cdot \sim D)]$　　　Pr
3)　$(E \supset F) \cdot (F \supset A)$　　　　Pr
4)　$\sim[\sim E \cdot \sim\sim(\sim G \cdot \sim H)]$　　Pr
5)　$E \supset F$
6)　$(F \supset A) \cdot (E \supset F)$
7)　$F \supset A$
8)　$\sim[B \vee (C \vee D)]$
9)　$\sim A$
10)　$E \vee \sim(\sim G \cdot \sim H)$
11)　$\sim F$
12)　$\sim E$
13)　$\sim(\sim G \cdot \sim H)$
14)　$G \vee H$
15)　$H \vee G$
16)　$\sim(\sim H \cdot \sim G)$
17)　$\sim(\sim H \cdot \sim G) \vee \sim(\sim I \cdot \sim J)$
18)　$\therefore \sim[\sim\sim(\sim H \cdot \sim G) \cdot \sim\sim(\sim I \cdot \sim J)]$

Group B:

Construct a proof of validity for each of the following.

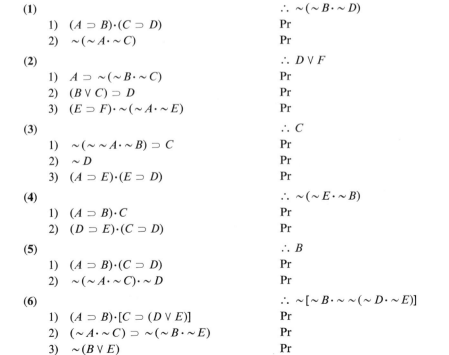

(1)　　　　　　　　　　　　　　　$\therefore \sim(\sim B \cdot \sim D)$
1)　$(A \supset B) \cdot (C \supset D)$　　Pr
2)　$\sim(\sim A \cdot \sim C)$　　　　　Pr

(2)　　　　　　　　　　　　　　　$\therefore D \vee F$
1)　$A \supset \sim(\sim B \cdot \sim C)$　　Pr
2)　$(B \vee C) \supset D$　　　　　Pr
3)　$(E \supset F) \cdot \sim(\sim A \cdot \sim E)$　Pr

(3)　　　　　　　　　　　　　　　$\therefore C$
1)　$\sim(\sim\sim A \cdot \sim B) \supset C$　　Pr
2)　$\sim D$　　　　　　　　　　Pr
3)　$(A \supset E) \cdot (E \supset D)$　　Pr

(4)　　　　　　　　　　　　　　　$\therefore \sim(\sim E \cdot \sim B)$
1)　$(A \supset B) \cdot C$　　　　　Pr
2)　$(D \supset E) \cdot (C \supset D)$　　Pr

(5)　　　　　　　　　　　　　　　$\therefore B$
1)　$(A \supset B) \cdot (C \supset D)$　　Pr
2)　$\sim(\sim A \cdot \sim C) \cdot \sim D$　　Pr

(6)　　　　　　　　　　　　　　　$\therefore \sim[\sim B \cdot \sim\sim(\sim D \cdot \sim E)]$
1)　$(A \supset B) \cdot [C \supset (D \vee E)]$　Pr
2)　$(\sim A \cdot \sim C) \supset \sim(\sim B \cdot \sim E)$　Pr
3)　$\sim(B \vee E)$　　　　　　　Pr

(7) $\therefore \sim[\sim E \cdot \sim \sim(\sim A \cdot \sim D)]$
    1) $(\sim A \cdot \sim B) \supset C$ Pr
    2) $\sim C \cdot \sim B$ Pr

(8) $\therefore \sim(\sim F \cdot \sim H)$
    1) $[A \supset \sim(\sim B \cdot \sim C)] \cdot [(B \vee C) \supset D]$ Pr
    2) $(A \supset D) \supset E$ Pr
    3) $(E \supset F) \cdot (G \supset H)$ Pr

(9) $\therefore A$
    1) $\sim[\sim(A \vee B) \cdot \sim C]$ Pr
    2) $(B \supset D) \cdot (D \supset E)$ Pr
    3) $\sim E \cdot \sim C$ Pr

(10) $\therefore E$
    1) $(A \cdot B) \supset \sim(\sim C \cdot \sim D)$ Pr
    2) $A \cdot (C \supset E)$ Pr
    3) $(\sim F \supset B) \cdot \sim F$ Pr
    4) $D \supset F$ Pr

Group C:

Give every exercise in Group B an interpretation by writing for each of the capital letters in a particular exercise an English statement—the same statement at each occurrence of the same capital letter in any given exercise—while also using appropriate English phrases for the logical operators.

Group D:

Symbolize the following arguments using the suggested notation, and then construct a proof of validity for each.

(1) Iodine is water soluble. So it isn't the case that alcohol isn't water soluble while iodine isn't soluble. (*I, A*)

(2) If alcohol isn't water soluble, iodine isn't water soluble and alcohol isn't. Iodine or alcohol is water soluble. Therefore, it isn't true that alcohol isn't soluble. (*A, I*)

(3) It isn't the case that bases aren't proton donors and acids aren't proton donors; moreover, acids aren't proton donors. Hence, bases are proton donors. (*B, A*)

(4) Acids are dangerous while bases sometimes aren't. It isn't true both that salts aren't dangerous and bases aren't sometimes dangerous. Thus, both acids and salts are dangerous. (*A, B, S*)

(5) That the study of sociology is without foundation is a necessary condition for human behavior being completely random. If human behavior isn't predictable and symbolic interaction analysis isn't meaningless, then human behavior is completely random. However, the study of sociology isn't without foundation and symbolic interaction analysis isn't meaningless. Human behavior, therefore, is predictable. (*F, R, P, M*)

(6) Sociology is concerned with rule-governed, but not chaotic, behavior; moreover, it isn't true that sociology isn't concerned with discovering the rules of group behavior while not being concerned with chaotic behavior. Consequently, the following isn't the case: It isn't true both that sociology is concerned with rule-governed behavior and with discovering rules of group behavior, even though theorists haven't clearly explicated social behavior. (*R, C, G, S*)

(7) That social workers aren't needed in slum sections and also aren't needed in upper-class areas implies they can be profitably employed in middle-class developments. But social workers can't be profitably employed in middle-class developments even though they aren't needed in upper-class areas. So, the following isn't true: Social workers can't contribute to any social group, and they are needed neither in slum sections nor in urban renewal programs. (*S, A, D, G, P*)

(8) That we aren't ignorant of various artistic styles suggests that we haven't overlooked the seventeenth-century Dutch masters. We aren't ignorant of various artistic styles and are familiar with the works of Jan Vermeer. The following isn't the case: We aren't ignorant of various artistic styles; furthermore, it isn't true that it isn't the case both that we haven't overlooked the seventeenth-century Dutch masters while also not being familiar with the works of Rembrandt van Ryn. Appreciating seventeenth-century Dutch painting is a necessary condition for being familiar with both the works of Vermeer and Rembrandt. Consequently, we appreciate seventeenth-century Dutch painting and are also familiar with the works of Vermeer. (*S, M, V, R, P*)

(9) Jan Vermeer wasn't well-known during his lifetime and certainly he wasn't appreciated as an artistic genius by his contemporaries. Also, it isn't true both that Vermeer wasn't well-known during his lifetime and neither was a prolific painter nor lived in relative solitude. Vermeer wasn't a prolific painter and furthermore he probably didn't sell many of his canvases. Either Vermeer probably sold many of his canvases or it isn't the case both that he wasn't appreciated as an artistic genius by his contemporaries and his greatness wasn't recognized until 200 years after his death. Therefore, either Vermeer lived in relative solitude or his greatness wasn't recognized until 200 years after his death; moreover, the greatness of Vermeer was recognized 200 years after his death or he didn't live in relative solitude. (*K, A, P, L, C, R*)

(10) If Marlene is energetic, it isn't true both that she doesn't invite us to dinner and isn't tired. Now, it isn't the case that Marlene isn't energetic and hasn't been feeling bad. If Marlene has been feeling bad, Tom will be worried; moreover, if Tom is worried, he will misplace the gin. But, if Marlene is giving a party, she isn't tired and Tom won't misplace the gin. Of course Marlene is giving a party. Hence, she invites us to dinner while also giving a party. (*E, I, T, F, W, M, G*)

D2: $\quad 'p \triangle q' = '\sim(p\cdot q)\cdot\sim(\sim p\cdot\sim q)'\quad$ Df

Suppose one were to argue

(1) If you pass this course, you've worked long hours and curtailed many social activities. Yet we know that you've either worked long hours or curtailed many social activities, but not both. You're not exhausted unless you've worked long hours; but, if you've curtailed many social activities, you're disappointed. So you haven't passed this course, while it is true that you're exhausted or disappointed. (*P, W, C, E, D*)

Let us construct a proof of validity for (1), first symbolizing the argument and then breaking down the third premiss into its various parts.

(2) $\qquad\qquad\qquad\qquad \therefore \sim P\cdot(E \vee D)$

1) $P \supset (H\cdot A)$ Pr
2) $H \triangle A$ Pr
3) $(H \supset E)\cdot(A \supset D)$ Pr
4) $H \supset E$ 3, Simp
5) $(A \supset D)\cdot(H \supset E)$ 3, Com
6) $A \supset D$ 5, Simp

Because the conclusion symbolized in (2) does not appear as such in the premiss set, we may read it as an overall conjunction and suppose that it will be reached by a use of Conjunction. In order to obtain '$\sim C\cdot(E \vee D)$' by Conjunction, however, '$\sim P$' and '$E \vee D$' first must be asserted as separate statements in the proof. Examining the premiss set of (2), we surmise that '$\sim P$' will come from line 1 by Modus Tollens, if we can first obtain '$\sim(H\cdot A)$' as a distinct statement in the proof. But, even so, how shall we assert '$E \vee D$'? We might use Constructive Dilemma with lines 4 and 6, provided we could state '$H \vee A$' on a separate line. Therefore, the completion of (2) rests upon asserting '$\sim(H\cdot A)$' and '$H \vee A$'.

Returning to the premiss set, we see that the second premiss, '$H \triangle A$', is an exclusive disjunctive statement. There is not much we can do with such statements except use Definition 2. Yet doing this will lead us quickly to '$\sim(H\cdot A)$' and '$H \vee A$'. Notice how this is accomplished in lines 7–11 in the following:

(3) $\qquad\qquad\qquad\qquad \therefore \sim P\cdot(E \vee D)$

1) $P \supset (H \cdot A)$ Pr
2) $H \triangle A$ Pr
3) $(H \supset E)\cdot(A \supset D)$ Pr
4) $H \supset E$ 3, Simp

5)	$(A \supset D) \cdot (H \supset E)$	3, Com
6)	$A \supset D$	5, Simp
7)	$\sim(H \cdot A) \cdot \sim(\sim H \cdot \sim A)$	2, D2
8)	$\sim(H \cdot A)$	7, Simp
9)	$\sim(\sim H \cdot \sim A) \cdot \sim(H \cdot A)$	7, Com
10)	$\sim(\sim H \cdot \sim A)$	9, Simp
11)	$H \lor A$	10, D1
12)	$\sim P$	1, 8, MT
13)	$E \lor D$	4, 6, 11, CD
14)	$\therefore \ \sim P \cdot (E \lor D)$	12, 13, Conj

Perhaps we should consider another example using Definition 2:

(4)   If game playing provides a man-machine contest, then machines can play games if game playing doesn't afford sufficient solution generation complexity to demand symbolic reasoning skills. Whenever game situations provide highly regular problem environments, then game situations provide well-defined problem boundaries only if game environments are useful task environments to study the nature and structure of complex problem-solving processes. Unless game situations provide highly regular problem environments, it isn't the case that game playing doesn't afford sufficient solution generation complexity to demand symbolic reasoning skills or game situations provide well-defined problem boundaries (but not both). But game situations provide highly regular problem environments and game playing also provides a man-machine contest. So it isn't the case both that game environments aren't useful task environments to study the nature and structure of complex problem-solving processes and machines can't play games. (C, G, S, E, B, P)

Symbolizing (4), we then continue constructing a proof by simplifying the fourth premiss into its conjuncts:

(5) $\hspace{4cm} \therefore \ \sim(\sim P \cdot \sim G)$

1)	$C \supset (\sim S \supset G)$	Pr
2)	$E \supset (B \supset P)$	Pr
3)	$E \supset (\sim S \triangle B)$	Pr
4)	$E \cdot C$	Pr
5)	E	4, Simp
6)	$C \cdot E$	4, Com
7)	C	6, Simp

Examining the desired conclusion, we see at once that '$\sim(\sim P \cdot \sim G)$' does not appear as a whole expression in any one premiss. Nor does, say, '$\sim P \cdot \sim G$' occur as an antecedent of a hypothetical statement. If it did, we might reach our conclusion by using Modus Tollens. We *do* notice that 'G' appears in the consequent of the statement on line 1 and 'P' in the consequent of line 2. Both of these consequents are themselves hypothetical statements having as their consequents 'G' and 'P'.

Two Modus Ponens moves yield the consequents of the first and second premisses on separate lines in our proof:

8) $\sim S \supset G$ 1, 7, MP
9) $B \supset P$ 2, 5, MP

But how do these statements further our proof? If we could now assert '$\sim S \lor B$', by a use of Constructive Dilemma we could justify '$G \lor P$', putting us within two steps of our conclusion! And, from where and by what means are we to obtain the needed '$\sim S \lor B$'? Upon '$\sim C \lor M$' the entire success of our proof now hinges!

The consequent of the third premiss is '$\sim S \triangle B$'. It is from this consequent— once it is on a separate line—that we derive '$\sim S \lor B$' by Definition 2, Commutation, Simplification, and then Definition 1. A complete proof of (4) may now be constructed:

(6) $\therefore \sim(\sim P \cdot \sim G)$

1)	$C \supset (\sim S \supset G)$		Pr
2)	$E \supset (B \supset P)$		Pr
3)	$E \supset (\sim S \triangle B)$		Pr
4)	$E \cdot C$		Pr
5)	E		4, Simp
6)	$C \cdot E$		4, Com
7)	C		6, Simp
8)	$\sim S \supset G$		1, 7, MP
9)	$B \supset P$		2, 5, MP
10)	$\sim S \triangle B$		3, 5, MP
11)	$\sim(\sim S \cdot B) \cdot \sim(\sim \sim S \cdot \sim B)$		10, D2
12)	$\sim(\sim \sim S \cdot \sim B) \cdot \sim(\sim S \cdot B)$		11, Com
13)	$\sim(\sim \sim S \cdot \sim B)$		12, Simp
14)	$\sim S \lor B$		13, D1
15)	$G \lor P$		8, 9, 14, CD
16)	$P \lor G$		15, Com
17)	$\therefore \sim(\sim P \cdot \sim G)$		16, D1

From the viewpoint of applying the Rules of Transformation, we want to remember that given any statement of the form '$p \triangle q$', we can always obtain '$p \lor q$'. This is *not* the *only* thing we can deduce, however. For example, we may also assert '$\sim(p \cdot q)$', given '$p \triangle q$'; moreover, as we continue in our studies, there will be more types of statements we can derive from a statement of the form '$p \triangle q$' than '$p \lor q$' and '$\sim(p \cdot q)$'.

Group A:

Give the correct justification for each unjustified line in the following.

(1)   ∴   ~A
  1) $A \supset (B \cdot C)$ Pr
  2) $B \triangle C$ Pr
  3) $\sim (B \cdot C) \cdot \sim (\sim B \cdot \sim C)$
  4) $\sim (B \cdot C)$
  5)   ∴ $\sim A$

(2)   ∴ B
  1) $\sim A$ Pr
  2) $B \triangle A$ Pr
  3) $\sim (B \cdot A) \cdot \sim (\sim B \cdot \sim A)$
  4) $\sim (\sim B \cdot \sim A) \cdot \sim (B \cdot A)$
  5) $\sim (\sim B \cdot \sim A)$
  6) $B \lor A$
  7) $A \lor B$
  8)   ∴ B

(3)   ∴ $A \triangle C$
  1) $A \cdot \sim B$ Pr
  2) $(A \cdot C) \supset B$ Pr
  3) A
  4) $\sim B \cdot A$
  5) $\sim B$
  6) $\sim (A \cdot C)$
  7) $A \lor C$
  8) $\sim (\sim A \cdot \sim C)$
  9) $\sim (A \cdot C) \cdot \sim (\sim A \cdot \sim C)$
  10)   ∴ $A \triangle C$

(4)   ∴ $C \triangle D$
  1) $A \lor B$ Pr
  2) $(\sim A \cdot \sim B) \lor C$ Pr
  3) $(C \cdot D) \supset (\sim A \cdot \sim B)$ Pr
  4) $\sim (\sim A \cdot \sim B)$
  5) $\sim (C \cdot D)$
  6) C
  7) $C \lor D$
  8) $\sim (\sim C \cdot \sim D)$
  9) $\sim (C \cdot D) \cdot \sim (\sim C \cdot \sim D)$
  10)   ∴ $C \triangle D$

(5) $\therefore\ D \lor \sim(\sim E \cdot \sim C)$

   1) $[\sim(A \cdot B) \cdot \sim(\sim A \cdot \sim B)] \supset C$ Pr

   2) $D \supset E$ Pr

   3) $F \supset (A \triangle B)$ Pr

   4) $(F \supset C) \supset D$ Pr

   5) $(A \triangle B) \supset C$

   6) $F \supset C$

   7) $(F \supset C) \supset E$

   8) E

   9) $E \lor C$

  10) $\sim(\sim E \cdot \sim C)$

  11) $\sim(\sim E \cdot \sim C) \lor D$

  12) $\therefore\ D \lor \sim(\sim E \cdot \sim C)$

(6) $\therefore\ C \lor E$

   1) $A \triangle (B \supset C)$ Pr

   2) $\sim A \cdot (B \triangle D)$ Pr

   3) $A \lor (D \supset E)$ Pr

   4) $\sim A$

   5) $(B \triangle D) \cdot \sim A$

   6) $B \triangle D$

   7) $\sim[A \cdot (B \supset C)] \cdot \sim[\sim A \cdot \sim(B \supset C)]$

   8) $\sim[\sim A \cdot \sim(B \supset C)] \cdot \sim[A \cdot (B \supset C)]$

   9) $\sim[\sim A \cdot \sim(B \supset C)]$

  10) $A \lor (B \supset C)$

  11) $B \supset C$

  12) $D \supset E$

  13) $\sim(B \cdot D) \cdot \sim(\sim B \cdot \sim D)$

  14) $\sim(\sim B \cdot \sim D) \cdot \sim(B \cdot D)$

  15) $\sim(\sim B \cdot \sim D)$

  16) $B \lor D$

  17) $\therefore\ C \lor E$

(7) $\therefore\ C \lor G$

   1) $A \supset (B \supset C)$ Pr

   2) $\sim D \supset (B \triangle E)$ Pr

   3) $F \supset (E \supset G)$ Pr

   4) $[D \lor (F \cdot A)] \cdot \sim D$ Pr

   5) $D \lor (F \cdot A)$

   6) $\sim D \cdot [D \lor (F \cdot A)]$

   7) $\sim D$

   8) $F \cdot A$

   9) F

  10) $A \cdot F$

  11) A

  12) $B \supset C$

13) $E \supset G$
14) $B \triangle E$
15) $\sim(B \cdot E) \cdot \sim(\sim B \cdot \sim E)$
16) $\sim(\sim B \cdot \sim E) \cdot \sim(B \cdot E)$
17) $\sim(\sim B \cdot \sim E)$
18) $B \vee E$
19) $\therefore \ C \vee G$

(8) $\therefore \ \sim[\sim F \cdot \sim \sim(\sim B \cdot \sim E)]$

    1) $(A \supset B) \cdot (C \supset D)$ Pr
    2) $\sim(\sim A \cdot \sim C)$ Pr
    3) $(B \triangle D) \supset E$ Pr
    4) $\sim(B \cdot D) \vee (\sim A \cdot \sim C)$ Pr
    5) $A \supset B$
    6) $(C \supset D) \cdot (A \supset B)$
    7) $C \supset D$
    8) $(\sim A \cdot \sim C) \vee \sim(B \cdot D)$
    9) $\sim(B \cdot D)$
   10) $A \vee C$
   11) $B \vee D$
   12) $\sim(\sim B \cdot \sim D)$
   13) $\sim(B \cdot D) \cdot \sim(\sim B \cdot \sim D)$
   14) $B \triangle D$
   15) E
   16) $E \vee B$
   17) $B \vee E$
   18) $\sim(\sim B) \cdot \sim E)$
   19) $\sim(\sim B \cdot \sim E) \vee F$
   20) $F \vee \sim(\sim B \cdot \sim E)$
   21) $\therefore \ \sim[\sim F \cdot \sim \sim(\sim B \cdot \sim E)]$

(9) $\therefore \ F \vee H$

    1) $(A \triangle B) \supset C$ Pr
    2) $\sim D \cdot (A \vee D)$ Pr
    3) $(A \cdot B) \supset D$ Pr
    4) $(E \supset F) \cdot (C \supset H)$ Pr
    5) $\sim D$
    6) $(A \vee D) \cdot \sim D$
    7) $A \vee D$
    8) $E \supset F$
    9) $(C \supset H) \cdot (E \supset F)$
   10) $C \supset H$
   11) $\sim(A \cdot B)$
   12) $D \vee A$
   13) A
   14) $A \vee B$

15) $\sim(\sim A \cdot \sim B)$
16) $\sim(A \cdot B) \cdot \sim(\sim A \cdot \sim B)$
17) $A \triangle B$
18) C
19) $C \lor E$
20) $E \lor C$
21) $\therefore F \lor H$

(10) $\therefore \sim(\sim C \cdot \sim F) \lor (C \cdot F)$

1) $A \supset (B \supset C)$ Pr
2) $(E \supset D) \cdot (A \lor E)$ Pr
3) $\sim D \cdot (D \supset F)$ Pr
4) $\sim E \supset (D \triangle B)$ Pr
5) $E \supset D$
6) $(A \lor E) \cdot (E \supset D)$
7) $A \lor E$
8) $\sim D$
9) $(D \supset F) \cdot \sim D$
10) $D \supset F$
11) $\sim E$
12) $E \lor A$
13) A
14) $B \supset C$
15) $D \triangle B$
16) $\sim(D \cdot B) \cdot \sim(\sim D \cdot \sim B)$
17) $\sim(\sim D \cdot \sim B) \cdot \sim(D \cdot B)$
18) $\sim(\sim D \cdot \sim B)$
19) $D \lor B$
20) $F \lor C$
21) $C \lor F$
22) $\sim(\sim C \cdot \sim F)$
23) $\therefore \sim(\sim C \cdot \sim F) \lor (C \cdot F)$

Group B:

Construct a proof of validity for each of the following.

(1) $\therefore A \triangle B$
1) $\sim(A \cdot B) \supset C$ Pr
2) $C \supset B$ Pr
3) $\sim(A \cdot B)$ Pr

(2) $\therefore B \cdot C$
1) $A \triangle B$ Pr
2) $C \cdot \sim A$ Pr

(3) $\therefore C \cdot A$

    1) $A \cdot \sim B$ Pr

    2) $A \supset (C \triangle B)$ Pr

(4) $\therefore B$

    1) $(A \supset B) \cdot (C \supset D)$ Pr

    2) $A \triangle C$ Pr

    3) $\sim D$ Pr

(5) $\therefore B \cdot \sim A$

    1) $A \supset (B \cdot C)$ Pr

    2) $\sim C \cdot (B \triangle C)$ Pr

(6) $\therefore D$

    1) $(A \supset B) \cdot \sim B$ Pr

    2) $C \supset D$ Pr

    3) $\sim A \supset (C \triangle A)$ Pr

(7) $\therefore \sim F \vee E$

    1) $(A \supset B) \cdot (C \supset D)$ Pr

    2) $A \triangle C$ Pr

    3) $(B \supset E) \cdot (D \supset \sim F)$ Pr

(8) $\therefore E$

    1) $A \supset \sim B$ Pr

    2) $C \triangle A$ Pr

    3) $(D \supset \sim C) \cdot D$ Pr

    4) $B \triangle E$ Pr

(9) $\therefore \sim [\sim G \cdot \sim \sim (\sim H \cdot \sim I)]$

    1) $\sim (A \vee B) \supset (\sim C \cdot \sim D)$ Pr

    2) $\sim \sim (\sim A \cdot \sim B)$ Pr

    3) $(C \triangle E) \cdot (D \vee F)$ Pr

    4) $(E \cdot F) \supset G$ Pr

(10) $\therefore \sim (\sim H \cdot \sim G)$

    1) $(A \cdot B) \supset (C \cdot D)$ Pr

    2) $(E \vee F) \vee (C \triangle D)$ Pr

    3) $\sim \sim (\sim E \cdot \sim F)$ Pr

    4) $B \vee (E \vee F)$ Pr

    5) $(A \triangle B) \supset [(C \supset G) \cdot (D \supset H)]$ Pr

Group C:

Give every exercise in Group B an interpretation by writing for each of the capital letters in a particular exercise an English statement—the same statement at each occurrence of the same capital letter in any given exercise—while also using appropriate English phrases for the logical operators.

Group D:

Symbolize the following arguments using the suggested notation, and then construct a proof of validity for each.

(1)   Either Ford or Porsche (but not both) won at Le Mans. Porsche didn't win. Therefore, Ford won. (*F, P*)

(2)   It isn't true that Austin Healeys and MG's have the same top speed of 140 mph. MG's have a top speed of 140 mph or Austin Healeys and MG's have a top speed of 140 mph. So, either Austin Healeys or MG's have a top speed of 140 mph (but not both). (*H, G*)

(3)   If an auto enthusiast appreciates style and classical design, he'll drive a Morgan. An auto enthusiast appreciates classical design or drives a Morgan. He doesn't drive a Morgan. Consequently, an auto enthusiast appreciates either style or classical design, but not both. (*S, D, M*)

(4)   That Merlin was always King Arthur's chief counselor suggests that the magician began the Knights of the Round Table. Merlin was always Arthur's chief counselor or he sometimes fell from the King's favor (but not both). Certainly Merlin didn't begin the Knights of the Round Table. Hence, Merlin sometimes fell from the King's favor and wasn't always Arthur's chief counselor; yet, also, Merlin didn't begin the Knights of the Round Table and he sometimes fell from the King's favor. (*C, T, F*)

(5)   It isn't true both that Merlin was lured into an enchanted forest while remaining loyal to King Arthur; moreover, it isn't true both that Merlin remained loyal to Arthur while possessing magical powers. That Merlin was lured into an enchanted forest is a necessary condition for Merlin either remaining loyal to Arthur or possessing magical powers (but not both). Merlin possessed magical powers or remained loyal to Arthur. Thus, Merlin was lured into an enchanted forest or he remained loyal to Arthur (but not both). (*F, L, P*)

(6)   If Merlin wanted King Arthur to marry the Princess of Carmalide, the King married Guinevere; but either Merlin wanted Arthur to marry the Princess of Carmalide or the tales concerning Lancelot were malicious court rumors (but not both). It isn't true both that Arthur married Guinevere and she was always faithful to him; yet if the tales concerning Lancelot were malicious court rumors, Guinevere was always faithful to Arthur. So Arthur married Guinevere or she was always faithful to him (but not both). (*C, G, L, F*)

(7)   Either King Arthur ruled in peace or Guinevere was always faithful to him (but not both), but also either Arthur was defeated in battle or he wasn't a coward (but not both). Arthur ruled in peace while Guinevere was always faithful to him, or Arthur wasn't defeated in battle. So it isn't true both that it isn't the case that Arthur wasn't a coward and yet didn't rule in peace. (*P, F, D, C*)

(8) Either it isn't the case that John Donne and Alfred Tennyson were metaphysical poets or Homer didn't write the *Republic* and Virgil didn't write *The Aeneid*. If Homer wrote the *Republic*, then Donne was a metaphysical poet; moreover, if Virgil wrote *The Aeneid*, Tennyson was also a metaphysical poet. Either Donne was a metaphysical poet or Tennyson was (but not both), only if Plato wrote the *Symposium*. It isn't the case that Homer didn't write the *Republic* and Virgil didn't write *The Aeneid*. Thus, Plato wrote the *Symposium*. (*D, T, H, V, P*)

(9) "The Song of Roland" is an early French epic only if it sings the glory of Charlemagne; moreover, either Ganelon was Roland's friend or "The Song of Roland" is an early French epic (but not both). That Ganelon was Roland's friend is a sufficient condition for Roland having remained alive; moreover, either Roland was killed by Ganelon or "The Song of Roland" is an early French epic. If Roland was killed by Ganelon, "The Song of Roland" doesn't sing the glory of Charlemagne and Roland didn't remain alive. Consequently, "The Song of Roland" is an early French epic and sings the glory of Charlemagne. (*E, G, F, A, K*)

(10) The following isn't the case: The author of *Beowulf* is unknown, and it isn't true that *Beowulf* is a Christian poem if it was written in the eighth century. Also, the following isn't true: *Beowulf* doesn't glorify the *comitatus* relationship, and moreover it isn't the case that *Beowulf* is an epic only if it begins *in medias res*. *Beowulf* doesn't glorify the *comitatus* relationship and doesn't begin *in medias res*. That the author of *Beowulf* is unknown implies that it is an epic or was written in the eighth century, but not both. The author of *Beowulf* is unknown or it begins *in medias res*, but not both. Therefore, *Beowulf* is a Christian poem. (*K, P, W, C, E, R*)

3. USING DEFINITION 3 IN PROOFS OF VALIDITY

D3:   '$p \supset q$' = '$\sim(p \cdot \sim q)$'   Df

We now must turn our attention to Definition 3. Notice how this definition permits us to construct a proof of validity for the next example:

(1)   That justice is in the interest of the stronger even though Glaucon isn't correct in his opinions is a sufficient condition for Thrasymachus being correct. Not only is Thrasymachus not correct, but further Glaucon isn't correct. So Socrates is correct in his position or justice isn't in the interest of the stronger. (*J, G, T, S*)

Symbolizing (1), we then proceed by breaking down the second premiss into its component parts:

(2) $\therefore S \vee \sim J$

    1) $(J \cdot \sim G) \supset T$ Pr

    2) $\sim T \cdot \sim G$ Pr

    3) $\sim T$ 2, Simp

    4) $\sim G \cdot \sim T$ 2, Com

    5) $\sim G$ 4, Simp

While examining both the conclusion and premiss set, we see that 'S' does not appear in the premiss set. Hence, we must use Addition somewhere in constructing the desired proof. For example, if '$\sim J$' could be obtained on a separate line, '$\sim J \vee S$' could be asserted by Addition and then '$S \vee \sim J$' by Commutation.

Clearly, the completion of (2) depends upon '$\sim J$'. While '$\sim J$' does not appear in any premiss of (2), nevertheless, 'J' is found in the antecedent of the first premiss. If we were able to use Modus Tollens with the first premiss, then '$\sim (J \cdot \sim G)$' could be asserted as a separate statement in the proof. But, how would such a Modus Tollens move help us in reaching our conclusion? Suppose we did have '$\sim (J \cdot \sim G)$' on a separate line. Then, viewing '$\sim (J \cdot \sim G)$' as an instance of '$\sim (p \cdot \sim q)$' and appealing to Definition 3, we could easily assert '$J \supset G$'. Another use of Modus Tollens would yield the much needed '$\sim J$'.

Our present strategy requires that we use Modus Tollens twice, once with '$(J \cdot \sim G) \supset T$' and then with '$J \supset G$'. We need, therefore, '$\sim T$' and '$\sim G$' as separate statements in the proof. But these statements are found on lines 3 and 5 of (2). Consequently, we are ready to construct a complete proof of the validity of (1):

(3) $\therefore S \vee \sim J$

    1) $(J \cdot \sim G) \supset T$ Pr

    2) $\sim T \cdot \sim G$ Pr

    3) $\sim T$ 2, Simp

    4) $\sim G \cdot \sim T$ 2, Com

    5) $\sim G$ 4, Simp

    6) $\sim (J \cdot \sim G)$ 1, 3, MT

    7) $J \supset G$ 6, D3

    8) $\sim J$ 7, 5, MT

    9) $\sim J \vee S$ 8, Add

  10) $\therefore S \vee \sim J$ 9, Com

Now, consider this more complicated argument:

(4)   That a man is temperate is a necessary condition for his being just; moreover, that a man is temperate is also a sufficient condition for his being good. A man is either just or evil, but not both. Now, it isn't true both that a man is evil and not wicked; furthermore, it isn't true both that a man is wicked and not deceiving. Hence, if a man isn't good, he is deceiving. (T, J, G, E, W, D)

Let us attempt to construct a proof of the validity of (4). As in all such proofs, we first symbolize the argument:

(5) $\therefore \sim G \supset D$

  1) $(J \supset T)\cdot(T \supset G)$ Pr
  2) $J \bigtriangleup E$ Pr
  3) $\sim(E\cdot\sim W)\cdot\sim(W\cdot\sim D)$ Pr

Perhaps after examining the conclusion and premiss set, we still do not grasp how the conclusion is related to the premises. Even so, we can call on two helpful rules of thumb. *First*, if any statement is viewed as an overall conjunction, and we see no reason to keep it in that form, break down that statement into its various conjuncts. *Second*, if there is a tilde on the outside of any punctuation marks, and we see no reason to keep that tilde there, remove it by using some Rule of Transformation. Following the first of these two rules of thumb, we easily generate the next lines in our proof:

  4) $J \supset T$ 1, Simp
  5) $(T \supset G)\cdot(J \supset T)$ 1, Com
  6) $T \supset G$ 5, Simp
  7) $\sim(E\cdot\sim W)$ 3, Simp
  8) $\sim(W\cdot\sim D)\cdot\sim(E\cdot\sim W)$ 3, Com
  9) $\sim(W\cdot\sim D)$ 8, Simp

Now, let us apply our second rule of thumb. Interpreting both '$\sim(E\cdot\sim W)$' and '$\sim(W\cdot\sim D)$' as instances of '$\sim(p\cdot\sim q)$' we use Definition 3 to move the tildes from before the punctuation marks:

 10) $E \supset W$ 7, D3
 11) $W \supset D$ 9, D3

Now what must we do? Consider the conclusion, '$\sim G \supset D$'. Since this statement does not appear as a complete element in the premiss set, we shall not use rules such as Modus Ponens or Disjunctive Syllogism to obtain it. But then, what rule shall we use? One answer is "Hypothetical Syllogism". Yet, given the premiss set of (5) and our present Rules of Transformation, '$\sim G \supset D$' cannot be reached by Hypothetical Syllogism. Why? Because nowhere do we discover '$\sim G$' as an antecedent of a hypothetical statement.

Then, how else may we obtain '$\sim G \supset D$'? Perhaps by appealing to Definition 3. If we were able to assert '$\sim(\sim G\cdot\sim D)$', Definition 3 would guarantee '$\sim G \supset D$'. It is important to notice that in this use of Definition 3, *we would interpret* '$\sim G$' *as an instance of* '*p*' *and* '*D*' *as an instance of* '*q*' *in* '*p* $\supset$ *q*'.

Very well, but how shall we reach '$\sim(\sim G\cdot\sim D)$'? Why not attempt a use of Definition 1? Let us imagine—shrewdly guess—that the last three lines in our proposed proof will be these:

) $G \lor D$
) $\sim(\sim G \cdot \sim D)$ D1
) $\therefore \sim G \supset D$ D3

The completion of (5) depends now on finding '$G \lor D$'. Since both 'G' and 'D' occur as consequents of hypothetical statements, we may decide to attempt a use of Constructive Dilemma. In that case we need these lines:

6) $T \supset G$
11) $W \supset D$
) $T \lor W$

How are we to obtain '$T \lor W$'? Once more, since both 'T' and 'W' appear as consequents of hypothetical statements, we suggest another use of Constructive Dilemma. Now, we need

4) $J \supset T$
10) $E \supset W$
) $J \lor E$

Where are we to find '$J \lor E$'? Simple! Look at the second premiss!

Having mapped out our overall plan of attack, we may now construct a complete proof of the validity of (4):

(6) $\therefore \sim G \supset D$

1)	$(J \supset T) \cdot (T \urcorner G)$	Pr
2)	$J \triangle E$	Pr
3)	$\sim(E \cdot \sim W) \cdot \sim(W \cdot \sim D)$	Pr
4)	$J \supset T$	1, Simp
5)	$(T \supset G) \cdot (J \supset T)$	1, Com
6)	$T \supset G$	5, Simp
7)	$\sim(E \cdot \sim W)$	3, Simp
8)	$\sim(W \cdot \sim D) \cdot \sim(E \cdot \sim W)$	3, Com
9)	$\sim(W \cdot \sim D)$	8, Simp
10)	$E \supset W$	7, D3
11)	$W \supset D$	9, D3
12)	$\sim(J \cdot E) \cdot \sim(\sim J \cdot \sim E)$	2, D2
13)	$\sim(\sim J \cdot \sim E) \cdot \sim(J \cdot E)$	12, Com
14)	$\sim(\sim J \cdot \sim E)$	13, Simp
15)	$J \lor E$	14, D1
16)	$T \lor W$	4, 10, 15, CD
17)	$G \lor D$	6, 11, 16, CD
18)	$\sim(\sim G \cdot \sim D)$	17, D1
19)	$\therefore \sim G \supset D$	18, D3

There is another proof of (4) which uses Hypothetical Syllogism twice and Constructive Dilemma once. Can you construct it?

It is important to notice in reading line 18 as ***coming from*** line 17 we appeal to Definition 1. But, when reading line 18 as ***leading to*** line 19, we use Definition 3. *Exactly what form we consider '$\sim(\sim G \cdot \sim D)$' to be exhibiting depends very much upon the uses to which we wish to put the statement at some particular occurrence in our proof.* But this, of course, is true of any statement in any proof of validity.

EXERCISES

Group A:

Give the correct justification for each unjustified line.

(1) $\therefore\ D \vee \sim C$

1)	$\sim(\sim A \cdot \sim B)$	Pr
2)	$A \supset \sim C$	Pr
3)	$\sim(B \cdot \sim D)$	Pr
4)	$B \supset D$	
5)	$A \vee B$	
6)	$\sim C \vee D$	
7)	$\therefore\ D \vee \sim C$	

(2) $\therefore\ C \cdot E$

1)	$\sim(A \cdot \sim B) \supset C$	Pr
2)	$D \supset (A \supset B)$	Pr
3)	$E \cdot D$	Pr
4)	E	
5)	$D \cdot E$	
6)	D	
7)	$(A \supset B) \supset C$	
8)	$D \supset C$	
9)	C	
10)	$\therefore\ C \cdot E$	

(3) $\therefore\ D \vee B$

1)	$\sim(A \cdot \sim B)$	Pr
2)	$\sim C \supset (\sim D \supset E)$	Pr
3)	$\sim C$	Pr
4)	$\sim(E \cdot \sim A)$	Pr
5)	$A \supset B$	
6)	$E \supset A$	
7)	$\sim D \supset E$	
8)	$E \supset B$	
9)	$\sim D \supset B$	
10)	$\sim(\sim D \cdot \sim B)$	
11)	$\therefore\ D \vee B$	

(4) $\therefore \sim B \supset D$

   1) $\sim(A \cdot \sim B)$ Pr
   2) $\sim(C \cdot \sim D) \cdot \sim(\sim A \cdot \sim C)$ Pr
   3) $\sim(C \cdot \sim D)$
   4) $\sim(\sim A \cdot \sim C) \cdot \sim(C \cdot \sim D)$
   5) $\sim(\sim A \cdot \sim C)$
   6) $A \supset B$
   7) $C \supset D$
   8) $A \lor C$
   9) $B \lor D$
  10) $\sim(\sim B \cdot \sim D)$
  11) $\therefore \sim B \supset D$

(5) $\therefore D \bigtriangleup \sim E$

   1) $A \supset (B \cdot \sim C)$ Pr
   2) $(D \cdot \sim E) \supset A$ Pr
   3) $(\sim D \supset \sim E) \cdot (B \supset C)$ Pr
   4) $\sim D \supset \sim E$
   5) $(B \supset C) \cdot (\sim D \supset \sim E)$
   6) $B \supset C$
   7) $\sim(B \cdot \sim C)$
   8) $\sim A$
   9) $\sim(D \cdot \sim E)$
  10) $\sim(\sim D \cdot \sim \sim E)$
  11) $\sim(D \cdot \sim E) \cdot \sim(\sim D \cdot \sim \sim E)$
  12) $\therefore D \bigtriangleup \sim E$

(6) $\therefore \sim C \supset D$

   1) $A \supset \sim(B \cdot \sim C)$ Pr
   2) $D \lor A$ Pr
   3) $D \supset \sim E$ Pr
   4) $B \cdot \sim \sim E$ Pr
   5) B
   6) $\sim \sim E \cdot B$
   7) $\sim \sim E$
   8) $\sim D$
   9) A
  10) $\sim(B \cdot \sim C)$
  11) $B \supset C$
  12) C
  13) $C \lor D$
  14) $\sim(\sim C \cdot \sim D)$
  15) $\therefore \sim C \supset D$

(7) $\therefore \; \sim F \supset B$

   1) $(A \cdot \sim B) \supset C$ Pr

   2) $\sim C \cdot \sim D$ Pr

   3) $(\sim A \cdot \sim E) \supset D$ Pr

   4) $\sim(E \cdot \sim F)$ Pr

   5) $\sim C$

   6) $\sim D \cdot \sim C$

   7) $\sim D$

   8) $E \supset F$

   9) $\sim(A \cdot \sim B)$

 10) $A \supset B$

 11) $\sim(\sim A \cdot \sim E)$

 12) $A \vee E$

 13) $B \vee F$

 14) $F \vee B$

 15) $\sim(\sim F \cdot \sim B)$

 16) $\therefore \; \sim F \supset B$

(8) $\therefore \; \sim(\sim G \cdot \sim F)$

   1) $A \triangle \sim B$ Pr

   2) $\sim(B \cdot \sim C)$ Pr

   3) $\sim(A \cdot \sim C) \supset \sim(\sim D \cdot \sim E)$ Pr

   4) $(D \supset F) \cdot (E \supset G)$ Pr

   5) $D \supset F$

   6) $(E \supset G) \cdot (D \supset F)$

   7) $E \supset G$

   8) $B \supset C$

   9) $\sim(A \cdot \sim B) \cdot \sim(\sim A \cdot \sim \sim B)$

 10) $\sim(A \cdot \sim B)$

 11) $A \supset B$

 12) $A \supset C$

 13) $\sim(A \cdot \sim C)$

 14) $\sim(\sim D \cdot \sim E)$

 15) $D \vee E$

 16) $F \vee G$

 17) $G \vee F$

 18) $\therefore \; \sim(\sim G \cdot \sim F)$

(9) $\therefore \; \sim E \supset B$

   1) $(\sim A \supset B) \cdot (B \supset C)$ Pr

   2) $(D \cdot \sim E) \supset (\sim F \cdot \sim G)$ Pr

   3) $(A \supset F) \cdot (C \supset G)$ Pr

   4) $\sim(\sim D \cdot \sim \sim A)$ Pr

   5) $\sim A \supset B$

   6) $(B \supset C) \cdot (\sim A \supset B)$

   7) $B \supset C$

   8) $A \supset F$

   9) $(C \supset G) \cdot (A \supset F)$

  10) $C \supset G$

  11) $D \vee \sim A$

  12) $\sim A \supset C$

  13) $\sim(\sim A \cdot \sim C)$

  14) $A \vee C$

  15) $F \vee G$

  16) $\sim(\sim F \cdot \sim G)$

  17) $\sim(D \cdot \sim E)$

  18) $D \supset E$

  19) $E \vee B$

  20) $\sim(\sim E \cdot \sim B)$

  21) $\therefore \sim E \supset B$

(10) $\therefore B \cdot \sim(\sim A \cdot \sim I)$

   1) $(A \cdot B) \vee (\sim C \cdot \sim D)$ Pr

   2) $(E \triangle \sim F) \supset \sim(\sim G \cdot \sim H)$ Pr

   3) $(H \supset D) \cdot (G \supset C)$ Pr

   4) $(E \supset F) \cdot (\sim F \vee E)$ Pr

   5) $H \supset D$

   6) $(G \supset C) \cdot (H \supset D)$

   7) $G \supset C$

   8) $E \supset F$

   9) $(\sim F \vee E) \cdot (E \supset F)$

  10) $\sim F \vee E$

  11) $\sim(E \cdot \sim F)$

  12) $E \vee \sim F$

  13) $\sim(\sim E \cdot \sim \sim F)$

  14) $\sim(E \cdot \sim F) \cdot \sim(\sim E \cdot \sim \sim F)$

  15) $E \triangle \sim F$

  16) $\sim(\sim G \cdot \sim H)$

  17) $G \vee H$

  18) $C \vee D$

  19) $\sim(\sim C \cdot \sim D)$

  20) $(\sim C \cdot \sim D) \vee (A \cdot B)$

  21) $A \cdot B$

  22) A

  23) $B \cdot A$

  24) B

  25) $A \vee I$

  26) $\sim(\sim A \cdot \sim I)$

  27) $\therefore B \cdot \sim(\sim A \cdot \sim I)$

Group B:

Construct a proof of validity for each of the following.

(1) $\therefore \ \sim(A \cdot \sim C)$
    1) $\sim(A \cdot \sim B) \cdot \sim(B \cdot \sim C)$ Pr

(2) $\therefore \ \sim C \supset B$
    1) $\sim(A \cdot \sim B) \cdot A$ Pr

(3) $\therefore \ A \lor D$
    1) $A \triangle B$ Pr
    2) $(B \cdot \sim D) \supset (A \cdot B)$ Pr

(4) $\therefore \ \sim F \supset D$
    1) $A \supset (B \supset C)$ Pr
    2) $\sim(B \cdot \sim C) \supset D$ Pr
    3) $(E \supset F) \cdot \sim(\sim E \cdot \sim A)$ Pr

(5) $\therefore \ A \supset E$
    1) $(A \cdot \sim B) \supset (\sim C \cdot \sim D)$ Pr
    2) $(C \lor D) \cdot F$ Pr
    3) $(B \cdot \sim E) \supset (\sim F \cdot \sim C)$ Pr

(6) $\therefore \ \sim A \supset D$
    1) $A \triangle \sim B$ Pr
    2) $B \triangle \sim C$ Pr
    3) $(A \cdot \sim B) \lor \sim(\sim C \cdot \sim D)$ Pr

(7) $\therefore \ C \cdot B$
    1) $\sim[A \cdot \sim \sim(B \cdot \sim C)]$ Pr
    2) $(A \cdot B) \lor (D \cdot E)$ Pr
    3) $\sim[(D \cdot E) \cdot \sim F] \cdot \sim F$ Pr

(8) $\therefore \ \sim B \supset D$
    1) $\sim A \triangle B$ Pr
    2) $\sim(\sim C \cdot \sim \sim B)$ Pr
    3) $\sim(\sim A \cdot \sim D) \cdot \sim C$ Pr

(9) $\therefore \ \sim F \supset G$
    1) $A \supset (B \triangle C)$ Pr
    2) $\sim D \cdot \sim[\sim D \cdot \sim(E \cdot A)]$ Pr
    3) $(B \cdot \sim F) \supset D$ Pr
    4) $E \supset \sim(C \cdot \sim G)$ Pr

(10) $\therefore \ H \cdot \sim(\sim G \cdot \sim \sim H)$
    1) $\sim[A \cdot \sim(\sim B \cdot C)]$ Pr
    2) $\sim[\sim \sim(D \cdot \sim E) \cdot \sim B]$ Pr
    3) $\sim(\sim A \cdot \sim F)$ Pr
    4) $\sim[\sim(D \cdot \sim E) \cdot \sim(G \cdot H)]$ Pr
    5) $\sim F \cdot \sim E$ Pr

Group C:

Give every exercise in Group B an interpretation by writing for each of the capital letters in a particular exercise an English statement—the same statement at each occurrence of the same capital letter in any given exercise—while also using appropriate English phrases for the logical operators.

Group D:

Symbolize the following arguments using the suggested notation, and then construct a proof of validity for each.

(1) Either Cupid was patient or Daphne was Apollo's first love. So Daphne was Apollo's first love if Cupid wasn't patient. (*C, D*)

(2) Daphne didn't love Apollo. It isn't the case both that Daphne's father forced her to marry though she didn't love Apollo. Hence, Daphne's father didn't force her to marry. (*D, F*)

(3) Daphne was transformed into a laurel tree or wasn't saved from Apollo, but not both. Thus, Daphne was transformed into a laurel tree only if she was saved from Apollo. (*D, A*)

(4) It isn't the case both that West opens with one no trump and East doesn't raise to six no trump; but also it isn't the case both that East raises to six no trump while game isn't made. Therefore, it isn't the case both that West opens with one no trump and game isn't made. (*W, E, G*)

(5) North doesn't have an opening bid and South doesn't have five honor count. The following isn't true: East is set even though South doesn't have five honor count; yet North doesn't have an opening bid. Wherefore, East isn't set. (*N, S, E*)

(6) Increases in real wages are needed to provide workers with an adequate share of benefits of the economy's progress or equity requires decreases in the buying power of wages, but not both. Equity requires decreases in the buying power of wages or a rise in real earnings isn't essential for the sustained growth of mass consumer markets, but not both. Consequently, increases in real wages are needed to provide workers with an adequate share of the benefits of the economy's progress or a rise in real earnings is essential for the sustained growth of mass consumer markets. (*I, E, R*)

(7) It isn't the case both that the quantity of economic goods produced gives rise to the supply of goods and services and that the personal choice of things wanted doesn't give rise to demand of goods and services; also, it isn't the case both that demand is influenced by a country's system of taxation and isn't affected by natural resources. The quantity of economic goods produced gives rise to the supply of goods and services or demand is influenced by a country's system of taxation, but not both. Wherefore, demand isn't affected by natural resources only if the personal choice of things wanted gives rise to demand of goods and services. (*Q, C, I, A*)

(8) If it isn't true both that the mechanisms of exchange include the credit system while the facilities for foreign exchange don't include natural resources, then the entire system of capitalism revolves around the price system. If natural resources influence the quantity of economic goods produced, then the facilities for foreign exchange include natural resources; moreover, if the entire system of capitalism revolves around the price system, then the mechanisms of exchange include the credit system. If natural resources don't influence the quantity of economic goods produced, then if the mechanisms of exchange include the credit system, the facilities for foreign exchange include natural resources. It isn't the case both that the facilities for foreign exchange include natural resources and the mechanisms of exchange include the credit system. Therefore, the facilities for foreign exchange include natural resources or the mechanisms of exchange include the credit system, but not both. (*M, F, S, R*)

(9) If Marlene doesn't go the Halloween party, Tom won't be pleased with her; yet it isn't true both that Marlene goes to the Halloween party while Grant isn't also there. It isn't the case both that Tom won't be pleased with Marlene and doesn't go to "The Chalet". That it isn't the case both that Tom doesn't go to "The Chalet" and Grant won't be there implies that everyone will then go to "The Red Barn" even though Tom won't be pleased with Marlene. Accordingly, Tom goes to "The Chalet" and everyone will then go to "The Red Barn". (*M, T, G, C, B*)

(10) Either Marlene joins "Little Women" or she is hunting her place in Harmony Grove society but won't dress for afternoon tea; yet Marlene doesn't join "Little Women". The following isn't true: Marlene is hunting her place in Harmony Grove society and it isn't true that it isn't the case both that Marlene is going to tea while not wearing a tweed suit. Furthermore, that Marlene won't dress for afternoon tea is a sufficient condition for it not being the case both that Marlene brings her feathered boa and doesn't carry her beaded bag. That it isn't true both that Marlene doesn't bring her feathered boa while not going to tea is a necessary condition for Marlene either not joining "Little Woman" or for bringing her feathered boa. It isn't true both that Marlene carries her beaded bag while wearing a tweed suit. So Marlene either carries her beaded bag or wears a tweed suit, but not both. (*J, H, D, G, W, B, C*)

4. USING DEFINITION 4 IN PROOFS OF VALIDITY

D4:   '$p \equiv q$' = '$\sim(p \cdot \sim q) \cdot \sim(q \cdot \sim p)$'   Df

The final logical definition we shall study in the Truth-Functional Calculus is applicable to statements exhibiting the form '$p \equiv q$'. For example, consider this argument:

(1)   Cassius won't be defeated if, and only if, the Senate doesn't meet. Yet that the people of Rome revolt is both a necessary and sufficient condition for Cassius not being defeated. So if the people of Rome revolt, the Senate won't meet. (C, S, P)

Reading both premisses as displaying the form '$p \equiv q$', (1) may be symbolized as

(2) $\therefore P \supset \sim S$
  1) $\sim C \equiv \sim S$ Pr
  2) $P \equiv \sim C$ Pr

Examining the premiss set and the conclusion, we see that '$P \supset \sim S$' does not appear as a complete statement in the premiss set. Nevertheless, 'P' appears in the second premiss and '$\sim S$' in the first, while '$\sim C$'—which does not appear in the conclusion—appears in both premisses. Obtaining '$P \supset \sim C$' and '$\sim C \supset \sim S$', the conclusion is at hand by a use of Hypothetical Syllogism. Each premiss in (2) may be regarded as a conjunction of two hypothetical statements. In particular we may view the first premiss of (2) as yielding '$\sim C \supset \sim S$' and '$\sim S \supset \sim C$', whereas the second premiss may be understood as producing '$P \supset \sim C$' and '$\sim C \supset P$'. Certainly, having '$P \supset \sim C$' and '$\sim C \supset \sim S$' as distinct statements in our proof, we assert '$P \supset \sim S$' by Hypothetical Syllogism. The question now is what rules do we have at our disposal permitting '$P \supset \sim C$' to be obtained from the second premiss and '$\sim C \supset \sim S$' from the first?

Converting the premisses into their definitional equivalences by Definition 4, we are in a much better position to see '$P \supset \sim C$' and '$\sim C \supset \sim S$'.

  3) $\sim(\sim C \cdot \sim \sim S) \cdot \sim(\sim S \cdot \sim \sim C)$ 1, D4
  4) $\sim(P \cdot \sim \sim C) \cdot \sim(\sim C \cdot \sim P)$ 2, D4

Using Simplification with the third statement followed by Definition 3, '$\sim C \supset \sim S$' is obtained. Similar remarks apply to the fourth statement in reaching '$\sim P \supset \sim C$'. As already noted, Hypothetical Syllogism yields the conclusion. The completed proof may now be constructed:

(3) $\therefore P \supset \sim S$
  1) $\sim C \equiv \sim S$ Pr
  2) $P \equiv \sim C$ Pr
  3) $\sim(\sim C \cdot \sim \sim S) \cdot \sim(\sim S \cdot \sim \sim C)$ 1, D4
  4) $\sim(P \cdot \sim \sim C) \cdot \sim(\sim C \cdot \sim P)$ 2, D4
  5) $\sim(\sim C \cdot \sim \sim S)$ 3, Simp
  6) $\sim(P \cdot \sim \sim C)$ 4, Simp
  7) $\sim C \supset \sim S$ 5, D3
  8) $P \supset \sim C$ 6, D3
  9) $\therefore P \supset \sim S$ 8, 7, HS

Even though both the third and fourth statements are read as conjunctions, nevertheless, Commutation followed by Simplification is not used in either case. The reason for this is fairly obvious. Our strategy was to use Hypothetical Syllogism to obtain '$P \supset \sim S$'. But this move necessitated having '$P \supset \sim C$' and '$\sim C \supset \sim S$'. Now, the *right-hand* conjuncts of the third and fourth statements do not yield these desired hypothetical statements.

Let us now consider a slightly different argument:

(4)　　　　Cassius won't be defeated if, and only if, the Senate doesn't meet. Yet that the people of Rome revolt is both a necessary and sufficient condition for Cassius not being defeated. So the people of Rome revolt if, and only if, the Senate won't meet. (C, S, P)

Statement (4) is exactly like (1) except for the conclusion and may be symbolized as

(5)　　　　　　　　　　　　$\therefore P \equiv \sim S$
　　1)　$\sim C \equiv \sim S$　　Pr
　　2)　$P \equiv \sim C$　　Pr

Not finding the conclusion, '$P \equiv \sim S$', as a whole statement in our premiss set, let us suppose that it will be derived by Definition 4. In order to use Definition 4, we shall first need the statement '$\sim (P \cdot \sim \sim S) \cdot \sim (\sim S \cdot \sim P)$'. Reading this statement as an overall conjunction, it can be obtained by Conjunction if previously we have asserted '$\sim (P \cdot \sim \sim S)$' and '$\sim (\sim S \cdot \sim P)$'. These statements in turn can be reached by Definition 3 provided we first obtain '$P \supset \sim S$' and '$\sim S \supset P$'. Working backward, our line of attack may be expressed in this way:

```
)       P ⊃ ~S
)       ~S ⊃ P
)       ~(P·~~S)                        D3
)       ~(~S·~P)                        D3
)       ~(P·~~S)·~(~S·~P)               Conj
)   ∴ P ≡ ~S                            D4
```

In (3) we see how to obtain '$P \supset \sim S$'. Now, using the right-hand conjuncts of the third and fourth statements of (3), we reach '$\sim S \supset P$' required in completing (5). Notice how the completed proof is constructed:

(6)　　　　　　　　　　　　　　　　　$\therefore P \equiv \sim S$
　　1)　　$\sim C \equiv \sim S$　　　　　　　　Pr
　　2)　　$P \equiv \sim C$　　　　　　　　　　Pr
　　3)　　$\sim (\sim C \cdot \sim \sim S) \cdot \sim (\sim S \cdot \sim \sim C)$　　　　1, D4
　　4)　　$\sim (P \cdot \sim \sim C) \cdot \sim (\sim C \cdot \sim P)$　　　　2, D4
　　5)　　$\sim (\sim C \cdot \sim \sim S)$　　　　　　3, Simp

6)	$\sim(\sim P \cdot \sim \sim C)$	4, Simp
7)	$\sim C \supset \sim S$	5, D3
8)	$P \supset \sim C$	6, D3
9)	$P \supset \sim S$	8, 7, HS
10)	$\sim(\sim S \cdot \sim \sim C) \cdot \sim(\sim C \cdot \sim \sim S)$	3, Com
11)	$\sim(\sim C \cdot \sim P) \cdot \sim(P \cdot \sim \sim C)$	4, Com
12)	$\sim(\sim S \cdot \sim \sim C)$	10, Simp
13)	$\sim(\sim C \cdot \sim P)$	11, Simp
14)	$\sim S \supset \sim C$	12, D3
15)	$\sim C \supset P$	13, D3
16)	$\sim S \supset P$	14, 15, HS
17)	$\sim(P \cdot \sim \sim S)$	9, D3
18)	$\sim(\sim S \cdot \sim P)$	16, D3
19)	$\sim(P \cdot \sim \sim S) \cdot \sim(\sim S \cdot \sim P)$	17, 18, Conj
20)	$\therefore P \equiv \sim S$	19, D4

Consider this perhaps slightly more difficult argument:

(7)   Unless money is tight and consumer spending doesn't increase, there won't be a financial recession. If stocks fall off or there isn't a financial recession, then it isn't the case both that dividends are paid on bonds and yet personal savings don't increase. Either dividends are paid on bonds or money is tight, but not both. Stocks fall off when, and only when, there is a financial recession, although stocks will not fall off. So, it isn't the case both that consumer spending doesn't increase while personal savings also don't increase. (M, C, R, S, D, P)

We shall symbolize (7) in this way:

(8) $\therefore \sim(\sim C \cdot \sim P)$

1)	$(M \cdot \sim C) \supset R$	Pr
2)	$(S \vee \sim R) \supset \sim(D \cdot \sim P)$	Pr
3)	$D \triangle M$	Pr
4)	$(S \equiv R) \cdot \sim S$	Pr

There are several moves we may want to make at once:

5)	$S \equiv R$	4, Simp
6)	$\sim S \cdot (S \equiv R)$	4, Com
7)	$\sim S$	6, Simp
8)	$\sim(D \cdot M) \cdot \sim(\sim D \cdot \sim M)$	3, D2
9)	$\sim(S \cdot \sim R) \cdot \sim(R \cdot \sim S)$	5, D4

Since the fourth premiss of (8) may be viewed as an overall conjunction and since there is no obvious reason to keep it in that form, we disjoint it into its various conjuncts. Reading the third premiss as an instance of '$p \triangle q$' and the statement at line 5 as an instance of '$p \equiv q$', we convert them into their definitional equivalences. Why? Because given the remainder of the premises in (8), it is not at all obvious what we could do with either an exclusive disjunctive statement or a material equivalence statement as such. On the other hand, it is likely that we shall use at least part of the definitional equivalences of each of these statements.

Now, notice the conclusion, '$\sim(\sim C \cdot \sim P)$'. This statement does not appear as a whole in the premiss set. Neither does '$\sim C \cdot \sim P$' appear as an antecedent of a hypothetical statement; if it did, we might use Modus Tollens to obtain the conclusion. As a matter of fact, 'C' appears in the first premiss while 'P' appears in the second. Examine very carefully how 'C' and 'P' do appear! If Modus Tollens could be used with the first premiss and Modus Ponens with the second, we could assert

) $\sim(M \cdot \sim C)$ MT
) $\sim(D \cdot \sim P)$ MP

These statements, by Definition 3, yield

) $M \supset C$ D3
) $D \supset P$ D3

Employing Constructive Dilemma, we could reach '$C \vee P$' and then our conclusion in one step. Yet, in order to carry out this plan, first we need '$M \vee D$'. However, this statement is simple enough to obtain from the third premiss.

Very well, let us suppose that we shall use Constructive Dilemma in reaching '$\sim(\sim C \cdot \sim P)$'. We still must have '$\sim R$' to use Modus Tollens with the first premiss and '$S \vee \sim R$' for a use of Modus Ponens with the second. Where shall we find these statements? They come from the only premiss we have yet to mention—the fourth! Surely, we can obtain both '$R \supset S$' and '$\sim S$' from line 4 in our proof. Modus Tollens then produces '$\sim R$', while Addition followed by Commutation yields '$S \vee \sim R$'.

Having worked through our maneuvers from the conclusion back to the premiss set, we can complete (8):

(9) $\therefore \sim(\sim C \cdot \sim P)$

1)	$(M \cdot \sim C) \supset R$	Pr	
2)	$(S \vee \sim R) \supset \sim(D \cdot \sim P)$	Pr	
3)	$D \triangle M$	Pr	
4)	$(S \equiv R) \cdot \sim S$	Pr	
5)	$S \equiv R$	4, Simp	
6)	$\sim S \cdot (S \equiv R)$	4, Com	
7)	$\sim S$	6, Simp	
8)	$\sim(D \cdot M) \cdot \sim(\sim D \cdot \sim M)$	3, D2	
9)	$\sim(S \cdot \sim R) \cdot \sim(R \cdot \sim S)$	5, D4	
10)	$\sim(R \cdot \sim S) \cdot \sim(S \cdot \sim R)$	9, Com	

11)	$\sim(R \cdot \sim S)$	10, Simp
12)	$R \supset S$	11, D3
13)	$\sim R$	12, 7, MT
14)	$\sim(M \cdot \sim C)$	1, 13, MT
15)	$M \supset C$	14, D3
16)	$\sim R \vee S$	13, Add
17)	$S \vee \sim R$	16, Com
18)	$\sim(D \cdot \sim P)$	2, 17, MP
19)	$D \supset P$	18, D3
20)	$\sim(\sim D \cdot \sim M) \cdot \sim(D \cdot M)$	8, Com
21)	$\sim(\sim D \cdot \sim M)$	20, Simp
22)	$D \vee M$	21, D1
23)	$P \vee C$	19, 15, 22, CD
24)	$C \vee P$	23, Com
25)	$\therefore \sim(\sim C \cdot \sim P)$	24, D1

EXERCISES

Group A:

Give the correct justification for each unjustified line.

(1) $\therefore D \cdot C$

1)	$A \cdot B$	Pr
2)	$(C \cdot D) \equiv (A \cdot B)$	Pr
3)	$\sim[(C \cdot D) \cdot \sim(A \cdot B)] \cdot \sim[(A \cdot B) \cdot \sim(C \cdot D)]$	
4)	$\sim[(A \cdot B) \cdot \sim(C \cdot D)] \cdot \sim[(C \cdot D) \cdot \sim(A \cdot B)]$	
5)	$\sim[(A \cdot B) \cdot \sim(C \cdot D)]$	
6)	$(A \cdot B) \supset (C \cdot D)$	
7)	$C \cdot D$	
8)	$\therefore D \cdot C$	

(2) $\therefore \sim \sim B$

1)	$A \equiv \sim B$	Pr
2)	$\sim(A \cdot \sim \sim C)$	Pr
3)	$\sim \sim C$	Pr
4)	$\sim(A \cdot \sim \sim B) \cdot \sim(\sim B \cdot \sim A)$	
5)	$A \supset \sim C$	
6)	$\sim(\sim B \cdot \sim A) \cdot \sim(A \cdot \sim \sim B)$	
7)	$\sim(\sim B \cdot \sim A)$	
8)	$\sim B \supset A$	
9)	$\sim A$	
10)	$\therefore \sim \sim B$	

(3) $\therefore \sim D$

   1) A Pr
   2) $(B \equiv C) \cdot \sim C$ Pr
   3) $(A \cdot \sim B) \supset \sim D$ Pr
   4) $B \equiv C$
   5) $\sim C \cdot (B \equiv C)$
   6) $\sim C$
   7) $\sim(B \cdot \sim C) \cdot \sim(C \cdot \sim B)$
   8) $\sim(B \cdot \sim C)$
   9) $B \supset C$
  10) $\sim B$
  11) $A \cdot \sim B$
  12) $\therefore \sim D$

(4) $\therefore \sim(A \cdot \sim D)$

   1) $A \equiv \sim B$ Pr
   2) $\sim(\sim B \cdot \sim \sim C)$ Pr
   3) $(B \supset C) \cdot (\sim C \supset D)$ Pr
   4) $B \supset C$
   5) $(\sim C \supset D) \cdot (B \supset C)$
   6) $\sim C \subset D$
   7) $\sim(A \cdot \sim \sim B) \cdot \sim(\sim B \cdot \sim A)$
   8) $\sim(A \cdot \sim \sim B)$
   9) $A \supset \sim B$
  10) $\sim B \supset \sim C$
  11) $A \supset \sim C$
  12) $A \supset D$
  13) $\therefore \sim(A \cdot \sim D)$

(5) $\therefore \sim C \supset D$

   1) $A \equiv \sim B$ Pr
   2) $B \triangle \sim C$ Pr
   3) $\sim(A \cdot \sim D)$ Pr
   4) $\sim(A \cdot \sim \sim B) \cdot \sim(\sim B \cdot \sim A)$
   5) $\sim(B \cdot \sim C) \cdot \sim(\sim B \cdot \sim \sim C)$
   6) $A \supset D$
   7) $\sim(B \cdot \sim C)$
   8) $B \supset C$
   9) $\sim(\sim B \cdot \sim A) \cdot \sim(A \cdot \sim \sim B)$
  10) $\sim(\sim B \cdot \sim A)$
  11) $B \vee A$
  12) $C \vee D$
  13) $\sim(\sim C \cdot \sim D)$
  14) $\therefore \sim C \supset D$

(6) $\therefore C \triangle B$

   1) $A \equiv B$ Pr

   2) $\sim(C \cdot A)$ Pr

   3) $\sim C \equiv B$ Pr

   4) $\sim(A \cdot \sim B) \cdot \sim(B \cdot \sim A)$

   5) $\sim(\sim C \cdot \sim B) \cdot \sim(B \cdot \sim \sim C)$

   6) $\sim(\sim C \cdot \sim B)$

   7) $\sim C \supset B$

   8) $\sim(B \cdot \sim A) \cdot \sim(A \cdot \sim B)$

   9) $\sim(B \cdot \sim A)$

 10) $B \supset A$

 11) $\sim C \supset A$

 12) $\sim(\sim C \cdot \sim A)$

 13) $\sim(C \cdot A) \cdot \sim(\sim C \cdot \sim A)$

 14) $\therefore C \triangle A$

(7) $\therefore E \vee D$

   1) $A \equiv B$ Pr

   2) $(A \vee C) \cdot \sim C$ Pr

   3) $B \supset D$ Pr

   4) $A \vee C$

   5) $\sim C \cdot (A \vee C)$

   6) $\sim C$

   7) $\sim(A \cdot \sim B) \cdot \sim(B \cdot \sim A)$

   8) $\sim(A \cdot \sim B)$

   9) $A \supset B$

 10) $C \vee A$

 11) A

 12) B

 13) D

 14) $D \vee E$

 15) $\therefore E \vee D$

(8) $\therefore \sim(E \cdot \sim F)$

   1) $A \triangle \sim B$ Pr

   2) $B \equiv C$ Pr

   3) $\sim[D \cdot \sim(A \cdot \sim C)]$ Pr

   4) $(E \supset F) \vee D$ Pr

   5) $D \supset (A \cdot \sim C)$

   6) $\sim(A \cdot \sim B) \cdot \sim(\sim A \cdot \sim \sim B)$

   7) $\sim(B \cdot \sim C) \cdot \sim(C \cdot \sim B)$

   8) $\sim(A \cdot \sim B)$

   9) $\sim(B \cdot \sim C)$

 10) $A \supset B$

 11) $B \supset C$

12)	$A \supset C$
13)	$\sim (A \cdot \sim C)$
14)	$\sim D$
15)	$D \vee (E \supset F)$
16)	$E \supset F$
17)	$\therefore \ \sim (E \cdot \sim F)$

(9) $\therefore \ \sim (C \cdot \sim E)$

1)	$\sim [(A \equiv B) \cdot \sim (C \equiv D)]$	Pr
2)	$D \triangle \sim E$	Pr
3)	$\sim (A \cdot \sim B) \cdot \sim B$	Pr
4)	$\sim [\sim \sim (B \cdot \sim A) \cdot \sim B]$	Pr
5)	$\sim (A \cdot \sim B)$	
6)	$\sim B \cdot \sim (A \cdot \sim B)$	
7)	$\sim B$	
8)	$(A \equiv B) \supset (C \equiv D)$	
9)	$\sim (B \cdot \sim A) \vee B$	
10)	$\sim (D \cdot \sim E) \cdot \sim (\sim D \cdot \sim \sim E)$	
11)	$B \vee \sim (B \cdot \sim A)$	
12)	$\sim (B \cdot \sim A)$	
13)	$\sim (A \cdot \sim B) \cdot \sim (B \cdot \sim A)$	
14)	$A \equiv B$	
15)	$C \equiv D$	
16)	$\sim (C \cdot \sim D) \cdot \sim (D \cdot \sim C)$	
17)	$\sim (C \cdot \sim D)$	
18)	$\sim (D \cdot \sim E)$	
19)	$C \supset D$	
20)	$D \supset E$	
21)	$C \supset E$	
22)	$\therefore \ \sim (C \cdot \sim E)$	

(10) $\therefore \ \sim (\sim A \cdot \sim \sim C) \cdot \sim (\sim E \cdot \sim \sim C)$

1)	$A \supset (B \equiv \sim C)$	Pr
2)	$(C \cdot \sim E) \vee (B \equiv \sim E)$	Pr
3)	$C \triangle \sim E$	Pr
4)	$(A \equiv E) \cdot E$	Pr
5)	$A \equiv E$	
6)	$E \cdot (A \equiv E)$	
7)	E	
8)	$\sim (A \cdot \sim E) \cdot \sim (E \cdot \sim A)$	
9)	$\sim (E \cdot \sim A) \cdot \sim (A \cdot \sim E)$	
10)	$\sim (E \cdot \sim A)$	
11)	$E \supset A$	
12)	A	
13)	$B \equiv \sim C$	

14) $\sim(C\cdot\sim E)\cdot\sim(\sim C\cdot\sim\sim E)$
15) $\sim(C\cdot\sim E)$
16) $B\equiv\sim E$
17) $\sim(B\cdot\sim\sim C)\cdot\sim(\sim C\cdot\sim B)$
18) $\sim(B\cdot\sim\sim E)\cdot\sim(\sim E\cdot\sim B)$
19) $\sim(B\cdot\sim\sim C)$
20) $B\supset\sim C$
21) $\sim(\sim E\cdot\sim B)\cdot\sim(B\cdot\sim\sim E)$
22) $\sim(\sim E\cdot\sim B)$
23) $E\lor B$
24) $A\lor\sim C$
25) $C\supset E$
26) $\sim(\sim C\cdot\sim B)\cdot\sim(B\cdot\sim\sim C)$
27) $\sim(\sim C\cdot\sim B)$
28) $C\lor B$
29) $E\lor\sim C$
30) $\sim(\sim A\cdot\sim\sim C)$
31) $\sim(\sim E\cdot\sim\sim C)$
32) $\therefore\ \sim(\sim A\cdot\sim\sim C)\cdot\sim(\sim E\cdot\sim\sim C)$

Group B:

Construct a proof of validity for each of the following.

(1) $\therefore\ A$
   1) $(A\equiv B)\cdot B$ Pr

(2) $\therefore\ \sim(A\cdot\sim C)$
   1) $A\bigtriangleup\sim B$ Pr
   2) $B\equiv C$ Pr

(3) $\therefore\ A\equiv B$
   1) $(A\supset C)\cdot(C\supset B)$ Pr
   2) $B\bigtriangleup\sim A$ Pr

(4) $\therefore\ \sim E$
   1) $\sim A\equiv\sim B$ Pr
   2) $(B\supset C)\cdot(\sim A\supset D)$ Pr
   3) $E\supset(\sim C\cdot\sim D)$ Pr

(5) $\therefore\ B\equiv A$
   1) $(A\lor\sim B)\supset\sim C$ Pr
   2) $A\bigtriangleup\sim B$ Pr
   3) $(B\supset A)\lor C$ Pr

(6) $\therefore\ B\supset D$
   1) $A\supset(B\equiv C)$ Pr
   2) $(C\cdot\sim D)\supset E$ Pr
   3) $\sim[\sim(A\cdot\sim E)\cdot\sim F]\cdot\sim F$ Pr

(7) $\therefore A \equiv D$

   1) $A \triangle \sim B$ Pr
   2) $B \equiv C$ Pr
   3) $\sim(C \cdot \sim D) \cdot \sim(D \cdot \sim A)$ Pr

(8) $\therefore B \equiv A$

   1) $(A \cdot \sim B) \triangle (B \equiv C)$ Pr
   2) $(A \supset D) \cdot (D \supset B)$ Pr
   3) $(B \cdot \sim A) \supset (D \cdot \sim C)$ Pr

(9) $\therefore F \lor C$

   1) $(A \equiv B) \supset C$ Pr
   2) $\sim(A \cdot \sim D) \cdot \sim(B \cdot \sim E)$ Pr
   3) $\sim(D \cdot \sim B) \cdot \sim(E \cdot \sim A)$ Pr

(10) $\therefore E \lor G$

   1) $A \supset (B \equiv \sim C)$ Pr
   2) $D \supset (B \equiv E)$ Pr
   3) $\sim F \cdot H$ Pr
   4) $\sim[\sim(A \cdot D) \cdot \sim F]$ Pr
   5) $H \supset (C \equiv G)$ Pr

Group C:

Give every exercise in Group B an interpretation by writing for each of the capital letters in a particular exercise an English statement—the same statement at each occurrence of the same capital letter in any given exercise—while also using appropriate English phrases for the logical operators.

Group D:

Symbolize the following arguments using the suggested notation, and then construct a proof of validity for each.

(1) The balance sheet is correct. Now, the balance sheet is correct if, and only if, the assets column total figure equals the liabilities and stockholders' equity column total figure. Therefore, the assets column total figure equals the liabilities and stockholders' equity column total figure. (S, A)

(2) In accounting, either the statement of retained earnings is correct or the income statement isn't correct, but not both. The income statement is correct only if the statement of retained earnings is correct. So, the statement of retained earnings is correct when, and only when, the income statement is correct. (E, I)

(3) Specific order cost accounting is used by a manufacturer or process cost accounting is used, but whenever process cost accounting is used by a manufacturer, specific order cost accounting isn't used. Consequently, specific order cost accounting isn't used by a manufacturer if, and only if, process cost accounting is. (S, P)

(4) A substance like interplanetary ether is assumed if, and only if, it is held that
     light must travel in a medium. Contemporary research is ignored when, and only
     when, a substance like interplanetary ether is assumed. Therefore, light must
     travel in a medium if contemporary research is ignored. (*S, L, R*)

(5) That Georg Stahl is right is a sufficient condition for the phlogiston theory being
     substantiated if his experiments are confirmed. The following isn't the case:
     The phlogiston theory is substantiated while Stahl's experiments aren't confirmed,
     but the phlogiston theory isn't substantiated. The phlogiston theory isn't sub-
     stantiated but Stahl is correct. So the phlogiston theory is substantiated if, and
     only if, Stahl's experiments are confirmed. (*S, P, E*)

(6) It isn't true both that Antoine Lavoisier was right and Georg Stahl wasn't wrong;
     furthermore, it isn't true both that phlogiston exists and contemporary chemistry
     isn't wrong. Lavoisier wasn't right if, and only if, phlogiston exists. Consequently,
     either it isn't true both that Lavoisier was right even though phlogiston doesn't
     exist or it isn't the case that Stahl wasn't wrong and also contemporary chemistry
     isn't wrong. (*L, S, P, C*)

(7) The following isn't the case: We follow the dictates of reason while it isn't true
     that we attend to the needs of others if, and only if, we wish to be happy. We
     wish either to be happy or not to be moral, but not both. Also, the following isn't
     the case: We don't follow the dictates of reason, but it isn't true that we wish to be
     happy and don't wish to be moral. So it isn't true both that we attend to the needs
     of others but don't wish to be moral. (*D, N, H, M*)

(8) The following isn't true: We are morally mature but not understanding, and we
     must not return evil for evil. It isn't the case both that we must do good for our
     enemies while it also isn't the case that we must not return evil for evil; moreover,
     we must do good for our enemies. It isn't true both that we must do good for
     our enemies and also not the case that it isn't true that we are understanding and
     not morally mature. That we are morally mature if, and only if, we are under-
     standing is a sufficient condition for loving our neighbor. Consequently, we must
     love our neighbor and do good for our enemies. (*M, U, R, G, L*)

(9) It isn't the case both that we hate someone but don't fall short of being morally
     good; furthermore, it isn't the case both that we are always loving and yet not
     continuously desirous of the good for others. That we both don't hate someone
     while not always being loving isn't true. Also it isn't the case both that we fall
     short of being morally good and must not continue to strive toward perfect love;
     but also it isn't the case both that we must continue to strive toward perfect love
     while it isn't true that we haven't reached our human fulfillment. It isn't true
     both that we are continuously desirous of the good for others but haven't reached
     our human fulfillment. Thus, we must continue to strive toward perfect love
     whenever, and only whenever, we haven't reached our human fulfillment. (*H, F,
     L, D, S, R*)

(10) We truly love a person when, and only when, we don't try to possess him as an object; moreover, that we don't try to possess a person as an object is a necessary and sufficient condition for desiring his good irrespective of our own. Now, that we truly love a person is a necessary and sufficient condition for desiring his good irrespective of our own only if we don't curtail his moral freedom while also not being unreasonable in our demands. We allow a person his moral freedom or curtail it; but also either we aren't reasonable in our demands or we follow the dictates of reason. Therefore, we allow a person his moral freedom while we also follow the dictates of reason. (L, P, D, C, R, A, F)

7

Proofs of Validity:

Logical Equivalences

In Chapter 4, Section 2, we discussed the notion of logical equivalences. Two statements are logically equivalent when, given exactly the same truth-conditions for both, they each have the same truth-value. Whenever two statements are logically equivalent, the conditions making one true also make the other true and the conditions making one false also make the other statement false. Now, we have at our disposal a completely mechanical method of determining whether any two truth-functional statements are, or are not, logically equivalent. Forming a biconditional statement from the two statements, we then construct a truth-table for this new statement. If the biconditional statement is tautological, the two original statements are logically equivalent. But, if the two original statements are not logically equivalent, the biconditional will be either contingent or contradictory.

Instead of speaking of logically equivalent statements, we may also talk of logically equivalent statement *forms*. Two statement forms are logically equivalent when any statements exhibiting these forms are logically equivalent. Such logically equivalent statement forms may be expressed in terms of the triple-bar; for example,

(1) $[(p \cdot q) \supset r] \equiv [p \supset (q \supset r)]$

In (1) we may understand '$(p \cdot q) \supset r$' is logically equivalent to '$p \supset (q \supset r)$'. This claim can be substantiated by truth-table procedures:

(2) $[(p \cdot q) \supset r] \equiv [p \supset (q \supset r)]$

```
1 1 1 1 1 1 1 1 1 1 1
1 1 1 0 0 1 1 0 1 0 0
1 0 0 1 1 1 1 1 0 1 1
1 0 0 1 0 1 1 1 0 1 0
0 0 1 1 1 1 0 1 1 1 1
0 0 1 1 0 1 0 1 1 0 0
0 0 0 1 1 1 0 1 0 1 1
0 0 0 1 0 1 0 1 0 1 0
          ↑
```

Since only '1's appear in the column under the triple-bar, (1) is a tautological statement form; that is, any statement of the form '$(p \cdot q) \supset r$' is logically equivalent to any statement of the form '$p \supset (q \supset r)$'.

As we find definitional equivalences helpful in constructing proofs of validity, so also we shall come to appreciate the usefulness of logical equivalences. Following is a list of logically equivalent statement forms *we shall use in proving the validity of arguments*. You should learn this list, for these forms will be used extensively in constructing proofs.

Association (*Assoc*)

$$[p \cdot (q \cdot r)] \equiv [(p \cdot q) \cdot r]$$
$$[p \vee (q \vee r)] \equiv [(p \vee q) \vee r]$$

Commutation (*Com*)

$$(p \vee q) \equiv (q \vee p)$$
$$(p \cdot q) \equiv (q \cdot p)$$
$$(p \triangle q) \equiv (q \triangle p)$$
$$(p \equiv q) \equiv (q \equiv p)$$

De Morgan's Laws (*De M*)

$$(\sim p \vee \sim q) \equiv \sim (p \cdot q)$$
$$(\sim p \cdot \sim q) \equiv \sim (p \vee q)$$

Distribution (*Dist*)

$$[p \vee (q \cdot r)] \equiv [(p \vee q) \cdot (p \vee r)]$$
$$[p \cdot (q \vee r)] \equiv [(p \cdot q) \vee (p \cdot r)]$$

Double Negation (DN)

$$p \equiv \sim \sim p$$

Exportation (Exp)

$$[(p \cdot q) \supset r] \equiv [p \supset (q \supset r)]$$

Material Implication (MI)

$$(p \supset q) \equiv (\sim p \vee q)$$

Tautology (Taut)

$$p \equiv (p \cdot p)$$
$$p \equiv (p \vee p)$$

Transposition (Trans)

$$(p \supset q) \equiv (\sim q \supset \sim p)$$

Once more note that we need the notions of both substitution and replacement in using logical equivalences. Any statement may be substituted for any statement variable in the logically equivalent statement forms above—provided, of course, the same statement is substituted at each occurrence of the same statement variable. Furthermore, we also may replace one statement by another—provided the statements are logically equivalent. Let us imagine the following argument:

(3) $\therefore A$
   1) $\sim A \supset B$ Pr
   2) $\sim B$ Pr
   3) $\sim \sim A$ 1, 2, MT
   4) $\therefore A$ 3, DN

The premiss set yields '$\sim \sim A$'. Making an appeal to Double Negation, we can assert 'A'. Of course in this move we read 'A' as an instance of 'p' in '$p \equiv \sim \sim p$'.

But we do not have to limit the use of our logical equivalences to entire statements.

(4) $\therefore A \supset D$
   1) $A \supset (B \supset C)$ Pr
   2) $(\sim B \vee C) \supset D$ Pr
   3) $(B \supset C) \supset D$ 2, MI
   4) $\therefore A \supset D$ 1, 3, HS

The conclusion in (4) does not appear as such in the premiss set. 'A', the antecedent of the conclusion, is also the antecedent of the first premiss. Moreover, '*D*', the consequent of the conclusion is also the consequent of the second premiss. If we could use Hypothetical Syllogism, the conclusion would be reached at once. Although the consequent of the first premiss and the antecedent of the second are different statements, they are still logically equivalent. Reading '*B*' as an instance of '*p*' and '*C*' as an instance of '*q*' in the second premiss, we may assert the third statement in (4) by Material Implication; or, given the premisses and conclusion of (4), we may construct another distinct proof using Material Implication.

(5) $\therefore A \supset D$

   1) $A \supset (B \supset C)$ Pr
   2) $(\sim B \lor C) \supset D$ Pr
   3) $A \supset (\sim B \lor C)$ 1, MI
   4) $\therefore A \supset D$ 3, 2, HS

Here Material Implication is used with the consequent of the first premiss by understanding '*B*' as an instance of '*p*' and '*C*' of '*q*'.

Still another point to grasp when using logical equivalences is this. We need not replace each occurrence of a statement by the same logical equivalence *if that statement appears more than once* in an overall statement. Consider this argument:

(6) $\therefore C \supset (A \supset B)$

   1) $(A \supset B) \supset [C \supset (A \supset B)]$ Pr
   2) $\sim A \lor B$ Pr
   3) $(\sim A \lor B) \supset [C \supset (A \supset B)]$ 1, MI
   4) $\therefore C \supset (A \supset B)$ 3, 2, MP

The desired conclusion is the consequent of the first premiss. Using Material Implication to obtain the third statement in (6), Modus Ponens is then used to reach the conclusion. Notice, while '$A \supset B$' appears twice in the first premiss, we use Material Implication just on the antecedent.

Thus, in connection with logical equivalences, replacement is understood in this way:

> *Any statement may be replaced by its logical equivalence. Such a replacement of logically equivalent statements may be performed on "parts" (these "parts" themselves being statements) of statements; moreover, replacement need not be performed at every occurrence of the same "part" of a statement.*

EXERCISES

Group A:

Construct a truth-table for each of the logically equivalent statement forms on pages 203–204.

Group B:

In Chapter 4, Section 2, you were asked to determine whether or not certain pairs of statements are logically equivalent. Of those pairs of statements which are logically equivalent, are there any instances of the logical statement forms on pages 203–204? If so, which statements are instances of which forms?

Group C:

Substituting statements at each statement variable, substituting the same statement at each occurrence of the same statement variable, and then construct at least three statements for each of the logically equivalent forms on pages 203–204.

1. USING DOUBLE NEGATION AND TRANSPOSITION IN PROOFS OF VALIDITY

DN

$$p \equiv {\sim}{\sim}p$$

Trans

$$(p \supset q) \equiv ({\sim}q \supset {\sim}p)$$

Let us consider this argument:

(1)   Acid is either bitter or sweet to the taste, but not both. So acid is either not bitter or not sweet to the taste. (B, S)

Argument (1) may be symbolized as

(2) $\therefore {\sim}B \lor {\sim}S$
    1) $B \triangle S$ Pr

There is not a great deal we can do with the premiss set of (2) except appeal to Definition 2. This may be done at line 2 of the proof:

    2) ${\sim}(B{\cdot}S){\cdot}{\sim}({\sim}B{\cdot}{\sim}S)$ 1, D2

But how are we to obtain '${\sim}B \lor {\sim}S$' from the second statement? We may attempt to use Commutation followed by Simplification. By these moves we could easily assert '${\sim}({\sim}B{\cdot}{\sim}S)$', and then, appealing to Definition 1, write '$B \lor S$'. Yet the conclusion we want is not '$B \lor S$' but, rather, '${\sim}B \lor {\sim}S$'.

Let us work "backward" from the conclusion to our premiss. Given the premiss set of (2), it is most unlikely that we shall use Addition or Constructive Dilemma to reach '$\sim B \lor \sim S$'. Utilizing Constructive Dilemma would require two hypothetical statements and also a disjunctive statement. But these are not obtainable from '$B \triangle S$'. On the other hand, Addition would require either '$\sim B$' or '$\sim S$' as a separate statement in the proof. Yet neither of these statements can be deduced from the premiss of (2). We might, however, use Definition 1 to reach '$\sim B \lor \sim S$'. In this case we need first '$\sim (\sim \sim B \cdot \sim \sim S)$'. Here we understand '$\sim B$' as an instance of '$p$' and '$\sim S$' as an instance of '$q$' in '$\sim(\sim p \cdot \sim q)$'. Our proof may be completed in the following manner:

(3) $\therefore \sim B \lor \sim S$

1)	$B \triangle S$	Pr
2)	$\sim (B \cdot S) \cdot \sim (\sim B \cdot \sim S)$	1, D2
3)	$\sim (B \cdot S)$	2, Simp
4)	$\sim (B \cdot \sim \sim S)$	3, DN
5)	$\sim (\sim \sim B \cdot \sim \sim S)$	4, DN
6)	$\therefore \sim B \lor \sim S$	5, D1

Notice in (3) that Double Negation is used twice. As always, *we shall never have more than one occurrence of one Rule of Transformation at any particular line in a proof.*

As another example, imagine an argument which, when symbolized, looks like this:

(4) $\therefore B \supset A$

1)	$\sim A \supset \sim B$	Pr

Constructing a proof for (4), we may proceed in this way:

(5) $\therefore B \supset A$

1)	$\sim A \supset \sim B$	Pr
2)	$\sim \sim B \supset \sim \sim A$	1, Trans
3)	$B \supset \sim \sim A$	2, DN
4)	$\therefore B \supset A$	3, DN

In moving by Transposition from the first to the second statement in (5), we interpreted '$\sim A$' as an instance of 'p' and '$\sim B$' as an instance of 'q' in '$(p \supset q) \equiv (\sim q \supset \sim p)$'. Or, notice another proof of (4):

(6) $\therefore B \supset A$

1)	$\sim A \supset \sim B$	Pr
2)	$\therefore B \supset A$	1, Trans

Now, when moving from the first to the second statement in (6) by Transposition, 'A' is read as an instance of 'q' in '$\sim q$' and 'B' as an instance of 'p' in '$\sim p$'. We are reading '$(p \supset q) \equiv (\sim q \supset \sim p)$' from right to left in (6). Notice both (5) and (6) are perfectly acceptable proofs of (4). However, (6) avoids the two appeals to Double Negation necessary in (5).

Suppose we were presented with this rather pessimistic argument:

(7)   It's a known fact that Nancy will develop lung cancer if, and only if, she continues with her present habit. Also, that Nancy won't stop smoking is a necessary condition for her developing lung cancer. That Nancy does stop smoking is both a necessary and sufficient condition for her reforming. Now, unless Nancy doesn't reform, she won't continue with her present habit. So Nancy will stop smoking or develop lung cancer, but not both. (C, H, S, R)

Statement (7) may symbolized as

(8) $\therefore S \triangle C$

1)	$C \equiv H$	Pr
2)	$C \supset \sim S$	Pr
3)	$S \equiv R$	Pr
4)	$\sim R \supset H$	Pr

Examining the symbolized premiss set of (7), we soon discover that there are several fairly obvious moves we might make. Since we can suppose that the first and third premisses will eventually be transformed into their definitional equivalences, let us do this at once:

5)	$\sim(C \cdot \sim H) \cdot \sim(H \cdot \sim C)$	1, D4
6)	$\sim(S \cdot \sim R) \cdot \sim(R \cdot \sim S)$	3, D4

Next, consider the conclusion, '$S \triangle C$', and various ways it might be reached. Since '$S \triangle C$' does not appear as a whole expression in our premiss set, we may suppose that it will be obtained by Definition 2. In that case, the statement immediately preceding the conclusion will be '$\sim(S \cdot C) \cdot \sim(\sim S \cdot \sim C)$'. This statement, read as a conjunction, may be asserted if we first have '$\sim(S \cdot C)$' and '$\sim(\sim S \cdot \sim C)$' at separate lines in the proof. Therefore, we attempt to find these statements:

)	$\sim(S \cdot C)$	
)	$\sim(\sim S \cdot \sim C)$	
)	$\sim(S \cdot C) \cdot \sim(\sim S \cdot \sim C)$	Conj
)	$\therefore S \triangle C$	D2

Noticing the second premiss, '$C \supset \sim S$', we find both 'S' and 'C' appearing in the same statement. Will this premiss lead us to '$\sim(S \cdot C)$'? Yes. Using Transposition, followed by Double Negation, we obtain '$S \supset \sim C$'. Definition 3 followed by another use of Double Negation then yields '$\sim(S \cdot C)$'. Let us write these new lines in our proof:

7)	$\sim\sim S \supset \sim C$	2, Trans
8)	$S \supset \sim C$	7, DN
9)	$\sim(S \cdot \sim \sim C)$	8, D3
10)	$\sim(S \cdot C)$	9, DN

Now, how are we to derive '$\sim(\sim S \cdot \sim C)$'? Reading '$\sim S$' as an instance of '$p$' and '$C$' of '$q$', if we obtain '$\sim S \supset C$', we could then assert '$\sim(\sim S \cdot \sim C)$' by Definition 3. Since '$\sim S \supset C$' does not appear as such in the premiss set, we might reach it by Hypothetical Syllogism. But, where in the premiss set of (8) can be found a hypothetical statement having '$\sim S$' as an antecedent? The third premiss! Employing Commutation and then Simplification at line 6—the definitional equivalence of the third premiss—'$\sim(R \cdot \sim S)$' is asserted. Then, using Definition 3 followed by Transposition, we obtain '$\sim S \supset \sim R$'. This sequence of statements can be added to our proof:

11)	$\sim(R \cdot \sim S) \cdot \sim(S \cdot \sim R)$	6, Com
12)	$\sim(R \cdot \sim S)$	11, Simp
13)	$R \supset S$	12, D3
14)	$\sim S \supset \sim R$	13, Trans

We must now obtain a hypothetical statement with 'C' as a consequent if we are to assert '$\sim S \supset C$' by Hypothetical Syllogism. Such a statement is derived easily from the fifth statement, the definitional equivalence of the first premiss. Using Commutation, followed by Simplification, we have '$\sim(H \cdot \sim C)$'. Definition 3 then gives us '$H \supset C$'. Writing these lines, we continue:

15)	$\sim(H \cdot \sim C) \cdot \sim(C \cdot \sim H)$	5, Com
16)	$\sim(H \cdot \sim C)$	15, Simp
17)	$H \supset C$	16, D3

Well and good! All we need to do now is discover some way of joining the antecedent of line 14 with the consequent of line 17. This problem is solved quite simply if we notice the fourth premiss and think of Hypothetical Syllogism. Thus, a completed proof of the validity of (4) is

(9) $\therefore S \triangle C$

1)	$C \equiv H$	Pr
2)	$C \supset \sim S$	Pr
3)	$S \equiv R$	Pr
4)	$\sim R \supset H$	Pr
5)	$\sim(C \cdot \sim H) \cdot \sim(H \cdot \sim C)$	1, D4
6)	$\sim(S \cdot \sim R) \cdot \sim(R \cdot \sim S)$	3, D4
7)	$\sim\sim S \supset \sim C$	2, Trans
8)	$S \supset \sim C$	7, DN
9)	$\sim(S \cdot \sim \sim C)$	8, D3

10)	$\sim(S \cdot C)$	9, DN
11)	$\sim(R \cdot \sim S) \cdot \sim(S \cdot \sim R)$	6, Com
12)	$\sim(R \cdot \sim S)$	11, Simp
13)	$R \supset S$	12, D3
14)	$\sim S \supset \sim R$	13, Trans
15)	$\sim(H \cdot \sim C) \cdot \sim(C \cdot \sim H)$	5, Com
16)	$\sim(H \cdot \sim C)$	15, Simp
17)	$H \supset C$	16, D3
18)	$\sim S \supset H$	14, 4, HS
19)	$\sim S \supset C$	18, 17, HS
20)	$\sim(\sim S \cdot \sim C)$	19, D3
21)	$\sim(S \cdot C) \cdot \sim(\sim S \cdot \sim C)$	10, 20, Conj
22)	$\therefore S \triangle C$	21, D2

EXERCISES

Group A:

In the following, justify each of the unjustified lines.

(1) $\therefore A$

1)	$\sim A \supset \sim B$	Pr
2)	$\sim B \supset C$	Pr
3)	$\sim D$	Pr
4)	$C \supset D$	Pr
5)	$\sim C$	
6)	$\sim \sim B$	
7)	$\sim \sim A$	
8)	$\therefore A$	

(2) $\therefore \sim(\sim B \cdot D)$

1)	$(A \supset B) \cdot (C \supset \sim D)$	Pr
2)	$\sim(\sim A \cdot \sim C)$	Pr
3)	$A \supset B$	
4)	$(C \supset \sim D) \cdot (A \supset B)$	
5)	$C \supset \sim D$	
6)	$A \vee C$	
7)	$B \vee \sim D$	
8)	$\sim(\sim B \cdot \sim \sim D)$	
9)	$\therefore \sim(\sim B \cdot D)$	

(3) $\therefore B \supset D$

1)	$\sim A \supset \sim B$	Pr
2)	$C \supset (\sim D \supset \sim A)$	Pr
3)	$\sim C \supset \sim E$	Pr

4) E Pr

5) $\sim\sim E$

6) $\sim\sim C$

7) C

8) $\sim D \supset \sim A$

9) $B \supset A$

10) $A \supset D$

11) $\therefore B \supset D$

(4) $\therefore D \lor E$

1) $(A \lor B) \supset C$ Pr

2) A Pr

3) $\sim(B \supset D) \supset \sim A$ Pr

4) $C \supset (A \supset E)$ Pr

5) $\sim\sim A$

6) $\sim\sim(B \supset D)$

7) $B \supset D$

8) $A \lor B$

9) C

10) $A \supset E$

11) $E \lor D$

12) $\therefore D \lor E$

(5) $\therefore \sim C \supset F$

1) $(A \supset B)\cdot(B \supset C)$ Pr

2) $\sim D \supset (\sim E \supset F)$ Pr

3) $\sim D$ Pr

4) $\sim(E\cdot\sim A)$ Pr

5) $A \supset B$

6) $(B \supset C)\cdot(A \supset B)$

7) $B \supset C$

8) $E \supset A$

9) $\sim E \supset F$

10) $A \supset C$

11) $E \supset C$

12) $\sim C \supset \sim E$

13) $\therefore \sim C \supset F$

(6) $\therefore \sim(\sim A \cdot D)$

1) $\sim A \equiv B$ Pr

2) $B \supset \sim C$ Pr

3) $D \triangle \sim C$ Pr

4) $\sim(\sim A \cdot \sim B)\cdot\sim(B\cdot\sim\sim A)$

5) $\sim(D\cdot\sim C)\cdot\sim(\sim D\cdot\sim\sim C)$

6) $\sim(\sim A \cdot \sim B)$

7) $\sim A \supset B$

8) $\sim A \supset \sim C$
9) $\sim(D \cdot \sim C)$
10) $D \supset C$
11) $\sim C \supset \sim D$
12) $\sim A \supset \sim D$
13) $\sim(\sim A \cdot \sim \sim D)$
14) $\therefore \sim(\sim A \cdot D)$

(7) $\therefore A \equiv B$

1) $\sim[(A \supset B) \supset C] \cdot \sim[\sim C \cdot \sim(\sim A \supset \sim B)]$ Pr
2) $\sim[(A \supset B) \supset C]$
3) $\sim[\sim C \cdot \sim(\sim A \supset \sim B)] \cdot \sim[(A \supset B) \supset C]$
4) $\sim[\sim C \cdot \sim(\sim A \supset \sim B)]$
5) $\sim \sim[(A \supset B) \cdot \sim C]$
6) $(A \supset B) \cdot \sim C$
7) $A \supset B$
8) $\sim C \cdot (A \supset B)$
9) $\sim C$
10) $C \vee (\sim A \supset \sim B)$
11) $\sim A \supset \sim B$
12) $B \supset A$
13) $\sim(A \cdot \sim B)$
14) $\sim(B \cdot \sim A)$
15) $\sim(A \cdot \sim B) \cdot \sim(B \cdot \sim A)$
16) $\therefore A \equiv B$

(8) $\therefore \sim(F \cdot \sim C)$

1) $A \supset (B \supset C)$ Pr
2) $\sim D \supset (E \supset \sim F)$ Pr
3) $\sim(A \cdot \sim D) \supset \sim(B \vee E)$ Pr
4) $\sim(\sim E \cdot \sim B)$ Pr
5) $E \vee B$
6) $B \vee E$
7) $\sim \sim(B \vee E)$
8) $\sim \sim(A \cdot \sim D)$
9) $A \cdot \sim D$
10) A
11) $\sim D \cdot A$
12) $\sim D$
13) $B \supset C$
14) $E \supset \sim F$
15) $C \vee \sim F$
16) $\sim F \vee C$
17) $\sim(\sim \sim F \cdot \sim C)$
18) $\therefore \sim(F \cdot \sim C)$

(9) $\therefore E$

1)	$(A \cdot B) \supset (C \vee D)$	Pr
2)	$A \cdot (C \supset E)$	Pr
3)	$(\sim B \supset \sim \sim F) \cdot \sim F$	Pr
4)	$D \supset F$	Pr
5)	A	
6)	$(C \supset E) \cdot A$	
7)	$C \supset E$	
8)	$\sim B \supset \sim \sim F$	
9)	$\sim F \cdot (\sim B \supset \sim \sim F)$	
10)	$\sim F$	
11)	$\sim \sim \sim F$	
12)	$\sim \sim B$	
13)	B	
14)	$A \cdot B$	
15)	$C \vee D$	
16)	$D \vee C$	
17)	$\sim D$	
18)	C	
19)	$\therefore E$	

(10) $\therefore \sim(C \cdot D)$

1)	$(A \equiv B) \cdot (B \equiv C)$	Pr
2)	$B \triangle \sim D$	Pr
3)	$A \supset \sim B$	Pr
4)	$A \equiv B$	
5)	$(B \equiv C) \cdot (A \equiv B)$	
6)	$B \equiv C$	
7)	$\sim(A \cdot \sim B) \cdot \sim(B \cdot \sim A)$	
8)	$\sim(B \cdot \sim C) \cdot \sim(C \cdot \sim B)$	
9)	$\sim(B \cdot \sim A) \cdot \sim(A \cdot \sim B)$	
10)	$\sim(C \cdot \sim B) \cdot \sim(B \cdot \sim C)$	
11)	$\sim(B \cdot \sim A)$	
12)	$\sim(C \cdot \sim B)$	
13)	$B \supset A$	
14)	$C \supset B$	
15)	$C \supset A$	
16)	$\sim A \supset \sim C$	
17)	$\sim(B \cdot \sim D) \cdot \sim(\sim B \cdot \sim \sim D)$	
18)	$\sim(\sim B \cdot \sim \sim D) \cdot \sim(B \cdot \sim D)$	
19)	$\sim(\sim B \cdot \sim \sim D)$	
20)	$\sim B \supset \sim D$	
21)	$\sim(A \cdot \sim \sim B)$	
22)	$\sim(\sim \sim A \cdot \sim \sim B)$	
23)	$\sim A \vee \sim B$	

24) $\sim C \lor \sim D$
25) $\sim(\sim \sim C \cdot \sim \sim D)$
26) $\sim(C \cdot \sim \sim D)$
27) $\therefore\ \sim(C \cdot D)$

Group B:

Construct a proof of validity for each of the following.

(1) $\therefore\ B \supset \sim A$
    1) $A \supset \sim B$ Pr

(2) $\therefore\ B$
    1) A Pr
    2) $\sim B \supset \sim A$ Pr

(3) $\therefore\ A \supset C$
    1) $(A \supset B) \cdot (\sim C \supset \sim B)$ Pr

(4) $\therefore\ \sim A \supset [\sim C \cdot (\sim B \supset \sim A)]$
    1) $[(A \supset B) \supset C] \supset A$ Pr

(5) $\therefore\ C \cdot \sim A$
    1) $A \equiv \sim B$ Pr
    2) $B \cdot C$ Pr

(6) $\therefore\ C \cdot A$
    1) $A \triangle B$ Pr
    2) $(A \supset \sim B) \supset C$ Pr
    3) $\sim B$ Pr

(7) $\therefore\ D$
    1) $A \cdot (B \lor C)$ Pr
    2) $B \triangle A$ Pr
    3) $C \supset D$ Pr

(8) $\therefore\ D \supset [C \supset (B \supset A)]$
    1) $[(\sim A \cdot B) \cdot C] \supset \sim D$ Pr

(9) $\therefore\ D \supset C$
    1) $\sim[(\sim B \supset \sim A) \cdot C]$ Pr
    2) $\sim A$ Pr
    3) $D \supset (\sim C \supset A)$ Pr

(10) $\therefore\ \sim B \supset D$
    1) $A \supset (\sim B \supset \sim C)$ Pr
    2) $\sim(D \equiv E) \supset F$ Pr
    3) $\sim(C \cdot \sim A) \cdot \sim(C \supset F)$ Pr

Group C:

Give every exercise in Group B an interpretation by substituting for each of the capital letters in a particular exercise an English statement—the same statement at each occurrence of the same capital letter in any given exercise—while also writing appropriate English phrases for the logical operators.

Group D:

Symbolize the following arguments using the suggested notation, and then construct a proof of validity for each.

(1) That this figure isn't a square is a sufficient condition for it not having four equal angles. But this figure does have four equal angles. Consequently, it is a square. (*S*, *A*)

(2) It isn't the case that this triangle is both equiangular and scalene. It is equiangular. Therefore, this triangle isn't scalene. (*E*, *S*)

(3) That the circumference of this figure is determined by '$2\pi r$' is a necessary condition for this figure being a circle; moreover, that this figure is an ellipse is a sufficient condition for its circumference not being determined by '$2\pi r$'. So a sufficient condition for this figure not being an ellipse is that it is a circle. (*D*, *C*, *E*)

(4) It isn't true both that this figure is conical and its volume is determined by '$\frac{4}{3}\pi r^3$'. The volume of this figure is determined by '$\frac{4}{3}\pi r^3$'. Thus, it isn't true that this figure is both conical and spherical. (*C*, *D*, *S*)

(5) It isn't the case both that we don't examine ruby-type lasers and yet do consider long-pulse solid state lasers; also it isn't the case both that we don't consider long-pulse solid state lasers and also are interested in a large potential industrial market. Hence, that we are interested in a large potential industrial market implies that we examine ruby-type lasers. (*E*, *C*, *I*)

(6) It isn't true both that glass is better than ruby in building lasers and it has a low thermal conductivity; yet glass does have a low thermal conductivity. Therefore, if glass is better than ruby in building lasers, it isn't susceptible to damage under high pump fluxes. (*L*, *C*, *F*)

(7) It isn't true that lasers producing ordinary incandescent light is a necessary condition for light being essentially of one wavelength whenever it is coherent; moreover, the following isn't true: namely, lasers don't produce ordinary incandescent light while it also isn't true that if light is incoherent, then it isn't essentially of one wavelength. Wherefore, light is coherent when, and only when, it is essentially of one wavelength. (*I*, *W*, *C*)

(8) The following isn't true: Laser radiation differs from other electromagnetic waves in length and frequency while it isn't the case that lasers emit wavelengths of approximately 1×10^{-5} to 5×10^{-2} cm if they don't produce gamma rays. Lasers beam x-rays only if they produce gamma rays, but they don't produce gamma rays. Laser radiation does differ from other electromagnetic waves in length and frequency. Therefore, lasers emit wavelengths of approximately 1×10^{-5} to 5×10^{-2} cm or beam x-rays, but not both. (*D*, *E*, *P*, *B*)

(9) If Rembrandt worked during the seventeenth century, he didn't execute the tomb

of Pope Julius III, and Michelangelo lived in the sixteenth century only if he didn't paint "Nude Descending a Staircase". Also, Michelangelo sketched "Aristotle Contemplating the Bust of Homer" only if he didn't live in the sixteenth century; furthermore, it isn't true both that Rembrandt didn't execute the tomb of Pope Julius III and Michelangelo didn't live in the sixteenth century. So the following isn't the case: Either Michelangelo painted "Nude Descending a Staircase" and Rembrandt worked during the seventeenth century or Rembrandt did work during the seventeenth century and Michelangelo sketched "Aristotle Contemplating the Bust of Homer". (*W, E, L, P, S*)

(10)   Michelangelo didn't want to paint the ceiling of the Sistine Chapel even though he was commissioned by Pope Julius III if, and only if, Donato Bramante pressured the Pope. It isn't the case that Michelangelo felt assured of himself as a painter in spite of Bramante pressuring the Pope; yet Michelangelo either felt assured of himself as a painter or didn't believe he had mastered painting (but not both). So if Michelangelo believed he had mastered painting, then he wanted to paint the ceiling of the Sistine Chapel if commissioned by Pope Julius III. (*W, C, P, F, B*)

2. USING ASSOCIATION AND COMMUTATION IN PROOFS OF VALIDITY

Assoc

$$[p \cdot (q \cdot r)] \equiv [(p \cdot q) \cdot r]$$
$$[p \vee (q \vee r)] \equiv [(p \vee q) \vee r]$$

Com

$$(p \vee q) \equiv (q \vee p)$$
$$(p \cdot q) \equiv (q \cdot p)$$
$$(p \triangle q) \equiv (q \triangle p)$$
$$(p \equiv q) \equiv (q \equiv p)$$

Association and Commutation are very helpful in rearranging the order of statements and in repunctuating statements. For example, consider this argument:

(1)   Either Mildred or Sharon will be at the library, or Mrs. Crosland will be there. Hence, Sharon will be at the library, or Mrs. Crosland or Mildred will. (*M, S, C*)

Symbolizing (1), we may write

(2) $\therefore\ S \vee (C \vee M)$
    1) $(M \vee S) \vee C$ Pr

Comparing the premiss set with the conclusion of (2), we see the only differences are the ordering of 'M', 'S', and 'C' from left to right and the punctuation—grouping—of these statements. Notice how we can apply Commutation and Association to reach our conclusion:

(3) $\therefore\ S \vee (C \vee M)$
    1) $(M \vee S) \vee C$ Pr
    2) $(S \vee M) \vee C$ 1, Com
    3) $S \vee (M \vee C)$ 2, Assoc
    4) $\therefore\ S \vee (C \vee M)$ 3, Com

Now, let us think about arguments in which we find only one premiss. If (1) there are exactly the same statements in the premiss as in the conclusion and (2) there are exactly the same number of occurrences of each of these statements in the premiss as in the conclusion, then it is often very helpful to order the statements in the premiss from left to right as they appear in the conclusion. Also, we may find it helpful to group the statements in the premiss as they are grouped in the conclusion. Statement (3) above is an example following this strategy, as is the next argument:

(4)   If $\sqrt{1}$ is a natural number, it's either odd or even. Thus, if $\sqrt{1}$ is neither even nor odd, it isn't a natural number. (N, O, E)

To symbolize (4), we may write

(5) $\therefore\ \sim(E \vee O) \supset \sim N$
    1) $N \supset (O \vee E)$ Pr

Following the suggestions above, the proof is completed:

    2) $\sim(O \vee E) \supset \sim N$ 1, Trans
    3) $\therefore\ \sim(E \vee O) \supset \sim N$ 2, Com

EXERCISES

Group A:

In the following, justify each of the unjustified lines.

(1) $\therefore\ B \vee (C \vee A)$
    1) $A \vee (B \vee C)$ Pr
    2) $(B \vee C) \vee A$
    3) $\therefore\ B \vee (C \vee A)$

(2) $\therefore (D \cdot A) \cdot (B \cdot C)$

  1) $(A \cdot B) \cdot (C \cdot D)$ Pr
  2) $[(A \cdot B) \cdot C] \cdot D$
  3) $D \cdot [(A \cdot B) \cdot C]$
  4) $D \cdot [A \cdot (B \cdot C)]$
  5) $\therefore (D \cdot A) \cdot (B \cdot C)$

(3) $\therefore \{C \vee [C \cdot (B \cdot A)]\} \vee D$

  1) $[(A \cdot B) \cdot C] \vee (D \vee C)$ Pr
  2) $[C \cdot (A \cdot B)] \vee (D \vee C)$
  3) $[C \cdot (B \cdot A)] \vee (D \vee C)$
  4) $[C \cdot (B \cdot A)] \vee (C \vee D)$
  5) $\{[C \cdot (B \cdot A)] \vee C\} \vee D$
  6) $\therefore \{C \vee [C \cdot (B \cdot A)]\} \vee D$

(4) $\therefore D \equiv E$

  1) $\therefore (A \triangle B) \supset C$ Pr
  2) $\sim (D \cdot \sim C) \supset (E \equiv D)$ Pr
  3) $D \supset (B \triangle A)$ Pr
  4) $(B \triangle A) \supset C$
  5) $D \supset C$
  6) $\sim (D \cdot \sim C)$
  7) $E \equiv D$
  8) $\therefore D \equiv E$

(5) $\therefore C \supset D$

  1) $A \equiv B$ Pr
  2) $\sim C \vee \sim (B \equiv A)$ Pr
  3) $\sim (B \equiv A) \vee \sim C$
  4) $B \equiv A$
  5) $\sim \sim (B \equiv A)$
  6) $\sim C$
  7) $\sim C \vee D$
  8) $\sim (\sim \sim C \cdot \sim D)$
  9) $\sim (C \cdot \sim D)$
  10) $\therefore C \supset D$

(6) $\therefore C \triangle A$

  1) $A \equiv B$ Pr
  2) $\sim C \equiv B$ Pr
  3) $\sim (C \cdot A)$ Pr
  4) $B \equiv A$
  5) $\sim (B \cdot \sim A) \cdot \sim (A \cdot \sim B)$
  6) $\sim (\sim C \cdot \sim B) \cdot \sim (B \cdot \sim \sim C)$
  7) $\sim (\sim C \cdot \sim B)$
  8) $\sim (B \cdot \sim A)$

9) $\sim C \supset B$
10) $B \supset A$
11) $\sim C \supset A$
12) $\sim(\sim C \cdot \sim A)$
13) $\sim(C \cdot A) \cdot \sim(\sim C \cdot \sim A)$
14) $\therefore\ C \triangle A$

(7) $\therefore\ \sim(A \supset \sim C)$

1) $B \supset \sim[A \lor (C \lor D)]$ Pr
2) A Pr
3) $\sim B \supset C$ Pr
4) $\sim C \supset \sim\sim B$
5) $\sim C \supset B$
6) $\sim C \supset \sim[A \lor (C \lor D)]$
7) $A \lor C$
8) $(A \lor C) \lor D$
9) $A \lor (C \lor D)$
10) $\sim\sim[A \lor (C \lor D)]$
11) $\sim\sim C$
12) $A \cdot \sim\sim C$
13) $\sim\sim(A \cdot \sim\sim C)$
14) $\therefore\ \sim(A \supset \sim C)$

(8) $\therefore\ \sim C \cdot (A \lor D)$

1) $C \supset \sim(A \supset B)$ Pr
2) $B \lor (\sim A \lor E)$ Pr
3) $\sim E \cdot (A \triangle D)$ Pr
4) $\sim E$
5) $(A \triangle D) \cdot \sim E$
6) $A \triangle D$
7) $\sim(A \cdot D) \cdot \sim(\sim A \cdot \sim D)$
8) $\sim(\sim A \cdot \sim D) \cdot \sim(A \cdot D)$
9) $\sim(\sim A \cdot \sim D)$
10) $A \lor D$
11) $(B \lor \sim A) \lor E$
12) $E \lor (B \lor \sim A)$
13) $B \lor \sim A$
14) $\sim A \lor B$
15) $\sim(\sim\sim A \cdot \sim B)$
16) $\sim(A \cdot \sim B)$
17) $A \supset B$
18) $\sim\sim(A \supset B)$
19) $\sim C$
20) $\therefore\ \sim C \cdot (A \lor D)$

(9) $\therefore\ B \lor F$

  1) $(A \cdot \sim B) \supset C$ Pr
  2) $(\sim D \equiv C) \cdot D$ Pr
  3) $(\sim D \lor \sim C) \supset\ \sim(E \cdot \sim F)$ Pr
  4) $E \triangle A$ Pr
  5) $\sim D \equiv C$
  6) $D \cdot (\sim D \equiv C)$
  7) D
  8) $C \equiv\ \sim D$
  9) $\sim(C \cdot \sim \sim D) \cdot \sim(\sim D \cdot \sim C)$
 10) $\sim(C \cdot \sim \sim D)$
 11) $C \supset\ \sim D$
 12) $\sim \sim D$
 13) $\sim C$
 14) $\sim(A \cdot \sim B)$
 15) $A \supset B$
 16) $\sim C \lor \sim D$
 17) $\sim D \lor \sim C$
 18) $\sim(E \cdot \sim F)$
 19) $E \supset F$
 20) $\sim(E \cdot A) \cdot \sim(\sim E \cdot \sim A)$
 21) $\sim(\sim E \cdot \sim A) \cdot \sim(E \cdot A)$
 22) $\sim(\sim E \cdot \sim A)$
 23) $E \lor A$
 24) $A \lor E$
 25) $\therefore\ B \lor F$

(10) $\therefore\ D \supset E$

  1) $A \supset (B \equiv C)$ Pr
  2) $\sim(B \cdot D) \cdot A$ Pr
  3) $(E \lor \sim A) \lor C$ Pr
  4) $\sim(B \cdot D)$
  5) $A \cdot \sim(B \cdot D)$
  6) A
  7) $B \equiv C$
  8) $\sim(B \cdot \sim \sim D)$
  9) $B \supset\ \sim D$
 10) $(\sim A \lor E) \lor C$
 11) $\sim A \lor (E \lor C)$
 12) $\sim \sim A$
 13) $E \lor C$
 14) $C \lor E$
 15) $\sim(\sim C \cdot \sim E)$
 16) $\sim C \supset E$
 17) $\sim(B \cdot \sim C) \cdot \sim(C \cdot \sim B)$

18) $\sim(C \cdot \sim B) \cdot \sim(B \cdot \sim C)$
19) $\sim(C \cdot \sim B)$
20) $\sim(\sim \sim C \cdot \sim B)$
21) $\sim C \vee B$
22) $E \vee \sim D$
23) $\sim D \vee E$
24) $\sim(\sim \sim D \cdot \sim E)$
25) $\sim(D \cdot \sim E)$
26) $\therefore D \supset E$

Group B:

Construct a proof of validity for each of the following.

(1) $\therefore (C \vee B) \vee (D \vee A)$
   1) $(A \vee B) \vee (C \vee D)$ Pr

(2) $\therefore [(\sim D \supset \sim C) \vee (B \equiv C)] \vee (B \bigtriangleup \sim A)$
   1) $[(\sim A \bigtriangleup B) \vee (C \equiv B)] \vee (C \supset D)$ Pr

(3) $\therefore (D \cdot B) \cdot (C \cdot A)$
   1) $(A \cdot B) \cdot (C \cdot D)$ Pr

(4) $\therefore [A \cdot (B \cdot C)] \supset (D \cdot C)$
   1) $(C \supset \sim D) \supset \sim[(B \cdot A) \cdot C]$ Pr

(5) $\therefore D \vee C$
   1) $[(A \equiv B) \supset C] \cdot [\sim(B \equiv A) \supset D]$ Pr

(6) $\therefore B \equiv C$
   1) $(A \supset \sim B) \cdot (\sim A \supset D)$ Pr
   2) $\sim C \supset \sim D$ Pr
   3) $\sim(C \cdot \sim B)$ Pr

(7) $\therefore C \supset (B \supset D)$
   1) $(A \vee \sim B) \vee \sim C$ Pr
   2) $D \cdot (A \supset \sim D)$ Pr

(8) $\therefore A \supset B$
   1) $(A \cdot \sim B) \supset (B \vee C)$ Pr
   2) $\sim(\sim D \cdot B) \cdot \sim(\sim E \cdot C)$ Pr
   3) $\sim D \cdot \sim E$ Pr

(9) $\therefore B \vee D$
   1) $(\sim A \bigtriangleup B) \cdot (D \equiv C)$ Pr
   2) $(E \vee A) \vee (B \vee C)$ Pr
   3) $\sim(E \vee B)$ Pr

(10) $\therefore E \bigtriangleup D$
   1) $(A \supset C) \cdot \sim B$ Pr
   2) $(C \supset D) \cdot (\sim E \supset A)$ Pr
   3) $\sim D \vee (B \vee \sim E)$ Pr

Group C:

Give every exercise in Group B an interpretation by writing for each of the capital letters in a particular exercise an English statement—the same statement at each occurrence of the same capital letter in any given exercise—while also using appropriate English phrases for the logical operators.

Group D:

Symbolize the following arguments using the suggested notation, and then construct a proof of validity for each.

(1) Randell Jarrell wrote either *The Lost World* or *Little Friend, Little Friend*, or *Blood for a Stranger*. Consequently, Jarrell wrote *Little Friend, Little Friend*, or either *The Lost World* or *Blood for a Stranger*. (*W, F, S*)

(2) Thomas Mann authored either *Doctor Faustus* or *The Magic Mountain* and *The Subterraneans*. But Mann didn't author both *The Subterraneans* and *The Magic Mountain*. Therefore, he authored *Doctor Faustus*. (*F, M, S*)

(3) Either William Faulkner didn't write *Sanctuary* or he did write *Of Human Bondage*, or he also wrote *As I Lay Dying;* moreover, he didn't write *Of Human Bondage*. So, if Faulkner wrote *Sanctuary*, he also wrote *As I Lay Dying*. (*S, B, D*)

(4) It isn't true both that Thomas Wolfe didn't write *Of Time and the River* while writing *Look Homeward, Angel;* but it also isn't true that he didn't write both *You Can't Go Home Again* and also *Of Time and the River*. Hence, it isn't true both that Wolfe didn't write *You Can't Go Home Again* while also writing *Look Homeward, Angel*. (*R, A, H*)

(5) The following isn't true: We don't question the existence of Priam's Troy; moreover, we read about Heinrich Schliemann's digs, while studying George Grote's *History of Greece* and being interested in the Homeric stories. So, that we're interested in the Homeric stories is a sufficient condition for studying Grote's *History of Greece* only if we question the existence of Priam's Troy whenever we read about Schliemann's digs. (*P, S, G, H*)

(6) That George Grote is correct implies that the Trojan War is an "interesting fable", although that Troy wasn't uncovered in the Hissarlik digs implies that Heinrich Schliemann's work doesn't cast light on the Homeric stories. It isn't true both that the Trojan War is an "interesting fable" while Troy was uncovered in the Hissarlik digs; yet also it isn't the case both that Grote isn't correct and Schliemann's work doesn't cast light on the Homeric stories. Therefore, either Troy was uncovered in the Hissarlik digs or the Trojan War is an "interesting fable", but not both. (*G, T, H, S*)

(7) That Rhys Carpenter is correct implies that something is wrong either with Heinrich Schliemann's Troy or with Homer's Troy, but not both. It isn't the case both that the clay tablets in Linear B don't add support to Schliemann's evidence even though something is wrong with Homer's Troy; yet Carpenter is correct and

the clay tablets in Linear B don't add support to Schliemann's evidence. So, something is wrong with Schliemann's Troy. (*C, S, H, B*)

(8) Winslow Homer painted either "Gross Clinic" or "Life Line" (but not both) only if he loved the sea. That Homer didn't paint "The Wreck" is a necessary condition for it not being true that he painted "Life Line" if, and only if, he didn't paint "Gross Clinic". Hence, that Homer painted "The Wreck" and "Kissing the Moon" implies that he loved the sea. (*C, L, S, W, M*)

(9) That Winslow Homer didn't paint "Jonah" is a necessary condition for his painting "Swimming Hole" if, and only if, he painted "Between Rounds". If Homer didn't paint "Temple of the Mind" and didn't paint "Jonah", he painted "Life Line". Homer painted "Swimming Hole" or he didn't paint "Between Rounds" (but not both), and he didn't paint "Swimming Hole". Consequently, Homer painted either "Temple of the Mind" or "Life Line"; yet he painted neither "Between Rounds" nor "Jonah". (*J, H, R, M, L*)

(10) Pinkham Ryder was a visionary, and furthermore the following isn't true: Namely, it isn't the case that he was a realist if, and only if, he didn't appreciate heroic music, even though he was a visionary. The following isn't the case: Either Ryder painted the "Flying Dutchman" while also being a realist or he wasn't impressed by Richard Wagner but did appreciate heroic music. Therefore, Ryder painted the "Flying Dutchman" only if he was impressed by Wagner. (*V, R, M, D, W*)

3. USING DE MORGAN'S LAWS
AND DISTRIBUTION
IN PROOFS OF VALIDITY

DeM

$$(\sim p \lor \sim q) \equiv \sim(p \cdot q)$$
$$(\sim p \cdot \sim q) \equiv \sim(p \lor q)$$

Dist

$$[p \lor (q \cdot r)] \equiv [(p \lor q) \cdot (p \lor r)]$$
$$[p \cdot (q \lor r)] \equiv [(p \cdot q) \lor (p \cdot r)]$$

Let us construct a proof of validity for this argument:

(1)   If we persist in our work, then we either are rewarded and honored or aren't faithful in our duties. We do persist in our work. So unless we are faithful in our duties, we shall not be honored. (*W, R, H, D*)

Statement (1) may be expressed symbolically as

(2) $\therefore D \supset H$
   1) $W \supset [(R \cdot H) \vee \sim D]$ Pr
   2) W Pr

Observing the conclusion and premiss set, we see that 'W' and 'R' appear in the premiss set but not in the conclusion. These statements must be "left behind" in the proof before reaching the conclusion. Using Modus Ponens, we rid ourselves of 'W'.

   3) $(R \cdot H) \vee \sim D$ 1, 2, MP

The statement at line 3 may be viewed as an overall disjunctive statement. Furthermore, the left-hand disjunct may be read as a conjunction. Suppose we use Commutation:

   4) $\sim D \vee (R \cdot H)$ 3, Com

The fourth statement exhibits the form '$p \vee (q \cdot r)$'; now, distribute:

   5) $(\sim D \vee R) \cdot (\sim D \vee H)$ 4, Dist

We find 'D' and 'H' of the conclusion appearing only in the right-hand conjunct of line 5. Therefore, we use Commutation followed by Simplification:

   6) $(\sim D \vee H) \cdot (\sim D \vee R)$ 5, Com
   7) $\sim D \vee H$ 6, Simp

But, how do we move from '$\sim D \vee H$' to '$D \supset H$'? Simple! Use Definition 1, Definition 3, and Double Negation. Thus, a completed proof of the validity of (1) may be constructed in this may:

(3) $\therefore D \supset H$
   1) $W \supset [(R \cdot H) \vee \sim D]$ Pr
   2) W Pr
   3) $(R \cdot H) \vee \sim D$ 1, 2, MP
   4) $\sim D \vee (R \cdot H)$ 3, Com
   5) $(\sim D \vee R) \cdot (\sim D \vee H)$ 4, Dist
   6) $(\sim D \vee H) \cdot (\sim D \vee R)$ 5, Com
   7) $\sim D \vee H$ 6, Simp
   8) $\sim (\sim \sim D \cdot \sim H)$ 7, D1
   9) $\sim \sim D \supset H$ 8, D3
  10) $\therefore D \supset H$ 9, DN

As a general rule of thumb, whenever there are statements appearing in only one premiss and not in the conclusion, attempt a Distribution move which will yield an overall conjunction. Given an overall conjunction, you may then use Simplification, or Commutation followed by Simplification, to obtain at a separate line those statements appearing in the conclusion. Statements not appearing in the conclusion are "left behind" in the use of Simplification. Notice how this strategy was carried out in (3), lines 4–7. On the other hand suppose some statement not appearing in the conclusion is found in two or more premisses. Then, think of such possible moves as Hypothetical Syllogism or Modus Ponens to "get rid of" unwanted statements.

As another general rule of thumb, we have suggested that if there is a tilde on the outside of some punctuation marks, remove it. Double Negation and our various logical definitions often remove tildes. De Morgan's laws, however, are also quite helpful. Consider the next argument:

(4) Our new computer will use punch cards or tapes, or it will use disks and be the most modern machine available. Our new computer will neither use punch cards nor be the most modern machine available. Hence, our computer will use tapes. (C, T, D, M)

We shall symbolize (4) as

(5) $\therefore T$
    1) $(C \lor T) \lor (D \cdot M)$ Pr
    2) $\sim (C \lor M)$ Pr

In (5), observe that 'C', 'D', and 'M' appear in the premiss set but not in the conclusion. Also notice that 'C' and 'M' occur in two premisses, but 'D' in only one. Furthermore, there is a tilde on the outside of the punctuation marks in the second premiss. Following our general rule of thumb concerning tildes on the outside of punctuation marks, we apply De Morgan's Law to the second premiss:

    3) $\sim C \cdot \sim M$ 2, DeM

Since the third statement may be viewed as a conjunction and there is no apparent reason to keep it in that form, disjoint the statement into its conjuncts.

    4) $\sim C$ 3, Simp
    5) $\sim M \cdot \sim C$ 3, Com
    6) $\sim M$ 5, Simp

Turning our attention to the first premiss, let us use Association to obtain

    7) $C \lor [T \lor (D \cdot M)]$ 1, Assoc

Of course we want to obtain 'T' on a line by itself. So, using Disjunctive Syllogism, we move to

   8) $T \vee (D \cdot M)$ 7, 4, DS

The statement at line 8 may be considered an overall disjunctive statement such that its right-hand disjunct is a conjunction. '$T \vee (D \cdot M)$' may be viewed, then, as an instance of '$p \vee (q \cdot r)$'. Using Distribution, we obtain

   9) $(T \vee D) \cdot (T \vee M)$ 8, Dist

Remembering '$\sim M$' at line 6, the remainder of the proof is rather simple. Commute the statement on line 9 and then use Simplification. Another use of Commutation, followed by an appeal to Disjunctive Syllogism, yields the conclusion. A complete proof of (4) now may be constructed:

(6) $\therefore T$

	1)	$(C \vee T) \vee (D \cdot M)$	Pr
	2)	$\sim (C \vee M)$	Pr
	3)	$\sim C \cdot \sim M$	2, DeM
	4)	$\sim C$	3, Simp
	5)	$\sim M \cdot \sim C$	3, Com
	6)	$\sim M$	5, Simp
	7)	$C \vee [T \vee (D \cdot M)]$	1, Assoc
	8)	$T \vee (D \cdot M)$	7, 4, DS
	9)	$(T \vee D) \cdot (T \vee M)$	8, Dist
	10)	$(T \vee M) \cdot (T \vee D)$	9, Com
	11)	$T \vee M$	10, Simp
	12)	$M \vee T$	11, Com
	13)	$\therefore T$	12, 6, DS

EXERCISES

Group A:

In the following, justify each of the unjustified lines.

(1) $\therefore \sim A$

	1)	$A \supset (B \vee C)$	Pr
	2)	$\sim C \cdot \sim B$	Pr
	3)	$\sim B \cdot \sim C$	
	4)	$\sim (B \vee C)$	
	5)	$\therefore \sim A$	

(2) $\therefore C$

	1)	$(A \cdot B) \vee C$	Pr
	2)	$\sim B$	Pr

  3) $\sim B \lor \sim A$
  4) $\sim A \lor \sim B$
  5) $\sim (A \cdot B)$
  6) $\therefore\ C$

(3) $\therefore\ C$

  1) $(A \cdot B) \lor C$ Pr
  2) $\sim B$ Pr
  3) $C \lor (A \cdot B)$
  4) $(C \lor A) \cdot (C \lor B)$
  5) $(C \lor B) \cdot (C \lor A)$
  6) $C \lor B$
  7) $B \lor C$
  8) $\therefore\ C$

(4) $\therefore\ A \cdot B$

  1) $(A \cdot B) \lor (C \cdot A)$ Pr
  2) $\sim C$ Pr
  3) $(A \cdot B) \lor (A \cdot C)$
  4) $A \cdot (B \lor C)$
  5) A
  6) $(B \lor C) \cdot A$
  7) $B \lor C$
  8) $C \lor B$
  9) B
 10) $\therefore\ A \cdot B$

(5) $\therefore\ \sim (D \lor A) \lor \sim (D \lor B)$

  1) $\sim A \lor (\sim B \cdot C)$ Pr
  2) $\sim D \lor (B \cdot A)$ Pr
  3) $(\sim A \lor \sim B) \cdot (\sim A \lor C)$
  4) $\sim A \lor \sim B$
  5) $\sim B \lor \sim A$
  6) $\sim (B \cdot A)$
  7) $(B \cdot A) \lor \sim D$
  8) $\sim D$
  9) $\sim D \cdot (\sim A \lor \sim B)$
 10) $(\sim D \cdot \sim A) \lor (\sim D \cdot \sim B)$
 11) $(\sim D \cdot \sim A) \lor \sim (D \lor B)$
 12) $\therefore\ \sim (D \lor A) \lor \sim (D \lor B)$

(6) $\therefore\ C \supset D$

  1) $\sim (A \lor B) \supset \sim C$ Pr
  2) $\sim B \cdot (B \lor \sim A)$ Pr
  3) $\sim B$
  4) $(B \lor \sim A) \cdot \sim B$
  5) $B \lor \sim A$

6) $\sim A$
7) $\sim A \cdot \sim B$
8) $\sim (A \lor B)$
9) $\sim C$
10) $\sim C \lor D$
11) $\sim (\sim \sim C \cdot \sim D)$
12) $\sim (C \cdot \sim D)$
13) $\therefore C \supset D$

(7) $\therefore A \triangle D$

1) $\sim A \lor (\sim D \cdot C)$ Pr
2) $(\sim D \supset B) \cdot (\sim A \supset \sim B)$ Pr
3) $(\sim A \lor \sim D) \cdot (\sim A \lor C)$
4) $\sim A \lor \sim D$
5) $\sim (A \cdot D)$
6) $\sim D \supset B$
7) $(\sim A \supset \sim B) \cdot (\sim D \supset B)$
8) $\sim A \supset \sim B$
9) $B \supset A$
10) $\sim D \supset A$
11) $\sim A \supset \sim \sim D$
12) $\sim A \supset D$
13) $\sim (\sim A \cdot \sim D)$
14) $\sim (A \cdot D) \cdot \sim (\sim A \cdot \sim D)$
15) $\therefore A \triangle D$

(8) $\therefore A \supset \sim D$

1) $[A \supset (B \supset C)] \cdot [A \supset (C \supset B)]$ Pr
2) $(C \equiv B) \supset \sim D$ Pr
3) $\sim [A \cdot \sim (B \supset C)] \cdot [A \supset (C \supset B)]$
4) $\sim [\sim \sim A \cdot \sim (B \supset C)] \cdot [A \supset (C \supset B)]$
5) $[\sim A \lor (B \supset C)] \cdot [A \supset (C \supset B)]$
6) $[\sim A \lor (B \supset C)] \cdot \sim [A \cdot \sim (C \supset B)]$
7) $[\sim A \lor (B \supset C)] \cdot \sim [\sim \sim A \cdot \sim (C \supset B)]$
8) $[\sim A \lor (B \supset C)] \cdot [\sim A \lor (C \supset B)]$
9) $\sim A \lor [(B \supset C) \cdot (C \supset B)]$
10) $\sim A \lor [\sim (B \cdot \sim C) \cdot (C \supset B)]$
11) $\sim A \lor [\sim (B \cdot \sim C) \cdot \sim (C \cdot \sim B)]$
12) $\sim A \lor (B \equiv C)$
13) $\sim [\sim \sim A \cdot \sim (B \equiv C)]$
14) $\sim [A \cdot \sim (B \equiv C)]$
15) $A \supset (B \equiv C)$
16) $A \supset (C \equiv B)$
17) $\therefore A \supset \sim D$

(9) $\therefore A \supset (C \supset E)$

1) $(\sim A \cdot B) \vee [(A \cdot \sim C) \vee (D \cdot E)]$ Pr
2) $(\sim A \cdot B) \vee \{[(A \cdot \sim C) \vee D] \cdot [(A \cdot \sim C) \vee E]\}$
3) $\{(\sim A \cdot B) \vee [(A \cdot \sim C) \vee D]\} \cdot \{(\sim A \cdot B) \vee [(A \cdot \sim C) \vee E]\}$
4) $\{(\sim A \cdot B) \vee [(A \cdot \sim C) \vee E]\} \cdot \{(\sim A \cdot B) \vee [(A \cdot \sim C) \vee D]\}$
5) $(\sim A \cdot B) \vee [(A \cdot \sim C) \vee E]$
6) $(\sim A \cdot B) \vee [E \vee (A \cdot \sim C)]$
7) $(\sim A \cdot B) \vee [(E \vee A) \cdot (E \vee \sim C)]$
8) $[(\sim A \cdot B) \vee (E \vee A)] \cdot [(\sim A \cdot B) \vee (E \vee \sim C)]$
9) $[(\sim A \cdot B) \vee (E \vee \sim C)] \cdot [(\sim A \cdot B) \vee (E \vee A)]$
10) $(\sim A \cdot B) \vee (E \vee \sim C)$
11) $(E \vee \sim C) \vee (\sim A \cdot B)$
12) $[(E \vee \sim C) \vee \sim A] \cdot [(E \vee \sim C) \vee B]$
13) $(E \vee \sim C) \vee \sim A$
14) $\sim A \vee (E \vee \sim C)$
15) $\sim A \vee (\sim C \vee E)$
16) $\sim A \vee \sim (\sim \sim C \cdot \sim E)$
17) $\sim A \vee \sim (C \cdot \sim E)$
18) $\sim A \vee (C \supset E)$
19) $\sim [\sim \sim A \cdot \sim (C \supset E)]$
20) $\sim [A \cdot \sim (C \supset E)]$
21) $\therefore A \supset (C \supset E)$

(10) $\therefore A \supset (C \vee E)$

1) $(\sim A \cdot B) \vee (C \cdot D)$ Pr
2) $(B \cdot E) \vee [(C \cdot \sim D) \vee C]$ Pr
3) $(\sim A \cdot B) \vee (D \cdot C)$
4) $[(\sim A \cdot B) \vee D] \cdot [(\sim A \cdot B) \vee C]$
5) $(\sim A \cdot B) \vee D$
6) $D \vee (\sim A \cdot B)$
7) $(D \vee \sim A) \cdot (D \vee B)$
8) $D \vee \sim A$
9) $\sim A \vee D$
10) $\sim (\sim \sim A \cdot \sim D)$
11) $\sim (A \cdot \sim D)$
12) $A \supset D$
13) $(B \cdot E) \vee [C \vee (C \cdot \sim D)]$
14) $(B \cdot E) \vee [C \vee (\sim D \cdot C)]$
15) $(B \cdot E) \vee [(C \vee \sim D) \cdot (C \vee C)]$
16) $[(B \cdot E) \vee (C \vee \sim D)] \cdot [(B \cdot E) \vee (C \vee C)]$
17) $(B \cdot E) \vee (C \vee \sim D)$
18) $(C \vee \sim D) \vee (B \cdot E)$
19) $(C \vee \sim D) \vee (E \cdot B)$
20) $[(C \vee \sim D) \vee E] \cdot [(C \vee \sim D) \vee B]$
21) $(C \vee \sim D) \vee E$

22) $(\sim D \vee C) \vee E$
23) $\sim D \vee (C \vee E)$
24) $\sim [\sim \sim D \cdot \sim (C \vee E)]$
25) $\sim [D \cdot \sim (C \vee E)]$
26) $D \supset (C \vee E)$
27) $\therefore A \supset (C \vee E)$

Group B:

Construct a proof of validity for each of the following.

(1) $\therefore \sim (B \vee A)$
   1) $\sim A \cdot (A \vee \sim B)$ Pr

(2) $\therefore \sim (C \cdot A)$
   1) $\sim A \vee (B \vee \sim C)$ Pr
   2) $\sim B$ Pr

(3) $\therefore \sim A$
   1) $(A \cdot B) \supset C$ Pr
   2) $\sim C \cdot B$ Pr

(4) $\therefore (A \cdot B) \supset D$
   1) $\sim A \vee [\sim B \vee (C \cdot D)]$ Pr

(5) $\therefore A \supset C$
   1) $(\sim A \cdot \sim B) \vee (C \cdot D)$ Pr

(6) $\therefore \sim (\sim D \vee \sim A)$
   1) $(A \cdot B) \vee (C \cdot A)$ Pr
   2) $(C \vee B) \supset D$ Pr

(7) $\therefore \sim (C \cdot D)$
   1) $(C \supset \sim A) \cdot (D \supset \sim B)$ Pr
   2) $(A \cdot E) \vee (E \cdot B)$ Pr

(8) $\therefore C \triangle \sim E$
   1) $A \vee [(\sim C \cdot B) \vee (E \cdot D)]$ Pr
   2) $\sim A \cdot \sim (E \cdot \sim C)$ Pr

(9) $\therefore A \supset \sim [(D \cdot B) \vee \sim E]$
   1) $A \supset [\sim D \vee (\sim B \cdot C)]$ Pr
   2) $A \supset (E \cdot F)$ Pr

(10) $\therefore (A \cdot E) \supset (C \cdot F)$
   1) $[A \supset (B \cdot C)] \cdot [A \supset (D \cdot \sim E)]$ Pr

Group C:

Give every exercise in Group B an interpretation by writing for each of the capital letters in a particular exercise an English statement—the same statement at each occurrence of the same capital letter in any given exercise—while also using appropriate English phrases for the logical operators.

Group D:

Symbolize the following arguments using the suggested notation, and then construct a proof of validity for each.

(1) Aristophanes contended that democracy was destroying Athens. Now, it isn't true both that Aristophanes expressed his political views in the "Knights" while also contending that democracy was destroying Athens, or he sided with the old oligarch. Therefore, Aristophanes' political views aren't expressed in the "Knights" or he sided with the old oligarch. (*C, E, S*)

(2) We may appreciate Euripides' dramatic style while also understanding the political events of his time if we study carefully the "Trojan Women". However, we don't understand the political events of Euripides' time. Consequently, we don't study carefully the "Trojan Women". (*A, U, S*)   *

(3) Euripides thought that either the gods are powerful, or they are helpless in the affairs of men and there isn't any objective moral order (but not both). So Euripides thought that the gods are powerful whenever there is an objective moral order. (*P, H, O*)

(4) We may gather from Sophocles that a man finds happiness when, and only when, the gods provide a divine law and a man obeys it. A man obeys the divine law only if he desires justice. Wherefore, a man finds happiness only if he also desires justice. (*F, P, O, D*)

(5) If we study Aristotle's writings, then it isn't the case both that we appreciate Plato's dialogues while not being infatuated with Socrates' life. The following isn't true: Neither do we appreciate Plato's dialogues nor pursue mediocrity, but we're infatuated with Socrates' life. We do study Aristotle's writings and don't pursue mediocrity. Thus, we're infatuated with Socrates' life if, and only if, we appreciate Plato's dialogues. (*S, A, I, P*)

(6) Either it isn't true both that many of the Platonic dialogues aren't tentative and also not conclusive, or neither are all the dialogues worthwhile nor always suggestive. Many Platonic dialogues aren't conclusive although they are always suggestive. Consequently, many of the Platonic dialogues are tentative. (*T, C, W, S*)

(7) That Aristotle studied with Gorgias is a necessary condition for the following not being true: Namely, Aristotle was influenced by Plato if, and only if, he wasn't molded by the Sophists. If Aristotle was influenced by Plato, then he was inconsistent in his writings if he studied with Gorgias. Neither was Aristotle not influenced by Plato nor was he inconsistent in his writings. Therefore, either Aristotle was influenced by Plato or he was molded by the Sophists, but not both. (*S, I, M, C*)

(8) It isn't the case that we either follow Aristotle's cosmology or accept his Unmoved Mover thesis (but not both). Hence, that we follow Aristotle's cosmology is both a necessary and sufficient condition for accepting his Unmoved Mover thesis. (*F, A*)

(9) It isn't true that we either don't accept Aristotle's cosmology or don't recognize his teleological viewpoint (but not both). So, that we accept Aristotle's cosmology is a sufficient and necessary condition for recognizing his teleological viewpoint. (*A, R*)

(10) Unless we wish to evaluate our society correctly, we need not read the ancient Greeks and seek to know ourselves. If we don't heed the ancient Greeks, we ignore problems of value although we do read the ancient Greeks; moreover, if we don't wish to evaluate our society correctly, we read the ancient Greeks while not heeding them. Thus, we either seek to know ourselves or ignore problems of value. (*W, R, S, H, I*)

4. USING EXPORTATION, MATERIAL IMPLICATION, AND TAUTOLOGY IN PROOFS OF VALIDITY

Exp

$$[(p \cdot q) \supset r] \equiv [p \supset (q \supset r)]$$

MI

$$(p \supset q) \equiv (\sim p \lor q)$$

Taut

$$p \equiv (p \cdot p)$$
$$p \equiv (p \lor p)$$

Consider this argument:

(1) A necessary condition for theories in psychology not being constructed is the following: Neither experimental nor clinical psychologists are interested in this type of work, or neither statistical nor quantitative measurement is satisfactory for representing psychological data. Consequently, if experimental psychologists are interested in this type of work, then theories in psychology will be constructed if statistical measurement is satisfactory in representing psychological data. (*T, E, C, S, Q*)

In symbols, (1) may be expressed as

(2) $\therefore E \supset (S \supset T)$

    1) $\sim T \supset [\sim (E \lor C) \lor \sim (S \lor Q)]$ Pr

We notice at once that there is only one premiss in the premiss set of (2). Furthermore, 'C' and 'Q' are found in the premiss while not in the conclusion. This being the case, we shall attempt to convert the first premiss into a statement of the form '$p \lor (q \cdot r)$' and then use Distribution. In order to carry out this plan, we appeal to Material Implication:

2) $\sim \sim T \lor [\sim (E \lor C) \lor \sim (S \lor Q)]$ 1, MI

Moving from the premiss to the second statement by Material Implication, read '$\sim T$' as an instance of 'p', '$\sim (E \lor C)$' an instance of 'q', and '$\sim (S \lor Q)$' as an instance of 'r'.

Since there is no apparent need to keep the two tildes in '$\sim \sim T$', we remove them by Double Negation:

3) $T \lor [\sim (E \lor C) \lor \sim (S \lor Q)]$ 2, DN

The next two moves are designed to remove the tildes appearing in front of the parentheses in the third statement:

4) $T \lor [(\sim E \cdot \sim C) \lor \sim (S \lor Q)]$ 3, DeM
5) $T \lor [(\sim E \cdot \sim C) \lor (\sim S \cdot \sim Q)]$ 4, DeM

Using Association, we may now obtain a statement displaying the form '$p \lor (q \cdot r)$'.

6) $[T \lor (\sim E \cdot \sim C)] \lor (\sim S \cdot \sim Q)$ 5, Assoc

Here we understand the statement '$T \lor (\sim E \cdot \sim C)$' as an instance of '$p$', '$\sim S$' as an instance of '$q$', and '$\sim C$' an instance of '$r$'. Distribution leads us to

7) $\{[T \lor (\sim E \cdot \sim C)] \lor \sim S\} \cdot \{[T \lor (\sim E \cdot \sim C)] \lor \sim Q\}$ 6, Dist

Now, using Simplification, the unwanted 'Q' is "left behind" in our proof:

8) $[T \lor (\sim E \cdot \sim C)] \lor \sim S$ 7, Simp

Once more, we want to move to a statement exhibiting the form '$p \lor (q \cdot r)$' in order to use Distribution followed by the appropriate Simplification move:

9) $\sim S \lor [T \lor (\sim E \cdot \sim C)]$ 8, Com
10) $(\sim S \lor T) \lor (\sim E \cdot \sim C)$ 9, Assoc
11) $[(\sim S \lor T) \lor \sim E] \cdot [(\sim S \lor T) \lor \sim C]$ 10, Dist
12) $(\sim S \lor T) \lor \sim E$ 11, Simp

Only those statements appearing in the conclusion are found in line 12 with exactly the same number of occurrences of each statement in both the conclusion and line 12. So, arrange the statements in line 12 in the same spatial order—from left to right—as they appear in the conclusion:

13) $\sim E \vee (\sim S \vee T)$ 12, Com

Two uses of Material Implication yield the desired conclusion:

14) $E \supset (\sim S \vee T)$ 13, MI
15) $\therefore E \supset (S \supset T)$ 14, MI

Putting all the lines above together, we construct a proof for (1):

(3) $\therefore E \supset (S \supset T)$
   1) $\sim T \supset [\sim(E \vee C) \vee \sim(S \vee Q)]$ Pr
   2) $\sim \sim T \vee [\sim(E \vee C) \vee \sim(S \vee Q)]$ 1, MI
   3) $T \vee [\sim(E \vee C) \vee \sim(S \vee Q)]$ 2, DN
   4) $T \vee [(\sim E \cdot \sim C) \vee \sim(S \vee Q)]$ 3, DeM
   5) $T \vee [(\sim E \cdot \sim C) \vee (\sim S \cdot \sim Q)]$ 4, DeM
   6) $[T \vee (\sim E \cdot \sim C)] \vee (\sim S \cdot \sim Q)$ 5, Assoc
   7) $\{[T \vee (\sim E \cdot \sim C)] \vee \sim S\} \cdot \{[T \vee (\sim E \cdot \sim C)] \vee \sim Q\}$ 6, Dist
   8) $[T \vee (\sim E \cdot \sim C)] \vee \sim S$ 7, Simp
   9) $\sim S \vee [T \vee (\sim E \cdot \sim C)]$ 8, Com
  10) $(\sim S \vee T) \vee (\sim E \cdot \sim C)$ 9, Assoc
  11) $[(\sim S \vee T) \vee \sim E] \cdot [(\sim S \vee T) \vee \sim C]$ 10, Dist
  12) $(\sim S \vee T) \vee \sim E$ 11, Simp
  13) $\sim E \vee (\sim S \vee T)$ 12, Com
  14) $E \supset (\sim S \vee T)$ 13, MI
  15) $\therefore E \supset (S \supset T)$ 14, MI

Let us examine another argument:

(4)   Unless Dottie comes, her car isn't working. That Dottie's car is working and
        she does come is a sufficient condition for Bo bringing the beer. A necessary
        condition for both Dottie's car working and her coming while Bo brings the
        beer is that the party will be a success. So Dottie comes only if the party will
        be a success. (C, W, B, S)

Symbolizing (4), we may write

(5) $\therefore C \supset S$
   1) $C \supset W$ Pr
   2) $(W \cdot C) \supset B$ Pr
   3) $[(W \cdot C) \cdot B] \supset S$ Pr

Examining the conclusion and premiss set of (5), we see first that statements
appearing in the premiss set do not appear in the conclusion. These statements
are 'W' and 'B'. Second, we notice that 'C', which appears in the conclusion, is
found three times in the premiss set. These observations suggest the strategy we
shall follow. 'W' and 'B' must be "left behind" in the proof before reaching '$C \supset S$'.

On the other hand, 'C' must appear in the conclusion. Here the problem is to reduce the number of occurrences of 'C' in the premiss set. As a general rule of thumb, whenever there is a statement found both in the conclusion and premiss set but occurring more in the premiss set than the conclusion, consider using Tautology.

How might we leave 'W' behind in the proof before reaching '$C \supset S$'? Since 'W' is found in at least two premisses, each of which may be read as an overall hypothetical statement, attempt to move toward possible uses of Hypothetical Syllogism. Hopefully, we shall be able to find 'W' as an antecedent in one hypothetical statement and as a consequent in another. Of course 'W' is the consequent of the first premiss. Can we obtain, perhaps, a hypothetical statement from the second premiss having 'W' as the antecedent? Yes, by using Exportation:

$$
\begin{array}{lll}
4) & W \supset (C \supset B) & 2, \text{Exp} \\
5) & C \supset (C \supset B) & 1, 4, \text{HS}
\end{array}
$$

'C' appears twice in line 5. Are we able to reduce the number of occurrences of 'C' here? Yes! First appeal to Exportation and then Tautology:

$$
\begin{array}{lll}
6) & (C \cdot C) \supset B & 5, \text{Exp} \\
7) & C \supset B & 6, \text{Taut}
\end{array}
$$

Having 'B' as the consequent of the statement in line 7, from the third premiss we obtain a hypothetical statement with 'B' as its antecedent. Carefully notice how the desired hypothetical statement is deduced at line 9:

$$
\begin{array}{lll}
8) & [B \cdot (W \cdot C)] \supset S & 3, \text{Com} \\
9) & B \supset [(W \cdot C) \supset S] & 8, \text{Exp} \\
10) & C \supset [(W \cdot C) \supset S] & 7, 9, \text{HS}
\end{array}
$$

Once more we find 'C' occurring twice in the same statement. Now, let us reduce the number of occurrences of 'C' in line 10 of the proof. Begin with a use of Exportation. Then, appealing to Commutation and Association, we are ready for a use of Tautology:

$$
\begin{array}{lll}
11) & [C \cdot (W \cdot C)] \supset S & 10, \text{Exp} \\
12) & [C \cdot (C \cdot W)] \supset S & 11, \text{Com} \\
13) & [(C \cdot C) \cdot W] \supset S & 12, \text{Assoc} \\
14) & (C \cdot W) \supset S & 13, \text{Taut}
\end{array}
$$

But we have yet to reach '$C \supset S$'. Using Commutation followed by Exportation, we obtain a hypothetical statement with 'W' as its antecedent. However, 'W' is also the consequent of the first premiss. Hypothetical Syllogism puts us within two lines of the conclusion. A completed proof of (1) may be constructed as follows:

(6) $\therefore C \supset S$

1)	$C \supset W$	Pr
2)	$(W \cdot C) \supset B$	Pr
3)	$[(W \cdot C) \cdot B] \supset S$	Pr
4)	$W \supset (C \supset B)$	2, Exp
5)	$C \supset (C \supset B)$	1, 4, HS
6)	$(C \cdot C) \supset B$	5, Exp
7)	$C \supset B$	6, Taut
8)	$[B \cdot (W \cdot C)] \supset S$	3, Com
9)	$B \supset [(W \cdot C) \supset S]$	8, Exp
10)	$C \supset [(W \cdot C) \supset S]$	7, 9, HS
11)	$[C \cdot (W \cdot C)] \supset S$	10, Exp
12)	$[C \cdot (C \cdot W)] \supset S$	11, Com
13)	$[(C \cdot C) \cdot W] \supset S$	12, Assoc
14)	$(C \cdot W) \supset S$	13, Taut
15)	$(W \cdot C) \supset S$	14, Com
16)	$W \supset (C \supset S)$	15, Exp
17)	$C \supset (C \supset S)$	1, 16, HS
18)	$(C \cdot C) \supset S$	17, Exp
19)	$\therefore C \supset S$	18, Taut

There are, of course, other distinct proofs of the validity of (1). For example, instead of asserting '$C \supset [(W \cdot C) \supset S]$' at line 10 as done in (6), proceed in this way:

(7)

10)	$(W \cdot C) \supset [(W \cdot C) \supset S]$	2, 9, HS
11)	$[(W \cdot C) \cdot (W \cdot C)] \supset S$	10, Exp
12)	$(W \cdot C) \supset S$	11, Taut
13)	$W \supset (C \supset S)$	12, Exp
14)	$C \supset (C \supset S)$	1, 13, HS
15)	$(C \cdot C) \supset S$	14, Exp
16)	$\therefore C \supset S$	15, Taut

Before proceeding to the Exercises, let us briefly review some of our various rules of thumb which help in applying Rules of Transformation.

(1) *If a statement is read as an overall conjunction and you see no reason to leave it in that form, disjoint it into its various conjuncts.*

(2) *If there is one tilde, or more, on the outside of punctuation marks and there seems to be no reason to keep it there, remove that tilde. In removing tildes from before punctuation marks, Double Negation, Definitions 1 and 3, and De Morgan's Laws are often helpful.*

(3) *If a statement, or statements, appears in the conclusion but not in the premiss set of an argument, Addition must be used somewhere in the proof.*

(4) *If statements appear in the premiss set and yet not in the conclusion, those statements must be "left behind" before reaching the conclusion. Whenever such statements are found in two or more premisses, attempt to move toward a use of Hypothetical Syllogism, Disjunctive Syllogism, Modus Ponens, or the like. If, however, such statements appear in only one premiss and that premiss is not an overall conjunction, attempt to use Distribution which will yield an overall conjunction. Then, use Simplification, or Commutation followed by Simplification, to obtain only those statements found in the conclusion.*

(5) *If there is only one premiss in the premiss set of an argument and that premiss contains both (1) the same statements as in the conclusion and (2) the same number of occurrences of each statement as in the conclusion, order the statements in the premiss as they are ordered in the conclusion.*

(6) *And, above all, whenever possible in planning a strategy, attempt to work from the conclusion toward the premiss set.*

EXERCISES

Group A:

In the following, justify each of the unjustified lines.

(1) $\therefore A \supset C$

   1) $(A \cdot B) \supset C$ Pr

   2) B Pr

   3) $(B \cdot A) \supset C$

   4) $B \supset (A \supset C)$

   5) $\therefore A \supset C$

(2) $\therefore \sim A$

   1) $A \supset (B \cdot C)$ Pr

   2) $\sim B$ Pr

   3) $\sim A \vee (B \cdot C)$

   4) $(\sim A \vee B) \cdot (\sim A \vee C)$

   5) $\sim A \vee B$

   6) $B \vee \sim A$

   7) $\therefore \sim A$

(3) $\therefore C$

   1) $A \supset (\sim C \supset \sim B)$ Pr

   2) $\sim C \supset (A \cdot B)$ Pr

   3) $A \supset (B \supset C)$

   4) $(A \cdot B) \supset C$

5) $\sim C \supset C$
6) $\sim \sim C \vee C$
7) $C \vee C$
8) $\therefore C$

(4) $\therefore B \supset D$
   1) $\sim(A \vee B) \vee C$ Pr
   2) $C \supset D$ Pr
   3) $(\sim A \cdot \sim B) \vee C$
   4) $C \vee (\sim A \cdot \sim B)$
   5) $(C \vee \sim A) \cdot (C \vee \sim B)$
   6) $(C \vee \sim B) \cdot (C \vee \sim A)$
   7) $C \vee \sim B$
   8) $\sim B \vee C$
   9) $B \supset C$
 10) $\therefore B \supset D$

(5) $\therefore A \supset (B \supset D)$
   1) $A \supset (B \supset C)$ Pr
   2) $(B \cdot C) \supset D$ Pr
   3) $(A \cdot B) \supset C$
   4) $(C \cdot B) \supset D$
   5) $C \supset (B \supset D)$
   6) $(A \cdot B) \supset (B \supset D)$
   7) $[(A \cdot B) \cdot B] \supset D$
   8) $[A \cdot (B \cdot B)] \supset D$
   9) $(A \cdot B) \supset D$
 10) $\therefore A \supset (B \supset D)$

(6) $\therefore C \triangle D$
   1) $(A \cdot B) \vee (C \vee D)$ Pr
   2) $\sim A$ Pr
   3) $C \supset (\sim A \supset \sim D)$ Pr
   4) $(C \vee D) \vee (A \cdot B)$
   5) $[(C \vee D) \vee A] \cdot [(C \vee D) \vee B]$
   6) $(C \vee D) \vee A$
   7) $A \vee (C \vee D)$
   8) $C \vee D$
   9) $\sim(\sim C \cdot \sim D)$
 10) $C \supset (D \supset A)$
 11) $(C \cdot D) \supset A$
 12) $\sim(C \cdot D)$
 13) $\sim(C \cdot D) \cdot \sim(\sim C \cdot \sim D)$
 14) $\therefore C \triangle D$

(7) $\therefore \sim C \supset D$

    1) $\sim A \equiv \sim B$ Pr

    2) $B \equiv C$ Pr

    3) A Pr

    4) $\sim(\sim A \cdot \sim \sim B) \cdot \sim(\sim B \cdot \sim \sim A)$

    5) $\sim(B \cdot \sim C) \cdot \sim(C \cdot \sim B)$

    6) $\sim(\sim B \cdot \sim \sim A) \cdot \sim(\sim A \cdot \sim \sim B)$

    7) $\sim(\sim B \cdot \sim \sim A)$

    8) $\sim B \supset \sim A$

    9) $\sim \sim A$

   10) $\sim \sim B$

   11) B

   12) $\sim(B \cdot \sim C)$

   13) $B \supset C$

   14) C

   15) $C \vee D$

   16) $\sim \sim C \vee D$

   17) $\therefore \sim C \supset D$

(8) $\therefore (A \vee B) \supset C$

    1) $[A \supset (B \cdot C)] \cdot [B \supset (D \cdot C)]$ Pr

    2) $A \supset (B \cdot C)$

    3) $[B \supset (D \cdot C)] \cdot [A \supset (B \cdot C)]$

    4) $B \supset (D \cdot C)$

    5) $\sim A \vee (B \cdot C)$

    6) $\sim B \vee (D \cdot C)$

    7) $(\sim A \vee B) \cdot (\sim A \vee C)$

    8) $(\sim B \vee D) \cdot (\sim B \vee C)$

    9) $(\sim A \vee C) \cdot (\sim A \vee B)$

   10) $\sim A \vee C$

   11) $(\sim B \vee C) \cdot (\sim B \vee D)$

   12) $\sim B \vee C$

   13) $C \vee \sim A$

   14) $C \vee \sim B$

   15) $(C \vee \sim A) \cdot (C \vee \sim B)$

   16) $C \vee (\sim A \cdot \sim B)$

   17) $C \vee \sim(A \vee B)$

   18) $\sim(A \vee B) \vee C$

   19) $\therefore (A \vee B) \supset C$

(9) $\therefore A \supset E$

    1) $(\sim A \supset \sim B) \supset (C \cdot D)$ Pr

    2) $D \supset (C \cdot E)$ Pr

    3) $\sim(\sim A \supset \sim B) \vee (C \cdot D)$

    4) $\sim \sim(\sim A \cdot \sim \sim B) \vee (C \cdot D)$

    5) $(\sim A \cdot \sim \sim B) \vee (C \cdot D)$

    6) $(\sim A \cdot B) \vee (C \cdot D)$

   7) $[(\sim A \cdot B) \vee C] \cdot [(\sim A \cdot B) \vee D]$
   8) $[(\sim A \cdot B) \vee D] \cdot [(\sim A \cdot B) \vee C]$
   9) $(\sim A \cdot B) \vee D$
  10) $D \vee (\sim A \cdot B)$
  11) $(D \vee \sim A) \cdot (D \vee B)$
  12) $D \vee \sim A$
  13) $\sim A \vee D$
  14) $A \supset D$
  15) $\sim D \vee (C \cdot E)$
  16) $(\sim D \vee C) \cdot (\sim D \vee E)$
  17) $(\sim D \vee E) \cdot (\sim D \vee C)$
  18) $\sim D \vee E$
  19) $D \supset E$
  20) $\therefore A \supset E$

(10) $\therefore E \cdot D$

   1) $A \supset (B \supset \sim C)$ Pr
   2) $C \supset (B \cdot A)$ Pr
   3) $(A \cdot C) \vee (D \cdot E)$ Pr
   4) $(A \cdot B) \supset \sim C$
   5) $(B \cdot A) \supset \sim C$
   6) $C \supset \sim C$
   7) $\sim C \vee \sim C$
   8) $\sim C$
   9) $[(A \cdot C) \vee D] \cdot [(A \cdot C) \vee E]$
  10) $(A \cdot C) \vee D$
  11) $[(A \cdot C) \vee E] \cdot [(A \cdot C) \vee D]$
  12) $(A \cdot C) \vee E$
  13) $D \vee (A \cdot C)$
  14) $(D \vee A) \cdot (D \vee C)$
  15) $(D \vee C) \cdot (D \vee A)$
  16) $D \vee C$
  17) $C \vee D$
  18) D
  19) $E \vee (A \cdot C)$
  20) $(E \vee A) \cdot (E \vee C)$
  21) $(E \vee C) \cdot (E \vee A)$
  22) $E \vee C$
  23) $C \vee E$
  24) E
  25) $\therefore E \cdot D$

Group B:

Construct a proof of validity for each of the following.

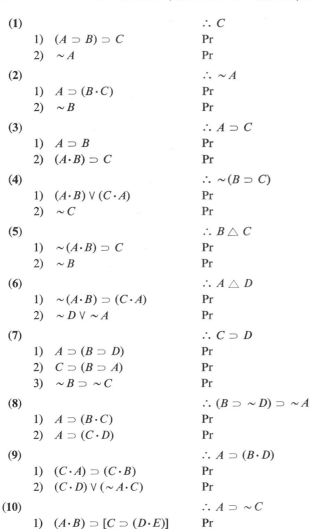

(1)   ∴ *C*
    1) (*A* ⊃ *B*) ⊃ *C*   Pr
    2) ~*A*   Pr

(2)   ∴ ~*A*
    1) *A* ⊃ (*B*·*C*)   Pr
    2) ~*B*   Pr

(3)   ∴ *A* ⊃ *C*
    1) *A* ⊃ *B*   Pr
    2) (*A*·*B*) ⊃ *C*   Pr

(4)   ∴ ~(*B* ⊃ *C*)
    1) (*A*·*B*) ∨ (*C*·*A*)   Pr
    2) ~*C*   Pr

(5)   ∴ *B* △ *C*
    1) ~(*A*·*B*) ⊃ *C*   Pr
    2) ~*B*   Pr

(6)   ∴ *A* △ *D*
    1) ~(*A*·*B*) ⊃ (*C*·*A*)   Pr
    2) ~*D* ∨ ~*A*   Pr

(7)   ∴ *C* ⊃ *D*
    1) *A* ⊃ (*B* ⊃ *D*)   Pr
    2) *C* ⊃ (*B* ⊃ *A*)   Pr
    3) ~*B* ⊃ ~*C*   Pr

(8)   ∴ (*B* ⊃ ~*D*) ⊃ ~*A*
    1) *A* ⊃ (*B*·*C*)   Pr
    2) *A* ⊃ (*C*·*D*)   Pr

(9)   ∴ *A* ⊃ (*B*·*D*)
    1) (*C*·*A*) ⊃ (*C*·*B*)   Pr
    2) (*C*·*D*) ∨ (~*A*·*C*)   Pr

(10)   ∴ *A* ⊃ ~*C*
    1) (*A*·*B*) ⊃ [*C* ⊃ (*D*·*E*)]   Pr
    2) ~(*B* ⊃ *E*)   Pr

Group C:

Give every exercise in Group B an interpretation by writing for each of the capital letters in a particular exercise an English statement—the same statement at each occurrence of the same capital letter in any given exercise—while also using appropriate English phrases for the logical operators.

Group D:

Symbolize the following arguments using the suggested notation, and then construct a proof of validity for each.

(1) If cells make up tissue, then that tissue forms an organ implies that homologues are discovered in pairs. Tissue forms an organ, So, unless cells make up tissue, homologues aren't discovered in pairs. (*M, F, D*)

(2) Either it isn't the case that a particular cell doesn't divide or can't carry out photosynthesis or we know it is a nerve cell. Thus, that a cell doesn't divide is a sufficient condition for knowing it is a nerve cell. (*D, C, K*)

(3) A cell doesn't plasmolyze whenever it doesn't undergo exosmosis. If a cell does undergo exosmosis but doesn't contract, it doesn't plasmolyze. Therefore, a cell plasmolyzes only if it contracts. (*P, U, C*)

(4) If a cell is placed in a hypertonic solution, it will lyse only if it doesn't remain unchanged. Also, whenever a cell is placed in a hypertonic solution, it will lyse whenever it doesn't remain unchanged. Hence, if a cell is placed in a hypertonic solution, then it will lyse when, and only when, it doesn't remain unchanged. (*P, L, R*)

(5) If Napoleon Bonaparte neither escaped from Elba nor lost at Waterloo, then the Duke of Wellington defeated Napoleon and saved Europe from French domination. If Wellington defeated Napoleon, then if Napoleon didn't lose at Waterloo, Wellington didn't save Europe from French domination. Consequently, either Napoleon escaped from Elba or he lost at Waterloo. (*E, L, D, S*)

(6) Either it isn't the case both that Napoleon Bonaparte escaped from Elba and didn't win at Waterloo or he was defeated even though he escaped from Elba. If Napoleon was defeated, then if he escaped from Elba, he didn't restore permanently the Empire. Wherefore, unless Napoleon escaped from Elba and restored permanently the Empire, he didn't win at Waterloo. (*E, W, D, R*)

(7) Napoleon Bonaparte was exiled to St. Helena only if he lost at Waterloo; moreover, that Napoleon didn't lose at Waterloo is a necessary condition for the following not being the case: Namely, if Alexander, the Czar of Russia, didn't form the Holy Alliance, Napoleon wasn't exiled to St. Helena. Either it isn't true both that Europe was jeopardized by Napoleon although Alexander formed the Holy Alliance or Europe wasn't jeopardized by Napoleon. So, if Napoleon was exiled to St. Helena, Europe wasn't jeopardized by him. (*E, L, F, J*)

(8) If we appreciate J. S. Bach's works and are fond of baroque music, then we'll also enjoy Antonio Vivaldi's compositions. Appreciating Bach's works while also enjoying Vivaldi's compositions implies that we're both fond of baroque music and delighted by ornamentation. Therefore, if we appreciate Bach's works, then we either enjoy Vivaldi's compositions or aren't fond of baroque music (but not both). (*A, F, E, D*)

(9) If we study either Antonio Vivaldi or Thomas Tallis, we are familiar with "The Seasons" or "The Lamentations of Jeremiah". That we are familiar with "With Weeping and Mourning" or "The Lamentations of Jeremiah" implies that we study Tallis and are familiar with "The Lamentations of Jeremiah". Consequently, if we are familiar with "With Weeping and Mourning", then we are also familiar with "The Seasons" or "The Lamentations of Jeremiah". (*V, T, S, L, M*)

(10) That we're students of Claudio Monteverdi implies that we're either interested in his laments and know "Amor" or appreciate his lyric style and are familiar with "Chiome d'oro". It isn't the case both that we know "Amor" while also being interested in Monteverdi's laments; moreover, it isn't the case both that we aren't interested in his laments but know "Amor". So, if we know "Amor" and are students of Monteverdi, then we're interested in his laments and are familiar with "Chiome d'oro". (*S, I, K, A, F*)

8

Completing the
Truth-Functional Calculus

Our methods for constructing proofs of validity are not yet completed. There are other valid truth-functional arguments whose validity can be established only by truth-table means. Consider this example:

(1) It isn't true both that our known enemies or covertly dangerous governments attack us while our allies don't come to our aid. Hence, either our known enemies or covertly dangerous governments attacking us is a sufficient condition for covertly dangerous governments or our known enemies attacking us and our allies coming to our aid. (E, G, A)

Symbolizing (1), we may demonstrate its validity by truth-table analysis:

(2) $\therefore (E \lor G) \supset [(G \lor E) \cdot A]$
  1) $\sim [(E \lor G) \cdot \sim A]$ Pr

Forming a hypothetical statement corresponding to (2), we then construct a truth-table:

(3) $\sim [(E \lor G) \cdot \sim A] \supset \{(E \lor G) \supset [(G \lor E) \cdot A]\}$

```
1  1 1 1 0 0 1  1  1 1 1  1  1 1 1  1 1
0  1 1 1 1 1 0  1  1 1 1  0  1 1 1  0 0
1  1 1 0 0 0 1  1  1 1 0  1  0 1 1  1 1
0  1 1 0 1 1 0  1  1 1 0  0  0 1 1  0 0
1  0 1 1 0 0 1  1  0 1 1  1  1 1 0  1 1
0  0 1 1 1 1 0  1  0 1 1  0  1 1 0  0 0
1  0 0 0 0 0 1  1  0 0 0  1  0 0 0  0 1
1  0 0 0 0 1 0  1  0 0 0  1  0 0 0  0 0
                ↑
```

Since the hypothetical statement, (3), corresponding to the argument, (2), is tautological, the argument is valid. Nevertheless, given our present methods of constructing proofs, a proof of validity cannot be constructed for (2). Our notion of a proof of validity must be augmented to include such arguments as (2).

Imagine an argument—any you wish—having a *hypothetical conclusion*. Letting '*P*' stand for the premiss set, '*A*' for the antecedent, and '*C*' for the consequent of the conclusion, we may picture the imagined argument as

(4) $\therefore A \supset C$
          P

Corresponding to every argument is a hypothetical statement. Given (4), we construct this hypothetical schema:

(5) $P \supset (A \supset C)$

If (5) were tautological, (4) would be valid; yet, if (5) were either contingent or contradictory, (4) would be invalid.

Now, if we let '*P*' stand for the same premiss set—whatever it may be—as in (4) and '*A*' and '*C*' also represent the same statements as in (4), we can imagine another argument:

(6) $\therefore C$
          P
          A

Once more we may form a hypothetical schema corresponding to the argument in question:

(7) $(P \cdot A) \supset C$

If (7) were tautological, (6) would be valid; and, if (7) were either contingent or contradictory, (6) would be invalid.

Now, inspect (5) and (7) very carefully. We see that '$P \supset (A \supset C)$' and '$(P \cdot A) \supset C$' are logically equivalent by Exportation. Consequently, if (5) is tautological, so is (7) and vice versa; whereas, if (5) is contingent or contradictory, so is (7) and vice versa. But since (5) corresponds to (4) and (7) corresponds to (6), if (4) is valid, so is (6), or if (4) is invalid, so is (6)—and vice versa. These logical facts may be put into the following schema:

$$\begin{array}{ccc}
 & \text{valid} & \\
\therefore A \supset C & \Longleftrightarrow & \therefore C \\
P & \text{invalid} & P \\
 & & A
\end{array}$$

$$\updownarrow \qquad\qquad \updownarrow$$

$$\begin{array}{ccc}
 & \text{tautology} & \\
P \supset (A \supset C) & \Longleftrightarrow & (P \cdot A) \supset C \\
 & \text{contingent} & \\
 & \textit{or} & \\
 & \text{contradictory} &
\end{array}$$

This schema may be viewed as a basis for the *Conditional Method of Proving Validity*. A result of using the Conditional Method of Proving Validity is a *Conditional Proof (CP)*.

Taking (2) as an example, let us use the Conditional Method of Proving Validity.

(8) $\therefore (E \lor G) \supset [(G \lor E) \cdot A]$

1)	$\sim[(E \lor G) \cdot \sim A]$	Pr
2)	$E \lor G$	CP, $\therefore (G \lor E) \cdot A$
3)	$(E \lor G) \supset A$	1, Df3
4)	A	3, 2, MP
5)	$G \lor E$	2, Com
6)	$(G \lor E) \cdot A$	5, 4, Conj
7)	$\therefore (E \lor G) \supset [(G \lor E) \cdot A]$	2–6, CP

Having symbolized (1), the original premiss set is augmented by assuming the antecedent of the hypothetical conclusion. Commencing with an instance of

$$\therefore A \supset C$$
$$P$$

we now have an instance of

$$\therefore C$$
$$P$$
$$A$$

in

$$\therefore (E \lor G) \supset [(G \lor E) \cdot A]$$

1)	$\sim[(E \lor G) \cdot \sim A]$	Pr
2)	$E \lor G$	CP, $\therefore (G \lor E) \cdot A$

Notice that our new statement—the assumption—is justified by writing to its right-hand side '*CP*, ∴ $(G \lor E) \cdot A$'. This justification may be read, " '$E \lor G$' is an assumption which, with the Conditional Method of Proving Validity and all the other premisses, will be used to deduce '$(G \lor E) \cdot A$' ". Of course '$(G \lor E) \cdot A$' is the consequent of the original hypothetical conclusion. The proof, (8), now proceeds straightforwardly until the statement of line 6 in the proof is reached. At this point we have proved the validity of an argument having the general schema

$$\therefore C$$

$$P$$

$$A$$

where 'P' is understood as '$\sim [(E \lor G) \cdot \sim A]$', '$A$' as '$E \lor G$', and '$C$' as '$(G \lor E) \cdot A$'.

Continuing (8), line 7 tells us that since '$\sim [(E \lor G) \cdot \sim A]$' and '$E \lor G$' imply '$(G \lor E) \cdot A$', then '$\sim [(E \lor G) \cdot \sim A]$' implies '$(E \lor G) \supset [(G \lor E) \cdot A]$' by the Conditional Method of Proving Validity. Notice that in the justification of line 7 we find '2–6, CP', *not* '2, 6, CP'. The *dash* used between '2' and '6' indicates that the Conditional Method of Proving Validity is employed in lines 2 *through* 6. The seventh statement is *not* justified by an appeal to lines 2 and 6 plus some Rule of Transformation. 'CP' indicates the results of using a particular method of proof—not a particular Rule of Transformation.

The vertical line to the left of the statements in (8) indicates the scope of the assumption. In particular, the statements in lines 3, 4, 5, and 6 depend on the assumption —at line 2—plus the original premiss set—in (8) only one premiss—for their derivation. The scope of an assumption used in a Conditional Proof never extends to the last statement of the completed proof; furthermore, the scope of any assumption introduced by a use of the Conditional Method of Proving Validity is always ended by a hypothetical statement not falling under the scope of the assumption.

Our new method of proving validity easily can be extended to arguments *whose conclusions are not hypothetical statements but which are logically equivalent to hypothetical statements*. Notice the following argument:

(9)   If James West appears whenever there is trouble, it doesn't pay to be the villain. So it isn't true that it pays to be the villain while James West appears. (W, T, V)

Translating (9) into our logical notation, we may write

(10) $\therefore \sim (V \cdot W)$
  1) $(T \supset W) \supset \sim V$ Pr

Even though '$\sim (V \cdot W)$' is not a hypothetical statement, it *is* logically equivalent to '$V \supset \sim W$'. Consequently, let us assume 'V' as a new premiss, prove for '$\sim W$', and then by use of Conditional Proof assert '$V \supset \sim W$'. The proof of the validity of (10) may then be completed in two lines.

(11) $\therefore \sim(V \cdot W)$
   1) $(T \supset W) \supset \sim V$ Pr
   2) V CP, $\therefore \sim W$
   3) $\sim \sim V$ 2, DN
   4) $\sim(T \supset W)$ 1, 3, MT
   5) $\sim(\sim T \vee W)$ 4, MI
   6) $\sim \sim T \cdot \sim W$ 5, DeM
   7) $\sim W \cdot \sim \sim T$ 6, Com
   8) $\sim W$ 7, Simp
   9) $V \supset \sim W$ 2–8, CP
  10) $\sim(V \cdot \sim \sim W)$ 9, Df3
  11) $\therefore \sim(V \cdot W)$ 10, DN

    The Conditional Method of Proving Validity also may be used several times in one overall proof.

(12)   Pat coming or Madge leaving and Grace going or Larry staying is a sufficient condition for the success of Bo's party. Hence, whenever Pat comes, Bo's party will be a success if Grace goes. (P, M, G, L, B)

First, let us symbolize (12) in this way:

(13) $\therefore P \supset (G \supset B)$
   1) $[(P \vee M) \cdot (G \vee L)] \supset B$ Pr

Second, we assume as a new premiss the antecedent of the conclusion and prove for the consequent.

(14) $\therefore P \supset (G \supset B)$
   1) $[(P \vee M) \cdot (G \vee L)] \supset B$ Pr
   2) P CP, $\therefore G \supset B$

But since '$G \supset B$' is a hypothetical statement, we may assume its antecedent as a new premiss and deduce 'B'.

(15) $\therefore P \supset (G \supset B)$
   1) $[(P \vee M) \cdot (G \vee L)] \supset B$ Pr
   2) P CP, $\therefore G \supset B$
   3) G CP, $\therefore B$
   4) $P \vee M$ 2, Add
   5) $G \vee L$ 3, Add
   6) $(P \vee M) \cdot (G \vee L)$ 4, 5, Conj
   7) B 1, 6, MP
   8) $G \supset B$ 3–7, CP
   9) $\therefore P \supset (G \supset B)$ 2–8, CP

Because the first three statements of (15) imply '*B*', the first two statements imply '*G* ⊃ *B*'. Then, by Conditional Proof, the original premiss implies '*P* ⊃ (*G* ⊃ *B*)'.

EXERCISES

Group A:

Without using the Conditional Method of Proving Validity, construct proofs for (10) and (13) in this section.

Group B:

Symbolize the following arguments, using the suggested notation. Then, utilizing the Conditional Method of Proving Validity, construct proofs for each of these arguments.

(1)   The following isn't the case: It isn't true that there isn't a stable economic development if the money supply doesn't respond to a growing economy; yet, the money supply is inelastic. There isn't a stable economic development, according to some authorities. If the 1913 Federal Reserve Act is observed, then unless the money supply is elastic, there isn't a stable economic development. So, that the 1913 Federal Reserve Act is observed implies that the money supply is inelastic. (*D, R, E, O*)

(2)   That the money supply is elastic is implied by the following: Namely, the flow of currency being regular is a necessary condition for the economy being balanced toward stable growth whenever the money supply is elastic. Hence, that the money supply is inelastic is a sufficient condition for the following: The flow of currency isn't regular, and if the economy isn't balanced toward stable growth, the money supply is inelastic. (*E, R, B*)

(3)   If the Federal Reserve performs its principal function, the flow of money is regulated and the economy is stable; moreover, if the economy is stable, both the flow of credit and money are regulated. Consequently, if either the Federal Reserve performs its principal function or the economy is stable, the flow of money is regulated (*F, M, E, C*)

(4)   Either money isn't considered as a means of payment but is thought of as a measure of value, or currency is a form of money while money is also considered as a store of purchasing power. Also, either money is thought of as a measure of value and demand deposits are a form of money, or either currency is a form of money but money isn't considered as a store of purchasing power or currency is a form of money. Therefore, that money is considered as a means of payment implies that either currency is a form of money or demand deposits are. (*P, V, C, S, D*)

(5)   It isn't the case both that a sociologist is interested in theory construction and doesn't know various systems of logic. Also, it isn't true both that a sociologist is

concerned only with collecting data while not being unable to make fruitful predictions; moreover, it isn't true both that a sociologist isn't interested in theory construction and not concerned only with collecting data. Therefore, that a sociologist won't be able to make fruitful predictions is implied by his not knowing various systems of logic. (*I, K, C, A*)

(6) It isn't true both that we desire to organize our data although various systems of logic don't prove helpful. If we don't want to fail in our theory construction, we may find digital computers helpful in our research whenever we can't ignore logical models. We don't want to fail in our theory construction. Further, it isn't true both that we may find digital computers helpful in our research while not desiring to organize our data. So we can ignore logical models and/or various systems of logic will prove helpful. (*D, P, W, F, I*)

(7) If we're interested in methodology, then unless logic proves helpful, our scientific language isn't completely analyzed; moreover, if we are interested in methodology, then logic proves helpful whenever our scientific language is completely analyzed. That we aren't concerned simply with collecting data is a necessary condition for the following: Namely, our scientific language is carefully analyzed when, and only when, logic proves helpful. Consequently, we're interested in methodology only if we aren't concerned simply with collecting data. (*I, P, A, C*)

(8) That there isn't a finite number of positions in a game of chess is a necessary condition for the following: Chess isn't a finite game albeit the rules of chess provide that any move will terminate in some final move and, further, each position in the game admits of a finite number of moves. Thus, that there is a finite number of positions in chess implies the following: If each position in the game admits of a finite number of moves, then the rules of chess provide that any move will terminate in some final move only if chess is a finite game. (*N, G, P, A*)

(9) Either chess isn't a finite game and no move ever terminates in a last move, or either chess is a finite game but in principle can't be completely described as a branching tree or one can in principle scan the branching tree and easily find the best move to make at any juncture in the game. Hence, if chess is a finite game, then it can in principle be completely described as a branching tree only if one can easily find the best move to make at any juncture in the game. (*G, T, D, S, F*)

(10) If heuristic programs are written for computers to play chess, then algorithmic methods suffice for all computer programming needs whenever, and only whenever, computers are massive enough to analyze all possible chess moves. It isn't true both that algorithmic methods will suffice for all computer programming needs while contemporary heuristic programming authorities are studied profitably, and yet heuristic programs are written so that computers can play chess. Either Claude Shannon's approach for programming computers to play chess is an important contribution to heuristic programming or heuristic programs aren't written so that computers can play chess, or our present computers are massive enough to analyze all possible chess moves. So it isn't true both that Shannon's approach for

programming computers to play chess isn't an important contribution to heuristics and contemporary heuristic programming authorities are studied. (P, M, C, A, S)

2. INDIRECT METHOD OF PROVING VALIDITY

There is another method of constructing proofs often used in logic. This is the *Indirect Method of Proving Validity,* and a proof constructed by this method is an *Indirect Proof (IP).*

Let '*P*' stand for any premiss set you please and '*C*' for any conclusion. In this case, '*C*' need not be a hypothetical statement. '*C*' represents *any type* of statement you wish. In general we may picture our imagined argument as

(1) $\therefore C$
        P

Corresponding to (1), we may form this hypothetical schema:

(2) $P \supset C$

Now, suppose we were to make an assumption, adding a new premiss to the original premiss set of (1). Let us *assume the denial of the entire conclusion* no matter what that conclusion is:

(3) $\therefore C$
        P
        $\sim C$

Again, we construct a hypothetical schema, but now corresponding to (3):

(4) $(P \cdot \sim C) \supset C$

If (2) were tautological, (1) would be valid; moreover, if (2) were contingent or contradictory, (1) would be invalid. In like manner if (4) were tautological, (3) would be valid; whereas if (4) were contingent or contradictory, (3) would be invalid. It is also a simple matter to establish that (2) and (4) are logically equivalent:

(5) $(P \supset C) \equiv [(P \cdot \sim C) \supset C]$
        1 1 1 1 1 0 0 1 1 1
        1 0 0 1 1 1 1 0 0 0
        0 1 1 1 0 0 0 1 1 1
        0 1 0 1 0 0 1 0 1 0
                 ↑

Thus, we can see if (4) is tautological, (3) is valid; but so is (1), for (2) and (4) are logically equivalent and (2) is the hypothetical corresponding to (1). Schematically, this information may be pictured in this way:

$$\begin{array}{ccc} & \text{valid} & \\ \therefore C & \Longleftrightarrow & \therefore C \\ P & \text{invalid} \quad P \end{array}$$

$$\updownarrow \qquad\qquad \updownarrow$$

$$\begin{array}{ccc} & \text{tautology} & \\ P \supset C & \Longleftrightarrow & (P \cdot \sim C) \supset C \\ & \text{contingent} & \\ & \textit{or} & \\ & \text{contradictory} & \end{array}$$

There is a close relation holding between the Conditional and Indirect Methods of Proving Validity. By Exportation, '$(P \cdot \sim C) \supset C$' is logically equivalent to

(6) $P \supset (\sim C \supset C)$

Yet, corresponding to (6), there is an argument which may be pictured as

(7) $\therefore \sim C \supset C$
        P

Using the Conditional Method of Proving Validity with (7), we assume the antecedent of the conclusion:

(8) $\therefore C$
        P
        $\sim C$

It is clear, however, that (8) and (3) are logically the same. Or, a Conditional Proof of (7) is the same as an Indirect Proof of (1).

In constructing an Indirect Proof, first symbolize the argument, and then assume as a new premiss the denial of the entire conclusion no matter what that conclusion might be. Justify this assumption by writing 'IP' to its right-hand side. Next, deduce both a statement 'p' and its denial '$\sim p$'. We want to show that if the original argument is valid, then assuming the denial of its conclusion leads to a contradiction. This is a *critical step* in any use of the Indirect Method of Proving Validity.

Imagine the following hypotheticals correspond to various arguments such that these conditions are met: In the first case there is both a consistent premiss set and a true conclusion; in the second case there is an inconsistent premiss set and a true conclusion; in the third case there is an inconsistent premiss set and a false conclusion.

(9) $1 \supset 1$

          $0 \supset 1$

          $0 \supset 0$

The following represent the same arguments using the Indirect Method of Proving Validity.

(10) $(1 \cdot 0) \supset 1$

          $(0 \cdot 0) \supset 1$

          $(0 \cdot 1) \supset 0$

The second conjunct in each of the antecedents above represents the *denial* of the conclusion of the original argument. Hence, if the original conclusion were true, its denial would be false as in the first case of (10). Each antecedent of (10) represents an inconsistent premiss set—a premiss set which will yield both some statement 'p' and also its denial '$\sim p$'.

Notice in (9) and (10) we omitted one possible case. Corresponding to any *invalid* argument, we find

(11) $1 \supset 0$

Here we have a consistent premiss set and a false conclusion. Assuming the denial of the conclusion as a new premiss, we still have an invalid argument represented by this hypothetical:

(12) $(1 \cdot 1) \supset 0$

Having assumed the denial of our conclusion and having deduced a contradiction in constructing an Indirect Proof, we proceed in this way. Using Addition, to the statement at 'p' add the original conclusion of the argument. Then, using the statement at '$\sim p$' and appealing to Disjunctive Syllogism, assert the original conclusion at the last line in the overall proof. Let us examine a particular argument:

(13)   James' behavior may be viewed as basically anticipatory rather than reactive or as being environmentally controlled. That James' behavior is environmentally controlled is a sufficient condition for his being mentally deficient; but, if his behavior is viewed as basically anticipatory rather than reactive, he is emotionally sensitive. It follows, then, that James is mentally deficient or emotionally sensitive. (A, C, D, S)

Symbolizing (13), we may write

(14) $\therefore D \lor S$

     1) $A \lor C$ Pr

     2) $(C \supset D) \cdot (A \supset S)$ Pr

Assuming the denial of '$D \lor S$', we move to an explicit contradiction; then we obtain the desired conclusion using Addition followed by Disjunctive Syllogism.

(15) $\therefore D \lor S$

1)	$A \lor C$	Pr
2)	$(C \supset D) \cdot (A \supset S)$	Pr
3)	$\sim(D \lor S)$	IP
4)	$\sim D \cdot \sim S$	3, DeM
5)	$C \supset D$	2, Simp
6)	$(A \supset S) \cdot (C \supset D)$	2, Com
7)	$A \supset S$	6, Simp
8)	$\sim D$	4, Simp
9)	$\sim S \cdot \sim D$	4, Com
10)	$\sim S$	9, Simp
11)	$\sim C$	5, 8, MT
12)	$C \lor A$	1, Com
13)	A	12, 11, DS
14)	S	7, 13, MP
15)	$S \lor (D \lor S)$	14, Add
16)	$\therefore D \lor S$	15, 10, DS

In justifying the assumption at line 3, we write only 'IP', indicating that we are using the Indirect Method of Proving Validity. We do not write 'IP, $\therefore$ $D \lor S$' because we have already indicated the conclusion to be proved when we symbolized the original argument. In general the assumption introduced by any use of the Indirect Method of Proving Validity will be justified by writing 'IP' to its right-hand side.

The contradiction in (15) is made explicit at lines 10 and 14 in terms of 'S' and '$\sim S$'. However, this is not the only contradiction we could obtain. For instance, note the next proof of the same argument, (13):

(16) $\therefore D \lor S$

1)	$A \lor C$	Pr
2)	$(C \supset D) \cdot (A \supset S)$	Pr
3)	$\sim(D \lor S)$	IP
4)	$\sim D \cdot \sim S$	3, DeM
5)	$C \supset D$	2, Simp
6)	$(A \supset S) \cdot (C \supset D)$	2, Com
7)	$A \supset S$	6, Simp
8)	$\sim D$	4, Simp
9)	$\sim S \cdot \sim D$	4, Com
10)	$\sim S$	9, Simp
11)	$\sim A$	7, 10, MT
12)	C	1, 11, DS
13)	D	5, 12, MP
14)	$D \lor (D \lor S)$	13, Add
15)	$\therefore D \lor S$	14, 8, DS

Here our contradiction appears at lines 8 and 13 in terms of 'D' and '$\sim D$'.

In both (15) and (16) the scope of the assumption is indicated by a vertical bar drawn to the left-hand side of the statements in the proof falling under that scope. *As we have developed the Indirect Method of Proving Validity, the last statement within the scope of the assumption is obtained by Addition, while the statement ending the scope of the assumption is deduced by a use of Disjunctive Syllogism.*

Both the Conditional and Indirect Methods of Proving Validity may be used in constructing a single proof. In Chapter 7, Section 4, we considered this argument:

(17)   A necessary condition for theories in psychology not being constructed is the following: Neither experimental nor clinical psychologists are interested in this type of work, or neither statistical nor quantitative measurement is satisfactory for representing psychological data. Consequently, if experimental psychologists are interested in this type of work, then theories in psychology will be constructed if statistical measurement is satisfactory in representing psychological data. (T, E, C, S, Q)

Let us first symbolize (17), and then make two assumptions. The first of these assumptions will be used in a Conditional Proof, and the second in an Indirect Proof.

(18) $\therefore E \supset (S \supset T)$

1)	$\sim T \supset [\sim(E \lor C) \lor \sim(S \lor Q)]$	Pr
2)	E	CP, $\therefore S \supset T$
3)	$\sim(S \supset T)$	IP
4)	$\sim\sim(S \cdot \sim T)$	3, Df3
5)	$S \cdot \sim T$	4, DN
6)	S	5, Simp
7)	$\sim T \cdot S$	5, Com
8)	$\sim T$	7, Simp
9)	$\sim(E \lor C) \lor \sim(S \lor Q)$	1, 8, MP
10)	$E \lor C$	2, Add
11)	$\sim\sim(E \lor C)$	10, DN
12)	$\sim(S \lor Q)$	9, 11, DS
13)	$\sim S \cdot \sim Q$	12, DeM
14)	$\sim S$	13, Simp
15)	$S \lor (S \supset T)$	6, Add
16)	$S \supset T$	15, 14, DS
17)	$\therefore E \supset (S \supset T)$	2–16, CP

Notice in (18) we first assumed the antecedent of our original conclusion at line 2. Given 'E', we now want to deduce '$S \supset T$' by Indirect Proof. Consequently, we assume the denial of '$S \supset T$' at line 3. It would have been incorrect to have asserted '$\sim[E \supset (S \supset T)]$' at line 3. We do not want to reach the original conclusion of (18) by the Indirect Method of Proving Validity. Rather, we want to obtain

'$S \supset T$' by Indirect Proof and, having '$S \supset T$', move to '$E \supset (S \supset T)$' by Conditional Proof.

Also notice, whenever utilizing both Conditional and Indirect Proofs in a single proof of validity, that the Conditional Proof assumption is always made first. If we had first used the Indirect Method of Proving Validity to establish the validity of (17), we should have written

(19) $\therefore E \supset (S \supset T)$

   1) $\sim T \supset [\sim(E \lor C) \lor \sim(S \lor Q)]$ Pr
   2) $\sim[E \supset (S \supset T)]$ IP

But, given (19), we cannot continue with a Conditional Proof, for line 2 has no antecedent which can be assumed for a Conditional Proof.

We could construct another proof for (17) by making three assumptions, as in the following:

(19) $\therefore E \supset (S \supset T)$

1)	$\sim T \supset [\sim(E \lor C) \lor \sim(S \lor Q)]$	Pr
2)	E	CP, $\therefore S \supset T$
3)	S	CP, $\therefore T$
4)	$\sim T$	IP
5)	$\sim(E \lor C) \lor \sim(S \lor Q)$	1, 4, MP
6)	$E \lor C$	2, Add
7)	$\sim\sim(E \lor C)$	6, DN
8)	$\sim(S \lor Q)$	5, 7, DS
9)	$\sim S \cdot \sim Q$	8, DeM
10)	$\sim S$	9, Simp
11)	$S \lor T$	3, Add
12)	T	11, 10, DS
13)	$S \supset T$	3–12, CP
14)	$\therefore E \supset (S \supset T)$	2–13, CP

EXERCISES

Group A:

Symbolize the following arguments, using the suggested notation. Then, utilizing the Indirect Method of Proving Validity, construct proofs for each of the arguments.

(1) Either information theory is a branch of probability theory with many applications to communication systems and was initiated by communication scientists, or information theory is an old discipline and yet is a branch of probability theory with many applications to communication systems. Information theory isn't an

old discipline. Consequently, information theory is a branch of probability theory with many applications to communication systems, having been initiated by communication scientists. (*B, I, D*)

(2) If a commodity is tangible and communication processes are concerned with the flow of a commodity in a network, information is a tangible commodity in communication processes. Information isn't a tangible commodity in communication processes, although communication processes are concerned with the flow of a commodity in a network. Therefore, a commodity doesn't need to be tangible. (*T, F, P*)

(3) A contrastive grammar is a teaching device if, and only if, it may be used as a tool in the preparation of teaching materials. Now, a contrastive grammar may be used as a tool in the preparation of teaching materials and is one in which descriptive grammars of two languages are tied together. Wherefore, while a contrastive grammar is one in which descriptive grammars of two languages are tied together, it is also a teaching device. (*D, T, L*)

(4) That Yiddish is basically a German dialect if, and only if, it has identifying characteristics making it a member of the Germanic language family implies that Yiddish as a written language uses the modified Hebrew alphabet; moreover, that it isn't true that Yiddish has identifying characteristics making it a member of the Germanic language family if, and only if, it is basically a German dialect implies that Yiddish is completely synonymous with Hebrew. So either Yiddish is completely synonymous with Hebrew or, as a written language, Yiddish uses the modified Hebrew alphabet. (*D, C, A, S*)

(5) Either Yiddish as a written language uses a modified Hebrew alphabet and, like Hebrew, is written from left to right, or Yiddish is basically a German dialect and as a written language uses a modified Hebrew alphabet. That Yiddish has identifying characteristics which make it a member of the Germanic language family is a necessary condition for either Yiddish being basically a German dialect or, like Hebrew, being written from left to right. Hence, neither Yiddish doesn't have identifying characteristics making it a member of the Germanic language family nor Yiddish as a written language doesn't use a modified Hebrew alphabet. (*A, W, D, C*)

(6) If risk is a measure of potential exposure to system failure in business systems analysis, then precise measures of risk aren't always quantifiable if high risk can be characterized by low statistical probability. That precise measures of risk are always quantifiable implies that both high risk can be characterized by low statistical probability and risk is a measure of potential exposure in system failure in business systems analysis. Either risk is a measure of potential exposure to system failure in business systems analysis and precise measures of risk are always quantifiable, or risk may be increased and emerge as a dominant characteristic of an alternative selected through miscalculation of an input-output feedback error. Thus, risk can emerge as a dominant characteristic of an alternative selected

through miscalculation of an input-output feedback error and risk may also be increased. (*M, Q, C, I, E*)

(7) That relationships are bonds linking objects and attributes in a system process and symbiosis is a first-order relationship is implied by it not being the case both that symbiosis is a first-order relationship while synergy is a second-order one. Now, either a vital relationship doesn't always hold between two similar organisms or symbiosis isn't a first-order relationship. Therefore, that symbiosis isn't a first-order relationship is a sufficient and necessary condition for a vital relationship always holding between two similar organisms. (*B, F, S, H*)

(8) Either it isn't the case both that an essential part of a communication system is a transmitter even though the system mustn't have a receiver, or a channel conveying information from a transmitter to a receiver is vital to a communication system and an essential part of such a system is a transmitter. That a channel conveying information from a transmitter to a receiver is vital to a communication system is a sufficient condition for both a transmitter being an essential part of a communication system although the simplest system isn't obliged to have a feedback loop. So a communication system mustn't have a receiver unless an essential part of such a system is a transmitter and the simplest communication system is obliged to have a feedback loop. (*T, R, C, L*)

(9) If both a total system may be comprised of numerous subsystems and system objectives may define organizational purposes, then real-world systems are ideal only if both constraints may limit system operation and system attributes should be sacrificed for seemingly optimal system relationships. It isn't the case that system attributes should be sacrificed for seemingly optimal system relationships whenever system objectives may define organizational purposes. Thus, a necessary condition for asserting that a total system may be comprised of numerous subsystems is that real-world systems aren't ideal. (*C, D, I, L, S*)

(10) Either phonemes are signs, or either various members of a writing system aren't signs of a given language's phonemes while writing systems are sign systems or writing systems can be interpreted as meaningful but phonemes are meaningless. Phonemes aren't signs even though it isn't true that writing systems can be interpreted as meaningful while various members of a writing system aren't signs of a given language's phonemes. Consequently, either various members of a writing system are signs of a given language's phonemes or writing systems can't be interpreted as meaningful, but not both. (*P, L, W, I, M*)

Group B:

Symbolize the following arguments using the suggested notation, and then construct a proof of validity such that each proof uses both the Conditional and Indirect Methods of Proving Validity.

(1) That the circumference of this figure is determined by '$2\pi r$' is implied by this figure being a circle; moreover, that this figure is an ellipse implies that its circumference

isn't determined by '$2\pi r$'. So a sufficient condition for this figure not being an ellipse is that it's a circle. (D, C, E)

(2) Either William Faulkner didn't write *Sanctuary* or he did write *Of Human Bondage*, or he also wrote *As I Lay Dying*; nevertheless, he didn't write *Of Human Bondage*. Hence, unless Faulkner wrote *Sanctuary*, he didn't write *As I Lay Dying*. (S, B, D)

(3) Winslow Homer painted either "Gross Clinic" or "Life Line" (but not both) only if he loved the sea. That Homer didn't paint "The Wreck" is a necessary condition for it not being true that he painted "Life Line" if, and only if, he didn't paint "Gross Clinic". Therefore, that Homer painted "The Wreck" and "Kissing the Moon" implies that he loved the sea. (C, L, S, W, M)

(4) The following isn't true: We don't question the existence of Priam's Troy; moreover, we read about Heinrich Schliemann's digs, while studying George Grote's *History of Greece* and being interested in the Homeric stories. So, that we're interested in the Homeric stories is a sufficient condition for studying Grote's *History of Greece* only if we question the existence of Priam's Troy whenever we read about Schliemann's digs. (P, S, G, H)

(5) Either it isn't the case both that Napoleon Bonaparte escaped from Elba and didn't win at Waterloo, or he was defeated even though he escaped from Elba. If Napoleon was defeated, he escaped from Elba but didn't restore permanently the Empire. Wherefore, unless Napoleon escaped from Elba and restored permanently the empire, he didn't win at Waterloo. (E, W, D, R)

3. PROOFS OF INCONSISTENCY

As we know, an argument is inconsistent if all its premisses can never be true. In an inconsistent argument no matter how the premisses are interpreted in terms of truth and falsity, at least one premiss will always be false. Truth-table methods were used in Chapter 3 to establish inconsistency. We may now devise other means to prove the inconsistency of an argument. The procedure is simple enough! Symbolizing the argument in question, we then move toward some statement, 'p', and its formal denial, '$\sim p$'. Now, our Rules of Transformation guarantee if all the premisses of an argument are true, any statement obtained from these premisses must also be true. But 'p' and '$\sim p$', while both deduced from the premisses, cannot both be true. Hence, all the premisses cannot be true. The premiss set, and the argument, is therefore inconsistent.

The inconsistency of the following argument was established in Chapter 3 by truth-table means:

(1)   Either my Zipper Gripper will hold or I'll be most embarrassed, but not both. It isn't true that my Zipper Gripper will hold and I shall not be most embarrassed. Further, either I shall not be most embarrassed or my Zipper

Gripper will hold. My Zipper Gripper isn't going to hold. Therefore, I'll be most embarrassed. (G, E)

Symbolizing (1), we may then prove its inconsistency by deducing a contradiction.

(2) $\therefore E$

1)	$G \triangle E$	Pr
2)	$\sim(G \cdot \sim E)$	Pr
3)	$\sim E \lor G$	Pr
4)	$\sim G$	Pr
5)	$\sim(G \cdot E) \cdot \sim(\sim G \cdot \sim E)$	1, Df2
6)	$\sim(\sim G \cdot \sim E) \cdot \sim(G \cdot E)$	5, Com
7)	$\sim(\sim G \cdot \sim E)$	6, Simp
8)	$G \lor E$	7, Df1
9)	$G \lor \sim E$	3, Com
10)	$\sim E$	9, 4, DS
11)	$E \lor G$	8, Com
12)	G	11, 10, DS

The desired contradiction appears at lines 4 and 12. Of course once having these two lines, *any conclusion we please can be deduced by using Addition followed by Disjunctive Syllogism. An inconsistent premiss set implies every possible statement!*

EXERCISES

Group A:

(1) Given the premisses of (1), prove the conclusion, 'Either my Zipper Gripper won't hold or the party will be a crashing bore.' (G, P)

(2) Given the premisses of (2), show that they are contradictory by deducing the statements 'E' and '$\sim E$'.

Group B:

Symbolize the following arguments, using the suggested notation. Then show each argument is inconsistent by deducing a contradiction from the premiss set. Once having obtained a contradiction, move to the desired conclusion of the argument.

(1) Either the principles of quantum mechanics are applied to the chemistry of molecules or molecular-orbital theory is an exciting development in chemistry (but not both), or Newtonian laws are the sole basis of contemporary chemistry. The principles of quantum mechanics are applied to the chemistry of molecules and molecular-orbital theory is an exciting development in contemporary chemistry.

Further, Newtonian laws aren't the sole basis of contemporary chemistry. Accordingly, that Newtonian laws are the sole basis of contemporary chemistry implies that the principles of quantum mechanics aren't applied to the chemistry of molecules. (P, O, L)

(2) Either molecular-orbital theory assumes a molecule is comprised of nuclei fixed in space, or the electrons introduced into the nuclei's electrostatic field travel over the entire molecule while molecular-orbital theory does assume a molecule is comprised of nuclei fixed in space. Neither do the electrons introduced into the nuclei's electrostatic field travel over the entire molecule nor does molecular-orbital theory assume a molecule is comprised of nuclei fixed in space. Hence, molecular-orbital theory assumes a molecule is comprised of nuclei fixed in space. (T, E)

(3) In molecular-orbital theory the energy levels of the electrons must be determined or their orbitals described. It isn't the case that whenever the orbitals of the electrons aren't described, their energy levels must be determined. Consequently, the orbitals of electrons must be described or their density established. (L, O, D)

(4) Accepting the basic assumptions of molecular-orbital theory is a sufficient condition for asserting that if a molecule isn't in the electrostatic field of several nuclei concurrently, then an eigenfunction isn't used to represent an electron. But, an eigenfunction is used to represent an electron. Further, the basic assumptions of molecular-orbital theory are accepted in spite of the fact that a molecule isn't in the electrostatic field of several nuclei concurrently. So, that the basic assumptions of molecular-orbital theory are accepted is a sufficient condition for a molecule being in the electrostatic field of several nuclei concurrently. (A, M, E)

(5) If a linear velocity v is associated with a particle mass m, a linear momentum p is also associated with m. v is associated with m even though the acceleration a of m hasn't been determined. We may use Newton's second law of mechanics provided that it isn't the case a of m has been determined whenever v is associated with m. A linear momentum p is also associated with m only if the acceleration a of m has been determined. Therefore, we don't use Newton's second law of mechanics, but a of m has been determined only if a linear momentum p is associated with m. (V, M, A, L)

(6) Either Coulomb's law is misleading, or the following is: The force of attraction between two charged bodies is either directly proportional to the product of their charges or inversely proportional to the square of the distance between them, but not both. Now, the force of attraction between two charged bodies is directly proportional to the product of their charges and inversely proportional to the square of the distance between them. Coulomb's law isn't misleading despite the fact that the force of attraction between two charged bodies is neither directly proportional to the product of their charges nor inversely proportional to the square of the distance between them. Thus, the force of attraction between two charged bodies is directly proportional to the product of their charges if, and only if, it is also inversely proportional to the square of the distance between them. (*M*, *D*, *I*)

(7)   If light waves are composed of photons and not atoms, we may still expect to discover an interstellar ether-type substance. Now, it isn't the case both that light waves aren't composed of photons even though we may not still expect to discover an interstellar ether-type substance. Not only are light waves not composed of atoms, but as well we may not still expect to discover an interstellar ether-type substance. If we still may expect to discover an interstellar ether-type substance, we aren't familiar with the 1887 Michelson-Morley experiments. So, it is obvious that we aren't familiar with the 1887 Michelson-Morley experiments. (*P*, *A*, *S*, *E*)

(8)   Either blackbody radiation can be explained whenever quantum mechanics is accepted, or Max Planck's 1901 interpretation of his experiments isn't correct and his constant, *h*, must be revised. Planck's 1901 interpretation of his experiments is correct and quantum mechanics is accepted, but even so blackbody radiation can't be explained. Accordingly, Planck's constant, *h*, must be revised even though blackbody radiation can be explained. (*R*, *M*, *I*, *C*)

(9)   In a photoelectric effect if the frequency of the incident of light on a metallic electrode changes but the intensity of radiation doesn't, then either the intensity of radiation changes or the electrons' energy changes. The electrons' energy changes only if neither they are emitted from a metallic electrode nor the radiation frequency passes the value v_0. Either the intensity of radiation doesn't change, or neither the electrons are emitted from a metallic electrode nor does the radiation frequency pass the value v_0. Now, the frequency of the incident of light on a metallic electrode changes and the radiation frequency passes the value of v_0. Accordingly, not only does the frequency of the incident of light change, but also the intensity of radiation. (*F*, *I*, *E*, *M*, *V*)

(10) That we can't accept Louis de Broglie's 1924 "Investigations into Quantum Theory" is a necessary condition for either Newtonian mechanics sufficing to explain Max Planck's findings or light phenomena being explained in terms of waves. If neither the photoelectric effect can be explained nor can light phenomena be explained in terms of particles, light phenomena can be explained in terms of waves. Light phenomena can be explained in terms of either particles or waves only if we can accept de Broglie's 1924 "Investigations into Quantum Theory". Neither can the photoelectric effect be explained nor light phenomena explained in terms of particles, or either Newtonian mechanics is sufficient to explain Planck's findings or Robert Millikan in 1916 produced experimental evidence for *h*. Newtonian mechanics doesn't suffice to explain Planck's findings and Millikan didn't produce experimental evidence for *h* in 1916. Hence, if the photoelectric effect can be explained, light phenomena can be explained in terms of particles. (*B*, *N*, *P*, *E*, *W*, *M*)

As seen in Chapter 3, truth-table techniques can be used to determine whether a particular truth-functional statement is tautological. Other methods, resembling proofs, can also be employed. For example, to demonstrate that a *hypothetical statement* is tautological, using the Conditional Method of Proving Validity, we assume the antecedent as a premiss and then by our various Rules of Transformation deduce the consequent as the conclusion. We then demonstrate that if the premiss (the antecedent) is true, the conclusion (the consequent) must also be true. We know that a hypothetical statement can be false only when the antecedent is true and the consequent false. But, if an argument corresponding to a hypothetical statement is valid, the hypothetical statement is tautological.

Let us determine whether the following hypothetical statement is tautological:

(1)   If the cost of living doesn't stabilize or building loans become more plentiful, while building loans become more plentiful only if there is more spending, then the cost of living will stabilize only if there is more spending. (C, B, S)

Symbolizing (1), a truth-table shows at once that the statement is tautological:

(2) $[(\sim C \lor B) \cdot (B \supset S)] \supset (C \supset S)$

```
0 1 1 1 1 1 1 1   1  1 1 1
0 1 1 1 0 1 0 0   1  1 0 0
0 1 0 0 0 0 1 1   1  1 1 1
0 1 0 0 0 0 1 0   1  1 0 0
1 0 1 1 1 1 1 1   1  0 1 1
1 0 1 1 0 1 0 0   1  0 1 0
1 0 1 0 1 0 1 1   1  0 1 1
1 0 1 0 1 0 1 0   1  0 1 0
              ↑
```

But, we can also demonstrate that (1) is tautological by our new method. Let the antecedent of (1) serve as a premiss and the consequent as a conclusion in the following manner:

(3)

1)	$(\sim C \lor B) \cdot (B \supset S)$	CP, $\therefore C \supset S$
2)	$\sim C \lor B$	1, Simp
3)	$(B \supset S) \cdot (\sim C \lor B)$	1, Com
4)	$B \supset S$	3, Simp
5)	$C \supset B$	2, MI
6)	$C \supset S$	5, 4, HS
7)	$[(\sim C \lor B) \cdot (B \supset S)] \supset (C \supset S)$	1–6, CP

Since line 1 of (3) does imply line 6, we may assert line 7. Furthermore, '$[(\sim C \vee B) \cdot (B \supset S)] \supset (C \supset S)$' must be tautological simply because '$(\sim C \vee B) \cdot (B \supset S)$' does imply '$C \supset S$'.

Notice the scope of line 1 of (3) extends only through line 6. The scope of line 1 does *not* extend through line 7; line 7 is *not* deduced from line 1 of (3). In fact, line 7 is *not deduced from any statement* in (3)! Line 7 is *not* the conclusion of *any* argument, although that it is tautological is established by a Conditional Proof in lines 1–6.

We also can ascertain whether some nonhypothetical statement is tautological. Assume the denial of the statement in question by using an Indirect Proof. Next, move to a contradiction; that is, obtain one statement, 'p', and another, '$\sim p$'. Deducing both 'p' and '$\sim p$' establishes that the *denial* of the original statement is a contradiction—it can never be true. But, if the denial of the original statement can never be true, the original statement must always be true. The original statement, then, must be tautological. Consider this example:

(4)   Either the computer won't function properly, or if the tapes are secured whenever the computer functions properly, the tapes are secured. (C, T)

That (4) is a tautology can be established quickly by truth-table means:

(5) $\sim C \vee [(C \supset T) \supset T]$

```
0 1 1   1 1 1   1 1
0 1 1   1 0 0   1 0
1 0 1   0 1 1   1 1
1 0 1   0 1 0   0 0
          ↑
```

But we may also demonstrate that (4) is tautological by using the method of Indirect Proof. Assume the denial of '$\sim C \vee [(C \supset T) \supset T]$' and work toward a contradiction:

(6)

1)	$\sim\{\sim C \vee [(C \supset T) \supset T]\}$	IP
2)	$\sim\sim C \cdot \sim[(C \supset T) \supset T]$	1, DeM
3)	$\sim\sim C$	2, Simp
4)	$\sim[(C \supset T) \supset T] \cdot \sim\sim C$	2, Com
5)	$\sim[(C \supset T) \supset T]$	4, Simp
6)	$\sim\sim[(C \supset T) \cdot \sim T]$	5, Df3
7)	$(C \supset T) \cdot \sim T$	6, DN
8)	$C \supset T$	7, Simp
9)	$\sim T \cdot (C \supset T)$	7, Com
10)	$\sim T$	9, Simp
11)	$\sim C$	8, 10, MT
12)	$\sim C \vee \{\sim C \vee [(C \supset T) \supset T]\}$	11, Add
13)	$\sim C \vee [(C \supset T) \supset T]$	12, 3, DS

The contradiction appears at lines 3 and 11. Since the denial of '$\sim C \vee [(C \supset T) \supset T]$' leads to a contradiction, '$\sim C \vee [(C \supset T) \supset T]$' must be tautological. We notice also that line 13 of (6) does *not* fall within the scope of line 1. In fact, line 13 does not fall within the scope of any previous line in (6). The thirteenth statement is *not* the conclusion of *any* argument, for it is *not deduced from any premiss set.*

EXERCISES

Symbolize the following statements, using the suggested notation. Then, employing the methods developed in this section, demonstrate that each of the statements is a tautology.

(1) If scientists are interested not only in prediction but also in explanation, then scientists are interested in either description or prediction while they are also interested in explanation. (*P, E, D*)

(2) If scientists organize their findings whenever they collect data as well as confirm their observations if they construct theories, then scientists either organize their findings or confirm their observations whenever they collect data or construct theories. (*F, D, O, T*)

(3) If scientists construct theories only if they are interested in explanation, then that scientists construct theories and organize their findings implies they are interested in explanation at the same time they organize their findings. (*T, E, F*)

(4) Either it isn't the case both that government supports research but taxpayers don't, or it isn't the case both that industry doesn't support research while government also doesn't support it. (*G, P, I*)

(5) If research is supported provided scientists collect data, then either scientists collect data or knowledge is increased whenever either research is supported or knowledge is increased. (*R, S, K*)

(6) The following isn't the case: It isn't true that unless knowledge increases with research, costly expenditures aren't important; however, costly expenditures are important. (*K, E*)

(7) Either costly expenditures are important to support new research, or a necessary condition for sources of revenue not being found is that costly expenditures aren't important to support new research. (*C, S*)

(8) Either it is not the case that sources of revenue will be found to finance research whenever, and only whenever, the public appreciates the value of knowledge, or either sources of revenue will be found to finance research or the public doesn't appreciate the value of knowledge (but not both). (*S, P*)

(9) Either the public appreciates the value of knowledge, or costly expenditures are

important to support new research only if either sources of revenue are found or the public doesn't appreciate the value of knowledge. (*P, E, S*)

(10) If scientists are interested in explanation and prediction while finances are found to support their work, scientists are interested in explanation and prediction; further, if finances are found to support scientists' work, then they are interested in explanation and prediction whenever they are interested in explanation and prediction. (*S, F*)

5. DEMONSTRATIONS OF LOGICAL EQUIVALENCES

Any two statements, '*p*' and '*q*', are logically equivalent if, and only if, they both have the same truth-values given the same truth-conditions. Therefore, '*p*' and '*q*' are logically equivalent if, and only if, '$p \equiv q$' is tautological. Another way of expressing this is to say that *any statements '*p*' and '*q*' are logically equivalent if '*p*' implies '*q*' and '*q*' implies '*p*'*. For example, these statements are logically equivalent:

(1) (a) There is a lightning discharge if, and only if, there is an electrical discharge. (*L, E*)

　　(b) If there isn't a lightning discharge, there won't be an electrical discharge; moreover, there isn't a lightning discharge or there is an electrical discharge. (*L, E*)

Of course we can show these statements are logically equivalent by truth-table methods. Symbolizing (a) and (b), we form a biconditional and then construct a truth-table for this biconditional.

(2)　　　$(L \equiv E) \equiv [(\sim L \supset \sim E) \cdot (\sim L \lor E)]$

　　　　1 1 1　1　0 1 1 0 1 1 0 1 1 1
　　　　1 0 0　1　0 1 1 1 0 0 0 1 0 0
　　　　0 0 1　1　1 0 0 0 1 0 1 0 1 1
　　　　0 1 0　1　1 0 1 1 0 1 1 0 1 0
　　　　　　　↑

Or we can also show that '$L \equiv E$' and '$(\sim L \supset \sim E) \cdot (\sim L \lor E)$' are logically equivalent by proving *both* that '$L \equiv E$' implies '$(\sim L \supset \sim E) \cdot (\sim L \lor E)$' *and* that '$(\sim L \supset \sim E) \cdot (\sim L \lor E)$' implies '$L \equiv E$'.

(3)　　　　　　　　　　　　　　　∴ $(\sim L \supset \sim E) \cdot (\sim L \lor E)$

　　1)　　$L \equiv E$　　　　　　　　　Pr
　　2)　　$\sim (L \cdot \sim E) \cdot \sim (E \cdot \sim L)$　　1, Df4
　　3)　　$\sim (E \cdot \sim L) \cdot \sim (L \cdot \sim E)$　　2, Com

4)	$(E \supset L) \cdot \sim (L \cdot \sim E)$	3, Df3
5)	$(\sim L \supset \sim E) \cdot \sim (L \cdot \sim E)$	4, Trans
6)	$(\sim L \supset \sim E) \cdot (\sim L \vee \sim \sim E)$	5, DeM
7)	$\therefore (\sim L \supset \sim E) \cdot (\sim L \vee E)$	6, DN

and

		$\therefore L \equiv E$
1)	$(\sim L \supset \sim E) \cdot (\sim L \vee E)$	Pr
2)	$(\sim L \vee E) \cdot (\sim L \supset \sim E)$	1, Com
3)	$(\sim L \vee E) \cdot (E \supset L)$	2, Trans
4)	$(L \supset E) \cdot (E \supset L)$	3, MI
5)	$\sim (L \cdot \sim E) \cdot (E \supset L)$	4, Df3
6)	$\sim (L \cdot \sim E) \cdot \sim (E \cdot \sim L)$	5, Df3
7)	$\therefore L \equiv E$	6, Df4

Example (3) establishes that '$L \equiv E$' does imply '$(\sim L \supset \sim E) \cdot (\sim L \vee E)$' while '$(\sim L \supset \sim E) \cdot (\sim L \vee E)$' also implies '$L \equiv E$'. Hence, '$L \equiv E$' and '$(\sim L \supset \sim E)$ $\cdot (L \vee E)$' are logically equivalent. In general *we may show any two statements are logically equivalent by showing they imply each other.*

EXERCISES

Symbolize the following pairs of statements, using the suggested notation. Then, employing the method developed in this section, demonstrate that the statements in each pair are logically equivalent.

(1) (a) If there is an atom, x, of high electronegativity, then if x approaches an atom, y, of low electronegativity, the very strong attraction for electrons exerted by x may suffice to remove an electron from y. (H, L, S)

(b) If an atom, x, approaches an atom of low electronegativity, y, then if the atom x is of high electronegativity, the very strong attraction for electrons exerted by x may suffice to remove an electron from y. (L, H, S)

(2) (a) If two simple ions are produced by oxidation and an energy input is required, then the two original ions are at a lower state of potential energy than the two produced ones. (P, R, S)

(b) Unless two simple ions are produced by oxidation, neither are the two original ions at a lower state of potential energy than the two produced ones nor is an energy input not required. (P, S, R)

(3) (a) It isn't the case that a chemical bond is ionic if, and only if, it is metallic. (I, M)

(b) Either a chemical bond is ionic but not metallic, or it isn't ionic while being metallic. (I, M)

(4) (a) If we're to understand the beginnings of Gothic architecture, we must study the life of Abbot Suger and the royal Abbey Church of Saint-Denis. (G, S, D)

(b) A necessary condition for understanding the beginnings of Gothic architecture is that we study the life of Abbot Suger; moreover, a sufficient condition for studying the royal Abbey Church of Saint-Denis is that we understand the beginnings of Gothic architecture. (*G, S, D*)

(5) (a) Either Abbot Suger was chief advisor to Louis VI or he played a small role in the creation of a powerful French monarch, but it isn't the case both that Abbot Suger played a small role in the creation of a powerful French monarch while also being chief advisor to Louis VI. (*A, M*)

(b) That Abbot Suger was chief advisor to Louis VI implies he didn't play a small role in the creation of a powerful French monarch; further, either Abbot Suger did play a small role in the creation of a powerful French monarch or he was chief advisor to Louis VI. (*A, M*)

(6) (a) If Abbot Suger brought the Church and monarch together against the nobility, Louis VI rewarded the Church either by supporting the Papacy against the German emperors or by rebuilding Saint-Denis in a lavish style. (*S, P, D*)

(b) Either Louis VI rewarded the Church by supporting the Papacy against the German emperors if Abbot Suger brought the Church and monarch together against the nobility, or Abbot Suger brought the Church and monarch together against the nobility only if Louis VI rewarded the Church by rebuilding Saint-Denis in a lavish style. (*P, S, D*)

(7) (a) The Saint-Denis of Abbot Suger is Gothic if, and only if, the edifice stresses geometric planning and light. (*D, E*)

(b) The Saint-Denis of Abbot Suger isn't Gothic if, and only if, the edifice doesn't stress geometric planning and light. (*D, E*)

(8) (a) The ambulatory of Saint-Denis is Byzantine or Romanesque (but not both) in style, or it is Gothic (but not both). (*B, R, G*)

(b) Either the ambulatory of Saint-Denis is Romanesque in style, or it isn't Byzantine in style if, and only if, it is Gothic (but not both). (*R, B, G*)

(9) (a) That Dottie tours Charleston is a necessary condition for her visiting Julia whenever, and only whenever, she sees Summerville. (*C, J, S*)

(b) If Dottie visits Julia whenever she sees Summerville, then she either tours Charleston or visits Julia but doesn't see Summerville. (*J, S, C*)

(10) (a) If Dottie visits the West Side and the Ansonborough areas of Charleston, then she'll see either the Brandford-Horry House or the William Rhett House. (*S, A, H, R*)

(b) Dottie doesn't see the William Rhett House but does visit the West Side area of Charleston only if she either sees the Brandford-Horry House or doesn't visit the Ansonborough area of Charleston. (*R, S, H, A*)

9

An Axiomatic System

Thus far, in our mastery of logic we have learned particular truth-table techniques, Rules of Transformation, various methods of proof, and some rules of thumb which may be helpful in applying our logical apparatus to individual arguments. Our Rules of Transformation have been based on truth-table techniques of one sort or another; our truth-table techniques have been developed in part from the common sense notion that a statement is either true or false but not both, given the same interpretation. Moreover, we have come to understand the use of our logical operators—for instance, the horseshoe—by appealing to various examples of different uses of descriptive language.

While a careful examination of various uses of descriptive languages may suggest how we might understand logical operators, Rules of Transformation, and the like, it is not the case that logic, as such, is altogether justified by such an examination. Since our basic approach to the Truth-Functional Calculus has been founded on a familiarity with our own use of descriptive language, our approach has been very intuitive. Let us attempt now to be more exact. Let us construct an *axiomatic system* which is, in itself, independent of how we commonly use descriptive language.

We must notice at once that the system we shall develop has no meaning in one very important sense of 'meaning'. The system "says" nothing about anything; it has no particular *interpretation*, although there are many interpretations we could give the system. Perhaps you may find it helpful to view the following system as analogous to certain types of games. For example, consider the game of chess. Here, we have a "board" marked off in a specified way and "pieces" which may be moved about on the board—or even taken off the board—by following the rules of chess. The movable pieces are given names such as 'king', 'queen', and 'bishop'. But, that the pieces have these names is not essential, for they do not represent kings, queens, or bishops. In fact, as such, *the pieces do not represent anything at all.* In this sense they have no meaning, no interpretation. Yet, even so, we can do things with the pieces—for example, move them—according to the rules of chess.

We could, however, imagine that the chess pieces did represent something. We could give the game a meaning by giving the pieces an interpretation. For example, we might let the chessboard represent a battlefield and the several pieces various divisions of armies. The game of chess might then be used to plan military tactics. We can also imagine that such "war games" may lead to the winning of wars. Yet, whether or not the game is useful for some given purpose is a different question from, say, whether or not the rules of the game are correctly followed.

We, too, shall play something of a "game". Our "board" will be sheets of paper ruled into lines. The "pieces" will be various marks we are permitted to jot on the lines according to the rules of the "game". Like chess pieces, we shall not understand our marks as standing for anything at all, although we could give our "game" various interpretations. But, even though our "game" will have no interpretation—no meaning—we may still play the "game" according to the rules. Yet, playing the "game" will have at least this very important feature: Besides being challenging and fun, we shall be able to see just how the various marks may or may not be arranged according to the rules of play. *We may see just how the various marks are related to each other in the system.*

We have, in speaking of chess, implicitly acknowledged three important ways of viewing the game: We may speak of how the pieces can be moved and arranged according to the rules of the game; we may speak of an interpretation of the game; and we may speak of a useful interpretation. In their study of descriptive language, logicians often introduce the terms '*syntax*', '*semantics*', and '*pragmatics*'. These terms indicate important ways of viewing descriptive language—ways similar to those of viewing chess. *Syntax* is concerned with the rules governing the ways uninterpreted marks in a given system may or may not be arranged. *Semantics* deals with the rules governing the interpretation of the uninterpreted marks as statements. Semantics is also concerned with the general conditions making a statement true or false. *Pragmatics* refers to the rules governing the ascertaining of whether a given statement actually is true or false. The actual confirmation or falsification of a statement by some individual is a matter of pragmatics.

When speaking of syntactical, semantical, and pragmatical rules of language, we may speak of syntax and semantics as being "parasitic" on pragmatics, and syntax as "parasitic" on semantics. Surely, we want to say things which are actually true about the world. But this demands that we clarify those conditions which would make a statement true or false. Yet we are now forced to put our grammar in order

—a matter of syntax. Only from an academic point of view are we able to speak of pure syntax, pure semantics, and pure pragmatics as isolated sorts of rules. However, it is this academic viewpoint we shall adopt in developing the following system—*a purely syntactical system.*

Roughly, we shall understand an axiomatic system contains some initial lines of marks—the axioms—from which other lines of marks are deduced by various syntactical rules of the system. Because our system is governed solely by syntactical rules, it is inappropriate to speak of the truth or falsity of the initial assumptions or axioms. The axioms are simply strings, or groups, of marks. They are formulae; not statements. Somewhat like a master chess player who is interested only in the moves and countermoves of the game, logicians and mathematicians may view their study not to be about the meaning, interpretation, or truth of their subject matter. Rather, they are very interested in ascertaining what moves can be made with certain marks, given a certain set of (syntactical) rules. Of course, this is not to say that the work of the logician and mathematician has no application to the world about us, for it does. But, such applications are a matter of semantics and pragmatics, not of syntax.

In constructing any axiomatic system, the following requirements must be met. (1) There must be a list of marks undefined in that system. These are the *primitive marks* of the system which, coupled with any other marks explicitly defined in terms of the primitives, are the only marks used in the system. (2) A purely formal (syntactical) method must be provided which allows the marks of (1) to be grouped in ways appropriate to the system. Without appealing to any interpretation of these marks, we must be able to distinguish which combinations of marks (formulae) are appropriate in the system and which are not. Those formulae (groups of marks) appropriate to the system are called the '*well-formed formulae*' (*wff*) of the system. (3) We must syntactically distinguish which of the wff are axioms of the system. (4) There must be a syntactical method for determining which sequence of lines of wff will count as well-constructed sequences of lines and which are not well-constructed within the system. How these conditions are realized is indicated in the following discussion.

In our axiomatic system there will be three types of primitive marks: (1) logical operators, (2) punctuation marks, and (3) variables. These primitive marks may be understood to be *analogous to* chess pieces which have no interpretation beyond their appropriate moves in the game. The marks are

(1) *Logical operators:* ' $\sim$, $\vee$'
(2) *Punctuation marks:* '$\{ [( )] \}$'
(3) *Variables:* '$p, q, r, s, \ldots$'

For convenience we shall call ' $\sim$ ' the tilde and ' $\vee$ ' the wedge. The punctuation marks shall be used in the system as they have been used in previous chapters to indicate scope of operators and avoid ambiguity. The "variables" are understood as having no range or values; in particular we do not understand them as statement variables, for that would give our system an interpretation. Therefore, in this chapter 'p', 'q', 'r', 's', $\cdots$ may be understood as "pseudovariables".

The following rules determine which combinations of primitive marks (which formulae) are well-formed formulae within the system and which are not.

WFF1:   Any *single* variable is a wff. Such a wff is called '*atomic*'. All other wff are called '*molecular*'.

WFF2:   Any two wff connected by the wedge is a wff, and the wedge must always be flanked on both its left- and right-hand sides by wff.

WFF3:   Any wff preceded by the tilde is a wff, and the tilde must always be flanked only on its right-hand side by wff.

WFF4:   No other formulae except those permitted by these rules, and the logical definitions to be presented below, are to count as wff.

Given these rules of well-formed formulae, an indefinitely large number of wff may be written in the system. These rules also serve to exclude just as many other groups of primitive marks as inappropriate formulae within the system.

The axioms of the system are

A1: $\sim (p \lor p) \lor p$

A2: $\sim p \lor (p \lor q)$

A3: $\sim (p \lor q) \lor (q \lor p)$

A4: $\sim (\sim p \lor q) \lor [\sim (r \lor p) \lor (r \lor q)]$

These axioms are consistent, independent, and complete. Axioms are consistent if some formulae 'p' and '$\sim p$' are not both deducible from the axioms. Any axiom is independent of the remaining axioms if it cannot be deduced from them. We may say that an axiom set is complete if, when we add another well-formed formula as a new axiom, either that new axiom is not independent or the expanded axiom set is inconsistent.

The ensuing rules are used to determine which sequence of lines of wff are to count as *well-constructed* in the system. Further, any wff obtainable from the axioms by the following rules is a *theorem* of the system. We assume R1, Modus Ponens, as the one primitive rule of inference in the system. R2 and R3 are rules of substitution, and R4 and R5 are rules of replacement.

R1:   If '$p \supset q$' appears as a wff in a sequence of wff and 'p' also appears in that sequence, we may then assert 'q' as a wff in that sequence. (MP)

R2:   In any rule of inference—MP or any derived rule of inference (DRI)—we may substitute any wff at any occurrence of a given atomic wff provided we make the same substitution at each occurrence of the given atomic wff throughout the entire rule of inference.

R3:   We may substitute any wff for any given atomic wff in an *axiom* or *theorem* provided we make the same substitution at each occurrence of the given atomic wff throughout the entire axiom or theorem.

R4: We may replace any wff by its definitional equivalence. Such a replacement of definitionally equivalent wff may be performed on "parts" of a wff, these "parts" themselves being wff. This replacement need not be performed at every occurrence of the same "part" of a wff.

R5: Given any theorem of the form '$p \equiv q$', then 'p' may be replaced by 'q' (and vice versa) in any wff. Such a replacement may be performed on "parts" of a wff, these "parts" themselves being wff. This replacement need not be performed at every occurrence of the same "part" of a wff.

Solely for the purpose of brevity in generating well-constructed sequences of wff, we adopt the following definitional equivalences:

D1:   '$p \cdot q$' = '$\sim(\sim p \vee \sim q)$'   Df

D2:   '$p \supset q$' = '$\sim p \vee q$'   Df

D3:   '$p \equiv q$' = '$\sim[\sim(\sim p \vee q) \vee \sim(\sim q \vee p)]$'   Df

Our task is to prove theorems and derive further rules of inference within the system. A *proof* is understood as any finite sequence of wff commencing with at least one axiom or theorem—and only axioms or theorems—and generated by appeals to R1–R5, D1–D3, or any derived rules of inference (DRI) previously obtained in the system. A *derivation* is understood as any finite sequence of wff commencing with at least one assumption which is a wff but not an axiom or a theorem. Like a proof, a derivation will be generated by appeals to R1–R5, D1–D3, or any previous axioms or theorems in the system, or derived rules of inference (DRI).

In proving theorems and deriving rules of inference in the system, we shall name each wff in a sequence of wff by writing a numeral to its left-hand side. The justification of each wff in a sequence of wff will be written to the right-hand side of that wff.

You will find in the following pages both unproved theorems and underived derived rules of inference. Some of these theorems and DRI are marked with an asterisk, '*'. You should construct a proof or derivation for these as exercises for this chapter. Those theorems not proved or rules of inference not derived *but not marked with an asterisk* are simply to be assumed as being theorems or rules of inference in the system. If you are brave, you may want to try your hand at these, too. Do not be surprised if you find them difficult.

A word to the wise: Since in the following proofs and derivations we have to select our beginning lines, it becomes even more important *to start with the conclusion and work backward until you see some previously established line you can use.*

T1:   '$(p \vee p) \supset p$' is a theorem.

Proof:

1) $\sim(p \lor p) \lor p$ A1
2) $(p \lor p) \supset p$ 1, D2, R4 $(p \lor p/p, p/q)$

The proof of Theorem 1 begins with Axiom 1 and then moves to the conclusion by an appeal to Definition 2. Yet, to use Definition 2 in this case, we must also make use of R4, substituting '$p \lor p$' for 'p' and 'p' for 'q' in the definition. This is indicated by the slash notation. However, *by convention, when using R2, R4, or R5 in constructing a sequence of lines of wff, we shall not note our substitution (or replacement) rules or substitution (or replacement) instances in our justifications.* Hence, by convention, the proof of Theorem 1 is constructed in this way:

1) $\sim(p \lor p) \lor p$ A1
2) $(p \lor p) \supset p$ 1, D2

*T2:   '$p \supset (p \lor q)$' is a theorem.

*T3:   '$(p \lor q) \supset (q \lor p)$' is a theorem.

*T4:   '$(p \supset q) \supset [(r \lor p) \supset (r \lor q)]$' is a theorem.

T5:   '$(p \supset q) \supset [(r \supset p) \supset (r \supset q)]$' is a theorem.

Proof:

1) $(p \supset q) \supset [(r \lor p) \supset (r \lor q)]$ T4
2) $(p \supset q) \supset [(\sim r \lor p) \supset (\sim r \lor q)]$ 1, $(\sim r/r)$
3) $(p \supset q) \supset [(r \supset p) \supset (\sim r \lor q)]$ 2, D2
4) $(p \supset q) \supset [(r \supset p) \supset (r \supset q)]$ 3, D2

The justification of line 2 in the proof above is understood as "line 2 comes from line 1 by an appeal to R3 and substituting '$\sim r$' for 'r'." Once more we use the slash notation to indicate our substitution instances—the wff on the left of the slash being substituted for the wff on the right of the slash. *By convention, when appealing to a use of R3, we shall not write 'R3' in our justification, but we shall indicate our substitution instances by using the slash notation.*

DRI 1 (HS):   If '$p \supset q$' and '$q \supset r$' are theorems, then '$p \supset r$' is also a theorem.

Derivation:

1) $p \supset q$ Assump
2) $q \supset r$ Assump
3) $(p \supset q) \supset [(r \supset p) \supset (r \supset q)]$ T5
4) $(q \supset r) \supset [(p \supset q) \supset (p \supset r)]$ 3, $(q/p, r/q, p/r)$
5) $(p \supset q) \supset (p \supset r)$ 4, 2, MP
6) $p \supset r$ 5, 1, MP

The first two lines in the derivation of DRI 1 are assumptions, as indicated by their justifications. Theorem 5 is then asserted in line 3 of the derivation. Appropriate substitutions in line 4, made possible by R3, followed by two uses of Modus Ponens, yield the desired line, '$p \supset r$'. Remember a derivation, as opposed to a proof, always makes use of at least one assumption, as in the first two lines of DRI 1.

T6:   '$\sim p \lor p$' is a theorem.

Proof:

1) $p \supset (p \lor q)$ T2
2) $p \supset (p \lor p)$ 1, (p/q)
3) $(p \lor p) \supset p$ T1
4) $p \supset p$ 2, 3, HS
5) $\sim p \lor p$ 4, D2

*DRI 2:   If '$p \lor q$' is a theorem, then '$q \lor p$' is also a theorem.

T7:   '$p \lor \sim p$' is a theorem.

Proof:

1) $\sim p \lor p$ T6
2) $p \lor \sim p$ 1, DRI 2

*T8:   '$p \supset \sim \sim p$' is a theorem.
    *DRI 3:   If '$p \supset q$' is a theorem and 'r' any wff, then '$(r \lor p) \supset (r \lor q)$' is also a theorem.

T9:   '$\sim \sim p \supset p$' is a theorem.

Proof:

1) $p \supset \sim \sim p$ T8
2) $\sim p \supset \sim \sim \sim p$ 1, $(\sim p/p)$
3) $(p \lor \sim p) \supset (p \lor \sim \sim \sim p)$ 2, DRI 3
4) $p \lor \sim p$ T7
5) $p \lor \sim \sim \sim p$ 3, 4, MP
6) $\sim \sim \sim p \lor p$ 5, DRI 2
7) $\sim \sim p \supset p$ 6, D2

In the proof above, line 3 comes from line 2 by a use of DRI 3. Here it is necessary to appeal to R2 using the substitutions, '$(\sim p/p, \sim \sim \sim p/q, p/r)$'. Similar comments may be made concerning the justification of line 6.

Complete each of the incomplete justifications in the following proof.

T10:   '$(p \cdot q) \supset p$' is a theorem.

Proof:

1) $p \supset (p \vee q)$ T2
2) $\sim p \supset (\sim p \vee \sim q)$ 1,
3) $\sim \sim p \vee (\sim p \vee \sim q)$ 2,
4) $(\sim p \vee \sim q) \vee \sim \sim p$ 3,
5) $\sim \sim (\sim p \vee \sim q) \vee \sim \sim p$ 4,
6) $\sim (p \cdot q) \vee \sim \sim p$ 5,
7) $(p \cdot q) \supset \sim \sim p$ 6,
8) $\sim \sim p \supset p$ T9
9) $(p \cdot q) \supset p$ 7, 8,

DRI 4 (Simp): If '$p \cdot q$' is a theorem, then 'p' is also a theorem.

DRI 5 (Add):   If 'p' is a theorem and 'q' any wff, then '$p \vee q$' is also a theorem.

T11:   '$(p \supset q) \supset (\sim q \supset \sim p)$' is a theorem.

Hint: Begin with Theorem 4.

DRI 6: If '$p \supset q$' is a theorem, then '$\sim q \supset \sim p$' is also a theorem.

DRI 7 (Conj): If 'p' and 'q' are theorems, then '$p \cdot q$' is also a theorem. (*In the following derivation, justify all the lines not yet justified.*)

Derivation:

1) p Assump
2) q Assump
3) $p \supset (p \vee q)$ T2
4) $\sim \sim q \supset (\sim \sim q \vee \sim p)$
5) $p \supset \sim \sim p$ T8
6) $q \supset \sim \sim q$
7) $q \supset (\sim \sim q \vee \sim p)$
8) $\sim \sim q \vee \sim p$
9) $\sim q \supset \sim p$
10) $(\sim p \vee \sim q) \supset (\sim p \vee \sim p)$
11) $\sim (\sim p \vee \sim p) \supset \sim (\sim p \vee \sim q)$
12) $(p \vee p) \supset p$ T1
13) $(\sim p \vee \sim p) \supset \sim p$
14) $\sim \sim p \supset \sim (\sim p \vee \sim p)$
15) $p \supset \sim \sim p$ T8
16) $p \supset \sim (\sim p \vee \sim p)$
17) $\sim (\sim p \vee \sim p)$
18) $\sim (\sim p \vee \sim q)$
19) $p \cdot q$

*T12:   '$(p \cdot q) \supset (q \cdot p)$' is a theorem.

   *DRI 8:   If 'p' is a theorem, then '$\sim \sim p$' is also a theorem.

   *DRI 9:   If '$\sim \sim p$' is a theorem, then 'p' is also a theorem.

Give the appropriate justification for each of the unjustified lines in the following proof.

T13 (DN):   '$p \equiv \sim \sim p$' is a theorem.

   Proof:

   1) $p \supset \sim \sim p$ T8
   2) $\sim \sim p \supset p$ T9
   3) $\sim p \lor \sim \sim p$
   4) $\sim \sim \sim p \lor p$
   5) $(\sim p \lor \sim \sim p) \cdot (\sim \sim \sim p \lor p)$
   6) $\sim [\sim (\sim p \lor \sim \sim p) \lor \sim (\sim \sim \sim p \lor p)]$
   7) $p \equiv \sim \sim p$

   *DRI 10:   If '$p \cdot q$' is a theorem, then '$q \cdot p$' is also a theorem.

   *DRI 11 (CD):   If '$p \supset q$', '$r \supset s$', and '$p \lor r$' are theorems, then '$q \lor s$' is also a theorem.

   *DRI 12 (MT):   If '$p \supset q$' is a theorem and '$\sim q$' is a theorem, then '$\sim p$' is also a theorem.

   *DRI 13 (DS):   If '$p \lor q$' and '$\sim p$' are theorems, then 'q' is also a theorem.

   *DRI 14:   If '$p \lor p$' is a theorem, then 'p' is also a theorem.

Justify each of the unjustified lines in the following proof.

T14 (Taut):   '$p \equiv (p \lor p)$' is a theorem.

   Proof:

   1) $p \supset (p \lor q)$ T2
   2) $p \supset (p \lor p)$
   3) $(p \lor p) \supset p$ T1
   4) $\sim p \lor (p \lor p)$
   5) $\sim (p \lor p) \lor p$
   6) $[\sim p \lor (p \lor p)] \cdot [\sim (p \lor p) \lor p]$
   7) $\sim \{\sim [\sim p \lor (p \lor p)] \lor \sim [\sim (p \lor p) \lor p]\}$
   8) $p \equiv (p \lor p)$

*T15 (Taut):   '$p \equiv (p \cdot p)$' is a theorem.

*T16 (Com):   '$(p \lor q) \equiv (q \lor p)$' is a theorem.

*T17 (Com):   '$(p \cdot q) \equiv (q \cdot p)$' is a theorem.

*T18 (Com):   '$(p \equiv q) \equiv (q \equiv p)$' is a theorem.

*T19 (Trans):   '$(p \supset q) \equiv (\sim q \supset \sim p)$' is a theorem.

Give the appropriate justification for each unjustified line in the following derivation.

DRI 15:   If '$p \equiv q$' is a theorem, then '$\sim p \equiv \sim q$' is also a theorem.

Derivation:

1) $p \equiv q$ Assump
2) $\sim[\sim(\sim p \lor q) \lor \sim(\sim q \lor p)]$
3) $\sim[\sim(q \lor \sim p) \lor \sim(\sim q \lor p)]$
4) $\sim[\sim(q \lor \sim p) \lor \sim(p \lor \sim q)]$
5) $\sim[\sim(p \lor \sim q) \lor \sim(q \lor \sim p)]$
6) $\sim[\sim(\sim \sim p \lor \sim q) \lor \sim(q \lor \sim p)]$
7) $\sim[\sim(\sim \sim p \lor \sim q) \lor \sim(\sim \sim q \lor \sim p)]$
8) $\sim p \equiv \sim q$

In constructing a derivation for DRI 15, we might have been tempted to do the following:

Derivation:

1) $p \equiv q$ Assump
2) $\sim p \equiv \sim q$ 1, $(\sim p/p, \sim q/q)$

The justification of line 2 suggests that it comes from line 1 by an appeal to R3 and substitutions of '$\sim p$' for 'p' and '$\sim q$' for 'q'. This, however, is a *misuse* of R3. R3 allows for certain sorts of substitutions in *axioms* or *theorems*. But, '$p \equiv q$' is neither an axiom nor a theorem of the system—it is an assumption.

*DRI 16:   If '$p \equiv q$' is a theorem and 'r' any wff, then '$(r \lor p) \equiv (r \lor q)$' is also a theorem.

*T20 (MI):   '$(\sim p \lor q) \equiv (p \supset q)$' is a theorem.

*T21 (DeM):   '$(p \lor q) \equiv \sim(\sim p \cdot \sim q)$' is a theorem.

*T22 (DeM):   '$\sim(p \lor q) \equiv (\sim p \cdot \sim q)$' is a theorem.

*T23 (DeM):   '$(p \cdot q) \equiv \sim(\sim p \lor \sim q)$' is a theorem.

*T24 (DeM):   '$\sim(p \cdot q) \equiv (\sim p \lor \sim q)$' is a theorem.

T25:   '$[p \lor (q \lor r)] \supset [q \lor (p \lor r)]$' is a theorem.

T26 (Assoc):   '$[p \lor (q \lor r)] \equiv [(p \lor q) \lor r]$' is a theorem.

T27 (Assoc):   '$[p \cdot (q \cdot r)] \equiv [(p \cdot q) \cdot r]$' is a theorem.

*__T28__ (Exp):   '$[(p \cdot q) \supset r] \equiv [p \supset (q \supset r)]$' is a theorem.

*__T29__: '$p \supset [q \supset (p \cdot q)]$' is a theorem.

T30 (Dist):   '$[p \lor (q \cdot r)] \equiv [(p \lor q) \cdot (p \lor r)]$' is a theorem.

T31 (Dist):   '$[p \cdot (q \lor r)] \equiv [(p \cdot q) \lor (p \cdot r)]$' is a theorem.

   While the axiomatic system we have developed allows an indefinitely large number of theorems and derived rules of inference to be generated, we shall end our present work with Theorem 31. Notice every argument form used in Chapter 5 now has associated with it either a primitive rule of inference or a derived rule of inference.

R1	Modus Ponens
DRI 1	Hypothetical Syllogism
DRI 4	Simplification
DRI 5	Addition
DRI 7	Conjunction
DRI 9	Constructive Dilemma
DRI 10	Modus Tollens
DRI 11	Disjunctive Syllogism

Also every logical equivalence used in Chapter 7, except those involving exclusive disjunction, appears as a theorem in our axiomatic system.

T13	Double Negation
T14 and T15	Tautology
T16–T18	Commutation
T19	Transposition
T20	Material Implication
T22 and T24	De Morgan's Laws
T26 and T27	Association
T29	Exportation
T30 and T31	Distribution

10

Categorical Statements and Syllogisms

Our present methods of constructing proofs are not sufficient to establish the validity of such arguments as

(1)   All mariners are pugnacious people.
        All sailors are mariners.
        So, all sailors are pugnacious people.

Letting '*M*' stand for 'All mariners are pugnacious people', '*S*' for 'All sailors are mariners', and '*P*' for 'All sailors are pugnacious people', we may symbolize (1) in this way:

(2)   ∴ *P*
    1) *M*   Pr
    2) *S*   Pr

But surely, none of the Rules of Transformation now at our disposal will allow us to move from the premiss set of (2) to its conclusion. Given only the Truth-Functional Calculus, we cannot prove the validity of (1), even though we no doubt *feel* it is valid. Surely, *if* the premises of (1) are all true, *then* the conclusion must also be true! So we must expand our logic.

The basic unit of analysis in the Truth-Functional Calculus is the statement. No matter how far we continue to analyze a statement into its component statements, we always end with statements. But, to establish the validity of such arguments as (1), we require more subtle methods of analysis. The validity of (1) depends upon the "inner" structure of the statements occurring in the argument. Exactly what this inner structure is can be clarified in several distinct, but related, ways. In this chapter we shall approach the problem from a rather traditional viewpoint. For clarification, however, we also shall introduce some more modern devices such as the concept of a *set* and the use of Venn diagrams.

1. CATEGORICAL STATEMENTS

Throughout the history of logic—from Aristotle into the nineteenth century— four particular *types* of statements have received special attention. These types of statements are called *'categorical statements'* to distinguish them from, say, hypothetical statements. Examples of categorical statements are

(1)   All cats are fish-eaters.
         No whales are fish.
         Some snakes are poisonous.
         Some people are not mendacious.

The *types*, of which these examples are instances, have been given the names 'A', 'E', 'I', and 'O'. These letter-names are taken from vowels of the Latin words *'affirmo'*—'I affirm', and *'nego'*—'I deny'. Thus, the **A** statement 'All cats are fish-eaters' and the **I** statement 'Some snakes are poisonous' both affirm something. However, the **E** statement 'No whales are fish' and the **O** statement 'Some people are not mendacious' deny something.

The various types of categorical statements are often represented in these ways:

(2) **A:**   All *S* are *P*.
    E: No *S* are *P*.
    I: Some *S* are *P*.
    O: Some *S* are not *P*.

Any categorical statement expressed in one of these four ways is said to be in *'standard form'*.

The '*S*' and '*P*' in (2) stand in place of **terms**. '*S*' designates a **subject term** and '*P*' a **predicate term** of a categorical statement. We should be careful here, for we must not understand 'subject term' and 'predicate term' grammatically, although words used in different grammatical ways may indicate a term of a categorical statement. For example, 'fish' grammatically functions as a substantive in 'All whales are fish', whereas 'mendacious' is used as an adjective in 'Some people are not mendacious'. Verbs also are used to express terms. 'All metals expand' may be expressed as 'All metals are expandable'. Furthermore, a subject or predicate term is *not* necessarily expressed by a single word. It is not uncommon to find the subject *or* predicate term indicated by clauses:

(3)   The soldiers who are on the front holding back the enemy onslaught are the best fighting men in the regiment.

Here the clause 'soldiers who are on the front holding back the enemy onslaught' expresses the subject term. The predicate term is indicated by 'the best fighting men in the regiment'. Remember, *subject term* and *predicate term* are concepts of logic and not grammar.

When categorical statements are in standard form, as in (1), we find the words 'all', 'no', or 'some' introducing the various statements. These words are called **'quantifiers'** because they answer the question 'how many?'. When categorical statements are *not* in standard form, we may find various words used in place of 'all', 'no', or 'some'. For instance, none of the following categorical statements is in standard form:

(4) a) A saint is a prayerful person.
  b) Any saint is a prayerful person.
  c) Anybody who is a saint is a prayerful person.
  d) Every saint is a prayerful person.
  e) Everyone who is a saint is a prayerful person.
  f) None but prayerful persons are saints.
  g) Only prayerful persons are saints.
  h) The saint is a prayerful person.
  i) Whatever is a saint is a prayerful person.
  j) Whoever is a saint is a prayerful person.

And, there are cases in which *no* word is used in place of 'all':

  k) Saints are prayerful persons.

Each of these examples, however, can be put into a *standard form* categorical statement:

  All saints are prayerful persons.

Instead of 'no', we might find 'never', 'nobody', 'none', or 'nothing' expressing the quantifier of an **E** statement. For example,

> A standard chemical substance never is phlogiston.
> None of the standard chemical substances is phlogiston.
> Nothing which is a standard chemical substance is phlogiston.

may all be put into standard form:

> No standard chemical substances are phlogiston.

In place of 'some' the words 'a', 'an', 'a certain', 'a few', 'a suitable', 'one', 'somebody', 'someone', 'something', 'the', 'there exists', 'there is', and 'there are' are frequently used. We must remember, however, that 'a', 'an', and 'the' are also used in place of the universal quantifier 'all'. *How* we interpret 'a', 'an', and 'the' is very much dependent upon the context and intended meaning of the statements in which these words appear:

> A mammal is warm-blooded.

or

> The mammal is warm-blooded.

surely means

> All mammals are warm-blooded.

On the other hand

> A thief is caught.

does not mean in any ordinary context

> All thieves are caught.

'A thief is caught' is usually understood as 'Some thief is caught'. There are cases not as clear, however. For instance, if we say 'A student is punctual', do we mean 'All students are punctual' or 'Some student is punctual'? To answer this question, we need more information about the context of 'A student is punctual'. So always remember, when putting a categorical statement into standard form, to read the statement carefully, consider its context, and capture in symbols the intended meaning.

> *When we put a categorical statement into STANDARD FORM, we shall use only 'all', 'no', or 'some' as our quantifiers, and the quantifier shall be the first word in the statement followed directly by the subject term.*

Not only are quantifiers and terms found in categorical statements, there is also the **copula** (Latin for 'bond', 'tie', or 'fastening'). When overtly expressed, the copula takes some grammatical form of the verb 'to be'. But, the copula may not be overtly expressed in a categorical statement. 'Whales breathe' makes no use of 'to be'. However, 'Whales breathe' may be rewritten as 'All whales are breathing things'. From a rhetorical viewpoint this statement is awkward, but it does retain the exact meaning of 'Whales breathe' *and* makes the copula explicit. *Any categorical statement can be expressed in such a way that some grammatical form of the verb 'to be' is used to express the copula.* Now, as logicians, we are not concerned with the tense of 'to be'. The example 'Categorical statements *were* the basis of much medieval logic' uses a past tense of 'to be'. For the purposes of *logical analysis* we may write 'Categorical statements *are* the basis of much medieval logic'. *The copula is tenseless in logic.* Neither shall we be interested in whether some grammatical form of 'to be' is singular or plural. 'The dodo bird is extinct' may be rephrased as 'All dodo birds are extinct'. *The logical copula is neither singular nor plural.*

> *To facilitate uniformity of expression, when putting a categorical statement into standard form we shall always use either 'are' or 'are not' to indicate the copula.*

For instance, the next example is *not* in standard form:

(5)   The duckbilled platypus lays eggs.

(5) may, however, be put into standard form:

(6)   All duckbilled platypuses are egg-laying things.

Summarizing, a categorical statement is considered in standard form when it is an instance of one of the following, where 'S' designates the subject term and 'P' the predicate term:

(7)   **A:**   All S are P.
      E: No S are P.
      I: Some S are P.
      O: Some S are not P.

Categorical statements also may be interpreted as making assertions about **sets** (class, collection, group, universe) and relations between sets, where a set is understood as any well-defined collection of distinguishable, individual things. In that a particular thing belongs to a set, it is a **member of** that set. In our present usage we are to understand the word 'thing' in a very broad sense. For example, persons, textbooks, chemicals, atoms, neutrinos, genes, and numbers all count as "things".

In that we interpret categorical statements as making assertions about sets and relations between sets, we understand both the subject and predicate terms as designating particular sets. Such sets may be related in one of the following ways. One set is **included in** another set if all the members of the first set are also members of the second set; however, all the members of the second set need not be members of the first set. One set is **excluded from** another set if the two sets have no common member. One set is **partially included in** another if some members of the first set are also members of the second. Finally, one set is **partially excluded from** another set if some members of the first are not also members of the second. A statements now may be interpreted as asserting set inclusion and E statements as asserting set exclusion; I statements may be read as asserting partial set inclusion and O statements as asserting partial set exclusion.

In speaking of sets, contemporary logicians carefully distinguish a set from the members of that set. From a contemporary viewpoint, sets need not have any members at all. While 'poltergeist' designates a set in 'All poltergeists are demons', it is an open question whether there are any poltergeists or not. *If* there is a poltergeist, *then* it will be a demon. But, there may not be any poltergeists. This contemporary viewpoint concerning sets and their members is the **hypothetical interpretation of categorical statements**—*if* there is a member of *S*, **then** it is also a member of *P*. In particular, whether or not the set indicated by the subject term of an A or E statement has a member is an open question. In contemporary logic, A and E statements are always given a hypothetical interpretation.

Prior to the nineteenth century the subject term of any categorical statement was always thought of as designating a set with at least one existing member. And certainly the subject terms of A and E statements were viewed this way. Such a reading of categorical statements is the **existential interpretation**. On the existential interpretation, A and E statements make straightforward assertions. 'All cats are fish-eaters', an A statement, asserts that anything which is a member of the set *cats* is also a member of the set *fish-eating things*. The E statement, 'No whales are fish', asserts that anything which is a member of the set *whales* is not a member of the set *fish*; that is, anything which is a member of the set *whales* fails to be a member of the set *fish*.

Now, let us turn our attention to I and O statements. To understand these statements, we must clarify how the word 'some' is employed in categorical statements. 'Some' is used rather loosely in ordinary discourse. If we are told 'Some friends are coming tonight', we are not at all certain *just how many* friends are coming. Should we prepare for one, two, three, or a hundred? We do not know. To avoid this vagueness in our more technical *a priori* study of the forms of descriptive language, we shall *stipulate* that *'some' is always understood as 'there is at least one'*. This stipulation provides the *minimal* answer to the question 'how many?' when answering 'some'. So to claim 'Some friends are coming tonight' is to claim 'There is at least one friend who is coming tonight'.

From the viewpoint of logic there is another difficulty in our more ordinary uses of 'some'. A person may say sarcastically '*Some* television programs are worthwhile'. It is not unreasonable to suppose that such a person is also intentionally suggesting 'Some television programs are *not* worthwhile'. But a person casually claiming 'Some students are average' may or may not be suggesting also that 'Some students are not average'. Let us avoid such ambiguous uses of 'some' by again *stipulating* a minimal meaning. *We stipulate that an* **I** *statement does not imply an* **O** *statement, nor an* **O** *statement an* **I***.*

Categorical statements have a **quantity** and **quality** *which, together, determine the form of such statements.* The quantity of a categorical statement is either *universal* or *particular.* If a categorical statement makes an assertion about all the members of the set designated by the subject term, its quantity is universal. Thus, the quantity of **A** and **E** statements is universal. On the other hand, a categorical statement making an assertion about at least one member designated by the subject term is particular. Hence, the quantity of **I** and **O** statements is particular.

A categorical statement makes an assertion in that it either *affirms* or *denies* certain relations holding between two sets. The quality of a categorical statement which affirms is *affirmative*, while the quality of a categorical statement which denies is *negative*. So, the quality of **A** and **I** statements is affirmative, but of **E** and **O** statements, negative. The quantity and quality, that is, the various forms, of categorical statements may be summarized:

> **A:**   universal affirmative
> **E:**   universal negative
> **I:**   particular affirmative
> **O:**   particular negative

Traditionally, some terms in categorical statements are said to be *distributed.* A term in a categorical statement is distributed when, and only when, because of the form of the statement, that term refers to every member of the set it designates. For instance in the **A** statement, 'All Puritans are bigots', the subject term is distributed. Here we are referring to each and every Puritan but not each and every bigot. While the subject term is distributed in **A** statements, the predicate term is not. In 'No reptiles are warm-blooded'—an **E** statement—*both* the subject and predicate terms are distributed. Any reptile at all is not a warm-blooded thing, and there are no warm-blooded things which are reptiles—no member of either set is a member of the other. **I** statements have no distributed terms. Neither of the terms in 'Some people are cruel' is distributed. The subject term does not refer to all people but only to at least one. Nor does the predicate term refer to all cruel things. And, what may we say of the terms in **O** statements such as 'Some reptiles are not snakes'? The subject term is not distributed in that we are not speaking of all reptiles. However, the predicate term is distributed. In a circumscribed manner the predicate term does say something about all snakes; namely, considering the entire set of snakes, there is at least one reptile excluded from it. The predicate term is distributed in **O** statements.

An easy way to remember which terms are distributed in a categorical statement is this. *The subject term of a universal categorical statement is distributed, and the predicate term of a negative categorical statement is distributed.*

	Subject	*Predicate*
A:	distributed	undistributed
E:	distributed	distributed
I:	undistributed	undistributed
O:	undistributed	distributed

John Venn, a nineteenth-century English logician and mathematician, developed a technique for pictorially representing the various relations holding between the sets designated by the terms of a categorical statement. Suppose we draw a circle and let that circle represent some set. Or, if considering two sets and the possible relations between them, we draw two overlapping circles:

Each *circle* represents a distinct set. The overlap of the circles forms a distinct area representing a *subset* of the original two sets. Numbering all the distinct areas created by the two overlapping circles, we now have four distinct subsets—each subset itself being a distinct set:

Let us say that if we put a cross, '×', in any one of these four areas, we indicate there is at least one member in the set pictured by that area. If, however, we shade in an entire area, we indicate that there are no members in the set represented by that area. If an area is neither shaded nor has a cross, we know nothing about the membership of the set it represents. This manner of representing sets and subsets is the basis of the **Venn diagram** method.

Let us draw a Venn diagram representing 'All cats are fish-eaters'. We first draw two overlapping circles. The circle on the left represents the set *cats*, while the one on the right represents the set *fish-eating things*.

Area 1 stands for the set of all cats; area 3 stands for the set of all things which are fish-eating; area 2—the overlap of areas 1 and 3—depicts the set of all those things which are both cats and fish-eating; and in area 4 we find everything else.

The statement 'All cats are fish-eaters' affirms that *anything* which is a cat is also a fish-eater. Nothing which is a cat fails to be a fish-eater. We therefore shade in area 1, showing the set *cats* has no members. If area 1 were not shaded, there might be cats which are not fish-eaters.

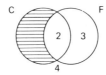

Assuming the existential interpretation of **A** statements, we would also put a cross in area 2:

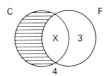

'No whales are fish' can also be represented by a Venn diagram. To claim that no whales are fish is to deny that any member of the set *whales* is also a member of the set *fish*. There is nothing which is both a whale and a fish. Once more, we draw two overlapping circles:

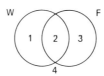

The left-hand circle represents the set *whales* and the right-hand one the set *fish*. Since there is nothing which is both a whale and a fish, the set represented by area 2 is empty—it has no members. Consequently, we shade in area 2:

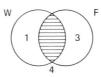

Assuming the existential interpretation of 'No whales are fish', a cross is put in area 1 indicating that whales do in fact exist.

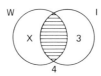

In utilizing Venn diagrams to picture **I** and **O** categorical statements, no areas are shaded. Only the cross is used. For example, to assert 'Some snakes are poisonous' is to affirm that there is at least one (there may be more) member of the set *snakes* which is also a member of the set *poisonous things*. It is an open question whether there are any snakes which are not poisonous. Our Venn diagram must show only the assertion made by 'Some snakes are poisonous'. This is done as follows:

Because there is a cross in area 2, we affirm that there is at least one snake which is also poisonous. By *not* shading in area 1 or putting a cross there, we *do* leave open the question of whether there are any snakes which are not poisonous.

The statement 'Some people are not mendacious' denies that *every* member of the set *people* is also a member of the set *mendacious things*. That is, there is at least one person who is not also mendacious. Of course we do not claim that there is any mendacious person—only that at least one person is not mendacious. The exact assertion of 'Some people are not mendacious' can be exhibited in this Venn diagram.

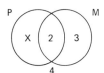

We may now generalize our discussion of representing assertions of categorical statements by Venn diagrams. Given the *hypothetical interpretation* of **A** and **E** statements, they are represented as follows:

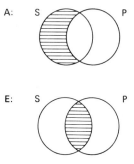

(Here '*S*' designates any subject term and '*P*' any predicate term.) Or, assuming the *existential viewpoint*, we draw

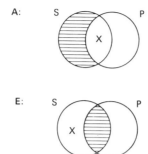

The assertions made by **I** and **O** categorical statements are diagrammed these ways in both the hypothetical and existential interpretations:

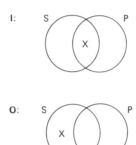

EXERCISES

Group A:

Translate the following categorical statements into standard form. Indicate for each whether it is an **A, E, I,** or **O** type statement.

(1) Cowards are cravens.

(2) Saints are never sinners.

(3) At night every cat is grey.

(4) Certain men who are well adjusted in their work are happy at home.

(5) There are goals of life not obtainable by everyone.

(6) A friend in need is a friend indeed.

(7) Certain people who are unloving never are forgiving.

(8) No ignorant person is ever truly free.

(9) A few professors who are sincere in their work show concern for their students.

(10) No person who hates anyone shall see the Kingdom of God.

(11) A patient person is God's friend.

(12) Few gossips are never vicious.

(13) Certain experiences of life are bitterly absurd.

(14)   The silent man still suffers wrong.

(15)   Many nosy people are lonely fools.

(16)   Few men are not belligerent toward their enemies.

(17)   There are those people who are rewarded by society without any real cause.

(18)   Try as they may, a few people never succeed.

(19)   No man who is wise and good can suffer real disgrace.

(20)   Any patient and understanding wife is more valuable than a thousand friends.

Group B:

Identify the quantity and quality of each categorical statement in Group A.

Group C:

Indicate which terms, if any, are distributed in the categorical statements of Group A.

Group D:

Using Venn diagrams, picture the exact assertion made by each statement in Group A. For any **A** and **E** statement draw two diagrams, letting the first indicate a hypothetical interpretation and the second an existential interpretation of that statement.

2. EXISTENTIAL SQUARE OF OPPOSITION

When adopting the existential viewpoint, several important relations hold between categorical statements having the same subject and predicate terms.

While **A** and **E** statements might both be false (given the same subject and predicate terms in each statement), they cannot both be true. Assuming the existence of at least one scientist, let us say 'All scientists are proficient' and also 'No scientists are proficient'. If 'All scientists are proficient' is true, 'No scientists are proficient' is false. Yet if 'No scientists are proficient' is true, then 'All scientists are proficient' must be false. On the other hand, 'All scientists are proficient' and 'No scientists are proficient' could both be false. Both statements could be false if either 'Some scientists are proficient' or 'Some scientists are not proficient' is true. This relation holding between **A** and **E** statements is indicated by calling them '*contraries*'. *Two statements are contraries when they cannot both be true but when both may be false.*

Further, we might suggest 'Some scientists are proficient' and also 'Some scientists are not proficient'. If 'Some scientists are proficient' is false, then 'Some scientists are not proficient' must be true. If 'Some scientists are not proficient' is false, however, then 'Some scientists are proficient' is certainly true. While

'Some scientists are proficient' and 'Some scientists are not proficient' cannot both be false, nevertheless they may both be true. Traditionally, this relation holding between **I** and **O** categorical statements is indicated by calling them '*subcontraries*'. *Two statements are subcontraries when they cannot both be false but they may both be true.*

Continuing to assume the existential viewpoint, an important relation links **A** and **I** categorical statements and **E** and **O** statements. Given the same subject and predicate terms in each, an **A** statement implies an **I** statement and an **E** statement implies an **O**. Granting the truth of 'All scientists are proficient', we must also acknowledge the truth of 'Some scientists are proficient'. Or, that 'All scientists are proficient' is false is sufficient to guarantee that 'Some scientists are proficient' is also false. Of course the truth of 'Some scientists are proficient' *does not guarantee* the truth of 'All scientists are proficient'. Notice also that if 'No scientists are proficient' is true, we must accept the truth of 'Some scientists are not proficient'. But, if 'No scientists are proficient' is false, we must also accept 'Some scientists are not proficient' as being false. On the other hand, the truth of 'Some scientists are not proficient' *does not guarantee* the truth of 'No scientists are proficient'. For our present purposes, *one statement implies another when its truth guarantees the truth of the second, but the truth of the second statement does not guarantee the truth of the first.* Thus, while an **A** statement implies an **I** and an **E** statement an **O**, an **I** statement does not imply an **A** nor does an **O** statement imply an **E**.

Another important relation is found among categorical statements having the same subject and predicate terms. Assume 'All scientists are proficient' is true. If it is true that *all* scientists are proficient, then the statement 'Some scientists are *not* proficient' must be false. Or, if it is false that 'All scientists are proficient', then at least one scientist must *not* be proficient and 'Some scientists are not proficient' is true. Given the same subject and predicate terms in both statements, **A** and **O** categorical statements have *opposite* truth-values—if one is true, the other must be false. The same relation holds between **E** and **I** categorical statements; that is, if one is true, the other must be false. Therefore, assuming the truth of 'No scientists are proficient', we must grant that 'Some scientists are proficient' is false. But, if 'No scientists are proficient' is false, then 'Some scientists are proficient' is true. This relation holding between **A** and **O** statements and **E** and **I** statements is indicated by calling them '*contradictory*'. *Two statements are contradictory when they can neither both be true nor both be false.*

The various relations holding between categorical statements, given the existential interpretation, are pictured in *The Traditional Square of Opposition* on page 293.

Granting the truth or falsity of one categorical statement, we can determine the truth or falsity of others. For example—assuming the same subject and predicate terms in each case—let an **E** statement be true. Then the **I** statement must be false because **E** and **I** statements are contradictories. The **O** statement, however, must be true since **E** statements imply **O** statements. Further, if the **E** statement is true, the **A** statement must be false because **E** and **A** statements are contraries. Here we can calculate the truth-value of all the categorical statements given the truth-value of one. In some cases we are not able to do this. Imagine that some **O** statement is true. We can say the corresponding **A** statement is false because **O** and **A** statements are contradictories—assuming the same subject and predicate terms in each. Yet, that the **A** statement is false does *not* guarantee the truth of the **E** statement, for **A** and **E** both may be false. Neither does the truth of an **O** statement establish either the truth or falsity of an **I** statement since **O** and **I** statements may both be true. That an **O** statement is true leaves the actual truth-value of an **E** or **I** statement an open question.

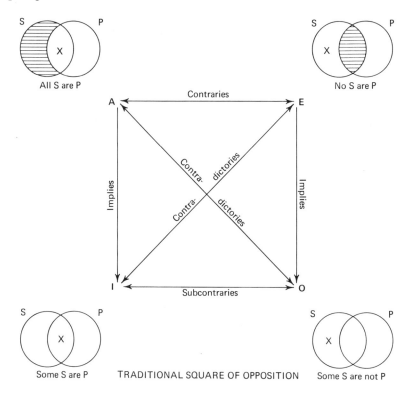

All S are P   No S are P

Contraries

A   Contradictories   E

Implies   Implies

I   Subcontraries   O

Some S are P   TRADITIONAL SQUARE OF OPPOSITION   Some S are not P

If we assume the more contemporary *hypothetical interpretation* of categorical statements, many of the relations holding between statements from the existential stance fail. For example, suppose we say 'All homophlants are heteromorphic' and 'No homophlants are heteromorphic'. These **A** and **E** statements would be considered contraries if given an existential interpretation. But if we assume there may not be any homophlants at all—that the set designated by the subject term of the statements has no members—*both statements may be true*. If there are no homophlants, it is equally true from the contemporary viewpoint to say that all homophlants are heteromorphic and that no homophlants are heteromorphic. Furthermore, if there are no homophlants, the truth of 'All homophlants are heteromorphic' does not imply the truth of 'Some homophlants are hetero-morphic'; and neither does the truth of 'No homophlants are heteromorphic' imply 'Some homophlants are not heteromorphic'. Also, 'Some homophlants are heteromorphic' and 'Some homophlants are not heteromorphic' cannot be considered subcontraries if we grant the hypothetical interpretation of categorical statements. **I** and **O** statements can no longer be considered subcontraries, for they may *both* be false if there are no members of the set designated by the subject term. Only the relation of being contradictory continues to hold. Hence, ***The Contemporary Square of Opposition*** may be pictured as follows:

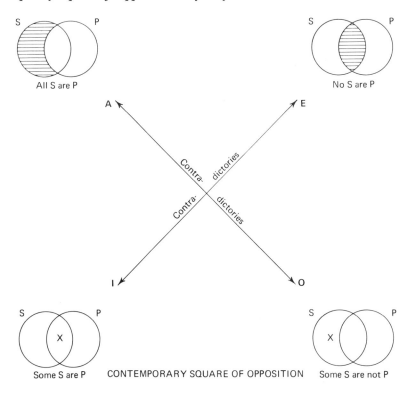

CONTEMPORARY SQUARE OF OPPOSITION

EXERCISES

Imagine some **A, E, I,** and **O** categorical statements such that each statement uses the same subject and predicate terms. Then answer the following questions, assuming an existential interpretation of categorical statements.

(1) If the **A** statement is true, what can we say about the truth-values of the remaining statements; what if the **A** statement is false?

(2) If the **E** statement is false, what are the truth-values of the other categorical statements?

(3) If the **I** statement is true, what can be determined concerning the truth-values of the remaining statements; what if the **I** statement is false?

(4) If the **O** statement is true, what can we say about the truth-values of the other three statements?

3. CONVERSION, OBVERSION, AND CONTRAPOSITION

We often want to know whether two categorical statements make the same assertion; that is, do they mean the same thing. There is a simple procedure for determining whether such statements do, or do not, have the same meaning. Put the statements into standard form and then draw a Venn diagram for each. If the two Venn diagrams are identical, the two statements make the same assertion; that is, they have the same meaning.

Consider this standard form **E** categorical statement:

(1)   No Moslems are Christians.

Would the meaning of (1) be preserved if we switched the terms? Replacing the subject term by the predicate and the predicate term by the subject, we obtain

(2)   No Christians are Moslems.

That (1) and (2) do convey the same meaning can be established by Venn diagrams. Assuming the hypothetical viewpoint, (3) represents (1), and (4), (2):

(3)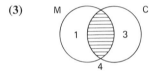

(4)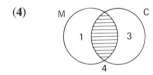

Clearly (3) and (4) are the same diagram in that both show nothing is a Moslem and also a Christian. The existential interpretation yields the same results.

In traditional discussions of categorical statements, (2) is said to be immediately inferred from (1) by **simple conversion,** where (1) is the convertant and (2) the converse. *The simple converse of a categorical statement is obtained by replacing the subject term with the predicate and the predicate term with the subject.*

Simple conversion may also be performed with **I** statements. Suppose we assert

(5)   Some students are punctual people.

Letting the subject and predicate terms trade places, we declare

(6)   Some punctual people are students.

That (5) and (6) make the same assertion may be established by Venn diagrams. Schematically, we represent (5) as

(7)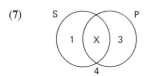

(7) shows there is at least one thing which is both a student and a punctual person. Diagramming (6), we have

(8)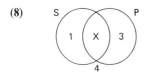

Or, there is at least one punctual person who is also a student. But (7) and (8) are the same diagram and so (5) and (6) make the same assertion.

While simple conversion is applicable to **E** and **I** statements, this is not the case when dealing with **A** and **O** statements. Consider this **A** statement:

(9)   All pines are coniferous trees.

The truth of (9) does *not* guarantee the truth of (10):

(10)   All coniferous trees are pines.

After all, spruce trees, while not pines, have cones. A pair of Venn diagrams (hypothetical interpretation) shows that (9) and (10) do not make the same assertion. Let (11) correspond to (9) and (12) to (10):

(11)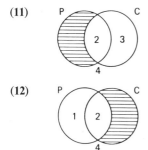

(12)

An existential interpretation of (9) and (10) would have the same results. To appreciate this, imagine a cross in area 2 of both (11) and (12).

Even though a simple conversion of **A** statements is not possible, *assuming an existential interpretation,* we can argue from (9) to

(13)   Some coniferous trees are pines.

Corresponding to (13) is this Venn diagram:

(14)
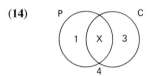

Given the existential interpretation of categorical statements, 'All pines are coniferous trees' *implies* 'Some coniferous trees are pines'. The move from (9) to (13) is an example of ***conversion by limitation***. To carry out this operation, begin with an **A** statement. Then, switch the subject and predicate terms and change the quantity of the statement from universal to particular—from 'all' to 'some'. It is important to remember that *conversion by limitation holds only under the existential interpretation.* In particular we can use conversion by limitation only if we assume there is a member of the set designated by the subject term of an **A** statement.

Neither simple conversion nor conversion by limitation preserves the meaning of an **O** statement. Consider this example:

(15)   Some taxes are not necessary.

The simple conversion of (15) produces

(16)   Some necessary things are not taxes.

That (15) and (16) do not assert the same thing can be substantiated by Venn diagrams. (15) may be pictured this way:

(17)
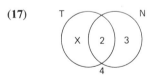

Sentence (16) is diagrammed as

(18)
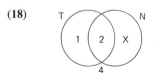

Here (17) and (18) are not identical; (15) and (16) do not make the same assertion. But, perhaps we may utilize conversion by limitation with (15) to obtain

(19)   No necessary things are taxes.

Such a move cannot preserve the meaning of (15) because a particular statement never implies a universal one. Venn diagrams also show that (15) and (19) make different assertions, even when assuming the existential interpretation of categorical statements. (19) is represented by

(20)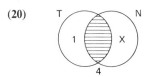

(The cross in area 3 indicates the existential viewpoint.)

But, certainly (17) and (20) are far from identical. Thus, our discussion shows that *an **O** categorical statement has no converse of any sort.*

In summary we can use simple conversion with **E** and **I** statements, conversion by limitation with **A** statements if we presuppose the existential viewpoint, and no conversion of any kind with **O** statements.

Another move often made with categorical statements is **obversion**. Before discussing obversion, however, we must first consider the *complement of a set. The complement of a set, designated by 'S', is that set, designated by 'non S', which has as its members all those things not a member of S.* For instance, the set indicated by 'man' contains as its members just those things which are men—Caesar, Dorian, Edward—and nothing else. The complement of this set, the set indicated by 'non-men', contains as its members *everything which is not a man*—desks, textbooks, atoms, and so on.

Some caution is necessary in discussing the complement of a set. A common mistake, for example, is to consider the complement of the set designated by 'white' to be the set designated by 'black'. Or, we might suppose the complement of the set indicated by 'good moral actions' is indicated by 'evil moral actions'. Both of these suppositions are incorrect. The set of white things contains *only* those things which are white and the set of black things *only* those things which are black. But, the complement of the set designated by 'white' contains not only black things but also red, blue, green, purple—in fact every colored thing except white ones. The set called 'good moral actions' does not have as its complement the set indicated by 'evil moral actions'. That some action is not morally good does not imply that it is morally evil. The act may be "morally neutral". We must be very careful in suggesting the *complement* of a set. *To indicate the complement of some set designated by 'S', we shall write 'non-S'; and, to indicate the complement of some set designated by 'non-S', we shall write 'S'.* Thus, the sets designated by 'white' and 'nonwhite' are complements, as are the sets indicated by 'good moral actions' and 'nongood moral actions'.

We may now describe the operation of *obversion: First, change the quality of the original categorical statement, the obvertant; and second, replace the predicate term by its complement.* If the quality of the statement is affirmative, change it to negative; if it is negative, change it to affirmative. If the predicate term of this categorical statement is designated by '*P*', replace it by 'non-*P*'; if this term is 'non-*P*', replace it by '*P*'. Thus, we obtain the obverse of the original statement.

Let us form the obverse of this **A** statement:

(21)　　　All enemies are pugnacious.

Following the steps of obversion, we first change the quality of (21):

(22)　　　No enemies are pugnacious.

Then, replacing the predicate term by its complement, we have the obverse of (21):

(23)　　　No enemies are nonpugnacious.

(23) claims that no member of the set *enemies* is excluded from the set *pugnacious things*. Assuming the hypothetical viewpoint, we may use Venn diagrams to show that (21) and (23) make the same assertion. Let (24) represent (21), and (25) picture (23):

(24)
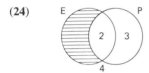

(25)
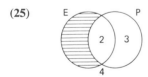

　　　(No *E* is excluded from *P*)

Clearly, (24) and (25) are identical; (21) and (23) make the same claim. An existential interpretation of (21) and (23) yields the same results. To appreciate this, simply imagine a cross in area 2 of both (24) and (25).

Obversion can be successfully used with **E** categorical statements:

(26)　　　No lunatics are sane people.

We change the quality of (26) and replace the predicate term by its complement to produce

(27)   All lunatics are nonsane people.

Under the hypothetical interpretation, the Venn diagram corresponding to (26) is

(28)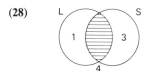

(27) claims that any member of the set *lunatics* is excluded from the set *sane people* or (hypothetical interpretation)

(29)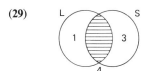

Granting the existential interpretation of (26) and (27), obversion retains their sameness of meaning. To grasp this, imagine a cross in area 1 of both (28) and (29).

The meaning of an **I** statement is also preserved by obversion, as in

(30)   Some chemicals are explosive.

Changing the quality of (30) and replacing its predicate term by the complement of that term, we have

(31)   Some chemicals are not nonexplosive.

Now, we draw (32) to represent (30):

(32)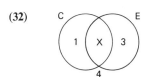

(31) claims that at least one member of the set *chemicals* is not excluded from the set *explosive things*. This assertion may be pictured as

(33)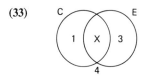

Since (32) and (33) are identical, the statements (30) and (31) make the same assertion.

Finally, obversion may also be used with **O** categorical statements:

(34)   Some politicians are not corrupt.

Proceeding through our now familiar steps, we change the quality of (34) and replace the predicate term by its complement:

(35)   Some politicians are noncorrupt.

Drawing a Venn diagram for (34), we have

(36)   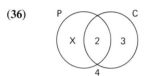

(35) asserts that at least one member of the set *politicians* is excluded from the set *corrupt things*, or

(37)   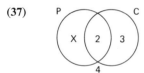

Once more, Venn diagrams help us literally to see that two statements—here, (34) and (35)—make the same assertion; they have the same meaning.

It is important to remember that every categorical statement has an obverse, although not every categorical statement has a converse.

The last operation we shall consider in this section is ***contraposition.*** In a sense contraposition is nothing more than a use of obversion, conversion, and a final use of obversion. For instance, suppose we are told

(38)   All saints are prayerful people.

By obversion we obtain

(39)   No saints are nonprayerful people.

Conversion guarantees

(40)   No nonprayerful people are saints.

And, a final appeal to obversion yields

(41)   All nonprayerful people are nonsaints.

Instead of going through these several steps, we may simply assert (42), given (38), by contraposition.

(42)   All nonprayerful people are nonsaints.

Contraposition may also be used with an **O** statement. For instance, the contrapositive of 'Some students are not Puritans' is 'Some non-Puritans are not nonstudents'. To see that we can use contraposition with **O** statements, consider

(43)   Some students are not Puritans.

Use obversion to obtain

(44)   Some students are non-Puritans.

Conversion of (44) results in

(45)   Some non-Puritans are students.

A final appeal to obversion yields the contrapositive of (43); namely,

(46)   Some non-Puritans are not nonstudents.

Next, let us examine an **E** statement:

(47)   No sailors are puritanical.

By obversion we obtain

(48)   All sailors are non-puritanical.

Here (48) is an **A** statement. But, only conversion by limitation can be used with **A** statements, and then we must assume the existential interpretation of terms. Granting this, we obtain from (48)

(49)   Some non-puritanical people are sailors.

Another appeal to obversion produces

(50)   Some non-puritanical people are not nonsailors.

While simple contraposition may be used with **A** and **O** statements, only contraposition by limitation (requiring the existential viewpoint) is correctly employed with **E** statements.

May either simple contraposition or contraposition by limitation be used with **I** statements? To answer this question, consider

(51)   Some Southerners are poor.

The obverse of (51) is

(52)   Some Southerners are not nonpoor.

(52) is an **O** statement, but **O** statements have no converse. Not being able to use conversion with (52), we cannot proceed to a concluding use of obversion and, thus, the contrapositive of 'Some Southerners are poor'. In general **I** statements have no contrapositive.

Instead of proceeding through obversion, conversion, and then obversion again, we can form the contrapositive of categorical statements this way. *Simple contraposition is used with* **A** *and* **O** *statements by replacing the subject term with the complement of the predicate and the predicate term with the complement of the subject. Contraposition by limitation is used with* **E** *statements (assuming the existential interpretation) by changing the quantity of the statement, and by replacing the subject term with the complement of the predicate and the predicate term with the complement of the subject. No use of contraposition is appropriate with* **I** *statements.*

EXERCISES

Group A:

Put each of the following statements into standard form. Then, when possible, state the converse of each. Indicate when conversion by limitation is used.

(1)   Certain chemical transformations are endothermic.
(2)   Each heat-releasing chemical transformation is exothermic.
(3)   There are chemical substances not in liquid form.
(4)   Chemical elements never represent an ambiguous species of matter.
(5)   Energy is the capability of a body to bring about changes in other bodies.

Group B:

Translate each of the following statements into standard form; then state the obverse of each.

(1)   Manometers measure vapor.
(2)   Nothing which is a barometer measures temperature.
(3)   Any microbalance is more accurate than an analytical one.
(4)   A suitable instrument for measuring the sun's temperature isn't a mercury column thermometer.
(5)   Some experiments require analytical balances.

Group C:

Put each of the following statements into standard form. Then, when possible, form the contrapositive of each. Indicate when contraposition by limitation is used.

(1)   There are nonpolar molecules.
(2)   A dipole moment can be determined experimentally.
(3)   Certain molecular structures aren't predictable by the "octet rule".
(4)   There are molecules which aren't homonuclear.
(5)   Polar molecules are never nonpolar.

Group D:

By using conversion, obversion, and contraposition, determine how (b) is derived from (a) in each of the following pairs of statements. Be certain to indicate any uses of conversion by limitation and contraposition by limitation.

(1)   (a)   Some chemical substances are homogeneous substances.
      (b)   Some homogeneous substances are not nonchemical substances.
(2)   (a)   All chemical substances are discretely structured.
      (b)   No nondiscretely structured things are chemical substances.
(3)   (a)   No chemical substances are phlogistic substances.
      (b)   Some nonphlogistic substances are chemical substances.
(4)   (a)   Some chemical substances are not heterogeneous substances.
      (b)   Some nonheterogeneous substances are chemical substances.
(5)   (a)   All atomic elements are chemical substances.
      (b)   Some chemical substances are not nonatomic elements.

4.   CATEGORICAL SYLLOGISMS

Categorical statements may be related in a *categorical syllogism* (in contrast to a hypothetical or disjunctive syllogism).

> *A categorical syllogism* (or simply *syllogism*) *is a deductive argument having a sequence of three and only three categorical statements such that three and only three terms appear in this sequence of statements, each term appearing in exactly two statements.*

An example of a syllogism is found at the beginning of this chapter:

(1)   All mariners are pugnacious people.

          All sailors are mariners.

          So, all sailors are pugnacious people.

Here (1) fulfills our defining characteristics of the syllogism. We find exactly three categorical statements in the example; there are three and only three terms, and each term appears in exactly two statements.

Some technical jargon becomes helpful in discussing syllogisms. The predicate term of the conclusion is the **major term** throughout the syllogism. The subject term of the conclusion is the **minor term** throughout the syllogism. The premiss in which the major term appears is the **major premiss** of the syllogism. The premiss in which the minor term appears is the **minor premiss**. Finally, that term which is found in both premisses, but not in the conclusion, is the **middle term** of the syllogism. Any syllogism is in *standard form* if, and only if, all the categorical statements are in standard form—the major premiss is mentioned first, then the minor premiss, and last the conclusion. Notice, (1) is in standard form. The major term of (1), 'pugnacious people', is the predicate of the conclusion and appears in the first premiss. Being the subject of the conclusion, 'sailors' is the minor term and appears in the second premiss. The middle term, 'mariners', appears in the premisses but not in the conclusion.

The validity of any syllogism, like all deductive arguments, depends solely on its logical form.

> **The logical form of a syllogism is determined by (1) the logical forms of the categorical statements in the syllogism, and (2) the ways the terms are arranged in those statements and, therefore, in the syllogism.**

Examining (1), notice that all the syllogism's statements are universal affirmative, or **A**, statements. *To name the forms of all the statements in a standard form syllogism is to give the mood of that syllogism.* The mood of (1) is specified by '**A A A**', writing first an '**A**' to designate the form of the major premiss, then the next '**A**' for the form of the minor premiss, and finally specifying the form of the conclusion by another '**A**'.

But, the validity of a syllogism is dependent upon more than its mood. For example, the mood of the following syllogism is **A A A**; yet the argument is invalid:

(2)   All pugnacious people are mariners.

All sailors are mariners.

So, all sailors are pugnacious people.

The only difference between (1) and (2) is the arrangement of the terms in each syllogism. Syllogism (1) may be pictured as

(3)   All M are P.

All S are M.

So, all S are P.

On the other hand, (2) is shown as

(4)   All P are M.

All S are M.

So, all S are P.

A quick glance at (3) and (4) shows the difference between them. The major premisses of (3) and (4) differ because of the arrangement of the terms in those statements. Consequently, since the two syllogisms are alike in every respect except the ordering of their terms, and since (3) is valid while (4) is not, we can appreciate the importance of the location of the several terms in a syllogism.

*The way in which the terms of a syllogism are arranged is the **figure** of that syllogism.* In that a syllogism is a sequence of three categorical statements, having exactly three terms such that each term appears in only two statements and the middle term is found in both premisses, *there are four possible figures a syllogism may have.* These four figures may be represented this way:

M—P	*P—M*	*M—P*	*P—M*
S—M	*S—M*	*M—S*	*M—S*
∴ *S—P*	∴ *S—P*	∴ *S—P*	∴ *S—P*
Figure 1	*Figure 2*	*Figure 3*	*Figure 4*

You may find the following device helpful in remembering the position of the middle term in the four figures:

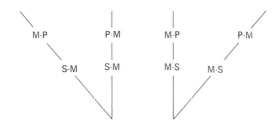

Just think of the outline of a conventional shirt collar.

Remember, *the form of a syllogism is a function of its mood and figure.* To indicate the form of any syllogism, we name both its mood and figure. Thus, the form of (1) is designated by 'A A A—1' but of (2) by 'A A A—2'.

We may now determine just how many categorical syllogistic forms there are. While there is an indefinitely large number of truth-functional argument forms, there is a finite number of syllogistic forms. The major premiss of any syllogism may be an **A, E, I,** or **O** statement, but so may the minor premiss. Thus, if the major premiss is an **A** statement, the minor premiss may be either an **A, E, I,** or **O** statement. This means there are *4 × 4* or *16* possible combinations of major and minor premisses. But, for each of these 16 possibilities, the conclusion may be an **A, E, I,** or **O** statement. Hence, there are *16 × 4* or *64* possible moods a syllogism may have. Yet, each mood may be in one of four figures. Consequently, we find *64 × 4* or *256 possible syllogistic forms.*

Group A:

Put the following arguments into standard form. Then, state the mood and figure for each.

(1) Some substances are nonprotoplasmic. Living things are never nonprotoplasmic. So, some substance isn't a living thing.

(2) No glucose is a double sugar. One of the simplest carbohydrates found in protoplasms is glucose. Thus, one of the simplest carbohydrates found in protoplasms isn't a double sugar.

(3) Everything which has the ability to metabolize is protoplasmic. Nothing having the ability to metabolize is nonorganic. Accordingly, nothing which is protoplasmic is nonorganic.

(4) Some metabolic processes aren't anabolic. Every organic growth process is metabolic. Therefore, there is an organic growth process which isn't anabolic.

(5) Only things composed of protoplasm are unicellular. Some organisms are unicellular. Accordingly, there are organisms composed of protoplasm.

(6) Some algae are unicellular things. Some algae are Euglenae. So, certain unicellular things are Euglenae.

(7) Euglenae never have an outer cellulose cell wall. Some flagellates don't have an outer cellulose cell wall. Thus, some flagellates aren't Euglenae.

(8) None of the species of green algae is without a definite nucleus. Some species of green algae are terrestrial. Hence, some terrestrial things aren't without a definite nucleus.

(9) Any Chordae are brown algae. Nothing which is brown algae survives in fresh water. Consequently, no Chordae survive in fresh water.

(10) Whatever is a thallophyte is classified in the subkingdom Thallophyta. An alga is a thallophyte. Therefore, algae are classified in the subkingdom Thallophyta.

Group B:

Given the following moods and figures, construct a syllogism for each form. Your syllogisms do not have to be in standard form.

(1) E A E—1		**(6)** E I O—2
(2) A E O—4		**(7)** A A I—3
(3) E A E—2		**(8)** A I I—4
(4) O A O—3		**(9)** A E O—1
(5) I O I—4		**(10)** A O O—2

5. ESTABLISHING THE VALIDITY OF CATEGORICAL SYLLOGISMS: VENN DIAGRAMS

In this section we shall adopt the hypothetical interpretation of categorical statements unless the existential interpretation is indicated.

Continuing to interpret terms as designating sets, we can expand our use of Venn diagrams to establish the validity or invalidity of syllogisms. Since a syllogism has exactly three distinct terms, we now need three overlapping circles. These circles must be drawn so that all possible combinations—all possible subsets of three sets—are realized. The following diagram serves our purpose.

(1)

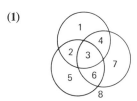

Counting the area outside the circles, the three overlapping circles create eight distinct areas, each area representing a distinct set.

The following syllogism is an instance of the form **A A A—1**:

(2)   All mathematicians are pliable people.
       All statisticians are mathematicians.
       So, all statisticians are pliable people.

Is this a valid syllogism? Does the truth of the premisses (if true) guarantee the truth of the conclusion? We can answer this question by drawing a Venn diagram, showing exactly what is asserted by the premisses. If the argument is valid, this Venn diagram will also represent exactly what is asserted by the conclusion. Let '*M*' stand for the set *mathematicians*, '*P*' for the set *pliable people*, and '*S*' for the set *statisticians*.

(3)

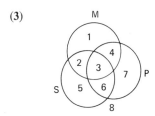

Area 1 represents mathematicians who are neither statisticians nor pliable people. In area 2 we find mathematicians who are statisticians but not pliable people.

Area 3 is made up of mathematicians who are both statisticians and pliable people. Area 4 designates mathematicians who are pliable people but not statisticians. Indicated by area 5 are statisticians who are neither mathematicians nor pliable people. Picturing those statisticians who are pliable people yet not mathematicians is area 6. Area 7 represents pliable people who are not statisticians and not mathematicians. Anything which is not a mathematician, statistician, nor a pliable person is designated by area 8.

The major premiss of (2) asserts that anything which is a mathematician is also a pliable person; no mathematicians fail to be pliable people. Hence, assuming the hypothetical viewpoint, we must shade areas 1 and 2 of our Venn diagram to show these areas have no members:

(4)

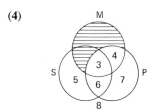

The minor premiss of (2) claims that anything which is a statistician is also a mathematician; or, no statisticians fail to be mathematicians. So, we shade in areas 5 and 6:

(5)

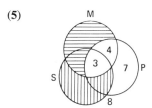

Here (5) represents exactly what is asserted, no more no less, by the premisses of (2). However, (5) also represents exactly what is asserted by the conclusion of (2); namely, all statisticians are pliable people. The only area represented by '*S*' not shaded is area 3, showing that all statisticians are, indeed, pliable people. Syllogism (2) is a valid syllogism.

Once more, assuming the hypothetical viewpoint, let us examine the following argument for validity:

(6) All philosophers are metaphysicians.

No scientists are metaphysicians.

Hence, no scientists are philosophers.

The form of (6) is **A E E—2**. Appealing to a Venn diagram, we draw

(7)

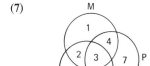

The major premiss of (6) claims that everything which is a philosopher is also a metaphysician. Areas 6 and 7 designate philosophers which are not metaphysicians. To picture the assertion of the major premiss, we shade these areas to indicate that they have no members:

(8)

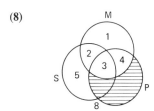

The minor premiss of (6) asserts that anything which is a scientist fails to be a metaphysician; that is, areas 2 and 3 are shaded:

(9)

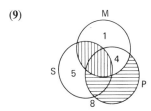

Is (6) valid? Yes, for (9) literally shows us that no scientists are philosophers. Anything which is a scientist fails to be a philosopher.

While the syllogisms (2) and (6) are valid, the following syllogism is not:

(10)   All philosophers are mentally alert people.

  All sagacious persons are mentally alert people.

  Thus, all sagacious persons are philosophers.

Like (2), the mood of (10) is **A A A**, but its figure is **2**. Using a Venn diagram, we begin to picture (10):

(11)

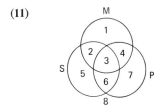

The major premiss of (10) claims that anything which is a philosopher is also mentally alert—any member of the set *philosophers* is also a member of the set *mentally alert people*, so we shade areas 6 and 7.

(12)

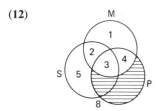

Since the minor premiss of (10) asserts that all sagacious persons are also mentally alert people, areas 5 and 6 are shaded to represent the assertion of the minor premiss.

(13)

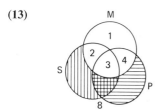

But, (13) does not picture 'All sagacious persons are philosophers'. If the premisses of (10) guaranteed the conclusion, *both* areas 5 *and* 2 would have to be shaded. However, in (13) area 2 is not shaded. There *may* be a sagacious person who is not a philosopher.

When constructing Venn diagrams corresponding to syllogisms which are sequences of only **A** and **E** categorical statements, always represent the major premiss first and then the minor premiss. In picturing the assertion of the major premiss, use *horizontal lines* to shade various areas. To represent the claim of the minor premiss, use *vertical lines* in shading. This *convention* allows us to distinguish between the assertions made by the major and minor premisses.

Thus far we have considered only syllogisms composed of **A** and **E** statements. Let us now examine a syllogism with **I** statements:

(14)   Some marine animals are porpoises.

    All marine animals are sea creatures.

    Accordingly, some sea creatures are porpoises.

The minor premiss of (14) asserts that nothing which is a marine animal fails to be a sea creature. Drawing a Venn diagram, we picture this information:

(15)

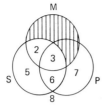

We learn from the *major premiss* there is at least one marine animal which is also a porpoise. Only area 3 of (15) represents just those things which are both marine animals and porpoises; thus, we place a cross in that section of our diagram:

(16)

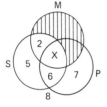

Notice (16) also indicates there is at least one sea creature which is also a porpoise. Syllogism (14) is a valid argument!

As a point of procedure in drawing Venn diagrams, *whenever diagramming a syllogism containing both a universal and a particular premiss, always picture the universal premiss first.* This is the procedure we followed in diagramming (14). But, suppose we had attempted to diagram first the particular statement of (14) and then the universal. Where would we have placed the cross? In area 3 or 4? These questions cannot be answered until after the universal statement—the minor premiss—has been pictured in our Venn diagram. In general, then, always diagram a universal premiss before a particular one.

Is the following argument utilizing an **O** statement valid or not?

(17)   Some philosophers are metaphysicians.

No metaphysicians are scientists.

So, some scientists are not philosophers.

Constructing a Venn diagram, we first represent the universal statement in (17)— the *minor premiss:*

(18)

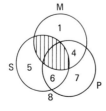

The *major premiss*, on the other hand, states there is at least one philosopher who is also a metaphysician. Since area 4 of (18) indicates all those things—if any—which are both philosophers and metaphysicians, we put a cross in that area:

(19)

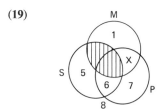

Examining (19), we see that the conclusion of (17), 'So, some scientists are not philosophers', is *not* diagrammed in (19). Area 5 represents all those things which are both scientists and also not philosophers. If (17) were a valid argument, we should find a cross in area 5. Since no cross appears there, we know (17) is invalid.

Consider this argument:

(20)   All puritanical people are malicious.

           Some malicious people are shrewd.

           Thus, some shrewd people are puritanical.

Let us establish the validity or invalidity of this syllogism by constructing a Venn diagram, first indicating the major premiss:

(21)

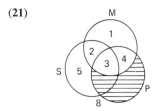

But now, how are we to represent the minor premiss of (20)? A difficulty arises here when we realize that *both* areas 2 and 3 represent 'Some malicious people are shrewd'. Are we to put a cross in area 2 or 3, both? The premisses of (20) afford no answer. In order to represent exactly what is asserted by the minor premiss of (20), let us draw a *bar* touching *both* of the areas in question:

(22)

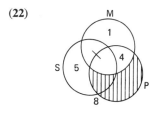

The bar indicates there is at least one (there may be more) malicious person who is also shrewd; we do not know whether this person—or persons—is represented by area 2 or 3, or both. Consequently, the premisses of (20) could all be true and the conclusion false, for our shrewd person *may* be represented by area 2—that area composed of persons who are both shrewd and malicious *but not puritanical*. The argument is invalid because the truth of all the premisses does not *guarantee* the truth of the conclusion. If an argument is valid, it is not possible for all the premisses to be true and the conclusion false.

There are some syllogisms invalid under the hypothetical interpretation of their premisses but valid when an existential viewpoint is adopted. Consider this example:

(23)   All psychopathic people are miserable.

No saints are miserable.

Therefore, some saints are not psychopathic people.

Drawing a Venn diagram for (23) and assuming the hypothetical viewpoint, we obtain

(24)

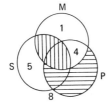

Syllogism (23) is invalid because area 5 of (24) is empty. There may or may not be any saint who is not a psychopathic person. If, however, we adopt the existential viewpoint and *assume the existence* of saints, the argument is valid, as indicated by this Venn diagram:

(25)

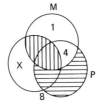

Another example of a syllogism, invalid given the hypothetical interpretation but valid from the existential viewpoint, is this:

(26)   All puritanical people are ethically misguided.

All ethically misguided people are sinners.

So, some sinners are puritanical people.

Assuming the hypothetical standpoint, a Venn diagram for (26) is

(27)

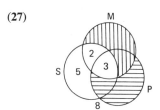

But, (27) does not show that the truth of the premisses of (26) guarantees the conclusion. Since area 3 is empty, there may or may not be sinners who are also puritanical people. Taking the existential viewpoint and *assuming the existence* of puritanical people, (26) becomes a valid argument:

(28)

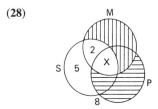

Diagram (28), by having a cross in area 5, clearly indicates there is at least one sinner who is also a puritanical person.

Notice in adopting the existential viewpoint with (23) we assume the existence of saints; that is, we assume the set indicated by the *minor term* has at least one member. On the other hand, taking an existential viewpoint with (26), we assume there is at least one member in the set indicated by the *major term*. There are also syllogisms valid under the existential stance—but not under a hypothetical standpoint—only if we assume the existence of at least one member of the set indicated by the *middle term* of the syllogism.

In summary, to establish the validity or invalidity of a syllogism by Venn diagram methods, first put the syllogism into standard form. Then draw three overlapping circles forming eight distinct areas (counting the area outside the circles); label these circles to correspond with the terms of the syllogism. Next, represent all universal premisses by appropriately shading the areas and then the particular premiss—if any—by using a cross or bar. If the completed Venn diagram is found to represent exactly the conclusion of the syllogism, the syllogism is valid; but, if the finished Venn diagram does not picture the conclusion exactly, the syllogism is invalid.

Group A:

Establish by Venn diagram methods which arguments are valid in Group A of the preceding Exercise, page 307; assume the hypothetical viewpoint. For those arguments invalid under the hypothetical viewpoint, determine which are valid if an existential interpretation is adopted.

Group B:

Translate each of the following syllogisms into standard form. Identify the form of each argument. Then, establish by Venn diagram methods which of the arguments are valid and which invalid, given the hypothetical interpretation. For those arguments invalid under the hypothetical viewpoint, determine which are valid if an existential interpretation is adopted.

(1) The termite is a colonial insect. None of the colonial insects is independent. So, there are termites which aren't independent.

(2) Every bee is a social insect. A spider never is a social insect. Therefore, spiders never are bees.

(3) Certain terrestrial worms are earthworms. There are annelids which are terrestrial worms. Consequently, some annelids aren't earthworms.

(4) Whatever is a centipede has one pair of appendages per segment. Only an arthropod is a centipede. Wherefore, there are arthropods having one pair of appendages per segment.

(5) Starfish are invertebrates. A few echinoderms are starfish. Hence, some invertebrate is an echinoderm.

(6) Nothing which is a salamander has scales. Many salamanders aren't brightly colored animals. Accordingly, some brightly colored animals don't have scales.

(7) The penguin has flipper-like wings. There are birds which don't have flipper-like wings. Thus, there are birds which are not penguins.

(8) Each mule is an outbred animal. No outbred animal is an inbred one. So, some inbred animals are not mules.

(9) Any trait present at birth is a congenital one. There are traits present at birth which aren't inherited. Therefore, there are congenital traits which aren't inherited.

(10) Some siblings are twins. There are girls who aren't siblings. Hence, some girls aren't twins.

6. ESTABLISHING THE VALIDITY OF CATEGORICAL SYLLOGISMS: CATEGORICAL RULES

If we were to construct a Venn diagram for each of the 256 possible syllogistic forms, we would find the following valid—assuming the hypothetical viewpoint:

Figure 1	Figure 2	Figure 3	Figure 4
A A A	A E E	A I I	A E E
E A E	E A E	E I O	E I O
A I I	A O O	I A I	I A I
E I O	E I O	O A O	

Not only are these fifteen forms valid, but the following nine are also valid if we assume the existential interpretation and grant the appropriate assumptions:

Figure 1	Figure 2	Figure 3	Figure 4	Assumption
A A I	A E O		A E O	There are S's
E A O	E A O			
		A A I	E A O	There are M's
		E A O		
			A A I	There are P's

Examining these valid syllogistic forms, we may generate several groups of rules such that if all the rules of any one group are followed, the validity of any particular syllogism is guaranteed. For example, in all twenty-four valid forms we find the middle term distributed—that is, the term refers to all the members of the set it designates—at least once. In such forms as **E A E**—2, the middle term is distributed in both premisses. We also discover if either the subject or predicate term (or both) is distributed in the conclusion, it is also distributed in the premisses.

The following rules are one group of several which guarantee the validity of *any* syllogism, whether considered from the hypothetical or existential standpoint:

Rule 1. *The middle term of a valid syllogism is distributed at least once.*

Rule 2. *If any term in the conclusion of a valid syllogism is distributed, that term is distributed in the premisses.*

Rule 3. *If any valid syllogism has one positive and one negative premiss, its conclusion is negative.*

Rule 4. *No syllogism is valid if it has two negative premisses.*

Expanding this list of rules to include the following will guarantee the validity of any valid syllogism under *only* the hypothetical interpretation.

Rule 5.   *If any valid syllogism has only universal premises, its conclusion is also universal.*

There are other rules we could have incorporated into our list of rules for valid syllogisms. For instance, we may notice that if both the premises of a valid syllogism are affirmative, the conclusion is also affirmative. But, we do not need to supplement our present list of rules this way, for this rule can be established from those we already have adopted. To do this, consider all possible cases of syllogistic forms having two affirmative premises *and* a negative conclusion. Then show, by appealing to our present rules, that none of these syllogistic forms can be valid. All possible syllogistic forms having affirmative premises and a negative conclusion are

(1)

Figure 1	Figure 2	Figure 3	Figure 4
A A E	A A E	A A E	A A E
A I E	A I E	A I E	A I E
I A E	I A E	I A E	I A E
I I E	I I E	I I E	I I E
A A O	A A O	A A O	A A O
A I O	A I O	A I O	A I O
I A O	I A O	I A O	I A O
I I O	I I O	I I O	I I O

Appealing to Rule 1, we *eliminate* the following candidates from the list above:

Figure 1	Figure 2	Figure 3	Figure 4
	A A E		
	A I E		A I E
I A E	I A E		
I I E	I I E	I I E	I I E
	A A O		
	A I O		A I O
I A O	I A O		
I I O	I I O	I I O	I I O

Citing Rule 2, these possibilities now remaining in (1) are also *eliminated*:

Figure 1	Figure 2	Figure 3	Figure 4
A A E		A A E	A A E
A I E		A I E	
		I A E	I A E
A A O		A A O	A A O
A I O		A I O	
		I A O	I A O

To establish the validity, or invalidity, of any syllogism by using Categorical Rules, put the syllogism into standard form and then carefully inspect it in relation to the rules. If the syllogism violates at least one of the rules, it is invalid; otherwise, it is valid.

EXERCISES

Group A:

Translate each of the following syllogisms into standard form. Indicate the form of each syllogism. Then, by appealing to your Categorical Rules, determine which syllogisms are valid and which invalid, assuming first the hypothetical and then the existential viewpoint. For those syllogisms that are invalid, state clearly which Cateogrical Rule(s) is violated.

(1) Some metabolic processes aren't anabolic. None but metabolic processes are organic growth processes. Consequently, certain organic growth processes aren't anabolic.

(2) The anabolic process is an organic growth process. There are metabolic processes which are anabolic. So there are metabolic processes which are also organic growth processes.

(3) There are algae which are also Euglenae. Some algae are unicellular. Therefore, there are unicellular things which are Euglenae.

(4) Any unicellular thing is composed of protoplasm. There are organisms which are unicellular. Accordingly, some organisms are composed of protoplasm.

(5) None of the Euglenae has outer cellulose cell walls. Some flagellates don't have outer cellulose cell walls. Thus, some flagellates aren't Euglenae.

(6) Any nonmetallic Group VIIB element is a halogen. Nothing which is a compound is also a halogen. Consequently, there is a compound which isn't a nonmetallic Group VIIB element.

(7) No elements are compound substances. No salt is an element. Therefore, some compound substances are salts.

(8) Chlorine is a halogen. Any chlorine is a nonmetallic Group VIIB element. So, each nonmetallic Group VIIB element is a halogen.

(9) Some compounds such as sodium chloride are salt. Salt is a chief natural source of chlorine. Wherefore, any compound such as sodium chloride is a chief natural source of chlorine.

(10) Salt is found widely in nature. Sodium chloride is salt. Thus, some sodium chloride is found widely in nature.

Group B:

Inspecting the twenty-four valid syllogistic forms, do the following need to be added as further rules to our present list of Categorical Rules, or does our present list cover these cases? Substantiate your answer for each case.

(1) No valid syllogism has two particular premisses.
(2) Every valid syllogism of Figure 2 has one, and only one, negative premiss.
(3) Every valid syllogism of Figure 3 has a particular conclusion.
(4) No valid syllogism of Figure 4 has an **A** conclusion.

11

Quantification and Symbols

Chapter 10 introduced the notion of *quantifiers* through a discussion of categorical statements and syllogisms. As we noted, quantifiers, expressed by 'all', 'no', and 'some' in standard form categorical statements, are necessary to establish the validity of an argument such as

(1)   All even numbers are natural numbers.

No natural numbers are imaginary numbers.

So, no even numbers are imaginary numbers.

Yet there are other arguments whose validity cannot be established by using only methods developed in preceding chapters. For example, we have not developed techniques for establishing the validity of such arguments as these:

(2)   Astronauts are highly trained and physically fit. Walter Schirra is an astronaut. Thus, Schirra is physically fit.

(3)   Every metal expands when heated. Certain metals are heated in kilns. Hence, some metals expand while in kilns.

(4)   Any artist is creative only if every poet is sensitive. Each artist is a poet, and every poet a creator. Accordingly, all artists are sensitive.

(5)   If Johnson speaks, every person at the meeting will be attentive. Johnson

will speak while some person at the meeting takes notes. Wherefore, some person at the meeting will be attentive and take notes.

Our deductive techniques must allow us to establish the validity of arguments like (2)–(5) as well as (1). To achieve this goal, we shall combine the Truth-Functional Calculus with some very important concepts used in Chapter 10. In this chapter a logical notation necessary for symbolizing arguments such as (1)–(5) will be developed, and various methods of translating back and forth from English to the notation will be examined. Later we shall apply these new techniques to establish the validity of deductive arguments.

1. SYMBOLIZING SINGULAR AND CATEGORICAL STATEMENTS

In ordinary speech it is not at all unusual to say some individual thing, or object, has (or does not have) a certain property, characteristic, or trait. To say 'Boston is a city' is to assert that the property of being a city is true of Boston. And, since it is true of Boston that it is a city, we may also say the individual, Boston, is a member of the set *city*. Or, we may say 'Boston is not a state' and assert that the property of being a state is false of Boston or that Boston is not a member of the set *state*. That a certain property is true of (or false of) an individual and that the individual is (or is not) a member of a specific set are closely related notions. So we can distinguish between an individual thing on the one hand and on the other a property said to be true of (or false of) that individual or a set to which the individual does (or does not) belong. This important distinction will be reflected in our expanded notation.

In our new notation, we shall let the capital letters '*A*' through '*Z*' be *predicate letters* used to designate predicates. For our purposes we may think of a predicate either as a property said to be true of (or false of) an individual or as a set of which an individual is (or is not) a member. Lower case letters '*a*' through '*w*' are used to designate specific individuals. Consequently, we may think of these letters as *individual constants*. In symbolizing a statement, we adopt the convention that, when possible, the individual constant corresponding to the first letter of the individual's name will be used. A similar convention guides us in selecting our predicate letters.

We may now begin to translate 'Boston is a city' into our notation. First, putting '*b*' in place of 'Boston', we have

(1)   *b* is a city.

Using '*C*' for 'city', we obtain

(2)   *b* is a *C*.

To remove the last vestige of English from (2), we follow this convention: The letter designating the individual is always written immediately to the right of the predicate letter. Thus, (2) becomes

(3) *Cb*

For our purposes, (3) may be read '*b* is a member of *C*' or '*C* is true of *b*'; that is, 'Boston is a city'.

But we may also want to say several things about a particular individual; for example,

(4) Boston is an industrial city.

To assert that Boston is an industrial city is to assert

(5) Boston is industrial *and* Boston is a city.

Symbolizing (5), we write

(6) *Ib · Cb*

Or, suppose we claim

(7) Boston is an industrial northern city.

(7) can be reexpressed

(8) Boston is industrial and Boston is northern and Boston is a city.

Grouping our predicate letters by twos, we associate to the left and write

(9) (*Ib · Nb*) · *Cb*

Another example of a statement mentioning a particular individual is

(10) If Boston is an industrial city, then it's wealthy.

And, (10) may be translated

(11) (*Ib · Cb*) ⊃ *Wb*

Returning to the use of one predicate, there are many cities besides Boston. We can say

(12) Athens is a city.

    Chicago is a city.

    Denver is a city.

and so on. The examples in (12) may be translated as

(13)   *Ca*

       Cc

       Cd

Glancing quickly at (13) reveals that, while '*C*' appears in each example, the lower case letter changes. This observation leads us to introduce *individual variables* into our notation. The lower case letters '*x*', '*y*', and '*z*' are considered *individual variables* replaceable by *individual constants*. Using our new variables, we now picture a form common to all the examples of (13):

(14)   *Cx*

Instead of '*x*', we could have used '*y*' or '*z*' and written '*Cy*' or '*Cz*'. But, for the sake of consistency, let us use '*x*' as our individual variable.

While each example in (13) is a statement, (14) is not. We can sensibly ask whether 'Athens is a city', 'Chicago is a city', or 'Denver is a city' is true or false; we cannot sensibly ask this question of '*x* is a city', that is '*Cx*'. '*Cx*' is roughly equivalent to 'it is a city' where 'it' is understood as a "pronoun" having no referent. Replacing 'it' by the name of an individual transforms 'it is a city' into a statement which may be either true or false. Here, we distinguish between a statement and a statement matrix [such as the statement matrix '*Cx*' which may be true of (or false of) an indefinitely large number of individuals and which becomes a statement when the individual variable either is replaced by the name of an individual or is given some referent].

Statements such as 'Boston is a city' may be called '*singular statements*'.

> *A singular statement asserts that a given property is true of (or false of) a particular individual or that a particular individual is (or is not) a member of a certain set.*

In contrast to singular statements we also speak of *general statements*.

> *A general statement asserts that a given property is true of (or false of) some or all individuals or that some or all individuals are (or are not) members of a certain set.*

Thus, such statements as 'Everyone who studies passes' and 'Some metals aren't precious' are general statements, as are all the categorical statements in Chapter 10. Consequently, categorical statements offer a convenient point of departure in our study of general statements.

In this chapter we shall devote our energy to mastering skills of translating English statements into our logical notation. Remember there are no mechanical rules we can follow in moving from English to the symbols of logic; we must rely on a careful and sensitive reading of what is to be translated. Then we must capture, and portray, the intended meaning in our symbolization. A very successful method of developing skills of translation is to proceed in a step-by-step fashion. We shall follow this method in the ensuing discussion. While somewhat time-consuming, you might also use this stepwise method of translation until you feel comfortable with the new symbolism and how it is used. Then, you may proceed directly from the English statement to its symbolization, and vice versa.

Let us first examine various **A** statements. Consider this example:

(15)   All astronauts are highly trained.

The contemporary hypothetical interpretation of statements such as (15) can be made more explicit:

(16)   Each thing in the universe is such that if it is an astronaut, then it is highly trained.

Clearly, such a hypothetical interpretation of (15) does not commit us to the existence of any astronaut, although astronauts do happen to exist. One reason contemporary logicians choose this interpretation of universal statements becomes more evident if we consider such statements as

(17)   All nymphs are graceful.

Here we certainly do not want our logic to commit us to the existence of nymphs. By (17), we understand only that *if* there are any nymphs, *then* they are graceful.

For the phrase 'each thing in the universe is such that' we introduce the symbol '(x)', called the ***universal quantifier***. The universal quantifier is a logical operator always followed by a statement matrix. Notice the grammatical subject of (16), 'each thing', may be viewed as an indefinite pronoun which becomes "embedded" in the universal quantifier, '(x)'. Using the universal quantifier, (16) may be reexpressed as

(18)   (x) if it is an astronaut, then it is highly trained.

Both occurrences of 'it' in (18) refer to the subject of the statement. In our new notation we use individual variables, instead of 'it', to refer to the subject embedded in the quantifier:

(19)   (x) if x is an astronaut, then x is highly trained.

Symbolizing 'astronaut' by 'A' and 'highly trained' by 'T', we obtain

(20)   (x) if x is an A, then x is T.

Rewriting (20), we place the individual variables to the immediate right-hand side of the predicate letters:

(21) (x) if Ax, then Tx.

Finally, the horseshoe may be used to symbolize the phrase 'if $\cdots$ then – – –':

(22) $(x)\ Ax \supset Tx$

But, (22) is ambiguous. If someone were to read only (22), he would not know whether the 'x' in 'Tx' refers back to the subject in the quantifier or not. The *scope* of the quantifier must be indicated by making use of appropriate punctuation marks:

(23) $(x)(Ax \supset Tx)$

In indicating the scope of any quantifier, we shall follow conventions similar to those indicating the scope of the tilde. These conventions may be stated as

> *Any quantifier shall operate over the smallest possible statement matrix following it. This statement matrix shall be indicated by parentheses, brackets, or braces. By convention, however, when the statement matrix following the quantifier employs no logical connectives, punctuation marks will be omitted.*

When individual variables are within the scope of a quantifier, they are said to be *bound* by that quantifier. Individual variables not within the scope of any quantifier are said to be *free*. Given the notions of bound and free individual variables, we can characterize a statement matrix this way:

> *A statement matrix is an expression containing at least one free individual variable such that when all occurrences of free variables are bound by a quantifier or replaced by an individual constant, the statement matrix becomes a statement.*

Assume 'A', 'B', and 'C' designate some particular predicates; then, the following expressions are all examples of statement matrixes:

    a) $\sim\ \sim Ax$
    b) $Ax \cdot Bx$
    c) $Ax \supset (Bx \supset Cx)$
    d) $(Ax \cdot Bx) \supset Cx$
    e) $Ax \lor (Bx \cdot Cx)$

Letting 'A' stand for 'athlete', 'B' for 'boxer', and 'C' for 'contestant', and replacing 'x' by 'Joe Lewis', we may convert (a)–(e) into the following statements:

    a)   It is not true that Joe Lewis is not an athlete.
    b)   The athlete, Joe Lewis, is a boxer.
    c)   If Joe Lewis is an athlete, then if he is a boxer, he is a contestant.
    d)   Unless Joe Lewis is both an athlete and a boxer, he is not a contestant.

    e)   Joe Lewis is either an athlete, or a boxer and contestant.

Before proceeding further, note this common translation mistake. Often in translating from English into logical notation someone will be careless in using punctuation marks. In particular, such carelessness is found in indicating the scope of a quantifier. It is very important to remember that every individual variable must be bound by a quantifier in a correctly translated statement. No statement can contain a free individual variable! For example, each of the following is a statement matrix; none is a statement, for each contains at least one free variable:

    a) $(x)Ax \supset Bx$
    b) $(x)(Ax \cdot Bx) \cdot \sim Cx$
    c) $(x)[Ax \cdot (Bx \lor Cx)] \supset \sim Dx$

Now, let us continue to analyze categorical statements in terms of quantificational notation. A slightly more complicated **A** statement than (18) is

(24)   Metal expands whenever heated.

With a little ingenuity, (24) may be rewritten as

(25)   Each thing in the universe is such that if it is metal, then if it is heated then it expands.

Using the universal quantifier, '(x)', and introducing the individual variable 'x' at every occurrence of 'it', we have

(26) (x) if x is metal, then if x is heated then x expands.

Continuing to symbolize (24) in a step-by-step fashion, we introduce appropriate predicate letters:

(27) (x) if x is M, then if x is H then x is E.

Placing the individual variables to the immediate right-hand side of the predicate letters yields

(28) (x) if Mx, then if Hx then Ex.

Finally, (29) is obtained by introducing the horseshoe and appropriate punctuation marks:

(29) $(x)[Mx \supset (Hx \supset Ex)]$

Notice it would be incorrect to symbolize (24) as '$(x)Mx \supset (Hx \supset Ex)$'. Why?
    A statement very similar to (24) is

(30)   Any heated metal expands.

Rewriting (30) produces

(31)   Each thing in the universe is such that if it is heated and it is metal, then it
          expands.

Once more, introducing the universal quantifier and individual variables, we have

(32) (x) if x is heated and x is metal, then x is E.

Using appropriate predicate letters gives us

(33) (x) if x is H and x is M, then x is E.

Writing the individual variables to the immediate right-hand side of the predicate
letters produces

(34) (x) if Hx and Mx, then Ex.

Replacing 'and' in (34) by the dot and 'if $\cdots$ then $---$' by the horseshoe, and
using appropriate punctuation marks, we write

(35) $(x)[(Hx \cdot Mx) \supset Ex]$

A comparison of (29) and (35) displays obvious differences in (24) and (30). While
both statement matrixes '$Mx \supset (Hx \supset Ex)$' and '$(Hx \cdot Mx) \supset Ex$' are hypothetical
in form, they differ in both their antecedents and consequents. These logical differences parallel grammatical differences found in (24) and (30).

  As a technique in translating from English to our logical notation, you may
want to follow this strategy. Whenever you find, from a grammatical viewpoint,
one or more modifiers of some subject, place the predicate letters corresponding
to those modifiers in conjunction. This procedure holds especially in connection
with adjectives, pronominal phrases, and appositives. Predicate nouns and adjectives are also put in conjunction with other modifiers in **I** and **O** statements, but not
in **A** and **E** statements. In an **A** or **E** statement we find predicate nouns and predicate
adjectives represented by the consequent of the hypothetical statement matrix in
the fully symbolized statement. For example, consider

          a) Gold metal is expensive.
          b) Gold, which is a metal, is expensive.
          c) Gold, a metal, is expensive.

Here (a)–(c) all may be symbolized

(36) $(x)[(Gx \cdot Mx) \supset Ex]$

A great advantage of combining quantificational and truth-functional notation is
that it allows us to symbolize more finely both the "subject terms" and "predicate
terms" of categorical statements. Suppose we were told

(37)   Any person who is either tolerant or understanding is happy if, and only if,
          he is not selfish.

From the viewpoint of Chapter 10 the subject term of (37) is 'person who is either tolerant or understanding', and the predicate term is 'happy if, and only if, he is not selfish'. The symbolism of (37), considered as a categorical statement, could be written

(38)   All P are H.

But now we can refine (38). Stepwise, let us translate (37) into our new notation. First, we write

(39)   Each thing in the universe is such that if it is a person and either it is tolerant or it is understanding, then it is happy if, and only if, it is not selfish.

Introducing the universal quantifier and replacing each instance of 'it' by the individual variable 'x', we have

(40)   (x) if x is a person and either x is tolerant or x is understanding, then x is happy if, and only if, x is not selfish.

Next, select appropriate predicate letters and write the individual variables to the right-hand side of them:

(41)   (x) if Px and Tx or Ux, then Hx if, and only if, not Sx.

Finally, we correctly punctuate (41), clearly indicating the "subject" and "predicate" terms and the scope of the quantifier, and also introduce truth-functional operators:

(42) $(x)\{[Px \cdot (Tx \lor Ux)] \supset (Hx \equiv \sim Sx)\}$

To move from (37) to (42) is straightforward if we proceed stepwise. The result is a clear, concise analysis of the logical form of (37).

Turning our attention to **E** categorical statements, let us analyze

(43)   No cowards are brave.

First, to say 'No cowards are brave' and 'All cowards fail to be brave' or 'All cowards are not brave' is to assert the same thing. Thus, (43) can be rewritten as

(44)   All cowards are not brave.

And (44) may be expressed

(45)   Each thing in the universe is such that if it is a coward, then it is not brave.

Continuing, we introduce the universal quantifier and individual variables:

(46)   (x) if x is a coward, then x is not brave.

Now, we write 'C' for 'coward' and 'B' for 'brave' and also place the individual variables to the immediate right-hand side of the predicate letters:

(47)   (x) if Cx, then not Bx.

Introducing truth-functional operators and punctuation marks, we have

(48) $(x)(Cx \supset \sim Bx)$

Consider another **E** statement:

(49)   Nothing which is expensive or beautiful goes unnoticed if it is a fine painting.

Reflecting on the meaning of (49) leads us to reformulate it this way:

(50)   Each thing in the universe is such that if it is expensive or it is beautiful, then if it is a fine painting then it does not go not noticed.

Again, moving step-by-step, we put (50) into quantificational notation:

(51)   (x) if x is expensive or x is beautiful, then if x is a fine painting then x does not go not noticed.

Predicate letters, followed by individual variables, are now inserted:

(52)   (x) if Ex or Bx, then if Px then not not Nx.

Completing the translation of (49), we introduce truth-functional operators and punctuation marks:

(53) $(x)[(Ex \lor Bx) \supset (Px \supset \sim \sim Nx)]$

Now let us analyze this **E** statement:

(54)   No drug which is habit-forming is either safe or beneficial if not prescribed by a physician.

(54) can be expressed, without changing meaning, as

(55)   All drugs which are habit-forming are not either safe or beneficial if not prescribed by a physician.

And (55) may be rewritten

(56)   Each thing in the universe is such that if it is a drug and it is habit forming, then if it is not prescribed by a physician then it is not the case that either it is safe or it is beneficial.

Replace 'Each thing in the universe is such that' by '(x)' and each occurrence of 'it' referring *to the subject*, 'each thing', by 'x':

(57) (x) if x is a drug and x is habit-forming, then if x is not prescribed by a physician then it is not the case that either x is safe or x is beneficial.

An occurrence of 'it' is still found in (57), but here the pronoun *does not refer* to the subject 'each thing'.

Introducing appropriate predicate letters and writing the individual variables to the right-hand side of these letters, we have

(58) (x) if Dx and Fx, then if not Px then it is not the case that either Sx or Bx.

Using truth-functional operators and appropriate punctuation marks, we write

(59) $(x)\{(Dx \cdot Fx) \supset [\sim Px \supset \sim (Sx \lor Bx)]\}$

Let us examine one more **E** statement:

(60)   No contestant will be either unnoticed or judged who is either not over twenty-one years old or unmarried.

First, we notice the pronominal clause 'who is either not over twenty-one years old or unmarried' modifies 'contestant'. To make this more evident, we may rewrite (60) as

(61)   No contestant who is either not over twenty-one years old or unmarried will be either unnoticed or judged.

The meaning of (61) is preserved by

(62)   All contestants who are either not over twenty-one years old or unmarried will not be either unnoticed or judged.

And (62) may be rewritten as

(63)   Each thing in the universe is such that if it is a contestant and either it is not over twenty-one years old or it is not married, it is not the case that either it is not noticed or it is judged.

The universal quantifier and individual variables allow

(64) (x) if x is a contestant and either x is not over twenty-one years old or x is not married, it is not the case that either x is not noticed or x is judged.

Selecting appropriate predicate letters and writing the individual variables to their right-hand side, we express (64) as

(65)   (*x*) if *Cx* and either not *Ox* or not *Mx*, it is not the case that either not *Nx* or *Jx*.

Using truth-functional operators and punctuation marks, we complete the symbolization of (60):

(66) $(x)\{[Cx \cdot (\sim Ox \lor \sim Mx)] \supset \sim (\sim Nx \lor Jx)\}$

While we do not interpret universally quantified statements as suggesting the existence of anything, this is not the case with **I** and **O** statements. To say 'Some students are clever' is to suggest that there is, in fact, at least one student who is also clever. Of course suggesting something does not make it so. Nevertheless, when using **I** and **O** statements, we do imply the existence of something. Hence, **I** and **O** statements are called *'existential statements'*.

Let us examine then

(67)   Some students are clever.

Continuing to interpret 'some' as we did in Chapter 10, page 285, the meaning of (67) is retained by

(68)   There is at least one thing in the universe such that it is a student and it is clever.

Corresponding to the phrase 'There is at least one thing in the universe such that', we introduce the symbol '$(\exists x)$', called the *'existential quantifier'*. Like the universal quantifier, the existential quantifier is a logical operator always followed by a statement matrix. Further, the subject 'thing', an indefinite pronoun, is "embedded" in the existential quantifier, '$(\exists x)$'. Still using the individual variable, '*x*', and also the existential quantifier, '$(\exists x)$', we begin to symbolize (68):

(69) $(\exists x)$ *x* is a student and *x* is clever.

Introducing predicate letters and writing the individual variables to the right of the predicate letters, we have

(70) $(\exists x)$ *Sx* and *Cx*.

The scope of the quantifier is indicated by appropriate punctuation marks and the dot replaces 'and':

(71) $(\exists x)(Sx \cdot Cx)$

Because 'All students are clever' is symbolized as '$(x)(Sx \supset Cx)$', you may be tempted to symbolize 'Some students are clever' as '$(\exists x)(Sx \supset Cx)$'. This is wrong! The truth of '$(\exists x)(Sx \supset Cx)$' is guaranteed if there is even one thing in the entire universe which is *not* a student or even one thing which *is* clever. To appreciate this observation, consider that '$(\exists x)(Sx \supset Cx)$' is logically equivalent to '$(\exists x)(\sim Sx \vee Cx)$'. But '$(\exists x)(\sim Sx \vee Cx)$' asserts that 'There is at least one thing in the universe such that either it is not a student or it is clever'. Surely, however, *this* statement is too weak to be of much interest. The statement 'Some students are clever' asserts that there does exist at least one clever student; and this is symbolized by '$(\exists x)(Sx \cdot Cx)$'.

Now, let us symbolize this **I** statement:

(72)   Some clever students are industrious.

The meaning of (72) is retained by

(73)   There is at least one thing in the universe such that it is clever and it is a student, and it is industrious.

Employing the existential quantifier and individual variables, we write

(74) $(\exists x)$ x is clever and x is a student, and x is industrious.

Now (75) is easily obtained by using appropriate predicate letters and writing the individual variables to the right-hand side of those letters:

(75) $(\exists x)$ Cx and Sx, and Ix.

We appeal to truth-functional operators and punctuation marks to obtain

(76) $(\exists x)[(Cx \cdot Sx) \cdot Ix]$

A more complicated **I** statement is

(77)   Certain students will pass or graduate who are neither clever nor industrious but lazy and dense.

Noting that 'who are neither clever nor industrious but lazy and dense' modifies 'student', we rewrite (77) as

(78)   Certain students who are neither clever nor industrious but lazy and dense will pass or graduate.

But, (78) can be reexpressed as

(79)   There is at least one thing in the universe such that it is a student and it is not the case that either it is clever or it is industrious, and it is lazy and it is dense; and either it will pass or it will graduate.

The existential quantifier and individual variables can now be employed:

(80) $(\exists x)$ x is a student and it is not the case that either x is clever or x is industrious, and x is lazy and x is dense; and either x will pass or x will graduate.

Using predicate letters and writing the individual variables to the right of them, we express (80) this way:

(81) $(\exists x)$ Sx and it is not the case that either Cx or Ix, and Lx and Dx; and either Px or Gx.

Now (82) is obtained by using truth-functional operators and punctuation marks:

(82) $(\exists x)(\{Sx\cdot[\sim(Cx \vee Ix)\cdot(Lx\cdot Dx)]\}\cdot(Px \vee Gx))$

Examining **O** statements, let us analyze

(83)   Some painters are not artists.

Example (83) may be reexpressed without changing the meaning as

(84)   There is at least one thing in the universe such that it is a painter and it is not an artist.

The existential quantifier and individual variables allow

(85) $(\exists x)$ x is a painter and x is not an artist.

Using predicate letters and placing the individual variables to the right of these letters, we form

(86) $(\exists x)$ Px and not Ax.

The complete symbolization of (83) is reached with truth-functional operators and punctuation marks:

(87) $(\exists x)(Px\cdot\sim Ax)$

Imagine you were told to put the following into quantificational notation:

(88)   There are painters who are not artists or craftsmen.

Sentence (88) is ambiguous, for it *may* be read two distinct ways:

(89)   There are painters who are either craftsmen or not artists.
(90)   There are painters who are neither artists nor craftsmen.

Example (89) is viewed as an **I** statement but (90) is an **O** statement. Which reading of (88) is correct can only be answered by supplying a context for the sentence. Not having such a context, but continuing our general examination of **O** statements, we shall analyze (90) this way:

(91)   There is at least one thing in the universe such that it is a painter and it is not the case that either it is an artist or it is a craftsman.

Once more we use the existential quantifier and individual variables in moving to our final symbolization of (90):

(92) $(\exists x)$ x is a painter and it is not the case that either x is an artist or x is a craftsman.

Employing predicate letters and writing the individual variables in their correct position produces

(93) $(\exists x)$ Px and it is not the case that either Ax or Cx.

Completing the symbolization of (90), we use truth-functional operators and punctuation marks:

(94) $(\exists x)[Px \cdot \sim (Ax \vee Cx)]$

As a final example of an **O** statement, let us consider

(95)   Some painters are not artists who, nevertheless, are craftsmen and decorators only if they have an eye for color balance.

Again, we find a pronominal clause—'who are craftsmen and decorators only if they have an eye for color balance'—modifying the subject, 'painters':

(96)   Some painters who are craftsmen and decorators only if they have an eye for color balance are not artists.

Preparing to put (96) into quantificational symbols, we rewrite it as

(97)   There is at least one thing in the universe such that it is a painter and if it is a craftsman and it is a decorator, then it has an eye for color balance; and it is not an artist.

We obtain (98) by introducing the existential quantifier and individual variables:

(98) $(\exists x)$ x is a painter and if x is a craftsman and x is a decorator, then x has an eye for color balance; and x is not an artist.

Statement (99) is written by using appropriate predicate letters and placing the individual variables to their right-hand side:

(99) $(\exists x)\ Px$ and if Cx and Dx, then Bx; and not Ax.

Lastly, properly place truth-functional operators and punctuation marks:

(100) $(\exists x)\big(\{Px\cdot[(Cx\cdot Dx) \supset Bx]\}\cdot \sim Ax\big)$

Remember, there are no mechanical rules we can follow to translate every quantification statement into the desired notation. The step-by-step technique does, however, prove helpful in translating. But as you become more facile in moving from English to symbols, you should be able to go directly from the English statement to its symbolic form and vice versa.

To become more facile in using our new notation, let us now translate from symbols to English. If we are given a "vocabulary" indicating an interpretation of the predicate letters, such translations are readily accomplished. Suppose we wish to render the following into English:

(101) $(x)\{[Px\cdot(Sx \vee Tx)] \supset [Rx \supset (Ex\cdot Kx)]\}$

Further, we are given the following "vocabulary", where the equals sign means 'is to be read':

$$\text{'}Ex\text{'} = \text{'}x \text{ is well-educated'}$$
$$\text{'}Kx\text{'} = \text{'}x \text{ is knowledgeable'}$$
$$\text{'}Px\text{'} = \text{'}x \text{ is a person'}$$
$$\text{'}Rx\text{'} = \text{'}x \text{ is respected'}$$
$$\text{'}Sx\text{'} = \text{'}x \text{ is a scientist'}$$
$$\text{'}Tx\text{'} = \text{'}x \text{ is a technician'}$$

Stepwise, we may now transform (101) to an English statement. We may first write

(102)   Each thing in the universe is such that if Px and either Sx or Tx, then if Rx then Ex and Kx.

Next, we can proceed to

(103)   Each thing in the universe is such that if it is a person and either it is a scientist or it is a technician, then if it is respected it is well-educated and it is knowledgeable.

And now, (103) goes quickly into

(104)   All persons who are either scientists or technicians are respected only if well-educated and knowledgeable.

Group A:

Translate the following singular statements into predicate notation, using the suggested symbols.

(1) W. H. Auden is an exciting poet. (*E, P; a*)

(2) T. S. Eliot is a dramatist or a poet. (*D, P; e*)

(3) Bowman Clarke will become a famous philosopher only if he is widely read. (*F, P, R; c*)

(4) A Harvard professor, Willard Quine, is an outstanding logician. (*P, O, L; q*)

(5) Norman Malcolm, who read philosophy under Ludwig Wittgenstein, studied in England and teaches at Cornell University. (*R, S, T; m*)

(6) The famous chef, Julia Child, appears regularly on television. (*F, C, A; c*)

(7) Unless Ludwig Wittgenstein is read and studied, he isn't an important philosopher. (*R, S, I, P; w*)

(8) Claes Oldenburg, born in Stockholm and educated at Yale, is a humorous artist. (*B, E, H, A; o*)

(9) D. L. Gordy, an information scientist, matriculated at Georgia Institute of Technology while engaging in research at the Engineering Experiment Station. (*I, S, M, E; g*)

(10) Edward Hopper was either an American realist painter or a French impressionist, but not both. (*A, R, P, F, I; h*)

Group B:

Translate the following categorical statements into predicate notation, using the suggested symbols.

(1) Behavior originates in stimuli. (*B, O; x*)

(2) Stimuli exist which aren't reinforced. (*S, R; x*)

(3) Behavior is never stimulus-free. (*B, S; x*)

(4) Whatever is an hallucinatory-producing drug is unsafe. (*P, D, S; x*)

(5) Drugs are unsafe if hallucinatory-producing. (*D, S, P; x*)

(6) No drug if hallucinatory-producing is safe. (*D, P, S; x*)

(7) There are investments which aren't both practical and sound. (*I, P, S; x*)

(8) Securities which are rapidly declining in value will never be purchased by small investors. (*S, D, P; x*)

(9) All growth investments are sound if, and only if, they produce a steady gain. (*I, S, P; x*)

(10)   No philosopher is an Idealist who is also a student of Ludwig Wittgenstein or a follower of Rudolf Carnap. (*P, I, W, C; x*)

(11)   Many Neo-Thomistic philosophers are Roman Catholics or Anglicans, but not both. (*N, P, C, A; x*)

(12)   Some philosophers who are neither Existentialists nor Thomists are, nonetheless, not Wittgensteinians. (*P, E, T, W; x*)

(13)   No philosopher is a sense-data theorist who is convinced by the arguments of J. L. Austin if he has read *Sense and Sensibilia*. (*P, T, C, R; x*)

(14)   If anyone is convinced by the arguments of J. L. Austin whenever he reads *Sense and Sensibilia*, then he is a philosopher only if he isn't a sense-data theorist. (*C, R, P, T; x*)

(15)   Any Euclidian figure is such that if it is a triangle, then it has equal angles if, and only if, it also has equal sides. (*E, F, T, A, S; x*)

(16)   Some triangles are neither isosceles nor scalene which are Euclidean or Riemannian. (*T, I, S, E, R; x*)

(17)   A triangle which has three angles whose sum is 180° is never both Riemannian and Lobachevskian. (*T, A, S, R, L; x*)

(18)   Some Euclidean traingles which are obtuse-angled or acute-angled aren't either right-angled or isosceles. (*E, T, O, A, R, I; x*)

(19)   Someone who is either an astronaut or successful entertainer is idolized only if he is heroic or talented. (*A, S, E, I, H, T; x*)

(20)   Anyone who is interesting or entertaining while also learned is admired and respected only if he isn't overbearing and pompous. (*I, E, L, A, R, O, P; x*)

Group C:

In each of the following exercises you will find a symbolized statement and a vocabulary giving the interpretation of the predicates. Translate each symbolized statement into smoothly flowing English.

(1) $(\exists x)(Sx \cdot Ix)$

>   '*Sx*' = '*x* is a stimuli'
>   '*Ix*' = '*x* is internal to the organism'

(2) $(\exists x)[Sx \cdot (Px \triangle Mx)]$

>   '*Sx*' = '*x* is stock'
>   '*Px*' = '*x* has a good growth potential'
>   '*Mx*' = '*x* has a rapid return market'

(3) $(x)[Sx \supset (Cx \supset \sim Fx)]$

>   '*Sx*' = '*x* is stock'
>   '*Cx*' = '*x* remains constant'
>   '*Fx*' = '*x* fluctuates'

(4) $(x)\{[Mx\cdot(Lx \lor Rx)] \supset Hx\}$

         'Mx' = 'x is a mammal'
         'Lx' = 'x is linguistic'
         'Rx' = 'x is rational'
         'Hx' = 'x is human'

(5) $(\exists x)\{[Mx\cdot(Hx \supset Rx)]\cdot(Lx\cdot Bx)\}$

         'Mx' = 'x is a mammal'
         'Hx' = 'x is human'
         'Rx' = 'x is risible'
         'Lx' = 'x is linguistic'
         'Bx' = 'x is a biped'

(6) $(x)\{[(Rx \lor Fx)\cdot(Cx\cdot Sx)] \supset {\sim} Vx\}$

         'Rx' = 'x is a reptile'
         'Fx' = 'x is a fish'
         'Cx' = 'x is cold-blooded'
         'Sx' = 'x is scaly'
         'Vx' = 'x is viviparous'

(7) $(\exists x)\{[Cx\cdot(Ax \lor Bx)]\cdot(Tx \supset {\sim} Sx)\}$

         'Cx' = 'x is a chemical'
         'Ax' = 'x is an acid'
         'Bx' = 'x is a base'
         'Tx' = 'x tastes bitter'
         'Sx' = 'x is sweet'

(8) $(\exists x)\{[(Sx\cdot Px) \supset Cx]\cdot {\sim}(Fx \lor Bx)\}$

         'Sx' = 'x is common salt'
         'Px' = 'x is produced by evaporation of seawater'
         'Cx' = 'x is a source of chlorine'
         'Fx' = 'x is a source of fluorine'
         'Bx' = 'x is a source of bromine'

(9) $(x)\big(\{Cx\cdot[Ax \supset (Px \lor Nx)]\} \supset {\sim}(Sx\cdot Hx)\big)$

         'Cx' = 'x is a chemical'
         'Ax' = 'x is an acid'
         'Px' = 'x is phosphoric'
         'Nx' = 'x is nitric'
         'Sx' = 'x is slick to the touch'
         'Hx' = 'x is high on the pH scale'

(10) $(x)\{[Ax\cdot(Cx\cdot Rx)] \supset [Dx \supset (Gx\cdot Sx)]\}$

         'Ax' = 'x is an acid'
         'Cx' = 'x corrodes the more electropositive metals'
         'Rx' = 'x releases hydrogen'
         'Dx' = 'x is a proton donor'
         'Gx' = 'x gives up protons easily'
         'Sx' = 'x is strong'

2. SYMBOLIZING NONCATEGORICAL STATEMENTS

Letting '(α)' represent any universal quantifier, '$(\exists\alpha)$' any existential quantifier, 'α' any individual variable, and 'Φ' and 'Ψ' any predicates, we may then represent the forms of **A, E, I,** and **O** categorical statements as follows:

$$\textbf{A:} \quad (\alpha)(\Phi\alpha \supset \Psi\alpha)$$
$$\textbf{E:} \quad (\alpha)(\Phi\alpha \supset \sim\Psi\alpha)$$
$$\textbf{I:} \quad (\exists\alpha)(\Phi\alpha \cdot \Psi\alpha)$$
$$\textbf{O:} \quad (\exists\alpha)(\Phi\alpha \cdot \sim\Psi\alpha)$$

Notice the statement matrixes, $\Phi\alpha \supset \Psi\alpha$ and $\Phi\alpha \supset \sim\Psi\alpha$, under the scope of the quantifier in **A** and **E** statements are hypothetical in form. But the corresponding statement matrixes of **I** and **O** statements are both conjunctions.

But, there are statements which are not translated straightforwardly as **A, E, I,** or **O** categorical statements. For instance, we might read

(1)   Either everything is red or it isn't.

(1) may be rewritten without changing its meaning as

(2)   Each thing in the universe is such that either it is red or it is not red.

(2) may be translated

(3) $(x)(Rx \lor \sim Rx)$

Or, we might discover this statement:

(4)   Some things are either squares or circles.

We can reexpress (4) as

(5)   There is at least one thing in the universe such that either it is a square or it is a circle.

And now (5) may be put into our notation:

(6) $(\exists x)(Sx \lor Cx)$

We may view (3) and (6) as displaying these forms, neither of which is displayed by any categorical statement:

$$(\alpha)(\Phi\alpha \lor \sim\Phi\alpha)$$
$$(\exists\alpha)(\Phi\alpha \lor \Psi\alpha)$$

We sometimes find the word 'except', or synonymous words or phrases, used in statements:

(7)   Anyone may enter the contest except employees.

(8)   Anyone may enter the contest but employees.

Carefully reading (7) and (8), we understand them to assert that anyone who may enter the contest is not an employee *and* anyone who is not an employee may enter the contest. This is to say, anyone may enter the contest if, and only if, he is not an employee. Using the universal quantifier and triple-bar, we may translate both (7) and (8) as

(9) $(x)(Cx \equiv \sim Ex)$

Continuing to characterize an atomic statement as any substitution instance of a single statement variable coupled with no truth-functional operator, all categorical statements, including (1), (4), (7), and (8) of this section, are considered atomic. In all these examples a quantifier ranges over the *entire* expression following it. But some statements involving quantifiers may be viewed as molecular statements. Suppose we are told

(10)   Any artist is creative only if every poet is sensitive.

Expanding (10), we write

(11)   If each thing in the universe is such that if it is an artist, then it is creative; then each thing in the universe is such that if it is a poet, then it is sensitive.

(11) may be interpreted as an overall hypothetical statement whose antecedent is

(12)   each thing in the universe is such that if it is an artist, then it is creative

which may be symbolized as

(13) $(x)(Ax \supset Cx)$

The consequent of (11) is

(14)   each thing in the universe is such that if it is a poet, then it is sensitive

and (14) goes into symbols as

(15) $(x)(Px \supset Sx)$

Having symbolized separately both the antecedent and consequent of (11), we connect them with the horseshoe:

(16) $(x)(Ax \supset Cx) \supset (x)(Px \supset Sx)$

(16) may be interpreted as a molecular statement by reading '$(x)(Ax \supset Cx)$' as an instance of 'p' and '$(x)(Px \supset Sx)$' as an instance of 'q' in '$p \supset q$'.

You may be tempted to symbolize such statements as (10) in this manner:

(17) $(x)[(Ax \supset Cx) \supset (Px \supset Sx)]$

But, such a move is incorrect, for (16) and (17) do not assert the same thing. (17) is equivalent to

(18) $(x)\{[Px \cdot (Ax \supset Cx)] \supset Sx\}$

which states

(19)   All poets who are artists only if they are creative are sensitive.

(19) is an **A** categorical statement, whereas (10) is a hypothetical statement making use of two distinct **A** statements—one the antecedent and the other the consequent. Or, from a grammatical viewpoint, we can say that while (10) is a compound statement, (19) is a complex one. Such distinctions may be reflected in our symbolization.

Consider this example:

(20)   Some figures are squares while other figures are circles.

Rephrasing (20), we write

(21)   There is at least one thing in the universe such that it is a figure and it is a square, and there is at least one thing in the universe such that it is a figure and it is a circle.

Let us interpret (21) as a conjunction of two **I** statements. Consequently, we symbolize it this way:

(22) $(\exists x)(Fx \cdot Sx) \cdot (\exists x)(Fx \cdot Cx)$

Carefully note that (20) cannot be correctly symbolized as either

(23) $(\exists x)[(Fx \cdot Sx) \cdot (Fx \cdot Cx)]$

or

(24) $(\exists x)[Fx \cdot (Sx \cdot Cx)]$

(23) and (24) both assert that some figures are both squares and circles, which is false. While (22) asserts a true statement, neither (23) nor (24) does.

An interesting type of statement is exemplified by

(25)   Flounder and shrimp are to be served for dinner.

How would we move stepwise to symbolize (25)? We might begin by saying

(26)   Each thing in the universe is such that if it is a flounder and it is a shrimp, then it is served for dinner.

Using the universal quantifier and individual variables, we would next proceed to

(27) (x) x is a flounder and x is a shrimp, then x is served for dinner.

Appropriate predicate letters, followed by individual variables, yields

(28) (x) if Fx and Sx, then Dx.

Using truth-functional connectives and punctuation marks, we write

(29) $(x)[(Fx \cdot Sx) \supset Dx]$

Given the conditions required to make (29) true, we should still be waiting for dinner! According to our symbolization of (25), what is to be served for dinner is a creature which is *both* a flounder *and* a shrimp. But, there are no such creatures. (25) is not properly expressed by (29). A straightforward way of rewriting (25) without changing its meaning is

(30)   Flounder are to be served for dinner and shrimp are to be served for dinner.

(30) is easily interpreted as an overall conjunction of two **A** statements, and it can be symbolized accordingly:

(31) $(x)(Fx \supset Dx) \cdot (x)(Sx \supset Dx)$

Another correct method of symbolizing (25) is this:

(32) $(x)[(Fx \lor Sx) \supset Dx]$

(32), an **A** statement, helps to stress the important point that simply because there is the occurrence of the word 'and' in a statement, this does not guarantee the use of the dot. We must remember there are no ironclad, mechanical rules of translation. A careful reading to grasp the intended meaning of a statement, or argument, is always required.

     Another important type of molecular statement is the denial, and, like all statements, quantified statements may be denied. We may be told

(33)   All hippies are kooks.

The denial of (33) can be expressed as

(34)   It is not the case that all hippies are kooks.

Symbolizing (33), we have

(35) $(x)(Hx \supset Kx)$

But, (34) goes into symbols this way:

(36) $\sim[(x)(Hx \supset Kx)]$

There are two important points we must notice about (36). *First*, (36) is not an **E** statement. The denial of (33) is *not*

(37)   No hippies are kooks.

Later in our work we shall see that (36) is equivalent to the **O** statement

(38)   Some hippies are not kooks.

And, we know from both Squares of Opposition that **A** and **O** statements are contradictories—denials—not **A** and **E** statements. *Second*, the tilde appearing in (36) denies the entire statement, '$(x)(Hx \supset Kx)$', as indicated by the brackets. No confusion will result in dropping the brackets and writing

(39) $\sim(x)(Hx \supset Kx)$

This practice shall be followed in the remainder of our studies. Punctuation marks are eliminated from our symbolization when their omission leads to no ambiguity.

Our notational techniques have now been expanded to include instances of the molecular statement forms

$$\sim p$$
$$p \cdot q$$
$$p \lor q$$
$$p \supset q$$
$$p \triangle q$$
$$p \equiv q$$

where the statement variables are replaced by quantified statements. We can extend even further the usefulness of our techniques by considering molecular statements in which both singular and quantified statements appear. Consider this example:

(40)   If Johnson speaks, every person at the meeting will be attentive.

Let (40) be interpreted as a hypothetical statement such that its antecedent is a singular statement symbolized by '*Sj*'. Then we may further translate (40) by rewriting its consequent:

(41)   each thing in the universe is such that if it is a person and it is at the meeting, then it is attentive.

The universal quantifier and individual variables are employed to express

(42) (x) x is a person and x is at the meeting, then x is attentive.

Using predicate letters followed by individual variables, we have

(43) (x) Px and Mx, then Ax

The final move in symbolizing the consequent of (40) is to introduce truth-functional connectives and appropriate punctuation marks:

(44) $(x)[(Px \cdot Mx) \supset Ax]$

Since (44) is the symbolized consequent of (40), the complete symbolization of (40) may be expressed as

(45) $Sj \supset (x)[(Px \cdot Mx) \supset Ax]$

We shall analyze one more molecular statement using both singular and quantified statements:

(46)   While a few people do the work, Madge receives the rewards.

(46) may be interpreted as an overall conjunction whose left-hand conjunct is the quantified statement

(47)   a few people do the work.

(47) can quite simply be translated as

(48) $(\exists x)(Px \cdot Wx)$

The right-hand conjunct of (46) is a singular statement symbolized

(49) Rm

With both (48) and (49) at hand, we may completely symbolize (46):

(50) $(\exists x)(Px \cdot Wx) \cdot Rm$

Group A:

Translate the following statements into appropriate symbols using the suggested notation.

(1) Not every war is just. ($W, J; x$)

(2) There aren't any just wars. ($J, W; x$)

(3) Either we don't believe Professor Murray Gell-Mann or quarks exist. ($B, Q; x, m$)

(4) Everything is ultimately composed of quarks or structured of pions, but not both. ($C, S; x$)

(5) Anything is composite except quarks. ($C, Q; x$)

(6) Everybody is happy whenever Mildred or Julia visits Carrs Hill. ($H, V; x, m, j$)

(7) If someone is rich, then someone is either influential and powerful or rich. ($R, I, P; x$)

(8) Not everyone is wise who is rich or powerful. ($W, R, P; x$)

(9) Solomon was wise or anyone who is rich is never wise. ($W, R; x, s$)

(10) If someone repents, the saints are joyful. ($R, S, J; x$)

(11) Unless a person repents, he cannot enter the Kingdom of Heaven. ($P, R, E; x$)

(12) Each student progresses rapidly whenever Professor Goode teaches the course. ($S, P, T; x, g$)

(13) Any act is good but a selfish or harmful one. ($A, G, S, H; x$)

(14) If all metals expand whenever heated, then heated copper expands. ($M, E, H, C; x$)

(15) That certain metals are conductors is a sufficient condition for some things being either electrical conductors or insulators. ($M, C, E, I; x$)

(16) If anything is gold, then it melts if heated to 1063°C, or some gold heated to 1063°C doesn't both vaporize and melt, but not both. ($G, M, H, V; x$)

(17) Each man and woman is equal under the law except those not having citizenship. ($M, W, E, C; x$)

(18) Not every philosopher who has come under the influence of Ludwig Wittgenstein finds the study of the history of philosophy worthless, although there aren't any philosophers coming under the influence of Wittgenstein who don't recognize the importance of language. ($P, I, S, R; x$)

(19) None of the philosophers influenced by Ludwig Wittgenstein is a metaphysician but those are who have been tempered by other thinkers. ($P, I, M, T; x$)

(20) No philosopher is an Idealist who is a strict follower of the Vienna Circle and adheres to American Pragmatism if, and only if, it isn't true that some philosophers are strict followers of the Vienna Circle while also adhering to American Pragmatism and being Idealists. ($P, I, F, A; x$)

Group B:

In each of the following exercises you will find a symbolized statement and a vocabulary giving the interpretation of the predicates. Translate each symbolized statement into smoothly flowing English.

(1) $\sim(x)(Px \supset Rx)$

'Px' = 'x is a poet'
'Rx' = 'x is ethically radical'

(2) $(\exists x)(Ex \cdot Px) \supset [(\exists x)Px \cdot (\exists x)Ex]$

'Ex' = 'x is exciting'
'Px' = 'x is a poet'

(3) $Ae \supset (\exists x)(Mx \cdot Nx)$

'Ae' = 'T. S. Eliot's views are accepted'
'Mx' = 'x is a man'
'Nx' = 'x is noble'

(4) $\sim(\exists x)[(Vx \cdot Cx) \cdot \sim Hx]$

'Vx' = 'x is a vertebrate'
'Cx' = 'x is a creature'
'Hx' = 'x has a heart'

(5) $(x)[Mx \supset (Lx \supset Bx)] \bigtriangleup (\exists x)[(Mx \cdot Lx) \cdot \sim Bx]$

'Mx' = 'x is a mammal'
'Lx' = 'x has lungs'
'Bx' = 'x has a blood stream'

(6) $(\exists x)[(Gx \cdot Sx) \cdot \sim Ox] \equiv \sim(x)[Sx \supset (Gx \supset Ox)]$

'Gx' = 'x is gaseous'
'Sx' = 'x is a substance'
'Ox' = 'x is odoriferous'

(7) $(x)[(Sx \cdot Gx) \supset \sim Bx] \lor (x)[(Lx \cdot Sx) \supset \sim Bx]$

'Sx' = 'x is a substance'
'Gx' = 'x is a gas'
'Bx' = 'x has a definite boundary of its own'
'Lx' = 'x is a liquid'

(8) $[(\exists x)(Gx \cdot Dx) \lor (\exists x)(Gx \cdot Cx)] \equiv (\exists x)[(Dx \lor Cx) \cdot (Gx \lor Lx)]$

'Gx' = 'x is a gas'
'Dx' = 'x is dense'
'Cx' = 'x is colorless'
'Lx' = 'x is a liquid'

(9) $Cg \supset (x)[(Ox \lor Cx) \supset (Hx \supset Ex)]$

‘*Cg*’ = ‘J. P. Goode is correct’
‘*Ox*’ = ‘*x* is oxygen’
‘*Cx*’ = ‘*x* is copper’
‘*Hx*’ = ‘*x* is heated’
‘*Ex*’ = ‘*x* expands’

(10) $\sim(\exists x)\{[Gx\cdot(Px \lor Mx)]\cdot\sim[Sx \equiv \sim(Hx\cdot Rx)]\}$

‘*Gx*’ = ‘*x* is a gas’
‘*Px*’ = ‘*x* is pure’
‘*Mx*’ = ‘*x* is mixed’
‘*Sx*’ = ‘*x* closely approaches the specifications of Boyle’s law’
‘*Hx*’ = ‘*x* is under high pressure’
‘*Rx*’ = ‘*x* can still be represented by the law’

3. SYMBOLIZING RELATIONAL STATEMENTS

Let us extend our present notation two ways to strengthen it for analyzing descriptive language. First, we may allow predicate letters to be followed by more than one individual constant or variable.* Heretofore, predicate letters have been interpreted indifferently in terms of properties or sets, but we shall now also consider them as representing relations holding (or not holding) between individuals and call such predicate letters ‘relational predicates’. Second, we may let quantifiers fall within the scope of other quantifiers.

Suppose we symbolize ‘talks to’ or ‘is talked to by’ as ‘*T*’, ‘Smith’ by ‘*s*’, and ‘Jones’ by ‘*j*’. Then we may put the following into our extended notation.

(1)   Smith talks to Jones.

Jones is talked to by Smith.

Both examples are rendered

(2)   *Tsj*

We must be careful in ordering the individual constants or variables following the predicate letter. It would be incorrect to express (1) as ‘*Tjs*’. ‘*Tjs*’ is translated

(3)   Jones talks to Smith.

Smith is talked to by Jones.

---

*While a predicate letter may be followed by any number of individual constants or variables, we shall limit our examples to “two-place predicates”. The procedures, however, applying to the examples in this section and in the following chapter are equally applicable to predicate letters followed by more than two individual constants or variables.

Instead of talking about Smith and Jones, we could as well symbolize 'Williams talks to Brown'. Here, we write

(4)   *Twb*

Once more, the order of the individual constants following the predicate letter is important. '*Tbw*' is not a correct symbolization of 'Williams talks to Brown'.

We do not need to limit ourselves to conversations between Smith and Jones, Williams and Brown, etc. We may speak of any individual talking to any other. Instead of individual constants, we must now use individual variables. Thus, in general, '*x* talks to *y*', or '*y* is talked to by *x*', may be expressed by the statement matrix

(5)   *Txy*

Two distinct individual variables are used in (5) to show the possibility of two distinct individuals, one talking to the other. (5), however, also permits such examples as 'Payne talks to Payne' when we mean 'Payne talks to himself'. While the same individual constant must be substituted at each occurrence of the same individual variable following the predicate letter, the same individual constant can also be substituted for different individual variables. Why distinct individual variables usually follow a predicate letter is more obvious in such examples as 'is the father of'. In such cases it would be incorrect to write

(6)   *Fxx*

(6) is incorrect because it suggests '*x* is the father of itself'. Yet, nothing is literally its own father!

If we combine individual constants and variables, we can then symbolize such statements as

(7)   Someone talks to Greene.

Moving stepwise, (7) is rewritten as

(8)   There is at least one thing in the universe such that it talks to Greene.

Introducing an existential quantifier and replacing 'it' by an individual variable, we proceed to

(9) $(\exists x)$ *x* talks to Greene.

A final symbolization of (7) is reached by introducing the predicate letter '*T*' and the individual constant '*g*':

(10) $(\exists x)Txg$

On the other hand, we can also symbolize

(11)   Greene talks to someone.

From (11) we move to

(12)   There is at least one thing in the universe such that Greene talks to it.

Using the existential quantifier, '$(\exists x)$', and individual variable, 'x', we write

(13) $(\exists x)$ Greene talks to x.

From (13) we obtain

(14) $(\exists x)\ Tgx$

Perhaps Greene is very popular—everyone talks to him; so

(15)   Everyone talks to Greene.

We may first go to

(16)   Each thing in the universe is such that it talks to Greene.

(16) may be rewritten

(17) $(x)\ x$ talks to Greene

Continuing to use 'T' and 'g', (17) is translated

(18) $(x)Txg$

Also, Greene might be gregarious—he talks to everyone, or

(19)   Greene talks to everyone.

The meaning of (19) is retained by

(20)   Each thing in the universe is such that Greene talks to it.

Using the universal quantifier, '(x)', and the individual variable, 'x', we write

(21) (x) Greene talks to x.

and (21) is completely symbolized:

(22) $(x)Tgx$

The second way our notation is expanded is by letting quantifiers fall within the scope of other quantifiers. Suppose we wish to symbolize this ambiguous example:

(23)   Everyone talks to someone.

(23) may be rewritten:

(24)   Everything in the universe is such that it talks to someone.

Moving from (24) to (25) is easily accomplished:

(25) (x) x talks to someone.

Our problem now becomes one of rendering into our notation the 'someone' of (25). The meaning of (25) is retained in

(26) (x) there is at least one thing in the universe such that x talks to it.

For 'there is at least one thing in the universe such that' we write '$(\exists y)$'; and for 'it', 'y'. A 'y', instead of an 'x', is chosen to distinguish clearly between the quantifier and individual variable introduced in (25) and (27):

(27) $(x)(\exists y)$ x talks to y.

Using the predicate letter 'T', we assert

(28) $(x)(\exists y)Txy$

In (28) one quantifier, '$(\exists y)$', falls within the scope of another, '(x)'. It is important to notice in (28) why the universal quantifier is written before the existential. Symbolizing (23), we might also write

(29) $(\exists y)(x)Txy$

(28) says that everyone talks to someone, but not necessarily the same person. Once any x is selected, some y is found such that 'x talks to y' is true even if the individual, x, talks to itself. But, (29) maintains

(30)   There is someone to whom everyone talks, and they all talk to the same individual.

Once some y is selected, then every x talks to that individual. So (28) and (29) are not logically equivalent statements; they are not interchangeable. While (29) logically implies (28), the reverse is not the case. (28) and (29) simply do not mean the same thing, although they may both be used to symbolize the ambiguous (23).

Whether we symbolize (23) as (28) or (29) depends upon the *context* of (23).

On the other hand, the ordering of the quantifiers is logically insignificant when they are all universal or all existential, as in

(31) $(x)(y)Txy$

(32) $(\exists x)(\exists y)Txy$

(31) says everyone talks to everyone, including himself, while (32) maintains that someone talks to someone. (31) is logically equivalent to

(33) $(y)(x)Txy$

and (32) to

(34) $(\exists y)(\exists x)Txy$

So far in our examples we have assumed that people, or persons, are talking—not, say, Martians. This assumption can be made explicit in our various symbolizations. Consider (23) which may be reexpressed as

(35)   Every person talks to someone.

Expand (35) then as:

(36)   Each thing in the universe is such that if it is a person, then it talks to someone.

Using a universal quantifier, individual variables, and parentheses to indicate the scope of the quantifier, (36) may be written

(37) (x) (if x is a person, then x talks to someone)

Introducing 'Px' for 'x is a person' and the horseshoe operator, we proceed to

(38) $(x)(Px \supset x$ talks to someone)

Moving on, we reexpress 'x talks to someone' by

(39)   There is at least one thing in the universe such that it is a person and x talks to it.

With an appropriate quantifier, individual variables, and punctuation marks to indicate scope, (39) may be written

(40) $(\exists y)(y$ is a person and x talks to $y)$

(40) then becomes

(41) $(\exists y)(Py \cdot Txy)$

Combining (38) and (41) and indicating the scope of the various quantifiers by appropriate punctuation marks, we obtain the complete symbolization of (35):

(42) $(x)[Px \supset (\exists y)(Py \cdot Txy)]$

Now, let's try another example:

(43)   Someone talks to everyone.

(43) may be rewritten

(44)   There is at least one thing in the universe such that it is a person and it talks to everyone.

Expressing (44) with the help of an existential quantifier, individual variables, and punctuation marks to display scope, we assert

(45) $(\exists x)(x$ is a person and x talks to everyone$)$

Letting 'Px' represent 'x is a person' and introducing the dot, we have

(46) $(\exists x)(Px \cdot x$ talks to everyone$)$

The phrase 'x talks to everyone' may be rendered

(47)   each thing in the universe is such that if it is a person, then x talks to it.

A universal quantifier, individual variables, and punctuation marks are used to obtain

(48) $(y)($if y is a person, then x talks to $y)$

(48) moves straightforwardly to

(49) $(y)(Py \supset Txy)$

Combining (46) and (49), we have a final symbolization of (43):

(50) $(\exists x)[Px \cdot (y)(Py \supset Txy)]$

A more complicated example than either (35) or (43) is

(51)   Whatever draws a circle draws a figure.

We may first expand (51) as

(52)   Each thing in the universe is such that if it draws a circle, then it draws a figure.

A universal quantifier, individual variables, and punctuation marks yield

(53) (x) (if x draws a circle, then x draws a figure)

Surely, in (53) 'a circle' is not understood as 'every circle' or 'all circles' but, rather, as 'some circle'. Similarly, 'a figure' is understood as 'some figure'. Therefore, we reexpress (53) this way:

(54) (x) (if x draws some circle, then x draws some figure)

Using the horseshoe operator, (54) is put in this form:

(55) (x) (x draws some circle $\supset$ x draws some figure)

How may we analyze 'x draws some circle' in terms of our expanded notation? This way:

(56)   there is at least one thing in the universe such that it is a circle and x draws it.

Following our familiar procedure, we move to

(57) $(\exists y)(Cy \cdot Dxy)$

Now, with (57), (55) is rewritten:

(58) $(x)[(\exists y)(Cy \cdot Dxy) \supset x$ draws some figure]

'x draws some figure' still remains to be symbolized. First, we move to

(59)   there is at least one thing in the universe such that it is a figure and x draws it.

And then, we write

(60) $(\exists y)(Fy \cdot Dxy)$

Combining (60) with (58) yields a final symbolization of (51):

(61) $(x)[(\exists y)(Cy \cdot Dxy) \supset (\exists y)(Fy \cdot Dxy)]$

Notice in (61) the existential quantifier, '$(\exists y)$', appears twice. The first of these quantifiers ranges over '$Cy \cdot Dxy$', while the second ranges over '$Fy \cdot Dxy$'. Since the 'y's in '$Cy \cdot Dxy$' and those in '$Fy \cdot Dxy$' fall under the scope of different quantifiers, they may or may not stand for the same thing. The situation we find in (61) is analogous to

(62)   Someone came and someone left.

and

(63)   Someone came and left.

In (62) it is an open question whether the same person both came and left. One person may have come, while another left. However, in (63) we understand that the same person both came and left. So, to clarify further the scope of the quantifiers in (61), we may use the individual variable, 'z', in place of 'y' in either '$Cy \cdot Dxy$' or '$Fy \cdot Dxy$'. Thus, we could write

(64) $(x)[(\exists y)(Cy \cdot Dxy) \supset (\exists z)(Fz \cdot Dxz)]$

Now, instead of moving from English statements to our expanded notation, let us reverse the procedure. For example, assume the following "vocabulary":

$$\begin{aligned}
'Gy' &= \text{'}y \text{ is glass'} \\
'Hy' &= \text{'}y \text{ is a house'} \\
'Px' &= \text{'}x \text{ is a person'} \\
'Sz' &= \text{'}z \text{ is a stone'} \\
'Lxy' &= \text{'}x \text{ lives in } y\text{'} \\
'Txz' &= \text{'}x \text{ should throw } z\text{'}
\end{aligned}$$

Systematically, let us render the following into idiomatic English:

(65) $(x)(\{Px \cdot (\exists y)[(Gy \cdot Hy) \cdot Lxy]\} \supset (z)(Sz \supset \sim Txz))$

Beginning with '$(z)(Sz \supset \sim Txz)$', the "smallest part" of (65), we assert

(66)   Each thing, z, in the universe is such that if Sz, then not Txz.

(66) becomes

(67)   Each thing, z, in the universe is such that if z is a stone, then x should not throw z.

'$(\exists y)[(Gy \cdot Hy) \cdot Lxy]$' may be translated

(68)   There is at least one thing, y, in the universe such that Gy and Hy, and Lxy.

Continuing, we move from (68) to

(69)   There is at least one thing, y, in the universe such that y is glass and y is a house, and x lives in y.

We may translate '$Px \cdot (\exists y)[(Gy \cdot Hy) \cdot Lxy]$' as

(70) Px and there is at least one thing, y, in the universe such that y is glass and y is a house, and x lives in y.

or

(71) x is a person and there is at least one thing, y, in the universe such that y is glass and y is a house, and x lives in y.

Using (67) and (71), we now render (65) into

(72)   Each thing, x, in the universe is such that if x is a person, and there is at least one thing, y, in the universe such that y is glass and y is a house and x lives in y, then each thing, z, in the universe is such that if z is a stone, then x should not throw z.

(72) is hardly in idiomatic English, but (73) is:

(73)   People who live in glass houses should not throw stones.

As you become familiar and comfortable with this expanded notation, you will want to move more directly both from statements to symbols and symbols to statements.

A common mistake in symbolizing any quantified statement is carelessness in indicating the exact scope of a quantifier. The possibility of such a mistake becomes even more acute in symbolizing relational predicates and quantifiers ranging over other quantifiers. For example, (42), '$(x)[Px \supset (\exists y)(Py \cdot Txy)]$', is not correctly symbolized as

(74) $(x)Px \supset (\exists y)(Py \cdot Txy)$

(74) is incorrect because there is a free 'x' in 'Txy'. The 'y' in 'Txy' is bound by '$(\exists y)$', but the 'x' does not fall under the scope of any quantifier. (42) would not be correctly symbolized as

(75) $(x)(Px \supset (\exists y)Py \cdot Txy)$

Here the 'x' is bound in 'Txy', but the 'y' is not. Remember, in any properly symbolized quantified statement, every individual variable must be bound by some quantifier. Note that we also may use different individual variables with correct punctuation marks to indicate the scope of various quantifiers.

Once more, it is important to realize that there are no mechanical rules which, if followed, guarantee a correct translation of a statement. It is necessary to read carefully every statement to be analyzed and then move step-by-step from, say, an English example to its symbolized form (or the reverse). What is required in going from English to our logical notation is a sensitivity to language rather than a set of mechanical rules.

Group A:

Assume we are speaking of people; using individual variables and '*R*' to represent 'respects', symbolize each of the following.

(1) Everyone respects himself.

(2) Someone respects someone or other.

(3) Someone respects everyone.

(4) Everyone respects someone or other.

(5) There is someone respected by everyone.

(6) No one respects everyone.

(7) There isn't someone whom everyone respects.

(8) There is someone whom everyone doesn't respect.

(9) No one respects nobody.

(10) Some don't respect themselves.

Group B:

Symbolize the following, using the suggested notation.

(1) Every natural number other than zero is a successor of zero.

> '*Nx*' = '*x* is a natural number other than zero'
> '*Fxa*' = '*x* is a successor of zero'

(2) Zero is not the successor of any natural number.

> '*Nx*' = '*x* is a natural number'
> '*Sax*' = 'zero is a successor of *x*'

(3) The successor of any number is a number.

> '*Nx*' = '*x* is a number'
> '*Ny*' = '*y* is a number'
> '*Sxy*' = '*x* is a successor of *y*'

(4) No successor of an even number is an even number.

> '*Nx*' = '*x* is an even number'
> '*Ny*' = '*y* is an even number'
> '*Sxy*' = '*x* is a successor of *y*'

(5) All numbers are succeeded by some number or another.

> '*Nx*' = '*x* is a number'
> '*Ny*' = '*y* is a number'
> '*Sxy*' = '*x* is succeeded by *y*'

357

(6)   A few students appreciate all their professors.

'*Py*' = '*y* is a professor'
'*Sx*' = '*x* is a student'
'*Axy*' = '*x* appreciates *y*'
'*Pyx*' = '*y* is a professor of *x*'

(7)   Most students do not like every course they take.

'*Cy*' = '*y* is a course'
'*Sx*' = '*x* is a student'
'*Lxy*' = '*x* likes *y*'
'*Txy*' = '*x* takes *y*'

(8)   Not all students entering a university will receive a degree.

'*Dz*' = '*z* is a degree'
'*Sx*' = '*x* is a student'
'*Uy*' = '*y* is a university'
'*Exy*' = '*x* enters *y*'
'*Rxz*' = '*x* receives *z*'

(9)   Certain materials used by scientists conduct electrical impulses.

'*Ly*' = '*y* is an electrical impulse'
'*Mx*' = '*x* is a material'
'*Sz*' = '*z* is a scientist'
'*Cxy*' = '*x* conducts *y*'
'*Uxz*' = '*x* is used by *z*'

(10) If any unbalanced force does not act on some body, that body continues in a state
of rest or uniform motion (but not both).

'*By*' = '*y* is a body'
'*Fx*' = '*x* is a force'
'*Mw*' = '*w* is a state of uniform motion'
'*Rz*' = '*z* is a state of rest'
'*Ux*' = '*x* is unbalanced'
'*Axy*' = '*x* acts on *y*'
'*Ixw*' = '*x* is in *w*'
'*Ixz*' = '*x* is in *z*'

Group C:

In each of the following exercises there is a symbolized statement and a vocabulary
giving an interpretation of its predicates. Translate each symbolized statement into
smoothly flowing English.

(1) $(x)(Px \supset Fxg)$

'*Px*' = '*x* is a patient person'
'*Fxg*' = '*x* is a friend of God'

(2) $(x)[Px \supset (\exists y)(Fy \cdot Nxy)]$

$\qquad\qquad\qquad$ 'Fy' = 'y is a friend'
$\qquad\qquad\qquad$ 'Px' = 'x is a person'
$\qquad\qquad\qquad$ 'Nxy' = 'x needs y'

(3) $(x)[Hx \supset (\exists y)(Ey \cdot Mxy)]$

$\qquad\qquad\qquad$ 'Ey' = 'y is an error'
$\qquad\qquad\qquad$ 'Hx' = 'x is human'
$\qquad\qquad\qquad$ 'Mxy' = 'x makes y'

(4) $(x)[Dx \supset (\exists y)(Ey \cdot Fxy)]$

$\qquad\qquad\qquad$ 'Ey' = 'y is an error'
$\qquad\qquad\qquad$ 'Dx' = 'x is divine'
$\qquad\qquad\qquad$ 'Fxy' = 'x forgives y'

(5) $(x)[(Sx \cdot Mx) \supset (\exists y)(Iy \cdot Exy)]$

$\qquad\qquad\qquad$ 'Iy' = 'y is injustice'
$\qquad\qquad\qquad$ 'Mx' = 'x is a man'
$\qquad\qquad\qquad$ 'Sx' = 'x is silent'
$\qquad\qquad\qquad$ 'Exy' = 'x still endures y'

(6) $(x)[(Lx \cdot Mx) \supset {\sim}(\exists y)(Fy \cdot Kxy)]$

$\qquad\qquad\qquad$ 'Fy' = 'y is a friend'
$\qquad\qquad\qquad$ 'Lx' = 'x is lonely'
$\qquad\qquad\qquad$ 'Mx' = 'x is a man'
$\qquad\qquad\qquad$ 'Kxy' = 'x knows y'

(7) $(x)\{[Px \cdot (\exists y)(Py \cdot Wxy)] \supset Wxx\}$

$\qquad\qquad\qquad$ 'Px' = 'x is a person'
$\qquad\qquad\qquad$ 'Py' = 'y is a person'
$\qquad\qquad\qquad$ 'Wxx' = 'x wrongs x'
$\qquad\qquad\qquad$ 'Wxy' = 'x wrongs y'

(8) $(x)(\{Px \cdot (\exists y)[(Py \cdot Nyx) \cdot Lxy]\} \supset Lxg)$

$\qquad\qquad\qquad$ 'Px' = 'x is a person'
$\qquad\qquad\qquad$ 'Py' = 'y is a person'
$\qquad\qquad\qquad$ 'Lxg' = 'x loves God'
$\qquad\qquad\qquad$ 'Lxy' = 'x loves y'
$\qquad\qquad\qquad$ 'Nyx' = 'y is the neighbor of x'

(9) $(x)\big(Px \supset (y)\{[(Py \cdot Fy) \cdot Nxy] \supset (Gy \cdot Fy)\}\big)$

$\qquad\qquad\qquad$ 'Fy' = 'y is a friend'
$\qquad\qquad\qquad$ 'Gy' = 'y is genuine'
$\qquad\qquad\qquad$ 'Px' = 'x is a person'
$\qquad\qquad\qquad$ 'Py' = 'y is a person'
$\qquad\qquad\qquad$ 'Nxy' = 'x is in need of y'

(10) $(x)\big(Wx \supset \{(\exists y)[Py \cdot (z)(Az \supset Fzy)] \cdot Gwy\}\big)$

'Az' = 'z is an angel'
'Py' = 'y is a person'
'Wx' = 'x is a woman'
'Fzy' = 'z fears to tread to y'
'Gwy' = 'w goes to y'

12

Arguments Involving Quantifiers

In Chapter 11 various statements using quantifiers were analyzed. We must now investigate how such statements can function in proofs of validity. Constructing proofs of validity involving quantifiers requires expansion of our Rules of Transformation. In the next two sections, four new argument forms will be introduced. Two of these forms are used with the universal quantifier and two with the existential quantifier.

To develop our argument forms, 'α' will stand for any individual variable and '$\Psi\alpha$' for any statement matrix containing at least one free occurrence of α. Thus, each of the following may be represented by '$\Psi\alpha$':

$$Ax$$
$$Ax \supset Bx$$
$$Ax \lor Bx$$
$$Ax \cdot Bx$$
$$(x)[Ax \cdot (Bx \lor Cx)] \equiv Dx$$

Further, let '(α)' represent any universal quantifier and '$(\exists\alpha)$' any existential quantifier. Then '$(\alpha)\Psi\alpha$' depicts any universally quantified statement and '$(\exists\alpha)\Psi\alpha$' any existentially quantified statement.

Initially, we shall also speak of substitution instances of a statement matrix Ψα this way:

> *A substitution instance of a statement matrix* **Ψα** *is the result of replacing every free occurrence of* **α** *in* **Ψα** *by the same individual constant.*

Thus, if '$Ax \supset Bx$' is a statement matrix, '$Aa \supset Ba$' is a substitution instance of it. However, '$Aa \supset Bx$' and '$Aa \supset Bc$' are not substitution instances of '$Ax \supset Bx$'. In '$Aa \supset Bx$' *every* free occurrence of α is not replaced by the same individual constant. On the other hand, '$Aa \supset Bc$' is not a substitution instance of '$Ax \supset Bx$' because every free occurrence of α is not replaced by the *same* individual constant.

1. UNIVERSAL INSTANTIATION AND PRELIMINARY UNIVERSAL GENERALIZATION

Suppose a statement $(\alpha)\Psi\alpha$ is true. If $(\alpha)\Psi\alpha$ is true, $\Psi\alpha$ must be true of everything in the universe. For example, assume the truth of

(1)   All men are risible.

This may be symbolized as

(2) $(x)(Mx \supset Rx)$

Here, we view (2) as represented by '$(\alpha)\Psi\alpha$', and '$Mx \supset Rx$' by '$\Psi\alpha$'. Since (1) and, consequently, (2) are accepted as true, '$Mx \supset Rx$' must be true of everything. For example, each of the following must be true:

(3)   If Alex is a man, then Alex is risible.

        If Bruce is a man, then Bruce is risible.

        If Carl is a man, then Carl is risible.

and so on. Each example of (3) may be symbolized as a substitution instance of '$Mx \supset Rx$':

(4) $Ma \supset Ra$

        $Mb \supset Rb$

        $Mc \supset Rc$

In general then

$(\alpha)\Psi\alpha$ *is true if for every substitution of the same individual constant at each free occurrence of α in $\Psi\alpha$, then $\Psi\alpha$ becomes a true statement.*

We may now formulate our first argument form, *Universal Instantiation*. Letting 'β' stand for any individual constant, we assert

Universal Instantiation (*UI*)

$$(\alpha)\ \Psi\alpha$$
$$\therefore \Psi\beta$$

Beginning with an overall universally quantified statement, we may assert any instance of that statement by (1) dropping the quantifier and (2) substituting at every free occurrence of α in $\Psi\alpha$ the same individual constant β. Following these steps, we *instantiate* the quantified statement.

Turning to a particular argument, let us see how Universal Instantiation is used to construct a proof of validity.

(5)   Every poet is a dreamer. W. H. Auden is a poet. Accordingly, Auden is also a dreamer.

Symbolizing (5), we continue:

(6) $\therefore Da$
    1) $(x)(Px \supset Dx)$ Pr
    2) Pa Pr

The first premiss declares something to be true of anything in the universe—namely, if it is a poet, then it is also a dreamer. And certainly, *if* the first premiss is true of anything, *then* it is true of the poet, Auden. Thus, (6) can be augmented by this line:

    3) $Pa \supset Da$ 1, UI

As the justification indicates, '$Pa \supset Da$' is obtained from line 1 by Universal Instantiation. Now, the conclusion, 'Da', is the consequent of line 3, while the antecedent of line 3 appears as a separate statement in line 2. Thus, Modus Ponens quickly leads to our conclusion:

(7) $\therefore Da$
    1) $(x)(Px \supset Dx)$ Pr
    2) Pa Pr
    3) $Pa \supset Da$ 1, UI
    4) $\therefore Da$ 3, 2, MP

Assuming the first premiss of (5) to be true of anything, we could have instantiated line 1 in terms of any individual we wish, say, S. F. Barker:

(8) $\therefore Da$
   1) $(x)(Px \supset Dx)$ Pr
   2) Pa Pr
   3) $Pb \supset Db$ 1, UI

Line 3 of (8) is acceptable in the sense that Universal Instantiation has been correctly used. However, '$Pb \supset Db$' will not help us obtain 'Da'. Only by instantiating the first premiss in terms of 'a' can we reach the conclusion of (5). And, as a general rule of thumb,

> *if the conclusion of a particular argument is a singular statement mentioning one individual, instantiate universally quantified premisses in terms of that individual mentioned in the conclusion.*

It is important to remember that Universal Instantiation is an argument form applying to whole lines of a proof. For example, the following move from the first to the second line is incorrect:

(9) $\therefore Aa \supset Ca$
   1) $(x)(Ax \supset Bx) \cdot (x)(Bx \supset Cx)$ Pr
   2) $(Aa \supset Ba) \cdot (x)(Bx \supset Cx)$ 1, UI

Universal Instantiation can never be used on a part of a line. Of course we can construct a proof for (9) this way:

(10) $\therefore Aa \supset Ca$
   1) $(x)(Ax \supset Bx) \cdot (x)(Bx \supset Cx)$ Pr
   2) $(x)(Ax \supset Bx)$ 1, Simp
   3) $(x)(Bx \supset Cx) \cdot (x)(Ax \supset Bx)$ 1, Com
   4) $(x)(Bx \supset Cx)$ 3, Simp
   5) $Aa \supset Ba$ 2, UI
   6) $Ba \supset Ca$ 4, UI
   7) $\therefore Aa \supset Ca$ 5, 6, HS

In instantiating a universally quantified statement, $(\alpha)\Psi\alpha$, we said that at every free occurrence of α in $\Psi\alpha$ we substitute the same individual *constant*. We now expand this notion of substitution by permitting the substitution of a free individual variable β at every free occurrence of α in $\Psi\alpha$. For example, the following are legitimate uses of Universal Instantiation:

(11)

  1) $(x)(Px \supset Dx)$ Pr
  2) $Px \supset Dx$ 1, UI

  1) $(x)(Px \supset Dx)$ Pr
  2) $Py \supset Dy$ 1, UI

  1) $(x)(Px \supset Dx)$ Pr
  2) $Pz \supset Dz$ 1, UI

Universal Instantiation permits us to move not only from statements to other statements, as in (7), but also from statements to statement matrixes, as in (11). Why?
If $(\alpha)\Psi\alpha$ is true, $\Psi\alpha$ is true of every individual in the universe. That is, no matter
what individual constant is substituted in $\Psi\alpha$, the substitution instance will convert
to a true statement. But imagine we are not concerned with any particular individual as such. Then we can indicate something of individuals by using individual
variables instead of individual constants. Consequently, statement matrixes may
become part of a proof of validity, as in (11). We revise, therefore, the rule of Universal Instantiation by saying 'β' may depict either an individual constant or an
individual variable.

Because statement matrixes, as well as statements, are allowed to function in
proofs of validity, the concept of a statement variable must be expanded. Heretofore, 'p', 'q', 'r', and 's' have ranged only over statements. We now augment the
range of statement variables to include statement matrixes. In effect, then, we may
substitute either statements or statement matrixes at any occurrence of a statement
variable. This expansion of the range of statement variables has the important
consequence of permitting the use of all truth-functional Rules of Transformation
—argument forms and equivalences—with statement matrixes.

The second argument form governing universally quantified statements is
Universal Generalization. Consider this argument:

(12) Every poet is an artist. None but dreamers are artists. So, each poet is a
    dreamer.

Symbolizing (12), we write

(13) $\therefore (x)(Px \supset Dx)$
  1) $(x)(Px \supset Ax)$ Pr
  2) $(x)(Ax \supset Dx)$ Pr

Using Universal Instantiation, the following statement matrixes are deduced from
the premises of (13):

  3) $Px \supset Ax$ 1, UI
  4) $Ax \supset Dx$ 2, UI

An appeal to Hypothetical Syllogism yields

> 5) $Px \supset Dx$ 3, 4, HS

The conclusion, '$(x)(Px \supset Dx)$', is the statement matrix at line 5 universally quantified. But, how is this conclusion reached? To answer this question, notice the statement matrix at line 5 is deduced from only universally quantified statements and accepted Rules of Transformation. Indeed, no individual variable is found in '$Px \supset Dx$' which is not introduced in the proof by a use of Universal Instantiation. Hence, while line 5 does not contain a true statement, '$Px \supset Dx$' is transformed into a true statement—assuming the truth of the premises—by substituting any individual constant at each occurrence of 'x', the same constant being substituted at each 'x'. Since '$Px \supset Dx$' can be converted to a true statement by mentioning any individual, it is true of all individuals. The Rule of Transformation needed to reach the conclusion of (13) can now be given a preliminary formulation, which will be expanded in Section 3 of this chapter:

Preliminary Universal Generalization (UG)

$$\Psi\beta$$
$$\therefore (\alpha)\Psi\alpha$$

where (1) β is a variable which occurs free in $\Psi\beta$ at all and only those places where α is a variable which occurs free in $\Psi\alpha$, and (2) $\Psi\beta$ is obtained from only statements in which β does not occur free. Notice that while α is bound in $(\alpha)\Psi\alpha$, it is free in $\Psi\alpha$. In $(\alpha)\Psi\alpha$ the first occurrence of α is part of the quantifier, while the second occurrence of α falls under the scope of the quantifier. Now, in $\Psi\alpha$ we find α neither as part of a quantifier nor under the scope of a quantifier, and, hence, α occurs free in $\Psi\alpha$.

A complete proof of (13) may now be constructed:

(14) $\therefore (x)(Px \supset Dx)$

1)	$(x)(Px \supset Ax)$	Pr
2)	$(x)(Ax \supset Dx)$	Pr
3)	$Px \supset Ax$	1, UI
4)	$Ax \supset Dx$	2, UI
5)	$Px \supset Dx$	3, 4, HS
6)	$\therefore (x)(Px \supset Dx)$	5, UG

Consider this more complicated proof using Universal Instantiation and Universal Generalization:

(15) $\therefore (x)\{[Ax \cdot (Bx \cdot Ex)] \supset Dx\}$

1)	$(x)\{[Ax \cdot (Bx \cdot Cx)] \supset Dx\}$	Pr
2)	$(x)[(Bx \cdot Ex) \supset Cx]$	Pr

Both premisses and conclusion in (15) are overall universally quantified statements. Since the conclusion is an overall universally quantified statement, it could be reached by Universal Generalization if we had this statement matrix:

(16) $[Ax \cdot (Bx \cdot Ex)] \supset Dx$

Now, in order to reach (16), we introduce the free variable, 'x', into our proof by Universal Instantiation:

(17) $\therefore (x)\{[Ax \cdot (Bx \cdot Ex)] \supset Dx\}$

1)	$(x)\{[Ax \cdot (Bx \cdot Cx)] \supset Dx\}$	Pr
2)	$(x)[(Bx \cdot Ex) \supset Cx]$	Pr
3)	$[Ax \cdot (Bx \cdot Cx)] \supset Dx$	1, UI
4)	$(Bx \cdot Ex) \supset Cx$	2, UI

Once the premisses have been instantiated, we may use all our truth-functional Rules of Transformation to reach (16).

Comparing lines 3 and 4 of (17) with (16), we see that 'Cx' must be left behind in the proof. Since both lines 3 and 4 may be viewed as hypotheticals and since 'Cx' appears in the antecedent of line 3 and the consequent of line 4, we move toward a use of Hypothetical Syllogism.

5)	$[Ax \cdot (Cx \cdot Bx)] \supset Dx$	3, Com
6)	$[(Cx \cdot Bx) \cdot Ax] \supset Dx$	5, Com
7)	$[Cx \cdot (Bx \cdot Ax)] \supset Dx$	6, Assoc
8)	$Cx \supset [(Bx \cdot Ax) \supset Dx]$	7, Exp
9)	$(Bx \cdot Ex) \supset [(Bx \cdot Ax) \supset Dx]$	4, 8, HS

Obtaining line 9 and still moving toward (16), we must reduce the occurrences of 'Bx'.

10)	$[(Bx \cdot Ex) \cdot (Bx \cdot Ax)] \supset Dx$	9, Exp
11)	$\{[(Bx \cdot Ex) \cdot Bx] \cdot Ax\} \supset Dx$	10, Assoc
12)	$\{[Bx \cdot (Bx \cdot Ex)] \cdot Ax\} \supset Dx$	11, Com
13)	$\{[(Bx \cdot Bx) \cdot Ex] \cdot Ax\} \supset Dx$	12, Assoc
14)	$[(Bx \cdot Ex) \cdot Ax] \supset Dx$	13, Taut

We are within two steps of the conclusion. Using Commutation followed by Universal Generalization, (17) is completed:

15)	$[Ax \cdot (Bx \cdot Ex)] \supset Dx$	14, Com
16)	$\therefore (x)\{[Ax \cdot (Bx \cdot Ex)] \supset Dx\}$	15, UG

A common mistake is the following:

15)	$[Ax \cdot (Bx \cdot Ex)] \supset Dx$	14, Com
16)	$\therefore (x)[Ax \cdot (Bx \cdot Ex)] \supset Dx$	15, UG

Line 16 here is incorrect because there is a free individual variable in '*Dx*'. In using Universal Generalization to move from $\Psi\alpha$ to $(\alpha)\Psi\alpha$, every free occurrence of α in $\Psi\alpha$ must fall under the scope of the quantifier in $(\alpha)\Psi\alpha$.

EXERCISES

Group A:

Give the correct justification for each of the following unjustified lines.

(1) $\therefore Ba$
1)	$(x)(Ax \supset Bx)$	Pr
2)	Aa	Pr
3)	$Aa \supset Ba$	
4)	$\therefore Ba$	

(2) $\therefore Aa$
1)	$\sim Ba$	Pr
2)	$(x)(Ax \lor Bx)$	Pr
3)	$Aa \lor Ba$	
4)	$Ba \lor Aa$	
5)	$\therefore Aa$	

(3) $\therefore Aa \supset Ca$
1)	$(x)(Ax \supset Bx)$	Pr
2)	$(x)(Bx \supset Cx)$	Pr
3)	$Aa \supset Ba$	
4)	$Ba \supset Ca$	
5)	$\therefore Aa \supset Ca$	

(4) $\therefore (x)(Ax \supset Cx)$
1)	$(x)(Bx \supset Cx)$	Pr
2)	$(x)(Ax \supset Bx)$	Pr
3)	$Ax \supset Bx$	
4)	$Bx \supset Cx$	
5)	$Ax \supset Cx$	
6)	$\therefore (x)(Ax \supset Cx)$	

(5) $\therefore \sim Aa \lor \sim Ba$
1)	$(x)[(Ax \cdot Bx) \supset \sim Cx]$	Pr
2)	Ca	Pr
3)	$(Aa \cdot Ba) \supset \sim Ca$	
4)	$\sim \sim Ca$	
5)	$\sim (Aa \cdot Ba)$	
6)	$\therefore \sim Aa \lor \sim Ba$	

(6) $\therefore Ca$

 1) $Aa \supset (x)(Bx \supset Cx)$ Pr
 2) $Ba \cdot Aa$ Pr
 3) $Aa \cdot Ba$
 4) Aa
 5) $(x)(Bx \supset Cx)$
 6) $Ba \supset Ca$
 7) Ba
 8) $\therefore Ca$

(7) $\therefore (x)(Bx \lor Dx)$

 1) $(x)(Ax \supset Bx) \cdot (x)(Cx \supset Dx)$ Pr
 2) $(x)(Cx \lor Ax)$ Pr
 3) $(x)(Ax \supset Bx)$
 4) $(x)(Cx \supset Dx) \cdot (x)(Ax \supset Bx)$
 5) $(x)(Cx \supset Dx)$
 6) $Cx \supset Dx$
 7) $Ax \supset Bx$
 8) $Cx \lor Ax$
 9) $Dx \lor Bx$
 10) $Bx \lor Dx$
 11) $\therefore (x)(Bx \lor Dx)$

(8) $\therefore (x)[(Ax \cdot Dx) \supset Bx]$

 1) $(x)[Ax \supset (Bx \lor Cx)]$ Pr
 2) $(x)(Cx \supset \sim Dx)$ Pr
 3) $Ax \supset (Bx \lor Cx)$
 4) $Cx \supset \sim Dx$
 5) $Ax \supset (\sim \sim Bx \lor Cx)$
 6) $Ax \supset (\sim Bx \supset Cx)$
 7) $(Ax \cdot \sim Bx) \supset Cx$
 8) $(Ax \cdot \sim Bx) \supset \sim Dx$
 9) $Ax \supset (\sim Bx \supset \sim Dx)$
 10) $Ax \supset (Dx \supset Bx)$
 11) $(Ax \cdot Dx) \supset Bx$
 12) $\therefore (x)[(Ax \cdot Dx) \supset Bx]$

(9) $\therefore (x)(Ax \supset Dx) \cdot (x)(Cx \supset Dx)$

 1) $(x)(Ax \supset Bx) \supset (x)(Bx \supset Dx)$ Pr
 2) $(x)(Ax \supset Cx) \cdot (x)(Cx \supset Bx)$ Pr
 3) $(x)(Ax \supset Cx)$
 4) $(x)(Cx \supset Bx) \cdot (x)(Ax \supset Cx)$
 5) $(x)(Cx \supset Bx)$
 6) $Ax \supset Cx$
 7) $Cx \supset Bx$
 8) $Ax \supset Bx$

9) $(x)(Ax \supset Bx)$
10) $(x)(Bx \supset Dx)$
11) $Bx \supset Dx$
12) $Cx \supset Dx$
13) $(x)(Cx \supset Dx)$
14) $Ax \supset Dx$
15) $(x)(Ax \supset Dx)$
16) $\therefore (x)(Ax \supset Dx) \cdot (x)(Cx \supset Dx)$

(10) $\therefore (x)[Ax \supset (Dx \supset Cx)]$
1) $(x)(Ax \supset Bx) \cdot (x)(Bx \supset Cx)$ Pr
2) $(x)(Ax \supset Bx)$
3) $(x)(Bx \supset Cx) \cdot (x)(Ax \supset Bx)$
4) $(x)(Bx \supset Cx)$
5) $Ax \supset Bx$
6) $Bx \supset Cx$
7) $Ax \supset Cx$
8) $\sim Ax \vee Cx$
9) $(\sim Ax \vee Cx) \vee \sim Dx$
10) $\sim Dx \vee (\sim Ax \vee Cx)$
11) $(\sim Dx \vee \sim Ax) \vee Cx$
12) $\sim (Dx \cdot Ax) \vee Cx$
13) $(Dx \cdot Ax) \supset Cx$
14) $(Ax \cdot Dx) \supset Cx$
15) $Ax \supset (Dx \supset Cx)$
16) $\therefore (x)[Ax \supset (Dx \supset Cx)]$

Group B:

Construct a proof of validity for each of the following.

(1) $\therefore \sim Aa$
1) $\sim Ba$ Pr
2) $(x)(Ax \supset Bx)$ Pr

(2) $\therefore \sim Aa \vee \sim Ba$
1) $(x)[(Ax \cdot Bx) \supset \sim Cx]$ Pr
2) Ca Pr

(3) $\therefore Ca$
1) $(x)(Ax \supset \sim Bx)$ Pr
2) Aa Pr
3) $(x)(Bx \vee Cx)$ Pr

(4) $\therefore (x)[(Ax \cdot Bx) \vee Cx]$
1) $(x)(Ax \vee Cx) \cdot (x)(Bx \vee Cx)$ Pr

(5) $\therefore (x)(Ax \supset Bx)$
1) $(x)[(Ax \cdot \sim Bx) \supset Cx]$ Pr
2) $(x)(Cx \supset Bx)$ Pr

(6) $\therefore \sim (Aa \cdot Ba)$
    1) $(x)[(Ax \supset Bx) \supset \sim Cx]$ Pr
    2) Ca Pr

(7) $\therefore \sim Ba$
    1) $(x)[(Ax \cdot Bx) \equiv \sim Cx]$ Pr
    2) $Aa \cdot Ca$ Pr

(8) $\therefore \sim Aa \cdot Ca$
    1) $(x)\{[Ax \cdot (Bx \lor Cx)] \supset \sim Dx\}$ Pr
    2) $(x)(\sim Dx \supset \sim Ax)$ Pr
    3) Ca Pr

(9) $\therefore (x)[(Ax \cdot Cx) \supset \sim Dx]$
    1) $(x)\{[Ax \cdot (Bx \lor Cx)] \equiv \sim Dx\}$ Pr

(10) $\therefore (x)[(Cx \lor Ax) \supset Dx]$
    1) $(x)[Ax \supset (Bx \cdot Cx)]$ Pr
    2) $(x)(Cx \supset Dx)$ Pr

Group C:

Construct an English argument corresponding to each of the exercises in Group B. Attempt to make each argument sound.

Group D:

Symbolize the following arguments using the suggested notation, and then construct a proof of validity for each.

(1)   Every logician is highly trained. Anyone who is highly trained is skillful. Alonzo Church is a logician. And, so, Church is skillful. ($L, T, S; x, c$)

(2)   Everything is extended or it isn't. Only those things having mass are extended. Nothing which isn't extended is physically locatable. Hence, anything has mass or isn't physically locatable. ($E, M, L; x$)

(3)   If every body is in motion, only those things changing are in motion. Whatever is a body is changing, while whatever is changing is in motion. Consequently, everything in motion is changing. ($B, M, C; x$)

(4)   Squares and circles are extended. Accordingly, circles are extended. ($S, C, E; x$)

(5)   The student who is both industrious and clever will pass. While Earl is a student, nonetheless he won't pass. Earl is clever. Therefore, Earl isn't industrious. ($S, P, I, C; x, e$)

(6)   No student will benefit from his work who is lazy when he is made to perform. Karl will benefit from his work, although he is lazy. Wherefore, Karl isn't a student. ($S, B, L, M; x, k$)

(7)   Anyone can use a computer who is facile with mathematical manipulations or interested in symbolic operations except those not trained in programming. Alex is neither trained in programming nor can't use a computer. Therefore, Alex is neither facile with mathematical manipulations nor trained in programming. (*U, F, I, T; x, a*)

(8)   Whoever is intemperate is neither slow to anger nor quick to forgive when aroused or contradicted. So whoever is contradicted is temperate when quick to forgive. (*T, S, Q, A, C; x*)

(9)   Everyone who isn't understanding when not compassionate is truly happy and beneficial to his fellow man. Anyone beneficial to his fellow man is both truly happy and forgiving. Consequently, whoever is compassionate is forgiving. (*U, C, H, B, F; x*)

(10) All persons who are 18 years old must register for the draft if they are males and not aliens. Whoever registers for the draft isn't exempt from military service if an 18-year-old male. Thus, all nonalien males are not exempt from the draft if they are persons 18 years old. (*P, O, R, M, A, E; x*)

2. EXISTENTIAL GENERALIZATION AND EXISTENTIAL INSTANTIATION

In Section 1, Rules of Transformation were developed which allow instantiation of universal statements and universal generalization of certain statement matrixes. Analogous rules must be introduced to govern the existential quantifier. The first of these rules is

Existential Generalization (EG)

$$\Psi\beta$$
$$\therefore (\exists\alpha)\Psi\alpha$$

where 'β' represents any individual constant or free variable and where $\Psi\beta$ is like $\Psi\alpha$ except for containing free occurrences of β wherever $\Psi\alpha$ contains free occurrences of α. If β is an individual constant and $\Psi\beta$ is a true statement, then it is also true that there is at least one individual having the property represented by 'Ψ' or belonging to the set depicted by 'Ψ'. If, on the other hand, β is an individual variable and $\Psi\beta$ is a statement matrix true of at least one individual, then $(\exists\alpha)\Psi\alpha$ is true.

A simple argument using Existential Generalization is

(1)   All saints are virtuous and Augustine is a saint. Therefore, virtuous things exist.

Symbolizing (1), we then construct a proof moving toward '*Va*':

(2) $\therefore (\exists x)Vx$

   1) $(x)(Sx \supset Vx)\cdot Sa$ Pr
   2) $(x)(Sx \supset Vx)$ 1, Simp
   3) $Sa \cdot (x)(Sx \supset Vx)$ 1, Com
   4) Sa 3, Simp
   5) $Sa \supset Va$ 2, UI
   6) Va 5, 4, MP

Assuming the truth of the premiss of (1), we can assert the truth of 'Augustine is virtuous'. But, since there is at least one thing—namely, Augustine—which is virtuous, (2) is completed by

   7) $\therefore (\exists x)Vx$ 6, EG

The next Rule of Transformation governing the existential quantifier may be pictured

Existential Instantiation (*EI*)

$$(\exists \alpha)\Psi\alpha$$

$$\therefore \Psi\beta$$

where β is free at every place, and only those places, and α is free in $\Psi\alpha$. Before using this rule in constructing proofs of validity, we must consider the following restrictions. What these restrictions are and why they are needed can be made clear through examples.

Imagine the following argument:

(3)   Some mammals are dangerous. Some lizards are dangerous. Consequently, some mammals are lizards.

Following exactly the Rules of Transformation at our disposal, we construct this "proof":

(4) $\therefore (\exists x)(Mx \cdot Lx)$

   1) $(\exists x)(Mx \cdot Dx)$ Pr
   2) $(\exists x)(Lx \cdot Dx)$ Pr
   3) $Mx \cdot Dx$ 1, EI
   4) $Lx \cdot Dx$ 2, EI
   5) Mx 3, Simp
   6) Lx 4, Simp
   7) $Mx \cdot Lx$ 5, 6, Conj
   8) $\therefore (\exists x)(Mx \cdot Lx)$ 7, EG

Surely, this is an invalid argument. While it is true there are dangerous mammals and dangerous lizards, it is not true there are mammals which are also lizards. [Since there are only three "terms" in (3), you may show its invalidity by a Venn diagram.]

Where has (4) gone astray? In the fourth line! To see why line 4 is incorrect, assume '$(\exists x)(Mx \cdot Dx)$' and '$(\exists x)(Lx \cdot Dx)$' are both *true*. Now, if '$(\exists x)(Mx \cdot Dx)$' is true, the range of 'x' is limited to only those individuals having *both* the properties indicated by 'M' *and* 'D'—or being a member of the set composed of *both* mammals *and* dangerous things. On the other hand, if '$(\exists x)(Lx \cdot Dx)$' is true, the range of 'x' is limited to only those individuals having *both* the properties indicated by 'L' *and* 'D'—or being a member of the set composed of *both* lizards *and* dangerous things. Since we have no guarantee that '$Mx \cdot Dx$' and '$Lx \cdot Dx$' are both true of exactly the same individuals—and in (4) they surely are not—we cannot use the same variable 'x' in both statement matrixes. Indeed, since 'x' has been used in line 3, it cannot also be used in line 4. Some other individual variable, such as 'y' or 'z', must be used in line 4. But, if the same variable cannot be used in both lines 3 and 4, the conclusion, '$(\exists x)(Mx \cdot Lx)$', cannot be reached. To avoid "proofs" such as (4), we must place a restriction on Existential Instantiation. *Assuming $(\exists\alpha)\Psi\alpha$ is a true statement, we cannot introduce any individual variable, β, into a proof by Existential Instantiation which has already appeared as a free variable in that proof.*

It is a common occurrence to hear or read that, statistically speaking, college graduates make more money during their lifetimes than people without a college degree. Having been indoctrinated with these statistical findings, Larry obtains a college degree so he will also make more money. Larry's argument might be

(5)   Some college graduates make more money than a person not holding a college degree. I'm a college graduate. Hence, I shall make more money than a person not having a college degree.

As many disgruntled college graduates have discovered, (5) is not a valid deductive argument. While all the premises of (5) may be true, nevertheless the conclusion can still be false. Examples, such as (5), suggest that we can never argue deductively from a statement about some individuals to a statement about a particular, specified individual. This second restriction on Existential Instantiation can be put somewhat more technically. *Assuming $(\exists\alpha)\Psi\alpha$ is a true statement, we cannot introduce an individual constant, β, into a proof by Existential Instantiation.*

Consider this argument:

(6)   All tensiometers measure tautness. Some of the tensiometers in this lab are accurately calibrated. Therefore, certain tensiometers in this lab measure tautness accurately.

Notice how Existential Instantiation and Existential Generalization are used to construct a proof for (6):

(7) $\therefore (\exists x)[(Tx \cdot Lx) \cdot (Mx \cdot Ax)]$

1)	$(x)(Tx \supset Mx)$	Pr
2)	$(\exists x)[(Tx \cdot Lx) \cdot (Ax \cdot Cx)]$	Pr
3)	$(Tx \cdot Lx) \cdot (Ax \cdot Cx)$	2, EI
4)	$Tx \supset Mx$	1, UI
5)	$Tx \cdot Lx$	3, Simp
6)	Tx	5, Simp
7)	Mx	4, 6, MP
8)	$(Ax \cdot Cx) \cdot (Tx \cdot Lx)$	3, Com
9)	$Ax \cdot Cx$	8, Simp
10)	Ax	9, Simp
11)	$Mx \cdot Ax$	7, 10, Conj
12)	$(Tx \cdot Lx) \cdot (Mx \cdot Ax)$	5, 11, Conj
13)	$\therefore (\exists x)[(Tx \cdot Lx) \cdot (Mx \cdot Ax)]$	12, EG

In (7), Existential Instantiation is used before Universal Instantiation so the first restriction on Existential Instantiation is not violated. Had we first instantiated '$(x)(Tx \supset Mx)$' by writing '$Tx \supset Mx$', we could not have again used 'x' to instantiate '$(\exists x)[(Tx \cdot Lx) \cdot (Ax \cdot Cx)]$'. *To help maintain the restrictions on Existential Instantiation, whenever a premiss set contains both an existentially quantified statement and one or more universally quantified statements, for the present, instantiate the existentially quantified statement first.*

In constructing any proof of validity, we begin with a statement, or statements, —our premiss set—and end with a statement—our conclusion. Consequently, the following is not a complete proof:

(8)

1)	$(\exists x)Ax$	Pr
2)	Ax	1, EI

Example (8) is not completed because line 2 contains a statement matrix and not a statement. We must never leave a proof uncompleted. To avoid the possibility of an uncompleted proof, let us stipulate that *the last line of a proof must never contain any free variable, nor must any free variables occur in the premiss set.*

Remember, as with Universal Generalization and Universal Instantiation, the Rules of Transformation governing the existential quantifier are argument forms applying to *entire* lines in a proof—never to parts of lines.

EXERCISES

Group A:

Justify each of the unjustified lines in the following.

(1) $\therefore (\exists x)[(Ax \lor Cx) \cdot Bx]$
   1) $(\exists x)(Ax \cdot Bx)$ Pr
   2) $Ax \cdot Bx$
   3) Ax
   4) $Ax \lor Cx$
   5) $Bx \cdot Ax$
   6) Bx
   7) $(Ax \lor Cx) \cdot Bx$
   8) $\therefore (\exists x)[(Ax \lor Cx) \cdot Bx]$

(2) $\therefore (\exists x)Cx$
   1) $(x)(Ax \supset Bx)$
   2) $(\exists x)Ax$ Pr
   3) $(x)(\sim Cx \supset \sim Bx)$ Pr
   4) Ax
   5) $Ax \supset Bx$
   6) $\sim Cx \supset \sim Bx$
   7) $Bx \supset Cx$
   8) $Ax \supset Cx$
   9) Cx
  10) $\therefore (\exists x)Cx$

(3) $\therefore (\exists x)(Bx \cdot Cx)$
   1) $(x)(Ax \supset Bx) \cdot (\exists x)(Ax \cdot Cx)$ Pr
   2) $(x)(Ax \supset Bx)$
   3) $(\exists x)(Ax \cdot Cx) \cdot (x)(Ax \supset Bx)$
   4) $(\exists x)(Ax \cdot Cx)$
   5) $Ax \cdot Cx$
   6) $Ax \supset Bx$
   7) Ax
   8) Bx
   9) $Cx \cdot Ax$
  10) Cx
  11) $Bx \cdot Cx$
  12) $\therefore (\exists x)(Bx \cdot Cx)$

(4) $\therefore (\exists x) \sim Ax$
   1) $(x)\{[Ax \cdot (Bx \lor Cx)] \supset Dx\}$ Pr
   2) $(\exists x)(Cx \cdot \sim Dx)$ Pr
   3) $Cx \cdot \sim Dx$
   4) $[Ax \cdot (Bx \lor Cx)] \supset Dx$
   5) Cx
   6) $\sim Dx \cdot Cx$
   7) $\sim Dx$
   8) $\sim [Ax \cdot (Bx \lor Cx)]$
   9) $\sim Ax \lor \sim (Bx \lor Cx)$

10) $\sim(Bx \lor Cx) \lor \sim Ax$
11) $Cx \lor Bx$
12) $Bx \lor Cx$
13) $\sim\sim(Bx \lor Cx)$
14) $\sim Ax$
15) $\therefore (\exists x) \sim Ax$

(5) $\therefore (\exists x) \sim (Dx \lor Ax)$

1) $(x)(Ax \supset Bx)$ Pr
2) $(\exists x)(\sim Bx \cdot Cx)$ Pr
3) $(x)(Dx \supset \sim Cx)$ Pr
4) $\sim Bx \cdot Cx$
5) $Ax \supset Bx$
6) $Dx \supset \sim Cx$
7) $\sim Bx$
8) $Cx \cdot \sim Bx$
9) Cx
10) $\sim Ax$
11) $\sim\sim Cx$
12) $\sim Dx$
13) $\sim Dx \cdot \sim Ax$
14) $\sim(Dx \lor Ax)$
15) $\therefore (\exists x) \sim (Dx \lor Ax)$

(6) $\therefore (\exists x)[Cx \lor (Dx \cdot Ax)]$

1) $(\exists x)(Ax \cdot \sim Bx)$ Pr
2) $(x)\{[Ax \cdot \sim(Cx \lor Dx)] \supset Bx\}$ Pr
3) $Ax \cdot \sim Bx$
4) $[Ax \cdot \sim(Cx \lor Dx)] \supset Bx$
5) Ax
6) $\sim Bx \cdot Ax$
7) $\sim Bx$
8) $\sim[Ax \cdot \sim(Cx \lor Dx)]$
9) $Ax \supset (Cx \lor Dx)$
10) $Cx \lor Dx$
11) $Ax \lor Cx$
12) $Cx \lor Ax$
13) $(Cx \lor Dx) \cdot (Cx \lor Ax)$
14) $Cx \lor (Dx \cdot Ax)$
15) $\therefore (\exists x)[Cx \lor (Dx \cdot Ax)]$

(7) $\therefore (\exists x)(Ax \cdot Dx)$

1) $(x)[(Ax \cdot Bx) \supset \sim Cx]$ Pr
2) $(\exists x)(Ax \cdot Cx)$ Pr
3) $(x)[(Ax \cdot \sim Bx) \supset Dx]$ Pr
4) $Ax \cdot Cx$

5) $(Ax \cdot Bx) \supset \sim Cx$
6) $(Ax \cdot \sim Bx) \supset Dx$
7) Ax
8) $Cx \cdot Ax$
9) Cx
10) $\sim \sim Cx$
11) $\sim (Ax \cdot Bx)$
12) $\sim Ax \lor \sim Bx$
13) $\sim \sim Ax$
14) $\sim Bx$
15) $Ax \cdot \sim Bx$
16) Dx
17) $Ax \cdot Dx$
18) $\therefore (\exists x)(Ax \cdot Dx)$

(8) $\therefore (\exists x)[Ax \cdot \sim (Dx \cdot Ex)]$

1) $(\exists x)[Ax \cdot \sim (\sim Bx \lor Cx)]$ Pr
2) $(x)[(Ax \cdot Dx) \equiv \sim Bx]$ Pr
3) $Ax \cdot \sim (\sim Bx \lor Cx)$
4) $(Ax \cdot Dx) \equiv \sim Bx$
5) Ax
6) $\sim (\sim Bx \lor Cx) \cdot Ax$
7) $\sim (\sim Bx \lor Cx)$
8) $\sim \sim Bx \cdot \sim Cx$
9) $\sim [(Ax \cdot Dx) \cdot \sim \sim Bx] \cdot \sim [\sim Bx \cdot \sim (Ax \cdot Dx)]$
10) $\sim [(Ax \cdot Dx) \cdot \sim \sim Bx]$
11) $(Ax \cdot Dx) \supset \sim Bx$
12) $Ax \supset (Dx \supset \sim Bx)$
13) $Dx \supset \sim Bx$
14) $\sim \sim Bx$
15) $\sim Dx$
16) $\sim Dx \lor \sim Ex$
17) $\sim (Dx \cdot Ex)$
18) $Ax \cdot \sim (Dx \cdot Ex)$
19) $\therefore (\exists x)[Ax \cdot \sim (Dx \cdot Ex)]$

(9) $\therefore (\exists x)(Ex \lor Gx)$

1) $(\exists x)[Ax \cdot (\sim Bx \cdot Cx)]$ Pr
2) $(x)[Ax \supset (Dx \supset Ex)]$ Pr
3) $(x)[(Cx \cdot Fx) \supset Gx]$ Pr
4) $(x)[(\sim Dx \cdot \sim Fx) \supset Bx]$ Pr
5) $Ax \cdot (\sim Bx \cdot Cx)$
6) $Ax \supset (Dx \supset Ex)$
7) $(Cx \cdot Fx) \supset Gx$
8) $(\sim Dx \cdot \sim Fx) \supset Bx$
9) Ax

10) $(\sim Bx \cdot Cx) \cdot Ax$
11) $\sim Bx \cdot Cx$
12) $\sim Bx$
13) $Cx \cdot \sim Bx$
14) Cx
15) $Dx \supset Ex$
16) $Cx \supset (Fx \supset Gx)$
17) $Fx \supset Gx$
18) $\sim (\sim Dx \cdot \sim Fx)$
19) $Dx \vee Fx$
20) $Ex \vee Gx$ •
21) $\therefore (\exists x)(Ex \vee Gx)$

(10) $\therefore (\exists x)[Bx \cdot (Hx \cdot \sim Fx)]$

1) $(x)[(Ax \vee Bx) \supset Cx]$ Pr
2) $(x)[(Cx \vee Dx) \supset Ex]$ Pr
3) $(\exists x)[Ax \cdot \sim (Gx \vee Hx)]$ Pr
4) $(x)[Ex \supset (Fx \cdot Gx)]$ Pr
5) $Ax \cdot \sim (Gx \vee Hx)$
6) $(Ax \vee Bx) \supset Cx$
7) $(Cx \vee Dx) \supset Ex$
8) $Ex \supset (Fx \cdot Gx)$
9) Ax
10) $\sim (Gx \vee Hx) \cdot Ax$
11) $\sim (Gx \vee Hx)$
12) $\sim Gx \cdot \sim Hx$
13) $Ax \vee Bx$
14) Cx
15) $Cx \vee Dx$
16) Ex
17) $Fx \cdot Gx$
18) $Gx \cdot Fx$
19) Gx
20) $\sim Gx$
21) $Gx \vee (\exists x)[Bx \cdot (Hx \cdot \sim Fx)]$
22) $\therefore (\exists x)[Bx \cdot (Hx \cdot \sim Fx)]$

Group B:

Construct a proof of validity for each of the following.

(1) $\therefore (\exists x) \sim Ax$
1) $(x)[Ax \supset (Bx \vee Cx)]$ Pr
2) $(\exists x)(\sim Cx \cdot \sim Bx)$ Pr

(2) $\therefore (\exists x)(Ax \cdot Cx)$
1) $(\exists x)(Ax \cdot Bx)$ Pr
2) $(x)(Bx \supset Cx)$ Pr

(3) $\therefore (\exists x) \sim Bx$

   1) $(x)[(Ax \cdot Bx) \supset Cx]$ Pr

   2) $(x)(Cx \supset \sim Bx)$ Pr

   3) $(\exists x)Ax$ Pr

(4) $\therefore (\exists x)[Bx \lor (Cx \cdot Dx)]$

   1) $(x)[Ax \supset (Bx \lor Cx)] \cdot (x)[Ax \supset (Bx \lor Dx)]$ Pr

   2) $(\exists x)Ax$ Pr

(5) $\therefore (\exists x)(Cx \lor Ax)$

   1) $[(\exists x)Ax \cdot (\exists x)Bx] \supset (\exists x)(Cx \lor Ax)$ Pr

   2) $(x)[Cx \supset (Ax \cdot Bx)]$ Pr

   3) $(x)(Dx \supset Cx)$ Pr

   4) $(\exists x)Dx$ Pr

(6) $\therefore (\exists x)[Ax \cdot (Bx \triangle Cx)]$

   1) $(x)\{Ax \supset [Bx \lor (Cx \cdot Dx)]\}$ Pr

   2) $(\exists x)(Ax \cdot \sim Cx)$ Pr

(7) $\therefore (\exists x) \sim (Dx \cdot Ax)$

   1) $(x)[(Ax \cdot Bx) \equiv \sim Cx]$ Pr

   2) $(\exists x)(Cx \cdot Bx)$ Pr

(8) $\therefore (\exists x)(\sim Cx \lor \sim Ax)$

   1) $(x)(Ax \supset Bx)$ Pr

   2) $(x)[(Bx \cdot Cx) \supset Dx]$ Pr

   3) $(x)[(Ax \cdot Dx) \supset Ex]$ Pr

   4) $(\exists x) \sim Ex$ Pr

(9) $\therefore (\exists x)[\sim Ax \cdot (Bx \lor Ex)]$

   1) $(x)[Ax \supset \sim (Bx \supset Cx)]$ Pr

   2) $(x)[Bx \supset (Cx \lor Dx)]$ Pr

   3) $(\exists x)[\sim Dx \cdot (Bx \triangle Ex)]$ Pr

(10) $\therefore (\exists x)(Ex \triangle Dx)$

   1) $(\exists x)[(Ax \supset Cx) \cdot \sim Bx]$ Pr

   2) $(x)(Cx \supset Dx) \cdot (x)(\sim Ex \supset Ax)$ Pr

   3) $(x)[Dx \supset (Ex \supset Bx)]$ Pr

Group C:

Construct an English argument corresponding to each of the exercises in Group B. Attempt to make each argument sound.

Group D:

Symbolize the following arguments using the suggested notation, and then construct a proof of validity for each.

(1) Artificial satellites are useful in meteorology and communications. There are artificial satellites. Therefore, there are artificial satellites useful in meteorology. $(S, M, C; x)$

(2) Every man-made satellite is an important technological achievement even though some man-made satellites aren't American inventions. So, certain important technological achievements aren't American inventions. (*S, A, I; x*)

(3) If some things are important or useful, then surely every advancement in human understanding is beneficial. Certain things are both important and also advancements in human understanding. Hence, some things are beneficial. (*I, U, A, B; x*)

(4) Any nation has either a large population of poverty or a substantial middle class. Every large population of poverty is accompanied by a high rate of suicide. Certain nations don't have a high rate of suicide. Consequently, some nations have a substantial middle class. (*N, P, C, R; x*)

(5) Nations are economically backward when poor. However, some poor nations are developing their resources. Wherefore, certain nations which are economically backward are developing their resources. (*N, B, P, D; x*)

(6) Anyone who isn't loving is ignorant to some degree only if selfish. Some people aren't selfish. Every person is ignorant to some degree. So, a few people are loving. (*L, I, S, P; x*)

(7) Succubi and incubi are demons. Now, demons and ghosts are occult things. But, some things are not occult. Thus, some things are neither ghosts nor incubi. (*S, I, D, G, O; x*)

(8) There exist Chordates which are mammals or reptiles only if every tortoise is a reptile. If some Chordates are mammals or vertebrates, then all reptiles are vertebrates. Certain Chordates are mammals. Hence, all tortoises are vertebrates. (*C, M, R, T, V; x*)

(9) Certain poetry is neither understandable nor readable. Further, no poetry or novel is factual. If anything is neither factual nor readable, it's hippie. Therefore, some poetry is hippie but neither readable nor understandable. (*P, U, R, N, F, H; x*)

(10) Anyone who wrote the Scriptures must have been either a good man or a bad one, or a Deity. Anyone who wrote the Scriptures preached virtue while saying "Thus saith the Lord." Whoever said "Thus saith the Lord" and wasn't a Deity was fabricating. No good man fabricates but no bad man preaches virtue. Obviously, someone wrote the Scriptures. Consequently, a Deity exists who wrote the Scriptures. (*S, G, B, D, V, L, F; x*)

3. THE CONDITIONAL METHOD OF PROVING VALIDITY

In Chapter 8 the Conditional Method of Proving Validity was developed. To use the Conditional Method of Proving Validity with an argument having a hypothetical statement as a conclusion, we assume the antecedent of the conclusion as a new premiss in our proof. Then, from the augmented premiss set, we deduce the consequent of the conclusion. Ending the Conditional Proof, we assert the original hypothetical conclusion as a new line in our proof. Every Conditional Proof is ended with a hypothetical statement which does not fall within the scope of the assumption introduced in that Conditional Proof. Hence, the scope of the assumption of a Conditional Proof is limited in the sense that it never extends through the last line of a proof.

But as pointed out in Chapter 8, the Conditional Method of Proving Validity can also be used with arguments whose conclusions are not hypothetical statements but are logically equivalent to hypothetical statements. Here, we assume the antecedent of the hypothetical statement which is equivalent to the conclusion and then prove for the consequent of that statement. The Conditional Proof is ended with the hypothetical statement equivalent to the conclusion and from this statement we move to the conclusion of the argument.

These same techniques may be used with arguments involving quantifiers whose conclusions are hypothetical statements or logically equivalent to hypothetical statements. For instance, the following example has a hypothetical statement as its conclusion:

(1) $\therefore (x)(Cx \supset Dx) \supset (\exists x)(Ax \cdot Dx)$

   1) $(x)(Ax \supset Bx)$ Pr
   2) $(x)(Bx \supset Cx)$ Pr
   3) $(\exists x)Ax$ Pr

Using the Conditional Method of Proving Validity, we assume '$(x)(Cx \supset Dx)$' and deduce '$(\exists x)(Ax \cdot Dx)$'. The proof is completed by appealing to CP.

(2) $\therefore (x)(Cx \supset Dx) \supset (\exists x)(Ax \cdot Dx)$

1)	$(x)(Ax \supset Bx)$	Pr
2)	$(x)(Bx \supset Cx)$	Pr
3)	$(\exists x)Ax$	Pr
4)	Ax	3, EI
5)	$Ax \supset Bx$	1, UI
6)	$Bx \supset Cx$	2, UI
7)	$Ax \supset Cx$	5, 6, HS
8)	Cx	7, 4, MP
9)	$(x)(Cx \supset Dx)$	CP, $\therefore (\exists x)(Ax \cdot Dx)$
10)	$Cx \supset Dx$	9, UI
11)	Dx	10, 8, MP
12)	$Ax \cdot Dx$	4, 11, Conj
13)	$(\exists x)(Ax \cdot Dx)$	12, EG
14)	$\therefore (x)(Cx \supset Dx) \supset (\exists x)(Ax \cdot Dx)$	9–13, CP

We can expand the Conditional Method of Proving Validity and Universal Generalization. Imagine an argument having as its conclusion some statement

$(\alpha)(\Phi\alpha \supset \Psi\alpha)$. Such a statement would not be a hypothetical, but the statement matrix leading to $(\alpha)(\Phi\alpha \supset \Psi\alpha)$ by Universal Generalization would be hypothetical in form. Consequently, as a new premiss, we may assume the antecedent of $\Phi\alpha \supset \Psi\alpha$ and then deduce $\Psi\alpha$ from the augmented premiss set. Having done this, $\Phi\alpha \supset \Psi\alpha$ is obtained by Conditional Proof and then $(\alpha)(\Phi\alpha \supset \Psi\alpha)$ by this expanded rule of Universal Generalization:

Universal Generalization (UG)

$$\Psi\beta$$
$$\therefore (\alpha)\,\Psi\alpha$$

where (1) β is a variable which occurs free in $\Psi\beta$ at all and only those places where α is a variable which occurs free in $\Psi\alpha$; (2) β does not occur free in any statement matrix, $\Psi\beta$, obtained by Existential Instantiation; and (3) β is a variable which does not occur free in any assumption within whose scope $\Psi\beta$ lies.

Examine carefully the following proof:

(3) $\therefore (x)[Ax \supset (Dx \supset Cx)]$

1)	$(x)(Ax \supset Bx)\cdot(x)(Bx \supset Cx)$	Pr
2)	$(x)(Ax \supset Bx)$	1, Simp
3)	$(x)(Bx \supset Cx)\cdot(x)(Ax \supset Bx)$	1, Com
4)	$(x)(Bx \supset Cx)$	3, Simp
5)	$Ax \supset Bx$	2, UI
6)	$Bx \supset Cx$	4, UI
7)	$Ax \supset Cx$	5, 6, HS
8)	Ax	CP, $\therefore Dx \supset Cx$
9)	Cx	7, 8, MP
10)	$Cx \lor \sim Dx$	9, Add
11)	$\sim Dx \lor Cx$	10, Com
12)	$Dx \supset Cx$	11, MI
13)	$Ax \supset (Dx \supset Cx)$	8–12, CP
14)	$\therefore (x)[Ax \supset (Dx \supset Cx)]$	13, UG

Or, if the statement matrix leading to the conclusion is logically equivalent to a hypothetical statement matrix, the Conditional Method of Proving Validity may be used. Notice this proof:

(4) $\therefore (x)[(Ax \supset Dx) \lor Bx]$

1)	$(x)[Ax \supset (Bx \lor Cx)]$	Pr
2)	$(x)(Cx \supset Dx)$	Pr
3)	$Ax \supset (Bx \lor Cx)$	1, UI
4)	$Cx \supset Dx$	2, UI

5)	$Ax \cdot \sim Dx$	CP, $\therefore Bx$
6)	Ax	5, Simp
7)	$\sim Dx \cdot Ax$	5, Com
8)	$\sim Dx$	7, Simp
9)	$Bx \lor Cx$	3, 6, MP
10)	$Cx \lor Bx$	9, Com
11)	$\sim Cx$	4, 8, MT
12)	Bx	10, 11, DS
13)	$(Ax \cdot \sim Dx) \supset Bx$	5–12, CP
14)	$\sim (Ax \cdot \sim Dx) \lor Bx$	13, MI
15)	$(Ax \supset Dx) \lor Bx$	14, D3
16)	$\therefore (x)[(Ax \supset Dx) \lor Bx]$	15, UG

While the statement matrix, '$(Ax \supset Dx) \lor Bx$', leading directly to the conclusion of (4) is not hypothetical in form, it is logically equivalent to '$(Ax \cdot \sim Dx) \supset Bx$' which may be read as displaying a hypothetical form. Hence, we assume '$Ax \cdot \sim Dx$' and then deduce 'Bx'. Having done this, the scope of '$Ax \cdot \sim Dx$' is ended with '$(Ax \cdot \sim Dx) \supset Bx$' and we move to '$(x)[(Ax \supset Dx) \lor Bx]$'.

EXERCISES

Symbolize the following arguments using the suggested notation, and then construct a proof for each using the Conditional Method of Proving Validity. Next construct a proof for each in which you do not use the Conditional Method of Proving Validity.

(1) No drug which is habit-forming is either safe or beneficial if not prescribed by a physician. Hence, any habit-forming drug is either prescribed by a physician or isn't beneficial. ($D, F, S, B, P; x$)

(2) Anything not safe to use without a prescription might not be harmful even though it isn't beneficial. Everything which is safe to use without a prescription is trustworthy. So, everything is trustworthy or not beneficial. ($S, H, B, T; x$)

(3) Every body is spatially extended. Any body is spatially extended only if it obeys the laws of physics. Each spatially extended body can be described and explained if it obeys the laws of physics. Thus, any body can be described and explained. ($B, S, O, D, E; x$)

(4) If anything is either knowable or understandable, it is a proper object of scientific study. Everything is either understandable or not explainable and not describable. Consequently, anything explainable is a proper object of scientific study. ($K, U, O, E, D; x$)

(5) No chemical which is an acid only if either phosphoric or nitric is both slick to the touch while also high on the pH scale. Therefore, no chemical which is slick to the touch and high on the pH scale is either phosphoric or nitric. (*C, A, P, N, S, H; x*)

(6) Acids which corrode the more electropositive metals while releasing hydrogen are proton donors only if they give up protons easily and are strong. Accordingly, acids which corrode the more electropositive metals release hydrogen only if they are strong whenever they are proton donors. (*A, C, R, D, G, S; x*)

(7) People who are either scientists or technicians are respected only if well-educated and knowledgeable. Therefore, people who are scientists are well-educated if respected. (*P, S, T, R, E, K; x*)

(8) Nothing which is both cold-blooded and has a shell is viviparous. Anything which isn't oviparous is viviparous. Turtles are cold-blooded. So, turtles are oviparous if they have shells. (*C, S, V, O, T; x*)

(9) Nothing which is either a reptile or fish while also being cold-blooded and scaly is viviparous. Hence, anything viviparous is both cold-blooded and scaly only if it isn't a fish. (*R, F, C, S, V; x*)

(10) No contestant will be either noticed or judged who is either not over 21 years old or married. Consequently, any noticed contestant isn't married. (*C, N, J, O, M; x*)

4. DEFINITION 5 AND QUANTIFICATIONAL DENIAL

In Chapter 4 we learned any truth-functional statement can be expressed in terms of the tilde and dot. Thus, we said the tilde and dot comprise a functionally complete set of operators for the Truth-Functional Calculus. Both operators are called 'primitives' because all other operators of the Calculus are explicitly defined in terms of them. Quantification Theory also has a functionally complete set of operators. For Quantification Theory not only do we need the tilde and dot but also a quantifier if we want to talk about a property true of an infinite number of things or about a set, or universe, with an infinite number of members.

But, for a moment, let us suppose we want to talk about a property true of a finite number of things or a set, or universe, having a finite number of members such that those members can be listed and named. In this case we do not need quantifiers. Imagine there are only three things in the set we wish to discuss, named '*a*', '*b*', and '*c*'. Thus, to say of this set

(1)   Everything is blue

is to say

(2)   *a* is blue, ***and*** *b* is blue, ***and*** *c* is blue.

Associating to the left, (2) may be symbolically represented as

(3) $(Ba \cdot Bb) \cdot Bc$

If 'Everything is blue' is true of our finite set, then each member of that set is blue. On the other hand, to say of this set

(4)   Something is blue

is to say

(5) a is blue, **or** b is blue, **or** c is blue.

Again, associating to the left, we depict (5) by

(6) $(Ba \lor Bb) \lor Bc$

If 'Something is blue' is true of our finite set, then one or another member of that set must be blue.

When discussing a finite number of things which can be named and listed, the universal quantifier can be expressed in terms of the dot and the existential quantifier in terms of the wedge. But we do not want to limit our language this way. For instance, we want to be able to say 'All prime numbers are divisible by unity or themselves' and allow for an infinite number of primes. Or we want to be able to say 'Some natural numbers are even' and consider an infinite number of even numbers. Thus, we shall define neither of the quantifiers solely in terms of truth-functional operators.

A question now arises: Is it necessary to count both the universal and existential quantifiers as primitive operators in Quantification Theory? No—just one of them. Furthermore, it does not logically matter which quantifier is selected as primitive. If the existential quantifier is chosen, then with the help of the tilde the universal quantifier can be explicitly defined. Or, if the universal quantifier is selected as primitive, with the use of the tilde, the existential quantifier can be explicitly defined.

To appreciate the relationship holding between quantifiers, we might consider these examples:

(7) (a)   Somebody is intelligent.
    (b)   Not everybody isn't intelligent.
(8) (a)   A few things are weightless.
    (b)   It isn't true that all things aren't weightless.

Examples (7) and (8) may be symbolized as

(9) (a) $(\exists x)Ix$
    (b) $\sim (x) \sim Ix$

(10)　(a)　$(\exists x)Wx$

　　　(b)　$\sim(x)\sim Wx$

Continuing to let '$(\exists\alpha)$' represent any existential quantifier and '$\Psi\alpha$' any statement matrix, the first statement of (7) and (8) may be interpreted as an instance of

(11)　　　$(\exists\alpha)\Psi\alpha$

Allowing '(α)' to picture any universal quantifier, the second statement in (7) and (8) may be interpreted as an instance of

(12)　　　$\sim(\alpha)\sim\Psi\alpha$

Further, in each example the two statements are equivalent in the sense that whatever conditions make one true, or false, also make the other true, or false. And, this observation holds for any quantified statements having the same statement matrix, $\Psi\alpha$, and the general forms $(\exists\alpha)\,\Psi\alpha$ and $\sim(\alpha)\sim\Psi\alpha$. Accordingly, we may define the existential quantifier in terms of the tilde and universal quantifier:

D5:　　　'$(\exists\alpha)\Psi\alpha$' = '$\sim(\alpha)\sim\Psi\alpha$'　Df

A functionally complete set of operators for Quantification Theory is, then,

$$\{\sim,\,\cdot,\,(\alpha)\}$$

where '(α)' represents any universal quantifier.

　　Definition 5, like Definitions 1–4, is a Rule of Transformation and may be used in constructing proofs of validity where

> *any statement or statement matrix may be replaced by its definitional equivalence. Such a replacement of definitionally equivalent statements or statement matrixes may be performed on "parts" of statements or statement matrixes; moreover, such replacement need not be performed at every occurrence of the same "part" of a statement or statement matrix.*

Thus, appealing to Definition 5 and the notion of replacement, the following proof is constructed:

(13)　　　　　　　　　　　　　　　　　$\therefore\ \sim(x)\sim(Ax\cdot Bx)$

　　1)　　$(x)\sim(Ax\cdot Bx)\supset(\exists x)\sim(Bx\lor Cx)$　　　Pr

　　2)　　$(x)(Bx\lor Cx)$　　　　　　　　　　　　　　　　Pr

　　3)　　$\sim(\exists x)\sim(Bx\lor Cx)$　　　　　　　　　　　2, D5

　　4)　$\therefore\ \sim(x)\sim(Ax\cdot Bx)$　　　　　　　　　　1, 3, MT

But for our purposes, Definition 5 is most useful in establishing the following logical equivalences—equivalences we must have in proving the validity of many quantificational arguments:

(14)   (a) $\sim(\exists\alpha) \sim \Psi\alpha \equiv (\alpha)\Psi\alpha$

      (b) $\sim(\exists\alpha)\Psi\alpha \equiv (\alpha) \sim \Psi\alpha$

      (c) $(\exists\alpha) \sim \Psi\alpha \equiv \sim(\alpha)\Psi\alpha$

      (d) $(\exists\alpha)\Psi\alpha \equiv \sim(\alpha) \sim \Psi\alpha$

Two statement forms, such as $\sim(\exists\alpha) \sim \Psi\alpha$ and $(\alpha)\Psi\alpha$ are logically equivalent when they mutually imply one another. Can we establish in each case of (14) that the left-hand statement form implies the right-hand and vise versa? Yes.

(a) $\therefore (\alpha)\Psi\alpha$

     1) $\sim(\exists\alpha) \sim \Psi\alpha$ Pr

     2) $\therefore (\alpha)\Psi\alpha$ 1, D5

                                       $\therefore \sim(\exists\alpha) \sim \Psi\alpha$

     1) $(\alpha)\Psi\alpha$ Pr

     2) $\therefore \sim(\exists\alpha) \sim \Psi\alpha$ 1, D5

Here, by appealing to Definition 5, we establish $\sim(\exists\alpha) \sim \Psi\alpha \equiv (\alpha)\Psi\alpha$. Similarly, we can establish that (b), (c), and (d) of (14) are logically equivalent statement forms and may all be accepted as new Rules of Transformation:

(b) $\therefore (\alpha) \sim \Psi\alpha$

     1) $\sim(\exists\alpha)\Psi\alpha$ Pr

     2) $\sim(\exists\alpha) \sim \sim \Psi\alpha$ 1, DN

     3) $\therefore (\alpha) \sim \Psi\alpha$ 2, D5

                                       $\therefore \sim(\exists\alpha)\Psi\alpha$

     1) $(\alpha) \sim \Psi\alpha$ Pr

     2) $\sim \sim(\alpha) \sim \Psi\alpha$ 1, DN

     3) $\therefore \sim(\exists\alpha)\Psi\alpha$ 2, D5

(c) $\therefore \sim(\alpha)\Psi\alpha$

     1) $(\exists\alpha) \sim \Psi\alpha$ Pr

     2) $\sim \sim(\exists\alpha) \sim \Psi\alpha$ 1, DN

     3) $\therefore \sim(\alpha)\Psi\alpha$ 2, D5

                                       $\therefore (\exists\alpha) \sim \Psi\alpha$

     1) $\sim(\alpha)\Psi\alpha$ Pr

     2) $\sim(\alpha) \sim \sim \Psi\alpha$ 1, DN

     3) $\therefore (\exists\alpha) \sim \Psi\alpha$ 2, D5

(d) $\therefore \sim(\alpha) \sim \Psi\alpha$

     1) $(\exists\alpha)\Psi\alpha$ Pr

     2) $\sim \sim(\exists\alpha)\Psi\alpha$ 1, DN

     3) $\sim \sim(\exists\alpha) \sim \sim \Psi\alpha$ 2, DN

     4) $\therefore \sim(\alpha) \sim \Psi\alpha$ 3, D5

$$\therefore (\exists\alpha)\Psi\alpha$$

1)	$\sim(\alpha) \sim \Psi\alpha$	Pr
2)	$\sim\sim(\exists\alpha) \sim \sim \Psi\alpha$	1, D5
3)	$(\exists\alpha) \sim \sim \Psi\alpha$	2, DN
4)	$\therefore (\exists\alpha)\Psi\alpha$	3, DN

We shall call every logical equivalence in (14) '***Quantificational Denial***' and refer to each as '***QD***' in proofs.

Why are the equivalences, Quantificational Denial, needed to construct proofs? Consider this argument:

(15)   Not all rodents are mice. So, certain rodents aren't mice.

Symbolizing (15),

(16) $\therefore (\exists x)(Rx \cdot \sim Mx)$

   1) $\sim(x)(Rx \supset Mx)$ Pr

Notice first the premiss of (16) cannot be instantiated because there is a tilde before the quantifier. If it were possible to instantiate '$\sim(x)(Rx \supset Mx)$', we could move to '$(x)(Rx \supset Mx)$' by Universal Generalization. But, surely, if 'Not all rodents are mice' is true, 'All rodents are mice' cannot also be true. In fact *we can never instantiate any quantified statement having a tilde before its quantifier.* We can remove such tildes, however, by Quantificational Denial. So, (16) may be completed:

(17) $\therefore (\exists x)(Rx \cdot \sim Mx)$

1)	$\sim(x)(Rx \supset Mx)$	Pr
2)	$(\exists x) \sim(Rx \supset Mx)$	1, QD
3)	$\sim(Rx \supset Mx)$	2, EI
4)	$\sim\sim(Rx \cdot \sim Mx)$	3, D3
5)	$Rx \cdot \sim Mx$	4, DN
6)	$\therefore (\exists x)(Rx \cdot \sim Mx)$	5, EG

Carefully notice the premiss of (15) and how it is symbolized in (16). A common error in moving from English to logical symbols is to confuse such phrases as 'not all', 'not every', and 'not any' with 'no', 'nothing', and the like. To say 'Not all rodents are mice' and 'No rodents are mice' is to make entirely different assertions, for while the former is true, the latter is not. Such distinctions must be pictured in our symbolic representation of statements.

Not only does Quantificational Denial permit us to remove tildes from before quantifiers, it also allows us to place tildes before quantifiers. For instance, we might argue

(18)   Only reptiles are snakes. Some snakes are poisonous. So, not every reptile isn't poisonous.

Example (18) may be symbolized as

(19) $\qquad\qquad\qquad\qquad\qquad\qquad\qquad \therefore \sim(x)(Rx \supset \sim Px)$

    1) $(x)(Sx \supset Rx)$ Pr

    2) $(\exists x)(Sx \cdot Px)$ Pr

How can '$\sim(x)(Rx \supset \sim Px)$' be obtained? Not by Universal Generalization. But, if we could deduce '$(\exists x) \sim (Rx \supset \sim Px)$', our conclusion would follow by Quantificational Denial. '$(\exists x) \sim (Rx \supset \sim Px)$' can be derived by Existential Generalization if we first have the statement matrix '$\sim(Rx \supset \sim Px)$'. '$\sim(Rx \supset \sim Px)$' could come quite easily from '$\sim \sim(Rx \cdot \sim \sim Px)$' by Definition 3. '$\sim \sim(Rx \cdot \sim \sim Px)$' in turn can be obtained from 'Rx' and 'Px' by Conjunction and various uses of Double Negation. Surely, however, we can deduce 'Rx' and 'Px' from the premiss set of (19).

(20) $\qquad\qquad\qquad\qquad\qquad\qquad\qquad \therefore \sim(x)(Rx \supset \sim Px)$

	1)	$(x)(Sx \supset Rx)$	Pr
	2)	$(\exists x)(Sx \cdot Px)$	Pr
	3)	$Sx \cdot Px$	2, EI
	4)	$Sx \supset Rx$	1, UI
	5)	Sx	3, Simp
	6)	$Px \cdot Sx$	3, Com
	7)	Px	6, Simp
	8)	Rx	4, 5, MP
	9)	$\sim \sim Px$	7, DN
	10)	$Rx \cdot \sim \sim Px$	8, 9, Conj
	11)	$\sim \sim (Rx \cdot \sim \sim Px)$	10, DN
	12)	$\sim (Rx \supset \sim Px)$	11, D3
	13)	$(\exists x) \sim (Rx \supset \sim Px)$	12, EG
	14)	$\therefore \sim(x)(Rx \supset \sim Px)$	13, QD

Since Quantificational Denial refers to various logical equivalences, the notion of replacement is applicable.

> ***Any statement or statement matrix may be replaced by its logical equivalence. Such a replacement of logically equivalent statements or statement matrixes may be performed on "parts" of statements or statement matrixes; moreover, replacement need not be performed at every occurrence of the same "part" of a statement or statement matrix.***

Consider this argument:

(21)   Either some people are vicious or there isn't a person who isn't kind. That all persons are kind isn't true. Wherefore, some people are vicious.

We may symbolize (21) as

(22) $\therefore (\exists x)(Px \cdot Vx)$

    1) $(\exists x)(Px \cdot Vx) \lor \sim(\exists x)(Px \cdot \sim Kx)$ Pr

    2) $\sim(x)(Px \supset Kx)$ Pr

Inspecting the premiss set and conclusion of (22), we see that the conclusion is the left-hand disjunct of the first premiss. Consequently, to obtain our conclusion, we shall first commute line 1 and then use Disjunctive Syllogism. Notice how this may be done:

(23) $\therefore (\exists x)(Px \cdot Vx)$

    1) $(\exists x)(Px \cdot Vx) \lor \sim(\exists x)(Px \cdot \sim Kx)$ Pr

    2) $\sim(x)(Px \supset Kx)$ Pr

    3) $\sim(\exists x)(Px \cdot \sim Kx) \lor (\exists x)(Px \cdot Vx)$ 1, Com

    4) $(x) \sim(Px \cdot \sim Kx) \lor (\exists x)(Px \cdot Vx)$ 3, QD

    5) $(x)(Px \supset Kx) \lor (\exists x)(Px \cdot Vx)$ 4, D3

    6) $\therefore (\exists x)(Px \cdot Vx)$ 5, 2, DS

EXERCISES

Group A:

Using the suggested notation and also appropriate quantifiers, symbolize each of the following. Then, assuming a finite universe consisting of only three members, '*a*', '*b*', and '*c*', resymbolize each of the following using only truth-functional operators.

(1)   Some numbers are positive integers. ($N, P, I; x$)

(2)   Even numbers are all divisible by two without a remainder. ($E, N, D; x$)

(3)   Rational numbers can be expressed as the ratio of integers. ($R, N, E; x$)

(4)   Certain trinomials are perfect squares. ($T, P, S; x$)

(5)   A sign is a constant if it has just one interpretation. ($S, C, I; x$)

(6)   Any lens is converging or diverging (but not both). ($L, C, D; x$)

(7)   Some converging lenses are plano-convex. ($C, L, P; x$)

(8)   Many diverging lenses are plano-concave. ($D, L, P; x$)

(9)   No concavo-convex lens is flat. ($C, L, F; x$)

(10) All diverging lenses are not convexo-concave. ($D, L, C; x$)

Group B:

In the following, justify each of the unjustified lines.

(1) $\therefore (\exists x)(Ax \cdot Bx)$

    1) $(x) \sim (Ax \cdot Bx) \supset (x)(Cx \supset Bx)$ Pr

    2) $(\exists x)(Cx \cdot \sim Bx)$ Pr

    3) $\sim (x) \sim (Cx \cdot \sim Bx)$

    4) $\sim (x)(Cx \supset Bx)$

    5) $\sim (x) \sim (Ax \cdot Bx)$

    6) $\therefore (\exists x)(Ax \cdot Bx)$

(2) $\therefore (x)(Ax \supset \sim Cx)$

    1) $\sim (\exists x)(Ax \cdot \sim Bx)$ Pr

    2) $(x)(Bx \supset \sim Cx)$ Pr

    3) $(x) \sim (Ax \cdot \sim Bx)$

    4) $Bx \supset \sim Cx$

    5) $\sim (Ax \cdot \sim Bx)$

    6) $Ax \supset Bx$

    7) $Ax \supset \sim Cx$

    8) $\therefore (x)(Ax \supset \sim Cx)$

(3) $\therefore (\exists x)Cx$

    1) $\sim (x) \sim (Ax \cdot Bx)$ Pr

    2) $(x)(Bx \supset Cx)$ Pr

    3) $(\exists x)(Ax \cdot Bx)$

    4) $Ax \cdot Bx$

    5) $Bx \supset Cx$

    6) $Bx \cdot Ax$

    7) Bx

    8) Cx

    9) $\therefore (\exists x)Cx$

(4) $\therefore (x)(Ax \supset Cx)$

    1) $\sim (\exists x)(Ax \cdot \sim Bx) \cdot \sim (\exists x)(Bx \cdot \sim Cx)$ Pr

    2) $\sim (\exists x)(Ax \cdot \sim Bx)$

    3) $\sim (\exists x)(Bx \cdot \sim Cx) \cdot \sim (\exists x)(Ax \cdot \sim Bx)$

    4) $\sim (\exists x)(Bx \cdot \sim Cx)$

    5) $(x) \sim (Ax \cdot \sim Bx)$

    6) $(x) \sim (Bx \cdot \sim Cx)$

    7) $\sim (Ax \cdot \sim Bx)$

    8) $\sim (Bx \cdot \sim Cx)$

    9) $Ax \supset Bx$

    10) $Bx \supset Cx$

    11) $Ax \supset Cx$

    12) $\therefore (x)(Ax \supset Cx)$

(5) $\therefore \sim (x)(Cx \lor Bx)$

    1) $\sim (x)(Ax \lor Bx)$ Pr

    2) $(x)(Cx \supset Bx)$ Pr

    3) $(\exists x) \sim (Ax \lor Bx)$

    4) $\sim (Ax \lor Bx)$

    5) $Cx \supset Bx$

    6) $\sim Ax \cdot \sim Bx$

    7) $\sim Bx \cdot \sim Ax$

    8) $\sim Bx$

    9) $\sim Cx$

   10) $\sim Cx \cdot \sim Bx$

   11) $\sim (Cx \lor Bx)$

   12) $(\exists x) \sim (Cx \lor Bx)$

   13) $\therefore \sim (x)(Cx \lor Bx)$

(6) $\therefore (x)(Bx \supset Dx)$

    1) $\sim (\exists x) \sim (Ax \lor \sim Bx)$ Pr

    2) $(x)[(Ax \lor Cx) \supset Dx]$ Pr

    3) $(x)(Ax \lor \sim Bx)$

    4) $(Ax \lor Cx) \supset Dx$

    5) $Ax \lor \sim Bx$

    6) $\sim Bx \lor Ax$

    7) $Bx \supset Ax$

    8) $\sim (Ax \lor Cx) \lor Dx$

    9) $(\sim Ax \cdot \sim Cx) \lor Dx$

   10) $Dx \lor (\sim Ax \cdot \sim Cx)$

   11) $(Dx \lor \sim Ax) \cdot (Dx \lor \sim Cx)$

   12) $Dx \lor \sim Ax$

   13) $\sim Ax \lor Dx$

   14) $Ax \supset Dx$

   15) $Bx \supset Dx$

   16) $\therefore (x)(Bx \supset Dx)$

(7) $\therefore (\exists x)(Ax \cdot \sim Bx)$

    1) $(x)(Ax \supset Bx) \supset (x)(Cx \supset Bx)$ Pr

    2) $(x)(Dx \supset Cx)$ Pr

    3) $\sim (x)(Dx \supset Bx)$ Pr

    4) $(\exists x) \sim (Dx \supset Bx)$

    5) $\sim (Dx \supset Bx)$

    6) $\sim \sim (Dx \cdot \sim Bx)$

    7) $Dx \cdot \sim Bx$

    8) $Dx \supset Cx$

    9) Dx

   10) $\sim Bx \cdot Dx$

   11) $\sim Bx$

   12) Cx

   13) $Cx \cdot \sim Bx$

14) $(\exists x)(Cx \cdot \sim Bx)$
15) $\sim (x) \sim (Cx \cdot \sim Bx)$
16) $\sim (x)(Cx \supset Bx)$
17) $\sim (x)(Ax \supset Bx)$
18) $(\exists x) \sim (Ax \supset Bx)$
19) $(\exists x) \sim \sim (Ax \cdot \sim Bx)$
20) $\therefore (\exists x)(Ax \cdot \sim Bx)$

(8) $\therefore \sim (\exists x)(Dx \cdot \sim Bx)$

1) $\sim (\exists x)[(Cx \lor Dx) \cdot \sim Ax]$ Pr
2) $\sim (\exists x)(Ax \cdot \sim Bx)$ Pr
3) $(x) \sim [(Cx \lor Dx) \cdot \sim Ax]$
4) $(x) \sim (Ax \cdot \sim Bx)$
5) $\sim [(Cx \lor Dx) \cdot \sim Ax]$
6) $\sim (Ax \cdot \sim Bx)$
7) $(Cx \lor Dx) \supset Ax$
8) $Ax \supset Bx$
9) $(Cx \lor Dx) \supset Bx$
10) $\sim (Cx \lor Dx) \lor Bx$
11) $(\sim Cx \cdot \sim Dx) \lor Bx$
12) $Bx \lor (\sim Cx \cdot \sim Dx)$
13) $(Bx \lor \sim Cx) \cdot (Bx \lor \sim Dx)$
14) $(Bx \lor \sim Dx) \cdot (Bx \lor \sim Cx)$
15) $Bx \lor \sim Dx$
16) $\sim Dx \lor Bx$
17) $Dx \supset Bx$
18) $(x)(Dx \supset Bx)$
19) $\sim (\exists x) \sim (Dx \supset Bx)$
20) $\sim (\exists x) \sim \sim (Dx \cdot \sim Bx)$
21) $\therefore \sim (\exists x)(Dx \cdot \sim Bx)$

(9) $\therefore \sim (\exists x)[(Ex \cdot Bx) \cdot \sim Dx]$

1) $\sim (\exists x)[Ax \cdot \sim (Bx \supset \sim Cx)]$ Pr
2) $\sim (\exists x)(\sim Dx \cdot \sim Cx) \cdot \sim (\exists x)(Ex \cdot \sim Ax)$ Pr
3) $\sim (\exists x)(\sim Dx \cdot \sim Cx)$
4) $\sim (\exists x)(Ex \cdot \sim Ax) \cdot \sim (\exists x)(\sim Dx \cdot \sim Cx)$
5) $\sim (\exists x)(Ex \cdot \sim Ax)$
6) $(x) \sim [Ax \cdot \sim (Bx \supset \sim Cx)]$
7) $(x) \sim (\sim Dx \cdot \sim Cx)$
8) $(x) \sim (Ex \cdot \sim Ax)$
9) $\sim [Ax \cdot \sim (Bx \supset \sim Cx)]$
10) $\sim (\sim Dx \cdot \sim Cx)$
11) $\sim (Ex \cdot \sim Ax)$
12) $Ax \supset (Bx \supset \sim Cx)$

13) $\sim Dx \supset Cx$
14) $Ex \supset Ax$
15) $Ex \supset (Bx \supset \sim Cx)$
16) $(Ex \cdot Bx) \supset \sim Cx$
17) $\sim Cx \supset \sim \sim \sim Dx$
18) $\sim Cx \supset Dx$
19) $(Ex \cdot Bx) \supset Dx$
20) $(x)[(Ex \cdot Bx) \supset Dx]$
21) $\sim (\exists x) \sim [(Ex \cdot Bx) \supset Dx]$
22) $\sim (\exists x) \sim \sim [(Ex \cdot Bx) \cdot \sim Dx]$
23) $\therefore \sim (\exists x)[(Ex \cdot Bx) \cdot \sim Dx]$

(10) $\therefore (x)[(Cx \lor Ax) \supset Dx]$

1) $(x)[Ax \supset (Bx \cdot Cx)]$ Pr
2) $\sim (\exists x)[Cx \cdot (\sim Dx \lor \sim Ex)]$ Pr
3) $(x) \sim [Cx \cdot (\sim Dx \lor \sim Ex)]$
4) $(x) \sim [Cx \cdot \sim (Dx \cdot Ex)]$
5) $Ax \supset (Bx \cdot Cx)$
6) $\sim [Cx \cdot \sim (Dx \cdot Ex)]$
7) $Cx \supset (Dx \cdot Ex)$
8) $\sim Ax \lor (Bx \cdot Cx)$
9) $(\sim Ax \lor Bx) \cdot (\sim Ax \lor Cx)$
10) $(\sim Ax \lor Cx) \cdot (\sim Ax \lor Bx)$
11) $\sim Ax \lor Cx$
12) $Ax \supset Cx$
13) $\sim Cx \lor (Dx \cdot Ex)$
14) $(\sim Cx \lor Dx) \cdot (\sim Cx \lor Ex)$
15) $\sim Cx \lor Dx$
16) $Cx \supset Dx$
17) $Ax \supset Dx$
18) $\sim Ax \lor Dx$
19) $Dx \lor \sim Cx$
20) $Dx \lor \sim Ax$
21) $(Dx \lor \sim Cx) \cdot (Dx \lor \sim Ax)$
22) $Dx \lor (\sim Cx \cdot \sim Ax)$
23) $(\sim Cx \cdot \sim Ax) \lor Dx$
24) $\sim (Cx \lor Ax) \lor Dx$
25) $(Cx \lor Ax) \supset Dx$
26) $\therefore (x)[(Cx \lor Ax) \supset Dx]$

Group C:

Construct a proof of validity for each of the following.

(1)   ∴ (∃x) ~ Ax
   1)   ~(∃x)(Ax · ~ Bx) · ~(x)Bx   Pr

(2)   ∴ (x)(Bx ⊃ Cx)
   1)   ~(∃x)[(Ax ⊃ Bx) · ~ Cx]   Pr

(3)   ∴ ~(x)(Cx ⊃ Ax)
   1)   ~(∃x) ~ (Ax ⊃ Bx)   Pr
   2)   ~(x)(Cx ⊃ Bx)   Pr

(4)   ∴ (x)[Ax ⊃ (Dx ⊃ ~ Bx)]
   1)   ~(∃x)[(Ax · Bx) · (Cx ∨ Dx)]   Pr

(5)   ∴ (∃x)[Bx · (Ax · ~ Dx)]
   1)   ~(∃x)[(Ax · Bx) · ~ Cx]   Pr
   2)   (x)[Cx ⊃ (Ax ⊃ Dx)]   Pr

(6)   ∴ ~(x)[(Cx ∨ Dx) ⊃ Bx]
   1)   ~(x) ~ Ax   Pr
   2)   ~(∃x)(Ax · Bx)   Pr
   3)   (x)(Bx · Cx)   Pr

(7)   ∴ (∃x)(Cx · Ax) ∨ (∃x)(Cx · Dx)
   1)   ~(∃x)[~ Ax · (~ Bx · Cx)]   Pr
   2)   ~(x)(Cx ⊃ Bx)   Pr

(8)   ∴ (∃x)[Ax · (Cx · Ex)]
   1)   ~(x)(Ax ⊃ Bx)   Pr
   2)   (x)(Ax ⊃ Cx)   Pr
   3)   ~(∃x)[(~ Bx · ~ Ex) · (Dx ∨ Cx)]   Pr

(9)   ∴ ~(∃x)(~ Cx · ~ Fx)
   1)   ~(∃x)(Ax · ~ Bx) · ~(∃x)(Bx · ~ Cx)   Pr
   2)   (x)(~ Ax ≡ Dx)   Pr
   3)   (x)(Dx ⊃ Ex) · (x)(Ex ⊃ Fx)   Pr

(10)   ∴ (x)(~ Cx ⊃ Fx)
   1)   ~(∃x)[(Ax · Bx) · ~ Cx]   Pr
   2)   (x)[Dx ⊃ (~ Bx ≡ Ex)]   Pr
   3)   ~(∃x)[(Dx · Ex) · ~ Fx]   Pr
   4)   ~(x)(Dx ⊃ ~ Ax)   Pr

Group D:

Construct an English argument corresponding to each of the exercises in Group C. Attempt to make each argument sound.

Group E:

Symbolize the following arguments using the suggested notation, and then construct a proof of validity for each.

(1) Everyone is basically an Aristotelian or Platonist in his world view; but not everyone is a Platonist in his world view. Consequently, there are those who are Aristotelian but not Platonists in their world view. (*A, P; x*)

(2) There aren't any Aristotelians who aren't also empiricists; but further there isn't anyone who isn't an Aristotelian but is a naturalist. So, there aren't any naturalists who aren't empiricists. (*A, E, N; x*)

(3) None but teleologists are Aristotelians. It isn't true that there are teleologists who aren't both interested in ethics while maintaining a doctrine of the supreme good for man. Thus, there aren't any Aristotelians who fail to be interested in ethics. (*T, A, I, M; x*)

(4) Anyone who is a Platonist holds that sets exist if he is a mathematician. Not everyone who is a mathematician holds that sets exist. Every Logicist is a Platonist or holds that sets exist. Therefore, someone isn't a Platonist and not a Logicist. (*P, S, M, L; x*)

(5) Any action is good if, and only if, it is neither selfish nor harmful. There are good actions. Hence, not every action is harmful. (*A, G, S, H; x*)

(6) It isn't the case that some harmful actions aren't selfish. Actions are harmful and mean when selfish. Wherefore, there isn't any action of which it isn't true to assert that it's selfish when, and only when, it's harmful. (*H, A, S, M; x*)

(7) There isn't something vicious which is an action but not mean. It isn't true that some action which is mean isn't both harmful as well as cruel. Consequently, all actions are harmful if vicious. (*V, A, M, H, C; x*)

(8) Not every person is compassionate who is understanding or tolerant. There isn't anyone who is understanding but either not virtuous or not compassionate. Accordingly, not all persons are compassionate who are tolerant. (*P, C, U, T, V; x*)

(9) There isn't any follower of *The Little Prince* of which it isn't true to say that he is morally innocent if, and only if, he doesn't act like a grown-up. Not any follower of *The Little Prince* is concerned with matters of consequent. There isn't anyone who acts like a grown-up but isn't concerned with matters of consequent; yet also, there isn't anyone who is morally innocent but not always self-sacrificing. So, there exists someone who is always self-sacrificing. (*F, I, A, C, S; x*)

(10) There is no one who truly loves his neighbor but doesn't either understand or gossip (but not both). Not everyone who truly loves his neighbor isn't compassionate. It isn't the case that there are those who are compassionate but of whom it isn't true that they understand when, and only when, they are virtuous. No one is compassionate who both gossips and is intolerant. Hence, not everyone is both not virtuous and intolerant. (*L, U, G, C, V, T; x*)

5. ARGUMENTS INVOLVING RELATIONS

To establish the validity of arguments using relational predicates, we shall not need to expand our Rules of Transformation. Rather, we must expand our notation. First, we shall permit predicate letters followed by more than one individual constant or variable; thus we shall obtain relational predicates. Second, we shall allow quantifiers to fall within the scope of other quantifiers. Imagine that our notation had not been extended and we wished to symbolize

(1) All circles are figures. Thus, whatever draws a circle draws a figure.

Let 'Cx' stand for 'x is a circle' and 'Fx' for 'x is a figure'; let 'Ax' symbolize 'x draws a circle' and 'Bx' represent 'x draws a figure'. We may put (1) in the following form:

(2) $\therefore (x)(Ax \supset Bx)$
    1) $(x)(Cx \supset Fx)$ Pr

Perhaps we "feel" that (1) is valid—if the premiss is true, the conclusion must also be true. Nevertheless, the symbolization of (2) displays no deductive relation between the premiss and conclusion. Given our Rules of Transformation, we cannot move from '$(x)(Cx \supset Fx)$' to '$(x)(Ax \supset Bx)$'.

On the other hand, let us use our extended notation and symbolize the conclusion of (1) as

(3) $(x)[(\exists y)(Cy \cdot Dxy) \supset (\exists y)(Fy \cdot Dxy)]$

A Conditional Proof now yields

(4) $\therefore (x)[(\exists y)(Cy \cdot Dxy)$
                                           $\supset (\exists y)(Fy \cdot Dxy)]$

1)	$(x)(Cx \supset Fx)$	Pr
2)	$(\exists y)(Cy \cdot Dxy)$	CP, $\therefore (\exists y)(Fy \cdot Dxy)$
3)	$Cy \cdot Dxy$	2, EI
4)	$Cy \supset Fy$	1, UI
5)	Cy	3, Simp
6)	Fy	4, 5, MP
7)	$Dxy \cdot Cy$	3, Com
8)	Dxy	7, Simp
9)	$Fy \cdot Dxy$	6, 8, Conj
10)	$(\exists y)(Fy \cdot Dxy)$	9, EG
11)	$(\exists y)(Fy \cdot Dxy) \supset (\exists y)(Cy \cdot Dxy)$	2–10, CP
12)	$\therefore (x)[(\exists y)(Fy \cdot Dxy) \supset (\exists y)(Cy \cdot Dxy)]$	11, UG

Going from the premiss to line 4 by Universal Instantiation, the bound individual variable, 'x', is changed to a free 'y'. Previously, when appealing to Universal Instantiation or Existential Instantiation, the bound variables have not been changed when the quantifier was dropped. However, this was only a matter of convenience. Our rules of instantiation certainly permit us to change a bound variable to any free variable we please. Of course we must continue to obey all the restrictions on the various rules of quantification.

But why make the change at all? To apply Modus Ponens at line 6 of (4), it is first necessary to substitute the free 'y' in line 4 at every occurrence of the bound 'x' in line 1. Not changing the variable this way would yield

(5)

    4) $Cx \supset Fx$ 1, UI
    5) Cy 3, Simp

While the statement matrix, '$Cx \supset Fx$', is correctly obtained by Universal Instantiation, we cannot now use Modus Ponens to reach 'Fy'. The statement matrix at line 5 is not the same as the antecedent of '$Cx \supset Fx$'.

The strategy involved in changing variables becomes slightly more complicated if we symbolize the conclusion of (1) as

(6) $(x)[(\exists y)(Cy \cdot Dxy) \supset (\exists z)(Fz \cdot Dxz)]$

Examine the following:

(7) $\therefore (x)[(\exists y)(Cy \cdot Dxy) \supset (\exists z)(Fz \cdot Dxz)]$

    1) $(x)(Cx \supset Fx)$ Pr
    2) $(\exists y)(Cy \cdot Dxy)$ CP, $\therefore (\exists z)(Fz \cdot Dxz)$
    3) $Cz \cdot Dxz$ 2, EI
    4) $Cz \supset Fx$ 1, UI
    5) Cz 3, Simp
    6) Fz 4, 5, MP
    7) $Dxz \cdot Cz$ 3, Com
    8) Dxz 7, Simp
    9) $Fz \cdot Dxz$ 6, 8, Conj
  10) $(\exists z)(Fz \cdot Dxz)$ 9, EG
  11) $(\exists y)(Cy \cdot Dxy) \supset (\exists z)(Fz \cdot Dxy)$ 2–10, CP
  12) $\therefore (x)[(\exists y)(Cy \cdot Dxy) \supset (\exists z)(Fz \cdot Dxz)]$ 11, UG

Moving from the statement in line 2 of (7) to the statement matrix in line 3, the bound variable, 'y', is transformed to 'z'. This is done to obtain the 'Dxz' appearing in the conclusion. Now, we must introduce 'z' in line 4. Why? So 'Cz' may be deduced. 'Cz' is needed to use Modus Ponens with '$Cz \supset Fz$', to obtain 'Fz'. In this way we may reach the 'Fz' found in the conclusion.

When using relational predicates and quantifiers falling within the scope of other quantifiers, we must avoid the following types of "proofs". Consider, first, this argument:

(8)   Every person has a mother. There are people. Therefore, something is its own mother.

We may symbolize and attempt to construct a "proof" for (8) this way:

(9) $\therefore (\exists y)(My \cdot Hyy)$

    1) $(x)[Px \supset (\exists y)(My \cdot Hxy)]$ Pr
    2) $(\exists x)Px$ Pr
    3) Py 2, EI
    4) $Py \supset (\exists y)(My \cdot Hyy)$ 1, UI
    5) $\therefore (\exists y)(My \cdot Hyy)$ 4, 3, MP

Now examine this argument:

(10)   Some people are wise in every act. Thus, every act is itself a wise one.

Putting (10) into our notation, again we attempt to construct a "proof":

(11) $\therefore (y)(Ay \supset Wyy)$

    1) $(\exists x)[Px \cdot (y)(Ay \supset Wxy)]$ Pr
    2) $Py \cdot (y)(Ay \supset Wyy)$ 1, EI
    3) $(y)(Ay \supset Wyy) \cdot Py$ 2, Com
    4) $\therefore (y)(Ay \supset Wyy)$ 3, Simp

What has gone wrong in both (9) and (11)? Roughly, in both examples an individual variable (or one substituted for it) originally bound by one quantifier has become bound by another. For instance, 'x' of the first premiss of (9) is under the scope of the universal quantifier, '(x)'. But in line 4 we changed 'x' to 'y' so that 'x' in 'Hxy' becomes 'y' and then falls under the scope of the existential quantifier, '$(\exists y)$'. The same sort of illegitimate move occurs in (11) in going from the premiss to the statement matrix in line 2. Such moves, however, break restrictions placed on Universal Instantiation and Existential Instantiation in *Sections 1 and 2*. The particular violated restriction may be restated as follows:

> *Let* $\Phi\alpha$ *be a statement matrix under the scope of either a universal quantifier, (α), or an existential quantifier, ($\exists\alpha$). Then, if* $\Phi\beta$ *is obtained by either Universal Instantiation or Existential Instantiation and β is some individual variable, then β must remain free in* $\Phi\beta$ *wherever α is free in* $\Phi\alpha$.

This important restriction is certainly violated in both (9) and (11).

Analogous to the mistakes in (9) and (11) are those sometimes made when appealing to Universal Generalization or Existential Generalization. Consider

(12)   Given anything you wish, there is something to which it is not identical. Hence, given anything you wish, it is not identical to itself.

Putting (12) into our notation and attempting a "proof", we proceed:

(13) $\therefore (y) \sim Iyy$

1)	$(x)(\exists y) \sim Ixy$	Pr
2)	$(\exists y) \sim Ixy$	1, UI
3)	$\sim Ixy$	2, EI
4)	$\therefore (y) \sim Iyy$	3, UG

The errors in (13) are not found in the use of Existential Instantiation. Even though Universal Instantiation is used before Existential Instantiation, 'y' does not appear free before line 3. Two restrictions placed on Universal Generalization have been violated. First, the statement matrix to be generalized, '$\sim Ixy$', was obtained by Existential Instantiation. Second, the free 'x' in '$\sim Ixy$' becomes bound in line 4 as does the free 'y'. In going from line 3 to the conclusion, we have allowed our quantifier to capture too much in its scope. A similar mistake is found in

(14) $\therefore (\exists y) \sim Iyy$

1)	$(x)(\exists y) \sim Ixy$	Pr
2)	$(\exists y) \sim Ixy$	1, UI
3)	$\sim Ixy$	2, EI
4)	$\therefore (\exists y) \sim Iyy$	3, EG

Roughly, too much becomes bound by the final quantifier in both (13) and (14). In both examples the free 'y' in line 3 becomes bound in line 4. Yet, in both (13) and (14)—ignoring for the moment the first violation in (13)—we want to bind only the 'x' in line 3.

The restrictions developed in Sections 1 and 2 actually prohibit the illicit moves taken in (13) and (14). The particular restriction violated in both examples may be restated this way:

> Let $\Phi\beta$ *be some statement matrix and* β *an individual variable. Now, if* $(\alpha)\Phi\alpha$ *is obtained from* $\Phi\beta$, *then* α *must be found in* $\Phi\alpha$ *only at those occurrences of free* β *in* $\Phi\beta$. *Or, if* $(\exists\alpha)\Phi\alpha$ *is obtained from* $\Phi\beta$ *by Existential Generalization, then* α *must be bound in* $\Phi\alpha$ *only at those occurrences of free* β *in* $\Phi\beta$.

Group A:

Construct a proof of validity for each of the following, using the Conditional Method of Proving Validity when appropriate.

(1) $\therefore \sim Bba$
    1) Aab Pr
    2) $(x)(Bxa \supset \sim Aax)$ Pr

(2) $\therefore (\exists z)Bzz$
    1) $(x)[(\exists y)Ayx \supset Bxx]$ Pr
    2) $(\exists x)[(\exists y)Ayx \cdot Bxy]$ Pr

(3) $\therefore (y)[Ay \supset (\exists w)Cyw]$
    1) $(x)[Ax \supset (\exists z)(Bz \cdot Cxz)]$ Pr

(4) $\therefore (z)(Dz \supset \sim Bz)$
    1) $(x)[Ax \supset (y)(By \supset Cxy)]$ Pr
    2) Aa Pr
    3) $(x)[Ax \supset (w)(Dw \supset \sim Cxw)]$ Pr

(5) $\therefore (\exists x)(y)(\sim Cx \supset \sim By)$
    1) $(\exists x)(y)[(Axy \supset By) \supset Cx]$ Pr

(6) $\therefore (w)[Cw \supset (z)(Bz \supset Awz)]$
    1) $(x)(y)(Axy \supset Ayx)$ Pr
    2) $(x)[Bx \supset (y)(Cy \supset Axy)]$ Pr

(7) $\therefore \sim (y)(Ay \supset Bxy)$
    1) $(x)\{[Ax \cdot (y)(Ay \supset Bxy)] \supset Bxx\}$ Pr
    2) $\sim (x)(Ax \supset (\exists y)Bxy)$ Pr

(8) $\therefore (\exists y)(By \cdot \sim Dy)$
    1) $(x)[Ax \supset (\exists y)(By \cdot Cxy)]$ Pr
    2) Aa Pr
    3) $(x)[Ax \supset (y)(Dy \supset \sim Cxy)]$ Pr

(9) $\therefore (\exists x)[Bx \cdot (y)(Ay \supset Cyx)]$
    1) $(x)[Ax \supset (\exists w)(Bw \cdot Cxw)]$ Pr
    2) $(\exists x)(Bx \cdot (y)\{[Ay \cdot (\exists z)(Bz \cdot Cyz)] \supset Cyx\})$ Pr

(10) $\therefore (y)\{(By \cdot Dy) \supset (x)[(Ax \cdot Dx) \supset Cyx]\}$
    1) $(x)(y)[(Ax \lor By) \supset (Cxy \equiv Cyx)]$ Pr
    2) $(x)\{(Ax \cdot Dx) \supset (y)[(By \cdot Dy) \supset Cxy]\}$ Pr
    3) $(\exists x)Ax \cdot (\exists y)By$ Pr

Group B:

Construct an English argument corresponding to each of the exercises in Group A. Attempt to make each argument sound.

Group C:

Using the suggested notation, symbolize the following arguments and construct a proof of validity for each. Remember to use the Conditional Method of Proving Validity when appropriate.

(1) Any friend of Julia's is a friend of Dottie's. Rella is Julia's friend. So, Rella is a friend of Dottie's.

$$\text{`}Frj\text{'} = \text{`Rella is a friend of Julia'}$$
$$\text{`}Fxd\text{'} = \text{`}x \text{ is a friend of Dottie'}$$
$$\text{`}Fxj\text{'} = \text{`}x \text{ is a friend of Julia'}$$

(2) Someone appreciates everything. Therefore, everything is appreciated by someone.

$$\text{`}Axy\text{'} = \text{`}x \text{ appreciates } y\text{'}$$

(3) For any two numbers 'x' and 'y', if 'x' is greater than 'y', 'y' is not greater than 'x'. Now 7 is greater than 3. Hence, 3 is not greater than 7.

$$\text{`}Gxy\text{'} = \text{`}x \text{ is greater than } y\text{'}$$
$$\text{`}Gyx\text{'} = \text{`}y \text{ is greater than } x\text{'}$$
$$\text{`}Gab\text{'} = \text{`7 is greater than 3'}$$

(4) Certain poets are appreciated by every poet. Consequently, some poets appreciate themselves.

$$\text{`}Px\text{'} = \text{`}x \text{ is a poet'}$$
$$\text{`}Py\text{'} = \text{`}y \text{ is a poet'}$$
$$\text{`}Ayx\text{'} = \text{`}y \text{ appreciates } x\text{'}$$

(5) Everyone who hates Smaug appreciates Bilbo. Anyone who trusts William the Troll isn't trusted by Bilbo. Thorin appreciates everyone who trusts Gandalf. Thus, Gandalf trusts William the Troll only if Thorin doesn't hate Smaug.

$$\text{`}Atx\text{'} = \text{`Thorin appreciates } x\text{'}$$
$$\text{`}Axb\text{'} = \text{`}x \text{ appreciates Bilbo'}$$
$$\text{`}Hxs\text{'} = \text{`}x \text{ hates Smaug'}$$
$$\text{`}Tbx\text{'} = \text{`Bilbo trusts } x\text{'}$$
$$\text{`}Txg\text{'} = \text{`}x \text{ trusts Gandalf'}$$
$$\text{`}Txw\text{'} = \text{`}x \text{ trusts William the Troll'}$$

(6) Every student enjoys some course or another. Lucia is a student, and, moreover, Lucia will work at anything if she enjoys it. So, Lucia will work at something.

$$\text{`}Cy\text{'} = \text{`}y \text{ is a course'}$$
$$\text{`}Sl\text{'} = \text{`Lucia is a student'}$$
$$\text{`}Sx\text{'} = \text{`}x \text{ is a student'}$$
$$\text{`}Exy\text{'} = \text{`}x \text{ enjoys } y\text{'}$$

(7) No person is his own father. Consequently, any person who was the father of every person would not be a person.

$$\text{'}Px\text{'} = \text{'}x \text{ is a person'}$$
$$\text{'}Py\text{'} = \text{'}y \text{ is a person'}$$
$$\text{'}Fxx\text{'} = \text{'}x \text{ is the father of } x\text{'}$$
$$\text{'}Fxy\text{'} = \text{'}x \text{ is the father of } y\text{'}$$

(8)   All lies are falsehoods. Thus, whoever tells a lie tells a falsehood.

$$\text{'}Fx\text{'} = \text{'}x \text{ is a falsehood'}$$
$$\text{'}Fy\text{'} = \text{'}y \text{ is a falsehood'}$$
$$\text{'}Lx\text{'} = \text{'}x \text{ is a lie'}$$
$$\text{'}Ly\text{'} = \text{'}y \text{ is a lie'}$$
$$\text{'}Txy\text{'} = \text{'}x \text{ tells } y\text{'}$$

(9)   Some people are critical of any new idea. Therefore, if anything is a new idea, not all people aren't critical of it.

$$\text{'}Iy\text{'} = \text{'}y \text{ is an idea'}$$
$$\text{'}Ny\text{'} = \text{'}y \text{ is new'}$$
$$\text{'}Px\text{'} = \text{'}x \text{ is a person'}$$
$$\text{'}Cxy\text{'} = \text{'}x \text{ is critical of } y\text{'}$$

(10)   Unless Michael's sister helps him trim his sails, he won't row a boat ashore. Only if he finds the land of milk and honey, Michael rows a boat ashore. Rachael, a person who is Michael's sister, helps him trim ∴is sails. Any person who trims Michael's sails helps him. So, Michael will find the land of milk and honey.

$$\text{'}By\text{'} = \text{'}y \text{ is a boat'}$$
$$\text{'}Lx\text{'} = \text{'}x \text{ is the land of milk and honey'}$$
$$\text{'}Px\text{'} = \text{'}x \text{ is a person'}$$
$$\text{'}Fmx\text{'} = \text{'Michael finds } x\text{'}$$
$$\text{'}Hxm\text{'} = \text{'}x \text{ helps Michael'}$$
$$\text{'}Rmy\text{'} = \text{'Michael rows } y\text{'}$$
$$\text{'}Srm\text{'} = \text{'Rachael is a sister of Michael'}$$
$$\text{'}Txm\text{'} = \text{'}x \text{ trims the sails of Michael'}$$

Forsan et haec olim meminisse invabit.

(Virgil, *Aeneid* I, 203)

APPENDIX A

The Truth-Functional Calculus

and Switching Networks

In developing the Truth-Functional Calculus, truth-tables were used to characterize such statement forms as '$\sim p$', '$p \cdot q$', and '$p \lor q$'. The truth-tables were constructed with '1's and '0's, and these numerals were given an *interpretation* in which '1' was read as 'is true' and '0' as 'is false'. But other interpretations may be given to both '1' and '0'—interpretations permitting us to model our logical relations in electronic switching networks. Since such networks are of fundamental importance in the construction and operation of electronic digital computers, we may glimpse the extreme importance of logic to the "computer revolution".

We begin with the notion of a switch. While there are many types of switches, we shall consider only those—no matter what their technical design—which function as two-state switches. Our switches are either "on" or "off", but not both, and can be in no other position. (We are ideally not allowing the possibility of any "mechanical failures" in our switches.) Switches having two states, "on" or "off", are often called 'bi-polar' or 'flip-flop' switches. These switches are the ones we need to depict our logical relations.

Having a bi-polar switch of some type, some wire, an electrical power supply, and a light bulb, we can construct this network:

(1)

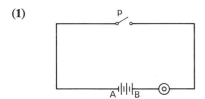

Given (1), when would the light bulb burn? Only when the current can pass from terminal *A* of the power supply to terminal *B*. But, that current can flow from *A* to *B* only when the switch, *p*, is in a closed position—only when the switch is "turned on":

(2)

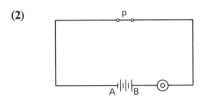

If the switch is opened—"turned off"—as in (1), the current will not pass through the network and the light bulb will not burn.

Instead of a single switch, suppose we had two or more. Again given wire, light bulb, and power supply, what kind of networks can we now build? There are just two. The switches may be put in "series" or "parallel" circuits. If the two switches are connected in series, our network is

(3)

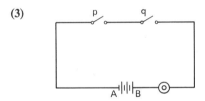

Under what conditions would the light bulb now burn? When would the current flow from terminal *A* of the power supply to terminal *B*? Only when both switches are in a closed position. If *p* is open, the current will not pass through the network no matter whether *q* is opened or closed. Or if *q* is opened, the current will not go through the network even if *p* is closed. Only in the case represented by the following diagram—only when both switches are closed—will the current flow and the light bulb burn.

(4)

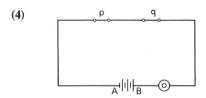

Having exactly two bi-polar switches in series, represented by '*p*' and '*q*', we can easily depict those conditions making the light bulb burn by the following "Switching Table":

(5) $p \cdot q$
       1 1 1
       0 0 1
       1 0 0
       0 0 0
          ↑

In (5) we interpret '1' as 'current flows' and '0' as 'current does not flow'. Thus, when the current flows through both p and q, the current flows through the series circuit. Notice (5) is the same table as that characterizing truth-functional conjunction in Chapter 2. But here, instead of interpreting the '1' as 'is true' and '0' as 'is false', they are interpreted in terms of current flow.

Two switches may also be put in parallel.

(6)

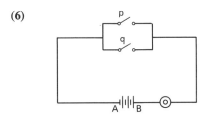

Given a network such as (6), when will the light bulb burn? If one or the other, or both, of the switches are closed, the current flows and so the light bulb will burn. If p is opened but q closed, the current will pass from A through q to B. When q is opened and p closed, the current will flow from A through p to B. Only when both p and q are open, as diagrammed in (6), will the current not flow. These conditions governing the flow of current in a switching network such as (6) may be represented in a "Switching Table".

(7) $p \lor q$
       1 1 1
       0 1 1
       1 1 0
       0 0 0
          ↑

Only when no current flows through both p and q does current not flow through the entire network. Once more our "Switching Table" is exactly the same table as that characterizing a truth-functional connective—here, the wedge.

Remember, *we can always represent a conjunction by a series circuit and a disjunction by a parallel circuit.*

It is now an easy matter to diagram a switching network representing any statement of this form:

(8) $p \cdot (q \lor r)$

Continuing to let each letter represent a switch, our network will have three switches. Since the overall statement form is a conjunction, the overall network will be in series. But, the right-hand conjunct is a disjunction represented by a parallel circuit. Thus, we draw

(9)

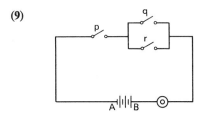

And now, what various possible positions of the switches in (9) would make the light bulb burn? To answer this question, the following "Switching Table" is constructed:

(10) $p \cdot (q \lor r)$

```
1 1  1 1 1
0 0  1 1 1
1 1  0 1 1
0 0  0 1 1
1 1  1 1 0
0 0  1 1 0
1 0  0 0 0
0 0  0 0 0
    ↑
```

Only when a '1' appears under the dot—rows 1, 3, and 5—does the current flow and the light bulb burn. A '0' under the dot indicates that current does not flow and the light bulb, therefore, does not burn.

A more complicated statement form than (10) is

(11) $(p \lor q) \cdot (r \lor s)$

Modeling (11) in a switching network, we draw

(12)

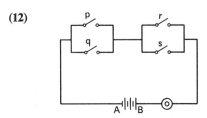

In that (11) is an overall conjunction, the basic circuit of (12) is in series. But, each conjunct in (11) is a disjunctive statement form which must be represented by parallel circuits. And what are the conditions necessary to make the light bulb burn in this switching network? Once more, a "Switching Table" is in order:

(13) $(p \lor q) \cdot (r \lor s)$

```
 1 1 1  1  1 1 1
 0 1 1  1  1 1 1
 1 1 0  1  1 1 1
 0 0 0  0  1 1 1
 1 1 1  1  0 1 1
 0 1 1  1  0 1 1
 1 1 0  1  0 1 1
 0 0 0  0  0 1 1
 1 1 1  1  1 1 0
 0 1 1  1  1 1 0
 1 1 0  1  1 1 0
 0 0 0  0  1 1 0
 1 1 1  0  0 0 0
 0 1 1  0  0 0 0
 1 1 0  0  0 0 0
 0 0 0  0  0 0 0
        ↑
```

Just in those rows in which a '1' appears under the dot will the light bulb burn.

Now, consider the following statement form and how it might be given a switching network interpretation:

(14) $(p \cdot q) \lor (p \cdot r)$

Because (14) is an overall disjunction, the network in which it is modeled will be in a parallel circuit. But, since each disjunction of (14) is a conjunction, two series circuits will also be used to represent it:

(15)

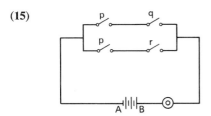

Notice that a p switch appears twice in (15), since p is in series with both q *and* r. In diagramming a switching network for (14), we must be careful to represent *all* the switches. In general *each occurrence of each letter in a statement form, or statement, must be represented by a single switch in a switching network.*

Of course (14) is logically equivalent to

(16) $p \lor (q \cdot r)$

However, the switching network corresponding to (16) is (17)—*not* (15):

(17)

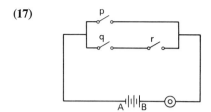

Imagine now that we want to represent an *argument* by a switching network. Corresponding to every argument is a hypothetical statement; corresponding to every argument form is a hypothetical statement form. Consider this simple valid argument:

(18)   ∴ C
   1) $A \supset B$ Pr
   2) $\sim B$ Pr
   3) $A \lor C$ Pr

From (18) we construct the statement

(19) $\{[(A \supset B) \cdot \sim B] \cdot (A \lor C)\} \supset C$

Is it possible to represent (19) by a switching network? Yes, but remember we have only parallel and series circuits and single switches permitting current to flow or not. We must reexpress (19) in a form which can be represented by our circuits and switches. Statement (19) must be reexpressed in such a way that the only connectives are the wedge and dot and so that if any tilde appears, it ranges over one letter only. Remember each letter, or letter coupled with a single tilde, represents a distinct switch. Further, (19) is a tautology if, and only if, (18) is valid. And, in terms of a switching network, (19) is a tautology if, and only if, there is no possible combination of switch positions which will cease the current flow.

Every truth-functional statement, or statement form, can be expressed as an overall disjunctive statement, or statement form, such that each disjunct is (1) a single letter, (2) a single letter governed by a tilde, (3) a conjunction of single letters, (4) a conjunction of single letters, each letter governed by a tilde, or both (3) and (4) together. We shall say that any truth-functional statement fulfilling these conditions is in 'Normal Disjunctive Form'. Using definitional and logical equivalences, we begin to reexpress (19) in Normal Disjunctive Form. Moving through a line-by-line sequence resembling a proof, we express each step of our transformation of (19) into Normal Disjunctive Form:

(20)
   1) $\{[(A \supset B) \cdot \sim B] \cdot (A \lor C)\} \supset C$
   2) $\sim\{[(A \supset B) \cdot \sim B] \cdot (A \lor C)\} \lor C$ 1, MI
   3) $\{\sim[(A \supset B) \cdot \sim B] \lor \sim(A \lor C)\} \lor C$ 2, DeM
   4) $\{[\sim(A \supset B) \lor \sim \sim B] \lor \sim(A \lor C)\} \lor C$ 3, DeM
   5) $\{[\sim \sim(A \cdot \sim B) \lor \sim \sim B] \lor \sim(A \lor C) \lor C$ 4, D3

6) $\{[\sim \sim (A \cdot \sim B) \vee \sim \sim B] \vee (\sim A \cdot \sim C)\} \vee C$ 5, DeM

7) $\{[(A \cdot \sim B) \vee \sim \sim B] \vee (\sim A \cdot \sim C)\} \vee C$ 6, DN

8) $\{[(A \cdot \sim B) \vee (\sim A \cdot \sim C)\} \vee C$ 7, DN

9) $(A \cdot \sim B) \vee B \vee (\sim A \cdot \sim C) \vee C$ 8, Assoc

Since Association asserts that the punctuation of a disjunctive statement is immaterial to its truth or falsity, we drop the braces and brackets from line 8 in moving to line 9. The statement at line 9 is in Normal Disjunctive Form.

Any statement in Normal Disjunctive Form can be modeled in a switching network. In particular, the statement at line 9 in (20) can be represented in the following switching network:

(21)

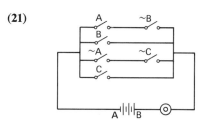

In a switching network, such as (21), we may find switches represented by, for example, both 'p' and '$\sim p$'. Here, if the current is flowing through p, it is not flowing through $\sim p$. Or, if the current is flowing through $\sim p$, it is not flowing through p.

Notice in a switching network as diagrammed by (21) the light bulb is always on. There is no possible combination of switch positions stopping the flow of current. This is interpreted as meaning the last statement in (20) is tautological. But if that statement is a tautology, so is (19). Yet if (19) is a tautology, the argument to which it corresponds, namely (18), is valid. Only when there is at least one possible combination of switch positions preventing the flow of electricity through the network would an argument modeled in that network be invalid. And so, we can model every truth-functional argument in a switching network by first reexpressing that argument in Normal Disjunctive Form. Then, depending on the various possible switch positions, we can determine whether the argument is valid or not.

Basically, electronic digital computers are really only very technically complicated switching networks through which current is either flowing or not. As we have seen, we can interpret such machines as modeling a two-valued logic—a logic dealing with statements which may be either true or false. In fact, the formal properties of the Truth-Functional Calculus can literally be built into the basic circuitry of digital computers. Consequently, logicians in studying the formal properties of their various systems can be of tremendous help to the computer engineer. And not only can the logician play a part in computer design, but, in turn, the digital computer becomes a powerful tool to help the logician—particularly in analyzing deductive systems and studying the logical forms of descriptive language. Using the digital computer as a tool, the logician can apply his knowledge to such rapidly expanding fields as information science, descriptive linguistics, mechanical translation, and cybernetics.

Glossary

analogical argument: An argument in which the truth of the premisses does not logically entail the truth of the conclusion, but neither is the conclusion confirmed or falsified by any evidence other than that used to establish the truth of the premisses.

a priori statement: A statement whose justification is independent of any particular sensory observations, experiments, or the like.

argument: A group of statements in which at least one is advanced by a person to provide evidence, or to give a reason, for accepting another statement as true.

atomic statement: Any statement substituted for a single statement variable.

atomic statement form: Any single statement variable not coupled with a logical operator.

axioms: The initial lines assumed in a particular deductive system and never proved within the system but simply accepted as starting points for that system.

bound individual variable: In Quantification Theory a variable falling under the scope of some quantifier.

categorical statements: A statement asserting that a certain relation does, or does not, hold between two sets.

categorical syllogism: A deductive argument having a sequence of three and only three categorical statements such that three and only three terms appear in this sequence of statements with each term appearing in exactly two statements.

complement of a set: That set, designated by '*non-S*', having as its members all those things not a member of the set designated '*S*'.

conclusion: That statement purportedly established as true given certain other statements of an argument.

consistent: When in a set of statements there is at least one interpretation making all those statements true.

constant: A sign having a fixed specific meaning: logical constants, including constants of punctuation, logical operators, and logical connectives to express a statement's form; empirical constants, including statement initials, predicate letters, and individual constants to determine a statement's content.

content: The elements ordered by the form of a particular thing.

contingent statement: A truth-functional statement having at least one '1' and one '0' in the final column of its truth-table analysis; a statement in which actual truth or falsity is not solely a function of logical form but must be ascertained by empirical investigations.

contradictory statement: A truth-functional statement having a '0' in every row in the final column of its truth-table analysis; a statement always false due to the logical form of the statement; any two statements of any type which can be neither both true nor both false.

contrary statements: Two statements which cannot both be true but which may both be false.

copula: In a categorical statement in standard form the words 'are' or 'are not' connecting the subject and predicate terms.

deductive argument: An argument in which the truth of the premises is sufficient to establish the truth of the conclusion if the premises logically entail the conclusion, where the conclusion of the deductive argument is not confirmed by any evidence other than that used to confirm the premises.

definiendum: That sign, or group of signs, to be defined in a definition.

definiens: That sign, or group of signs, defining some other sign, or group of signs, in a definition.

definition: A formula by which new signs in a system are given a meaning in terms of signs already used in that system.

derivation: Any finite sequence of well-formed formulae (wff) commencing with at least one assumption which is a wff but not an axiom or a theorem.

distributed term: A term in a categorical statement which, because of the form of the statement, refers to every member of the set it designates.

empirical statement: A statement whose truth or falsity is known by means of sensory observations, experiments, or the like.

equivalent statements: When, and only when, two statements are both true under exactly the same conditions and both false under exactly the same conditions.

existential interpretation: When there is at least one member in any set designated by the terms of categorical statements; represented in the Traditional Square of Opposition.

existential quantifier: The sign '$(\exists \alpha)$' when 'α' is replaced by any individual variable; '$(\exists \alpha)$' is read as 'There is at least one α in the universe such that . . .'.

figure: The arrangement of terms of a categorical syllogism in standard form; known as the figure of that syllogism.

form: The way, or ways, in which the elements of a particular thing are arranged for a specific purpose.

formal fallacy: A deductive argument form such that the truth of the premisses of any argument having that form would not guarantee the truth of that argument's conclusion.

free individual variable: In Quantification Theory a variable not falling under the scope of some quantifier.

general statement: Asserts that a given property is true of (or false of) some or all individuals or that some or all individuals are (or are not) members of a certain set.

hypothetical interpretation: In **A** and **E** categorical statements, leaving undecided whether there are or are not any members in the set designated by the subject term; represented in the Contemporary Square of Opposition.

inconsistent argument: An argument having no interpretation of its premiss set which would make all the premisses true.

individual constants: In Quantification Theory the lowercase letters '*a*' through '*w*' designating specific individuals.

individual variables: In Quantification Theory the lower case letters '*x*', '*y*', and '*z*' used as individual variables and replaceable by individual constants.

inductive argument: An argument in which the truth of the premisses does not logically entail the truth of the conclusion, where the conclusion is confirmed or falsified by evidence other than that evidence used to establish the premisses.

instance: In any quantified statement in Quantification Theory, a statement exactly like the quantified statement except the quantifier is removed and the same individual constant is substituted at each occurrence of the same individual variable; a statement matrix resulting from removal of the quantifier of the first statement.

invalidity: In a deductive argument if all the premisses could be true and the conclusion false.

logic: The *a priori* study of the forms of descriptive language.

logical entailment: One (or more) statement(s) logically entailing another if when the former is true, the latter must also be true.

logical form: The structure of a statement or argument indicated by such words as 'all', 'no', 'some', 'not', 'and', 'either . . . or . . . ', etc.

major premiss: In a categorical syllogism that premiss in which the major term appears.

major term: In a categorical syllogism the predicate term of the conclusion; also any other appearance of this term throughout the syllogism.

metalanguage: Any language used to talk about some linguistic element in relation to that linguistic element.

middle term: In a categorical syllogism the term found in both premisses but not in the conclusion.

minor premiss: In a categorical syllogism the premiss in which the minor term appears.

minor term: In a categorical syllogism the subject term of the conclusion; also any other appearance of this term throughout the syllogism.

molecular statement: Any statement substituted for a single statement variable governed by a logical operator.

molecular statement form: Any statement variable, or variables, coupled with a logical operator.

mood: In a categorical syllogism a function of the forms of the categorical statements in the syllogism.

necessary condition: Expressed by the consequent of a hypothetical statement; some state of affairs, *B*, being a necessary condition for another state of affairs, *A*, if, and only if, an occurrence of *A* guarantees an occurrence of *B*, although an occurrence of *B* does not guarantee an occurrence of *A*; *B* being a necessary condition for *A* if, and only if, all cases of *A* are also cases of *B*, although all cases of *B* are not cases of *A*.

pragmatics: An investigation of language as it is related to a speaker; an investigation of those relations holding between signs and the user of those signs.

predicate: A property, characteristic, trait, or the like said to be true of (or false of) an individual; a set of which an individual is (or is not) a member.

predicate letters: In Quantification Theory the capital letters '*A*' through '*Z*' used to designate predicates.

predicate term: In a standard form categorical statement the term following the copula.

premiss: Any statement assumed in an argument to provide evidence, or to give a reason, for accepting another statement.

premiss set: The collection of all the premisses (even if only one) of an argument.

primitive marks: Those marks, or signs, of some system undefined in that system but in terms of which every other mark in the system is defined.

proof: Any finite sequence of lines which is either a premiss (or axiom) or is obtained from a premiss, or previous line, by some Rule of Transformation or by Conditional or Indirect Methods of Proving Validity.

quality: A property of a categorical statement when it is viewed as either affirming or denying certain relations holding between two sets; thus a categorical statement which affirms (or denies) has the quality of being affirmative (or negative).

quantifier: Any word or sign indicating how many things are being referred to by a given statement; in standard form categorical statements, quantifiers are 'all', 'no', and 'some', while in Quantification Theory they are '(α)' and '$(\exists \alpha)$' where 'α' is replaced by any individual variable.

quantity: A property of a categorical statement when it is either universal or particular; if a categorical statement is viewed as making an assertion about all the members of the set designated by its subject term, its quantity is universal; the quantity of a categorical statement making an assertion about at least one member of the set designated by its subject term is particular.

Rules of Transformation: Rules allowing moves from one (or more) statement(s), or line(s), in a proof to another statement, or line; types of Rules of Transformation include argument forms (rules of inference) and definitional and logical equivalences.

scope of an operator: That part of a statement, or statement form, governed by a logical operator.

semantics: An investigation of language as it relates to the world independently of any speaker.

sentence: A specifiable class of speech-types of a particular word-language.

set: Also called 'class', 'collection', or 'universe'; a well-defined collection of distinguishable things or individuals.

singular statement: Asserts that a given property is true of (or false of) a particular individual or that a particular individual is (or is not) a member of a certain set.

soundness: A property of a deductive argument if, and only if, the argument is valid and all its premises are true; notice a deductive argument may be valid but unsound.

speech-token: A particular sound utterance or line of marks used in the act of speaking.

speech-types: Expressed by speech-tokens; unlike speech-tokens since they are not spatial or temporal and are not printed, written, or uttered.

Square of Opposition: A diagram depicting various logical relationships holding between categorical statements having the same subject and predicate terms; the Traditional Square of Opposition is based on the existential interpretation of categorical statements and the Contemporary Square of Opposition is based on the hypothetical interpretation of categorical statements.

standard form categorical statement: Any categorical statement having the form 'All *S* are *P*', 'No *S* are *P*', 'Some *S* are *P*', or 'Some *S* are not *P*', where '*S*' designates a subject term and '*P*' a predicate term.

standard form categorical syllogism: Any categorical syllogism if, and only if, all the categorical statements are in standard form and the major premiss is mentioned first, followed by the minor premiss and then the conclusion.

statement: An assertion which is either true or false, but not both.

statement matrix: An expression containing at least one free individual variable such that when all occurrences of free variables are properly bound by a quantifier or replaced by an individual constant, the statement matrix becomes a statement.

statement variables: The lowercase letters '*p*', '*q*', '*r*', and '*s*' replaceable by statements, statement initials, statement matrixes, or other statement variables.

subcontrary statements: When two statements cannot both be false but when they may both be true.

subject term: In a standard form categorical statement the term following the quantifier and preceding the copula.

sufficient condition: Expressed by the antecedent of a hypothetical statement; some state of affairs, *A*, being a sufficient condition for another state of affairs, *B*, if, and only if, an occurrence of A guarantees an occurrence of B; A being a sufficient condition for B if, and only if, all cases of A are also cases of B.

syllogistic form: Determined by the logical forms of the categorical statements in the syllogism and the way terms are arranged in the syllogism; note that the logical form of a categorical syllogism is a function of its mood and figure.

syntax: An investigation of the purely formal properties of language, independent of how it relates to the world or to any speaker.

tautological statement: A truth-functional statement having a '1' in every row in the final column of its truth-table analysis; that a tautological statement is always true is due to its logical form.

terms: In a categorical syllogism those words or clauses designating sets.

theorem: Any well-formed formula in a specific deductive system obtained solely from the axioms of the system by the Rules of Transformation of the system.

Truth-Functional Calculus: The *a priori* study of the forms of statements whose truth or falsity is a function of the truth or falsity of their component parts and/or the way these parts are ordered by certain logical operators; the study of arguments constructed out of truth-functional statements.

truth-table: Any diagram, or picture, systematically displaying all truth-functional conditions making a statement true or false.

universal quantifier: The sign '(α)' when 'α' is replaced by any individual variable; '(α)' is read as 'Each thing in the universe is such that . . . '.

validity: The property of a deductive argument if the premises logically entail the conclusion—that is, if all the premises are true, the conclusion must also be true.

variable: Any sign acting as a place holder replaceable by some empirical constant; types of variables include statement variables and individual variables.

Venn diagram: A figure of overlapping circles—each circle representing a distinct set— used to picture all possible relations holding, or not holding, between those sets.

well-formed formula (wff): Any single line of signs which is appropriately formed, according to certain rules, in a given system.

APPENDIX C

Selected Answers

The following answers do not purport to be the only ones possible, nor are they necessarily the shortest or the simplest; they are guides.

Chapter 1

Group A: (page 19)

In defining terms here, Appendix B may be helpful.

Group B: (page 19)

(3) a) Is the cabinet in the other room?
   b) Is the fingernail file in the other room?
(5) a) Break the last listed achievement!
   b) Break the phonograph disk!
(7) a) Are the flowers flourishing?
   b) Are the manufacturing establishments flourishing?
(9) a) Go to the side of a river!
   b) Go to a financial institution!
(11) a) Is that really a reasonable argument?
   b) Is that really a sound argument?

Group C: (page 20)

(3) The name of Boston is 'Boston'.
(5) Let us define 'logic' as 'the *a priori* study of the forms of descriptive language'.
(7) 'Saul wrote a term paper' uses the active voice of the verb, while 'A term paper was written by Saul' uses the passive voice.
(9) '$P(x, y)$' is to be read 'the probability of x given y'.
(11) The curve of any elliptical motion can be depicted by '$(x - h)^2/a^2 + (y - k)^2/b^2 = 1$'.

Group D: (page 20)

(1) Empirical: Empirical observations are necessary to establish the truth or falsity of this statement.

(3) *A priori*: The truth of this statement is guaranteed by the ways we use the words 'all', 'some', 'not', and 'if · · · then – – –'.

(5), (7), (9), (11) Empirical: Empirical observations, collections of documents, etc., are necessary to establish the truth or falsity of this statement.

(13) *A priori*: A moral maxim, or rule, asserting how men ought to act.

(15) *A priori*: 'Lying' is being defined in terms of 'sinning'.

Group E: (page 21)

Only conclusions are cited; other statements are premisses.

(1) Therefore, the litmus paper turned red.

(3) Hence, the platypus is a mammal and not a fowl.

(5) So, it stands to reason that they will probably support him on this appointment, too.

(7) All exergonic reactions are heat-producing reactions.

(9) But, on this account, computers are also able to think and are, as man, distinguished from the lower animals because of this ability.

Group F: (page 22)

(1) Deductive: The truth of the premisses would guarantee the truth of the conclusion.

(3) Analogical: While the truth of the premiss would not guarantee the truth of the conclusion, no observations or data other than that used to establish the truth of the premiss are needed to establish the truth of the conclusion.

(5) Inductive: The truth of the premiss would not guarantee the truth of the conclusion. Evidence other than that used to establish the truth of the premiss is needed to establish the truth of the conclusion.

(7), (9) Deductive: The truth of the premisses would guarantee the truth of the conclusion.

Chapter 2

SECTION 1 (page 26)

(1) PTF (purely truth-functional)

(3) PTF

(5) NPTF (not purely truth-functional): That the experimenters are careless is a causal factor in the lab blowing up.

(7) NPTF: That there is a financial recession is a causal factor in stocks falling off.

(9) NPTF: That we do not build up our military strength is a causal factor in our having to fight an all-out war.

(11) NPTF: The implication is that because Mrs. Jordan was asleep at the wheel, she collided with another car.

(13) PTF **(15)**, **(17)**, **(19)**, **(21)**, **(23)**

(25) NPTF: Certainly a temporal priority is being suggested in that we must know a man's anatomy, etc., before we can explain his behavior.

SECTION 2

Group B: (page 30)

(2) a) John comes.
   b) Bill will leave.
(6) a) Individuals will all learn to live with one another.
   b) We will live.
(14) a) I'm going to San Francisco next summer.
   b) I'm going to Los Angeles next summer.
(18) a) The distance between two electrical charges is doubled.
   b) The force between them is decreased to one-quarter of its original value.
(22) a) The Kinsey Reports are read seriously by our lawmakers.
   b) Many now existing laws will be modified.
   c) Many now existing laws will be abrogated completely.

SECTION 4

Group C: (page 37)

(1) $\sim P$ **(5)** $\sim L$ **(9)** $\sim G$
(3) $\sim P$ **(7)** $\sim K$

SECTION 5

Group B: (page 41)

(1) $F \cdot \sim O$ **(11)** $\sim J \cdot \sim S$
(3) $A \cdot V$ **(13)** $D \cdot S$
(5) $G \cdot \sim W$ **(15)** $V \cdot P$
(7) $G \cdot R$ **(17)** $P \cdot A$
(9) $F \cdot \sim W$ **(19)** $C \cdot R$

SECTION 6

Group A: (page 45)

(1) $P \triangle V$ **(3)** $I \vee C$ **(5)** $M \triangle S$

Group B: (page 46)

(1) $H \vee F$ **(11)** $S \vee H$
(3) $C \vee H, C \triangle H$ **(13)** $C \vee D$
(5) $D \triangle P$ **(15)** $D \vee H, D \triangle H$
(7) $M \vee O$ **(17)** $H \vee M, H \triangle M$
(9) $A \vee L, A \triangle L$ **(19)** $P \vee A, P \triangle A$

SECTION 7 (page 51)

(1) $\sim C \vee G$

(3) $\sim(C \vee \sim G)$

(5) $\sim(A \cdot S)$

(7) $\sim(\sim S \cdot P)$

(9) $\sim(\sim A \cdot E)$

(11) $D \vee (\sim P \cdot \sim M)$

(13) $(G \cdot E) \triangle H$

(15) $\sim(O \cdot E) \vee \sim N$

(17) $(K \cdot A) \triangle S$

(19) $\sim(S \vee D) \vee H$

(21) $\sim[\sim(\sim S \cdot \sim D) \cdot \sim H]$

(23) $T \vee [\sim(E \vee C) \vee \sim(S \vee Q)]$

(25) $\sim\{\sim T \cdot \sim[(E \vee C) \cdot (S \vee Q)]\}$

SECTION 8

Group B: (page 58)

(1) $P \supset D$

(3) $(I \supset A) \cdot P$

(5) $\sim C \supset P$

(7) $\sim C \supset P$

(9) $\sim D \supset (\sim C \vee B)$

(11) $(N \supset F) \cdot (Q \supset S)$

(13) $(S \supset H) \cdot (F \supset M)$

(15) $(N \vee Q) \supset (N \supset P)$

(17) $(M \supset N) \cdot Q$

(19) $(S \triangle \sim R) \supset \sim(D \cdot \sim P)$

(21) $(E \supset D) \cdot (D \supset \sim F)$

(23) $\sim[T \supset \sim(C \cdot \sim E)]$

(25) $[\sim(\sim C \cdot \sim E) \triangle \sim Q] \supset S$

SECTION 9

Group A: (page 63)

(1) $P \equiv C$

(3) $(O \vee S) \equiv B$

(5) $(C \triangle D) \equiv (L \triangle N)$

(7) $\sim(A \triangle B) \equiv (\sim W \cdot \sim P)$

(9) $(A \supset I) \equiv [(S \cdot T) \supset (A \cdot \sim B)]$

Chapter 3

SECTION 1

Group A: (page 71)

(1)

A
1
0

(3)

A	B	$A \cdot B$	$\sim(A \cdot B)$
1	1	1	0
1	0	0	1
0	1	0	1
0	0	0	1

(5)

A	B	$A \vee B$
1	1	1
1	0	1
0	1	1
0	0	0

(7)

A	B	$\sim A$	$\sim B$	$\sim A \vee \sim B$
1	1	0	0	0
1	0	0	1	1
0	1	1	0	1
0	0	1	1	1

(9)

A	B	$\sim B$	$A \cdot \sim B$	$\sim (A \cdot \sim B)$	$\sim \sim (A \cdot \sim B)$
1	1	0	0	1	0
1	0	1	1	0	1
0	1	0	0	1	0
0	0	1	0	1	0

(11)

A	B	C	$\sim B$	$\sim C$	$\sim B \supset \sim C$	$A \supset (\sim B \supset \sim C)$
1	1	1	0	0	1	1
1	1	0	0	1	1	1
1	0	1	1	0	0	0
1	0	0	1	1	1	1
0	1	1	0	0	1	1
0	1	0	0	1	1	1
0	0	1	1	0	0	1
0	0	0	1	1	1	1

(13)

A	B	C	$B \cdot C$	$A \triangle (B \cdot C)$
1	1	1	1	0
1	1	0	0	1
1	0	1	0	1
1	0	0	0	1
0	1	1	1	1
0	1	0	0	0
0	0	1	0	0
0	0	0	0	0

(15)

A	B	C	$A \vee B$	$A \cdot C$	$\sim (A \cdot C)$	$(A \vee B) \vee \sim (A \cdot C)$
1	1	1	1	1	0	1
1	1	0	1	0	1	1
1	0	1	1	1	0	1
1	0	0	1	0	1	1
0	1	1	1	0	1	1
0	1	0	1	0	1	1
0	0	1	0	0	1	1
0	0	0	0	0	1	1

(17)

A	B	C	B⊃C	A⊃(B⊃C)	~[A⊃(B⊃C)]	A·B	(A·B)⊃C	~[A⊃(B⊃C)]△[(A·B)⊃C]
1	1	1	1	1	0	1	1	1
1	1	0	0	0	1	1	0	1
1	0	1	1	1	0	0	1	1
1	0	0	1	1	0	0	1	1
0	1	1	1	1	0	0	1	1
0	1	0	0	1	0	0	1	1
0	0	1	1	1	0	0	1	1
0	0	0	1	1	0	0	1	1

(19)

A	B	C	D	B∨C	~(B∨C)	A⊃~(B∨C)	C·D	[A⊃~(B∨C)]∨(C·D)
1	1	1	1	1	0	0	1	1
1	1	1	0	1	0	0	0	0
1	1	0	1	1	0	0	0	0
1	1	0	0	1	0	0	0	0
1	0	1	1	1	0	0	1	1
1	0	1	0	1	0	0	0	0
1	0	0	1	0	1	1	0	1
1	0	0	0	0	1	1	0	1
0	1	1	1	1	0	1	1	1
0	1	1	0	1	0	1	0	1
0	1	0	1	1	0	1	0	1
0	1	0	0	1	0	1	0	1
0	0	1	1	1	0	1	1	1
0	0	1	0	1	0	1	0	1
0	0	0	1	0	1	1	0	1
0	0	0	0	0	1	1	0	1

Group C: (page 72)

(Truth-tables remain for you to construct for each case.)

(1) $O \cdot \sim N$

(3) $\sim (B \cdot \sim B)$

(5) $\sim (G \lor D)$

(7) $(O \cdot R) \supset (\sim O \supset \sim R)$

(9) $\sim (B \equiv \sim H) \equiv (B \equiv H)$

(11) $Y \supset (N \equiv W)$

(13) $[(W \cdot N) \lor (W \cdot E)] \lor \sim (W \lor S)$

(15) $[(Q \supset K) \cdot (A \supset T)] \cdot [G \equiv \sim (K \lor T)]$

SECTION 3

Group B: (page 81)

In the following answers the statement is symbolized and classified as tautological, contingent, or contradictory. In all cases, however, the truth-tables remain for you to construct.

(1) $S \lor \sim S$; tautological.

(5) $\sim (E \cdot N) \supset (\sim E \lor \sim N)$; tautological.

(3) $S \supset \sim B$; contingent.

(7) $[(A \lor E) \cdot \sim A] \cdot \sim E$; contradictory.

(9) $[B \cdot (F \lor T)] \supset [(B \cdot F) \lor (B \cdot T)]$; tautological.

(11) $[(B \supset O) \cdot (V \supset C)] \cdot \sim (B \supset C)$; contingent.

(13) $[(E \lor N) \lor S] \equiv \sim W$; contingent.

(15) $\sim \{[\sim (K \cdot N) \lor \sim (T \cdot A)] \lor [(T \cdot A) \supset (N \cdot K)]\}$; contradictory.

SECTION 4 (page 86)

Each argument is classified as valid or invalid; you are to construct the appropriate truth-table for each argument.

(1)	I (invalid)	(5)	I	(9)	V	(13)	V	(17)	I
(3)	V (valid)	(7)	V	(11)	I	(15)	V	(19)	V

SECTION 5

Group B: (page 91)

(1) V (valid)

(11) V

(3) V

(13) I Let $A = 1, B = 0, C = 1, D = 0.$

(5) I (invalid). Let $A = 0, B = 0.$

(15) I Let $A = 1, B = 1, C = 0, D = 0.$

(7) I Let $A = 1, B = 0, C = 1.$

(17) V

(9) V

(19) V

SECTION 6 (page 96)

(Truth-tables remain for you to construct.)

(1) Consistent, valid.

(11) Inconsistent.

(3) Consistent, invalid.

(13) Consistent, valid.

(5) Inconsistent.

(15) Inconsistent

(7) Consistent, valid.

(17) Consistent, invalid.

(9) Consistent, invalid.

(19) Consistent, invalid.

Chapter 4

SECTION 1

Group B: (page 105)

(1)   ‘$p \triangle q$’ = ‘$\sim[\sim(\sim p \vee \sim q) \vee \sim(p \vee q)]$’   Df
      ‘$p \equiv q$’ = ‘$\sim[\sim(\sim p \vee q) \vee \sim(\sim q \vee p)]$’   Df

Group C: (page 105)

(1)
- 1) $A \vee E$
- 2) $\sim(\sim A \cdot \sim E)$

(3)
- 1) $\sim U \triangle L$
- 2) $\sim(\sim U \cdot L) \cdot \sim(\sim \sim U \cdot \sim L)$

(5)
- 1) $\sim(\sim D \vee \sim M)$
- 2) $\sim \sim(\sim \sim D \cdot \sim \sim M)$

(7)
- 1) $T \supset (C \cdot W)$
- 2) $\sim[T \cdot \sim(C \cdot W)]$

(9)
- 1) $C \vee (P \supset B)$
- 2) $C \vee \sim(P \cdot \sim B)$
- 3) $\sim[\sim C \cdot \sim \sim(P \cdot \sim B)]$

(11)
- 1) $W \supset \sim(L \cdot \sim M)$
- 2) $\sim[W \cdot \sim \sim(L \cdot \sim M)]$

(13)
- 1) $[(M \vee V) \cdot A] \supset [(A \cdot M) \vee (A \cdot V)]$
- 2) $[\sim(\sim M \cdot \sim V) \cdot A] \supset [(A \cdot M) \vee (A \cdot V)]$
- 3) $[\sim(\sim M \cdot \sim V) \cdot A] \supset \sim[\sim(A \cdot M) \cdot \sim(A \cdot V)]$
- 4) $\sim\{[\sim(\sim M \cdot \sim V) \cdot A] \cdot \sim \sim[\sim(A \cdot M) \cdot \sim(A \cdot V)]\}$

(15)
- 1) $[L \equiv (B \supset W)] \supset [(B \cdot W) \supset L]$
- 2) $[L \equiv \sim(B \cdot \sim W)] \supset [(B \cdot W) \supset L]$
- 3) $\{\sim[L \cdot \sim \sim(B \cdot \sim W)] \cdot \sim[\sim(B \cdot \sim W) \cdot \sim L]\} \supset [(B \cdot W) \supset L]$
- 4) $\{\sim[L \cdot \sim \sim(B \cdot \sim W)] \cdot \sim[\sim(B \cdot \sim W) \cdot \sim L]\} \supset \sim[(B \cdot W) \cdot \sim L]$
- 5) $\sim(\{\sim[L \cdot \sim \sim(B \cdot \sim W)] \cdot \sim[\sim(B \cdot \sim W) \cdot \sim L]\} \cdot \sim \sim[(B \cdot W) \cdot \sim L])$

SECTION 2   (page 107)

(Truth-tables are for you to construct.)

(1) LE (logically equivalent)	**(11)**	LE
(3) LE	**(13)**	NLE
(5) LE	**(15)**	NLE
(7) NLE (not logically equivalent)	**(17)**	NLE
(9) LE	**(19)**	LE

Chapter 5

SECTION 2

Group A: (page 115)

(1) $A \supset (B \supset C)$

(3) $A \equiv (B \cdot C)$

(5) $\sim(A \supset B) \cdot C$

(7) $(A \bigtriangleup \sim B) \bigtriangleup C$

(9) $\sim[A \supset (B \lor \sim C)]$

(1) $(A \supset B) \supset \{\sim(C \cdot \sim B) \supset [(D \supset B) \cdot (E \supset B)]\}$

(3) $(A \supset B) \equiv \{\sim(C \cdot \sim B) \cdot [(D \supset B) \cdot (E \supset B)]\}$

(5) $\sim[(A \supset B) \supset \sim(C \cdot \sim B)] \cdot [(D \supset B) \cdot (E \supset B)]$

(7) $[(A \supset B) \bigtriangleup \sim \sim(C \cdot \sim B)] \bigtriangleup [(D \supset B) \cdot (E \supset B)]$

(9) $\sim((A \supset B) \supset \{\sim(C \cdot \sim B) \lor \sim[(D \supset B) \cdot (E \supset B)]\})$

Group B: (page 116)

(1) $A \cdot (B \cdot C)$
    $\therefore A$

(3) $(A \cdot B) \lor C$
    $\therefore B \lor C$

(5) $A \supset (B \supset C)$
    $\sim(B \supset C)$
    $\therefore \sim A$

(7) $(A \lor B) \cdot \sim C$
    $\therefore \sim C \cdot (A \lor B)$

(9) $A \lor B$
    $\therefore \sim C \lor (B \lor A)$

(1) $(A \lor B) \cdot \{\sim(C \lor D) \cdot \sim[C \supset (D \supset B)]\}$
    $\therefore A \lor B$

(3) $[(A \lor B) \cdot \sim(C \lor D)] \lor \sim[C \supset (D \supset B)]$
    $\therefore \sim(C \lor D) \lor \sim[C \supset (D \supset B)]$

(5) $(A \lor B) \supset \{\sim(C \lor D) \supset \sim[C \supset (D \supset B)]\}$
    $\sim\{\sim(C \lor D) \supset \sim[C \supset (D \supset B)]\}$
    $\therefore \sim(A \lor B)$

(7) $[(A \lor B) \lor \sim(C \lor D)] \cdot \sim \sim[C \supset (D \supset B)]$
    $\therefore \sim \sim[C \supset (D \supset B)] \cdot [(A \lor B) \lor \sim(C \lor D)]$

(9) $(A \lor B) \lor \sim(C \lor D)$
    $\therefore \sim \sim[C \supset (D \supset B)] \lor [\sim(C \lor D) \lor (A \lor B)]$

SECTION 3

Group A: (page 122)

(1)
    1) Pr
    2) 1, Simp

(3)
  1) Pr
  2) 1, Com
  3) 2, Simp
  4) 3, Simp

(5)
  1) Pr
  2) 1, Simp
  3) 1, Com
  4) 3, Simp
  5) 2, Com
  6) 5, Simp
  7) 6, 4, Conj

(7)
  1) Pr
  2) Pr
  3) 2, Simp
  4) 2, Com
  5) 4, Simp
  6) 3, Com
  7) 6, Simp
  8) 7, 5, Conj
  9) 8, 1, Conj

(9)
  1) Pr
  2) 1, Simp
  3) 1, Com
  4) 3, Simp
  5) 2, Simp
  6) 2, Com
  7) 6, Simp
  8) 4, Simp
  9) 4, Com
  10) 9, Simp
  11) 10, 7, Conj
  12) 8, 5, Conj
  13) 11, 12, Conj

Group B: (page 124)

(1) $\therefore A$
  1) $A \cdot B$ Pr
  2) $\therefore A$ 1, Simp

(3) $\therefore B$
  1) $A \cdot B$ Pr
  2) $B \cdot A$ 1, Com
  3) $\therefore B$ 2, Simp

(5) $\therefore C \cdot B$

   1) $A \cdot B$ Pr

   2) C Pr

   3) $B \cdot A$ 1, Com

   4) B 3, Simp

   5) $\therefore C \cdot B$ 2, 4, Conj

(7) $\therefore (C \vee D) \cdot (A \vee B)$

   1) $(A \vee B) \cdot (C \vee D)$ Pr

   2) $\therefore (C \vee D) \cdot (A \vee B)$ 1, Com

(9) $\therefore (B \supset C) \cdot (C \supset D)$

   1) $(A \supset B) \cdot (B \supset C)$ Pr

   2) $C \supset D$ Pr

   3) $(B \supset C) \cdot (A \supset B)$ 1, Com

   4) $B \supset C$ 3, Simp

   5) $\therefore (B \supset C) \cdot (C \supset D)$ 4, 2, Conj

Group D: (page 125)

(1) $\therefore T$

   1) $T \cdot N$ Pr

   2) $\therefore T$ 1, Simp

(3) $\therefore T \cdot M$

   1) T Pr

   2) M Pr

   3) $\therefore T \cdot M$ 1, 2, Conj

(5) $\therefore D \cdot N$

   1) $(T \cdot N) \cdot D$ Pr

   2) $T \cdot N$ 1, Simp

   3) $D \cdot (T \cdot N)$ 1, Com

   4) D 3, Simp

   5) $N \cdot T$ 2, Com

   6) N 5, Simp

   7) $\therefore D \cdot N$ 4, 6, Conj

(7) $\therefore (P \cdot M) \cdot (T \cdot R)$

   1) $(R \cdot P) \cdot (T \cdot M)$ Pr

   2) $R \cdot P$ 1, Simp

   3) $(T \cdot M) \cdot (R \cdot P)$ 1, Com

   4) $T \cdot M$ 3, Simp

   5) R 2, Simp

   6) $P \cdot R$ 2, Com

   7) P 6, Simp

   8) T 4, Simp

   9) $M \cdot T$ 4, Com

  10) M 9, Simp

  11) $P \cdot M$ 7, 10, Conj

  12) $T \cdot R$ 8, 5, Conj

  13) $\therefore (P \cdot M) \cdot (T \cdot R)$ 11, 12, Conj

(9)   ∴ $(S \supset M) \cdot (C \cdot L)$

1)	$(S \supset M) \cdot C$	Pr
2)	$N \cdot L$	Pr
3)	$S \supset M$	1, Simp
4)	$C \cdot (S \supset M)$	1, Com
5)	C	4, Simp
6)	$L \cdot N$	2, Com
7)	L	6, Simp
8)	$C \cdot L$	5, 7, Conj
9)	∴ $(S \supset M) \cdot (C \cdot L)$	3, 8, Conj

SECTION 4

Group A: (page 130)

(1)

1) Pr
2) Pr
3) 2, Com
4) 3, 1, DS

(3)

1) Pr
2) 1, Simp
3) 1, Com
4) 3, Simp
5) 2, Com
6) 5, 4, DS

(5)

1) Pr
2) Pr
3) 1, Simp
4) 1, Com
5) 4, Simp
6) 2, Com
7) 6, 3, DS
8) 5, Add
9) 8, Com
10) 9, 7, Conj

(7)

1) Pr
2) Pr
3) 2, Simp
4) 2, Com
5) 4, Simp
6) 1, Com

7) 6, 5, DS
8) 7, Com
9) 8, 3, DS
10) 9, Add
11) 10, Add
12) 11, Com
13) 12, Add
14) 13, Com

(9)

1) Pr
2) Pr
3) Pr
4) Pr
5) 1, Simp
6) 1, Com
7) 6, Simp
8) 4, Simp
9) 4, Com
10) 9, Simp
11) 2, 5, DS
12) 11, 8, DS
13) 12, Add
14) 13, Com
15) 3, 10, DS
16) 15, 7, DS
17) 16, Add
18) 14, 17, Conj

Group B: (page 133)

(1)   ∴ $B \lor A$

1) $A \lor B$ Pr
2)   ∴ $B \lor A$ 1, Com

(3)   ∴ A

1) $A \lor B$ Pr
2) $\sim B$ Pr
3) $B \lor A$ 1, Com
4)   ∴ A 3, 2, DS

(5)   ∴ $(C \lor D) \lor (B \lor A)$

1) $A \lor B$ Pr
2) $B \lor A$ 1, Com
3) $(B \lor A) \lor (C \lor D)$ 2, Add
4)   ∴ $(C \lor D) \lor (B \lor A)$ 3, Com

(7)   ∴ *D* ∨ *C*
   1)   *A* ∨ [*B* ∨ (*C* ∨ *D*)]   Pr
   2)   ~ *B* · ~ *A*   Pr
   3)   ~ *B*   2, Simp
   4)   ~ *A* · ~ *B*   2, Com
   5)   ~ *A*   2, Com
   6)   *B* ∨ (*C* ∨ *D*)   1, 5, DS
   7)   *C* ∨ *D*   6, 3, DS
   8)   ∴ *D* ∨ *C*   7, Com

(9)   ∴ (*B* ∨ *E*) · (*C* ∨ *F*)
   1)   (*A* ∨ *B*) · (*C* ∨ *D*)   Pr
   2)   ~ *A* · ~ *D*   Pr
   3)   *A* ∨ *B*   1, Simp
   4)   (*C* ∨ *D*) · (*A* ∨ *B*)   1, Com
   5)   *C* ∨ *D*   4, Simp
   6)   ~ *A*   2, Simp
   7)   ~ *D* · ~ *A*   2, Com
   8)   ~ *D*   7, Simp
   9)   *B*   3, 6, DS
   10)   *D* ∨ *C*   5, Com
   11)   *C*   10, 8, DS
   12)   *B* ∨ *E*   9, Add
   13)   *C* ∨ *F*   11, Add
   14)   ∴ (*B* ∨ *E*) · (*C* ∨ *F*)   12, 13, Conj

Group D: (page 134)

(1)   ∴ *A* ∨ *P*
   1)   *P* ∨ *A*   Pr
   2)   ∴ *A* ∨ *P*   1, Com

(3)   ∴ *L* ∨ *S*
   1)   (*S* ∨ *E*) · ~ *E*   Pr
   2)   *S* ∨ *E*   1, Simp
   3)   ~ *E* · (*S* ∨ *E*)   1, Com
   4)   ~ *E*   3, Simp
   5)   *E* ∨ *S*   2, Com
   6)   *S*   5, 4, DS
   7)   *S* ∨ *L*   6, Add
   8)   ∴ *L* ∨ *S*   7, Com

(5)   ∴ *E* ∨ *D*
   1)   (~ *P* · ~ *E*) · (~ *A* ∨ *P*)   Pr
   2)   *A* ∨ *D*   Pr
   3)   ~ *P* · ~ *E*   1, Simp
   4)   (~ *A* ∨ *P*) · (~ *P* · ~ *E*)   1, Com
   5)   ~ *A* ∨ *P*   4, Simp

	6)	$P \lor \sim A$	5, Com
	7)	$\sim P$	3, Simp
	8)	$\sim A$	6, 7, DS
	9)	D	2, 8, DS
	10)	$D \lor E$	9, Add
	11)	$\therefore E \lor D$	10, Com
(7)		$\therefore \sim(P \cdot R) \lor (R \lor L)$	
	1)	$\sim P \lor (T \cdot R)$	Pr
	2)	$(R \lor L) \lor M$	Pr
	3)	$\sim(T \cdot R)$	Pr
	4)	$(\sim M \cdot \sim R) \lor P$	Pr
	5)	$(T \cdot R) \lor \sim P$	1, Com
	6)	$\sim P$	5, 3, DS
	7)	$P \lor (\sim M \cdot \sim R)$	4, Com
	8)	$\sim M \cdot \sim R$	7, 6, DS
	9)	$\sim M$	8, Simp
	10)	$M \lor (R \lor L)$	2, Com
	11)	$R \lor L$	10, 9, DS
	12)	$(R \lor L) \lor \sim(P \cdot R)$	11, Add
	13)	$\therefore \sim(P \cdot R) \lor (R \lor L)$	12, Com
(9)		$\therefore (E \supset \sim P) \lor (A \cdot S)$	
	1)	$(\sim T \cdot C) \cdot (\sim E \cdot S)$	Pr
	2)	$\sim X \lor T$	Pr
	3)	$E \lor (A \lor X)$	Pr
	4)	$\sim T \cdot C$	1, Simp
	5)	$(\sim E \cdot S) \cdot (\sim T \cdot C)$	1, Com
	6)	$\sim E \cdot S$	5, Simp
	7)	$\sim E$	6, Simp
	8)	$S \cdot \sim E$	6, Com
	9)	S	8, Simp
	10)	$A \lor X$	3, 7, DS
	11)	$X \lor A$	10, Com
	12)	$T \lor \sim X$	2, Com
	13)	$\sim T$	4, Simp
	14)	$\sim X$	12, 13, DS
	15)	A	11, 14, DS
	16)	$A \cdot S$	15, 9, Conj
	17)	$(A \cdot S) \lor (E \supset \sim P)$	16, Add
	18)	$\therefore (E \supset \sim P) \lor (A \cdot S)$	17, Com

SECTION 5

Group A: (page 141)

(1)
- 1) Pr
- 2) Pr
- 3) 1, 2, MP

(3)
- 1) Pr
- 2) 1, Simp
- 3) 1, Com
- 4) 3, Simp
- 5) 4, 2, MP

(5)
- 1) Pr
- 2) Pr
- 3) Pr
- 4) 1, Simp
- 5) 1, Com
- 6) 5, Simp
- 7) 4, 3, MP
- 8) 6, 7, MP
- 9) 2, 8, MP

(7)
- 1) Pr
- 2) Pr
- 3) Pr
- 4) Pr
- 5) 2, Com
- 6) 5, 4, DS
- 7) 1, 6, MP
- 8) 3, 7, MP
- 9) 8, Add
- 10) 9, Com

(9)
- 1) Pr
- 2) Pr
- 3) Pr
- 4) 2, Simp
- 5) 2, Com
- 6) 5, Simp
- 7) 3, Simp
- 8) 3, Com
- 9) 8, Simp
- 10) 1, 4, MP

11)	7, 4, DS
12)	11, 10, DS
13)	6, 12, Conj
14)	9, 13, MP
15)	14, Add
16)	15, Com

Group B: (page 143)

(1)   ∴ $C \cdot \sim A$

1)	$(A \supset B) \cdot C$	Pr
2)	$\sim B$	Pr
3)	$A \supset B$	1, Simp
4)	$C \cdot (A \supset B)$	1, Com
5)	C	4, Simp
6)	$\sim A$	3, 2, MT
7)	∴ $C \cdot \sim A$	5, 6, Conj

(3)   ∴ $D \lor C$

1)	$(A \lor B) \lor C$	Pr
2)	$(A \lor B) \supset E$	Pr
3)	$\sim E$	Pr
4)	$\sim (A \lor B)$	2, 3, MT
5)	C	1, 4, DS
6)	$C \lor D$	5, Add
7)	∴ $D \lor C$	6, Com

(5)   ∴ C

1)	$(A \cdot B) \supset C$	Pr
2)	$(D \supset A) \cdot (E \supset B)$	Pr
3)	$E \cdot D$	Pr
4)	$D \supset A$	2, Simp
5)	$(E \supset B) \cdot (D \supset A)$	2, Com
6)	$E \supset B$	5, Simp
7)	E	3, Simp
8)	$D \cdot E$	3, Com
9)	D	8, Simp
10)	A	4, 9, MP
11)	B	6, 7, MP
12)	$A \cdot B$	10, 11, Conj
13)	∴ C	1, 12, MP

(7)   ∴ $(A \lor B) \cdot (A \cdot E)$

1)	$(A \lor \sim B) \supset \sim (C \lor D)$	Pr
2)	$(C \lor D) \lor (A \cdot E)$	Pr
3)	$(B \supset F) \cdot \sim F$	Pr
4)	$B \supset F$	3, Simp
5)	$\sim F \cdot (B \supset F)$	3, Com

	6)	$\sim F$	5, Simp
	7)	$\sim B$	4, 6, MT
	8)	$\sim B \vee A$	7, Add
	9)	$A \vee \sim B$	8, Com
	10)	$\sim (C \vee D)$	1, 9, MP
	11)	$A \cdot E$	2, 10, DS
	12)	A	11, Simp
	13)	$A \vee B$	12, Add
	14)	$\therefore (A \vee B) \cdot (A \cdot E)$	13, 11, Conj
(9)			$\therefore \sim G$
	1)	$(A \cdot B) \cdot (C \cdot D)$	Pr
	2)	$[(B \cdot D) \supset E] \cdot [(A \cdot C) \supset F]$	Pr
	3)	$(E \cdot F) \supset \sim G$	Pr
	4)	$A \cdot B$	1, Simp
	5)	A	4, Simp
	6)	$B \cdot A$	4, Com
	7)	B	6, Simp
	8)	$(C \cdot D) \cdot (A \cdot B)$	1, Com
	9)	$C \cdot D$	8, Simp
	10)	C	9, Simp
	11)	$D \cdot C$	9, Com
	12)	D	11, Simp
	13)	$(B \cdot D) \supset E$	2, Simp
	14)	$[(A \cdot C) \supset F] \cdot [(B \cdot D) \supset E]$	2, Com
	15)	$(A \cdot C) \supset F$	14, Simp
	16)	$B \cdot D$	7, 12, Conj
	17)	E	13, 16, MP
	18)	$A \cdot C$	5, 10, Conj
	19)	F	15, 18, MP
	20)	$E \cdot F$	17, 19, Conj
	21)	$\therefore \sim G$	3, 20, MP

Group D: (page 145)

(1)			$\therefore M$
	1)	$B \supset M$	Pr
	2)	B	Pr
	3)	$\therefore M$	1, 2, MP
(3)			$\therefore L \cdot U$
	1)	$L \supset B$	Pr
	2)	$B \supset T$	Pr
	3)	$L \cdot (T \supset U)$	Pr
	4)	L	3, Simp
	5)	$(T \supset U) \cdot L$	3, Com
	6)	$T \supset U$	5, Simp
	7)	B	1, 4, MP

	8)	T	2, 7, MP
	9)	U	6, 8, MP
	10)	$\therefore L \cdot U$	4, 9, Conj
(5)			$\therefore B \cdot S$
	1)	$P \cdot B$	Pr
	2)	$(M \lor P) \supset S$	Pr
	3)	P	1, Simp
	4)	$B \cdot P$	1, Com
	5)	B	4, Simp
	6)	$P \lor M$	3, Add
	7)	$M \lor P$	6, Com
	8)	S	2, 7, MP
	9)	$\therefore B \cdot S$	5, 8, Conj
(7)			$\therefore E \cdot \sim C$
	1)	$(S \supset P) \supset \sim M$	Pr
	2)	$(\sim \sim M \lor B) \cdot (\sim B \lor C)$	Pr
	3)	$\sim C$	Pr
	4)	$(S \supset P) \lor E$	Pr
	5)	$\sim \sim M \lor B$	2, Simp
	6)	$(\sim B \lor C) \cdot (\sim \sim M \lor B)$	2, Com
	7)	$\sim B \lor C$	6, Simp
	8)	$C \lor \sim B$	7, Com
	9)	$\sim B$	8, 3, DS
	10)	$B \lor \sim \sim M$	5, Com
	11)	$\sim \sim M$	10, 9, DS
	12)	$\sim (S \supset P)$	1, 11, MT
	13)	E	4, 12, DS
	14)	$\therefore E \cdot \sim C$	13, 3, Conj
(9)			$\therefore \sim (S \cdot C) \lor (C \cdot S)$
	1)	$\sim (\sim T \lor \sim R) \supset C$	Pr
	2)	$(\sim R \lor C) \supset M$	Pr
	3)	$\sim (\sim T \lor \sim R) \lor (A \lor \sim D)$	Pr
	4)	$\sim (A \lor \sim D)$	Pr
	5)	$(M \lor \sim A) \supset S$	Pr
	6)	$(A \lor \sim D) \lor \sim (\sim T \lor \sim R)$	3, Com
	7)	$\sim (\sim T \lor \sim R)$	6, 4, DS
	8)	C	1, 7, MP
	9)	$C \lor \sim R$	8, Add
	10)	$\sim R \lor C$	9, Com
	11)	M	2, 10, MP
	12)	$M \lor \sim A$	11, Add
	13)	S	5, 12, MP
	14)	$C \cdot S$	8, 13, Conj
	15)	$(C \cdot S) \lor \sim (S \cdot C)$	14, Add
	16)	$\therefore \sim (S \cdot C) \lor (C \cdot S)$	15, Com

SECTION 6

Group A: (page 151)

(1)

    1) Pr
    2) Pr
    3) 2, 1, HS

(3)

    1) Pr
    2) Pr
    3) Pr
    4) 2, Simp
    5) 2, Com
    6) 5, Simp
    7) 3, 6, MP
    8) 1, 4, MP
    9) 7, 8, HS

(5)

    1) Pr
    2) Pr
    3) Pr
    4) 1, Simp
    5) 1, Com
    6) 5, Simp
    7) 3, 2, HS
    8) 6, Add
    9) 7, 4, 8, CD
   10) 9, Com

(7)

    1) Pr
    2) Pr
    3) Pr
    4) Pr
    5) 1, Simp
    6) 1, Com
    7) 6, Simp
    8) 2, 7, MP
    9) 3, 5, MP
   10) 8, 4, 9, CD

(9)

    1) Pr
    2) Pr
    3) Pr
    4) Pr
    5) Pr

6) 4, Simp
7) 4, Com
8) 7, Simp
9) 2, 8, MP
10) 9, Simp
11) 9, Com
12) 11, Simp
13) 1, 10, MP
14) 6, 12, Conj
15) 3, 14, MP
16) 15, Com
17) 5, 13, 16, CD

Group B: (page 154)

(1) $\therefore B \lor D$

1) $A \supset B$ Pr
2) $C \supset D$ Pr
3) $A \lor C$ Pr
4) $\therefore B \lor D$ 1, 2, 3, CD

(3) $\therefore D \lor B$

1) $A \supset B$ Pr
2) $A \lor C$ Pr
3) $C \supset D$ Pr
4) $B \lor D$ 1, 3, 2, CD
5) $\therefore D \lor B$ 4, Com

(5) $\therefore C \lor E$

1) $(A \supset B) \cdot (B \supset C)$ Pr
2) $D \supset E$ Pr
3) $D \lor A$ Pr
4) $A \supset B$ 1, Simp
5) $(B \supset C) \cdot (A \supset B)$ 1, Com
6) $B \supset C$ 5, Simp
7) $A \supset C$ 4, 6, HS
8) $E \lor C$ 2, 7, 3, CD
9) $\therefore C \lor E$ 8, Com

(7) $\therefore (G \cdot H) \lor (G \lor H)$

1) $[A \supset (B \cdot C)] \supset (D \lor E)$ Pr
2) $[A \supset (B \supset F)] \cdot [(B \supset F) \supset (B \cdot C)]$ Pr
3) $(D \lor E) \supset [(D \supset G) \cdot (E \supset H)]$ Pr
4) $A \supset (B \supset F)$ 2, Simp
5) $[(B \supset F) \supset (B \cdot C)] \cdot [A \supset (B \supset F)]$ 2, Com
6) $(B \supset F) \supset (B \cdot C)$ 5, Simp
7) $A \supset (B \cdot C)$ 4, 6, HS
8) $D \lor E$ 1, 7, MP

9)	$(D \supset G) \cdot (E \supset H)$	3, 8, MP
10)	$D \supset G$	9, Simp
11)	$(E \supset H) \cdot (D \supset G)$	9, Com
12)	$E \supset H$	11, Simp
13)	$G \lor H$	10, 12, 8, CD
14)	$(G \lor H) \lor (G \cdot H)$	13, Add
15)	$\therefore (G \cdot H) \lor (G \lor H)$	14, Com

(9) $\therefore G \lor E$

1)	$[A \lor (B \cdot \sim C)] \cdot \sim A$	Pr
2)	$[B \supset (D \supset E)] \cdot [\sim C \supset (F \supset G)]$	Pr
3)	$(\sim A \lor F) \supset (F \lor D)$	Pr
4)	$A \lor (B \cdot \sim C)$	1, Simp
5)	$\sim A \cdot [A \lor (B \cdot \sim C)]$	1, Com
6)	$\sim A$	5, Simp
7)	$B \supset (D \supset E)$	2, Simp
8)	$[\sim C \supset (F \supset G)] \cdot [B \supset (D \supset E)]$	2, Com
9)	$\sim C \supset (F \supset G)$	8, Simp
10)	$B \cdot \sim C$	4, 6, DS
11)	B	10, Simp
12)	$\sim C \cdot B$	10, Com
13)	$\sim C$	12, Simp
14)	$D \supset E$	7, 11, MP
15)	$F \supset G$	9, 13, MP
16)	$\sim A \lor F$	6, Add
17)	$F \lor D$	3, 16, MP
18)	$\therefore G \lor E$	15, 14, 17, CD

Group D: (page 154)

(1) $\therefore \sim (L \lor F) \lor (F \lor L)$

1)	$A \supset L$	Pr
2)	$A \lor B$	Pr
3)	$B \supset F$	Pr
4)	$L \lor F$	1, 3, 2, CD
5)	$F \lor L$	4, Com
6)	$(F \lor L) \lor \sim (L \lor F)$	5, Add
7)	$\therefore \sim (L \lor F) \lor (F \lor L)$	6, Com

(3) $\therefore T \supset E$

1)	$(T \supset S) \cdot (S \supset F)$	Pr
2)	$(F \supset M) \cdot (M \supset E)$	Pr
3)	$T \supset S$	1, Simp
4)	$(S \supset F) \cdot (T \supset S)$	1, Com
5)	$S \supset F$	4, Simp
6)	$F \supset M$	2, Simp
7)	$(M \supset E) \cdot (F \supset M)$	2, Com

	8)	$M \supset E$	7, Simp
	9)	$T \supset F$	3, 5, HS
	10)	$T \supset M$	9, 6, HS
	11)	$\therefore T \supset E$	10, 8, HS
(5)			$\therefore M \supset W$
	1)	$K \supset (T \cdot C)$	Pr
	2)	$T \supset (M \supset P)$	Pr
	3)	$C \supset (P \supset W)$	Pr
	4)	K	Pr
	5)	$T \cdot C$	1, 4, MP
	6)	T	5, Simp
	7)	$C \cdot T$	5, Com
	8)	C	7, Simp
	9)	$M \supset P$	2, 6, MP
	10)	$P \supset W$	3, 8, MP
	11)	$\therefore M \supset W$	9, 10, HS
(7)			$\therefore I \vee O$
	1)	$\sim(G \cdot A) \supset (P \supset C)$	Pr
	2)	$(G \cdot A) \supset I$	Pr
	3)	$\sim I \cdot (M \vee P)$	Pr
	4)	$(C \supset I) \cdot (M \supset O)$	Pr
	5)	$\sim I$	3, Simp
	6)	$(M \vee P) \cdot \sim I$	3, Com
	7)	$M \vee P$	6, Simp
	8)	$C \supset I$	4, Simp
	9)	$(M \supset O) \cdot (C \supset I)$	4, Com
	10)	$M \supset O$	9, Simp
	11)	$\sim(G \cdot A)$	2, 5, MT
	12)	$P \supset C$	1, 11, MP
	13)	$P \supset I$	12, 8, HS
	14)	$O \vee I$	10, 13, 7, CD
	15)	$\therefore I \vee O$	14, Com
(9)			$\therefore (T \vee S) \cdot (C \vee M)$
	1)	$(O \supset T) \cdot (F \supset S)$	Pr
	2)	$(O \vee F) \cdot (B \vee \sim P)$	Pr
	3)	$(B \supset C) \cdot (\sim P \supset M)$	Pr
	4)	$O \supset T$	1, Simp
	5)	$(F \supset S) \cdot (O \supset T)$	1, Com
	6)	$F \supset S$	5, Simp
	7)	$O \vee F$	2, Simp
	8)	$(B \vee \sim P) \cdot (O \vee F)$	2, Com
	9)	$B \vee \sim P$	8, Simp
	10)	$B \supset C$	3, Simp
	11)	$(\sim P \supset M) \cdot (B \supset C)$	3, Com

12)	$\sim P \supset M$	11, Simp
13)	$T \lor S$	4, 6, 7, CD
14)	$C \lor M$	10, 12, 9, CD
15)	$\therefore (T \lor S) \cdot (C \lor M)$	13, 14, Conj

SECTION 7

Group A: (page 158)

- **(1)** GV (guarantees validity)
- **(3)** GV
- **(5)** GV
- **(7)** GV
- **(9)** NGV (does not guarantee validity)
- **(11)** GV
- **(13)** GV
- **(15)** NGV
- **(17)** NGV
- **(19)** GV

Chapter 6

SECTION 1

Group A: (page 164)

(1)

1) Pr
2) Pr
3) 1, D1
4) 3, Com
5) 2, 4, MP

(3)

1) Pr
2) Pr
3) 1, Simp
4) 1, Com
5) 4, Simp
6) 2, 3, MT
7) 6, D1
8) 7, 5, DS

(5)

1) Pr
2) Pr
3) 2, Add
4) 3, Com
5) 4, D1

6) 1, 5, MP
7) 6, Add
8) 7, Com
9) 8, D1

(7)

1) Pr
2) Pr
3) Pr
4) Pr
5) 4, Simp
6) 4, Com
7) 6, Simp
8) 2, D1
9) 3, D1
10) 1, 8, HS
11) 5, 7, HS
12) 10, 11, 9, CD

(9)

1) Pr
2) Pr
3) Pr
4) 3, Simp
5) 3, Com
6) 5, Simp
7) 1, D1
8) 7, 2, MT
9) 8, D1
10) 9, Com
11) 10, 4, DS
12) 6, 11, MP
13) 12, Add
14) 13, Com
15) 14, D1
16) 15, Add

Group B: (page 167)

(1) $\therefore \sim (\sim B \cdot \sim D)$

1)	$(A \supset B) \cdot (C \supset D)$	Pr
2)	$\sim (\sim A \cdot \sim C)$	Pr
3)	$A \supset B$	1, Simp
4)	$(C \supset D) \cdot (A \supset B)$	1, Com
5)	$C \supset D$	4, Simp
6)	$A \lor C$	2, D1
7)	$B \lor D$	3, 5, 6, CD
8)	$\therefore \sim (\sim B \cdot \sim D)$	7, D1

(3)

		$\therefore\ C$
1)	$\sim(\sim\sim A\cdot\sim B)\supset C$	Pr
2)	$\sim D$	Pr
3)	$(A\supset E)\cdot(E\supset D)$	Pr
4)	$A\supset E$	3, Simp
5)	$(E\supset D)\cdot(A\supset E)$	3, Com
6)	$E\supset D$	5, Simp
7)	$(\sim A\lor B)\supset C$	1, D1
8)	$A\supset D$	4, 6, HS
9)	$\sim A$	8, 2, MT
10)	$\sim A\lor B$	9, Add
11)	$\therefore\ C$	7, 10, MP

(5)

		$\therefore\ B$
1)	$(A\supset B)\cdot(C\supset D)$	Pr
2)	$\sim(\sim A\cdot\sim C)\cdot\sim D$	Pr
3)	$A\supset B$	1, Simp
4)	$(C\supset D)\cdot(A\supset B)$	1, Com
5)	$C\supset D$	4, Simp
6)	$\sim(\sim A\cdot\sim C)$	2, Simp
7)	$\sim D\cdot\sim(\sim A\cdot\sim C)$	2, Com
8)	$\sim D$	7, Simp
9)	$A\lor C$	6, D1
10)	$B\lor D$	3, 5, 9, CD
11)	$D\lor B$	10, Com
12)	$\therefore\ B$	11, 8, DS

(7)

		$\therefore\ \sim[\sim E\cdot\sim\sim(\sim A\cdot\sim D)]$
1)	$(\sim A\cdot\sim B)\supset C$	Pr
2)	$\sim C\cdot\sim B$	Pr
3)	$\sim C$	2, Simp
4)	$\sim B\cdot\sim C$	2, Com
5)	$\sim B$	4, Simp
6)	$\sim(\sim A\cdot\sim B)$	1, 3, MT
7)	$A\lor B$	6, D1
8)	$B\lor A$	7, Com
9)	A	8, 5, DS
10)	$A\lor D$	9, Add
11)	$\sim(\sim A\cdot\sim D)$	10, D1
12)	$\sim(\sim A\cdot\sim D)\lor E$	11, Add
13)	$E\lor\sim(\sim A\cdot\sim D)$	12, Com
14)	$\therefore\ \sim[\sim E\cdot\sim\sim(\sim A\cdot\sim D)]$	13, D1

(9)

		$\therefore\ A$
1)	$\sim[\sim(A\lor B)\cdot\sim C]$	Pr
2)	$(B\supset D)\cdot(D\supset E)$	Pr
3)	$\sim E\cdot\sim C$	Pr

4)	$B \supset D$	2, Simp
5)	$(D \supset E) \cdot (B \supset D)$	2, Com
6)	$D \supset E$	5, Simp
7)	$\sim E$	3, Simp
8)	$\sim C \cdot \sim E$	3, Com
9)	$\sim C$	8, Simp
10)	$(A \lor B) \lor C$	1, D1
11)	$C \lor (A \lor B)$	10, Com
12)	$A \lor B$	11, 9, DS
13)	$B \lor A$	12, Com
14)	$B \supset E$	4, 6, HS
15)	$\sim B$	14, 7, MT
16)	$\therefore A$	13, 15, DS

Group D: (page 168)

(1) $\therefore \sim (\sim A \cdot \sim I)$

1)	I	Pr
2)	$I \lor A$	1, Add
3)	$A \lor I$	2, Com
4)	$\therefore \sim (\sim A \cdot \sim I)$	3, D1

(3) $\therefore B$

1)	$\sim (\sim B \cdot \sim A) \cdot \sim A$	Pr
2)	$\sim (\sim B \cdot \sim A)$	1, Simp
3)	$\sim A \cdot \sim (\sim B \cdot \sim A)$	1, Com
4)	$\sim A$	3, Simp
5)	$B \lor A$	2, D1
6)	$A \lor B$	5, Com
7)	$\therefore B$	6, 4, DS

(5) $\therefore P$

1)	$R \supset F$	Pr
2)	$(\sim P \cdot \sim M) \supset R$	Pr
3)	$\sim F \cdot \sim M$	Pr
4)	$\sim F$	3, Simp
5)	$\sim M \cdot \sim F$	3, Com
6)	$\sim M$	5, Simp
7)	$\sim R$	1, 4, MT
8)	$\sim (\sim P \cdot \sim M)$	2, 7, MT
9)	$P \lor M$	8, D1
10)	$M \lor P$	9, Com
11)	$\therefore P$	10, 6, DS

(7) $\sim [\sim G \cdot \sim (S \lor P)]$

1)	$(\sim S \cdot \sim A) \supset D$	Pr
2)	$\sim D \cdot \sim A$	Pr
3)	$\sim D$	2, Simp

	4)	$\sim A \cdot \sim D$	2, Com
	5)	$\sim A$	4, Simp
	6)	$\sim(\sim S \cdot \sim A)$	1, 3, MT
	7)	$S \lor A$	6, D1
	8)	$A \lor S$	7, Com
	9)	S	8, 5, DS
	10)	$S \lor P$	9, Add
	11)	$(S \lor P) \lor G$	10, Add
	12)	$G \lor (S \lor P)$	11, Com
	13)	$\therefore \sim[\sim G \cdot \sim(S \lor P)]$	12, D1
(9)			$\therefore (L \lor \sim R) \cdot (R \lor \sim L)$
	1)	$\sim K \cdot \sim A$	Pr
	2)	$\sim[\sim K \cdot \sim(P \lor L)]$	Pr
	3)	$\sim P \cdot \sim C$	Pr
	4)	$C \lor \sim(\sim A \cdot \sim R)$	Pr
	5)	$\sim K$	1, Simp
	6)	$\sim A \cdot \sim K$	1, Com
	7)	$\sim A$	6, Simp
	8)	$\sim P$	3, Simp
	9)	$\sim C \cdot \sim P$	3, Com
	10)	$\sim C$	9, Simp
	11)	$K \lor (P \lor L)$	2, D1
	12)	$P \lor L$	11, 5, DS
	13)	L	12, 8, DS
	14)	$L \lor \sim R$	13, Add
	15)	$\sim(\sim A \cdot \sim R)$	4, 10, DS
	16)	$A \lor R$	15, D1
	17)	R	16, 7, DS
	18)	$R \lor \sim L$	17, Add
	19)	$\therefore (L \lor \sim R) \cdot (R \lor \sim L)$	14, 18, Conj

SECTION 2

Group A: (page 173)

(1)

1) Pr
2) Pr
3) 2, D2
4) 3, Simp
5) 1, 4, MT

(3)

1) Pr
2) Pr
3) 1, Simp

4) 1, Com
5) 4, Simp
6) 2, 5, MT
7) 3, Add
8) 7, D1
9) 6, 8, Conj
10) 9, D2

(5)

1) Pr
2) Pr
3) Pr
4) Pr
5) 1, D2
6) 3, 5, HS
7) 4, 2, HS
8) 7, 6, MP
9) 8, Add
10) 9, D1
11) 10, Add
12) 11, Com

(7)

1) Pr
2) Pr
3) Pr
4) Pr
5) 4, Simp
6) 4, Com
7) 6, Simp
8) 5, 7, DS
9) 8, Simp
10) 8, Com
11) 10, Simp
12) 1, 11, MP
13) 3, 9, MP
14) 2, 7, MP
15) 14, D2
16) 15, Com
17) 16, Simp
18) 17, D1
19) 12, 13, 18, CD

(9)

1)	Pr
2)	Pr
3)	Pr
4)	Pr
5)	2, Simp
6)	2, Com
7)	6, Simp
8)	4, Simp
9)	4, Com
10)	9, Simp
11)	3, 5, MT
12)	7, Com
13)	12, 5, DS
14)	13, Add
15)	14, D1
16)	11, 15, Conj
17)	16, D2
18)	1, 17, MP
19)	18, Add
20)	19, Com
21)	8, 10, 20, CD

Group B: (page 176) $\therefore A \triangle B$

1)	$\sim(A \cdot B) \supset C$	Pr
2)	$C \supset B$	Pr
3)	$\sim(A \cdot B)$	Pr
4)	C	1, 3, MP
5)	B	2, 4, MP
6)	$B \lor A$	5, Add
7)	$A \lor B$	6, Com
8)	$\sim(\sim A \cdot \sim B)$	7, D1
9)	$\sim(A \cdot B) \cdot \sim(\sim A \cdot \sim B)$	3, 8, Conj
10)	$\therefore A \triangle B$	9, D2

(3) $\therefore C \cdot A$

1)	$A \cdot \sim B$	Pr
2)	$A \supset (C \triangle B)$	Pr
3)	A	1, Simp
4)	$\sim B \cdot A$	1, Com
5)	$\sim B$	4, Simp
6)	$C \triangle B$	2, 3, MP
7)	$\sim(C \cdot B) \cdot \sim(\sim C \cdot \sim B)$	6, D2
8)	$\sim(\sim C \cdot \sim B) \cdot \sim(C \cdot B)$	7, Com
9)	$\sim(\sim C \cdot \sim B)$	8, Simp

10)	$C \lor B$	9, D1
11)	$B \lor C$	10, Com
12)	C	11, 5, DS
13)	$\therefore \ C \cdot A$	12, 3, Conj

(5) $\therefore \ B \cdot \sim A$

1)	$A \supset (B \cdot C)$	Pr
2)	$\sim C \cdot (B \triangle C)$	Pr
3)	$\sim C$	2, Simp
4)	$(B \triangle C) \cdot \sim C$	2, Com
5)	$B \triangle C$	4, Simp
6)	$\sim (B \cdot C) \cdot \sim (\sim B \cdot \sim C)$	5, D2
7)	$\sim (B \cdot C)$	6, Simp
8)	$\sim (\sim B \cdot \sim C) \cdot \sim (B \cdot C)$	6, Com
9)	$\sim (\sim B \cdot \sim C)$	8, Simp
10)	$B \lor C$	9, D1
11)	$C \lor B$	10, Com
12)	B	11, 3, DS
13)	$\sim A$	1, 7, MT
14)	$\therefore \ B \cdot \sim A$	12, 13, Conj

(7) $\therefore \ \sim F \lor E$

1)	$(A \supset B) \cdot (C \supset D)$	Pr
2)	$A \triangle C$	Pr
3)	$(B \supset E) \cdot (D \supset \sim F)$	Pr
4)	$A \supset B$	1, Simp
5)	$(C \supset D) \cdot (A \supset B)$	1, Com
6)	$C \supset D$	5, Simp
7)	$B \supset E$	3, Simp
8)	$(D \supset \sim F) \cdot (B \supset E)$	3, Com
9)	$D \supset \sim F$	8, Simp
10)	$\sim (A \cdot C) \cdot \sim (\sim A \cdot \sim C)$	2, D2
11)	$\sim (\sim A \cdot \sim C) \cdot \sim (A \cdot C)$	10, Com
12)	$\sim (\sim A \cdot \sim C)$	11, Simp
13)	$A \lor C$	12, D1
14)	$A \supset E$	4, 7, HS
15)	$C \supset \sim F$	6, 9, HS
16)	$E \lor \sim F$	14, 15, 13, CD
17)	$\therefore \ \sim F \lor E$	16, Com

(9) $\therefore \ \sim [\sim G \cdot \sim \sim (\sim H \cdot \sim I)]$

1)	$\sim (A \lor B) \supset (\sim C \cdot \sim D)$	Pr
2)	$\sim \sim (\sim A \cdot \sim B)$	Pr
3)	$(C \triangle E) \cdot (D \lor F)$	Pr
4)	$(E \cdot F) \supset G$	Pr
5)	$C \triangle E$	3, Simp
6)	$(D \lor F) \cdot (C \triangle E)$	3, Com

7)	$D \lor F$	6, Simp
8)	$\sim(A \lor B)$	2, D1
9)	$\sim C \cdot \sim D$	1, 8, MP
10)	$\sim C$	9, Simp
11)	$\sim D \cdot \sim C$	9, Com
12)	$\sim D$	11, Simp
13)	F	7, 12, DS
14)	$\sim(C \cdot E) \cdot \sim(\sim C \cdot \sim E)$	5, D2
15)	$\sim(\sim C \cdot \sim E) \cdot \sim(C \cdot E)$	14, Com
16)	$\sim(\sim C \cdot \sim E)$	15, Simp
17)	$C \lor E$	16, D1
18)	E	17, 10, DS
19)	$E \cdot F$	18, 13, Conj
20)	G	4, 19, MP
21)	$G \lor \sim(\sim H \cdot \sim I)$	20, Add
22)	$\therefore \sim[\sim G \cdot \sim \sim(\sim H \cdot \sim I)]$	21, D1

Group D: (page 178)

(1) $\qquad \qquad \qquad \qquad \qquad \qquad \qquad \qquad \therefore F$

1)	$F \triangle P$	Pr
2)	$\sim P$	Pr
3)	$\sim(F \cdot P) \cdot \sim(\sim F \cdot \sim P)$	1, D2
4)	$\sim(\sim F \cdot \sim P) \cdot \sim(F \cdot P)$	3, Com
5)	$\sim(\sim F \cdot \sim P)$	4, Simp
6)	$F \lor P$	5, D1
7)	$P \lor F$	6, Com
8)	$\therefore F$	7, 2, DS

(3) $\qquad \qquad \qquad \qquad \qquad \qquad \qquad \qquad \therefore S \triangle D$

1)	$(S \cdot D) \supset M$	Pr
2)	$D \lor M$	Pr
3)	$\sim M$	Pr
4)	$\sim(S \cdot D)$	1, 3, MT
5)	$M \lor D$	2, Com
6)	D	5, 3, DS
7)	$D \lor S$	6, Add
8)	$S \lor D$	7, Com
9)	$\sim(\sim S \cdot \sim D)$	8, D1
10)	$\sim(S \cdot D) \cdot \sim(\sim S \cdot \sim D)$	4, 9, Conj
11)	$\therefore S \triangle D$	10, D2

(5) $\qquad \qquad \qquad \qquad \qquad \qquad \qquad \qquad \therefore F \triangle L$

1)	$\sim(F \cdot L) \cdot \sim(L \cdot P)$	Pr
2)	$(L \triangle P) \supset F$	Pr
3)	$P \lor L$	Pr
4)	$\sim(F \cdot L)$	1, Simp

	5)	$\sim(L\cdot P)\cdot\sim(F\cdot L)$	1, Com
	6)	$\sim(L\cdot P)$	5, Simp
	7)	$L \vee P$	3, Com
	8)	$\sim(\sim L\cdot\sim P)$	7, D1
	9)	$\sim(L\cdot P)\cdot\sim(\sim L\cdot\sim P)$	6, 8, Conj
	10)	$L \triangle P$	9, D2
	11)	F	2, 10, MP
	12)	$F \vee L$	11, Add
	13)	$\sim(\sim F\cdot\sim L)$	12, D1
	14)	$\sim(F\cdot L)\cdot\sim(\sim F\cdot\sim L)$	4, 13, Conj
	15)	$\therefore\ F \triangle L$	14, D2

(7) $\therefore\ \sim(\sim\sim C\cdot\sim P)$

	1)	$(P \triangle F)\cdot(D \triangle \sim C)$	Pr
	2)	$(P\cdot F) \vee \sim D$	Pr
	3)	$P \triangle F$	1, Simp
	4)	$(D \triangle \sim C)\cdot(P \triangle F)$	1, Com
	5)	$D \triangle \sim C$	4, Simp
	6)	$\sim(P\cdot F)\cdot\sim(\sim P\cdot\sim F)$	3, D2
	7)	$\sim(P\cdot F)$	6, Simp
	8)	$\sim D$	2, 7, DS
	9)	$\sim(D\cdot\sim C)\cdot\sim(\sim D\cdot\sim\sim C)$	5, D2
	10)	$\sim(\sim D\cdot\sim\sim C)\cdot\sim(D\cdot\sim C)$	9, Com
	11)	$\sim(\sim D\cdot\sim\sim C)$	10, Simp
	12)	$D \vee \sim C$	11, D1
	13)	$\sim C$	12, 8, DS
	14)	$\sim C \vee P$	13, Add
	15)	$\therefore\ \sim(\sim\sim C\cdot\sim P)$	14, D1

(9) $\therefore\ E\cdot G$

	1)	$(E \supset G)\cdot(F \triangle E)$	Pr
	2)	$(F \supset A)\cdot(K \vee E)$	Pr
	3)	$K \supset (\sim G\cdot\sim A)$	Pr
	4)	$E \supset G$	1, Simp
	5)	$(F \triangle E)\cdot(E \supset G)$	1, Com
	6)	$F \triangle E$	5, Simp
	7)	$F \supset A$	2, Simp
	8)	$(K \vee E)\cdot(F \supset A)$	2, Com
	9)	$K \vee E$	8, Simp
	10)	$\sim(F\cdot E)\cdot\sim(\sim F\cdot\sim E)$	6, D2
	11)	$\sim(\sim F\cdot\sim E)\cdot\sim(F\cdot E)$	10, Com
	12)	$\sim(\sim F\cdot\sim E)$	11, Simp
	13)	$F \vee E$	12, D1
	14)	$A \vee G$	7, 4, 13, CD
	15)	$G \vee A$	14, Com
	16)	$\sim(\sim G\cdot\sim A)$	15, D1

17)	~K	3, 16, MT
18)	E	9, 17, DS
19)	G	4, 18, MP
20)	∴ E·G	18, 19, Conj

SECTION 3

Group A: (page 183)

(1)

1)	Pr
2)	Pr ·
3)	Pr
4)	3, D3
5)	1, D1
6)	2, 4, 5, CD
7)	6, Com

(3)

1)	Pr
2)	Pr
3)	Pr
4)	Pr
5)	1, D3
6)	4, D3
7)	2, 3, MP
8)	6, 5, HS
9)	7, 8, HS
10)	9, D3
11)	10, D1

(5)

1)	Pr
2)	Pr
3)	Pr
4)	3, Simp
5)	3, Com
6)	5, Simp
7)	6, D3
8)	1, 7, MT
9)	2, 8, MT
10)	4, D3
11)	9, 10, Conj
12)	11, D2

(7)

    1)   Pr
    2)   Pr
    3)   Pr
    4)   Pr
    5)   2, Simp
    6)   2, Com
    7)   6, Simp
    8)   4, D3
    9)   1, 5, MT
  10)   9, D3
  11)   3, 7, MT
  12)   11, D1
  13)   10, 8, 12, CD
  14)   13, Com
  15)   14, D1
  16)   15, D3

(9)

    1)   Pr
    2)   Pr
    3)   Pr
    4)   Pr
    5)   1, Simp
    6)   1, Com
    7)   6, Simp
    8)   3, Simp
    9)   3, Com
  10)   9, Simp
  11)   4, D3
  12)   5, 7, HS
  13)   12, D1
  14)   13, D1
  15)   8, 10, 14, CD
  16)   15, D1
  17)   2, 16, MT
  18)   17, D3
  19)   18, 5, 11, CD
  20)   19, D1
  21)   20, D3

Group B: (page 187)

(1) $\therefore \sim(A \cdot \sim C)$

1)	$\sim(A \cdot \sim B) \cdot \sim(B \cdot \sim C)$	Pr
2)	$\sim(A \cdot \sim B)$	1, Simp
3)	$\sim(B \cdot \sim C) \cdot \sim(A \cdot \sim B)$	1, Com
4)	$\sim(B \cdot \sim C)$	3, Simp
5)	$A \supset B$	2, D3
6)	$B \supset C$	4, D3
7)	$A \supset C$	5, 6, HS
8)	$\therefore \sim(A \cdot \sim C)$	7, D3

(3) $\therefore A \vee D$

1)	$A \triangle B$	Pr
2)	$(B \cdot \sim D) \supset (A \cdot B)$	Pr
3)	$\sim(A \cdot B) \cdot \sim(\sim A \cdot \sim B)$	1, D2
4)	$\sim(A \cdot B)$	3, Simp
5)	$\sim(\sim A \cdot \sim B) \cdot \sim(A \cdot B)$	3, Com
6)	$\sim(\sim A \cdot \sim B)$	5, Simp
7)	$\sim(B \cdot \sim D)$	2, 4, MT
8)	$\sim A \supset B$	6, D3
9)	$B \supset D$	7, D3
10)	$\sim A \supset D$	8, 9, HS
11)	$\sim(\sim A \cdot \sim D)$	10, D3
12)	$\therefore A \vee D$	11, D1

(5) $\therefore A \supset E$

1)	$(A \cdot \sim B) \supset (\sim C \cdot \sim D)$	Pr
2)	$(C \vee D) \cdot F$	Pr
3)	$(B \cdot \sim E) \supset (\sim F \cdot \sim C)$	Pr
4)	$C \vee D$	2, Simp
5)	$F \cdot (C \vee D)$	2, Com
6)	F	5, Simp
7)	$\sim(\sim C \cdot \sim D)$	4, D1
8)	$\sim(A \cdot \sim B)$	1, 7, MT
9)	$A \supset B$	8, D3
10)	$F \vee C$	6, Add
11)	$\sim(\sim F \cdot \sim C)$	10, D1
12)	$\sim(B \cdot \sim E)$	3, 11, MT
13)	$B \supset E$	12, D3
14)	$\therefore A \supset E$	9, 13, HS

(7) $\therefore C \cdot B$

1)	$\sim[A \cdot \sim \sim(B \cdot \sim C)]$	Pr
2)	$(A \cdot B) \vee (D \cdot E)$	Pr
3)	$\sim[(D \cdot E) \cdot \sim F] \cdot \sim F$	Pr
4)	$\sim[(D \cdot E) \cdot \sim F]$	3, Simp
5)	$\sim F \cdot \sim[(D \cdot E) \cdot \sim F]$	3, Com

6)	$\sim F$	5, Simp
7)	$A \supset \sim(B \cdot \sim C)$	1, D3
8)	$(D \cdot E) \supset F$	4, D3
9)	$\sim(D \cdot E)$	8, 6, MT
10)	$(D \cdot E) \lor (A \cdot B)$	2, Com
11)	$A \cdot B$	10, 9, DS
12)	A	11, Simp
13)	$B \cdot A$	11, Com
14)	B	13, Simp
15)	$\sim(B \cdot \sim C)$	7, 12, MP
16)	$B \supset C$	15, D3
17)	C	16, 14, MP
18)	$\therefore\ C \cdot B$	17, 14, Conj

(9) $\therefore\ \sim F \supset G$

1)	$A \supset (B \triangle C)$	Pr
2)	$\sim D \cdot \sim[\sim D \cdot \sim(E \cdot A)]$	Pr
3)	$(B \cdot \sim F) \supset D$	Pr
4)	$E \supset \sim(C \cdot \sim G)$	Pr
5)	$\sim D$	2, Simp
6)	$\sim[\sim D \cdot \sim(E \cdot A)] \cdot \sim D$	2, Com
7)	$\sim[\sim D \cdot \sim(E \cdot A)]$	6, Simp
8)	$\sim D \supset (E \cdot A)$	7, D3
9)	$E \cdot A$	8, 5, MP
10)	E	9, Simp
11)	$A \cdot E$	9, Com
12)	A	11, Simp
13)	$B \triangle C$	1, 12, MP
14)	$\sim(C \cdot \sim G)$	4, 10, MP
15)	$C \supset G$	14, D3
16)	$\sim(B \cdot \sim F)$	3, 5, MT
17)	$B \supset F$	16, D3
18)	$\sim(B \cdot C) \cdot \sim(\sim B \cdot \sim C)$	13, D2
19)	$\sim(\sim B \cdot \sim C) \cdot \sim(B \cdot C)$	18, Com
20)	$\sim(\sim B \cdot \sim C)$	19, Simp
21)	$B \lor C$	20, D1
22)	$F \lor G$	17, 15, 21, CD
23)	$\sim(\sim F \cdot \sim G)$	22, D1
24)	$\therefore\ \sim F \supset G$	23, D3

Group D: (page 188)

(1) $\therefore\ \sim C \supset D$

1)	$C \lor D$	Pr
2)	$\sim(\sim C \cdot \sim D)$	1, D1
3)	$\therefore\ \sim C \supset D$	2, D3

(3)

		$\therefore\ D \supset A$
1)	$D \bigtriangleup \sim A$	Pr
2)	$\sim(D \cdot \sim A) \cdot \sim(\sim D \cdot \sim \sim A)$	1, D2
3)	$\sim(D \cdot \sim A)$	2, Simp
4)	$\therefore\ D \supset A$	3, D3

(5)

		$\therefore\ \sim E$
1)	$\sim N \cdot \sim S$	Pr
2)	$\sim[(E \cdot \sim S) \cdot \sim N]$	Pr
3)	$\sim N$	1, Simp
4)	$\sim S \cdot \sim N$	1, Com
5)	$\sim S$	4, Simp
6)	$(E \cdot \sim S) \supset N$	2, D3
7)	$\sim(E \cdot \sim S)$	6, 3, MT
8)	$E \supset S$	7, D3
9)	$\therefore\ \sim E$	8, 5, MT

(7)

		$\therefore\ \sim A \supset C$
1)	$\sim(Q \cdot \sim C) \cdot \sim(I \cdot \sim A)$	Pr
2)	$Q \bigtriangleup I$	Pr
3)	$\sim(Q \cdot \sim C)$	1, Simp
4)	$\sim(I \cdot \sim A) \cdot \sim(Q \cdot \sim C)$	1, Com
5)	$\sim(I \cdot \sim A)$	4, Simp
6)	$Q \supset C$	3, D3
7)	$I \supset A$	5, D3
8)	$\sim(Q \cdot I) \cdot \sim(\sim Q \cdot \sim I)$	2, D2
9)	$\sim(\sim Q \cdot \sim I) \cdot \sim(Q \cdot I)$	8, Com
10)	$\sim(\sim Q \cdot \sim I)$	9, Simp
11)	$Q \lor I$	10, D1
12)	$C \lor A$	6, 7, 11, CD
13)	$A \lor C$	12, Com
14)	$\sim(\sim A \cdot \sim C)$	13, D1
15)	$\therefore\ \sim A \supset C$	14, D3

(9)

		$\therefore\ C \cdot B$
1)	$(\sim M \supset \sim T) \cdot \sim(M \cdot \sim G)$	Pr
2)	$\sim(\sim T \cdot \sim C)$	Pr
3)	$\sim(\sim C \cdot \sim G) \supset (B \cdot \sim T)$	Pr
4)	$\sim M \supset \sim T$	1, Simp
5)	$\sim(M \cdot \sim G) \cdot (\sim M \supset \sim T)$	1, Com
6)	$\sim(M \cdot \sim G)$	5, Simp
7)	$\sim T \supset C$	2, D3
8)	$M \supset G$	6, D3
9)	$\sim(\sim M \cdot \sim \sim T)$	4, D3
10)	$M \lor \sim T$	9, D1
11)	$G \lor C$	8, 7, 10, CD

12)	$C \lor G$	11, Com
13)	$\sim(\sim C \cdot \sim G)$	12, D1
14)	$B \cdot \sim T$	3, 13, MP
15)	B	14, Simp
16)	$\sim T \cdot B$	14, Com
17)	$\sim T$	16, Simp
18)	C	7, 17, MP
19)	$\therefore C \cdot B$	18, 15, Conj

SECTION 4

Group A: (page 194)

(1)

1) Pr
2) Pr
3) 2, D4
4) 3, Com
5) 4, Simp
6) 5, D3
7) 6, 1, MP
8) 7, Com

(3)

1) Pr
2) Pr
3) Pr
4) 2, Simp
5) 2, Com
6) 5, Simp
7) 4, D4
8) 7, Simp
9) 8, D3
10) 9, 6, MT
11) 1, 10, Conj
12) 3, 11, MP

(5)

1) Pr
2) Pr
3) Pr
4) 1, D4
5) 2, D2
6) 3, D3
7) 5, Simp
8) 7, D3
9) 4, Com

10) 9, Simp
11) 10, D1
12) 8, 6, 11, CD
13) 12, D1
14) 13, D3

(7)

1) Pr
2) Pr
3) Pr
4) 2, Simp
5) 2, Com
6) 5, Simp
7) 1, D4
8) 7, Simp
9) 8, D3
10) 4, Com
11) 10, 6, DS
12) 9, 11, MP
13) 3, 12, MP
14) 13, Add
15) 14, Com

(9)

1) Pr
2) Pr
3) Pr
4) Pr
5) 3, Simp
6) 3, Com
7) 6, Simp
8) 1, D3
9) 4, D1
10) 2, D2
11) 9, Com
12) 11, 7, DS
13) 5, 12, Conj
14) 13, D4
15) 8, 14, MP
16) 15, D4
17) 16, Simp
18) 10, Simp
19) 17, D3
20) 18, D3
21) 19, 20, HS
22) 21, D3

Group B: (page 198)

(1) $\therefore A$

1)	$(A \equiv B)\cdot B$	Pr
2)	$A \equiv B$	1, Simp
3)	$B\cdot(A \equiv B)$	1, Com
4)	B	3, Simp
5)	$\sim(A\cdot\sim B)\cdot\sim(B\cdot\sim A)$	2, D4
6)	$\sim(B\cdot\sim A)\cdot\sim(A\cdot\sim B)$	5, Com
7)	$\sim(B\cdot\sim A)$	6, Simp
8)	$B \supset A$	7, D3
9)	$\therefore A$	8, 4, MP

(3) $\therefore A \equiv B$

1)	$(A \supset C)\cdot(C \supset B)$	Pr
2)	$B \bigtriangleup \sim A$	Pr
3)	$A \supset C$	1, Simp
4)	$(C \supset B)\cdot(A \supset C)$	1, Com
5)	$C \supset B$	4, Simp
6)	$A \supset B$	3, 5, HS
7)	$\sim(A\cdot\sim B)$	6, D3
8)	$\sim(B\cdot\sim A)\cdot\sim(\sim B\cdot\sim\sim A)$	2, D2
9)	$\sim(B\cdot\sim A)$	8, Simp
10)	$\sim(A\cdot\sim B)\cdot\sim(B\cdot\sim A)$	7, 9, Conj
11)	$\therefore A \equiv B$	10, D4

(5) $\therefore B \equiv A$

1)	$(A \lor \sim B) \supset \sim C$	Pr
2)	$A \bigtriangleup \sim B$	Pr
3)	$(B \supset A) \lor C$	Pr
4)	$\sim(A\cdot\sim B)\cdot\sim(\sim A\cdot\sim\sim B)$	2, D2
5)	$\sim(A\cdot\sim B)$	4, Simp
6)	$\sim(\sim A\cdot\sim\sim B)\cdot\sim(A\cdot\sim B)$	4, Com
7)	$\sim(\sim A\cdot\sim\sim B)$	6, Simp
8)	$A \lor \sim B$	7, D1
9)	$\sim C$	1, 8, MP
10)	$C \lor (B \supset A)$	3, Com
11)	$B \supset A$	10, 9, DS
12)	$\sim(B\cdot\sim A)$	11, D3
13)	$\sim(B\cdot\sim A)\cdot\sim(A\cdot\sim B)$	12, 5, Conj
14)	$\therefore B \equiv A$	13, D4

(7) $\therefore A \equiv D$

1)	$A \bigtriangleup \sim B$	Pr
2)	$B \equiv C$	Pr
3)	$\sim(C\cdot\sim D)\cdot\sim(D\cdot\sim A)$	Pr
4)	$\sim(C\cdot\sim D)$	3, Simp
5)	$\sim(D\cdot\sim A)\cdot\sim(C\cdot\sim D)$	3, Com
6)	$\sim(D\cdot\sim A)$	5, Simp

7)	$C \supset D$	4, D3
8)	$\sim(A \cdot \sim B) \cdot \sim(\sim A \cdot \sim \sim B)$	1, D2
9)	$\sim(B \cdot \sim C) \cdot \sim(C \cdot \sim B)$	2, D4
10)	$\sim(A \cdot \sim B)$	8, Simp
11)	$\sim(B \cdot \sim C)$	9, Simp
12)	$A \supset B$	10, D3
13)	$B \supset C$	11, D3
14)	$A \supset C$	12, 13, HS
15)	$A \supset D$	14, 7, HS
16)	$\sim(A \cdot \sim D)$	15, D3
17)	$\sim(A \cdot \sim D) \cdot \sim(D \cdot \sim A)$	16, 6, Conj
18)	$\therefore A \equiv D$	17, D4

(9)

		$\therefore F \lor C$
1)	$(A \equiv B) \supset C$	Pr
2)	$\sim(A \cdot \sim D) \cdot \sim(B \cdot \sim E)$	Pr
3)	$\sim(D \cdot \sim B) \cdot \sim(E \cdot \sim A)$	Pr
4)	$\sim(A \cdot \sim D)$	2, Simp
5)	$\sim(B \cdot \sim E) \cdot \sim(A \cdot \sim D)$	2, Com
6)	$\sim(B \cdot \sim E)$	5, Simp
7)	$\sim(D \cdot \sim B)$	3, Simp
8)	$\sim(E \cdot \sim A) \cdot \sim(D \cdot \sim B)$	3, Com
9)	$\sim(E \cdot \sim A)$	8, Simp
10)	$A \supset D$	4, D3
11)	$D \supset B$	7, D3
12)	$A \supset B$	10, 11, HS
13)	$\sim(A \cdot \sim B)$	12, D3
14)	$B \supset E$	6, D3
15)	$E \supset A$	9, D3
16)	$B \supset A$	14, 15, HS
17)	$\sim(B \cdot \sim A)$	16, D3
18)	$\sim(A \cdot \sim B) \cdot \sim(B \cdot \sim A)$	13, 17, Conj
19)	$A \equiv B$	18, D4
20)	C	1, 19, MP
21)	$C \lor F$	20, Add
22)	$\therefore F \lor C$	21, Com

Group D: (page 199)

(1)

		$\therefore A$
1)	S	Pr
2)	$S \equiv A$	Pr
3)	$\sim(S \cdot \sim A) \cdot \sim(A \cdot \sim S)$	2, D4
4)	$\sim(S \cdot \sim A)$	3, Simp
5)	$S \supset A$	4, D3
6)	$\therefore A$	5, 1, MP

(3) $\therefore \sim S \equiv P$

   1) $(S \lor P) \cdot (P \supset \sim S)$ Pr

   2) $S \lor P$ 1, Simp

   3) $(P \supset \sim S) \cdot (S \lor P)$ 1, Com

   4) $P \supset \sim S$ 3, Simp

   5) $\sim (\sim S \cdot \sim P)$ 2, D1

   6) $\sim (P \cdot \sim \sim S)$ 4, D3

   7) $\sim (\sim S \cdot \sim P) \cdot \sim (P \cdot \sim \sim S)$ 5, 6, Conj

   8) $\therefore \sim S \equiv P$ 7, D4

(5) $\therefore P \equiv E$

   1) $S \supset (E \supset P)$ Pr

   2) $\sim [(P \cdot \sim E) \cdot \sim P]$ Pr

   3) $\sim P \cdot S$ Pr

   4) $\sim P$ 3, Simp

   5) $S \cdot \sim P$ 3, Com

   6) S 5, Simp

   7) $(P \cdot \sim E) \supset P$ 2, D3

   8) $\sim (P \cdot \sim E)$ 7, 4, MT

   9) $E \supset P$ 1, 6, MP

   10) $\sim (E \cdot \sim P)$ 9, D3

   11) $\sim (P \cdot \sim E) \cdot \sim (E \cdot \sim P)$ 8, 10, Conj

   12) $\therefore P \equiv E$ 11, D4

(7) $\therefore \sim (N \cdot \sim M)$

   1) $\sim [D \cdot \sim (N \equiv H)]$ Pr

   2) $H \triangle \sim M$ Pr

   3) $\sim [\sim D \cdot \sim (H \cdot \sim M)]$ Pr

   4) $D \supset (N \equiv H)$ 1, D3

   5) $D \lor (H \cdot \sim M)$ 3, D1

   6) $\sim (H \cdot \sim M) \cdot \sim (\sim H \cdot \sim \sim M)$ 2, D2

   7) $\sim (H \cdot \sim M)$ 6, Simp

   8) $(H \cdot \sim M) \lor D$ 5, Com

   9) D 8, 7, DS

   10) $N \equiv H$ 4, 9, MP

   11) $\sim (N \cdot \sim H) \cdot \sim (H \cdot \sim N)$ 10, D4

   12) $\sim (N \cdot \sim H)$ 11, Simp

   13) $N \supset H$ 12, D3

   14) $H \supset M$ 7, D3

   15) $N \supset M$ 13, 14, HS

   16) $\therefore \sim (N \cdot \sim M)$ 15, D3

(9) $\therefore S \equiv \sim R$

   1) $\sim (H \cdot \sim F) \cdot \sim (L \cdot \sim D)$ Pr

   2) $\sim (\sim H \cdot \sim L)$ Pr

   3) $\sim (F \cdot \sim S) \cdot \sim (S \cdot \sim \sim R)$ Pr

   4) $\sim (D \cdot \sim R)$ Pr

   5) $\sim (H \cdot \sim F)$ 1, Simp

6)	$\sim(L \cdot \sim D) \cdot \sim (H \cdot \sim F)$	1, Com
7)	$\sim(L \cdot \sim D)$	6, Simp
8)	$\sim(F \cdot \sim S)$	3, Simp
9)	$\sim(S \cdot \sim \sim R) \cdot \sim (F \cdot \sim S)$	3, Com
10)	$\sim(S \cdot \sim \sim R)$	9, Simp
11)	$H \lor L$	2, D1
12)	$D \supset R$	4, D3
13)	$H \supset F$	5, D3
14)	$L \supset D$	7, D3
15)	$F \supset S$	8, D3
16)	$H \supset S$	13, 15, HS
17)	$L \supset R$	14, 12, HS
18)	$S \lor R$	16, 17, 11, CD
19)	$R \lor S$	18, Com
20)	$\sim(\sim R \cdot \sim S)$	19, D1
21)	$\sim(S \cdot \sim \sim R) \cdot \sim (\sim R \cdot \sim S)$	10, 20, Conj
22)	$\therefore S \equiv \sim R$	21, D4

Chapter 7

SECTION 1

Group A: (page 210)

(1)

- 1) Pr
- 2) Pr
- 3) Pr
- 4) Pr
- 5) 4, 3, MT
- 6) 2, 5, MT
- 7) 1, 6, MT
- 8) 7, DN

(3)

- 1) Pr
- 2) Pr
- 3) Pr
- 4) Pr
- 5) 4, DN
- 6) 3, 5, MT
- 7) 6, DN
- 8) 2, 7, MP
- 9) 1, Trans
- 10) 8, Trans
- 11) 9, 10, HS

(5)

1) Pr
2) Pr
3) Pr
4) Pr
5) 1, Simp
6) 1, Com
7) 6, Simp
8) 4, D3
9) 2, 3, MP
10) 5, 7, HS
11) 8, 10, HS
12) 11, Trans
13) 12, 9, HS

(7)

1) Pr
2) 1, Simp
3) 1, Com
4) 3, Simp
5) 2, D3
6) 5, DN
7) 6, Simp
8) 6, Com
9) 8, Simp
10) 4, D1
11) 10, 9, DS
12) 11, Trans
13) 7, D3
14) 12, D3
15) 13, 14, Conj
16) 15, D4

(9)

1) Pr
2) Pr
3) Pr
4) Pr
5) 2, Simp
6) 2, Com
7) 6, Simp
8) 3, Simp
9) 3, Com
10) 9, Simp

11) 10, DN
12) 8, 11, MT
13) 12, DN
14) 5, 13, Conj
15) 1, 14, MP
16) 15, Com
17) 4, 10, MT
18) 16, 17, DS
19) 7, 18, MP

Group B: (page 214)

(1) $\therefore B \supset \sim A$

1) $A \supset \sim B$ Pr
2) $\sim \sim B \supset \sim A$ 1, Trans
3) $\therefore B \supset \sim A$ 2, DN

(3) $\therefore A \supset C$

1) $(A \supset B)\cdot(\sim C \supset \sim B)$ Pr
2) $A \supset B$ 1, Simp
3) $(\sim C \supset \sim B)\cdot(A \supset B)$ 1, Com
4) $\sim C \supset \sim B$ 3, Simp
5) $B \supset C$ 4, Trans
6) $\therefore A \supset C$ 2, 5, HS

(5) $\therefore C \cdot \sim A$

1) $A \equiv \sim B$ Pr
2) $B \cdot C$ Pr
3) $\sim(A \cdot \sim \sim B)\cdot\sim(\sim B \cdot \sim A)$ 1, D4
4) B 2, Simp
5) $C \cdot B$ 2, Com
6) C 5, Simp
7) $\sim(A \cdot \sim \sim B)$ 3, Simp
8) $A \supset \sim B$ 7, D3
9) $\sim \sim B$ 4, DN
10) $\sim A$ 8, 9, MT
11) $\therefore C \cdot \sim A$ 6, 10, Conj

(7) $\therefore D$

1) $A \cdot (B \vee C)$ Pr
2) $B \triangle A$ Pr
3) $C \supset D$ Pr
4) A 1, Simp
5) $(B \vee C)\cdot A$ 1, Com
6) $B \vee C$ 5, Simp
7) $\sim(B \cdot A)\cdot\sim(\sim B \cdot \sim A)$ 2, D2
8) $\sim(B \cdot A)$ 7, Simp

	9)	$\sim(\sim\sim B\cdot A)$	8, DN
	10)	$\sim(\sim\sim B\cdot\sim\sim A)$	9, DN
	11)	$\sim B \vee \sim A$	10, D1
	12)	$\sim A \vee \sim B$	11, Com
	13)	$\sim\sim A$	4, DN
	14)	$\sim B$	12, 13, DS
	15)	C	6, 14, DS
	16)	$\therefore D$	3, 15, MP
(9)			$\therefore D \supset C$
	1)	$\sim[(\sim B \supset \sim A)\cdot C]$	Pr
	2)	$\sim A$	Pr
	3)	$D \supset (\sim C \supset A)$	Pr
	4)	$\sim[(\sim B \supset \sim A)\cdot\sim\sim C]$	1, DN
	5)	$(\sim B \supset \sim A) \supset \sim C$	4, D3
	6)	$(A \supset B) \supset \sim C$	5, Trans
	7)	$\sim A \vee B$	2, Add
	8)	$\sim(\sim\sim A\cdot\sim B)$	7, D1
	9)	$\sim(A\cdot\sim B)$	8, DN
	10)	$A \supset B$	9, D3
	11)	$\sim C$	6, 10, MP
	12)	$\sim C\cdot\sim A$	11, 2, Conj
	13)	$\sim\sim(\sim C\cdot\sim A)$	12, DN
	14)	$\sim(\sim C \supset A)$	13, D3
	15)	$\sim D$	3, 14, MT
	16)	$\sim D \vee C$	15, Add
	17)	$\sim(\sim\sim D\cdot\sim C)$	16, D1
	18)	$\sim(D\cdot\sim C)$	17, DN
	19)	$\therefore D \supset C$	18, D3

Group D: (page 215)

(1)			$\therefore S$
	1)	$\sim S \supset \sim A$	Pr
	2)	A	Pr
	3)	$\sim\sim A$	2, DN
	4)	$\sim\sim S$	1, 3, MT
	5)	$\therefore S$	4, DN
(3)			$\therefore C \supset \sim E$
	1)	$(C \supset D)\cdot(E \supset \sim D)$	Pr
	2)	$C \supset D$	1, Simp
	3)	$(E \supset \sim D)\cdot(C \supset D)$	1, Com
	4)	$E \supset \sim D$	3, Simp
	5)	$\sim\sim D \supset \sim E$	4, Trans
	6)	$D \supset \sim E$	5, DN
	7)	$\therefore C \supset \sim E$	2, 6, HS

(5)

		$\therefore I \supset E$
1)	$\sim(\sim E \cdot C) \cdot \sim(\sim C \cdot I)$	Pr
2)	$\sim(\sim E \cdot C)$	1, Simp
3)	$\sim(\sim C \cdot I) \cdot \sim(\sim E \cdot C)$	1, Com
4)	$\sim(\sim C \cdot I)$	3, Simp
5)	$\sim(\sim E \cdot \sim \sim C)$	2, DN
6)	$\sim(\sim C \cdot \sim \sim I)$	4, DN
7)	$\sim E \supset \sim C$	5, D3
8)	$\sim C \supset \sim I$	6, D3
9)	$\sim E \supset \sim I$	7, 8, HS
10)	$\therefore I \supset E$	9, Trans

(7)

		$\therefore C \equiv W$
1)	$\sim[(C \supset W) \supset I] \cdot \sim[\sim I \cdot \sim(\sim C \supset \sim W)]$	Pr
2)	$\sim[(C \supset W) \supset I]$	1, Simp
3)	$\sim[\sim I \cdot \sim(\sim C \supset \sim W)] \cdot \sim[(C \supset W) \supset I]$	1, Com
4)	$\sim[\sim I \cdot \sim(\sim C \supset \sim W)]$	3, Simp
5)	$\sim\sim[(C \supset W) \cdot \sim I]$	2, D3
6)	$(C \supset W) \cdot \sim I$	5, DN
7)	$I \vee (\sim C \supset \sim W)$	4, D1
8)	$C \supset W$	6, Simp
9)	$\sim I \cdot (C \supset W)$	6, Com
10)	$\sim I$	9, Simp
11)	$\sim C \supset \sim W$	7, 10, DS
12)	$W \supset C$	11, Trans
13)	$\sim(C \cdot \sim W)$	8, D3
14)	$\sim(W \cdot \sim C)$	12, D3
15)	$\sim(C \cdot \sim W) \cdot \sim(W \cdot \sim C)$	13, 14, Conj
16)	$\therefore C \equiv W$	15, D4

(9)

		$\therefore \sim[(P \cdot W) \vee (W \cdot S)]$
1)	$(W \supset \sim E) \cdot (L \supset \sim P)$	Pr
2)	$(S \supset \sim L) \cdot \sim(\sim E \cdot \sim L)$	Pr
3)	$W \supset \sim E$	1, Simp
4)	$(L \supset \sim P) \cdot (W \supset \sim E)$	1, Com
5)	$L \supset \sim P$	4, Simp
6)	$S \supset \sim L$	2, Simp
7)	$\sim(\sim E \cdot \sim L) \cdot (S \supset \sim L)$	2, Com
8)	$\sim(\sim E \cdot \sim L)$	7, Simp
9)	$E \vee L$	8, D1
10)	$\sim\sim E \supset \sim W$	3, Trans
11)	$E \supset \sim W$	10, DN
12)	$\sim W \vee \sim P$	11, 5, 9, CD
13)	$\sim P \vee \sim W$	12, Com

14)	$\sim(\sim\sim P\cdot\sim\sim W)$	13, D1
15)	$\sim(P\cdot\sim\sim W)$	14, DN
16)	$\sim(P\cdot W)$	15, DN
17)	$\sim\sim L\supset\ \sim S$	6, Trans
18)	$L\supset\ \sim S$	17, DN
19)	$\sim W\vee\sim S$	11, 18, 9, CD
20)	$\sim(\sim\sim W\cdot\sim\sim S)$	19, D1
21)	$\sim(W\cdot\sim\sim S)$	20, DN
22)	$\sim(W\cdot S)$	21, DN
23)	$\sim(P\cdot W)\cdot\sim(W\cdot S)$	16, 22, Conj
24)	$\sim\sim[\sim(P\cdot W)\cdot\sim(W\cdot S)]$	23, DN
25)	$\therefore\ \sim[(P\cdot W)\vee(W\cdot S)]$	24, D1

SECTION 2

Group A: (page 217)

(1)

1) Pr
2) 1, Com
3) 2, Assoc

(3)

1) Pr
2) 1, Com
3) 2, Com
4) 3, Com
5) 4, Assoc
6) 5, Com

(5)

1) Pr
2) Pr
3) 2, Com
4) 1, Com
5) 4, DN
6) 3, 5, DS
7) 6, Add
8) 7, D1
9) 8, DN
10) 9, D3

(7)

1) Pr
2) Pr
3) Pr
4) 3, Trans
5) 4, DN

6) 5, 1, HS
7) 2, Add
8) 7, Add
9) 8, Assoc
10) 9, DN
11) 6, 10, MT
12) 2, 11, Conj
13) 12, DN
14) 13, D3

(9)

1) Pr
2) Pr
3) Pr
4) Pr
5) 2, Simp
6) 2, Com
7) 6, Simp
8) 5, Com
9) 8, D4
10) 9, Simp
11) 10, D3
12) 7, DN
13) 11, 12, MT
14) 1, 13, MT
15) 14, D3
16) 13, Add
17) 16, Com
18) 3, 17, MP
19) 18, D3
20) 4, D2
21) 20, Com
22) 21, Simp
23) 22, D1
24) 23, Com
25) 15, 19, 24, CD

Group B: (page 221)

(1)

		∴ $(C \lor B) \lor (D \lor A)$
1)	$(A \lor B) \lor (C \lor D)$	Pr
2)	$[(A \lor B) \lor C] \lor D$	1, Assoc
3)	$[A \lor (B \lor C)] \lor D$	2, Assoc
4)	$[(B \lor C) \lor A] \lor D$	3, Com
5)	$(B \lor C) \lor (A \lor D)$	4, Assoc
6)	$(C \lor B) \lor (A \lor D)$	5, Com
7)	∴ $(C \lor B) \lor (D \lor A)$	6, Com

(3) $\therefore (D \cdot B) \cdot (C \cdot A)$

   1) $(A \cdot B) \cdot (C \cdot D)$ Pr

   2) $(A \cdot B) \cdot (D \cdot C)$ 1, Com

   3) $[(A \cdot B) \cdot D] \cdot C$ 2, Assoc

   4) $[A \cdot (B \cdot D)] \cdot C$ 3, Assoc

   5) $[(B \cdot D) \cdot A] \cdot C$ 4, Com

   6) $(B \cdot D) \cdot (A \cdot C)$ 5, Assoc

   7) $(D \cdot B) \cdot (A \cdot C)$ 6, Com

   8) $\therefore (D \cdot B) \cdot (C \cdot A)$ 7, Com

(5) $\therefore D \vee C$

   1) $[(A \equiv B) \supset C] \cdot [\sim(B \equiv A) \supset D]$ Pr

   2) $(A \equiv B) \supset C$ 1, Simp

   3) $[\sim(B \equiv A) \supset D] \cdot [(A \equiv B) \supset C]$ 1, Com

   4) $\sim(B \equiv A) \supset D$ 3, Simp

   5) $\sim D \supset \sim\sim(B \equiv A)$ 4, Trans

   6) $\sim D \supset (B \equiv A)$ 5, DN

   7) $\sim D \supset (A \equiv B)$ 6, Com

   8) $\sim D \supset C$ 7, 2, HS

   9) $\sim(\sim D \cdot \sim C)$ 8, D3

  10) $\therefore D \vee C$ 9, D1

(7) $\therefore C \supset (B \supset D)$

   1) $(A \vee \sim B) \vee \sim C$ Pr

   2) $D \cdot (A \supset \sim D)$ Pr

   3) D 2, Simp

   4) $(A \supset \sim D) \cdot D$ 2, Com

   5) $A \supset \sim D$ 4, Simp

   6) $\sim\sim D$ 3, DN

   7) $\sim A$ 5, 6, MT

   8) $A \vee (\sim B \vee \sim C)$ 1, Assoc

   9) $\sim B \vee \sim C$ 8, 7, DS

  10) $(\sim B \vee \sim C) \vee D$ 9, Add

  11) $(\sim C \vee \sim B) \vee D$ 10, Com

  12) $\sim C \vee (\sim B \vee D)$ 11, Assoc

  13) $\sim[\sim\sim C \cdot \sim(\sim B \vee D)]$ 12, D1

  14) $\sim[C \cdot \sim(\sim B \vee D)]$ 13, DN

  15) $C \supset (\sim B \vee D)$ 14, D3

  16) $C \supset \sim(\sim\sim B \cdot \sim D)$ 15, D1

  17) $C \supset \sim(B \cdot \sim D)$ 16, DN

  18) $\therefore C \supset (B \supset D)$ 17, D3

(9) $\therefore B \vee D$

   1) $(\sim A \triangle B) \cdot (D \equiv C)$ Pr

   2) $(E \vee A) \vee (B \vee C)$ Pr

   3) $\sim(E \vee B)$ Pr

   4) $\sim A \triangle B$ 1, Simp

   5) $(D \equiv C) \cdot (\sim A \triangle B)$ 1, Com

6)	$D \equiv C$	5, Simp
7)	$\sim(\sim A \cdot B) \cdot \sim(\sim \sim A \cdot \sim B)$	4, D2
8)	$C \equiv D$	6, Com
9)	$\sim(C \cdot \sim D) \cdot \sim(D \cdot \sim C)$	8, D4
10)	$E \lor [A \lor (B \lor C)]$	2, Assoc
11)	$E \lor [A \lor (C \lor B)]$	10, Com
12)	$E \lor [(A \lor C) \lor B]$	11, Assoc
13)	$E \lor [B \lor (A \lor C)]$	12, Com
14)	$(E \lor B) \lor (A \lor C)$	13, Assoc
15)	$A \lor C$	14, 3, DS
16)	$\sim(\sim \sim A \cdot \sim B) \cdot \sim(\sim A \cdot B)$	7, Com
17)	$\sim(\sim \sim A \cdot \sim B)$	16, Simp
18)	$\sim(A \cdot \sim B)$	17, DN
19)	$A \supset B$	18, D3
20)	$\sim(C \cdot \sim D)$	9, Simp
21)	$C \supset D$	20, D3
22)	$\therefore B \lor D$	19, 21, 15, CD

Group D: (page 222)

(1)

		$\therefore F \lor (W \lor S)$
1)	$(W \lor F) \lor S$	Pr
2)	$(F \lor W) \lor S$	1, Com
3)	$\therefore F \lor (W \lor S)$	2, Assoc

(3)

		$\therefore S \supset D$
1)	$[(\sim S \lor B) \lor D] \cdot \sim B$	Pr
2)	$(\sim S \lor B) \lor D$	1, Simp
3)	$\sim B \cdot [(\sim S \lor B) \lor D]$	1, Com
4)	$\sim B$	3, Simp
5)	$(B \lor \sim S) \lor D$	2, Com
6)	$B \lor (\sim S \lor D)$	5, Assoc
7)	$\sim S \lor D$	6, 4, DS
8)	$\sim(\sim \sim S \cdot \sim D)$	7, D1
9)	$\sim(S \cdot \sim D)$	8, DN
10)	$\therefore S \supset D$	9, D3

(5)

		$\therefore H \supset [G \supset (S \supset P)]$
1)	$\sim\{\sim P \cdot [S \cdot (G \cdot H)]\}$	Pr
2)	$\sim[(\sim P \cdot S) \cdot (G \cdot H)]$	1, Assoc
3)	$\sim[(S \cdot \sim P) \cdot (G \cdot H)]$	2, Com
4)	$\sim[(S \cdot \sim P) \cdot (H \cdot G)]$	3, Com
5)	$\sim[(H \cdot G) \cdot (S \cdot \sim P)]$	4, Com
6)	$\sim\{H \cdot [G \cdot (S \cdot \sim P)]\}$	5, Assoc
7)	$\sim\{H \cdot [G \cdot \sim \sim (S \cdot \sim P)]\}$	6, DN
8)	$\sim\{H \cdot [G \cdot \sim (S \supset P)]\}$	7, D3
9)	$\sim\{H \cdot \sim \sim [G \cdot \sim (S \supset P)]\}$	8, DN
10)	$\sim\{H \cdot \sim [G \supset (S \supset P)]\}$	9, D3
11)	$\therefore H \supset [G \supset (S \supset P)]$	10, D3

(7)

		∴ S
1)	$C \supset (S \triangle H)$	Pr
2)	$\sim(\sim B \cdot H) \cdot (C \cdot \sim B)$	Pr
3)	$\sim(\sim B \cdot H)$	2, Simp
4)	$(C \cdot \sim B) \cdot \sim(\sim B \cdot H)$	2, Com
5)	$C \cdot \sim B$	4, Simp
6)	C	5, Simp
7)	$\sim B \cdot C$	5, Com
8)	$\sim B$	7, Simp
9)	$S \triangle H$	1, 6, MP
10)	$\sim(S \cdot H) \cdot \sim(\sim S \cdot \sim H)$	9, D2
11)	$\sim(\sim S \cdot \sim H) \cdot \sim(S \cdot H)$	10, Com
12)	$\sim(\sim S \cdot \sim H)$	11, Simp
13)	$S \lor H$	12, D1
14)	$H \lor S$	13, Com
15)	$\sim(\sim B \cdot \sim \sim H)$	3, DN
16)	$B \lor \sim H$	15, D1
17)	$\sim H$	16, 8, DS
18)	∴ S	14, 17, DS

(9)

		∴ $(M \lor L) \cdot \sim(R \lor J)$
1)	$(H \equiv R) \supset \sim J$	Pr
2)	$(\sim M \cdot \sim J) \supset L$	Pr
3)	$(H \triangle \sim R) \cdot \sim H$	Pr
4)	$H \triangle \sim R$	3, Simp
5)	$\sim H \cdot (H \triangle \sim R)$	3, Com
6)	$\sim H$	5, Simp
7)	$\sim(H \cdot \sim R) \cdot \sim(\sim H \cdot \sim \sim R)$	4, D2
8)	$\sim(\sim H \cdot \sim \sim R) \cdot \sim(H \cdot \sim R)$	7, Com
9)	$\sim(\sim H \cdot \sim \sim R)$	8, Simp
10)	$H \lor \sim R$	9, D1
11)	$\sim R$	10, 6, DS
12)	$\sim(H \cdot \sim R) \cdot \sim(\sim \sim R \cdot \sim H)$	7, Com
13)	$\sim(H \cdot \sim R) \cdot \sim(R \cdot \sim H)$	12, DN
14)	$H \equiv R$	13, D4
15)	$\sim J$	1, 14, MP
16)	$\sim R \cdot \sim J$	11, 15, Conj
17)	$\sim(R \lor J)$	16, DeM
18)	$\sim(\sim M \cdot \sim J) \lor L$	2, MI
19)	$(M \lor J) \lor L$	18, D1
20)	$(J \lor M) \lor L$	19, Com
21)	$J \lor (M \lor L)$	20, Assoc
22)	$M \lor L$	21, 15, DS
23)	∴ $(M \lor L) \cdot \sim(R \lor J)$	22, 17, Conj

SECTION 3
Group A: (page 226)
(1)

   1) Pr
   2) Pr
   3) 2, Com
   4) 3, DeM
   5) 1, 4, MT

(3)

   1) Pr
   2) Pr
   3) 1, Com
   4) 3, Dist
   5) 4, Com
   6) 5, Simp
   7) 6, Com
   8) 7, 2, DS

(5)

   1) Pr
   2) Pr
   3) 1, Dist
   4) 3, Simp
   5) 4, Com
   6) 5, DeM
   7) 2, Com
   8) 7, 6, DS
   9) 8, 4, Conj
   10) 9, Dist
   11) 11, DeM
   12) 12, DeM

(7)

   1) Pr
   2) Pr
   3) 1, Dist
   4) 3, Simp
   5) 4, DeM
   6) 2, Simp
   7) 2, Com
   8) 7, Simp
   9) 8, Trans
   10) 6, 9, HS
   11) 10, Trans
   12) 11, DN
   13) 12, D1
   14) 5, 13, Conj
   15) 14, D2

(9)

1)	Pr
2)	1, Dist
3)	2, Dist
4)	3, Com
5)	4, Simp
6)	5, Com
7)	6, Dist
8)	7, Dist
9)	8, Com
10)	9, Simp
11)	10, Com
12)	11, Dist
13)	12, Simp
14)	13, Com
15)	14, Com
16)	15, D1
17)	16, DN
18)	17, D3
19)	18, D1
20)	19, DN
21)	20, D3

Group B: (page 230)

(1)

		$\therefore \sim (B \lor A)$
1)	$\sim A \cdot (A \lor \sim B)$	Pr
2)	$\sim A$	1, Simp
3)	$(A \lor \sim B) \cdot \sim A$	1, Com
4)	$A \lor \sim B$	3, Simp
5)	$\sim B$	4, 2, DS
6)	$\sim B \cdot \sim A$	5, 2, Conj
7)	$\therefore \sim (B \lor A)$	6, DeM

(3)

		$\therefore \sim A$
1)	$(A \cdot B) \supset C$	Pr
2)	$\sim C \cdot B$	Pr
3)	$\sim C$	2, Simp
4)	$B \cdot \sim C$	2, Com
5)	B	4, Simp
6)	$\sim (A \cdot B)$	1, 3, MT
7)	$\sim A \lor \sim B$	6, DeM
8)	$\sim B \lor \sim A$	7, Com
9)	$\sim \sim B$	5, DN
10)	$\therefore \sim A$	8, 9, DS

(5)

			$\therefore A \supset C$
	1)	$(\sim A \cdot \sim B) \vee (C \cdot D)$	Pr
	2)	$[(\sim A \cdot \sim B) \vee C] \cdot [(\sim A \cdot \sim B) \vee D]$	1, Dist
	3)	$(\sim A \cdot \sim B) \vee C$	2, Simp
	4)	$C \vee (\sim A \cdot \sim B)$	3, Com
	5)	$(C \vee \sim A) \cdot (C \vee \sim B)$	4, Dist
	6)	$C \vee \sim A$	5, Simp
	7)	$\sim A \vee C$	6, Com
	8)	$\sim (\sim \sim A \cdot \sim C)$	7, D1
	9)	$\sim (A \cdot \sim C)$	8, DN
	10)	$\therefore A \supset C$	9, D3

(7)

			$\therefore \sim (C \cdot D)$
	1)	$(C \supset \sim A) \cdot (D \supset \sim B)$	Pr
	2)	$(A \cdot E) \vee (E \cdot B)$	Pr
	3)	$C \supset \sim A$	1, Simp
	4)	$(D \supset \sim B) \cdot (C \supset \sim A)$	1, Com
	5)	$D \supset \sim B$	4, Simp
	6)	$\sim \sim A \supset \sim C$	3, Trans
	7)	$\sim \sim B \supset \sim D$	5, Trans
	8)	$A \supset \sim C$	6, DN
	9)	$B \supset \sim D$	7, DN
	10)	$(E \cdot A) \vee (E \cdot B)$	2, Com
	11)	$E \cdot (A \vee B)$	10, Dist
	12)	$(A \vee B) \cdot E$	11, Com
	13)	$A \vee B$	12, Simp
	14)	$\sim C \vee \sim D$	8, 9, 13, CD
	15)	$\therefore \sim (C \cdot D)$	14, DeM

(9)

			$\therefore A \supset \sim [(D \cdot B) \vee \sim E]$
	1)	$A \supset [\sim D \vee (\sim B \cdot C)]$	Pr
	2)	$A \supset (E \cdot \Gamma)$	Pr
	3)	$\sim \{A \cdot \sim [\sim D \vee (\sim B \cdot C)]\}$	1, D3
	4)	$\sim \{\sim \sim A \cdot \sim [\sim D \vee (\sim B \cdot C)]\}$	3, DN
	5)	$\sim A \vee [\sim D \vee (\sim B \cdot C)]$	4, D1
	6)	$\sim A \vee [(\sim D \vee \sim B) \cdot (\sim D \vee C)]$	5, Dist
	7)	$[\sim A \vee (\sim D \vee \sim B)] \cdot [\sim A \vee (\sim D \vee C)]$	6, Dist
	8)	$\sim A \vee (\sim D \vee \sim B)$	7, Simp
	9)	$\sim [A \cdot \sim (E \cdot F)]$	2, D3
	10)	$\sim [\sim \sim A \cdot \sim (E \cdot F)]$	9, DN
	11)	$\sim A \vee (E \cdot F)$	10, D1
	12)	$(\sim A \vee E) \cdot (\sim A \vee F)$	11, Dist
	13)	$\sim A \vee E$	12, Simp
	14)	$[\sim A \vee (\sim D \vee \sim B)] \cdot (\sim A \vee E)$	8, 13, Conj
	15)	$\sim A \vee [(\sim D \vee \sim B) \cdot E]$	14, Dist
	16)	$\sim A \vee [\sim (D \cdot B) \cdot E]$	15, DeM
	17)	$\sim \{\sim \sim A \cdot \sim [\sim (D \cdot B) \cdot E]\}$	16, D1

18)	$\sim\{A\cdot\sim[\sim(D\cdot B)\cdot E]\}$	17, DN
19)	$A \supset [\sim(D\cdot B)\cdot E]$	18, D3
20)	$A \supset [\sim(D\cdot B)\cdot \sim\sim E]$	19, DN
21)	$\therefore A \supset \sim[(D\cdot B) \vee \sim E]$	20, DeM

Group D: (page 231)

(1) | | | $\therefore \sim E \vee S$ |
|---|---|---|
| 1) | C | Pr |
| 2) | $\sim(E\cdot C) \vee S$ | Pr |
| 3) | $(\sim E \vee \sim C) \vee S$ | 2, DeM |
| 4) | $(\sim C \vee \sim E) \vee S$ | 3, Com |
| 5) | $\sim C \vee (\sim E \vee S)$ | 4, Assoc |
| 6) | $\sim\sim C$ | 1, DN |
| 7) | $\therefore \sim E \vee S$ | 5, 6, DS |

(3) | | | $\therefore O \supset P$ |
|---|---|---|
| 1) | $P \triangle (H\cdot \sim O)$ | Pr |
| 2) | $\sim[P\cdot(H\cdot \sim O)]\cdot \sim[\sim P\cdot \sim(H\cdot \sim O)]$ | 1, D2 |
| 3) | $\sim[\sim P\cdot \sim(H\cdot \sim O)]\cdot \sim[P\cdot(H\cdot \sim O)]$ | 2, Com |
| 4) | $\sim[\sim P\cdot \sim(H\cdot \sim O)]$ | 3, Simp |
| 5) | $P \vee (H\cdot \sim O)$ | 4, D1 |
| 6) | $P \vee (\sim O\cdot H)$ | 5, Com |
| 7) | $(P \vee \sim O)\cdot(P \vee H)$ | 6, Dist |
| 8) | $P \vee \sim O$ | 7, Simp |
| 9) | $\sim O \vee P$ | 8, Com |
| 10) | $\sim(\sim\sim O\cdot \sim P)$ | 9, D1 |
| 11) | $\sim(O\cdot \sim P)$ | 10, DN |
| 12) | $\therefore O \supset P$ | 11, D3 |

(5) | | | $\therefore I \equiv A$ |
|---|---|---|
| 1) | $S \supset \sim(A\cdot \sim I)$ | Pr |
| 2) | $\sim[\sim(A \vee P)\cdot I]$ | Pr |
| 3) | $S\cdot \sim P$ | Pr |
| 4) | S | 3, Simp |
| 5) | $\sim P\cdot S$ | 3, Com |
| 6) | $\sim P$ | 5, Simp |
| 7) | $\sim[\sim(A \vee P)\cdot \sim\sim I]$ | 2, DN |
| 8) | $(A \vee P) \vee \sim I$ | 7, D1 |
| 9) | $(P \vee A) \vee \sim I$ | 8, Com |
| 10) | $P \vee (A \vee \sim I)$ | 9, Assoc |
| 11) | $A \vee \sim I$ | 10, 6, DS |
| 12) | $\sim(A\cdot \sim I)$ | 1, 4, MP |
| 13) | $\sim I \vee A$ | 11, Com |
| 14) | $\sim(\sim\sim I\cdot \sim A)$ | 13, D1 |
| 15) | $\sim(I\cdot \sim A)$ | 14, DN |
| 16) | $\sim(I\cdot \sim A)\cdot \sim(A\cdot \sim I)$ | 15, 12, Conj |
| 17) | $\therefore I \equiv A$ | 16, D4 |

(7) $\therefore I \triangle M$

   1) $\sim (I \equiv \sim M) \supset S$ Pr

   2) $I \supset (S \supset \sim C)$ Pr

   3) $\sim (\sim I \vee \sim C)$ Pr

   4) $\sim \sim (I \cdot C)$ 3, DeM

   5) $I \cdot C$ 4, DN

   6) I 5, Simp

   7) $C \cdot I$ 5, Com

   8) C 7, Simp

   9) $S \supset \sim C$ 2, 6, MP

 10) $\sim \sim C$ 8, DN

 11) $\sim S$ 9, 10, MT

 12) $\sim \sim (I \equiv \sim M)$ 1, 11, MT

 13) $I \equiv \sim M$ 12, DN

 14) $\sim (I \cdot \sim \sim M) \cdot \sim (\sim M \cdot \sim I)$ 13, D4

 15) $\sim (I \cdot M) \cdot \sim (\sim M \cdot \sim I)$ 14, DN

 16) $\sim (I \cdot M) \cdot \sim (\sim I \cdot \sim M)$ 15, Com

 17) $\therefore I \triangle M$ 16, D2

(9) $\therefore A \equiv R$

   1) $\sim (\sim A \triangle \sim R)$ Pr

   2) $\sim [\sim (\sim A \cdot \sim R) \cdot \sim (\sim \sim A \cdot \sim \sim R)]$ 1, D2

   3) $(\sim A \cdot \sim R) \vee (\sim \sim A \cdot \sim \sim R)$ 2, D1

   4) $(\sim A \cdot \sim R) \vee (A \cdot \sim \sim R)$ 3, DN

   5) $(\sim A \cdot \sim R) \vee (A \cdot R)$ 4, DN

   6) $(A \cdot R) \vee (\sim A \cdot \sim R)$ 5, Com

   7) $[(A \cdot R) \vee \sim A] \cdot [(A \cdot R) \vee \sim R]$ 6, Dist

   8) $(A \cdot R) \vee \sim A$ 7, Simp

   9) $[(A \cdot R) \vee \sim R] \cdot [(A \cdot R) \vee \sim A]$ 7, Com

 10) $(A \cdot R) \vee \sim R$ 9, Simp

 11) $\sim A \vee (A \cdot R)$ 8, Com

 12) $\sim R \vee (A \cdot R)$ 10, Com

 13) $\sim A \vee (R \cdot A)$ 11, Com

 14) $(\sim A \vee R) \cdot (\sim A \vee A)$ 13, Dist

 15) $\sim A \vee R$ 14, Simp

 16) $(\sim R \vee A) \cdot (\sim R \vee R)$ 12, Dist

 17) $\sim R \vee A$ 16, Simp

 18) $\sim (\sim \sim A \cdot \sim R)$ 15, D1

 19) $\sim (A \cdot \sim R)$ 18, DN

 20) $\sim (\sim \sim R \cdot \sim A)$ 17, D1

 21) $\sim (R \cdot \sim A)$ 20, DN

 22) $\sim (A \cdot \sim R) \cdot \sim (R \cdot \sim A)$ 19, 21, Conj

 23) $\therefore A \equiv R$ 22, D4

SECTION 4

Group A: (page 237)

(1)
    1) Pr
    2) Pr
    3) 1, Com
    4) 3, Exp
    5) 4, 2, MP

(3)
    1) Pr
    2) Pr
    3) 1, Trans
    4) 3, Exp
    5) 2, 4, HS
    6) 5, MI
    7) 6, DN
    8) 7, Taut

(5)
    1) Pr
    2) Pr
    3) 1, Exp
    4) 2, Com
    5) 4, Exp
    6) 3, 5, HS
    7) 6, Exp
    8) 7, Assoc
    9) 8, Taut
   10) 9, Exp

(7)
    1) Pr
    2) Pr
    3) Pr
    4) 1, D4
    5) 2, D4
    6) 4, Com
    7) 6, Simp
    8) 7, D3
    9) 3, DN
   10) 8, 9, MT
   11) 10, DN
   12) 5, Simp
   13) 12, D3
   14) 13, 11, MP
   15) 14, Add
   16) 15, DN
   17) 16, MI

(9)

1)	Pr	
2)	Pr	
3)	1, MI	
4)	3, D3	
5)	4, DN	
6)	5, DN	
7)	6, Dist	
8)	7, Com	
9)	8, Simp	
10)	9, Com	
11)	10, Dist	
12)	11, Simp	
13)	12, Com	
14)	13, MI	
15)	2, MI	
16)	15, Dist	
17)	16, Com	
18)	17, Simp	
19)	18, MI	
20)	14, 19, HS	

Group B: (page 240)

(1) $\therefore C$

1)	$(A \supset B) \supset C$	Pr
2)	$\sim A$	Pr
3)	$\sim A \lor B$	2, Add
4)	$A \supset B$	3, MI
5)	$\therefore C$	1, 4, MP

(3) $\therefore A \supset C$

1)	$A \supset B$	Pr
2)	$(A \cdot B) \supset C$	Pr
3)	$(B \cdot A) \supset C$	2, Com
4)	$B \supset (A \supset C)$	3, Exp
5)	$A \supset (A \supset C)$	1, 4, HS
6)	$(A \cdot A) \supset C$	5, Exp
7)	$\therefore A \supset C$	6, Taut

(5) $\therefore B \triangle C$

1)	$\sim(A \cdot B) \supset C$	Pr
2)	$\sim B$	Pr
3)	$\sim \sim(A \cdot B) \lor C$	1, MI
4)	$(A \cdot B) \lor C$	3, DN
5)	$C \lor (A \cdot B)$	4, Com
6)	$C \lor (B \cdot A)$	5, Com
7)	$(C \lor B) \cdot (C \lor A)$	6, Dist
8)	$C \lor B$	7, Simp

9)	$B \lor C$	8, Com
10)	$\sim(\sim B \cdot \sim C)$	9, D1
11)	$\sim B \lor \sim C$	2, Add
12)	$\sim(B \cdot C)$	11, DeM
13)	$\sim(B \cdot C) \cdot \sim(\sim B \cdot \sim C)$	12, 10, Conj
14)	$\therefore B \triangle C$	13, D2

(7) $\therefore C \supset D$

1)	$A \supset (B \supset D)$	Pr
2)	$C \supset (B \supset A)$	Pr
3)	$\sim B \supset \sim C$	Pr
4)	$(C \cdot B) \supset A$	2, Exp
5)	$(C \cdot B) \supset (B \supset D)$	4, 1, HS
6)	$[(C \cdot B) \cdot B] \supset D$	5, Exp
7)	$[C \cdot (B \cdot B)] \supset D$	6, Assoc
8)	$(C \cdot B) \supset D$	7, Taut
9)	$(B \cdot C) \supset D$	8, Com
10)	$B \supset (C \supset D)$	9, Exp
11)	$C \supset B$	3, Trans
12)	$C \supset (C \supset D)$	11, 10, HS
13)	$(C \cdot C) \supset D$	12, Exp
14)	$\therefore C \supset D$	13, Taut

(9) $\therefore A \supset (B \cdot D)$

1)	$(C \cdot A) \supset (C \cdot B)$	Pr
2)	$(C \cdot D) \lor (\sim A \cdot C)$	Pr
3)	$(C \cdot D) \lor (C \cdot \sim A)$	2, Com
4)	$C \cdot (D \lor \sim A)$	3, Dist
5)	C	4, Simp
6)	$(D \lor \sim A) \cdot C$	4, Com
7)	$D \lor \sim A$	6, Simp
8)	$\sim A \lor D$	7, Com
9)	$C \supset [A \supset (C \cdot B)]$	1, Exp
10)	$A \supset (C \cdot B)$	9, 5, MP
11)	$\sim A \lor (C \cdot B)$	10, MI
12)	$\sim A \lor (B \cdot C)$	11, Com
13)	$(\sim A \lor B) \cdot (\sim A \lor C)$	12, Dist
14)	$\sim A \lor B$	13, Simp
15)	$(\sim A \lor B) \cdot (\sim A \lor D)$	14, 8, Conj
16)	$\sim A \lor (B \cdot D)$	15, Dist
17)	$\therefore A \supset (B \cdot D)$	16, MI

Group D: (page 241)

(1) $\therefore M \supset D$

1)	$M \supset (F \supset D)$	Pr
2)	F	Pr

3)	$(M \cdot F) \supset D$	1, Exp
4)	$(F \cdot M) \supset D$	3, Com
5)	$F \supset (M \supset D)$	4, Exp
6)	$\therefore M \supset D$	5, 2, MP

(3) $\therefore P \supset C$

1)	$\sim U \supset \sim P$	Pr
2)	$(U \cdot \sim C) \supset \sim P$	Pr
3)	$P \supset U$	1, Trans
4)	$U \supset (\sim C \supset \sim P)$	2, Exp
5)	$P \supset (\sim C \supset \sim P)$	3, 4, HS
6)	$P \supset (P \supset C)$	5, Trans
7)	$(P \cdot P) \supset C$	6, Exp
8)	$\therefore P \supset C$	7, Taut

(5) $\therefore E \vee L$

1)	$\sim(E \vee L) \supset (D \cdot S)$	Pr
2)	$D \supset (\sim L \supset \sim S)$	Pr
3)	$D \supset (S \supset L)$	2, Trans
4)	$(D \cdot S) \supset L$	3, Exp
5)	$\sim(E \vee L) \supset L$	1, 4, HS
6)	$(\sim E \cdot \sim L) \supset L$	5, DeM
7)	$\sim E \supset (\sim L \supset L)$	6, Exp
8)	$\sim E \supset (\sim \sim L \vee L)$	7, MI
9)	$\sim E \supset (L \vee L)$	8, DN
10)	$\sim E \supset L$	9, Taut
11)	$\sim \sim E \vee L$	10, MI
12)	$\therefore E \vee L$	11, DN

(7) $\therefore E \supset \sim J$

1)	$(E \supset L) \cdot [\sim(\sim F \supset \sim E) \supset \sim L]$	Pr
2)	$\sim(J \cdot F) \vee \sim J$	Pr
3)	$E \supset L$	1, Simp
4)	$[\sim(\sim F \supset \sim E) \supset \sim L] \cdot (E \supset L)$	1, Com
5)	$\sim(\sim F \supset \sim E) \supset \sim L$	4, Simp
6)	$L \supset (\sim F \supset \sim E)$	5, Trans
7)	$L \supset (E \supset F)$	6, Trans
8)	$E \supset (E \supset F)$	3, 7, HS
9)	$(E \cdot E) \supset F$	8, Exp
10)	$E \supset F$	9, Taut
11)	$(\sim J \vee \sim F) \vee \sim J$	2, DeM
12)	$\sim J \vee (\sim J \vee \sim F)$	11, Com
13)	$(\sim J \vee \sim J) \vee \sim F$	12, Assoc
14)	$\sim J \vee \sim F$	13, Taut
15)	$\sim F \vee \sim J$	14, Com
16)	$F \supset \sim J$	15, MI
17)	$\therefore E \supset \sim J$	10, 16, HS

(9) $\therefore M \supset (S \vee L)$

1)	$(V \vee T) \supset (S \vee L)$	Pr
2)	$(M \vee L) \supset (T \cdot L)$	Pr
3)	$\sim(V \vee T) \vee (S \vee L)$	1, MI
4)	$(\sim V \cdot \sim T) \vee (S \vee L)$	3, DeM
5)	$(S \vee L) \vee (\sim V \cdot \sim T)$	4, Com
6)	$(S \vee L) \vee (\sim T \cdot \sim V)$	5, Com
7)	$[(S \vee L) \vee \sim T] \cdot [(S \vee L) \vee \sim V]$	6, Dist
8)	$(S \vee L) \vee \sim T$	7, Simp
9)	$\sim T \vee (S \vee L)$	8, Com
10)	$T \supset (S \vee L)$	9, MI
11)	$\sim(M \vee L) \vee (T \cdot L)$	2, MI
12)	$[\sim(M \vee L) \vee T] \cdot [\sim(M \vee L) \vee L]$	11, Dist
13)	$\sim(M \vee L) \vee T$	12, Simp
14)	$(M \vee L) \supset T$	13, MI
15)	$(M \vee L) \supset (S \vee L)$	14, 10, HS
16)	$\sim(M \vee L) \vee (S \vee L)$	15, MI
17)	$(\sim M \cdot \sim L) \vee (S \vee L)$	16, DeM
18)	$(S \vee L) \vee (\sim M \cdot \sim L)$	17, Com
19)	$[(S \vee L) \vee \sim M] \cdot [(S \vee L) \vee \sim L]$	18, Dist
20)	$(S \vee L) \vee \sim M$	19, Simp
21)	$\sim M \vee (S \vee L)$	20, Com
22)	$\therefore M \supset (S \vee L)$	21, MI

Chapter 8

SECTION 1

Group A: (page 249)

(10) $\therefore \sim(V \cdot W)$

1)	$(T \supset W) \supset \sim V$	Pr
2)	$\sim\sim V \supset \sim(T \supset W)$	1, Trans
3)	$V \supset \sim(T \supset W)$	2, DN
4)	$V \supset \sim\sim(T \cdot \sim W)$	3, D3
5)	$V \supset (T \cdot \sim W)$	4, DN
6)	$\sim V \vee (T \cdot \sim W)$	5, MI
7)	$\sim V \vee (\sim W \cdot T)$	6, Com
8)	$(\sim V \vee \sim W) \cdot (\sim V \vee T)$	7, Dist
9)	$\sim V \vee \sim W$	8, Simp
10)	$\therefore \sim(V \cdot W)$	9, DeM

Group B: (page 249)

(1) $\therefore O \supset \sim E$

1)	$\sim[\sim(\sim R \supset \sim D) \cdot \sim E]$	Pr
2)	$\sim D$	Pr
3)	$O \supset (E \supset D)$	Pr

	4)	O	CP, $\therefore \sim E$
	5)	$E \supset D$	3, 4, MP
	6)	$\sim E$	5, 2, MT
	7)	$\therefore O \supset \sim E$	4–6, CP
(3)			$\therefore (F \lor E) \supset M$
	1)	$[F \supset (M \cdot E)] \cdot [E \supset (C \cdot M)]$	Pr
	2)	$F \lor E$	CP, $\therefore M$
	3)	$F \supset (M \cdot E)$	1, Simp
	4)	$[E \supset (C \cdot M)] \cdot [F \supset (M \cdot E)]$	1, Com
	5)	$E \supset (C \cdot M)$	4, Simp
	6)	$(M \cdot E) \lor (C \cdot M)$	3, 5, 2, CD
	7)	$(M \cdot E) \lor (M \cdot C)$	6, Com
	8)	$M \cdot (E \lor C)$	7, Dist
	9)	M	8, Simp
	10)	$\therefore (F \lor E) \supset M$	2–9, CP
(5)			$\therefore \sim K \supset \sim A$
	1)	$\sim (I \cdot \sim K)$	Pr
	2)	$\sim (C \cdot \sim \sim A) \cdot \sim (\sim I \cdot \sim C)$	Pr
	3)	$\sim K$	CP, $\therefore \sim A$
	4)	$\sim (C \cdot \sim \sim A)$	2, Simp
	5)	$\sim (\sim I \cdot \sim C) \cdot \sim (C \cdot \sim \sim A)$	2, Com
	6)	$\sim (\sim I \cdot \sim C)$	5, Simp
	7)	$I \supset K$	1, D3
	8)	$C \supset \sim A$	4, D3
	9)	$I \lor C$	6, D1
	10)	$K \lor \sim A$	7, 8, 9, CD
	11)	$\sim A$	10, 3, DS
	12)	$\therefore \sim K \supset \sim A$	3–11, CP
(7)			$\therefore I \supset \sim C$
	1)	$[I \supset (P \supset A)] \cdot [I \supset (A \supset P)]$	Pr
	2)	$(A \equiv P) \supset \sim C$	Pr
	3)	I	CP, $\therefore \sim C$
	4)	$I \supset (P \supset A)$	1, Simp
	5)	$[I \supset (A \supset P)] \cdot [I \supset (P \supset A)]$	1, Com
	6)	$I \supset (A \supset P)$	5, Simp
	7)	$P \supset A$	4, 3, MP
	8)	$A \supset P$	6, 3, MP
	9)	$\sim (P \cdot \sim A)$	7, D3
	10)	$\sim (A \cdot \sim P)$	8, D3
	11)	$\sim (A \cdot \sim P) \cdot \sim (P \cdot \sim A)$	10, 9, Conj
	12)	$A \equiv P$	11, D4
	13)	$\sim C$	2, 12, MP
	14)	$\therefore I \supset \sim C$	3–13, CP
(9)			$\therefore G \supset (D \supset F)$
	1)	$(\sim G \cdot T) \lor [(G \cdot \sim D) \lor (S \cdot F)]$	Pr

2)	G	CP, $\therefore$ $D \supset F$
3)	D	CP, $\therefore$ F
4)	$G \lor \sim T$	2, Add
5)	$\sim (\sim G \cdot \sim \sim T)$	4, D1
6)	$\sim (\sim G \cdot T)$	5, DN
7)	$(G \cdot \sim D) \lor (S \cdot F)$	1, 6, DS
8)	$D \lor \sim G$	3, Add
9)	$\sim G \lor D$	8, Com
10)	$\sim (\sim \sim G \cdot \sim D)$	9, D1
11)	$\sim (G \cdot \sim D)$	10, DN
12)	$S \cdot F$	7, 11, DS
13)	$F \cdot S$	12, Com
14)	F	13, Simp
15)	$D \supset F$	3–14, CP
16)	$\therefore$ $G \supset (D \supset F)$	2–15, CP

SECTION 2

Group A: (page 256)

(1)

		$\therefore$ $B \cdot I$
1)	$(B \cdot I) \lor (D \cdot B)$	Pr
2)	$\sim D$	Pr
3)	$\sim (B \cdot I)$	IP
4)	$D \cdot B$	1, 3, DS
5)	D	4, Simp
6)	$D \lor (B \cdot I)$	5, Add
7)	$\therefore$ $B \cdot I$	6, 2, DS

(3)

		$\therefore$ $L \cdot D$
1)	$D \equiv T$	Pr
2)	$T \cdot L$	Pr
3)	$\sim (L \cdot D)$	IP
4)	T	2, Simp
5)	$L \cdot T$	2, Com
6)	L	5, Simp
7)	$\sim L \lor \sim D$	3, DeM
8)	$\sim \sim L$	6, DN
9)	$\sim D$	7, 8, DS
10)	$\sim (D \cdot \sim T) \cdot \sim (T \cdot \sim D)$	1, D4
11)	$\sim (T \cdot \sim D) \cdot \sim (D \cdot \sim T)$	10, Com
12)	$\sim (T \cdot \sim D)$	11, Simp
13)	$T \supset D$	12, D3
14)	D	13, 4, MP
15)	$D \lor (L \cdot D)$	14, Add
16)	$\therefore$ $L \cdot D$	15, 9, DS

(5)

		$\therefore \sim (\sim C \lor \sim A)$
1)	$(A \cdot W) \lor (D \cdot A)$	Pr
2)	$(D \lor W) \supset C$	Pr
3)	$\sim \sim (\sim C \lor \sim A)$	IP
4)	$\sim C \lor \sim A$	3, DN
5)	$(A \cdot W) \lor (A \cdot D)$	1, Com
6)	$A \cdot (W \lor D)$	5, Dist
7)	A	6, Simp
8)	$(W \lor D) \cdot A$	6, Com
9)	$W \lor D$	8, Simp
10)	$\sim A \lor \sim C$	4, Com
11)	$\sim \sim A$	7, DN
12)	$\sim C$	10, 11, DS
13)	$D \lor W$	9, Com
14)	C	2, 13, MP
15)	$C \lor \sim (\sim C \lor \sim A)$	14, Add
16)	$\therefore \sim (\sim C \lor \sim A)$	15, 12, DS

(7)

		$\therefore \sim F \equiv H$
1)	$\sim (F \cdot S) \supset (B \cdot F)$	Pr
2)	$\sim H \lor \sim F$	Pr
3)	$\sim (\sim F \equiv H)$	IP
4)	$\sim [\sim (\sim F \cdot \sim H) \cdot \sim (H \cdot \sim \sim F)]$	3, D4
5)	$(\sim F \cdot \sim H) \lor (H \cdot \sim \sim F)$	4, D1
6)	$\sim \sim (F \cdot S) \lor (B \cdot F)$	1, MI
7)	$(F \cdot S) \lor (B \cdot F)$	6, DN
8)	$(F \cdot S) \lor (F \cdot B)$	7, Com
9)	$F \cdot (S \lor B)$	8, Dist
10)	F	9, Simp
11)	$F \lor H$	10, Add
12)	$\sim (\sim F \cdot \sim H)$	11, D1
13)	$H \cdot \sim \sim F$	5, 12, DS
14)	$\sim F \lor \sim H$	2, Com
15)	$\sim \sim F \cdot H$	13, Com
16)	$\sim \sim F$	15, Simp
17)	H	13, Simp
18)	$\sim H$	14, 16, DS
19)	$H \lor (\sim F \equiv H)$	17, Add
20)	$\therefore \sim F \equiv H$	19, 18, DS

(9)

		$\therefore C \supset \sim I$
1)	$(C \cdot D) \supset [I \supset (L \cdot S)]$	Pr
2)	$\sim (D \supset S)$	Pr

3)	$\sim(C \supset \sim I)$	IP
4)	$\sim\sim(D \cdot \sim S)$	2, D3
5)	$D \cdot \sim S$	4, DN
6)	D	5, Simp
7)	$\sim S \cdot D$	5, Com
8)	$\sim S$	7, Simp
9)	$\sim\sim(C \cdot \sim \sim I)$	3, D3
10)	$C \cdot \sim \sim I$	9, DN
11)	$C \cdot I$	10, DN
12)	C	11, Simp
13)	$I \cdot C$	11, Com
14)	I	13, Simp
15)	$C \cdot D$	12, 6, Conj
16)	$I \supset (L \cdot S)$	1, 15, MP
17)	$L \cdot S$	16, 14, MP
18)	$S \cdot L$	17, Com
19)	S	18, Simp
20)	$S \vee (C \supset \sim I)$	19, Add
21)	$\therefore C \supset \sim I$	20, 8, DS

Group B: (page 258)

(1) $\qquad\qquad\qquad\qquad\qquad\qquad\qquad \therefore C \supset \sim E$

1)	$(C \supset D) \cdot (E \supset \sim D)$	Pr
2)	C	CP, $\therefore \sim E$
3)	$\sim\sim E$	IP
4)	$C \supset D$	1, Simp
5)	$(E \supset \sim D) \cdot (C \supset D)$	1, Com
6)	$E \supset \sim D$	5, Simp
7)	E	3, DN
8)	D	4, 2, MP
9)	$\sim D$	6, 7, MP
10)	$D \vee \sim E$	8, Add
11)	$\sim E$	10, 9, DS
12)	$\therefore C \supset \sim E$	2–11, CP

(3) $\qquad\qquad\qquad\qquad\qquad\qquad\qquad \therefore (W \cdot M) \supset S$

1)	$(C \triangle L) \supset S$	Pr
2)	$\sim(L \equiv \sim C) \supset \sim W$	Pr
3)	$W \cdot M$	CP, $\therefore S$
4)	$\sim S$	IP
5)	$\sim(C \triangle L)$	1, 4, MT
6)	W	3, Simp
7)	$\sim\sim W$	6, DN
8)	$\sim\sim(L \equiv \sim C) \cdot$	2, 7, MT
9)	$L \equiv \sim C$	8, DN
10)	$\sim(L \cdot \sim \sim C) \cdot \sim(\sim C \cdot \sim L)$	9, D4
11)	$\sim(L \cdot C) \cdot \sim(\sim C \cdot \sim L)$	10, DN
12)	$\sim(C \cdot L) \cdot \sim(\sim C \cdot \sim L)$	11, Com
13)	$C \triangle L$	12, D2
14)	$(C \triangle L) \vee S$	13, Add
15)	S	14, 5, DS
16)	$\therefore (W \cdot M) \supset S$	3–15, CP

(5)

			$\therefore (E \cdot R) \supset W$
1)	$\sim (E \cdot \sim W) \vee (D \cdot E)$	Pr	
2)	$D \supset (E \cdot \sim R)$	Pr	
3)	$E \cdot R$	CP, $\therefore W$	
4)	$\sim W$	IP	
5)	E	3, Simp	
6)	$R \cdot E$	3, Com	
7)	R	6, Simp	
8)	$E \cdot \sim W$	5, 4, Conj	
9)	$\sim \sim (E \cdot \sim W)$	8, DN	
10)	$D \cdot E$	1, 9, DS	
11)	D	10, Simp	
12)	$E \cdot \sim R$	2, 11, MP	
13)	$\sim R \cdot E$	12, Com	
14)	$\sim R$	13, Simp	
15)	$R \vee W$	7, Add	
16)	W	15, 14, DS	
17)	$\therefore (E \cdot R) \supset W$	3–16, CP	

SECTION 3

Group A: (page 260)

(1)

			$\therefore \sim G \vee P$
1)	$G \triangle E$	Pr	
2)	$\sim (G \cdot \sim E)$	Pr	
3)	$\sim E \vee G$	Pr	
4)	$\sim G$	Pr	
5)	$\sim (G \cdot E) \cdot \sim (\sim G \cdot \sim E)$	1, D2	
6)	$\sim (\sim G \cdot \sim E) \cdot \sim (G \cdot E)$	5, Com	
7)	$\sim (\sim G \cdot \sim E)$	6, Simp	
8)	$G \vee E$	7, D1	
9)	$G \vee \sim E$	3, Com	
10)	$\sim E$	9, 4, DS	
11)	$E \vee G$	8, Com	
12)	G	11, 10, DS	
13)	$G \vee (\sim G \vee P)$	12, Add	
14)	$\therefore \sim G \vee P$	13, 4, DS	

Group B: (page 260)

(1)

			$\therefore L \supset \sim P$
1)	$(P \triangle O) \vee L$	Pr	
2)	$P \cdot O$	Pr	
3)	$\sim L$	Pr	
4)	$L \vee (P \triangle O)$	1, Com	

5)	$P \triangle O$	4, 3, DS
6)	$\sim(P \cdot O) \cdot \sim(\sim P \cdot \sim O)$	5, D2
7)	$\sim(P \cdot O)$	6, Simp
8)	$(P \cdot O) \lor (L \supset \sim Q)$	2, Add
9)	$\therefore L \supset \sim P$	8, 7, DS

(3) $\therefore O \lor D$

1)	$L \lor O$	Pr
2)	$\sim(\sim O \supset L)$	Pr
3)	$\sim\sim(\sim O \cdot \sim L)$	2, D3
4)	$\sim O \cdot \sim L$	3, DN
5)	$\sim O$	4, Simp
6)	$O \lor L$	1, Com
7)	L	6, 5, DS
8)	$\sim L \cdot \sim O$	4, Com
9)	$\sim L$	8, Simp
10)	$L \lor (O \lor D)$	7, Add
11)	$\therefore O \lor D$	10, 9, DS

(5) $\therefore \sim L \cdot (A \supset M)$

1)	$V \supset M$	Pr
2)	$V \cdot \sim A$	Pr
3)	$L \supset \sim(V \supset A)$	Pr
4)	$M \supset A$	Pr
5)	V	2, Simp
6)	$\sim A \cdot V$	2, Com
7)	$\sim A$	6, Simp
8)	M	1, 5, MP
9)	$\sim M$	4, 7, MT
10)	$M \lor [\sim L \cdot (A \supset M)]$	8, Add
11)	$\therefore \sim L \cdot (A \supset M)$	10, 9, DS

(7) $\therefore \sim E$

1)	$(P \cdot \sim A) \supset S$	Pr
2)	$\sim(\sim P \cdot \sim S)$	Pr
3)	$\sim A \cdot \sim S$	Pr
4)	$S \supset \sim E$	Pr
5)	$\sim A$	3, Simp
6)	$\sim S \cdot \sim A$	3, Com
7)	$\sim S$	6, Simp
8)	$\sim(P \cdot \sim A)$	1, 7, MT
9)	$P \supset A$	8, D3
10)	$\sim P$	9, 5, MT
11)	$P \lor S$	2, D1
12)	S	11, 10, DS
13)	$S \lor \sim E$	12, Add
14)	$\therefore \sim E$	13, 7, DS

(9) $\therefore F \cdot I$

1)	$(F \cdot \sim I) \supset (I \vee E)$	Pr
2)	$E \supset \sim(M \vee V)$	Pr
3)	$\sim I \vee \sim(M \vee V)$	Pr
4)	$F \cdot V$	Pr
5)	F	4, Simp
6)	$V \cdot F$	4, Com
7)	V	6, Simp
8)	$V \vee M$	7, Add
9)	$M \vee V$	8, Com
10)	$\sim \sim(M \vee V)$	9, DN
11)	$\sim(M \vee V) \vee \sim I$	3, Com
12)	$\sim I$	11, 10, DS
13)	$F \cdot \sim I$	5, 12, Conj
14)	$I \vee E$	1, 13, MP
15)	E	14, 12, DS
16)	$\sim E$	2, 10, MT
17)	$E \vee (F \cdot I)$	15, Add
18)	$\therefore F \cdot I$	17, 16, DS

SECTION 4   (page 265)

(1) $(P \cdot E) \supset [(D \vee P) \cdot E]$

1)	$P \cdot E$	CP, $\therefore (D \vee P) \cdot E$
2)	P	1, Simp
3)	$E \cdot P$	1, Com
4)	E	3, Simp
5)	$P \vee D$	2, Add
6)	$D \vee P$	5, Com
7)	$(D \vee P) \cdot E$	6, 4, Conj
8)	$(P \cdot E) \supset [(D \vee P) \cdot E]$	1–7, CP

(3) $(T \supset E) \supset [(T \cdot F) \supset (E \cdot F)]$

1)	$T \supset E$	CP, $\therefore (T \cdot F) \supset (E \cdot F)$
2)	$T \cdot F$	CP, $\therefore E \cdot F$
3)	T	2, Simp
4)	$F \cdot T$	2, Com
5)	F	4, Simp
6)	E	1, 3, MP
7)	$E \cdot F$	6, 5, Conj
8)	$(T \cdot F) \supset (E \cdot F)$	2–7, CP
9)	$(T \supset E) \supset [(T \cdot F) \supset (E \cdot F)]$	1–8, CP

(5) $(R \supset S) \supset [(R \lor K) \supset (S \lor K)]$

1)	$R \supset S$	CP, $\therefore$ $(R \lor K) \supset (S \lor K)$
2)	$R \lor K$	CP, $\therefore$ $S \lor K$
3)	$K \lor R$	2, Com
4)	$\sim\sim K \lor R$	3, DN
5)	$\sim K \supset R$	4, MI
6)	$\sim K \supset S$	5, 1, HS
7)	$\sim\sim K \lor S$	6, MI
8)	$K \lor S$	7, DN
9)	$S \lor K$	8, Com
10)	$(R \lor K) \supset (S \lor K)$	2–9, CP
11)	$(R \supset S) \supset [(R \lor K) \supset (S \lor K)]$	1–10, CP

(7) $C \lor (\sim S \supset \sim C)$

1)	$\sim[C \lor (\sim S \supset \sim C)]$	IP
2)	$\sim C \cdot \sim(\sim S \supset \sim C)$	1, DeM
3)	$\sim C$	2, Simp
4)	$\sim(\sim S \supset \sim C) \cdot \sim C$	2, Com
5)	$\sim(\sim S \supset \sim C)$	4, Simp
6)	$\sim\sim(\sim S \cdot \sim\sim C)$	5, D3
7)	$\sim S \cdot \sim\sim C$	6, DN
8)	$\sim\sim C \cdot \sim S$	7, Com
9)	$\sim\sim C$	8, Simp
10)	$\sim C \lor [C \lor (\sim S \supset \sim C)]$	3, Add
11)	$C \lor (\sim S \supset \sim C)$	10, 9, DS

(9) $P \lor [E \supset (S \lor \sim P)]$

1)	$\sim\{P \lor [E \supset (S \lor \sim P)]\}$	IP
2)	$\sim P \cdot \sim[E \supset (S \lor \sim P)]$	1, DeM
3)	$\sim P$	2, Simp
4)	$\sim[E \supset (S \lor \sim P)] \cdot \sim P$	2, Com
5)	$\sim[E \supset (S \lor \sim P)]$	4, Simp
6)	$\sim\sim[E \cdot \sim(S \lor \sim P)]$	5, D3
7)	$E \cdot \sim(S \lor \sim P)$	6, DN
8)	$\sim(S \lor \sim P) \cdot E$	7, Com
9)	$\sim(S \lor \sim P)$	8, Simp
10)	$\sim S \cdot \sim\sim P$	9, DeM
11)	$\sim\sim P \cdot \sim S$	10, Com
12)	$\sim\sim P$	11, Simp
13)	$\sim P \lor \{P \lor [E \supset (S \lor \sim P)]\}$	3, Add
14)	$P \lor [E \supset (S \lor \sim P)]$	13, 12, DS

SECTION 5   (page 267)

(1) a) $H \supset (L \supset S)$
   b) $L \supset (H \supset S)$

		$\therefore L \supset (H \supset S)$
1)	$H \supset (L \supset S)$	Pr
2)	$(H \cdot L) \supset S$	1, Exp
3)	$(L \cdot H) \supset S$	2, Com
4)	$\therefore L \supset (H \supset S)$	3, Exp
		$\therefore H \supset (L \supset S)$
1)	$L \supset (H \supset S)$	Pr
2)	$(L \cdot H) \supset S$	1, Exp
3)	$(H \cdot L) \supset S$	2, Com
4)	$\therefore H \supset (L \supset S)$	3, Exp

(3) a) $\sim (I \equiv M)$
   b) $(I \cdot \sim M) \vee (\sim I \cdot M)$

		$\therefore (I \cdot \sim M) \vee (\sim I \cdot M)$
1)	$\sim (I \equiv M)$	Pr
2)	$\sim [\sim (I \cdot \sim M) \cdot \sim (M \cdot \sim I)]$	1, D4
3)	$(I \cdot \sim M) \vee (M \cdot \sim I)$	2, D1
4)	$\therefore (I \cdot \sim M) \vee (\sim I \cdot M)$	3, Com
		$\therefore \sim (I \equiv M)$
1)	$(I \cdot \sim M) \vee (\sim I \cdot M)$	Pr
2)	$(I \cdot \sim M) \vee (M \cdot \sim I)$	1, Com
3)	$\sim [\sim (I \cdot \sim M) \cdot \sim (M \cdot \sim I)]$	2, D1
4)	$\therefore \sim (I \equiv M)$	3, D4

(5) a) $(A \vee M) \cdot \sim (M \cdot A)$
   b) $(A \supset \sim M) \cdot (M \vee A)$

		$\therefore (A \supset \sim M) \cdot (M \vee A)$
1)	$(A \vee M) \cdot \sim (M \cdot A)$	Pr
2)	$(A \vee M) \cdot (\sim M \vee \sim A)$	1, DeM
3)	$(A \vee M) \cdot (\sim A \vee \sim M)$	2, Com
4)	$(A \vee M) \cdot (A \supset \sim M)$	3, MI
5)	$(A \supset \sim M) \cdot (A \vee M)$	4, Com
6)	$\therefore (A \supset \sim M) \cdot (M \vee A)$	5, Com
		$\therefore (A \vee M) \cdot \sim (M \cdot A)$
1)	$(A \supset \sim M) \cdot (M \vee A)$	Pr
2)	$\sim (A \cdot \sim \sim M) \cdot (M \vee A)$	1, D3
3)	$\sim (A \cdot M) \cdot (M \vee A)$	2, DN
4)	$\sim (M \cdot A) \cdot (M \vee A)$	3, Com
5)	$(M \vee A) \cdot \sim (M \cdot A)$	4, Com
6)	$\therefore (A \vee M) \cdot \sim (M \cdot A)$	5, Com

(7) a) $D \equiv E$
     b) $\sim D \equiv \sim E$

$\qquad\qquad\qquad\qquad\qquad\qquad\qquad$ $\therefore \sim D \equiv \sim E$

1)	$D \equiv E$	Pr
2)	$\sim(D \cdot \sim E) \cdot \sim(E \cdot \sim D)$	1, D4
3)	$\sim(\sim \sim D \cdot \sim E) \cdot \sim(E \cdot \sim D)$	2, DN
4)	$\sim(\sim \sim D \cdot \sim E) \cdot \sim(\sim \sim E \cdot \sim D)$	3, DN
5)	$\sim(\sim \sim E \cdot \sim D) \cdot \sim(\sim \sim D \cdot \sim E)$	4, Com
6)	$\sim(\sim D \cdot \sim \sim E) \cdot \sim(\sim \sim D \cdot \sim E)$	5, Com
7)	$\sim(\sim D \cdot \sim \sim E) \cdot \sim(\sim E \cdot \sim \sim D)$	6, Com
8)	$\therefore \sim D \equiv \sim E$	7, D4

$\qquad\qquad\qquad\qquad\qquad\qquad\qquad$ $\therefore D \equiv E$

1)	$\sim D \equiv \sim E$	Pr
2)	$\sim(\sim D \cdot \sim \sim E) \cdot \sim(\sim E \cdot \sim \sim D)$	1, D4
3)	$\sim(\sim D \cdot E) \cdot \sim(\sim E \cdot \sim \sim D)$	2, DN
4)	$\sim(\sim D \cdot E) \cdot \sim(\sim E \cdot D)$	3, DN
5)	$\sim(E \cdot \sim D) \cdot \sim(\sim E \cdot D)$	4, Com
6)	$\sim(E \cdot \sim D) \cdot \sim(D \cdot \sim E)$	5, Com
7)	$\sim(D \cdot \sim E) \cdot \sim(E \cdot \sim D)$	6, Com
8)	$\therefore D \equiv E$	7, D4

(9) a) $(J \equiv S) \supset C$
     b) $(S \supset J) \supset [C \lor (J \cdot \sim S)]$

$\qquad\qquad\qquad\qquad\qquad\qquad\qquad$ $\therefore (S \supset J) \supset [C \lor (J \cdot \sim S)]$

1)	$(J \equiv S) \supset C$	Pr
2)	$[\sim(J \cdot \sim S) \cdot \sim(S \cdot \sim J)] \supset C$	1, D4
3)	$[(J \supset S) \cdot \sim(S \cdot \sim J)] \supset C$	2, D3
4)	$[(J \supset S) \cdot (S \supset J)] \supset C$	3, D3
5)	$[(S \supset J) \cdot (J \supset S)] \supset C$	4, Com
6)	$(S \supset J) \supset [(J \supset S) \supset C]$	5, Exp
7)	$(S \supset J) \supset [\sim C \supset \sim(J \supset S)]$	6, Trans
8)	$(S \supset J) \supset [\sim \sim C \lor \sim(J \supset S)]$	7, MI
9)	$(S \supset J) \supset [C \lor \sim(J \supset S)]$	8, DN
10)	$(S \supset J) \supset [C \lor \sim \sim(J \cdot \sim S)]$	9, D3
11)	$\therefore (S \supset J) \supset [C \lor (J \cdot \sim S)]$	10, DN

$\qquad\qquad\qquad\qquad\qquad\qquad\qquad$ $\therefore (J \equiv S) \supset C$

1)	$(S \supset J) \supset [C \lor (J \cdot \sim S)]$	Pr
2)	$(S \supset J) \supset [C \lor \sim \sim(J \cdot \sim S)]$	1, DN
3)	$(S \supset J) \supset [C \lor \sim(J \supset S)]$	2, D3
4)	$(S \supset J) \supset [\sim \sim C \lor \sim(J \supset S)]$	3, DN
5)	$(S \supset J) \supset [\sim C \supset \sim(J \supset S)]$	4, MI
6)	$(S \supset J) \supset [(J \supset S) \supset C]$	5, Trans
7)	$[(S \supset J) \cdot (J \supset S)] \supset C$	6, Exp
8)	$[(J \supset S) \cdot (S \supset J)] \supset C$	7, Com
9)	$[\sim(J \cdot \sim S) \cdot (S \supset J)] \supset C$	8, D3
10)	$[\sim(J \cdot \sim S) \cdot \sim(S \cdot \sim J)] \supset C$	9, D3
11)	$\therefore (J \equiv S) \supset C$	10, D4

Chapter 9

T2: '$p \supset (p \lor q)$' is a theorem.

Proof:

1) $\sim p \lor (p \lor q)$ A2
2) $p \supset (p \lor q)$ 1, D2

T4: '$(p \supset q) \supset [(r \lor p) \supset (r \lor q)]$' is a theorem.

Proof:

1) $\sim(\sim p \lor q) \lor [\sim(r \lor p) \lor (r \lor q)]$ A4
2) $(\sim p \lor q) \supset [\sim(r \lor p) \lor (r \lor q)]$ 1, D2
3) $(p \supset q) \supset [\sim(r \lor p) \lor (r \lor q)]$ 2, D2
4) $(p \supset q) \supset [(r \lor p) \supset (r \lor q)]$ 3, D2

DRI 2: If '$p \lor q$' is a theorem, then '$q \lor p$' is also a theorem.

Derivation:

1) $p \lor q$ Assump
2) $(p \lor q) \supset (q \lor p)$ T3
3) $q \lor p$ 2, 1, MP

T10: '$(p \cdot q) \supset p$' is a theorem.

Proof:

1) T2
2) 1, $(\sim p/p, \sim q/q)$
3) 2, D2
4) 3, DRI 2
5) 4, $[\sim\sim(\sim p \lor \sim q)/(\sim p \lor \sim q)]$
6) 5, D1
7) 6, D2
8) T9
9) 7, 8, HS

DRI 5 (Add): If 'p' is a theorem and 'q' any wff, then '$p \lor q$' is also a theorem.

Derivation:

1) p Assump
2) $p \supset (p \lor q)$ T2
3) $p \lor q$ 2, 1, MP

DRI 7 (Conj): If 'p' and 'q' are theorems, then '$p \cdot q$' is also a theorem.

Derivation:

1) Assump
2) Assump
3) T2
4) 3, $(\sim\sim q/p, \sim p/q)$
5) T8
6) 5, (q/p)
7) 6, 4, HS
8) 7, 2, MP
9) 8, D2

10)   9, DRI 3
11)   10, DRI 6
12)   T1
13)   12, $(\sim p/p)$
14)   13, DRI 6
15)   T8
16)   15, 14, HS
17)   16, 1, MP
18)   11, 17, MP
19)   18, D1

DRI 8: If 'p' is a theorem, then '$\sim \sim p$' is also a theorem.

Derivation:

1) p Assump
2) $p \supset \sim \sim p$ T8
3) $\sim \sim p$ 2, 1, MP

T13 (DN): '$p \equiv \sim \sim p$' is a theorem.

Proof:

1) $p \supset \sim \sim p$ T8
2) $\sim \sim p \supset p$ T9
3) $\sim p \lor \sim \sim p$ 1, D2
4) $\sim \sim \sim p \lor p$ 2, D2
5) $(\sim p \lor \sim \sim p) \cdot (\sim \sim \sim p \lor p)$ 3, 4, Conj
6) $\sim [\sim (\sim p \lor \sim \sim p) \lor \sim (\sim \sim \sim p \lor p)]$ 5, D1
7) $p \equiv \sim \sim p$ 6, D3

DRI 11 (CD): If '$p \supset q$', '$r \supset s$', and '$p \lor r$' are theorems, then '$q \lor s$' is also a theorem.

Derivation:

1) $p \supset q$ Assump
2) $r \supset s$ Assump
3) $p \lor r$ Assump
4) $\sim \sim p \lor r$ 3, $(\sim \sim p/p)$
5) $\sim p \supset r$ 4, MI
6) $\sim q \supset \sim p$ 1, DRI 6
7) $\sim q \supset r$ 6, 5, HS
8) $\sim q \supset s$ 7, 2, HS
9) $\sim \sim q \lor s$ 8, D2
10) $q \lor s$ 9, DN

DRI 14: If '$p \lor p$' is a theorem, then 'p' is also a theorem.

Derivation:

1) $p \lor p$ Assump
2) $(p \lor p) \supset p$ T1
3) p 2, 1, MP

T15 (Taut): '$p \equiv (p \cdot p)$' is a theorem.

Proof:

1)	$(p \lor p) \supset p$	T1
2)	$(\sim p \lor \sim p) \supset \sim p$	1, $(\sim p/p)$
3)	$\sim \sim p \supset \sim(\sim p \lor \sim p)$	2, DRI 6
4)	$p \supset \sim(\sim p \lor \sim p)$	3, DN
5)	$p \supset (p \cdot p)$	4, D1
6)	$\sim p \lor (p \cdot p)$	5, D2
7)	$(p \cdot q) \supset p$	T10
8)	$(p \cdot p) \supset p$	7, (p/q)
9)	$\sim(p \cdot p) \lor p$	8, D2
10)	$[\sim p \lor (p \cdot p)] \cdot [\sim(p \cdot p) \lor p]$	6, 9, Conj
11)	$\sim\{\sim[\sim p \lor (p \cdot p)] \lor \sim[\sim(p \cdot p) \lor p]\}$	10, D1
12)	$p \equiv (p \cdot p)$	11, D3

T17 (Com): '$(p \cdot q) \equiv (q \cdot p)$' is a theorem.

Proof:

1)	$(p \cdot q) \supset (q \cdot p)$	T12
2)	$(q \cdot p) \supset (p \cdot q)$	1, $(q/p, p/q)$
3)	$\sim(p \cdot q) \lor (q \cdot p)$	1, D2
4)	$\sim(q \cdot p) \lor (p \cdot q)$	2, D2
5)	$[\sim(p \cdot q) \lor (q \cdot p)] \cdot [\sim(q \cdot p) \lor (p \cdot q)]$	3, 4, Conj
6)	$\sim\{\sim[\sim(p \cdot q) \lor (q \cdot p)] \lor \sim[\sim(q \cdot p) \lor (p \cdot q)]\}$	5, D1
7)	$(p \cdot q) \equiv (q \cdot p)$	6, D3

T19 (Trans): '$(p \supset q) \equiv (\sim q \supset \sim p)$' is a theorem.

Proof:

1)	$(p \supset q) \supset (\sim q \supset \sim p)$	T11
2)	$(\sim q \supset \sim p) \supset (\sim \sim p \supset \sim \sim q)$	1, $(\sim q/p, \sim p/q)$
3)	$(\sim q \supset \sim p) \supset (p \supset \sim \sim q)$	2, DN
4)	$(\sim q \supset \sim p) \supset (p \supset q)$	3, DN
5)	$\sim(p \supset q) \lor (\sim q \supset \sim p)$	1, D2
6)	$\sim(\sim q \supset \sim p) \lor (p \supset q)$	4, D2
7)	$[\sim(p \supset q) \lor (\sim q \supset \sim p)] \cdot [\sim(\sim q \supset \sim p) \lor (p \supset q)]$	5, 6, Conj
8)	$\sim\{\sim[\sim(p \supset q) \lor (\sim q \supset \sim p)] \lor \sim[\sim(\sim q \supset \sim p) \lor (p \supset q)]\}$	7, D1
9)	$(p \supset q) \equiv (\sim q \supset \sim p)$	8, D3

DRI 16:   If '$p \equiv q$' is a theorem and 'r' any wff, then '$(r \lor p) \equiv (r \lor q)$' is also a theorem.

Derivation:

1)	$p \equiv q$	Assump
2)	$\sim[\sim(\sim p \lor q) \lor \sim(\sim q \lor p)]$	1, D3
3)	$(\sim p \lor q) \cdot (\sim q \lor p)$	2, D1
4)	$\sim p \lor q$	3, Simp
5)	$(\sim q \lor p) \cdot (\sim p \lor q)$	3, Com
6)	$\sim q \lor p$	5, Simp
7)	$p \supset q$	4, D2
8)	$q \supset p$	6, D2

9)	$(r \lor p) \supset (r \lor q)$	7, DRI 3
10)	$(r \lor q) \supset (r \lor p)$	8, DRI 3
11)	$\sim (r \lor p) \lor (r \lor q)$	9, D2
12)	$\sim (r \lor q) \lor (r \lor p)$	10, D2
13)	$[\sim (r \lor p) \lor (r \lor q)] \cdot [\sim (r \lor q) \lor (r \lor p)]$	11, 12, Conj
14)	$\sim \{\sim [\sim (r \lor p) \lor (r \lor q)] \lor \sim [\sim (r \lor q) \lor (r \lor p)]\}$	13, D1
15)	$(r \lor p) \equiv (r \lor q)$	14, D3

T21 (DeM):   '$(p \lor q) \equiv \sim (\sim p \cdot \sim q)$' is a theorem.

Proof:

1)	$(p \lor q) \equiv (q \lor p)$	T16
2)	$(p \lor q) \equiv (p \lor q)$	1, Com
3)	$(p \lor q) \equiv (p \lor \sim \sim q)$	2, DN
4)	$(p \lor q) \equiv (\sim \sim p \lor \sim \sim q)$	3, DN
5)	$(p \lor q) \equiv \sim \sim (\sim \sim p \lor \sim \sim q)$	4, DN
6)	$(p \lor q) \equiv \sim (\sim p \cdot \sim q)$	5, D1

T23 (DeM):   '$(p \cdot q) \equiv \sim (\sim p \lor \sim q)$' is a theorem.

Proof:

1)	$(p \cdot q) \equiv (q \cdot p)$	T17
2)	$(p \cdot q) \equiv (p \cdot q)$	1, Com
3)	$(p \cdot q) \equiv \sim (\sim p \lor \sim q)$	2, D1

T28 (Exp):   '$[(p \cdot q) \supset r] \equiv [p \supset (q \supset r)]$' is a theorem.

Proof:

1)	$[p \lor (q \lor r)] \equiv [(p \lor q) \lor r]$	T26
2)	$[(p \lor q) \lor r] \equiv [p \lor (q \lor r)]$	1, Com
3)	$[(\sim p \lor \sim q) \lor r] \equiv [\sim p \lor (\sim q \lor r)]$	2, $(\sim p/p, \sim q/q)$
4)	$[\sim \sim (\sim p \lor \sim q) \lor r] \equiv [\sim p \lor (\sim q \lor r)]$	3, DN
5)	$[\sim (p \cdot q) \lor r] \equiv [\sim p \lor (\sim q \lor r)]$	4, D1
6)	$[(p \cdot q) \supset r] \equiv [\sim p \lor (\sim q \lor r)]$	5, D2
7)	$[(p \cdot q) \supset r] \equiv [p \supset (\sim q \lor r)]$	6, D2
8)	$[(p \cdot q) \supset r] \equiv [p \supset (q \supset r)]$	7, D2

T29:   '$p \supset [q \supset (p \cdot q)]$' is a theorem.

Proof:

1)	$p \lor \sim p$	T7
2)	$(\sim p \lor \sim q) \lor \sim (\sim p \lor \sim q)$	1, $[(\sim p \lor \sim q)/p]$
3)	$\sim p \lor [\sim q \lor \sim (\sim p \lor \sim q)]$	2, Assoc
4)	$p \supset [\sim q \lor \sim (\sim p \lor \sim q)]$	3, D2
5)	$p \supset [q \supset \sim (\sim p \lor \sim q)]$	4, D2
6)	$p \supset [q \supset (p \cdot q)]$	5, D1

T31 (Dist): '$[p\cdot(q \vee r)] \equiv [(p\cdot q) \vee (p\cdot r)]$' is a theorem.

Proof:

1)	$[p \vee (q\cdot r)] \equiv [(p \vee q)\cdot(p \vee r)]$	T30
2)	$[\sim p \vee (\sim q\cdot \sim r)] \equiv [(\sim p \vee \sim q)\cdot(\sim p \vee \sim r)]$	1,$(\sim p/p, \sim q/q, \sim r/r)$
3)	$[\sim p \vee \sim(\sim \sim q \vee \sim \sim r)] \equiv [(\sim p \vee \sim q)\cdot(\sim p \vee \sim r)]$	2, D1
4)	$[\sim p \vee \sim(q \vee \sim \sim r)] \equiv [(\sim p \vee \sim q)\cdot(\sim p \vee \sim r)]$	3, DN
5)	$[\sim p \vee \sim(q \vee r)] \equiv [(\sim p \vee \sim q)\cdot(\sim p \vee \sim r)]$	4, DN
6)	$[\sim p \vee \sim(q \vee r)] \equiv [\sim(p\cdot q)\cdot(\sim p \vee \sim r)]$	5, DeM
7)	$[\sim p \vee \sim(q \vee r)] \equiv [\sim(p\cdot q)\cdot \sim(p\cdot r)]$	6, DeM
8)	$\sim[\sim p \vee \sim(q \vee r)] \equiv \sim[\sim(p\cdot q)\cdot \sim(p\cdot r)]$	7, DRI 15
9)	$[p\cdot(q \vee r)] \equiv \sim[\sim(p\cdot q)\cdot \sim(p\cdot r)]$	8, DeM
10)	$[p\cdot(q \vee r)] \equiv [(p\cdot q) \vee (p\cdot r)]$	9, DeM

Chapter 10

SECTION 1

Group A: (page 290)

(1) All cowards are cravens. **A**

(3) All cats are grey at night. **A**

(5) Some goals of life are not obtainable by everyone. **O**

(7) Some people who are unloving are not forgiving. **O**

(9) Some professors who are sincere in their work are those who show concern for their students. **I**

(11) All patient persons are God's friends. **A**

(13) Some experiences of life are bitterly absurd. **I**

(15) Some nosy people are lonely fools. **I**

(17) Some people are rewarded by society without any real cause. **I**

(19) No men who are wise and good are those who can suffer real disgrace. **E**

Group B: (page 290)

[U (universal), P (particular), A (affirmative), N (negative)]

(1)	UA	(11)	UA
(3)	UA	(13)	PA
(5)	PN	(15)	PA
(7)	PN	(17)	PA
(9)	PA	(19)	UN

Group C: (page 290)

[ST (subject term), PT (predicate term), SPT (subject and predicate terms), NT (no term)]

(1)	ST	(11)	ST
(3)	ST	(13)	NT
(5)	PT	(15)	NT
(7)	PT	(17)	NT
(9)	NT	(19)	SPT

SECTION 2   (page 294)

(1) a) **A** is true.   b) **A** is false.
            E is false.   **E** is undetermined.
            I is true.   **I** is undetermined.
            O is false.   **O** is true.

(2) **E** is false.
          A is undetermined.
          I is true.
          O is undetermined.

(3) b) **I** is false.
            A is false.
            E is true.
            O is true.

SECTION 3

Group A: (page 303)

(1) a) Some chemical transformations are endothermic.
         b) Some endothermic transformations are chemical.

(3) a) Some chemical substances are not in liquid form.
         b) (No converse of **O** statements.)

(5) a) All energies are those capabilities of a body to bring about changes in other bodies.
         b) Some capabilities of a body to bring about changes in other bodies are energies. (Conversion by limitation.)

Group B: (page 303)

(1) a) All manometers are measurers of vapor.
         b) No manometers are nonmeasurers of vapor.

(3) a) All microbalances are more accurate than analytical ones.
         b) No microbalances are more accurate than nonanalytical ones.

(5) a) Some experiments are those requiring analytical balances.
         b) Some experiments are not those requiring nonanalytical balances.

Group C: (page 303)

(1) a) Some things are nonpolar molecules.
         b) (No contrapositive of **I** statements.)

(3) a) Some molecular structures are not predictable by the "octet rule".
         b) Some things nonpredictable by the "octet rule" are nonmolecular structures.

(5) a) No polar molecules are nonpolar.
         b) Some polar things are nonpolar molecules. (Contraposition by limitation.)

Group D: (page 304)

(1) a) Some chemical substances are homogeneous substances.
         b) Some homogeneous substances are chemical substances. (Conversion.)
         c) Some homogeneous substances are not nonchemical substances. (Obversion.)

(3) a) No chemical substances are phlogistic substances.

b) Some nonphlogistic substances are not nonchemical substances. (Contraposition by limitation.)

c) Some nonphlogistic substances are chemical substances. (Obversion.)

(5) a) All atomic elements are chemical substances.

b) Some chemical substances are atomic elements. (Conversion by limitation.)

c) Some chemical substances are not nonatomic elements. (Obversion.)

SECTION 4

Group A: (page 307)

(1) No living things are nonprotoplasmic.
Some substances are nonprotoplasmic.
So, some substances are not living things.

E I O—2

(3) No things having the ability to metabolize are nonorganic.
All things having the ability to metabolize are protoplasmic.
Accordingly, no protoplasmic things are nonorganic.

E A E—3

(5) All unicellular things are composed of protoplasm.
Some organisms are unicellular things.
Accordingly, some organisms are composed of protoplasm.

A I I—1

(7) No Euglenae are things having an outer cellulose wall.
Some flagellates are not things having an outer cellulose wall.
Thus, some flagellates are not Euglenae.

E O O—2

(9) All Chordae are brown algae.
No things which are brown algae are things which survive in fresh water.
Consequently, no Chordae are things which survive in fresh water.

A E E—4

SECTION 5

Group A: (page 316)

(1)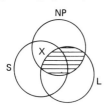

Valid

(3)

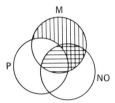

Invalid

(5)

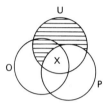

Valid

(7)

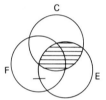

Invalid

(9)

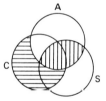

Valid

Group B: (page 316)

(1)   No colonial insects are independent.
All termites are colonial insects.
So, some termites are not independent.

E A O—1

Invalid

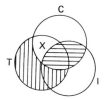

Valid, if we assume
the existence of termites.

(3) Some terrestrial worms are earthworms.
Some annelids are terrestrial worms.
Consequently, some annelids are not earthworms.

I I O—1

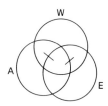

Invalid
There is no existential assumption
making this argument valid.

(5) Some echinoderms are starfish.
All starfish are invertebrates.
Hence, some invertebrates are echinoderms.

I A I—4

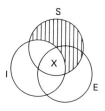

Valid

(7) All penguins are things having flipper-like wings.
Some birds are not things having flipper-like wings.
Thus, some birds are not penguins.

A O O—2

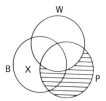

Valid

(9) Some traits present at birth are not inherited.
All traits present at birth are congenital ones.
Therefore, some congenital traits are not inherited.

O A O—3

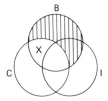

Valid

SECTION 6

Group A: (page 319)

(1) Some metabolic processes are not anabolic.
All organic growth processes are metabolic.
Consequently, some organic growth processes are not anabolic.
O A O—1, invalid, Rule 1.

(3) Some algae are Euglenae.
Some algae are unicellular.
Therefore, some unicellular things are Euglenae.
I I I—3, invalid, Rule 1.

(5) No Euglenae are things having outer cellulose cell walls.
Some flagellates are not things having outer cellulose cell walls.
Thus, some flagellates are not Euglenae.
E O O—2, invalid, Rule 4.

(7) No salts are elements.
No elements are compound substances.
Therefore, some compound substances are salts.
E E I—4, invalid, Rules 4 and 5.

(9) All salts are the chief natural sources of chlorine.
Some compounds such as sodium chloride are salts.
Wherefore, all compounds such as sodium chloride are the chief natural sources of chlorine.
A I A—1, invalid, Rule 2.

Group B: (page 320)

(1) No syllogism with two **O** premisses can be valid (Rule 4). No syllogism with two **I** premisses can be valid (Rule 1). No syllogism with both an **I** and **O** premiss can have an **A** or **I** conclusion (Rule 3). No syllogism having an **I** major premiss and an **O** minor can be valid in Figures 3 and 4 (Rule 1). No syllogism having an **I** major premiss, an **O** minor, an **E** conclusion, and in Figures 1 or 2 can be valid (Rule 2). No syllogism having an **I** major premiss, an **O** minor, an **O** conclusion, and in Figures 1 or 2 can be valid (Rule 2). No syllogism having an **O** major premiss, an **I** minor, and in Figure 1 can be valid (Rule 1). No syllogism having an **O** major premiss, an **I** minor, either an **E** or **O** conclusion, and in Figure 2 can be valid (Rule 2). Hence, our present set of rules is sufficient to establish the invalidity of any syllogism having two particular premisses.

(3) If the conclusion of a syllogism in Figure 3 were an **A** statement, the minor term would have to be distributed in the minor premiss. If the minor term is distributed in the minor premiss, that premiss must be either an **E** or **O** statement. But no valid syllogism can have a positive conclusion if it has a negative premiss (Rule 3). Thus, no valid syllogism in Figure 3 can have an **A** conclusion. On the other hand, if the conclusion of a syllogism in Figure 3 were an **E** statement, then one of the premisses must be negative (Rule 3) and both the major and minor terms must be distributed in the premisses (Rule 2). Since no terms are distributed in an **I** statement, no premiss can be an **I** statement. But, no syllogism can have two **E** premisses (Rule 4). Hence, our present set of rules is sufficient to establish that every valid syllogism of Figure 3 has a particular conclusion.

Chapter 11

SECTION 1

Group A: (page 337)

(1) $Ea \cdot Pa$

(3) $(Fc \cdot Pc) \supset Rc$

(5) $Rm \cdot (Sm \cdot Tm)$

(7) $(Rw \cdot Sw) \supset (Iw \cdot Pw)$

(9) $(Ig \cdot Sg) \cdot (Mg \cdot Eg)$

Group B: (page 337)

(1) $(x)(Bx \supset Ox)$

(3) $(x)(Bx \supset \sim Sx)$

(5) $(x)[Dx \supset (Px \supset \sim Sx)]$

(7) $(\exists x)[Ix \cdot \sim (Px \cdot Sx)]$

(9) $(x)[Ix \supset (Sx \equiv Px)]$

(11) $(\exists x)[(Nx \cdot Px) \cdot (Cx \bigtriangleup Ax)]$

(13) $(x)\{[Px \cdot (Rx \supset Cx)] \supset \sim Tx\}$

(15) $(x)\{(Ex \cdot Fx) \supset [Tx \supset (Ax \equiv Sx)]\}$

(17) $(x)\{[Tx \cdot (Ax \cdot Sx)] \supset \sim(Rx \cdot Lx)\}$

(19) $(\exists x)\{[Ax \vee (Sx \cdot Ex)] \cdot [Ix \supset (Hx \vee Tx)]\}$

Group C: (page 338)

Each of the following is only one of the many English translations.

(1) Certain stimuli are internal to the organism.

(3) Stocks never fluctuate if they remain constant.

(5) Most mammals, which are risible if humans, are linguistic bipeds.

(7) Some chemicals which are acids or bases taste bitter only if they aren't sweet.

(9) No chemical which is either phosphoric or nitric if acid is both slick to the touch and high on the pH scale.

SECTION 2

Group A: (page 346)

(1) $\sim(x)(Wx \supset Jx)$

(3) $\sim Bm \vee (\exists x) Qx$

(5) $(x)(Cx \equiv \sim Qx)$

(7) $(\exists x)Rx \supset (\exists x)[(Ix \cdot Px) \vee Rx]$

(9) $Ws \vee (x)(Rx \supset \sim Wx)$

(11) $(x)[(Px \cdot Rx) \equiv \sim\sim Ex]$

(13) $(x)\{Ax \supset [Gx \equiv \sim(Sx \vee Hx)]\}$

(15) $(\exists x)(Mx \cdot Cx) \supset (\exists x)[(Ex \cdot Cx) \vee Ix]$

(17) $(x)\{[(Mx \vee Wx) \supset Ex] \equiv \sim\sim Cx\}$

(19) $(x)\{[(Px \cdot Ix) \supset Mx] \equiv \sim\sim Tx\}$

Group B: (page 347)

Each of the following is only one of the many English translations.

(1) Not every poet is ethically radical.

(3) T. S. Eliot's views are accepted only if a few men are noble.

(5) Each mammal has lungs only if it also has a blood stream, or certain mammals with lungs don't have a blood stream—but not both.

(7) A substance which is a gas never has a definite boundary of its own or no liquid substance has a definite boundary of its own.

(9) That oxygen or copper expands when heated is a necessary condition for J. P. Goode being correct.

SECTION 3

Group A: (page 357)

(1) $(x)Rxx$

(3) $(\exists x)(y)Rxy$

(5) $(\exists y)(x)Rxy$

(7) $\sim(\exists x)(y)Rxy$

(9) $\sim(\exists x)(\exists y)Rxy$

Group B: (page 357)

(1) $(x)(Nx \supset Sxa)$

(3) $(x)(y)[(Ny \cdot Sxy) \supset Nx]$

(5) $(x)[Nx \supset (\exists y)(Ny \cdot Sxy)]$

(7) $(\exists x)\{Sx \cdot (\exists y)[(Cy \cdot Txy) \cdot \sim Lxy]\}$

(9) $(\exists x)\{[Mx \cdot (\exists y)(Iy \cdot Cxy)] \cdot (\exists z)(Sz \cdot Uxz)\}$

Group C: (page 358)

Each of the following is only one of the many English translations.

(1) A patient person is God's friend.

(3) To err is human.

(5) The silent man still endures injustice.

(7) Those who wrong others wrong themselves.

(9) A friend in need is a friend indeed.

Chapter 12

SECTION 1

Group A: (page 368)

(1)
    1) Pr
    2) Pr
    3) 1, UI
    4) 3, 2, MP

(3)
    1) Pr
    2) Pr
    3) 1, UI
    4) 2, UI
    5) 3, 4, HS

(5)
    1) Pr
    2) Pr
    3) 1, UI
    4) 2, DN
    5) 3, 4, MT
    6) 5, DeM

(7)
    1) Pr
    2) Pr
    3) 1, Simp
    4) 1, Com
    5) 4, Simp

   6) 5, UI
   7) 3, UI
   8) 2, UI
   9) 6, 7, 8, CD
  10) 9, Com
  11) 10, UG

(9)

   1) Pr
   2) Pr
   3) 2, Simp
   4) 2, Com
   5) 4, Simp
   6) 3, UI
   7) 5, UI
   8) 6, 7, HS
   9) 8, UG
  10) 1, 9, MP
  11) 10, UI
  12) 7, 11, HS
  13) 12, UG
  14) 8, 11, HS
  15) 14, UG
  16) 15, 13, Conj

Group B: (page 370)

(1) $\therefore \sim Aa$

   1) $\sim Ba$ Pr

   2) $(x)(Ax \supset Bx)$ Pr

   3) $Aa \supset Ba$ 2, UI

   4) $\therefore \sim Aa$ 3, 1, MT

(3) $\therefore Ca$

   1) $(x)(Ax \supset \sim Bx)$ Pr

   2) Aa Pr

   3) $(x)(Bx \lor Cx)$ Pr

   4) $Aa \supset \sim Ba$ 1, UI

   5) $Ba \lor Ca$ 3, UI

   6) $\sim Ba$ 4, 2, MP

   7) $\therefore Ca$ 5, 6, DS

(5) $\therefore (x)(Ax \supset Bx)$

   1) $(x)[(Ax \cdot \sim Bx) \supset Cx]$ Pr

   2) $(x)(Cx \supset Bx)$ Pr

   3) $(Ax \cdot \sim Bx) \supset Cx$ 1, UI

   4) $Cx \supset Bx$ 2, UI

   5) $(Ax \cdot \sim Bx) \supset Bx$ 3, 4, HS

   6) $Ax \supset (\sim Bx \supset Bx)$ 5, Exp

   7) $Ax \supset (\sim \sim Bx \lor Bx)$ 6, MI

8)		$Ax \supset (Bx \lor Bx)$	7, DN
9)		$Ax \supset Bx$	8, Taut
10)	$\therefore$	$(x)(Ax \supset Bx)$	9, UG

(7) $\therefore \sim Ba$

1)		$(x)[(Ax \cdot Bx) \equiv \sim Cx]$	Pr
2)		$Aa \cdot Ca$	Pr
3)		$(Aa \cdot Ba) \equiv \sim Ca$	1, UI
4)		$\sim[(Aa \cdot Ba) \cdot \sim \sim Ca] \cdot \sim[\sim Ca \cdot \sim (Aa \cdot Ba)]$	3, D4
5)		$\sim[(Aa \cdot Ba) \cdot \sim \sim Ca]$	4, Simp
6)		$(Aa \cdot Ba) \supset \sim Ca$	5, D3
7)		Aa	2, Simp
8)		$Ca \cdot Aa$	2, Com
9)		Ca	8, Simp
10)		$\sim \sim Ca$	9, DN
11)		$\sim(Aa \cdot Ba)$	6, 10, MT
12)		$\sim Aa \lor \sim Ba$	11, DeM
13)		$\sim \sim Aa$	7, DN
14)	$\therefore$	$\sim Ba$	12, 13, DS

(9) $\therefore (x)[Ax \cdot Cx) \supset \sim Dx]$

1)		$(x)\{[Ax \cdot (Bx \lor Cx)] \equiv \sim Dx\}$	Pr
2)		$[Ax \cdot (Bx \lor Cx)] \equiv \sim Dx$	1, UI
3)		$\sim\{[Ax \cdot (Bx \lor Cx)] \cdot \sim \sim Dx\} \cdot \sim\{\sim Dx \cdot \sim[Ax \cdot (Bx \lor Cx)]\}$	2, D4
4)		$\sim\{[Ax \cdot (Bx \lor Cx)] \cdot \sim \sim Dx\}$	3, Simp
5)		$[Ax \cdot (Bx \lor Cx)] \supset \sim Dx$	4, D3
6)		$\sim \sim Dx \supset \sim[Ax \cdot (Bx \lor Cx)]$	5, Trans
7)		$Dx \supset \sim[Ax \cdot (Bx \lor Cx)]$	6, DN
8)		$Dx \supset [\sim Ax \lor \sim (Bx \lor Cx)]$	7, DeM
9)		$Dx \supset [\sim Ax \lor (\sim Bx \cdot \sim Cx)]$	8, DeM
10)		$\sim Dx \lor [\sim Ax \lor (\sim Bx \cdot \sim Cx)]$	9, MI
11)		$\sim Dx \lor [(\sim Ax \lor \sim Bx) \cdot (\sim Ax \lor \sim Cx)]$	10, Dist
12)		$\sim Dx \lor [(\sim Ax \lor \sim Cx) \cdot (\sim Ax \lor \sim Bx)]$	11, Com
13)		$[\sim Dx \lor (\sim Ax \lor \sim Cx)] \cdot [\sim Dx \lor (\sim Ax \lor \sim Bx)]$	12, Dist
14)		$\sim Dx \lor (\sim Ax \lor \sim Cx)$	13, Simp
15)		$(\sim Ax \lor \sim Cx) \lor \sim Dx$	14, Com
16)		$\sim(Ax \cdot Cx) \lor \sim Dx$	15, DeM
17)		$(Ax \cdot Cx) \supset \sim Dx$	16, MI
18)	$\therefore$	$(x)[(Ax \cdot Cx) \supset \sim Dx]$	17, UG

Group D: (page 371)

(1) $\therefore Sc$

1)	$(x)(Lx \supset Tx)$	Pr
2)	$(x)(Tx \supset Sx)$	Pr
3)	Lc	Pr
4)	$Lc \supset Tc$	1, UI

	5)	$Tc \supset Sc$	2, UI
	6)	$Lc \supset Sc$	4, 5, HS
	7)	$\therefore\ Sc$	6, 3, MP
(3)			$\therefore\ (x)(Mx \supset Cx)$
	1)	$(x)(Bx \supset Mx) \supset (x)(Mx \supset Cx)$	Pr
	2)	$(x)(Bx \supset Cx)\cdot(x)(Cx \supset Mx)$	Pr
	3)	$(x)(Bx \supset Cx)$	2, Simp
	4)	$(x)(Cx \supset Mx)\cdot(x)(Bx \supset Cx)$	2, Com
	5)	$(x)(Cx \supset Mx)$	4, Simp
	6)	$Bx \supset Cx$	3, UI
	7)	$Cx \supset Mx$	5, UI
	8)	$Bx \supset Mx$	6, 7, HS
	9)	$(x)(Bx \supset Mx)$	8, UG
	10)	$\therefore\ (x)(Mx \supset Cx)$	1, 9, MP
(5)			$\therefore\ \sim Ie$
	1)	$(x)\{[Sx\cdot(Ix\cdot Cx)] \supset Px\}$	Pr
	2)	$Se\cdot\sim Pe$	Pr
	3)	Ce	Pr
	4)	$[Se\cdot(Ie\cdot Ce)] \supset Pe$	1, UI
	5)	Se	2, Simp
	6)	$\sim Pe\cdot Se$	2, Com
	7)	$\sim Pe$	6, Simp
	8)	$\sim[Se\cdot(Ie\cdot Ce)]$	4, 7, MT
	9)	$\sim Se \lor \sim(Ie\cdot Ce)$	8, DeM
	10)	$\sim\sim Se$	5, DN
	11)	$\sim(Ie\cdot Ce)$	9, 10, DS
	12)	$\sim Ie \lor \sim Ce$	11, DeM
	13)	$\sim Ce \lor \sim Ie$	12, Com
	14)	$\sim\sim Ce$	3, DN
	15)	$\therefore\ \sim Ie$	13, 14, DS
(7)			$\therefore\ \sim(Fa \lor Ta)$
	1)	$(x)\{[Ux\cdot(Fx \lor Ix)] \equiv\ \sim\sim Tx\}$	Pr
	2)	$\sim(Ta \lor \sim Ua)$	Pr
	3)	$[Ua\cdot(Fa \lor Ia)] \equiv\ \sim\sim Ta$	1, UI
	4)	$\sim Ta\cdot\sim\sim Ua$	2, DeM
	5)	$[Ua\cdot(Fa \lor Ia)] \equiv Ta$	3, DN
	6)	$\sim\{[Ua\cdot(Fa \lor Ia)]\cdot\sim Ta\}\cdot\sim\{Ta\cdot\sim[Ua\cdot(Fa \lor Ia)]\}$	5, D4
	7)	$\sim\{[Ua\cdot(Fa \lor Ia)]\cdot\sim Ta\}$	6, Simp
	8)	$[Ua\cdot(Fa \lor Ia)] \supset Ta$	7, D3
	9)	$\sim Ta$	4, Simp
	10)	$\sim[Ua\cdot(Fa \lor Ia)]$	8, 9, MT
	11)	$\sim Ua \lor \sim(Fa \lor Ia)$	10, DeM
	12)	$\sim\sim Ua\cdot\sim Ta$	4, Com
	13)	$\sim\sim Ua$	12, Simp

14)	$\sim (Fa \lor Ia)$	11, 13, DS
15)	$\sim Fa \cdot \sim Ia$	14, DeM
16)	$\sim Fa$	15, Simp
17)	$\sim Fa \cdot \sim Ta$	16, 9, Conj
18)	$\therefore \sim (Fa \lor Ta)$	17, DeM

(9)

		$\therefore (x)(Cx \supset Fx)$
1)	$(x)[(\sim Cx \supset \sim Ux) \supset (Hx \cdot Bx)]$	Pr
2)	$(x)[Bx \supset (Hx \cdot Fx)]$	Pr
3)	$(\sim Cx \supset \sim Ux) \supset (Hx \cdot Bx)$	1, UI
4)	$Bx \supset (Hx \cdot Fx)$	2, UI
5)	$\sim (\sim Cx \supset \sim Ux) \lor (Hx \cdot Bx)$	3, MI
6)	$\sim (\sim Cx \supset \sim Ux) \lor (Bx \cdot Hx)$	5, Com
7)	$[\sim (\sim Cx \supset \sim Ux) \lor Bx] \cdot [\sim (\sim Cx \supset \sim Ux) \lor Hx]$	6, Dist
8)	$\sim (\sim Cx \supset \sim Ux) \lor Bx$	7, Simp
9)	$(\sim Cx \supset \sim Ux) \supset Bx$	8, MI
10)	$\sim Bx \lor (Hx \cdot Fx)$	4, MI
11)	$\sim Bx \lor (Fx \cdot Hx)$	10, Com
12)	$(\sim Bx \lor Fx) \cdot (\sim Bx \lor Hx)$	11, Dist
13)	$\sim Bx \lor Fx$	12, Simp
14)	$Bx \supset Fx$	13, MI
15)	$(\sim Cx \supset \sim Ux) \supset Fx$	9, 14, HS
16)	$\sim Fx \supset \sim (\sim Cx \supset \sim Ux)$	15, Trans
17)	$\sim Fx \supset \sim \sim (\sim Cx \cdot \sim \sim Ux)$	16, D3
18)	$\sim Fx \supset (\sim Cx \cdot \sim \sim Ux)$	17, DN
19)	$\sim \sim Fx \lor (\sim Cx \cdot \sim \sim Ux)$	18, MI
20)	$(\sim \sim Fx \lor \sim Cx) \cdot (\sim \sim Fx \lor \sim \sim Ux)$	19, Dist
21)	$\sim \sim Fx \lor \sim Cx$	20, Simp
22)	$\sim Fx \supset \sim Cx$	21, MI
23)	$Cx \supset Fx$	22, Trans
24)	$\therefore (x)(Cx \supset Fx)$	23, UG

SECTION 2

Group A: (page 375)

(1)

1)	Pr
2)	1, EI
3)	2, Simp
4)	3, Add
5)	2, Com
6)	5, Simp
7)	4, 6, Conj
8)	7, EG

(3)

1) Pr
2) 1, Simp
3) 1, Com
4) 3, Simp
5) 4, EI
6) 2, UI
7) 5, Simp
8) 6, 7, MP
9) 5, Com
10) 9, Simp
11) 8, 10, Conj
12) 11, EG

(5)

1) Pr
2) Pr
3) Pr
4) 2, EI
5) 1, UI
6) 3, UI
7) 4, Simp
8) 4, Com
9) 8, Simp
10) 5, 7, MT
11) 9, DN
12) 6, 11, MT
13) 12, 10, Conj
14) 13, DeM
15) 14, EG

(7)

1) Pr
2) Pr
3) Pr
4) 2, EI
5) 1, UI
6) 3, UI
7) 4, Simp
8) 4, Com
9) 8, Simp
10) 9, DN
11) 5, 10, MT
12) 11, DeM
13) 7, DN
14) 12, 13, DS

15) 7, 14, Conj
16) 6, 15, MP
17) 7, 17, Conj
18) 17, EG

(9)

1) Pr
2) Pr
3) Pr
4) Pr
5) 1, EI
6) 2, UI
7) 3, UI
8) 4, UI
9) 5, Simp
10) 5, Com
11) 10, Simp
12) 11, Simp
13) 11, Com
14) 13, Simp
15) 6, 9, MP
16) 7, Exp
17) 16, 14, MP
18) 8, 12, MT
19) 18, D1
20) 15, 17, 19, CD
21) 20, EG

Group B: (page 379)

(1)

		$\therefore (\exists x) \sim Ax$
1)	$(x)[Ax \supset (Bx \lor Cx)]$	Pr
2)	$(\exists x)(\sim Cx \cdot \sim Bx)$	Pr
3)	$\sim Cx \cdot \sim Bx$	2, EI
4)	$Ax \supset (Bx \lor Cx)$	1, UI
5)	$\sim Bx \cdot \sim Cx$	3, Com
6)	$\sim (Bx \lor Cx)$	5, DeM
7)	$\sim Ax$	4, 6, MT
8)	$\therefore (\exists x) \sim Ax$	7, EG

(3)

		$\therefore (\exists x) \sim Bx$
1)	$(x)[(Ax \cdot Bx) \supset Cx]$	Pr
2)	$(x)(Cx \supset \sim Bx)$	Pr
3)	$(\exists x)Ax$	Pr
4)	Ax	3, EI
5)	$(Ax \cdot Bx) \supset Cx$	1, UI
6)	$Cx \supset \sim Bx$	2, UI

7)	$(Ax \cdot Bx) \supset \sim Bx$	5, 6, HS
8)	$Ax \supset (Bx \supset \sim Bx)$	7, Exp
9)	$Ax \supset (\sim Bx \lor \sim Bx)$	8, MI
10)	$Ax \supset \sim Bx$	9, Taut
11)	$\sim Bx$	10, 4, MP
12)	$\therefore (\exists x) \sim Bx$	11, EG

(5)

		$\therefore (\exists x)(Cx \lor Ax)$
1)	$[(\exists x)Ax \cdot (\exists x)Bx] \supset (\exists x)(Cx \lor Ax)$	Pr
2)	$(x)[Cx \supset (Ax \cdot Bx)]$	Pr
3)	$(x)(Dx \supset Cx)$	Pr
4)	$(\exists x)Dx$	Pr
5)	Dx	4, EI
6)	$Cx \supset (Ax \cdot Bx)$	2, UI
7)	$Dx \supset Cx$	3, UI
8)	$Dx \supset (Ax \cdot Bx)$	7, 6, HS
9)	$Ax \cdot Bx$	8, 5, MP
10)	Ax	9, Simp
11)	$Bx \cdot Ax$	9, Com
12)	Bx	11, Simp
13)	$(\exists x)Ax$	10, EG
14)	$(\exists x)Bx$	12, EG
15)	$(\exists x)Ax \cdot (\exists x)Bx$	13, 14, Conj
16)	$\therefore (\exists x)(Cx \lor Ax)$	1, 15, MP

(7)

		$\therefore (\exists x) \sim (Dx \cdot Ax)$
1)	$(x)[(Ax \cdot Bx) \equiv \sim Cx]$	Pr
2)	$(\exists x)(Cx \cdot Bx)$	Pr
3)	$Cx \cdot Bx$	2, EI
4)	$(Ax \cdot Bx) \equiv \sim Cx$	1, UI
5)	Cx	3, Simp
6)	$Bx \cdot Cx$	3, Com
7)	Bx	6, Simp
8)	$\sim [(Ax \cdot Bx) \cdot \sim \sim Cx] \cdot \sim [\sim Cx \cdot \sim (Ax \cdot Bx)]$	4, D4
9)	$\sim [(Ax \cdot Bx) \cdot \sim \sim Cx]$	8, Simp
10)	$(Ax \cdot Bx) \supset \sim Cx$	9, D3
11)	$\sim \sim Cx$	5, DN
12)	$\sim (Ax \cdot Bx)$	10, 11, MT
13)	$\sim Ax \lor \sim Bx$	12, DeM
14)	$\sim Bx \lor \sim Ax$	13, Com
15)	$\sim \sim Bx$	7, DN
16)	$\sim Ax$	14, 15, DS
17)	$\sim Ax \lor \sim Dx$	16, Add
18)	$\sim Dx \lor \sim Ax$	17, Com
19)	$\sim (Dx \cdot Ax)$	18, DeM
20)	$\therefore (\exists x) \sim (Dx \cdot Ax)$	19, EG

(9)

		∴ (∃x)[~ Ax·(Bx ∨ Ex)]
1)	(x)[Ax ⊃ ~(Bx ⊃ Cx)]	Pr
2)	(x)[Bx ⊃ (Cx ∨ Dx)]	Pr
3)	(∃x)[~ Dx·(Bx △ Ex)]	Pr
4)	~ Dx·(Bx △ Ex)	3, EI
5)	Ax ⊃ ~(Bx ⊃ Cx)	1, UI
6)	Bx ⊃ (Cx ∨ Dx)	2, UI
7)	~ Dx	4, Simp
8)	(Bx △ Ex)· ~ Dx	4, Com
9)	Bx △ Ex	8, Simp
10)	~ Bx ∨ (Cx ∨ Dx)	6, MI
11)	(~ Bx ∨ Cx) ∨ Dx	10, Assoc
12)	Dx ∨ (~ Bx ∨ Cx)	11, Com
13)	~ Bx ∨ Cx	12, 7, DS
14)	Bx ⊃ Cx	13, MI
15)	~ ~(Bx ⊃ Cx)	14, DN
16)	~ Ax	5, 15, MT
17)	~(Bx·Ex)· ~(~ Bx· ~ Ex)	9, D2
18)	~(~ Bx· ~ Ex)· ~(Bx·Ex)	17, Com
19)	~(~ Bx· ~ Ex)	18, Simp
20)	Bx ∨ Ex	19, D1
21)	~ Ax·(Bx ∨ Ex)	16, 20, Conj
22)	∴ (∃x)[~ Ax·(Bx ∨ Ex)]	21, EG

Group D: (page 380)

(1)

		∴ (∃x)(Sx·Mx)
1)	(x)[Sx ⊃ (Mx·Cx)]	Pr
2)	(∃x)Sx	Pr
3)	Sx	2, EI
4)	Sx ⊃ (Mx·Cx)	1, UI
5)	Mx·Cx	4, 3, MP
6)	Mx	5, Simp
7)	Sx·Mx	3, 6, Conj
8)	∴ (∃x)(Sx·Mx)	7, EG

(3)

		∴ (∃x)Bx
1)	(∃x)(Ix ∨ Ux) ⊃ (x)(Ax ⊃ Bx)	Pr
2)	(∃x)(Ix·Ax)	Pr
3)	Ix·Ax	2, EI
4)	Ix	3, Simp
5)	Ax·Ix	3, Com
6)	Ax	5, Simp
7)	Ix ∨ Ux	4, Add
8)	(∃x)(Ix ∨ Ux)	7, EG
9)	(x)(Ax ⊃ Bx)	1, 8, MP
10)	Ax ⊃ Bx	9, UI
11)	Bx	10, 6, MP
12)	∴ (∃x)Bx	11, EG

(5)

		$\therefore\ (\exists x)[(Nx \cdot Bx) \cdot Dx]$
1)	$(x)[Nx \supset (Px \supset Bx)]$	Pr
2)	$(\exists x)[(Px \cdot Nx) \cdot Dx]$	Pr
3)	$(Px \cdot Nx) \cdot Dx$	2, EI
4)	$Nx \supset (Px \supset Bx)$	1, UI
5)	$Px \cdot Nx$	3, Simp
6)	$Dx \cdot (Px \cdot Nx)$	3, Com
7)	Dx	6, Simp
8)	Px	5, Simp
9)	$Nx \cdot Px$	5, Com
10)	Nx	9, Simp
11)	$Px \supset Bx$	4, 10, MP
12)	Bx	11, 8, MP
13)	$Nx \cdot Bx$	10, 12, Conj
14)	$(Nx \cdot Bx) \cdot Dx$	13, 7, Conj
15)	$\therefore\ (\exists x)[(Nx \cdot Bx) \cdot Dx]$	14, EG

(7)

		$\therefore\ (\exists x) \sim (Gx \lor Ix)$
1)	$(x)[(Sx \lor Ix) \supset Dx]$	Pr
2)	$(x)[(Dx \lor Gx) \supset Cx]$	Pr
3)	$(\exists x) \sim Cx$	Pr
4)	$\sim Cx$	3, EI
5)	$(Sx \lor Ix) \supset Dx$	1, UI
6)	$(Dx \lor Gx) \supset Cx$	2, UI
7)	$\sim (Dx \lor Gx)$	6, 4, MT
8)	$\sim Dx \cdot \sim Gx$	7, DeM
9)	$\sim Dx$	8, Simp
10)	$\sim Gx \cdot \sim Dx$	8, Com
11)	$\sim Gx$	10, Simp
12)	$\sim (Sx \lor Ix)$	5, 9, MT
13)	$\sim Sx \cdot \sim Ix$	12, DeM
14)	$\sim Ix \cdot \sim Sx$	13, Com
15)	$\sim Ix$	14, Simp
16)	$\sim Gx \cdot \sim Ix$	11, 15, Conj
17)	$\sim (Gx \lor Ix)$	16, DeM
18)	$\therefore\ (\exists x) \sim (Gx \lor Ix)$	17, EG

(9)

		$\therefore\ (\exists x)[(Px \cdot Hx) \cdot \sim (Rx \lor Ux)]$
1)	$(\exists x)[Px \cdot \sim (Ux \lor Rx)]$	Pr
2)	$(x)[(Px \lor Nx) \supset \sim Fx]$	Pr
3)	$(x)[\sim (Fx \lor Rx) \supset Hx]$	Pr
4)	$Px \cdot \sim (Ux \lor Rx)$	1, EI
5)	$(Px \lor Nx) \supset \sim Fx$	2, UI
6)	$\sim (Fx \lor Rx) \supset Hx$	3, UI
7)	Px	4, Simp
8)	$\sim (Ux \lor Rx) \cdot Px$	4, Com

9)	$\sim(Ux \lor Rx)$	8, Simp
10)	$\sim Ux \cdot \sim Rx$	9, DeM
11)	$\sim Rx \cdot \sim Ux$	10, Com
12)	$\sim Rx$	11, Simp
13)	$Px \lor Nx$	7, Add
14)	$\sim Fx$	5, 13, MP
15)	$\sim Fx \cdot \sim Rx$	14, 12, Conj
16)	$\sim(Fx \lor Rx)$	15, DeM
17)	Hx	6, 16, MP
18)	$Px \cdot Hx$	7, 17, Conj
19)	$\sim(Rx \lor Ux)$	9, Com
20)	$(Px \cdot Hx) \cdot \sim(Rx \lor Ux)$	18, 19, Conj
21)	$\therefore (\exists x)[(Px \cdot Hx) \cdot \sim(Rx \lor Ux)]$	20, EG

SECTION 3 (page 384)

(1-a) $\therefore (x)[(Fx \cdot Dx) \supset (Px \lor \sim Bx)]$

1)	$(x)\{(Dx \cdot Fx) \supset [\sim Px \supset \sim(Sx \lor Bx)]\}$	Pr
2)	$(Dx \cdot Fx) \supset [\sim Px \supset \sim(Sx \lor Bx)]$	1, UI
3)	$Fx \cdot Dx$	CP, $\therefore Px \lor \sim Bx$
4)	$Dx \cdot Fx$	3, Com
5)	$\sim Px \supset \sim(Sx \lor Bx)$	2, 4, MP
6)	$\sim \sim Px \lor \sim(Sx \lor Bx)$	5, MI
7)	$Px \lor \sim(Sx \lor Bx)$	6, DN
8)	$Px \lor (\sim Sx \cdot \sim Bx)$	7, DeM
9)	$Px \lor (\sim Bx \cdot \sim Sx)$	8, Com
10)	$(Px \lor \sim Bx) \cdot (Px \lor \sim Sx)$	9, Dist
11)	$Px \lor \sim Bx$	10, Simp
12)	$(Fx \cdot Dx) \supset (Px \lor \sim Bx)$	3–11, CP
13)	$\therefore (x)[(Fx \cdot Dx) \supset (Px \lor \sim Bx)]$	12, UG

(1-b) $\therefore (x)[(Fx \cdot Dx) \supset (Px \lor \sim Bx)]$

1)	$(x)\{(Dx \cdot Fx) \supset [\sim Px \supset \sim(Sx \lor Bx)]\}$	Pr
2)	$(Dx \cdot Fx) \supset [\sim Px \supset \sim(Sx \lor Bx)]$	1, UI
3)	$(Dx \cdot Fx) \supset [\sim Px \supset (\sim Sx \cdot \sim Bx)]$	2, DeM
4)	$(Dx \cdot Fx) \supset [\sim \sim Px \lor (\sim Sx \cdot \sim Bx)]$	3, MI
5)	$(Dx \cdot Fx) \supset [Px \lor (\sim Sx \cdot \sim Bx)]$	4, DN
6)	$(Dx \cdot Fx) \supset [Px \lor (\sim Bx \cdot \sim Sx)]$	5, Com
7)	$(Dx \cdot Fx) \supset [(Px \lor \sim Bx) \cdot (Px \lor \sim Sx)]$	6, Dist
8)	$\sim(Dx \cdot Fx) \lor [(Px \lor \sim Bx) \cdot (Px \lor \sim Sx)]$	7, MI
9)	$[\sim(Dx \cdot Fx) \lor (Px \lor \sim Bx)] \cdot [\sim(Dx \cdot Fx) \lor (Px \lor \sim Sx)]$	8, Dist
10)	$\sim(Dx \cdot Fx) \lor (Px \lor \sim Bx)$	9, Simp
11)	$\sim(Fx \cdot Dx) \lor (Px \lor \sim Bx)$	10, Com

12)	$(Fx \cdot Dx) \supset (Px \lor \sim Bx)$	11, MI
13)	$\therefore (x)[(Fx \cdot Dx) \supset (Px \lor \sim Bx)]$	12, UG

(3-a) $\therefore (x)[Bx \supset (Dx \cdot Ex)]$

1)	$(x)(Bx \supset Sx)$	Pr
2)	$(x)[(Bx \cdot Sx) \supset Ox]$	Pr
3)	$(x)\{(Sx \cdot Bx) \supset [Ox \supset (Dx \cdot Ex)]\}$	Pr
4)	$Bx \supset Sx$	1, UI
5)	$(Bx \cdot Sx) \supset Ox$	2, UI
6)	$(Sx \cdot Bx) \supset [Ox \supset (Dx \cdot Ex)]$	3, UI
7)	Bx	CP, $\therefore Dx \cdot Ex$
8)	Sx	4, 7, MP
9)	$Bx \cdot Sx$	7, 8, Conj
10)	Ox	5, 9, MP
11)	$Sx \cdot Bx$	9, Com
12)	$Ox \supset (Dx \cdot Ex)$	6, 11, MP
13)	$Dx \cdot Ex$	12, 10, MP
14)	$Bx \supset (Dx \cdot Ex)$	7–13, CD
15)	$\therefore (x)[Bx \supset (Dx \cdot Ex)]$	14, UG

(3-b) $\therefore (x)[Bx \supset (Dx \cdot Ex)]$

1)	$(x)(Bx \supset Sx)$	Pr
2)	$(x)[(Bx \cdot Sx) \supset Ox]$	Pr
3)	$(x)\{(Sx \cdot Bx) \supset [Ox \supset (Dx \cdot Ex)]\}$	Pr
4)	$Bx \supset Sx$	1, UI
5)	$(Bx \cdot Sx) \supset Ox$	2, UI
6)	$(Sx \cdot Bx) \supset [Ox \supset (Dx \cdot Ex)]$	3, UI
7)	$[(Sx \cdot Bx) \cdot Ox] \supset (Dx \cdot Ex)$	6, Exp
8)	$[Ox \cdot (Sx \cdot Bx)] \supset (Dx \cdot Ex)$	7, Com
9)	$Ox \supset [(Sx \cdot Bx) \supset (Dx \cdot Ex)]$	8, Exp
10)	$(Bx \cdot Sx) \supset [(Sx \cdot Bx) \supset (Dx \cdot Ex)]$	5, 9, HS
11)	$(Bx \cdot Sx) \supset [(Bx \cdot Sx) \supset (Dx \cdot Ex)]$	10, Com
12)	$[(Bx \cdot Sx) \cdot (Bx \cdot Sx)] \supset (Dx \cdot Ex)$	11, Exp
13)	$(Bx \cdot Sx) \supset (Dx \cdot Ex)$	12, Taut
14)	$(Sx \cdot Bx) \supset (Dx \cdot Ex)$	13, Com
15)	$Sx \supset [Bx \supset (Dx \cdot Ex)]$	14, Exp
16)	$Bx \supset [Bx \supset (Dx \cdot Ex)]$	4, 15, HS
17)	$(Bx \cdot Bx) \supset (Dx \cdot Ex)$	16, Exp
18)	$Bx \supset (Dx \cdot Ex)$	17, Taut
19)	$\therefore (x)[Bx \supset (Dx \cdot Ex)]$	18, UG

(5-a) $\therefore (x)\{[Cx \cdot (Sx \cdot Hx)]$ $\supset \sim (Px \lor Nx)\}$

1)	$(x)(\{Cx \cdot [Ax \supset (Px \lor Nx)]\} \supset \sim (Sx \cdot Hx))$	Pr
2)	$\{Cx \cdot [Ax \supset (Px \lor Nx)]\} \supset \sim (Sx \cdot Hx)$	1, UI

3)	$Cx \cdot (Sx \cdot Hx)$	CP, $\therefore \sim(Px \lor Nx)$
4)	Cx	3, Simp
5)	$(Sx \cdot Hx) \cdot Cx$	3, Com
6)	$Sx \cdot Hx$	5, Simp
7)	$\sim\sim(Sx \cdot Hx)$	6, DN
8)	$\sim\{Cx \cdot [Ax \supset (Px \lor Nx)]\}$	2, 7, MT
9)	$\sim Cx \lor \sim[Ax \supset (Px \lor Nx)]$	8, DeM
10)	$\sim\sim Cx$	4, DN
11)	$\sim[Ax \supset (Px \lor Nx)]$	9, 10, DS
12)	$\sim\sim[Ax \cdot \sim(Px \lor Nx)]$	11, D3
13)	$Ax \cdot \sim(Px \lor Nx)$	12, DN
14)	$\sim(Px \lor Nx) \cdot Ax$	13, Com
15)	$\sim(Px \lor Nx)$	14, Simp
16)	$[Cx \cdot (Sx \cdot Hx)] \supset \sim(Px \lor Nx)$	3–15, CP
17)	$\therefore (x)\{[Cx \cdot (Sx \cdot Hx)] \supset \sim(Px \lor Nx)\}$	16, UG

(5-b) $\therefore (x)\{[Cx \cdot (Sx \cdot Hx)] \supset \sim(Px \lor Nx)\}$

1)	$(x)(\{Cx \cdot [Ax \supset (Px \lor Nx)]\} \supset \sim(Sx \cdot Hx))$	Pr
2)	$\{Cx \cdot [Ax \supset (Px \lor Nx)]\} \supset \sim(Sx \cdot Hx)$	1, UI
3)	$\{Cx \cdot [Ax \supset (Px \lor Nx)]\} \supset (\sim Sx \lor \sim Hx)$	2, DeM
4)	$\sim\{Cx \cdot [Ax \supset (Px \lor Nx)]\} \lor (\sim Sx \lor \sim Hx)$	3, MI
5)	$\{\sim Cx \lor \sim[Ax \supset (Px \lor Nx)]\} \lor (\sim Sx \lor \sim Hx)$	4, DeM
6)	$\{\sim Cx \lor \sim\sim[Ax \cdot \sim(Px \lor Nx)]\}$ $\lor (\sim Sx \lor \sim Hx)$	5, D3
7)	$\{\sim Cx \lor [Ax \cdot \sim(Px \lor Nx)]\} \lor (\sim Sx \lor \sim Hx)$	6, DN
8)	$\{\sim Cx \lor [Ax \cdot (\sim Px \cdot \sim Nx)]\} \lor (\sim Sx \lor \sim Hx)$	7, DeM
9)	$\{(\sim Cx \lor Ax) \cdot [\sim Cx \lor (\sim Px \cdot \sim Nx)]\}$ $\lor (\sim Sx \lor \sim Hx)$	8, Dist
10)	$(\sim Sx \lor \sim Hx) \lor \{(\sim Cx \lor Ax)$ $\cdot [\sim Cx \lor (\sim Px \cdot \sim Nx)]\}$	9, Com
11)	$(\sim Sx \lor \sim Hx) \lor \{[\sim Cx \lor (\sim Px \cdot \sim Nx)]$ $\cdot (\sim Cx \lor Ax)\}$	10, Com
12)	$\{(\sim Sx \lor \sim Hx) \lor [\sim Cx \lor (\sim Px \cdot \sim Nx)]\}$ $\cdot [(\sim Sx \lor \sim Hx) \cdot (\sim Cx \lor Ax)]$	11, Dist
13)	$(\sim Sx \lor \sim Hx) \lor [\sim Cx \lor (\sim Px \cdot \sim Nx)]$	12, Simp
14)	$[(\sim Sx \lor \sim Hx) \lor \sim Cx] \lor (\sim Px \cdot \sim Nx)$	13, Assoc
15)	$[\sim Cx \lor (\sim Sx \lor \sim Hx)] \lor (\sim Px \cdot \sim Nx)$	14, Com
16)	$[\sim Cx \lor \sim(Sx \cdot Hx)] \lor (\sim Px \cdot \sim Nx)$	15, DeM
17)	$\sim[Cx \cdot (Sx \cdot Hx)] \lor (\sim Px \cdot \sim Nx)$	16, DeM
18)	$\sim[Cx \cdot (Sx \cdot Hx)] \lor \sim(Px \lor Nx)$	17, DeM
19)	$[Cx \cdot (Sx \cdot Hx)] \supset \sim(Px \lor Nx)$	18, MI
20)	$\therefore (x)\{[Cx \cdot (Sx \cdot Hx)] \supset \sim(Px \lor Nx)\}$	19, UG

(7-a)
$\therefore (x)[(Px \cdot Sx)$
$\supset (Rx \supset Ex)]$

1)	$(x)\{[Px \cdot (Sx \lor Tx)] \supset [Rx \supset (Ex \cdot Kx)]\}$	Pr
2)	$[Px \cdot (Sx \lor Tx)] \supset [Rx \supset (Ex \cdot Kx)]$	1, UI
3)	$Px \cdot Sx$	CP, $\therefore Rx \supset Ex$
4)	Rx	CP, $\therefore Ex$
5)	Px	3, Simp
6)	$Sx \cdot Px$	3, Com
7)	Sx	6, Simp
8)	$Sx \lor Tx$	7, Add
9)	$Px \cdot (Sx \lor Tx)$	5, 8, Conj
10)	$Rx \supset (Ex \cdot Kx)$	2, 9, MP
11)	$Ex \cdot Kx$	10, 4, MP
12)	Ex	11, Simp
13)	$Rx \supset Ex$	4–12, CP
14)	$(Px \cdot Sx) \supset (Rx \supset Ex)$	3–13, CP
15)	$\therefore (x)[(Px \cdot Sx) \supset (Rx \supset Ex)]$	14, UG

(7-b)
$\therefore (x)[(Px \cdot Sx)$
$\supset (Rx \supset Ex)]$

1)	$(x)\{[Px \cdot (Sx \lor Tx)] \supset [Rx \supset (Ex \cdot Kx)]\}$	Pr
2)	$[Px \cdot (Sx \lor Tx)] \supset [Rx \supset (Ex \cdot Kx)]$	1, UI
3)	$[Px \cdot (Sx \lor Tx)] \supset [\sim Rx \lor (Ex \cdot Kx)]$	2, MI
4)	$[Px \cdot (Sx \lor Tx)] \supset [(\sim Rx \lor Ex) \cdot (\sim Rx \lor Kx)]$	3, Dist
5)	$\sim [Px \cdot (Sx \lor Tx)] \lor [(\sim Rx \lor Ex)$ $\cdot (\sim Rx \lor Kx)]$	4, MI
6)	$[\sim Px \lor \sim (Sx \lor Tx)] \lor [(\sim Rx \lor Ex)$ $\cdot (\sim Rx \lor Kx)]$	5, DeM
7)	$[\sim Px \lor (\sim Sx \cdot \sim Tx)] \lor [(\sim Rx \lor Ex)$ $\cdot (\sim Rx \lor Kx)]$	6, DeM
8)	$\{[\sim Px \lor (\sim Sx \cdot \sim Tx)] \lor (\sim Rx \lor Ex)\}$ $\cdot \{[\sim Px \lor (\sim Sx \cdot \sim Tx)] \lor (\sim Rx \lor Kx)$	7, Dist
9)	$[\sim Px \lor (\sim Sx \cdot \sim Tx)] \lor (\sim Rx \lor Ex)$	8, Simp
10)	$(\sim Rx \lor Ex) \lor [\sim Px \lor (\sim Sx \cdot \sim Tx)]$	9, Com
11)	$(\sim Rx \lor Ex) \lor [(\sim Px \lor \sim Sx) \cdot (\sim Px \lor \sim Tx)]$	10, Dist
12)	$[(\sim Rx \lor Ex) \lor (\sim Px \lor \sim Sx)]$ $\cdot [(\sim Rx \lor Ex) \lor (\sim Px \lor \sim Tx)]$	11, Dist
13)	$(\sim Rx \lor Ex) \lor (\sim Px \lor \sim Sx)$	12, Simp
14)	$(\sim Px \lor \sim Sx) \lor (\sim Rx \lor Ex)$	13, Com
15)	$\sim (Px \cdot Sx) \lor (\sim Rx \lor Ex)$	14, DeM
16)	$(Px \cdot Sx) \supset (\sim Rx \lor Ex)$	15, MI
17)	$(Px \cdot Sx) \supset (Rx \supset Ex)$	16, MI
18)	$\therefore (x)[(Px \cdot Sx) \supset (Rx \supset Ex)]$	17, UG

(9-a)

		∴ $(x)\{Vx ⊃$
		$[(Cx \cdot Sx) ⊃ \sim Fx]\}$
1)	$(x)\{[(Rx \lor Fx) \cdot (Cx \cdot Sx)] ⊃ \sim Vx\}$	Pr
2)	$[(Rx \lor Fx) \cdot (Cx \cdot Sx)] ⊃ \sim Vx$	1, UI
3)	Vx	CP, ∴ $(Cx \cdot Sx) ⊃ \sim Fx$
4)	$Cx \cdot Sx$	CP, ∴ $\sim Fx$
5)	$\sim \sim Vx$	3, DN
6)	$\sim [(Rx \lor Fx) \cdot (Cx \cdot Sx)]$	2, 5, MT
7)	$\sim (Rx \lor Fx) \lor \sim (Cx \cdot Sx)$	6, DeM
8)	$\sim (Cx \cdot Sx) \lor \sim (Rx \lor Fx)$	7, Com
9)	$\sim \sim (Cx \cdot Sx)$	4, DN
10)	$\sim (Rx \lor Fx)$	8, 9, DS
11)	$\sim Rx \cdot \sim Fx$	10, DeM
12)	$\sim Fx \cdot \sim Rx$	11, Com
13)	$\sim Fx$	12, Simp
14)	$(Cx \cdot Sx) ⊃ \sim Fx$	4–13, CP
15)	$Vx ⊃ [(Cx \cdot Sx) ⊃ \sim Fx]$	3–14, CP
16)	∴ $(x)\{Vx ⊃ [(Cx \cdot Sx) ⊃ \sim Fx]\}$	15, UG

(9-b)

		∴ $(x)\{Vx ⊃$
		$[(Cx \cdot Sx) ⊃ \sim Fx]\}$
1)	$(x)\{[(Rx \lor Fx) \cdot (Cx \cdot Sx)] ⊃ \sim Vx\}$	Pr
2)	$[(Rx \lor Fx) \cdot (Cx \cdot Sx)] ⊃ \sim Vx$	1, UI
3)	$\sim \sim Vx ⊃ \sim [(Rx \lor Fx) \cdot (Cx \cdot Sx)]$	2, Trans
4)	$Vx ⊃ \sim [(Rx \lor Fx) \cdot (Cx \cdot Sx)]$	3, DN
5)	$Vx ⊃ \sim [(Cx \cdot Sx) \cdot (Rx \lor Fx)]$	4, Com
6)	$Vx ⊃ [\sim (Cx \cdot Sx) \lor \sim (Rx \lor Fx)]$	5, DeM
7)	$Vx ⊃ [\sim (Cx \cdot Sx) \lor (\sim Rx \cdot \sim Fx)]$	6, DeM
8)	$Vx ⊃ [\sim (Cx \cdot Sx) \lor (\sim Fx \cdot \sim Rx)]$	7, Com
9)	$Vx ⊃ \{[\sim (Cx \cdot Sx) \lor \sim Fx]$	
	$\quad \cdot [\sim (Cx \cdot Sx) \lor \sim Rx]\}$	8, Dist
10)	$\sim Vx \lor \{[\sim (Cx \cdot Sx) \lor \sim Fx]$	
	$\quad \cdot [\sim (Cx \cdot Sx) \lor \sim Rx]\}$	9, MI
11)	$\{\sim Vx \lor [\sim (Cx \cdot Sx) \lor \sim Fx]\}$	
	$\quad \cdot \{\sim Vx \lor [\sim (Cx \cdot Sx) \lor \sim Rx]\}$	10, Dist
12)	$\sim Vx \lor [\sim (Cx \cdot Sx) \lor \sim Fx]$	11, Simp
13)	$Vx ⊃ [\sim (Cx \cdot Sx) \lor \sim Fx]$	12, MI
14)	$Vx ⊃ [(Cx \cdot Sx) ⊃ \sim Fx]$	13, MI
15)	∴ $(x)\{Vx ⊃ [(Cx \cdot Sx) ⊃ \sim Fx]\}$	14, UG

SECTION 4

Group A: (page 391)

(1) $(\exists x)[Nx \cdot (Px \cdot Ix)]$

$[Na \cdot (Pa \cdot Ia)] \lor [Nb \cdot (Pb \cdot Ib)] \lor [Nc \cdot (Pc \cdot Ic)]$

(3) $(x)[(Rx \cdot Nx) \supset Ex]$
$[(Ra \cdot Na) \supset Ea] \cdot [(Rb \cdot Nb) \supset Eb] \cdot [(Rc \cdot Nc) \supset Ec]$

(5) $(x)[Sx \supset (Ix \supset Cx)]$
$[Sa \supset (Ia \supset Ca)] \cdot [Sb \supset (Ib \supset Cb)] \cdot [Sc \supset (Ic \supset Cc)]$

(7) $(\exists x)[(Cx \cdot Lx) \cdot Px]$
$[(Ca \cdot La) \cdot Pa] \lor [(Cb \cdot Lb) \cdot Pb] \lor [(Cc \cdot Lc) \cdot Pc]$

(9) $(x)[(Cx \cdot Lx) \supset \sim Fx]$
$[(Ca \cdot La) \supset \sim Fa] \cdot [(Cb \cdot Lb) \supset \sim Fb] \cdot [(Cc \cdot Lc) \supset \sim Fc]$

Group B: (page 391)

(1)

    1) Pr
    2) Pr
    3) 2, QD
    4) 3, D3
    5) 1, 4, MT
    6) 5, QD

(3)

    1) Pr
    2) Pr
    3) 1, QD
    4) 3, EI
    5) 2, UI
    6) 4, Com
    7) 6, Simp
    8) 5, 7, MP
    9) 8, EG

(5)

    1) Pr
    2) Pr
    3) 1, QD
    4) 3, EI
    5) 2, UI
    6) 4, DeM
    7) 6, Com
    8) 7, Simp
    9) 5, 8, MT
   10) 9, 8, Conj
   11) 10, DeM
   12) 11, EG
   13) 12, QD

(7)

    1) Pr
    2) Pr
    3) Pr
    4) 3, QD
    5) 4, EI
    6) 5, D3
    7) 6, DN
    8) 2, UI
    9) 7, Simp
  10) 7, Com
  11) 10, Simp
  12) 8, 9, MP
  13) 12, 11, Conj
  14) 13, EG
  15) 14, QD
  16) 15, D3
  17) 1, 16, MT
  18) 17, QD
  19) 18, D3
  20) 19, DN

(9)

    1) Pr
    2) Pr
    3) 2, Simp
    4) 2, Com
    5) 4, Simp
    6) 1, QD
    7) 3, QD
    8) 5, QD
    9) 6, UI
  10) 7, UI
  11) 8, UI
  12) 9, D3
  13) 10, D3
  14) 11, D3
  15) 14, 12, HS
  16) 15, Exp
  17) 13, Trans
  18) 17, DN
  19) 16, 18, HS
  20) 19, UG
  21) 20, QD
  22) 21, D3
  23) 22, DN

Group C: (page 395)

(1)   ∴ (∃x) ~ Ax

1)	~(∃x)(Ax · ~ Bx) · ~(x)Bx	Pr
2)	~(∃x)(Ax · ~ Bx)	1, Simp
3)	~(x)Bx · ~(∃x)(Ax · ~ Bx)	1, Com
4)	~(x)Bx	3, Simp
5)	(x) ~(Ax · ~ Bx)	2, QD
6)	(∃x) ~ Bx	4, QD
7)	~ Bx	6, EI
8)	~(Ax · ~ Bx)	5, UI
9)	Ax ⊃ Bx	8, D3
10)	~ Ax	9, 7, MT
11)	∴ (∃x) ~ Ax	10, EG

(3)   ∴ ~(x)(Cx ⊃ Ax)

1)	~(∃x) ~(Ax ⊃ Bx)	Pr
2)	~(x)(Cx ⊃ Bx)	Pr
3)	(x)(Ax ⊃ Bx)	1, QD
4)	(∃x) ~(Cx ⊃ Bx)	2, QD
5)	~(Cx ⊃ Bx)	4, EI
6)	Ax ⊃ Bx	3, UI
7)	~ ~(Cx · ~ Bx)	5, D3
8)	Cx · ~ Bx	7, DN
9)	Cx	8, Simp
10)	~ Bx · Cx	8, Com
11)	~ Bx	10, Simp
12)	~ Ax	6, 11, MT
13)	Cx · ~ Ax	9, 12, Conj
14)	(∃x)(Cx · ~ Ax)	13, EG
15)	~(x) ~(Cx · ~ Ax)	14, QD
16)	∴ ~(x)(Cx ⊃ Ax)	15, D3

(5)   ∴ (∃x)[Bx · (Ax · ~ Dx)]

1)	~(∃x)[(Ax · Bx) · ~ Cx]	Pr
2)	(x)[Cx ⊃ (Ax ⊃ Dx)]	Pr
3)	(x) ~[(Ax · Bx) · ~ Cx]	1, QD
4)	Cx ⊃ (Ax ⊃ Dx)	2, UI
5)	~[(Ax · Bx) · ~ Cx]	3, UI
6)	(Ax · Bx) ⊃ Cx	5, D3
7)	(Ax · Bx) ⊃ (Ax ⊃ Dx)	6, 4, HS
8)	[(Ax · Bx) · Ax] ⊃ Dx	7, Exp
9)	[Ax · (Ax · Bx)] ⊃ Dx	8, Com
10)	[(Ax · Ax) · Bx] ⊃ Dx	9, Assoc
11)	(Ax · Bx) ⊃ Dx	10, Taut
12)	(x)[(Ax · Bx) ⊃ Dx]	11, UG
13)	~(∃x) ~[(Ax · Bx) ⊃ Dx]	12, QD

14)	$\sim(\exists x) \sim \sim[(Ax \cdot Bx) \cdot \sim Dx]$	13, D3
15)	$\sim(\exists x)[(Ax \cdot Bx) \cdot \sim Dx]$	14, DN
16)	$\sim(\exists x)[(Bx \cdot Ax) \cdot \sim Dx]$	15, Com
17)	$\therefore \sim(\exists x)[Bx \cdot (Ax \cdot \sim Dx)]$	16, Assoc

(7)

$\therefore (\exists x)(Cx \cdot Ax)$
$\lor (\exists x)(Cx \cdot Dx)$

1)	$\sim(\exists x)[\sim Ax \cdot (\sim Bx \cdot Cx)]$	Pr
2)	$\sim(x)(Cx \supset Bx)$	Pr
3)	$(x) \sim[\sim Ax \cdot (\sim Bx \cdot Cx)]$	1, QD
4)	$(\exists x) \sim (Cx \supset Bx)$	2, QD
5)	$\sim(Cx \supset Bx)$	4, EI
6)	$\sim[\sim Ax \cdot (\sim Bx \cdot Cx)]$	3, UI
7)	$\sim \sim(Cx \cdot \sim Bx)$	5, D3
8)	$Cx \cdot \sim Bx$	7, DN
9)	Cx	8, Simp
10)	$\sim Bx \cdot Cx$	8, Com
11)	$\sim Bx$	10, Simp
12)	$\sim[(\sim Ax \cdot \sim Bx) \cdot Cx]$	6, Assoc
13)	$\sim[Cx \cdot (\sim Ax \cdot \sim Bx)]$	12, Com
14)	$\sim[Cx \cdot \sim(Ax \lor Bx)]$	13, DeM
15)	$Cx \supset (Ax \lor Bx)$	14, D3
16)	$Ax \lor Bx$	15, 9, MP
17)	$Bx \lor Ax$	16, Com
18)	Ax	17, 11, DS
19)	$Cx \cdot Ax$	9, 18, Conj
20)	$(\exists x)(Cx \cdot Ax)$	19, EG
21)	$\therefore (\exists x)(Cx \cdot Ax) \lor (\exists x)(Cx \cdot Dx)$	20, Add

(9)

$\therefore \sim(\exists x)(\sim Cx \cdot \sim Fx)$

1)	$\sim(\exists x)(Ax \cdot \sim Bx) \cdot \sim(\exists x)(Bx \cdot \sim Cx)$	Pr
2)	$(x)(\sim Ax \equiv Dx)$	Pr
3)	$(x)(Dx \supset Ex) \cdot (x)(Ex \supset Fx)$	Pr
4)	$\sim(\exists x)(Ax \cdot \sim Bx)$	1, Simp
5)	$\sim(\exists x)(Bx \cdot \sim Cx) \cdot \sim(\exists x)(Ax \cdot \sim Bx)$	1, Com
6)	$\sim(\exists x)(Bx \cdot \sim Cx)$	5, Simp
7)	$(x)(Dx \supset Ex)$	3, Simp
8)	$(x)(Ex \supset Fx) \cdot (x)(Dx \supset Ex)$	3, Com
9)	$(x)(Ex \supset Fx)$	8, Simp
10)	$(x) \sim(Ax \cdot \sim Bx)$	4, QD
11)	$(x) \sim(Bx \cdot \sim Cx)$	6, QD
12)	$\sim Ax \equiv Dx$	2, UI
13)	$Dx \supset Ex$	7, UI
14)	$Ex \supset Fx$	9, UI
15)	$\sim(Ax \cdot \sim Bx)$	10, UI
16)	$\sim(Bx \cdot \sim Cx)$	11, UI

17)	$\sim(\sim Ax \cdot \sim Dx) \cdot \sim(Dx \cdot \sim \sim Ax)$	12, D4
18)	$Ax \supset Bx$	15, D3
19)	$Bx \supset Cx$	16, D3
20)	$Ax \supset Cx$	18, 19, HS
21)	$Dx \supset Fx$	13, 14, HS
22)	$\sim(\sim Ax \cdot \sim Dx)$	17, Simp
23)	$Ax \lor Dx$	22, D1
24)	$Cx \lor Fx$	20, 21, 23, CD
25)	$\sim(\sim Cx \cdot \sim Fx)$	24, D1
26)	$(x) \sim(\sim Cx \cdot \sim Fx)$	25, UG
27)	$\therefore \sim(\exists x)(\sim Cx \cdot \sim Fx)$	26, QD

Group E: (page 396)

(1)

		$\therefore (\exists x)(Ax \cdot \sim Px)$
1)	$(x)(Ax \lor Px) \cdot \sim(x)Px$	Pr
2)	$(x)(Ax \lor Px)$	1, Simp
3)	$\sim(x)Px \cdot (x)(Ax \lor Px)$	1, Com
4)	$\sim(x)Px$	3, Simp
5)	$(\exists x) \sim Px$	4, QD
6)	$\sim Px$	5, EI
7)	$Ax \lor Px$	2, UI
8)	$Px \lor Ax$	7, Com
9)	Ax	8, 6, DS
10)	$Ax \cdot \sim Px$	9, 6, Conj
11)	$\therefore (\exists x)(Ax \cdot \sim Px)$	10, EG

(3)

		$\therefore \sim(\exists x)(Ax \cdot \sim Ix)$
1)	$(x)(Ax \supset Tx)$	Pr
2)	$\sim(\exists x)[Tx \cdot \sim(Ix \cdot Mx)]$	Pr
3)	$(x) \sim[Tx \cdot \sim(Ix \cdot Mx)]$	2, QD
4)	$Ax \supset Tx$	1, UI
5)	$\sim[Tx \cdot \sim(Ix \cdot Mx)]$	3, UI
6)	$Tx \supset (Ix \cdot Mx)$	5, D3
7)	$Ax \supset (Ix \cdot Mx)$	4, 6, HS
8)	$\sim Ax \lor (Ix \cdot Mx)$	7, MI
9)	$(\sim Ax \lor Ix) \cdot (\sim Ax \lor Mx)$	8, Dist
10)	$\sim Ax \lor Ix$	9, Simp
11)	$\sim(\sim \sim Ax \cdot \sim Ix)$	10, D1
12)	$\sim(Ax \cdot \sim Ix)$	11, DN
13)	$(x) \sim(Ax \cdot \sim Ix)$	12, UG
14)	$\therefore \sim(\exists x)(Ax \cdot \sim Ix)$	13, QD

(5)

		$\therefore \sim(x)(Ax \supset Hx)$
1)	$(x)\{Ax \supset [Gx \equiv \sim(Sx \lor Hx)]\}$	Pr
2)	$(\exists x)(Gx \cdot Ax)$	Pr
3)	$Gx \cdot Ax$	2, EI

4)	$Ax \supset [Gx \equiv \sim(Sx \lor Hx)]$	1, UI
5)	Gx	3, Simp
6)	$Ax \cdot Gx$	3, Com
7)	Ax	6, Simp
8)	$Gx \equiv \sim(Sx \lor Hx)$	4, 7, MP
9)	$\sim[Gx \cdot \sim\sim(Sx \lor Hx)] \cdot \sim[\sim(Sx \lor Hx) \cdot \sim Gx]$	8, D4
10)	$\sim[Gx \cdot \sim\sim(Sx \lor Hx)]$	9, Simp
11)	$Gx \supset \sim(Sx \lor Hx)$	10, D3
12)	$\sim(Sx \lor Hx)$	11, 5, MP
13)	$\sim Sx \cdot \sim Hx$	12, DeM
14)	$\sim Hx \cdot \sim Sx$	13, Com
15)	$\sim Hx$	14, Simp
16)	$Ax \cdot \sim Hx$	7, 15, Conj
17)	$(\exists x)(Ax \cdot \sim Hx)$	16, EG
18)	$\sim(x) \sim(Ax \cdot \sim Hx)$	17, QD
19)	$\therefore \sim(x)(Ax \supset Hx)$	18, D3

(7)

		$\therefore (x)[Ax \supset (Vx \supset Hx)]$
1)	$\sim(\exists x)[Vx \cdot (Ax \cdot \sim Mx)]$	Pr
2)	$\sim(\exists x)[(Ax \cdot Mx) \cdot \sim(Hx \cdot Cx)]$	Pr
3)	$(x) \sim[Vx \cdot (Ax \cdot \sim Mx)]$	1, QD
4)	$(x) \sim[(Ax \cdot Mx) \cdot \sim(Hx \cdot Cx)]$	2, QD
5)	$\sim[Vx \cdot (Ax \cdot \sim Mx)]$	3, UI
6)	$\sim[(Ax \cdot Mx) \cdot \sim(Hx \cdot Cx)]$	4, UI
7)	$\sim[Vx \cdot \sim\sim(Ax \cdot \sim Mx)]$	5, DN
8)	$\sim[Vx \cdot \sim(Ax \supset Mx)]$	7, D3
9)	$Vx \supset (Ax \supset Mx)$	8, D3
10)	$(Ax \cdot Mx) \supset (Hx \cdot Cx)$	6, D3
11)	$(Vx \cdot Ax) \supset Mx$	9, Exp
12)	$(Mx \cdot Ax) \supset (Hx \cdot Cx)$	10, Com
13)	$Mx \supset [Ax \supset (Hx \cdot Cx)]$	12, Exp
14)	$(Vx \cdot Ax) \supset [Ax \supset (Hx \cdot Cx)]$	11, 13, HS
15)	$[(Vx \cdot Ax) \cdot Ax] \supset (Hx \cdot Cx)$	14, Exp
16)	$[Vx \cdot (Ax \cdot Ax)] \supset (Hx \cdot Cx)$	15, Assoc
17)	$(Vx \cdot Ax) \supset (Hx \cdot Cx)$	16, Taut
18)	$\sim(Vx \cdot Ax) \lor (Hx \cdot Cx)$	17, MI
19)	$[\sim(Vx \cdot Ax) \lor Hx] \cdot [\sim(Vx \cdot Ax) \lor Cx]$	18, Dist
20)	$\sim(Vx \cdot Ax) \lor Hx$	19, Simp
21)	$(Vx \cdot Ax) \supset Hx$	20, MI
22)	$(Ax \cdot Vx) \supset Hx$	21, Com
23)	$Ax \supset (Vx \supset Hx)$	22, Exp
24)	$\therefore (x)[Ax \supset (Vx \supset Hx)]$	23, UG

(9) $\therefore (\exists x)Sx$

1)	$\sim(\exists x)[Fx \cdot \sim(Ix \equiv \sim Ax)]$	Pr
2)	$\sim(x)(Fx \supset Cx)$	Pr
3)	$\sim(\exists x)(Ax \cdot \sim Cx) \cdot \sim(\exists x)(Ix \cdot \sim Sx)$	Pr
4)	$\sim(\exists x)(Ax \cdot \sim Cx)$	3, Simp
5)	$\sim(\exists x)(Ix \cdot \sim Sx) \cdot \sim(\exists x)(Ax \cdot \sim Cx)$	3, Com
6)	$\sim(\exists x)(Ix \cdot \sim Sx)$	5, Simp
7)	$(x) \sim[Fx \cdot \sim(Ix \equiv \sim Ax)]$	1, QD
8)	$(\exists x) \sim(Fx \supset Cx)$	2, QD
9)	$(x) \sim(Ax \cdot \sim Cx)$	4, QD
10)	$(x) \sim(Ix \cdot \sim Sx)$	6, QD
11)	$\sim(Fx \supset Cx)$	8, EI
12)	$\sim[Fx \cdot \sim(Ix \equiv \sim Ax)]$	7, UI
13)	$\sim(Ax \cdot \sim Cx)$	9, UI
14)	$\sim(Ix \cdot \sim Sx)$	10, UI
15)	$\sim \sim(Fx \cdot \sim Cx)$	11, D3
16)	$Fx \cdot \sim Cx$	15, DN
17)	Fx	16, Simp
18)	$\sim Cx \cdot Fx$	16, Com
19)	$\sim Cx$	18, Simp
20)	$Fx \supset (Ix \equiv \sim Ax)$	12, D3
21)	$Ax \supset Cx$	13, D3
22)	$Ix \supset Sx$	14, D3
23)	$Ix \equiv \sim Ax$	20, 17, MP
24)	$\sim(Ix \cdot \sim \sim Ax) \cdot \sim(\sim Ax \cdot \sim Ix)$	23, D4
25)	$\sim(\sim Ax \cdot \sim Ix) \cdot \sim(Ix \cdot \sim \sim Ax)$	24, Com
26)	$\sim(\sim Ax \cdot \sim Ix)$	25, Simp
27)	$Ax \lor Ix$	26, D1
28)	$\sim Ax$	21, 19, MT
29)	Ix	27, 28, DS
30)	Sx	22, 29, MP
31)	$\therefore (\exists x)Sx$	30, EG

SECTION 5
Group A: (page 402)

(1) $\therefore \sim Bba$

1)	Aab	Pr
2)	$(x)(Bxa \supset \sim Aax)$	Pr
3)	$Bba \supset \sim Aab$	2, UI
4)	$\sim \sim Aab$	1, DN
5)	$\therefore \sim Bba$	3, 4, MT

(3)

1)	$(x)[Ax \supset (\exists z)(Bz \cdot Cxz)]$	
2)	$Ay \supset (\exists z)(Bz \cdot Cyz)$	
3)	Ay	
4)	$(\exists z)(Bz \cdot Cyz)$	
5)	$Bw \cdot Cyw$	
6)	$Cyw \cdot Bw$	
7)	Cyw	
8)	$(\exists w)Cyw$	
9)	$Ay \supset (\exists w)Cyw$	
10)	$\therefore (y)[Ay \supset (\exists w)Cyw]$	

∴ $(y)[Ay \supset (\exists w)Cyw]$
Pr
1, UI
CP, ∴ $(\exists w)Cyw$
2, 3, MP
4, EI
5, Com
6, Simp
7, EG
3–8, CP
9, UG

(5)

1)	$(\exists x)(y)[(Axy \supset By) \supset Cx]$
2)	$(y)[(Axy \supset By) \supset Cx]$
3)	$(Axy \supset By) \supset Cx$
4)	$\sim Cx$
5)	$\sim (Axy \supset By)$
6)	$\sim \sim (Axy \cdot \sim By)$
7)	$Axy \cdot \sim By$
8)	$\sim By \cdot Axy$
9)	$\sim By$
10)	$\sim Cx \supset \sim By$
11)	$(y)(\sim Cx \supset \sim By)$
12)	$\therefore (\exists x)(y)(\sim Cx \supset \sim By)$

∴ $(\exists x)(y)(\sim Cx \supset \sim By)$
Pr
1, EI
2, UI
CP, ∴ $\sim By$
3, 4, MT
5, D3
6, DN
7, Com
8, Simp
4–9, CP
10, UG
11, EG

(7)

1)	$(x)\{[Ax \cdot (y)(Ay \supset Bxy)] \supset Bxx\}$
2)	$\sim (x)[Ax \supset (\exists y)Bxy]$
3)	$(\exists x) \sim [Ax \supset (\exists y)Bxy]$
4)	$(\exists x) \sim \sim [Ax \cdot \sim (\exists y)Bxy]$
5)	$(\exists x)[Ax \cdot \sim (\exists y)Bxy]$
6)	$(\exists x)[Ax \cdot (y) \sim Bxy]$
7)	$Ax \cdot (y) \sim Bxy$
8)	Ax
9)	$(y) \sim Bxy \cdot Ax$
10)	$(y) \sim Bxy$
11)	$[Ax \cdot (y)(Ay \supset Bxy)] \supset Bxx$
12)	$\sim Bxx$
13)	$\sim [Ax \cdot (y)(Ay \supset Bxy)]$
14)	$\sim Ax \lor \sim (y)(Ay \supset Bxy)$
15)	$\sim \sim Ax$
16)	$\therefore \sim (y)(Ay \supset Bxy)$

∴ $\sim (y)(Ay \supset Bxy)$
Pr
Pr
2, QD
3, D3
4, DN
5, QD
6, EI
7, Simp
7, Com
9, Simp
1, UI
10, UI
11, 12, MT
13, DeM
8, DN
14, 15, DS

(9)

		$\therefore (\exists x)[Bx \cdot (y)(Ay \supset Cyx)]$
1)	$(x)[Ax \supset (\exists w)(Bw \cdot Cxw)]$	Pr
2)	$(\exists x)\big(Bx \cdot (y)\{[Ay \cdot (\exists z)(Bz \cdot Cyz)] \supset Cyx\}\big)$	Pr
3)	$Ay \supset (\exists w)(Bw \cdot Cyw)$	1, UI
4)	Ay	CP, $\therefore Cyx$
5)	$(\exists w)(Bw \cdot Cyw)$	3, 4, MP
6)	$Bz \cdot Cyz$	5, EI
7)	$(\exists z)(Bz \cdot Czz)$	6, EG
8)	$Bx \cdot (y)\{[Ay \cdot (\exists z)(Bz \cdot Czz)] \supset Cyx\}$	2, EI
9)	$(y)\{[Ay \cdot (\exists z)(Bz \cdot Czz)] \supset Cyx\} \cdot Bx$	8, Com
10)	$(y)\{[Ay \cdot (\exists z)(Bz \cdot Czz)] \supset Cyx\}$	9, Simp
11)	$[Ay \cdot (\exists z)(Bz \cdot Czz)] \supset Cyx$	10, UI
12)	$Ay \cdot (\exists z)(Bz \cdot Czz)$	4, 7, Conj
13)	Cyx	11, 12, MP
14)	$Ay \supset Cyx$	4–13, CP
15)	$(y)(Ay \supset Cyx)$	14, UG
16)	Bx	8, Simp
17)	$Bx \cdot (y)(Ay \supset Cyx)$	16, 15, Conj
18)	$\therefore (\exists x)[Bx \cdot (y)(Ay \supset Cyx)]$	17, EG

Group C: (page 403)

(1)

		$\therefore Frd$
1)	$(x)(Fxj \supset Fxd)$	Pr
2)	Frj	Pr
3)	$Frj \supset Frd$	1, UI
4)	$\therefore Frd$	3, 2, MP

(3)

		$\therefore \sim Gba$
1)	$(x)(y)(Gxy \supset \sim Gyx)$	Pr
2)	Gab	Pr
3)	$(y)(Gay \supset \sim Gyz)$	I, UI
4)	$Gab \supset \sim Gba$	3, UI
5)	$\therefore \sim Gba$	4, 2, MP

(5)

		$\therefore Tgw \supset \sim Hts$
1)	$(x)(Hxs \supset Axb)$	Pr
2)	$(x)(Txw \supset \sim Tbx)$	Pr
3)	$(x)(Atx \supset Txg)$	Pr
4)	$Hts \supset Atb$	1, UI
5)	$Tgw \supset \sim Tbg$	2, UI
6)	$Atb \supset Tbg$	3, UI
7)	$\sim Atb \supset \sim Hts$	4, Trans
8)	$\sim Tbg \supset \sim Atb$	6, Trans
9)	$\sim Tbg \supset \sim Hts$	8, 7, HS
10)	$\therefore Tgw \supset \sim Hts$	5, 9, HS

(7)

		∴ (x){[Px·(y)(Py ⊃ Fxy)] ⊃ ~ Px}
1)	(x)(Px ⊃ ~ Fxx)	Pr
2)	Px ⊃ ~ Fxx	1, UI
3)	Px·(y)(Py ⊃ Fxy)	CP, ∴ ~ Px
4)	Px	3, Simp
5)	(y)(Py ⊃ Fxy)·Px	3, Com
6)	(y)(Py ⊃ Fxy)	5, Simp
7)	Px ⊃ Fxx	6, UI
8)	Fxx	7, 4, MP
9)	~ ~ Fxx	8, DN
10)	~ Px	2, 9, MT
11)	[Px·(y)(Py ⊃ Fxy)] ⊃ ~ Px	3–10, CP
12)	∴ (x){[Px·(y)(Py ⊃ Fxy)] ⊃ ~ Px}	11, UG

(9)

		∴ (y)[(Ny·Iy) ⊃ ~ (x)(Px ⊃ ~ Cxy)]
1)	(∃x){Px·(y)[(Ny·Iy) ⊃ Cxy]}	Pr
2)	Px·(y)[(Ny·Iy) ⊃ Cxy]	1, EI
3)	Px	2, Simp
4)	(y)[(Ny·Iy) ⊃ Cxy]·Px	2, Com
5)	(y)[(Ny·Iy) ⊃ Cxy]	4, Simp
6)	(Ny·Iy) ⊃ Cxy	5, UI
7)	Ny·Iy	CP, ∴ ~ (x)(Px ⊃ ~ Cxy)
8)	Cxy	6, 7, MP
9)	Px·Cxy	3, 8, Conj
10)	(∃x)(Px·Cxy)	9, EG
11)	~ (x) ~ (Px·Cxy)	10, QD
12)	~ (x) ~ (Px· ~ ~ Cxy)	11, DN
13)	~ (x)(Px ⊃ ~ Cxy)	12, D3
14)	(Ny·Iy) ⊃ ~ (x)(Px ⊃ ~ Cxy)	7–13, CP
15)	∴ (y)[(Ny·Iy) ⊃ ~ (x)(Px ⊃ ~ Cxy)]	14, UG

Index

The following index should be used in conjunction with both the table of contents and the glossary of technical terms (*Appendix B*) of this book.